D1617546

WITHDRAWN
UTSA LIBRARIES

Nonconformist Writing in Nazi Germany

Studies in German Literature, Linguistics, and Culture

Nonconformist Writing in Nazi Germany

in Nazi Germany

The Literature of Inner Emigration

John Klapper

 CAMDEN HOUSE
Rochester, New York

First published 2015
by Camden House

Camden House is an imprint of Boydell & Brewer Inc.
668 Mt. Hope Avenue, Rochester, NY 14620, USA
www.camden-house.com
and of Boydell & Brewer Limited
PO Box 9, Woodbridge, Suffolk IP12 3DF, UK
www.boydellandbrewer.com

ISBN-13: 978-1-57113-909-2
ISBN-10: 1-57113-909-5

Library of Congress Cataloging-in-Publication Data

CIP data applied for.

This publication is printed on acid-free paper.
Printed in the United States of America.

Contents

List of Illustrations

About the Cover Image

T HE IMAGE IS FROM A PAINTING by the Swiss writer Friedrich Dürrenmatt (1921–90) entitled *Engel und Heilige stoben davon – Da setzte sich auf Gottes Thron der Täuferkönig Bockelson* (Angels and saints fled the scene, then Baptist King Bockelson took his seat on God's throne, 1966). The title is a quotation from Dürrenmatt's play *Die Wiedertäufer* (The Anabaptists), scene 18, "Der Tanz" (The Dance). It is a parodic judgment-day scene in which God has "resigned" and been replaced by the usurper Bockelson and the Anabaptists. It shows the king with a naked female figure on his lap, to the right the damned heading for hell (seen at the bottom of the picture) in a procession reminiscent of the Inquisition's march of sinners to the funeral pyre, while to the left the blessed ascend to heaven. The picture evokes the typical inner emigrant use of camouflaged historical subject matter to create parallels to the Nazi present, in particular the use of historical despots as Hitler figures.

Acknowledgments

I WOULD LIKE TO THANK the British Academy and Deutscher Akademischer Austauschdienst for their funding of the research that led to this book, and the University of Birmingham for granting me a year's research leave to work on it. I am particularly grateful to the journal *German Life and Letters* and the College of Arts and Law, University of Birmingham, for their financial support of the publication.

I would like to express my gratitude to the staff of the library, the manuscript archive, and the photograph archive of the Deutsches Literaturarchiv in Marbach for their patient assistance with tracking down materials, as well as to the Centre Dürrenmatt Neuchâtel, Switzerland, for permission to use the painting on the front cover. I am also grateful to Frau Irene Maria Röhrscheid-Andres and Dr. Freimund Röhrscheid for providing the photograph of Stefan Andres and for granting me permission to use it; similarly Frau Andrea Clemen and Frau Viktoria Reck-Malleczewen, daughters of Friedrich Reck-Malleczewen, for kindly sending me the photograph of their father.

Thanks are further extended to: my colleague Professor Bill Dodd for reading and commenting on sections of the manuscript, my colleagues Professor Ronald Speirs and Dietmar Wozniak for insights into translation difficulties, the readers of the manuscript for their very helpful comments, and Jim Walker for his enthusiastic and unstinting support throughout the project.

Most important, for her support and considerable forbearance over many years and for her attentive proofreading, I would like to thank Jan, to whom the book is dedicated.

John Klapper
Birmingham, UK
April 2015

Introduction

Das war ein Vorspiel nur, dort wo man Bücher
Verbrennt, verbrennt man auch am Ende Menschen.

[That was but a prelude; where they burn books,
they will eventually burn people too.]
 —Heinrich Heine, *Almansor: Eine Tragödie*

HEINRICH HEINE'S FAMOUS and, with regard to Nazi Germany, chillingly prophetic words from 1821 might be used to suggest a direct linear development from the book burnings of spring 1933 to the implementation of the "Final Solution" of mass killings of Jews and others, following decisions taken at the Wannsee Conference in January 1942, and to imply a monolithic draconian policing of writing and writers under the regime. In fact, reality was more complex: censorship was undermined by the existence of competing state and party organs, a far from consistent or foolproof system of control of writers, a failure to recognize the potential oppositional content and significance of many works, and also a degree of official tactical tolerance of dissonant writing. Nevertheless, the room for maneuver for those writers opposed to the regime, who after 1933 did not choose the often harsh and uncertain path of emigration but opted to continue their literary careers under the regime, was severely constrained. In order to be published by journals and publishing houses that had been systematically brought under the control of party and state, and to lend expression to their opposition, such writers had to deal in ambiguity and employ a range of techniques to disguise their real intent, thereby running the risk that success in fooling a censor might also mean target readers failed to see the intended message.

The publication in 2002 of Carl Zuckmayer's *Geheimreport* (Secret report), a set of character sketches on leading figures in German cultural life under the Nazi regime prepared for the American authorities in 1943–44, constituted a significant milestone in the reappraisal of literary and cultural production under National Socialism.[1] It demonstrated that any view based on a simple dichotomy between opposition and dissent, on the one hand, and collaboration and "fellow traveling" on the other, is simply not tenable. The writer's nuanced and differentiated appraisal of fellow authors who, unlike Zuckmayer himself, had decided to stay in Germany reflects the reality of life, writing, and publishing under the regime. Many such authors could, in the words of the Austrian writer Erika Mitterer's self-characterization, be said to be "zwischen Protest, Mitfühlen und Anpassung" (between protest, compassion, and conformity).[2] And in the eyes of the Nazi authorities they were accordingly thought to belong to a twilight "intermediate realm," neither openly dissenting from nor clearly aligning themselves with the Nazi regime.[3]

Nonconformist writing published in Nazi Germany is indeed marked by an essential ambiguity; it has the potential to be read and understood simultaneously as both a form of tacit opposition to and acquiescence in the regime. Although several nonconformist writers evince in their work a deep-seated sense of morality, as well as at times personal courage, and see it as their role to defend humanist values in the face of Nazi cultural barbarism, it is not difficult also to find in their writing preconceptions, ideas, or implications that can be accommodated with Nazi thinking or mythology, to the extent that they could be readily exploited by the Nazi state for propaganda purposes abroad.

Such apparent ambivalence is very often also the result of deliberate camouflage on the part of authors. The act of targeting oppositional messages at a predisposed inner circle of readers, while simultaneously avoiding obvious hostages to fortune with censors, required a permanent state of virtual schizophrenia among oppositionally minded writers;[4] material needed to be interpretable at one and the same time as conformist and potentially nonconformist, ideologically neutral and potentially dissident. This demanded a corresponding form of "dual vision" on the part of readers, or, to borrow and adapt Ernst Jünger's metaphor, a "stereoscopic," 3-D view, a form of new, deep perception resulting from simultaneous modes of observing a phenomenon.[5]

The broad review undertaken by Karl-Heinz Schoeps in his revised history of literature in Nazi Germany is organized largely according to ideological considerations, and in his introduction the author states: "In order to reach a general and comprehensive verdict on the literature within the Third Reich, more detailed studies of individual works . . . are necessary"; he further suggests the need for the subcategory of "inner emigration" (and that of others) to be broken down and organized around aesthetic and literary-historical principles.[6] This book is an example of such a "drilling down" to the literary context and aesthetic concerns of individual writers and to a thorough analysis of key representative works. It explores the inevitable ambiguity of inner emigration and in doing so eschews the limitations of an exclusively "text immanent" approach—that is, an approach that focuses solely on the literary work itself as an entity independent of biographical, social, and historical content—but also avoids the sort of a priori moral standpoints according to which writers who wrote under Nazism were automatically considered complicit in the regime, and which for several years after the Second

World War characterized much writing on the topic in Germany. Instead, it employs close reading as just one element alongside a broader critical examination of writers' biographies; their personal, political, and literary development; their intellectual influences; their association with other writers; their economic situation (for example, book sales); and their relationship with the Third Reich,[7] including their engagement with state and party institutions, their membership in writers' organizations, and their standing in the eyes of the regime. In short, it seeks to capture what Neil H. Donahue has called that contingent "mosaic of circumstances" that attends each individual writer's life and literary production, while remaining alert to the dangers of post hoc revision and self-stylization.[8] In examining selected texts it further studies each work's origins, the history and circumstances of its publication, and its critical reception, in an effort to read the particular text in the spirit of the time, to understand it in its historical context rather than that of a very different postwar or even postunification world. In addition, in each case a detailed analysis is undertaken of the dissident or oppositional message and the camouflage techniques employed to disguise it from censors, with a view to evaluating the work's standing as a piece of nonconformist writing.

A vast array of terms have been used throughout history to denote writing that seeks to distance itself from an oppressive regime and its author's stance in so doing.[9] In the case of National Socialism, these include: "Rückzug" (withdrawal), "inneres Reich" (inner realm), "Innerlichkeit" (inwardness), "das heimliche Deutschland" (the secret Germany), "das andere Deutschland" (the other Germany), "Dissens" (dissent), "Regimekritik" (criticism of the regime), "Nonkonformität" (nonconformity), "Verweigerung" (refusal), "Protest," "Opposition," "Resistenz" (immunity/resistance), and "Widerstand" (resistance). A good deal of confusion has been caused by indiscriminate use, especially by postwar apologists, of this final term in connection with nonconformist writers living and working in Nazi Germany or Austria. The actions of a writer such as Jan Petersen, who for a while after 1933 remained active in Germany as leader of the illegal Bund proletarisch-revolutionärer Schriftsteller Deutschlands (Union of German Proletarian-Revolutionary Writers), or of exiled writers who actively campaigned against Nazism from outside the country, belong in a quite different category from the necessarily veiled publications under the regime of such Christian writers as Stefan Andres, Werner Bergengruen, Erika Mitterer, Reinhold Schneider, or Ernst Wiechert. The debate over the appropriate terms is not helped by the fact that the Nazis themselves perceived the attitude of these and similar Christian writers toward National Socialism to be precisely a form of resistance, as is clear from camp reports by the *Sicherheitsdienst* (intelligence services) of the SS, where there is repeated talk of "oppositional resistance," especially among Catholic philosophers and writers.[10]

With regard to the rhetorical techniques employed by oppositionally minded writers, the concept of "verdeckte/verdeckende Schreibweise" (concealed/concealing writing style) has gained ground, and this too has become a source of terminological confusion with alternative names for the intended camouflage including: "Tarnung" (disguise), "Zwischen den Zeilen" (between the lines), "Sklavensprache" (the language of slaves), "Katakombensprache" (language of the catacombs), "Geheimsprache" (secret language), "indirektes Schreiben" (indirect writing), "sublime Rede" (sublime speech), "enzyklopädischer Stil" (encyclopaedic style), "Äsopische Sprache" (Aesopian language), and "versteckte Schreibweise" (veiled writing style). The specific techniques underpinning the concealed writing style denoted by these various synonyms are discussed in chapter 2.

For reasons to be discussed in detail in chapter 1, the term "inner emigration" has become the established designation for writers in Germany opposed to the Nazi regime. The term has a troubled history and many would dispute its meaningfulness and legitimacy as a designation of an intellectual stance under National Socialism, of a readily identifiable grouping, or of a single coherent literary approach. Fundamentally, of course, the "emigration" element is misleading since it runs the risk of confusing those writers and artists who stayed in Germany with those who felt compelled to leave the country because they feared for their lives, or at least for their liberty and ability to pursue their work. Most acknowledge the term "inner emigration" is problematic, but the alternatives are also unsatisfactory in different ways, being overinclusive ("nonfascist," "the other Germany"), unduly restrictive ("antifascist"), misleading ("dissident"), or incomplete ("oppositional").[11] The phrase "innerer Widerstand" (inner resistance) is one favored by some and there is indeed much to be said for it.

However, "inner emigration" and its derivative "inner emigrant" have become firmly established in the literature and, when suitably qualified, are perceived as much less tainted than fifty or so years ago. As Günter Scholdt, one of the most active German researchers in the field, has affirmed:

"Innere Emigration" ist ein brauchbarer literaturwissenschaftlicher Terminus für eine Schreib- und Lebensform von Autoren, die mit Hitlers Politik nicht einverstanden waren, gleichwohl aber in Deutschland blieben und in ihren dort erscheinenden Werken oder ihrer publizistischen Zurückhaltung eine antitotalitäre Gesinnung erkennen ließen. Der Begriff bleibt sinnvoll, auch wo er nach Ende des Dritten Reiches zuweilen apologetisch mißbraucht wurde, auch wo die ihm zugehörigen Autoren nur selten dem reinen Typus entsprachen und der Übergang zu Opportunismus und Kollaboration fließend war.[12]

["Inner Emigration" is a viable term in literary studies to denote a form of writing and way of life among authors who disagreed with Hitler's policies but nevertheless remained in Germany and who in their works published there, or indeed in their reluctance to publish, revealed an antitotalitarian mindset. The concept is still meaningful, even though after the end of the Third Reich it was from time to time misused for apologist purposes, and even though the authors that belonged to it only seldom corresponded to the pure inner emigrant type and the line dividing it from opportunism and collaboration was a fluid one.]

Similarly, in one of the latest volumes on the theme, the term is said to be so well established that scholarship can use it "sachlich und sinnvoll" (objectively and meaningfully).[13] Since, furthermore, many writers in Germany saw themselves as leading a form of emigrant existence, and because a good number also suffered for their art (through bans, book burnings, loss of livelihood, even imprisonment),[14] the phrases "inner emigration" and "inner emigrant" remain meaningful descriptors and are the ones used in this book.

It says much about the controversial nature of discussions of nonconformist writing in Nazi Germany that the insertion or omission of quotes around the term "inner emigration" should have become so significant.[15] When used, they indicate continuing skepticism toward and a distancing from the term, while their omission assumes the term is being treated as an established literary historical category. The decision not to enclose the term in quotes here is not intended to imply formal or aesthetic homogeneity (the writers this study is concerned with were undeniably diverse in terms of ideology and literary approach and cannot aspire to the status of an "-ism"); rather, it is the contention of this book that there has been sufficient demarcation over the years to allow us to identify a (loose) literary grouping, and that research into literary context and forms of writing under National Socialism has progressed sufficiently far to allow us to dispense with the "scare quotes" and the attendant skeptical distancing.

Clarity about the status and significance of a nonconformist work can only be gained by considering its genesis, its original stimulus, and its public and critical reception, and by analyzing the text in the relevant biographical, literary-political, and political context. To take just one example, such contextual detail is essential in understanding Stefan Andres's nonconformist short works of historical fiction:[16] first, they owe their origin to the author's use of a French officer's memoirs about his time in Napoleon's army in the early nineteenth century;[17] second, Andres shapes the raw historical material to themes relevant to the circumstances of Nazi Germany, including spying, denunciation, blind obedience, inner resistance, restrictions on freedom, and abuses of justice, and he uses

Napoleon and the French Revolution as ciphers for Hitler and National Socialism; third, they owe their publication and republication in a range of newspapers to the liberal inclinations of the latter's feuilleton editors; and fourth, as hard as it is to believe, their appearance in the Nazi publication *Völkischer Beobachter* followed from Andres's personal acquaintance with the feuilleton editor of that paper's Munich edition, Hans Gstettner. Only access to the biographical, contextual, and historical background allows appreciation of the full nonconformist import of such texts.

This is a book about creative writing under National Socialism and it focuses primarily on narrative prose, supported by reference to writers' contemporaneous diaries and essayistic work, as well as later memoirs. Lyric poetry—for some a key mode of expressing the inevitable inner emigrant ambiguity referred to above and the subject of a surprisingly small number of studies[18]—is also discussed, especially in chapter 2 in connection with the work of Albrecht Haushofer, Oskar Loerke, Rudolf Alexander Schröder, Günter Eich, and the controversial Gottfried Benn and Hans Carossa; in chapter 3 in relation to Werner Bergengruen; and in chapter 7 in connection with Reinhold Schneider's sonnets. Drama is largely excluded from the study since it tended to be more conformist than other genres, it was subjected to stricter controls, and dramatists were fewer in number and less varied in their approach and ideological stance. Nonliterary publicist work and journalism in general, on the other hand, played a significant nonconformist role in the Third Reich and is addressed, where relevant to the work of the writers under discussion, but it too is not a prime concern.

The book is divided into two parts. Part 1 comprises two contextual chapters. The first of these looks at the intellectual and historical background to nonconformist writing, the Nazi system of literary censorship and control, the origins of the term "inner emigration," and its critical reception and evaluation. The second chapter provides short characterizations and evaluations of a varied range of nonconformist writers and offers a categorization of authors based on Grimm's scale or continuum stretching from open resistance to passive refusal;[19] it also considers the options facing writers who wished to publish under National Socialism, the various literary techniques of camouflage they employed, and the problems associated with these. Part 2, the more substantial portion of the book, comprises eight chapters, each of which offers a detailed study of a leading writer. These studies present a cross-section of the inner emigration, to illustrate the diversity within what is often seen as a narrow or undifferentiated grouping. They provide detailed biographical information; chart the various authors' literary development up to, but especially after, 1933; establish the conditions facing them during the Third Reich, in particular the personal implications of National Socialist cultural policy; and trace how their variously national conservative, conservative Christian, or Christian humanist worldview, political orientation, and approach to German history informed their individual oppositional stance. Each chapter also includes a detailed discussion of the context of publication and the critical reception of a key novel, novella, or story by the writer, and offers a fresh close reading of this often neglected text. The order in which authors are presented in part 2 is not intended to indicate any degree or scale of nonconformity but is dictated by the year of publication of the key work discussed in each case.

A first criterion for selection of these detailed textual analyses is that the writer stayed and published in his or her native country, whether Germany or Austria, for a substantial proportion of the Nazi years. A second is that the writer published a work that can be considered to be at variance with and to undermine in some way Nazi orthodoxy or to offer an alternative to the reality of the Third Reich. Third, this had to be a work whose sales figures suggest that, for whatever reason, it caught the public's imagination. These criteria clearly exclude the many oppositional writers who sought exile abroad and individual works whose explicit oppositional content meant they could only be published after 1945—for example, Wiechert's *Der Totenwald* (1946, translated into English in 1947 as *Forest of the Dead*). They also exclude from detailed discussion texts such as Elisabeth Langgässer's *Das unauslöschliche Siegel* (The indelible seal, 1946), which, though written during the Nazi period and very much fitting with the general tenor and approach of inner emigrant literature, could only be published after the war.

While offering a contribution to the inner emigration debate that will be of interest to Germanists, the book is intended to allow non-Germanist readers access to this material too. This has two consequences. First, all terms, titles, and quotations are provided in the original German but are also translated into English. Unless otherwise indicated, translations are my own and provide a working sense of meaning; this means that poems are reproduced in prose form. Published English translations of key primary texts, where available, are indicated at relevant points in the text. Second, I have provided summaries of content for the books discussed in chapters 3 through 10 since none of the texts is likely to be well known to a non-Germanist audience and even Germanists may not be entirely familiar with some of them.

Notes

Epigraph. Heinrich Heine, *Almansor: Eine Tragödie,* in *Heinrich Heine: Historisch-kritische Gesamtausgabe der Werke,* ed. Manfred Windfuhr, vol. 5 (Hamburg: Hoffmann and Campe, 1994), 16.

[1] Carl Zuckmayer, *Geheimreport,* ed. Gunther Nickel and Johanna Schrön (Göttingen: Wallstein, 2002).

2 Erika Mitterer, "'Sie gehören doch auch zu uns. . . .': Zwischen Protest, Mitfühlen und Anpassung—Eine Schriftstellerin erinnert sich an 1938," *Die Presse*, January 30–31, 1988, http://www.erika-mitterer.org/dokumente/mitterer_gehoerenzuuns.pdf (accessed February 20, 2014).

3 Hauptlektorat Schöngeistiges Schrifttum, "Jahresbericht 1940," *Lektoren-Brief* 4, nos. 5–6 (1941): 7, cited in Heidrun Ehrke-Rotermund and Erwin Rotermund, *Zwischenreiche und Gegenwelten: Texte und Vorstudien zur "verdeckten Schreibweise" im "Dritten Reich"* (Munich: Fink, 1999), 14. See also the section "A Watertight System of Control?" in chapter 1 of this book.

4 It is interesting that Benno von Wiese identified this same state of mind in the average citizen under National Socialism, depending on whether they were acting in the private or the public sphere. See Benno von Wiese, "Gegen den Hitler in uns selbst," in *Romane von gestern heute gelesen*, ed. Marcel Reich-Ranicki (Frankfurt am Main: Fischer, 1990), 65.

5 See Ernst Jünger, "Sizilischer Brief an den Mann im Mond," in *Ernst Jünger: Sämtliche Werke*, vol. 9 (Stuttgart: Klett-Cotta, 1978–2003), 22. See also the section "Weimar and Political Publicist Activity" in chapter 8 of this book.

6 Karl-Heinz Schoeps, *Literature and Film in the Third Reich* (Rochester, NY: Camden House, 2004), 4.

7 This term ("das Dritte Reich") reportedly originated in the work of the publicist and early Hitler mentor Dietrich Eckart, although it is most commonly associated with Arthur Moeller van den Bruck's publication of that name. See Claus-Ekkehard Bärsch, *Die politische Religion des Nationalsozialismus: Die religiöse Dimension der NS-Ideologie in den Schriften von Dietrich Eckart, Joseph Goebbels, Alfred Rosenberg und Adolf Hitler* (Munich: Fink, 1998), 50. Although the Nazi government formally withdrew use of the term on July 10, 1939, it is used in this book as shorthand to refer to the whole of 1933–45, as is common in German writing on the period.

8 Neil H. Donahue, "Introduction: 'Coming to Terms with' the German Past," in *Flight of Fantasy: New Perspectives on Inner Emigration in German Literature, 1933–1945*, ed. Neil H. Donahue and Doris Kirchner (New York: Berghahn, 2003), 6.

9 The following is based on larger selections in Wilhelm Haefs, "Einleitung," in *Nationalsozialismus und Exil 1933–1945* (Munich: Carl Hanser, 2009), 48; and Karl-Wolfgang Mirbt, *Methoden publizistischen Widerstandes im Dritten Reich, nachgewiesen an der "Deutschen Rundschau" Rudolf Pechels*, PhD diss., Freie Universität Berlin, 1958, 33–34.

10 Heinz Boberach, ed., *Meldungen aus dem Reich 1938–1945: Die geheimen Lagerberichte des Sicherheitsdienstes der SS* (Herrsching: Pawlak, 1984).

11 A particularly interesting exception is a recent attempt to focus on the similarities of inner emigration and exile by building on the Spanish example of an extended cultural diaspora to posit "inner exile" and territorial exile as "dialectal variations" of a broader oppositional discourse on Nazism. See William J. Dodd, "Dolf Sternberger's *Panorama*: Approaches to a Work of (Inner) Exile in the National Socialist Period," *Modern Language Review* 198, no. 1 (2013): 180–201.

[12] Günter Scholdt, "'Ein Geruch von Blut und Schande': Zur Kritik an dem Begriff und an der Literatur über die Emigranten im Innern," *Wirtschaft und Wissenschaft* 1 (1994): 27.

[13] Hans-Dieter Zimmermann, "'Innere Emigration': Ein historischer Begriff und seine Problematik," in *Schriftsteller im Widerstand: Facetten und Probleme der "Inneren Emigration*," ed. Frank-Lothar Kroll and Rüdiger von Voss (Göttingen: Wallstein, 2012), 60.

[14] See Annette Schmollinger, *"Intra muros et extra": Deutsche Literatur im Exil und in der inneren Emigration: Ein exemplarischer Vergleich* (Heidelberg: Winter, 1999), 62–64.

[15] See Ralf Schnell, *Literarische innere Emigration 1933–1945* (Stuttgart: Metzler, 1976), 4.

[16] These are discussed in greater detail in chapter 4. The various anecdotes and short stories are contained in Stefan Andres, *Stefan Andres: Wir sind Utopia: Prosa aus den Jahren 1933–1945*, ed. Erwin Rotermund, Heidrun Ehrke-Rotermund, with Thomas Hilsheimer (Göttingen: Wallstein, 2010).

[17] See Heidrun Ehrke-Rotermund, "Anekdoten aus den Napoleonischen Kriegen: Zu Stefan Andres' Rezeption von Johann Konrad Friederichs 'Hinterlassenen Papieren eines französisch-preußischen Offiziers' (1848/49)," *Mitteilungen der Stefan-Andres-Gesellschaft* 31 (2010): 26–51.

[18] See, for example, Theodore Ziolkowski, "Form als Protest: Das Sonett in der Literatur des Exils und der Inneren Emigration," in *Exil und innere Emigration: Third Wisconsin Workshop*, ed. Reinhold Grimm and Jost Hermand (Frankfurt am Main: Athenäum, 1972), 153–72; Charles Wesley Hoffmann, *Opposition Poetry in Nazi Germany* (Berkeley: University of California Press, 1962); Glenn R. Cuomo, *Career at the Cost of Compromise: Günter Eich's Life and Work in the Years 1933– 1945* (Amsterdam: Rodopi, 1989); Neil H. Donahue, *Karl Krolow and the Poetics of Amnesia in Postwar Germany* (Rochester, NY: Camden House, 2002), especially 28–33; and Leonard Olschner, "Absences of Time and History: Poetry of Inner Emigration," in Donahue and Kirchner, *Flight of Fantasy*, 131–52.

[19] Reinhold Grimm, "Innere Emigration als Lebensform," in Grimm and Hermand, *Exil und innere Emigration*, 48. See "Critical Reception" in chapter 1 of this book.

Part I

1: Nazi Germany and Literary Nonconformism

THE DEVELOPMENT OF literary nonconformism in the Third Reich needs to be understood particularly in the context of its intellectual roots in the Weimar Republic and of National Socialism's literary policies and organizational structures, which impinged on writers' freedom in different ways. This chapter will consider both these areas before discussing the origins of the term "inner emigration," reviewing the history of its critical reception and evaluating its status as a literary-historical category.

The Intellectual Background

The Conservative Revolution

The intellectual origins of inner emigrant writing are complex, owing not least to the diversity of the writers involved and their varied social, political, and religious backgrounds. This section and the following highlight two key common influences.

The sense of disorientation experienced by many Germans after the First World War gave rise to an intellectual and political movement known as the Conservative Revolution. Although the paradoxical use of the term "conservative" in connection with "revolutionary" can be traced back to the immediate post–World War I period, it became an umbrella term—for, variously, patriotic, nationalist, young conservative, *völkisch* (racist nationalist), and national revolutionary strands of thought—only in the second half of the 1920s. It was made famous by the cultural historian Arthur Moeller van den Bruck's book *Das dritte Reich* (The third empire, 1923) and the writer Hugo von Hofmannsthal's lecture on "Das Schrifttum als geistiger Raum der Nation" (Literature as the spiritual space of the nation, 1927).[1] The other principal figures associated with the movement were the lawyer, politician, and later adviser to Franz von Papen, Edgar Jung, who was subsequently murdered in the so-called Röhm putsch; Hermann Rauschning, a former army officer who was briefly to become an NSDAP (National Socialist German Workers' Party) member but later emigrated to the United States; and the historian and philosopher of history Oswald Spengler, who was initially seen as a potential intellectual collaborator by the Nazis but who had little time for their racial policy. The Conservative Revolution was strongly opposed to all socialist and liberal forms of government and was deeply suspicious of democracy in general. The movement also distanced itself from the internationalist spirit of the Paris Peace Conference of 1919 and the embryonic League of Nations, advocating instead an authoritarian nationalism with pronounced militarist tones. Many of its adherents saw themselves as belonging to a new generation of patriots, and perceived in the war and the November Revolution[2] the opportunity to break completely with the Wilhelmine past and forge a different form of nationalism.[3] Besides rejecting the conservatism of Wilhelmine Germany and the parliamentary democracy of the Weimar Republic (seen as a decadent and alien form of government that had been unjustly imposed on Germany), the intellectuals of the Conservative Revolution sought to address the challenge of socialism by reconceiving it as a racial and ethnic mass movement modeled on the community of the frontline soldier, as part of a broader German *Volksgemeinschaft* (national community) governed by a dictatorial regime, in which the type of military hierarchy established in the First World War would play a prominent role.[4] The Conservative Revolution has come to be seen by historians as a significant factor in preparing the ideological ground for National Socialism.

For Edgar Jung, the Conservative Revolution was less a political ideology than the expression of a whole philosophy of life that sought to reconnect man with God and nature through respect for the basic, "eternal" values and laws required for a lasting social order. This was to be a lengthy transformation, as gradual as the Reformation, rather than a sudden violent eruption like the French Revolution, and it would emanate from Germany, "das biologisch kräftigste Volk Europas" (biologically Europe's strongest nation). He believed it essential to resist the notions of equality and the "massification" of society typical of left-wing revolutions, and argued for a hierarchical social structure, within which strong leadership could be provided through the development of new elites in society.[5] For Arthur Moeller van den Bruck, the Conservative Revolution meant a rejection of the internecine squabbling of the parties in a parliamentary democracy, which he believed merely served to sow discord and instability.[6] The challenge that all proponents of the Conservative Revolution saw facing them was to stem the chaotic tide of modern human affairs, illustrated by Oswald Spengler's *Der Untergang des Abendlandes* (1918, English translation *The Decline of the West*, 1926), and the pernicious effect of the spread of base and immoral "mass-man," as outlined in the influential *La rebelión de las masas* (1930, English translation *The Revolt of the Masses*, 1932) by the Spanish philosopher José Ortega y Gasset. They believed that to attain these goals what Germany needed was a new *Reich* headed by a strong leader, and a social structure based around a hierarchically ordered corporative state in which human happiness was subordinated to the rights and needs of the whole *Volksgemeinschaft*.

Moeller van den Bruck's "third empire" was not, however, the political creation of the Nazis, nor was it just the successor to the Holy Roman and the Bismarck empires. Rather, it was an attempt to bring together revolutionary ideas and the notion of a continually self-renewing conservatism (his conservatism seems to have little to do with a narrowly conceived preservation of the existing or the traditional). It was a *Reich* in which thesis and antithesis of Left and Right, socialism and nationalism, could be overcome and brought together in a final synthesis, and it is significant in this regard that the original title for *Das dritte Reich* was *Der dritte Standpunkt* (The third viewpoint).[7]

Several conservative literary figures who were to go on and write nonconformist works in the Third Reich were influenced by this body of thought, and although none of these writers can be termed Nazis, the similarities between their thinking and some of the *völkisch*-nationalist notions of the new regime now seem considerable, since many of the ideas of the Conservative Revolution were appropriated by National Socialist ideologues. Thus, Christian writers such as Werner Bergengruen, Gertrud von le Fort, and Reinhold Schneider picked up on the specifically Christian nationalism of the likes of the political publicist, Protestant, and anti-Semite Wilhelm Stapel; they came to associate the *Reich* very much with the "Kingdom of God,"[8] and in their fiction duly depicted strong, often autocratic leaders whose actions are motivated by Christian ideals.[9] Although many conservative intellectuals distanced themselves from Hitler, they still adhered to the notion of a "strong leader" who would help Germany achieve a fundamental change of direction, but neither this nor the utopian concept of the *Reich* should be equated with the way these ideals were realized politically under National Socialism.

Inwardness

One of the most striking and also controversial aspects of nonconformist writing published in Nazi Germany is that, besides conveying dissident content, most works also displayed features that were at best ambiguous and lent themselves to a conformist reading or interpretation. On the one hand, this can be explained by the requirements of camouflaged writing, the need to overcome the barriers to publication presented by Nazi censorship by targeting (veiled) critical messages at an initiated readership, while simultaneously offering an uninitiated and potentially resistant readership the opportunity of a more conformist interpretation. (These ideas are discussed more fully in chapter 2.) On the other hand, and notwithstanding this pragmatic, tactical explanation for the works' ambiguity, it is also the case that fundamental to the inner emigrant mindset was the traditional bourgeois adherence to *Innerlichkeit* (inwardness), a tradition that played a fateful role in both the demise of the Weimar Republic and the rise of National Socialism.

Inwardness has deep roots in German history and can be viewed from two perspectives. First, the historically disenfranchised German middle classes derived their humanist ideals from the Enlightenment and classicism; however, lacking any political dimension, these ideals served the cultivation of an inward-looking mentality that led to a separation of humanity from historical reality, of the private from the political, resulting in the split between *Geist* (thought/spirit) and *Tat* (action) that the writer Heinrich Mann was later to argue against.[10] This inwardness came in due course to be accepted as a norm or model of existence. Second, one can seek an explanation in Luther's teaching. Lutheran morality knows no absolute human right to resist. The key text of Romans 13:1–2 exercises an almost debilitating influence here: "Let everyone be subject to the governing authorities, for there is no authority except that which God has established. The authorities that exist have been established by God. Consequently, whoever rebels against the authority is rebelling against what God has instituted, and those who do so will bring judgment on themselves."[11] Luther's interpretation of these verses and the lesson of the two realms or kingdoms, with its insistence on obedience even to a social or political order to which one is opposed, constitutes a potential ideological basis of inner emigration. Inwardness as "a way of life" for inner emigrants, as formulated by critics in the early 1970s, is held responsible for producing in many Germans a sort of double life.[12] Grimm sees the absence in Lutheran belief of any right to resist as having a paralyzing effect and by way of example draws attention to the characteristic affirmation of the Protestant inner emigrant writer and journalist Jochen Klepper: "Es bleibt bei Römer 13, dem Gehorsam gegen eine mir auch noch so entgegengesetzte Obrigkeit" (Romans 13 remains valid: obedience to an authority no matter how opposed I am to it).[13]

The embodiment of this inwardness can be seen in the existence led by the central characters in the "Rautenklause" (Rue retreat) in Ernst Jünger's *Auf den Marmorklippen* (1939, translated into English in 1947 as *On the Marble Cliffs*). It is also reflected in the title of Ernst Wiechert's novel *Das einfache Leben* (1939, translated into English in 1954 as *The Simple Life*), a work dominated by the images of the island and the asylum as places in which to find refuge from the world. In Erika Mitterer's *Der Fürst der Welt* (1940, translated into English in 2004 as *The Prince of Darkness*), the circle of enlightened thinkers in Nuremberg similarly constitutes for Dr. Fabri a welcome escape to the world of the intellect. Whereas in Stefan Andres's *Wir sind Utopia* (1942, translated into English in 1950 as *We Are God's Utopia*) one finds the escapist "Insel der Acht Seligkeiten" (island of the eight beatitudes), here, however, ultimately criticized as an *inappropriate* flight from the affairs of the world.

Instructive though these thoughts on inwardness are, however, not all writers of the inner emigration were primarily religiously motivated, and they certainly did not all share Klepper's authoritarian fixation. We would also do well to heed Schnell's words of warning that it is dangerous to posit inwardness as a universal phenomenon, to ignore the specific historical circumstances of the Third Reich, or to equate these with Luther's interpretation of the biblical source.[14] Although clearly relevant to inner emigration, the generalizing tendency evident in Grimm's analysis of inwardness does little to help us understand the *function* of literary works in Nazi society; for this, close attention to writers' biographies, their relationship with the Nazi state, the development of their ideas, and the background and reception of their individual works is essential.

The Literary-Historical Background

Gleichschaltung in the Literary Field

Following Hitler's appointment as chancellor on January 30, 1933, one of the top priorities for the new regime was the *Gleichschaltung*, or enforced conformity, to be imposed on all areas of political and cultural life. As far as literary life was concerned, laws passed in the early weeks of the regime began the process of exercising control over all writing published in Germany. The "Verordnung des Reichspräsidenten zum Schutz von Volk und Staat" (Decree of the *Reich* President on the Protection of People and State) of February 28 effectively abolished all constitutional rights; with regard to literature specifically, it proscribed all Marxist writings and arranged for their removal from bookshops and libraries. Later, in September 1933, the law establishing the Reichskulturkammer (Chamber of Culture) and the "Gesetz zum Schutze des deutschen Blutes und der deutschen Ehre" (Law to Protect German Blood and Honor) were enacted. These laws banned writings by Jewish authors and brought all other writers, publishers, booksellers, and librarians under state control.

In the wake of the Reichstag fire on February 27, 1933 and the decree of February 28, writers became caught up in the more general wave of arrests of left-wing opponents of the regime; this included the likes of Willi Bredel, later editor of the exile journal *Das Wort*; the pacifist essayist and journalist Kurt Hiller; the communist and Berlin-based Czech journalist and writer Egon Erwin Kisch; the anarchist and anti-militarist writer Erich Mühsam, who died in Oranienburg concentration camp a year later; Carl von Ossietzky, editor of the journal *Die Weltbühne*; and the writers and Communist Party members Ludwig Renn, who later escaped to Spain, and Anna Seghers, who fled to France.[15] Within the first two months of the regime several writers opted for exile, realizing they had no future under National Socialist rule; these included

the poet and playwright Bertolt Brecht, the novelist and author of
Berlin Alexanderplatz (1929) Alfred Döblin, the novelist and dramatist
Hermann Kesten, the actress and writer Erika Mann and her novelist
brother Klaus, as well as Arnold Zweig, best known for his cycle of anti-
war novels. In addition, Germany's most famous Nobel Prize-winning
writer, Thomas Mann, took up residence in Sanary-sur-Mer in the south
of France before moving to Switzerland and subsequently, in 1938, the
United States. It is estimated that within just the first few months of the
regime, over a thousand writers left Germany, including almost all the
internationally known ones.[16]

As a further aspect of this "cleansing" of cultural life, Education
Minister Bernhard Rust oversaw the restructuring of the Prussian
Academy of the Arts, which led, in the literature section (Sektion
Dichtkunst), to a large number of members leaving the Academy, includ-
ing Thomas Mann, the writer and historian Ricarda Huch (in protest
against the exclusion of Alfred Döblin), the pacifist writer Leonhard
Frank, the leading Expressionist dramatist Georg Kaiser, Heinrich Mann
(the former president of the section, ousted for allegedly abusing his
role for political purposes), the Austrian Expressionist Franz Werfel, the
German-French writer and essayist René Schickele, the Expressionist dramatist Fritz von Unruh, and the Jewish novelist Jakob Wassermann.[17]
The election in their place of Nazi-friendly *völkisch* writers—such as
Werner Beumelburg, Hans Friedrich Blunck, Paul Ernst, Hans Grimm,
Hanns Johst, Erwin Guido Kolbenheyer, Agnes Miegel, Wilhelm Schäfer,
Emil Strauß, and Will Vesper—reflected the strategy of neutralizing exist-
ing bodies by removing from them political opponents of the regime,
while simultaneously creating parallel state or party bodies invested with
greater powers (in this case, the Reichsschrifttumskammer, Chamber of
Literature, or RSK).[18]

The Schutzverband deutscher Schriftsteller (Association for the
Protection of German Writers) was the leading writers' organization in
the Weimar Republic and had been established in 1909 to defend writers
from state interference in their work. In spring 1933, its leadership also
fell victim to enforced restructuring. On Goebbels's orders, in June 1933,
it and other literary associations then became part of a new Reichsverband
Deutscher Schriftsteller (National Association of German Writers), which,
in contrast to its forerunners, was designed as an organization in which
membership was compulsory for those hoping to publish in Germany,
a permission-to-practice principle that served as one of the cornerstones
of the legislation on the creation of a Reich Chamber of Culture.[19]
Thereafter the National Association became an insignificant player in
the literary landscape of the Third Reich, and in September 1935 the
Propaganda Ministry and the RSK brought about its dissolution, its
twelve thousand members becoming direct members of the RSK.[20]

The German section of PEN, the international writers' organization, also fell victim to Nazi interference. Its president, the theater critic and dramatist Alfred Kerr, went into exile in February 1933, and the subsequent withdrawal of other members of its board gave rise to heated debates about the future of the section, as Nazi cultural officials sought to make use of the group to promote German foreign-policy goals. After Germany's withdrawal from the League of Nations in October 1933, the new board issued a public declaration of loyalty to Hitler, followed on November 18 by the section's withdrawal from International PEN. The German PEN section was subsequently reformed in January 1934 as the Union Nationaler Schriftsteller (Union of Nationalist Writers) with an anticommunist, nationalist, and racist agenda and with Hanns Johst as president and Gottfried Benn, a subsequent inner emigrant, as his deputy.[21]

The first major public act in the sphere of culture was the burning of books on May 10, 1933. The ritual was the same at all German universities and was organized by the Deutsche Studentenschaft (German Students' Union), a body founded in 1919, which throughout its history had been anti-Semitic and reactionary. The Union's use of the term "auto-da-fé" was intended to act as a reminder of the act of public penance—in its most extreme form, execution by burning—imposed on heretics and other sinners by the Catholic Spanish and Portuguese Inquisitions from the fifteenth to the eighteenth centuries, while the burning of books rested on a long tradition dating back at least to Roman times. By way of preparation, on April 12, students put up posters containing twelve theses entitled "Wider den Undeutschen Geist" (Against the un-German spirit)—an act modeled on Luther's historic nailing of his ninety-five theses on the door of the Schloßkirche in Wittenberg in 1517—which were also published in several newspapers. The main thrust of them was that literature should be exclusively German, meaning the exclusion of all foreign elements, especially Jewish ones; intellectualism and liberal decadence were condemned; and universities were to be the exclusive preserve of German students and German staff.[22] "Un-German" books were to be removed from libraries and bookshops; indeed shortly before the burnings, newspapers had begun to publish lists of specific books that deserved to be destroyed. At each of the burnings around the country, so-called *Feuersprüche* (fire oaths) were read out, which condemned authors considered enemies of the *Volksgemeinschaft*.[23] Among the hundreds of writers whose work was destroyed, the most famous were Bertolt Brecht, Alfred Döblin, Siegmund Freud, Heinrich Mann, Erich Maria Remarque, Kurt Tucholsky, and Stefan Zweig. The whole nation was to be made aware of the significance of the event and, to this end, radio, film, and all other forms of propaganda were employed. However, the Propaganda Ministry was also keen to ensure it retained overall control of the situation and, in collaboration with the professional organization of the book trade, the Börsenverein der deutschen Buchhändler (German Booksellers and Publishers Association), it sought a more coordinated and regulated attack on "un-German" writing. This put an end to the students' involvement in Nazi literary policy, and in due course the first *official*, regularly updated blacklists of books to be removed from libraries began to appear.[24] Such targeted "cleansing" of libraries resulted in some losing up to half their holdings.[25]

Nazi Literary Ideals

Like National Socialism itself, Nazi literature was not a coherent, clearly definable, and self-contained phenomenon but rather a loose combination of different ideological strands, including *völkisch* and anti-Semitic influences, national conservative and social revolutionary ideas, and anti-democratic and anticapitalist resentment.[26] The one common aim for Nazi literary authorities was the elimination of all left-wing, Jewish, democratic literature and the concomitant aspiration to clear the way for a racially and biologically based literature that would serve the Nazi cause.

Nazi literary historians and censors tended to divide writers simplistically into two camps: those friendly to the regime and those not. Books were also largely judged by the extent to which they could be used as weapons in the regime's propaganda battle, as a training instrument serving Nazi ideology. This meant support for themes such as struggle, sacrifice, blood, the soil, race, and the Führer; it also meant approval of what was healthy, ethnic, heroic, instinctive, and the harmonious organic *Volksgemeinschaft*, which united bourgeois, peasant, and worker. At the same time, it meant disapproval and rejection of the intellectual, rootless, skeptical, ironic, and divisive culture of the big city with its supposed connotations of disease and decay, and its literature, which was associated with weak or sickly heroes, psychologization of characters, class conflict, and a tendency toward experimentation with literary form.[27]

A typical view from 1933 onward was that there was, on the one hand, an "official" literature of the middle classes ranging across a political spectrum from communism to social democracy; this was a false literature of psychology, analysis, and eroticism, a literature concentrating on problems that had no real life outside of magazines with aesthetic pretensions. On the other hand, there was the real, truly German literature, firmly rooted in the localities and everyday concerns of average Germans. If names such as Erich Maria Remarque, Lion Feuchtwanger, Heinrich Mann, and Arnold Zweig were associated with the first type, then the second was represented by little-known figures such as Paul Ernst, Hans Grimm, Will Vesper, and Agnes Miegel, who often lived in the provinces, far removed from the literary cliques of the big city, and who concerned themselves with themes that were largely alien to mainstream Weimar literature.

National Socialism tried to show its line of descent through German intellectual history, and literary historians were encouraged to reshape literary history and identify some of Nazism's roots in German romanticism, for example, the poet and nationalist Ernst Moritz Arndt, the influential lyric poet Friedrich Hölderlin, and in Weimar classicism, Goethe and Schiller, especially for a while *Wilhelm Tell* (1804), which was seen as a drama of national liberation, although it was later banned since it deals with the murder of a tyrant.[28] The nineteenth-century dramatist Christian Dietrich Grabbe was seen as a key figure because his work dealt with the problematic relationship between leader and people (and his occasional anti-Semitic utterances no doubt also helped in identifying a kindred spirit). The dramatist and poet Friedrich Hebbel was considered a Nordic figure who developed Germanic themes such as the *Nibelungen*. Richard Wagner was celebrated for both his treatment of Germanic mythology and his anti-Semitic writings. Among the antiliberal philosophers and thinkers who could be linked with the nationalist cause was above all Nietzsche (although selectively, in view of his criticism of German culture and admiration for the French). Other less well-known influences were the French aristocrat and man of letters Joseph Arthur Gobineau, especially for his anti-Semitic *Essai sur l'inégalité des races humaines* (Essay on the inequality of the human races, 1853), or the English political philosopher and later son-in-law of Wagner, Houston Stewart Chamberlain, who wrote the highly popular and influential *Die Grundlagen des neunzehnten Jahrhunderts* (1899, translated into English in 1911 as *The Foundations of the Nineteenth Century*).[29]

One of the great enemies for Nazi literary commentators was naturalism, whose representatives were said to be good only at being negative, accusing, and criticizing: they offered no ideals, there were no heroes in their works, and they had nothing positive to offer, no hope for the future. True German art could never be naturalistic, as this was seen as the literary expression of the positivistic, rationalist age, which made it prone to "Jewish intellectualism." Furthermore, although many Nazi literary figures saw themselves as part of a cultural revolution and some were tempted to align themselves with the radical avant-garde, embracing modernism in general and expressionism in particular (the latter being supported by Goebbels as a potentially Germanic art form), cultural modernity was eventually denounced in strong terms by Hitler at the Party Congress in September 1934.[30] After this, *völkisch* elements in the party dominated literary developments.

The requirement to portray in literature "gesundes Volkstum" (healthy national traditions) gave rise to, in particular, historical writing based on *völkisch* blood-and-soil mysticism, nationalistic war novels, self-sacrificial heroism, and of course the cult of the strong leader.[31] Officially sanctioned literature came to involve regression into biological and mythical areas, a focus on the local, on the village and the community, and the lot of the honest German farmer, worker, and mother. A representative sample of headings in two standard literary works of the time illustrates the new literary norms: "The front soldier as leader and comrade," "The village," "The farmers' struggle for existence," "The honor of work," "Toward a new image of the Reich," "Hitler's Reich," "The image of wife and mother," "German farmers," "People and poets," "German workers," "The new way of life of the German people."[32] At the same time, although literary handbooks and histories were clear about their rejection of Jewish and communist writers, there was inconsistency in identifying what should be considered the Nazi literary canon and precisely which "Nazi writers" were to be promoted. Thus, Ketelsen's review of ten literary histories of the time shows that of the total of about two thousand writers mentioned, only twenty-five appear in all ten books.[33]

The Regulation of Literature in Nazi Germany

The new Nazi state had a tendency to create huge bureaucratic organizations and in its first two years in power it proceeded to deprive the *Länder* of their traditional sovereignty in cultural matters, to centralize control so as to turn culture into a weapon to further national identity and coherence, and to promote German racial purity. There were four major bodies whose work impinged on the activity of writers.

Reich Ministry of Public Enlightenment and Propaganda

Following a decree issued by President Hindenburg on March 13, 1933, Joseph Goebbels was appointed Reichsminister für Volksaufklärung und Propaganda (Reich Minister of Public Enlightenment and Propaganda) and charged with establishing what was to become the most influential and powerful body within Nazi literary policy, the Ministry of Propaganda. According to a further decree issued by Hitler on June 30, the ministry assumed responsibility for news coverage, information at home and abroad, the press, radio, advertising, film, national holidays, and for counteracting "harmful" writing.[34] The ministry consisted initially of seven departments, rising to seventeen by 1943, and its power and reach were further enhanced by the introduction of Landesstellen (regional offices) in the thirty-one NSDAP Gaus (Nazi administrative regions of government), which, from September 1933, were called Reichspropagandaämter (Reich Propaganda Offices).[35] A key first step in establishing the ministry's authority was taken at the end of June when the existing national departments for various spheres of culture were ordered by the chancellor to pass on a range of responsibilities, including those for radio, the press, theater, film, and literature. With this legal basis and with the income from radio, over which the state had a monopoly, Goebbels was subsequently able to build a ministry that eventually employed more than five hundred people and, by 1939, had a budget of 97 million Reichsmark.

Department VIII of the ministry was entitled Schrifttum (Literature), also known as Schrifttumsabteilung (Literature Department). It was only established in October 1934 and developed out of the existing section for literature and publishing in the Propaganda Department. It had responsibility for overseeing all literature written in the German language, both at home and abroad, as well as for publishers, the book trade, and libraries. After several years of territorial disputes with other agencies, in 1942, under the leadership of Wilhelm Haegert, the department eventually managed to centralize all censorship by bringing it under its control, and during wartime assumed responsibility for the crucial issue of paper supplies to publishers. Besides limiting the spread of publications deemed "unerwünscht" (undesirable), the ministry was also keen to promote select groups of writers loyal to the regime and to deploy them to further the aims of the Nazi state. Thus the department sent writers on lecture tours and organized the so-called Weimarer Dichtertreffen (Weimar Writers' Meetings), which, as invitation-only events, were almost only ever attended by writers loyal to the regime and were designed to lay down literary guidelines that conformed with Nazi aims and thus to exercise control over writers.[36]

Reich Chamber of Culture and Reich Chamber of Literature

Another important cultural body, also associated with the name of Goebbels, was the Reichskulturkammer (Reich Chamber of Culture, or RKK). The RKK was created by a law passed on September 22, 1933, following Goebbels's proposal to bring together all cultural professions under one organizational roof in an institution that would look after the interests of artists, writers, and performers; Goebbels became its president. The aim was to place all cultural activities at the service of the nation; the artist thereby was given a political task. Based in Berlin, it consisted of seven separate chambers for the press, radio, theater, music, film, fine arts, and literature. Membership, with an appropriate fee, was compulsory for all those wishing to ply their trade in one of the seven areas, and all applicants had to commit themselves to serving the Nazi state. When deciding on accepting or rejecting someone for membership, the presidents of the individual chambers had to make their decision on the basis of a person's reliability and suitability. If anyone was unable to produce proof of Aryan descent (a so-called *Ariernachweis*), they were either not admitted or, if already members, they were excluded from the particular chamber. This was effectively a ban on trade, which affected, above all, Jewish artists, writers, and actors, as well as those who were "jüdisch versippt" (denoting an unspecified relationship to a Jewish person, for example, a Jewish spouse). After the passing of the Nuremberg Race Laws in September 1935, Hans Hinkel of the Propaganda Ministry issued guidelines in April 1936 that clarified and extended these rules, stating that the ban on membership would henceforth apply to all "full, three-quarters, half, and quarter Jews" who were married to a "full, three-quarter, half, or quarter" Jew.[37] Besides deciding on membership, the chambers' presidents also had the power to lay down conditions for the running of cultural enterprises, to influence agreements on employment and social aspects of cultural activities in their field, to impose penalties on members in contravention of the RKK rules, and to involve the police authorities where they saw fit.

In an order of November 1, 1933 on the implementation of the RKK, the recently created Reichsverband Deutscher Schriftsteller (National Association of German Writers) was declared a public body and became a subsection of the Reichsschrifttumskammer (RSK) with the role of regulating and surveying literary activity. The Börsenverein, the book trade association, was also integrated into the RSK. The new president of this chamber was the writer Hans Friedrich Blunck (succeeded in 1935 by the dramatist and writer Hanns Johst). Significantly, its vice president was Dr. Heinz Wismann, an employee of the Propaganda Ministry and soon to be head of the latter's Department VIII (Literature), whose role was, among other things, to ensure a meshing of chamber and ministry policies.[38] This use of members of the most important state and party monitoring bodies in the leadership of the various chambers was a significant factor in bringing together state and party in the area of cultural leadership.[39] The RSK was responsible for producing the important lists of harmful and undesirable writing ("Listen des schädlichen und unerwünschten Schrifttums") based on the Propaganda Ministry's censorship decisions, but it also published a number of journals such as *Das Börsenblatt für den deutschen Buchhandel* (Journal for the German Book Trade) and *Der deutsche Schriftsteller* (The German Writer). Although membership in the RSK was essential for a writer to be published, there were exceptions in the form of a special permit, which could be issued by Goebbels for the publication of individual works by writers or other artists who were not members of their respective chamber.

Reich Office for the Promotion of German Writing

Alfred Rosenberg had become an important figure in Germany thanks to the publication of his *Mythus des 20. Jahrhunderts* (The myth of the twentieth century, 1930).[40] He belonged to the *völkisch* wing of the party and wanted literature to become a means of developing *völkisch* nationalist ideology, in contrast to Goebbels, who preferred other means of propaganda and saw literature more as entertainment and representative art.[41] In a decree of January 24, 1934, Hitler entrusted Rosenberg, as Beauftragter des Führers für die gesamte geistige und weltanschauliche Erziehung der NSDAP (Head of All Intellectual and Ideological Education for the Nazi Party), with leadership of the Reichsstelle zur Förderung des deutschen Schrifttums (Reich Office for the Promotion of German Writing—hereafter "Reichsstelle").[42] The Reichsstelle, which arose out of Rosenberg's nationalistic, anti-Semitic Kampfbund für deutsche Kultur (Militant League for German Culture) established in 1929,[43] was the most important and the largest of all the state and party organizations but, unlike the Ministry and the Party Inspection Commission, or PPK (see below), it had no powers of censorship and could not independently ban any publications. Nevertheless, through it Rosenberg sought to exert an authority over the party that was equal to that of Goebbels's Propaganda Ministry over the state sector. The role of the Reichsstelle was to scrutinize the whole of German culture to see that it conformed with official ideology and to work to disseminate Nazi thought throughout both the party and public life, ensuring uniform ideological development of the German people.[44] This brief inevitably meant that the Reichsstelle found itself at times in direct competition with the PPK. The absence of "real teeth" in the sense of censorship powers also meant its negative verdicts sometimes led nowhere since it was entirely dependent on the Propaganda Ministry for ultimate action.[45]

The Reichsstelle originally had four departments, of which the most important in literary matters was the Hauptstelle Schrifttumspflege (Main Office for the Cultivation of Literature), headed by Hans Hagemayer; in April 1936 this became the Amt Schrifttumspflege and then, in 1941, Hauptamt Schrifttumspflege. In due course Rosenberg formally put the whole Reichsstelle under the jurisdiction of this department, and Reichsstelle and Amt effectively became identical under the leadership of Hagemayer. By 1941, the Amt Schrifttumspflege had one Reichsamt (national office), four main offices, twenty-one offices, and one auxiliary office.[46] The bulk of the monitoring was performed by a team of full-time and honorary editors; in 1934, Rosenberg's office had twenty senior and four hundred junior editors; by 1941 the respective numbers were fifty and fourteen hundred.[47] Almost no book could be published in Germany between 1933 and 1945 if it had not been checked by Rosenberg's experts. This is clearly a major factor when we are considering what constituted "oppositional" writing under National Socialism and the possibilities of free literary expression in general.

After the initial period in which the Reichsstelle was concerned with suppressing literature, its machinery was intended not just to filter out undesirable publications but also to promote more "positive" writing. The Reichsstelle published the fortnightly and monthly journal *Bücherkunde*, which reported on the results of its examination of new publications and indicated those that were to be promoted and those deemed undesirable.[48] It also published an annual *Jahres-Gutachtenanzeiger*, for each of the years 1936–41, which presented alphabetical listings of all the publications reviewed over the year, both the positive and the negative. Through its extensive reach and this thorough system of review and recommendation, the Reichsstelle sought to compensate for its inability to issue actual bans on publications.

Party Inspection Commission

The Parteiamtliche Prüfungskommission (Party Inspection Commission, or PPK) under the direction of Philipp Bouhler, formerly senior leader (Reichsleiter) of the NSDAP and the head of the Chancellery of the Führer, was set up in April 1934 following a decree issued on March 15 of that year by Deputy Führer Rudolf Heß. The Nazi leadership's aim here was in part to limit the influence of Rosenberg's Reichsstelle,[49] and the PPK gradually extended its original brief and sphere of influence to cover all writings in Nazi Germany. By concluding work agreements with other party offices and centers of power, especially with Department VIII in Goebbels's Propaganda Ministry and with the Ministry of Science, Education, and National Culture (Reichsministerium für Wissenschaft, Erziehung und Volksbildung) headed by the zealous Nazi Bernhard Rust,[50] Bouhler managed by the outbreak of war to build up a huge bureaucracy devoted to the monitoring of writing and to secure considerable influence over the shaping of literary policy, becoming the second most significant authority of ideological control after the Propaganda Ministry. Rosenberg's office was outflanked by the two censorship bodies of state and party, and thus lost a lot of its power.

The PPK had the principal tasks of examining the party's philosophical and political publications in order to eliminate ideological misconceptions, and of compiling the party index and a National Socialist bibliography.[51] In its publications, it listed only those party literature titles that were to be recommended—unlike the more comprehensive Rosenberg publications. It also had to check all academic publications, including schoolbooks, fiction, journal, and newspaper articles, to make sure Nazi ideology was properly and forcefully presented in them. By June 1938 it had to approve in advance of publication all manuscripts containing extracts from Hitler's speeches or from *Mein Kampf*.[52] In general, the PPK undertook systematic examination of the book market, independently of the Propaganda Ministry and the Reichsstelle, and made increasing use of its power of censorship to ban publications. This involved both postpublication censorship, whereby the PPK could instruct the Gestapo to confiscate all published copies of works identified as problematic, and prepublication or preventative censorship through the requirement that all publications related to the NSDAP be approved by the PPK in advance of publication.

A Watertight System of Control?

The overall aim of *Gleichschaltung* of these various organizations' activities was to ensure that all aspects of cultural activity served to further the cause of National Socialism. This comprehensive coverage of cultural production was to be achieved by a variety of methods. In the case of writers it involved: outright bans on those deemed to be incompatible with Nazi ideals; repressive censorship in the shape of compulsory membership of the RSK to prevent other undesirable writers from publishing; prepublication censorship of particular book types and certain authors; comprehensive postpublication censorship to prevent the distribution of preexisting "harmful" writing; the use of propaganda and publicity; control of publishing houses, which were expected to seek prepublication approval from state or party censors for any works of uncertain ideological content; the maintenance of indexes of prohibited and permitted books; and regulation of paper supplies.[53] In addition, from November 1936, book reviews were regulated, with reviewers required to limit themselves to a summary of content and a summative recommendation, thereby eschewing aesthetic judgments and restricting themselves to an assessment of ideological content.[54] These controls and checks applied to all writers, publishers, booksellers, and librarians. Once the hated Jews, cultural Bolshevists, modernists, political turncoats, and opportunists had been removed, the way was to be clear for the creation of a new literature, one suited to the aspirations of the new Germany; and writers, in particular, were to be frontline fighters for this new Reich.

Any writer who wished to join the RSK had to undergo a bureaucratic procedure, which demanded exact information about the applicant's political past, racial origins, publications, and income. In addition, two guarantors had to be named who could testify to the character and the political reliability of the person as well as his or her professional suitability. From 1935, the RSK demanded from its members and their spouses an *Ariernachweis* dating back to 1800, leading to a sharp increase in the number of "problem cases." From April 1938, membership became an even more complex process with the requirement of a "politisches Führungszeugnis" (certificate of political good conduct) from the regional (Gau) leadership of the party. If this raised any doubts about political reliability, then reports were requested from the Gestapo or the Sicherheitsdienst (or SD, the intelligence services of the SS and the

Nazi Party).[55] The consequence of this new process was that the Gestapo, the SD, and the party organization at regional and local levels began to regularly monitor writers in their sphere of influence. Writers therefore lived in a constant state of uncertainty as a result of the combined effects of exclusion from the RSK,[56] outright bans on books by the Ministry of Propaganda, confiscation of material by the Gestapo, and instances of NSDAP groups intervening to get individual books banned or rewritten. After the start of the war this climate of profound uncertainty and fear became noticeably worse.

It might be thought, in view of this substantial state and party system of control, that writers in Nazi Germany were left powerless and unable to publish anything other than the most strictly conformist texts. This would be wrong, however. The confusion that reigned in the field of literary policy as a result of competing offices and overlapping competences meant that the apparently all-embracing system of monitoring and control was not as reliable or as faultless as it might appear, at least up until 1938 during the lengthy consolidation phase of state and party control. Indeed, even in that year, Hitler noted at the Party Congress that the regulation of culture in the Third Reich lagged a long way behind that of political, social, and economic spheres of life.[57] Only in 1938, for example, was a clear division made between the relative areas of competence of the Schrifttumsabteilung and the RSK. And, in view of competing activities in the Ministry of Education, PPK, Reichsstelle, Deutsche Arbeitsfront (German Labor Front), SD, NS-Lehrerbund (the National Socialist Teachers' Association), Reichsjugendführung (the Leadership of the Hitler-Jugend), and office of the Reichsleiter für die Presse der NSDAP (Head of the Nazi Press and thus also Head of the Press Chamber, Max Amann), it never proved possible to centralize completely responsibilities for literary matters and to provide a uniform direction for literary policy.[58] The various state and party offices competed intensely with one another to extend their area of influence, a situation not helped by the fact that Hitler reserved the power to make final decisions, denying any one cultural body the right to become sole arbiter.[59] The lack of clarity in the division of responsibilities for literary policy, especially between state and party offices, contributed to a confusing and excessively bureaucratized network of supervision and control.

This is seen especially in the area of censorship. Even after a clear division of competences had been established between the ministry and the PPK, there was much confusion surrounding the RSK-administered list of harmful and undesirable writing, which was the responsibility of nonspecialists and contained numerous inaccuracies. This situation was only improved when responsibility for censorship passed to the Literature Department of the ministry, and specialists in the Deutsche Bücherei (German Library) in Leipzig took over the processing of the banned list.[60]

Nazi control of writing and publication was undermined not just by such lack of clarity over areas of competence and censorship but also by the structure and nature of the book market. The Nazis left German publishing largely in the hands of private publishing houses[61] (in part to retain the myth of a system free from state control), which allowed individuals such as Peter Suhrkamp, editor of the journal *Die Neue Rundschau* and, from 1936, head of the now split publishing company S. Fischer Verlag,[62] to publish works that did not conform to Nazi ideals. Even publishers who had been brought under Nazi control were able to publish texts with nonconformist content; for example, Langen-Müller and the Hanseatische Verlagsanstalt were both controlled by the Deutsche Arbeitsfront, and yet the former still published Ernst Wiechert's *Das einfache Leben* (1939, translated into English in 1954 as *The Simple Life*) and the latter Werner Bergengruen's *Der Großtyrann und das Gericht* (The great tyrant and the court, 1935), Bergengruen's *Am Himmel wie auf Erden* (In heaven as on earth, 1940), and Ernst Jünger's *Auf den Marmorklippen* (1939, translated into English in 1947 as *On the Marble Cliffs*), while the reformed (that is, aryanized) Paul Zsolnay Verlag published Frank Thiess's novel *Das Reich der Dämonen* (The empire of demons, 1941). Other publishers of non-Nazi, nonconformist, and undesirable literature included the Deutsche Verlags-Anstalt, Diederichs, Goverts, Insel, List, Kösel & Pustet, Piper, Rowohlt, and Schünemann.[63]

Monitoring was also far from complete or foolproof. Owing to a lack of personnel and inadequate organizational structures, comprehensive precensoring of the enormous German nonpolitical book production industry simply was not possible, with the result that numerous narrative works, poetry collections, and essay volumes but also philosophical, theological, and historical works, which did not in any way conform to the spirit of National Socialism, could be freely published. Meanwhile the editorial scrutiny of newspapers and journals was also not as stringent as might have been expected, often as a result of such mundane facts as workload and delegation to less experienced or more sympathetic subordinates.[64] To take just one example of a book publication, the decision to allow Stefan Andres's *Wir sind Utopia*—first serialized in the *Frankfurter Zeitung* in 1942—to be published in 1943 by Riemerschmidt was made by junior censors on the pretext or in the belief that the novella represented an attack on communism; it has been claimed that, later, when a more senior official examined the work, now already published in book form, it was banned and all copies were withdrawn.[65]

It is significant in this connection that as late as 1940, in its annual report on, inter alia, new publications, the Hauptlektorat Schöngeistiges Schrifttum (Main Editorial Office for Belletristic Writing) in Rosenberg's Reichsstelle should be showing concern about a "literary clique," whose ideals had nothing to do with Nazi *völkisch* ideals but harked back to the literary world of the Weimar Republic. It expressed surprise at the popularity of these "Zwischenreichautoren" (authors of an intermediate realm), including Stefan Andres, Werner Bergengruen, Horst Lange, and Wolfgang Weyrauch, and at the unduly positive reviews of their work in the press, including Nazi publications.[66]

Writers were able to benefit from this combination of institutional overlap and lack of uniformity and consistency in the application of literary policy. Provided a writer did not indulge in open criticism of the Nazi state or the NSDAP, it was possible to find various niches ("Freiräume," free spaces) and to exploit weaknesses in the system. Thus, although Jewish and "half-Jewish" writers were ruthlessly excluded from the RSK, many others who had been known for their modernist, especially Expressionist, work or for left-wing views were still able to gain membership in the Chamber of Literature and to publish their writing—for example, Erich Kästner, Ernst Glaeser, and Arnolt Bronnen, who had all been viewed with suspicion in 1933 because of their left-wing affiliations in the Weimar Republic but who were given various special dispensations to write and publish in Nazi Germany.[67] Similarly, a writer and actor such as Günther Weisenborn, a noted communist sympathizer and resistance fighter, became a member of the RSK in 1933 and up to 1942 was able to lead a secret double life.[68] Moreover, as studies of authors with books on the official index show, the banning of one or more books did not necessarily lead to exclusion from the RSK.[69] The state bureaucracy applied postpublication censorship in many cases less rigidly than party offices wished; thus, the administration of the RSK did not always exclude writers on the basis of negative reports from the Gestapo, SD, or party offices, which frequently led to heated disputes between the state authority and the latter.[70]

Even when writers had been excluded from the RSK, it was sometimes still possible for them to publish their work, thanks to a so-called "Sondergenehmigung" (special permission), which had to be issued by the Propaganda Ministry and signed off by Goebbels himself. According to an RSK list prepared for the Propaganda Ministry in September 1938, the number of such special permissions had risen to thirty-four.[71] This applied, for example, to Jochen Klepper, who, despite having a Jewish wife, was granted permission to publish, no doubt in part because his successful novel *Der Vater* (The father, 1937) had been positively reviewed in Nazi newspapers.[72] Special permission was also granted to Bergengruen, who was married to a "three-quarters" Jew, and to Andres, who was "jüdisch versippt" (related to a Jew) through his half-Jewish wife.[73]

An important "free space" in the system was to be found in journals such as *Das Innere Reich, Deutsche Rundschau, Die Weißen Blätter, Eckart, Europäische Revue, Hochland, Die Neue Rundschau, Stimmen der Zeit,* in magazines such as *Die Dame, Die Neue Linie, Koralle,* and in the newspapers *Berliner Tageblatt, Deutsche Allgemeine Zeitung, Frankfurter Zeitung, Kölnische Zeitung,* and *Münchner Neueste Nachrichten.* Furthermore, publications more known for their *völkisch-*national tendency such as *Das Reich* and, remarkably, the feuilleton section of Nazi papers, such as the official party organ *Völkischer Beobachter* and the paper of the Generalgouvernement in occupied Eastern Europe, the *Krakauer Zeitung,* also allowed oppositionally minded writers space for publication. These were crucial outlets, as they enabled writers to serialize their longer nonconformist works with the agreement of liberal-minded editors, even though in some cases problems were subsequently encountered with censors when an attempt was made to publish the work in book form—for example, Alexander Lernet-Holenia's *Mars im Widder* (Mars in Aries, 1940, 1947), which had first appeared in *Die Dame,* or Andres's *Wir sind Utopia* in the *Frankfurter Zeitung.* Journals and newspapers also provided an important outlet for shorter prose works, poems, and articles. This has been a well-researched area with a range of studies devoted to nonconformist imaginative literature, literary critical work, and journalistic writing.[74]

A factor in the Nazis' decision to tolerate former political opponents and writers who did not seem to conform to the regime's ideological standpoint was the hope that they could act as a form of advertisement to the outside world (an "Aushängeschild"), demonstrating the supposedly generous and broad-minded cultural stance of the Nazi state. This was why such tolerance was shown toward the *Frankfurter Zeitung,* in particular, even though at least some of its subversive tactics were well known to the Propaganda Ministry and to regional censors.[75] In general, in response to criticism from abroad of barbaric behavior, the regime did all it could to present itself as a patron of the arts: books were promoted through prizes and conferences; Goebbels's Ministry set up a National Book and Film Prize; Hitler personally established a National Prize for Arts and Sciences; there were Berlin Book Weeks, and promotion of books reached a climax during the Week of the German Book.[76] This concern for the country's image abroad is also reflected in the decision to keep the contents of the lists of harmful and undesirable writing strictly confidential, after the public fuss caused in the Alsace region when it became known in early 1936 that the work of René Schickele had been placed on the index.[77] In countenancing the publication of strictly non-Nazi writing, the authorities were also pragmatically acknowledging the need to offer the reading public something other than political propaganda or fiction and poetry with Nazi themes. But they were also recognizing that to ban the works of sometimes well-known writers, who had not sought exile, would create a cultural vacuum immediately evident to foreign observers. Furthermore, officials faced the tricky question of how they could justify banning good writing that did not overtly offend against approved political norms, how they could prove

definitively that a work was nonconformist. Effectively what was being created and tolerated was a "politics-free sphere" in the cultural life of the
Third Reich:[78] provided writers and publishers did not overstep the mark,
works of nonconformist content that did not focus on Nazi ideals or the
achievements of the regime were condoned, though this was clearly motivated more by political calculation than benign tolerance. This meant that
writers could exercise veiled opposition, but only within strictly defined
limits, and that published works had to engage in an, at times, ambiguous
discourse that, of course, laid them open to misunderstanding, appropria-
tion, and later charges of conformity. The dynamics of this discourse are
explored in chapter 2.

Inner Emigration

The concept of "inner emigration" is much disputed in the history of
German literature but it is crucial to the self-understanding of nonconformist writers in Nazi Germany. The contradiction contained in the
term—the notion of removing oneself from a country while remaining
inside it—points to the idea of simultaneous spiritual distancing and physical proximity, to the aspiration to retain moral integrity and keep ideals
intact by maintaining a distance from the poisonous ideas and actions of
a surrounding repressive regime. In the context of the Third Reich, the
term "inner emigration" suggests it was possible to stay in Germany and
avoid compromise with and complicity in National Socialism, and that
furthermore a writer could continue to publish work that might be considered a form of dissent from or even opposition to the regime.

Origins and Issues

Far from being a term first used after the war, as many have assumed,
"inner emigration" seems to have been current from as early as 1933,
with claims from Frank Thiess that he coined the phrase in that year.[79] Be
that as it may, it is clear that the term was a familiar one at this time: it is
known that Thomas Mann himself used it as early as 1933 in his diary;[80] it
appeared in Lion Feuchtwanger's novel *Die Geschwister Oppenheim* (The
Oppenheims) in 1933;[81] Schnell cites various examples of the term being
used or implied throughout the 1930s, including in Klaus Mann's novel
Der Vulkan (The volcano, published in Amsterdam in 1939);[82] Brekle also
cites prewar use of the term in literary critical articles;[83] in 1937 Alfred
Döblin wrote in the emigrant journal *Das Wort*: "Man kann Emigrant im
eigenen Land sein" (One can be an emigrant in one's own country);[84]
and in 1943, in a speech in the Library of Congress in Washington, DC,
Thomas Mann talked about "millions" in Germany living in an "inner
emigration," waiting, like exiles, for the end of the regime.[85]

The term became much more current as a result of what was later to be called "the great controversy."[86] This pitted emigrants against those who had remained in Germany under National Socialism in what was at times a bitter and polemical exchange that explored the problematic questions associated with the concept "inner emigration." The substantial exodus of cultural talent, as writers went into exile, raised the question of whether "German culture" could still be identified as belonging within the borders of Germany or whether it denoted the intellectual life of those abroad. This notion of a broad *Kulturnation* versus the more narrowly defined *Staatsnation* became a particularly controversial question after the war, when both exiles and nonexiles struggled to bring together the various German cultures that had been split by the Nazi experience and its aftermath.

The initial focus of the debate was Thomas Mann, Germany's best-known living writer, who had left Germany in 1933 and had eventually settled in Santa Monica, California, where he continued to write and broadcast to Germany on behalf of the Allies, and who came to represent in this context all exiled writers. It was not unusual around the end of the war, and indeed under National Socialism, for people to distinguish a noble and pure German culture from the evil Nazi state with its cultural distortions and deceit. Mann adopted a different view: he rejected the supposed purity of German culture and insisted on the unity of the nation on *all* levels. His view was that German culture was itself implicated in Hitler's crimes and he was therefore reluctant to join the ranks of those who rejected out of hand the widespread idea of a collective responsibility for the crimes of National Socialism. He believed that the very aspects that were best in German culture and had attracted the admiration of the world had also helped to make possible that which was worst in German culture: Germany's evil and Germany's good were intertwined and could not be separated out this easily.[87]

The view that ordinary Germans were in part responsible for Hitler and his crimes was not a welcome one in Germany at the end of the war. Although Mann made no moral distinction between emigrants and non-emigrants in his broadcasts and speeches, many nonemigrant writers saw in his words an attack on them for not distancing themselves from the regime and for not leaving Germany. On August 13, 1945, Walter von Molo, a national conservative author who during the Nazi years had written historical novels about such figures as Frederick the Great, duly published in a number of newspapers an open letter that also appeared in the United States, in which he begged the exiled writer to return to Germany and to help in the reconstruction. He said the vast majority of Germans were not guilty of Nazi crimes, that they had remained in Germany during the Third Reich because they had nowhere else to go rather than because they supported Hitler. Germany was one large

"Konzentrationslager" (concentration camp), suggesting most Germans had themselves been victims of the Nazis.[88] He also implied that, far from being a burden, life in exile had been a privilege for the lucky few, thus ignoring completely the deprivation, the physical and psychological suffering of German exiles.[89] Finally, he invoked the cultural greats of German history to suggest that the unblemished *Kulturnation*, the "real Germany," was not identical with the recent *Staatsnation*.

Before Mann could publish his response to von Molo in Germany, a provocative essay by the writer Frank Thiess appeared on August 18, 1945, also in the *Münchner Zeitung*. Thiess, an author of historical novels who, like von Molo, belonged to the national conservative literary camp, linked the goodness of those writers in Nazi Germany who refused to conform to the regime with the supposed essential goodness of the German people as a whole. Inner emigrants occupied an "inner space" that Hitler could not conquer, he said, arguing for the spiritual existence of an alternative Germany that had been fully capable of existing physically within an evil and corrupt Nazi Germany. He contradicted Mann's ideas that German culture could transcend national barriers, reminding the great man of German letters of Erich Ebermayer's words that a German writer needed "de[n] deutschen Raum, [die] deutsche Erde und de[n] Widerhall deutscher Menschen" (German space, German earth, and the echo of German people). He went even further, however, implying that inner emigrants were the real patriots because they suffered alongside the German people, suggesting emigrants had had it comparatively easy, that they had almost been able to enjoy the spectacle of their fellow countrymen suffering, as if in the theater.[90]

The venting of spleen against not just Mann but the whole German exile community, which was implicit in von Molo's and Thiess's contributions to the debate, was linked to the desire to avoid the stigma of "collective guilt": anyone who had "emigrated spiritually" from Germany, it was thought, could claim to be free from responsibility for the rise of Nazism and for the events committed under the regime; indeed, the term "inner emigration" could be used to falsify the whole idea of collective guilt.

Mann replied to von Molo to emphasize the suffering of German exiles and to deny the possibility at all of "inner emigration," arguing that any cultural production had served to lend legitimacy to the National Socialist regime and claiming infamously: "Es mag Aberglaube sein, aber in meinen Augen sind Bücher, die von 1933 bis 1945 in Deutschland überhaupt gedruckt werden konnten, weniger als wertlos und nicht gut in die Hand zu nehmen. Ein Geruch von Blut und Schande haftet ihnen an: sie sollten alle eingestampft werden." (It may be superstition but in my eyes books that could be printed at all in Germany from 1933 to 1945 are less than worthless and should not be touched. A smell of blood and disgrace clings to them. They should all be pulped.)[91] That this was not Mann's real belief, that he had been riled by Thiess's polemic, can be seen from a letter in 1936, when he sought to mediate between writers "Drinnen" (within) and "Draußen" (without), encouraging the latter to withhold moral judgment: "[Die Emigrierten] leiden; aber gelitten wird auch im Innern, und sie sollten sich vor der Selbstgerechtigkeit hüten, die oft ein Erzeugnis des Leidens ist" (Emigrants are suffering, but there is also suffering within Germany, and they should beware of self-righteousness, which is often a product of suffering).[92]

It is one of the ironies of the "controversy" that such an extreme pronouncement as Mann's "pulping" recommendation served to undermine the valid criticism already made of the inner emigrant positions of von Molo (and Thiess) and actually made it easier for defenders of those positions to adduce evidence in the form of works that were clearly not tainted by "blood and disgrace." In fact, Mann's fiery hyperbole caused the controversy to rumble on for another year or so in the German cultural press, and it spread thereafter to France and America, with further contributions from, among others, Arnold Bauer, Johannes Becher, Alfred Döblin, Gottfried Benn, Max Frisch, Wilhelm Hausenstein, Hermann Hesse, Ricarda Huch, Erich Kästner, Otto Flake, and Luise Rinser. Exiled writers' evident disdain for them caused inner emigrants to justify their role under National Socialism, which inevitably entailed criticism of the exiled and forced the latter to respond to reproaches and make renewed accusations, in an increasingly unproductive vicious circle.[93] As a sign of the longevity of the debate, in 1973 Ernst Jünger was asked to respond to Mann's postwar comments and criticized him for having left Germany, saying emigrants could not understand, since they did not share the "tragedy," and in response to a subsequent objection that Mann would have ended up in a camp had he stayed, Jünger offered the example of Ernst Niekisch as someone who had faced up to his fate by staying and being imprisoned.[94]

Following the creation of the two German states in 1949, the controversy contributed to the subsequent "simplistic split between a largely apolitical literature in the German West and a politicized literature in the German East."[95] This not only damaged the notion of an apolitical *Kulturnation* but also cemented the divide in the literary world between writers who had stayed in Germany and those who had gone into exile. It also led to the political tainting of the term "inner emigration," the reluctance of scholars to engage in depth with its literary products, and the subsequent neglect of the latter by generations of postwar readers. Indeed the reason for the longevity of the debate over inner emigration is that it went to the heart of the issue that was to preoccupy Germany for many years: the question of guilt and responsibility for National Socialism.

Critical Reception

In the wake of the immediate postwar debate, the history of the critical reception of inner emigration was a chequered one. First, there appeared attempts at self-justification from fellow travelers or emotionally charged vilifications of Hitler from those who had suffered in one way or another at the hands of National Socialism.[96] With regard more specifically to writers who had remained in Germany between 1933 and 1945, there was the extreme example of Hans Blunck, who tried to present his severely compromised role under National Socialism as a form of resistance.[97] However, there were also less extreme but nevertheless apologist essays and books that sought to paint a simplistic and largely undifferentiated picture of the "other Germany" of nonfascist literary figures, of inner emigrants as the true resisters of National Socialism.[98] This aim to present a different image of Germans to the one assumed in apparent external calls for an admission of collective guilt is also reflected in compilations of oppositional texts from Nazi Germany.[99]

Numerous diaries and memoirs by former inner emigrants were also published.[100] Among the more prominent contributions from writers were those of Elisabeth Langgässer and Werner Bergengruen. In an address to the inaugural All German Writers' Congress in 1947, Langgässer was one of the first to call into question the claims to the moral high ground made by many writers who had stayed in Germany. She is here damning in her criticism of those who retrospectively engage in "das Spiel mit sechserlei Bällen" (the game with six types of ball), a juggling act of self-deception and deceit, and who claim for themselves a reputation not only as brave victims of the Nazi regime but also as writers of oppositional fiction whose every move was watched by the authorities and whose fiction somehow "deceived" the censors into overlooking their supposed criticism of the regime. She also rejects the tendency for such writers to use their "undesirable" status under National Socialism as a badge of honor.[101]

Bergengruen's views were also largely expressed in reasoned tones but he did betray a certain residual resentment. In 1947, when the reverberations from the fierce mutual recriminations of the Mann–von Molo–Thiess exchanges could still be felt, he evinced sympathy for the lot of exiled writers, respecting Mann's motives and decisions[102] and affirming his admiration of Mann's writing.[103] However, at the same time, he criticizes the Nobel laureate's broadcasts to Germany on behalf of the Allies, accusing him of misdirected reproaches delivered in a "schoolmasterly" tone and talking of Mann's "professorial doctrinarism" and lack of any sense of political reality.[104]

Over the next couple of decades, literary scholarship tended to adopt a more critical attitude to inner emigrant writers. Writers who had stayed in Germany, even when they had mostly kept their distance from the Nazi state, were increasingly accused of conformism to the regime, in contrast to exiled writers, who now came to be viewed as morally superior, as representatives of an unequivocal antifascism, and the literary value of whose works was contrasted favorably with the more limited, traditional approaches of inner emigrants.[105] Among condemnations of published writing in Nazi Germany, the most striking was Schonauer's deliberately polemical book, which argued against what he considered to be cultural and ideological restoration, a continuity of inner emigrant inwardness, and a flight from Nazi Germany.[106] Despite offering some valid insights, Schonauer's text is devalued by repeated generalizations, a failure to examine individual writers' circumstances, and an underplaying of both the limits on self-expression and writers' tactics in subverting the state and party censorship.

The reappraisal of the Nazi past, precipitated in West Germany in the early to mid-1960s by the younger generation's questioning of the extent to which the country had "dealt with" the legacy of National Socialism and by the subsequent student revolts of 1968, gave rise to further works that questioned critically the notion of "inner emigration." Most significant here was Schnell's focus on the *function* of inner emigrant writing and in particular authors' tendency toward inwardness and historical irrationality.[107] Dealing in the black-and-white moral currency of opposition versus conformity, of overt criticism versus intellectual withdrawal, some studies paid scant attention to the particular conditions of life and writing between 1933 and 1945.[108] Certain inner emigrant writers and specific works were thought to provide evidence of deliberate flight from the reality of the Third Reich. There was a tendency to accuse such writers of offering a public disinterested in politics the sort of escapist world they craved, a world of cultural values that served as a private antidote to the Nazis' relentless and crude propaganda offensive; and it was felt that this had the (unintended) function of deflecting readers from thoughts of resistance and thus effectively helped to stabilize or legitimize the regime.[109] On the other hand, the 1960s still saw studies, such as Wiesner's substantial essay on the "inner emigration," which reduced the term to an aesthetic one based largely on literary criteria and a writer's forced or intentional personal "emigration" from Nazi rule.[110]

It was not until the 1970s and 1980s that literary scholars began to get beyond the troubled debate over exile versus inner emigration, beyond the virtual hagiographies on the one hand and the near philippics on the other, and to explore in any great detail the realities of the lives and writing of a broad spectrum of writers. Brekle, for example, sought to establish a literary grouping under the unifying heading of "resistance," proposing "inner emigration" as a value-free overarching concept encompassing those writers who were not influenced by Nazi ideology, wrote "humanist works," and resisted enforced conformity; within this grouping, he identifies an "inner-German antifascist literature" and an "inner-German nonfascist literature." His main interest is the former, which constituted resistance or contained a specifically anti-Nazi stance, regardless of whether it was disseminated illegally, published openly, or written without intent to publish.[111] This is, however, a far from watertight division; it also takes no account of the significant differences between published and nonpublishable work, of the key issue of authors' official reputation and standing in Nazi Germany, or of the reception of the various works discussed. In his later book, Brekle abandoned the umbrella term, reserving "inner emigration" as a descriptor of nonfascist literature.[112]

Reinhold Grimm's essay "Innere Emigration als Lebensform" (Inner emigration as a way of life)[113] was a significant contribution to scholarship in the field, offering a more nuanced understanding of the work of such writers. The study marked a move away from the position that anything between support for National Socialism and active opposition was to be viewed as inner emigration. Criticizing Brekle's division, Grimm shows that simple compartmentalization is inappropriate and that we should be thinking, rather, in terms of a sliding scale from active resistance to passive refusal, from open action to total silence, and that, within that, inner emigration has to equate to a recognizable posture of opposition.[114] In avoiding all attempts to pigeonhole writers, the key criterion should be whether the refusal to conform is unambiguous and demonstrative: the mere fact that a writer refrained from writing in a fascist manner did not mean that his or her work was nonfascist or even antifascist. Inner emigration was to be seen as a way of life, in particular a German way of life, and its writers as representatives of a broad range of political, ideological, religious, and social perspectives. In pointing, for example, to the involvement of the conservative Catholic Bergengruen in such activities as distributing the leaflets of the Weiße Rose (White Rose) resistance group or copies of Bishop Galen's speeches critical of Nazi policies, Grimm notes: "Die Front der 'inneren Emigration' verlief bis zum Ende quer durch die weltanschaulichen und politischen Lager hindurch" (Up until the end, the front of the "inner emigration" ran right across the various philosophical and political camps).[115]

Following several years in which the phenomenon was rather neglected and scholarship did not really advance, new studies began to build on Grimm's example. Moving away from earlier prejudiced positions, moral judgments, and ideologically charged studies, certain scholars sought—as part of a general move toward historicization of National Socialism[116]—to explore the sociohistorical and social contexts of writing under the Nazi regime.[117] A good example of this approach is Michael Philipp's essay, which explores social circumstances and perceptions in an effort to get away from the simplistic distinction between fascist literature, on the one hand, and exile or oppositional writing on the other. He highlights factors relating to the mentality and "perceptual horizon" of people living under the regime and uses the historian Martin Broszat's term "Resistenz" to denote a wide-ranging intellectual stance that spans all points between resistance to and conformity with National Socialism. This social-historical extension of the term leads to a more appropriate recognition of the reality of the relationship between opposition and regime, which involved an often complex pattern of shifting phases and a paradoxical fluctuating process of simultaneous dissent and conformity, of distance and adaptation.[118]

Against this background, the past twenty-five years or so have seen a general burgeoning of critical interest in writers of the inner emigration, with particular attention being paid to the modes of communication possible in the Third Reich, to detailed exploration of publication context and reception, as well as to a reappraisal of function.[119] A major contribution to the field has been the work of the Rotermunds, in particular their substantial analysis-cum-anthology, which will be discussed at greater length in chapter 2.[120] The publication of Zuckmayer's *Geheimreport*,[121] with its examination of the particular circumstances of cultural life in the Third Reich and its recognition of the possibilities and limits of cultural production under a dictatorship, has lent momentum and conviction to such studies. Important investigations have explored the techniques and function of Sternberger's so-called *verdeckte Schreibweise* (concealed writing)[122] and the associated "reading between the lines," as practiced by informed and educated readers of both imaginative literature and journalistic writing,[123] whereas others have sought aesthetic and formal parallels between what German writers abroad were doing and the literary products of writers who remained in the country.[124]

Evaluating the Inner Emigration

Exile versus Inner Emigration

One of the flaws of the exile–inner emigration debate was the way some seemed to assume literature must play a decisive social role and imposed retrospectively on writers an expectation of open opposition and heroic public action. This wholly unrealistic standpoint gives rise to a suspicion of all who remained in Germany, as if staying in the country had not been the normal scenario for the overwhelming majority of Germans but rather something that needed to be justified, or as if exile had been exclusively a voluntary step rather than, for the vast majority, a necessary response to an immediate threat.[125]

A further assumption relates to the relative effects of literature written in Germany and abroad. Ernst Fischer, in the first issue of the

Prague-based exile journal *Neue Deutsche Blätter*, summed up the situation facing writers who wanted to pursue their career under a fascist regime and at the same time to use their writing to fight that regime. They could: stay in Germany and attack the regime in an artistically veiled manner, mindful that sooner or later they would be silenced; produce, anonymously, illegal literature and work for the antifascist press abroad; or leave the country and speak to Germans from abroad through whatever channels were available to them.[126] Increasingly, only options one and three were realistic alternatives. And in practice, nonconformist literature published legally in Germany and all oppositional literature produced in exile and then illicitly disseminated in Germany had a very limited effect on the regime, for all writers had to contend with the permanent threat of being arrested, all literary products faced the constant prospect of being destroyed, and all publishers and writers had to negotiate an increasingly complex system of censorship and propaganda. As the writer Otto Flake noted: "Vorträge waren uns verboten; am Radio durften wir nicht reden; keine Parteibuchhandlung führte unsere Bücher, keine Parteizeitung zeigte sie an. Aus den Weihnachtskatalogen sahen wir uns gestrichen, für Neuauflagen gab es kein Papier." (We were forbidden from giving talks; we were not allowed to speak on the radio; party bookshops did not stock our books and party newspapers did not announce their publication. We were removed from Christmas book catalogues and there was no paper to reprint our works.)[127] Though, as we have seen, this system of exclusion was not foolproof or infallible, it involved an interlocking network of prerequisites, barriers, and checks that made life extremely difficult for those who wished to register a protest that could be read by Germans, and who wanted at the same time to continue to write and publish. If one accepts the genuine nonconformist mindset of *most* inner emigrants, the moral higher ground claimed by apologists of exile becomes less significant, since literature produced in exile too, in practical terms, resulted in hopeless inefficacy. In both cases, the value of literary opposition lay in sustaining the nonconformist and in alerting readers—the sensitized and sometimes even the not-yet-sensitized—to the existence of like-minded non-Nazis determined to preserve and propagate variously socialist, humanist, liberal, Christian, and conservative values. In this sense, Dodd is surely right to propose that the two should be seen as variations on a common theme and that it is high time we sought the "homologies between inner and territorial exile."[128]

A frequent accusation leveled at inner emigrants is that by staying in Germany and publishing there they compromised themselves by coming to an arrangement with the regime, whereby they tacitly agreed to withdraw to a position of inwardness in order to be able to continue to ply their trade. This ignores, however, the fact that in exile, too, numerous texts were written for income to allow writers to survive in an alien environment, and that many of these had little direct link to contemporary events in Germany. In Scholdt's words: "Sie handelten von Liebe und Leidenschaft, von den Schönheiten der Natur, von Musikern und Malern oder der guten alten Zeit, die nichts mit der aktuellen Politik zu tun hatte" (They dealt with love and passion, the beauties of nature, with musicians and painters or the good old times that had nothing to do with contemporary politics).[129]

The most significant genre here was the historical novel, which gave rise to much controversy. Despite the absence of any external compulsion to engage in historically camouflaged writing, many exiled writers produced works of historical fiction, which left them open to the charge of fleeing from the reality of Nazi Germany, a charge that was potentially more damaging than the equivalent one leveled at those who had remained.[130] Historical fiction came to be seen by some as an intellectual emigration to parallel the political one, a failure to counter developments in Germany on the part of writers of the "other Germany," who sought instead to adapt themselves to the commercial potential of the international book market.[131] Although these criticisms prompted responses from the likes of Alfred Döblin, Ludwig Marcuse, and Georg Lukács,[132] the sheer number of historical works in exile is striking and can perhaps be explained by writers' existential need to remain connected to the literary traditions of their native land, their feeling as time progressed of not being able to re-create from afar the atmosphere, concerns, and even the language of life under National Socialism, and perhaps most significantly the need to secure their material existence through the use of tried and tested styles and forms. What it shows is that, in some key respects, the polarization of exile and inner emigration is a less than helpful or productive exercise.

It is true that the inner emigration remains a problematic phenomenon in German literature, partly because its usage after 1945 originated as a form of (often dubious) post hoc justification. Resented by many emigrants for its implication of parity of experience and standing between those who stayed and those who left, the term has over the years come to be considered by some as politically tainted and discredited. However, as indicated in the Introduction, it does denote a very real phenomenon and a distinct aspect of literary life under National Socialism. As, furthermore, the review of key inner emigrants in chapter 2 shows, there was a substantial and varied range of writers who distanced themselves from the values of National Socialism and adopted oppositional positions through their work, encompassing the rejection of violence, the championing of justice, or the establishment of positive counterimages and ideals, based on either religiously informed or humanist value systems. This broad nonconformist church features works that are the product of Christian, Christian humanist, national conservative, monarchist, or even pacifist standpoints.

The relatively narrow political base of the writers concerned and the fact that most were outwardly apolitical is often a further focus of criticism, but this ignores the fact that liberal democrat, socialist, and communist writers either left Germany in 1933–34 or, where they remained, almost without exception had no opportunity to publish and thus fell silent. Given the restrictions on literary activity and the limitations on public protest in the established Nazi state, to charge inner emigrants with political impotence is, as Löwenthal notes, unfair and, actually, irrelevant.[133]

The Muddy Waters of Opposition and Conformism

In view of the problematic conditions of literary production in the Third Reich and of the impossibility of establishing in most cases an incontrovertible, "demonstrative" oppositional stance, the gradual move over the past forty years away from an exclusive focus on the political content of texts toward a greater concern with sociohistorical issues has been a sensible and desirable development. Moreover, as Philipp points out, just as the term "exile literature" does not automatically denote that all such books contain antifascist content, it is important to broaden our understanding of inner emigration, to seek a more differentiated analysis, since the simple black-and-white contrast suggested by the dichotomy opposition/conformity fails to do justice to the complex nature of life in Nazi Germany.[134]

This idea derives in part from Broszat's rejection of simplistic moralizing about the Nazi period, the contrasting of demonized Nazi villains with selected virtuous heroes. Broszat calls instead for a "normalization" of the historical understanding of the Nazi era, for detailed scholarship on everyday life (*Alltagsgeschichte*) in the Third Reich, which, he argues, would reveal a fuzzier, grayer picture, would acknowledge the complexity of people's lives, and would show the way National Socialism and opposition to it were mutually dependent.[135] In his tripartite, largely chronological division of resistance to National Socialism, he identifies the substantial grouping of "Resistenz" between 1934–35 and 1940–41. This grouping did not display any fundamental or principle opposition to the regime, was by no means always politically motivated, and was frequently most concerned with preserving autonomy in religious, intellectual, cultural, economic, or professional matters.[136] However, it did manage in the face of the spread of Nazi ideology and sociopolitical structures to preserve spheres of "relativer Immunität und Selbstbestimmung" (relative immunity and self-determination) in which non-Nazi values were upheld, thanks in part to the degree of plurality of opinions and the limited "free space" that the Nazis were prepared to tolerate once left-wing opposition had been stamped out (299–300). It is in this sphere of inner "resistance to" Nazi values that Broszat locates inner emigrants, to whose criticism of National Socialism he attributes successes in undermining loyalty to the regime, "disturbing" the achievement of its aims, and contributing to partial long-term immunization from it (302, 304). However debatable this last point, Broszat's ideas provide the sort of broad framework within which one can locate inner emigration as a way of life hovering between opposition and conformity and can accommodate the full range of inner emigrants' varied responses to National Socialism.

This framework allows Philipp to employ "inner emigration" as a descriptive (as opposed to moral evaluative) term that encompasses large sections of the non-Nazi literature produced in the Third Reich and to argue that any writer who refused to accept the state's demand for authors to engage with Nazi ideals, who withdrew from society or published "unpolitical" literature, was affirming his or her distance from and rejection of the regime.[137] The implications of this definition through omission are explored in chapter 2.

Analyzing the nature and function of inner emigrant literature is made more complicated by the fact that contrary tendencies can sometimes be depicted in individual writers themselves. As Müller and Holzner note, society at the time could not simply be divided into fellow travelers and opponents, for "Der Riß geht nicht selten durch ein und dieselbe Person" (the split frequently goes through one and the same person).[138] On the one hand, many texts demonstrate their authors' moral integrity and their determination to promote humanist values and thereby to offer readers consolation and reassurance, while on the other, these same writers betray elements of conservative thinking very close to that of the Nazis, which allowed their work to be appropriated or willfully misinterpreted by the regime. The classic example of this is Ernst Wiechert, whose attitude toward the *ideas* of National Socialism is not always unequivocal, whereas his distaste for Nazi *methods* and tactics is unreservedly negative. Similarly, again with reference to Wiechert, but also the early Reinhold Schneider, Friedrich Reck-Malleczewen, and even Luise Rinser and Gottfried Benn, one needs to be alert to the way ideological views developed and changed over time. Indeed, the very nature of existence and literary activity under National Socialism means that for most, life inevitably involved a series of "pendulum swings" between opposition and adaptation to the regime, with writers forced to limit themselves to veiled utterances, sometimes vaguely and therefore ambiguously formulated, which on occasions could give the impression of compromise and conformity.[139]

It was also the case that the regime deliberately encouraged and tolerated nonaligned writers' contributions of light fiction, entertainment films, and children's literature as part of a politics-free zone at the heart of German culture, and as a result several writers can be accused, especially in the war years, of having served the regime's agenda of deploying cultural output to distract and "anaesthetize" the public. It is furthermore an uncomfortable fact that a small number of inner emigrants earned considerable amounts of money from the success of their published work under National Socialism (most notably Wiechert and, for a while, Mitterer and Lernet-Holenia) and thus owed their rise to literary prominence to the very system they sought to oppose. This raises the issue of whether such income earned from work published under National Socialism can ever qualify the writer as anything other than a fellow traveler, although, as Dür argues, the logical consequence of this is to deny the possibility of all publishing under Nazism,[140] almost in the spirit of Mann's postwar polemic.

For these reasons of internal contradiction, individual ideological development, and the treading of the line between opposition and conformism, it is a deeply problematic undertaking to seek to produce wholesale evaluations of writers. Inner emigration was essentially a social response characterized by differing forms of withdrawal from or rejection of the reality of National Socialism. Keeping one's distance from the regime could mean a range of things: from complete silence at one end of Grimm's sliding scale to clearly identifiable critical acts at the other, with in between the escape to genres such as nature poetry, children's literature, or travel writing, and works that exercised criticism of the regime with varying degrees of overtness (the focus of chapters 3–10). This makes a differentiated approach to inner emigration essential, one based on consideration of the everyday reality of life under National Socialism, of the extent to which writers were able to negotiate an (inevitably limited) social and political space between the necessities of outward conformity and inner rejection of the regime. In forming a view on individual writers' status after 1933, we cannot be restricted to whether or not they were members of a particular institution, whether or not they ever signed a declaration of loyalty, or whether they earned a living from writing under the regime; nor, conversely, can we rely too heavily on what may have been said in self-justifying post hoc autobiographical reflections. Rather, we need to explore nonassimilated writers' intellectual development before and during the Third Reich, together with relevant aspects of their biography after 1933, in relation to the aesthetic aspects of their nonconformity, as revealed by detailed examination of the publication context and reception of their work and a close reading of the texts themselves.

Notes

[1] Armin Mohler and Karlheinz Weißmann, *Die Konservative Revolution in Deutschland 1918–1932: Ein Handbuch*, 6th ed. (Graz: ARES, 2005), 93–94. See also Anna Guillemin, "The Conservative Revolution of Philologists and Poets:

Repositioning Hugo von Hofmannsthal's Speech 'Das Schrifttum als geistiger Raum der Nation,'" *Modern Language Review* 107, no. 2 (2012): 501–21.

[2] The term "November Revolution" refers not to the Bolshevik Revolution of 1917 but to the political conflict in Germany at the end of the First World War, especially the period November 1918 until the suppression of the Spartacist Uprising in January 1919 and the election of a Constituent National Assembly, which eventually led to the establishment of a republic in place of Germany's imperial government. See Richard Müller, *Eine Geschichte der Novemberrevolution: Vom Kaiserreich zur Republik—Die Novemberrevolution—Der Bürgerkrieg in Deutschland* (Berlin: Die Buchmacherei, 2011).

[3] Roger Woods, *The Conservative Revolution in the Weimar Republic* (Basingstoke, London: Macmillan, 1996), 1.

[4] Ibid., 2.

[5] Edgar J. Jung, "Deutschland und die Konservative Revolution," in *Deutsche über Deutschland: Die Stimme des unbekannten Politikers*, ed. Edgar J. Jung (Munich: Langen-Müller, 1932), 380.

[6] Arthur Moeller van den Bruck, *Das dritte Reich* (Hamburg: Hanseatische Verlagsanstalt, 1931), 7–8.

[7] Mohler and Weißmann, *Die Konservative Revolution*, 94–95.

[8] See on this especially "Schneider and National Socialism" in chapter 7 of this book.

[9] For example, the Great Tyrant in Bergengruen's *Der Großtyrann und das Gericht* (The great tyrant and the court), and Philip II and Charles V in Schneider's *Las Casas vor Karl V.* (Las Casas before Charles V, 1938, translated into English in 1948 as *Imperial Mission*).

[10] In the 1915 essay "Zola"—in Heinrich Mann, *Geist und Tat: Franzosen 1780–1930* (Frankfurt am Main: Suhrkamp, 1981), 149–255—which had prompted Thomas Mann to write his infamous *Betrachtungen eines Unpolitischen* (Reflections of an unpolitical man, 1918).

[11] *The Bible: New International Version*, https://www.biblegateway.com/passage/?search=Romans+13&version=NIV (accessed July 15, 2014).

[12] Grimm, "Innere Emigration als Lebensform," 70–71.

[13] Jochen Klepper, diary entry of August 6, 1937, *Unter dem Schatten deiner Flügel: Aus den Tagebüchern der Jahre 1932–1942*, ed. Hildegard Klepper (Stuttgart: Deutsche Verlags-Anstalt, 1956), 479.

[14] Schnell, *Literarische innere Emigration*, 11; see also 49–50.

[15] Sebastian Graeb-Könneker, ed., *Literatur im Dritten Reich: Dokumente und Texte* (Stuttgart: Reclam, 2001), 373.

[16] Erwin Rotermund and Heidrun Ehrke-Rotermund, "Literatur im 'Dritten Reich,'" in *Geschichte der deutschen Literatur vom 18. Jahrhundert bis zur Gegenwart*, vol. 3, part 1, *1918–1945*, 2nd ed., ed. Viktor Žmegač (Königstein/Ts.: Athenäum, 1994), 322.

[17] Dietrich Strothmann, *Nationalsozialistische Literaturpolitik: Ein Beitrag zur Publizistik im Dritten Reich* (Bonn: Bouvier Verlag, 1960), 67–68; and Inge Jens, *Dichter zwischen rechts und links: Die Geschichte der Sektion für Dichtkunst*

der Preußischen Akademie der Künste, dargestellt nach den Dokumenten (Munich: Piper, 1971).

18 Theo Buck, Hans-Peter Franke, Ulrich Staehle, Dietrich Steinbach, and Dietmar Wenzelburger, *Von der Weimarer Republik bis 1945: Geschichte der deutschen Literatur 5* (Stuttgart: Klett, 1985), 93–94; and Jan-Pieter Barbian, *Literaturpolitik im "Dritten Reich": Institutionen, Kompetenzen, Betätigungsfelder*, 2nd ed. (Munich: Deutscher Taschenbuch Verlag, 1995), 75.

19 Barbian, *Literaturpolitik*, 94–95.

20 Ibid., 209–10.

21 Ibid., 80–88.

22 Ulrich Walberer, ed., *10. Mai 1933: Bücherverbrennung in Deutschland und die Folgen* (Frankfurt: Fischer-Taschenbuch-Verlag, 1983).

23 Rotermund and Ehrke-Rotermund, "Literatur im 'Dritten Reich,'" 322.

24 Barbian, *Literaturpolitik*, 140.

25 Johannes Jungmichl, *Nationalsozialistische Literaturlenkung und bibliothekarische Buchbesprechung* (Berlin: Deutscher Bibliotheksverband, Arbeitsstelle für das Bibliothekswesen, 1974), 15.

26 See Klaus Vondung, "Der literarische Nationalismus: Ideologische, politische und sozial-historische Wirkungszusammenhänge," in *Die deutsche Literatur im Dritten Reich: Themen—Traditionen—Wirkungen*, ed. Horst Denkler and Karl Prümm (Stuttgart: Reclam, 1976), 44–46.

27 Strothmann, *Nationalsozialistische Literaturpolitik*, 324–32; and Karl-Heinz Schoeps, *Literatur im Dritten Reich (1933–1945)*, 2nd ed. (Berlin: Weidler, 2000), 51–52.

28 An astonishing fifty literary histories, some of them of considerable size, appeared between 1930 and 1945. Uwe-Karsten Ketelsen, *Literatur und Drittes Reich*, 2nd ed. (Schernfeld: SH-Verlag, 1994), 76). See also *Klassiker in finsteren Zeiten 1933–1945: Eine Ausstellung des Deutschen Literaturarchivs im Schiller-Nationalmuseum Marbach am Neckar*, vol. 1, ed. Bernhard Zeller (Marbach: Deutsche Schillergesellschaft, 1983), 409–22.

29 Schoeps, *Literatur im Dritten Reich*, 34–35.

30 Hildegard Brenner, *Die Kunstpolitik des Nationalsozialismus* (Reinbek bei Hamburg: Rowohlt, 1963), 64–65 and 82–86.

31 Frank Westenfelder, *Genese, Problematik und Wirkung nationalsozialistischer Literatur am Beispiel des historischen Romans zwischen 1890 und 1945* (Frankfurt am Main: Lang, 1989), 198.

32 Arno Mulot, *Die deutsche Dichtung unserer Zeit*, 2nd ed. (Stuttgart: Metzler, 1944); and Hellmuth Langenbucher, *Volkhafte Dichtung der Zeit* (Berlin: Junker und Dünnehaupt, 1941), cited in Strothmann, *Nationalsozialistische Literaturpolitik*, 334.

33 Ketelsen, *Literatur und Drittes Reich*, 86–87.

34 Strothmann, *Nationalsozialistische Literaturpolitik*, 23.

35 Barbian, *Literaturpolitik*, 159.

[36] Ibid., 436–50.

[37] Ibid, 372.

[38] Ibid., 197.

[39] Strothmann, *Nationalsozialistische Literaturpolitik*, 28.

[40] Alfred Rosenberg, *Der Mythus des 20. Jahrhunderts: Eine Wertung der seelisch-geistigen Gestaltenkämpfe unserer Zeit*, 3rd ed. (Munich: Hoheneichen, 1932).

[41] Westenfelder, *Genese, Problematik und Wirkung*, 196.

[42] It had originally been set up in 1933 as an authority that acted as an unofficial department of the Ministry of Propaganda.

[43] Strothmann, *Nationalsozialistische Literaturpolitik*, 38.

[44] Bernhard Payr, "Aufgaben des Amtes Schrifttumspflege," in *Die Welt des Buches: Eine Kunde vom Buch*, ed. Hellmuth Langenbucher, with Will Vesper (Ebenhausen near Munich: Langewiesche-Brandt, 1938), 204.

[45] Barbian cites critical reviews in the *Bücherkunde* and elsewhere of such writers as Stefan Andres, Werner Bergengruen, Hans Fallada, Horst Lange, Walter von Molo, Frank Thiess, Wolfgang Weyrauch, and Ernst Wiechert, none of which led to the outright bans that Reichsstelle staff proposed (*Literaturpolitik*, 289).

[46] Bernhard Payr, *Das Amt Schrifttumspflege: Eine Entwicklungsgeschichte und seine Organisation* (Berlin: Junker und Dunnhaupt, 1941), 10.

[47] Barbian, *Literaturpolitik*, 278.

[48] A so-called Ausgabe B (B edition) of the *Bücherkunde* listed reviews of publications from the weekly digest (*Gutachtenanzeiger*) produced by the central editorial office of the Reichsstelle. This "B" version was intended for internal consumption only and was not generally available.

[49] Strothmann, *Nationalsozialistische Literaturpolitik*, 44.

[50] For example, in 1939 the PPK secured Rust's agreement to the requirement that all university dissertations on questions relating to National Socialism should be submitted to the PPK in advance of printing (Barbian, *Literaturpolitik*, 315).

[51] The monthly *NS-Bibliographie* was established in 1936 to publish the results of the PPK's examination of the most important book publications and newspaper and journal articles, so as to indicate to publishers the type of literature deemed desirable and to inform booksellers which books were to be promoted as embodying Nazi ideals (Strothmann, *Nationalsozialistische Literaturpolitik*, 45–46).

[52] Barbian, *Literaturpolitik*, 311.

[53] Strothmann, *Nationalsozialistische Literaturpolitik*, 81.

[54] Westenfelder, *Genese, Problematik und Wirkung*, 195; and Strothmann, *Nationalsozialistische Literaturpolitik*, 326–32.

[55] Barbian, *Literaturpolitik*, 848. The Sicherheitsdienst des Reichsführers-SS was charged with building a central library covering all undesirable political writing, reviewing and reporting on all publications confiscated by local police authorities, and scrutinizing the activities of certain publishing houses (Barbian, *Literaturpolitik*, 261–63).

[56] Among writers excluded from the RSK were Stefan Andres, Werner Bergengruen, Wilhelm Hausenstein, and Jochen Klepper. Outright bans on writing were issued to Gottfried Benn and Elisabeth Langgässer, while Reinhold Schneider was not allowed to publish his work from 1941 on.

[57] Ketelsen, *Literatur und Drittes Reich*, 296.

[58] Barbian, *Literaturpolitik*, 332–64 and 842–43.

[59] Brenner, *Die Kunstpolitik des Nationalsozialismus*, 77–86. It has indeed been suggested that such territorial disputes were deliberately encouraged by Hitler (Strothmann, *Nationalsozialistische Literaturpolitik*, 44 n59, and 57). Schäfer further suggests that tactical motives were involved when Nazi authorities sometimes chose not to take action against individuals or artistic works considered distant from the official ideology of the regime. Hans-Dieter Schäfer, *Das gespaltene Bewußtsein: Über deutsche Kultur und Lebenswirklichkeit 1933–1945* (Munich: Hanser, 1981), 18–21.

[60] Barbian, *Literaturpolitik*, 519–27.

[61] This is not to underestimate the increasing domination of the publishing market by the central NSDAP publisher, Franz-Eher-Verlag, which as early as 1934 acquired the much larger Ullstein empire and by 1943 had taken over thirty-seven additional publishers, including Deutsche Verlags-Anstalt, Knorr & Hirth, Langen-Müller, and Rowohlt (Barbian, *Literaturpolitik*, 696–97). Eher was headed by the powerful and influential Reichsleiter Max Amann.

[62] The business was split when the founder Samuel Fischer's successor, his son-in-law Gottfried Bermann Fischer, was forced into exile, initially to Vienna, and took a share of the business with him. Suhrkamp led the remaining business until 1944 when he was arrested, accused of high treason, and imprisoned in Sachsenhausen concentration camp.

[63] Strothmann, *Nationalsozialistische Literaturpolitik*, 447–48.

[64] See, for example, the case of the feuilleton of the *Kölnische Zeitung*, discussed in Klaus-Dieter Oelze, *Das Feuilleton der Kölnischen Zeitung im Dritten Reich* (Frankfurt am Main: Lang, 1990), 62–63.

[65] Michael Hadley, "Resistance in Exile: Publication, Context and Reception of Stefan Andres's *Wir sind Utopia* (1942)," *Seminar* 19, no. 3 (1983): 166. But see also chapter 4, "Wir sind Utopia," for doubts about this version of events.

[66] Hauptlektorat Schöngeistiges Schrifttum, "Jahresbericht 1940," *Lektoren-Brief* 4, nos. 5–6 (1941): 7, cited in Ehrke-Rotermund and Rotermund, *Zwischenreiche*, 14.

[67] Barbian, *Literaturpolitik*, 375–86.

[68] See "Oppositional Writers" in chapter 2 of this book.

[69] See, for example, Strothmann, *Nationalsozialistische Literaturpolitik*, 444–46.

[70] See in this chapter the section "Reich Office for the Promotion of German Writing"; see also Barbian, *Literaturpolitik*, 289.

[71] Jan-Pieter Barbian, "Zwischen Anpassung und Widerstand: Regimekritische Autoren in der Literaturpolitik des Dritten Reiches," in Kroll and von Voss, *Schriftsteller und Widerstand*, 69.

[72] In his diary, Klepper explains the nature of this special permission: it required him to submit manuscripts in advance of publication and to restrict himself to nonpolitical content; he further notes that the permission could be withdrawn at any time (Klepper, *Unter dem Schatten deiner Flügel*, 445).

[73] The exclusion from the RSK in 1936 of Elisabeth Langgässer, designated a "half Jew" owing to her father's Jewish origins, suggests that such special permission was more likely to be granted in the case of Aryans married to Jews rather than those who were themselves of Jewish origin.

[74] See Konrad Ackermann, *Der Widerstand der Monatsschrift Hochland gegen den Nationalsozialismus* (Munich: Kösel, 1965); Maria Theodora von dem Bottlenberg-Landsberg, *Die Weißen Blätter: Eine konservative Zeitschrift im und gegen den Nationalsozialismus* (Berlin: Lukas, 2012); Bottlenberg-Landsberg, "Lautlose Stimmen?: Zeitschriften der 'Inneren Emigration,'" in Kroll and von Voss, *Schriftsteller und Widerstand*, 185–204; William J. Dodd, *"Jedes Wort wandelt die Welt": Dolf Sternbergers politische Sprachkritik* (Göttingen: Wallstein, 2007); Dodd, *"Der Mensch hat das Wort": Der Sprachdiskurs in der Frankfurter Zeitung 1933–1943* (Berlin: De Gruyter, 2013); Günther Gillessen, *Auf verlorenem Posten: Die Frankfurter Zeitung im Dritten Reich* (Berlin: Siedler, 1986); Marion Mallmann, *"Das Innere Reich": Analyse einer konservativen Kulturzeitschrift im Dritten Reich* (Bonn: Bouvier, 1978); Oelze, *Das Feuilleton*; and Hubert Orlowski, "Krakauer Zeitung 1939–1945: Nichtnationalsozialistische Literatur im Generalgouvernement?," in *"Das war ein Vorspiel nur. . . .": Berliner Colloquium zur Literaturpolitik im Dritten Reich*, ed. Eberhard Lämmert (Berlin: Akademie der Künste, 1985), 136–58.

[75] See Gillessen, *Auf verlorenem Posten*, 481 and 178.

[76] Service as public representatives of "German culture" promised not just financial security but also the opportunity for a degree of prestige from membership in key groups, invitations to high-profile events, and public honors that writers could otherwise not aspire to. For those struggling to make a living after 1933, especially the young generation, who had known little else than Nazi cultural policy, the enticements were not always easy to ignore (see chapter 2 of this book, especially the section "The Apolitical and the Young Generation").

[77] Barbian, *Literaturpolitik*, 525.

[78] See Schäfer, *Das gespaltene Bewußtsein*, 135–36.

[79] It has not proved possible to verify these claims. See Frank Thiess, "Innere Emigration," in Thomas Mann, Frank Thiess, and Walter von Molo, *Ein Streitgespräch über die äußere und die innere Emigration* (Dortmund: Crüwell, 1946), 3. See also Grimm, "Innere Emigration als Lebensform," 42–43.

[80] "Die innere Emigration, zu der ich im Grunde gehöre" (The inner emigration to which I basically belong), Thomas Mann, entry for November 7, 1933, in *Tagebücher, 1933–1934*, ed. Peter de Mendelssohn (Frankfurt am Main: Fischer, 1997), 243.

[81] Lion Feuchtwanger, *Die Geschwister Oppenheim* (Amsterdam: Querido, 1933). The title was originally intended to be *Die Geschwister Oppermann*, but Feuchtwanger was forced to change it temporarily owing to threats from a Nazi of

this name. After two editions, the original title was restored. See *Die Geschwister Oppermann* (Franfurt am Main: Fischer Taschenbuch, 1984), 329.

[82] Schnell, *Literarische innere Emigration*, 3.

[83] Wolfgang Brekle, "Die antifaschistische Literatur in Deutschland (1933–1945): Probleme der inneren Emigration am Beispiel deutscher Erzähler (Krauss, Kuckhoff, Petersen, Huch, Barlach, Wiechert u.a.)," *Weimarer Beiträge* 16, no. 6 (1970): 70–71.

[84] Alfred Döblin, "Der Historische Roman und wir," *Das Wort* 1, no. 4 (1936): 70.

[85] Thomas Mann, "Schicksal und Aufgabe," in *Gesammelte Werke in Einzelbänden: Frankfurter Ausgabe*, ed. Peter de Mendelssohn, vol. 18, *An die gesittete Welt: Politische Schriften und Reden im Exil* (Frankfurt am Main: S. Fischer, 1986), 650.

[86] For readable, balanced discussions, see Gerhard Kurz, "'Innere Emigration': Zur öffentlichen Kontroverse zwischen Walter v. Molo, Thomas Mann und Frank Thieß," in *Öffentlicher Sprachgebrauch: Praktische, theoretische und historische Perspektiven*, ed. Karin Böke, Matthias Jung, and Martin Wengeler (Opladen: Westdeutscher Verlag, 1996), 221–35; and Stephen Brockmann, "Inner Emigration: The Term and Its Origins in Postwar Debates," in Donahue and Kirchner, *Flight of Fantasy*, 11–26. The documentation edited by J. F. G. Grosser, *Die große Kontroverse: Ein Briefwechsel um Deutschland* (Hamburg: Nagel, 1963), adopts a more biased and very anti-Mann stance.

[87] Mann, "Schicksal und Aufgabe," 651.

[88] Mann, Thiess, and von Molo, *Ein Streitgespräch*, 2.

[89] It is interesting that this unjust accusation had already been made by Friedrich Reck-Malleczewen in his diary written during the Third Reich, where he refers to the writer's daily task of hiding manuscripts, the sense of constant fear of denunciation in the "leidgeladene Katakombenluft" (misery-laden air of the catacombs). He wonders if those in exile, when they return, will ever be able to understand the fate of those writers who had stayed in Germany: "Solltet Ihr es wirklich begreifen, daß die Flucht in die Zivilisation bequemer war als das Verharren auf dem gefahrvollen Vorposten und dieses illegale und beobachtende Verbleiben in der Barbarei?" (Will you really be able to understand that the flight to civilization was more comfortable than remaining at this dangerous outpost, than this illegal watching and waiting among barbarians?) Friedrich Percyval Reck-Malleczewen, entry for September 9, 1937, *Tagebuch eines Verzweifelten*, ed. Bernt Engelmann (Berlin: Dietz, 1981), 40.

[90] Mann, Thiess, and von Molo, *Ein Streitgespräch*, 3.

[91] Thomas Mann, "Warum ich nicht nach Deutschland zurückgehe," in *Gesammelte Werke*, vol. 18, *An die gesittete Welt*, 732. The article was originally published in New York's German-language exile newspaper *Aufbau* and also appeared two weeks later in Germany.

[92] Thomas Mann, "[An Eduard Korrodi]," in *Gesammelte Werke*, vol. 18, *An die gesittete Welt*, 147.

[93] See Schmollinger, *"Intra muros et extra,"* 12–19; also Grosser, *Die große Kontroverse.*

[94] Ernst Jünger, "Ältere Herrn-Heroiker," *Frankfurter Rundschau*, March 10, 1973, cited in Eliot Y. Neaman, *A Dubious Past: Ernst Jünger and the Politics of Literature after Nazism* (Berkeley: University of California Press, 1999), 106.

[95] Brockmann, "Inner Emigration," 22.

[96] See Thomas Koebner, "Die Schuldfrage: Vergangenheitsverweigerung und Lebenslügen in der Diskussion 1945–1949," in Thomas Koebner, *Unbehauste: Zur deutschen Literatur in der Weimarer Republik, im Exil und in der Nachkriegszeit* (Munich: text + kritik, 1992), 320–51.

[97] Hans Friedrich Blunck, *Unwegsame Zeiten: Lebensbericht*, vol. 2 (Mannheim: Kessler, 1952).

[98] For example, Karl O. Paetel, *Deutsche innere Emigration: Antinationalsozialistische Zeugnisse aus Deutschland* (New York: Krause, 1946); and Harald von Koenigswald, *Die Gewaltlosen: Dichtung im Widerstand gegen den Nationalsozialismus* (Herborn: Oranien, 1962).

[99] For example, Richard Drews and Alfred Kantorowicz, eds., *verboten und verbrannt: Deutsche Literatur—12 Jahre unterdrückt* (Berlin: Ullstein, 1947); and Günther Weisenborn, ed., *Der lautlose Aufstand: Bericht über die Widerstandsbewegung des deutschen Volkes 1933–1945* (Hamburg: Rowohlt, 1953).

[100] For example, Ernst Wiechert, *Jahre und Zeiten: Erinnerungen* (Erlenbach-Zürich: Rentsch, 1949); Hans Carossa, *Ungleiche Welten* (Wiesbaden: Insel, 1951); and Oskar Loerke, *Tagebücher 1903–1939*, ed. Hermann Kasack (Heidelberg, Darmstadt: Schneider, 1955).

[101] Elisabeth Langgässer, "Schriftsteller unter der Hitler-Diktatur," in *Deutsche Literatur im Exil 1933–1945*, vol. 1, *Dokumente*, ed. Heinz-Ludwig Arnold (Frankfurt am Main: Athenäum-Fischer-Taschenbuch-Verlag, 1974), 284–85.

[102] Entry no. 952, in Werner Bergengruen, *Schriftstellerexistenz in der Diktatur: Aufzeichnungen und Reflexionen zu Politik, Geschichte und Kultur 1940–1963*, ed. Frank-Lothar Kroll, N. Luise Hackelsberger, and Sylvia Taschka (Munich: Oldenbourg, 2005), 176–81. As early as 1942, Bergengruen had sympathized with the real difficulties faced by exiled writers and acknowledged the exile experience as a genuine test of character (entry no. 123, 32).

[103] Cf. Bergengruen's later obituary for Mann, broadcast on Norddeutscher Rundfunk and the Sender Freies Berlin on August 13, 1955: "Zum Tode Thomas Manns," in Bergengruen, *Werner Bergengruen: Mündlich gesprochen: Ansprache, Vorträge und Reden* (Zurich: Arche; Munich: Nymphenburger Verlags-Buchhandlung, 1963), 158–61.

[104] Bergengruen, *Schriftstellerexistenz*, entry no. 951, 175.

[105] See, for example, Walter A. Berendsohn, "Emigrantenliteratur," in *Reallexikon der deutschen Literaturgeschichte*, vol. 1, ed. Eckehard Catholy (Berlin: de Gruyter, 1958), 336, who denies the possibility of writers "emigrating within," rejecting the use of the term "emigration" for something that is more properly considered inner or private resistance.

[106] Franz Schonauer, *Deutsche Literatur im Dritten Reich: Versuch einer Darstellung in polemisch-didaktischer Absicht* (Freiburg im Breisgau: Walter, 1961).

[107] Schnell, *Literarische innere Emigration.*

[108] For example, Denkler and Prümm, *Die deutsche Literatur im Dritten Reich.*

[109] See, for example, Ernst Loewy, *Literatur unterm Hakenkreuz: Das Dritte Reich und seine Dichtung: Eine Dokumentation* (Frankfurt am Main: Europäische Verlagsanstalt, 1966). Also Wolfgang Emmerich's discussion of, inter alia, Werner Bergengruen, in "Die Literatur des antifaschistischen Widerstandes in Deutschland," in Denkler and Prümm, *Die deutsche Literatur im Dritten Reich*, 448–50.

[110] Herbert Wiesner, "'Innere Emigration': Die innerdeutsche Literatur im Widerstand 1933–1945," in *Handbuch der deutschen Gegenwartsliteratur*, 2nd ed., vol. 2, ed. Hermann Kunisch (Munich: Nymphenburger Verlagshandlung, 1970), 383–408.

[111] Brekle, "Die antifaschistische Literatur," 71–72.

[112] Wolfgang Brekle, *Schriftsteller im antifaschistischen Widerstand 1933–1945 in Deutschland* (Berlin, Weimar: Aufbau Verlag, 1985).

[113] Grimm, "Innere Emigration als Lebensform," 31–73. A revised version appeared under the title "Im Dickicht der inneren Emigration," in Denkler and Prümm, *Die deutsche Literatur im Dritten Reich*, 406–26.

[114] Grimm, "Innere Emigration als Lebensform," 48.

[115] Ibid., 51.

[116] See especially Martin Broszat, "Zur Sozialgeschichte des deutschen Widerstands," *Vierteljahreshefte für Zeitgeschichte* 34, no. 3 (1986): 293–309; also Ian Kershaw, *The Nazi Dictatorship* (London: Edward Arnold, 2000), 220–21.

[117] See in this context Schäfer, *Das gespaltene Bewußtsein* (1981), and the new edition, *Das gespaltene Bewußtsein: Vom Dritten Reich bis zu den langen fünfziger Jahren* (Göttingen: Wallstein, 2009). Also relevant are two studies by Ralf Schnell: "Innere Emigration und kulturelle Dissidenz," in *Widerstand und Verweigerung in Deutschland 1933–1945*, ed. Richard Löwenthal and Patrik von zur Mühlen (Bonn: Dietz, 1984), 211–25; and "Zwischen Anpassung und Widerstand: Zur Literatur der Inneren Emigration im Dritten Reich," in *Europäische Literatur gegen den Faschismus 1922–1945*, ed. Thomas Bremer (Munich: C. H. Beck, 1986), 15–32.

[118] Michael Philipp, "Distanz und Anpassung: Sozialgeschichtliche Aspekte der Inneren Emigration," in *Aspekte der künstlerischen Inneren Emigration 1933–1945*, ed. Claus Dieter Krohn, Erwin Rotermund, Lutz Winkler, and Wulf Koepke (Munich: text + kritik, 1994), 28.

[119] Examples include: Michael Braun, Georg Guntermann, and Christiane Gandner, eds., *"Gerettet und zugleich von Scham verschlungen": Neue Annäherungen an die Literatur der "inneren Emigration"* (Frankfurt am Main: Lang, 2007); Friedrich Denk, *Die Zensur der Nachgeborenen: Zur regimekritischen Literatur im Dritten Reich* (Weilheim i. Ob.: Denk, 1995); Donahue and Kirchner, *Flight of Fantasy*; Frank-Lothar Kroll, ed., *Die totalitäre Erfahrung: Deutsche Literatur und Drittes Reich* (Berlin: Duncker & Humblot, 2003); Kroll and

von Voss, *Schriftsteller und Widerstand*; Günter Scholdt, *Autoren über Hitler: Deutschsprachige Schriftsteller 1910–1945 und ihr Bild vom Führer* (Bonn: Bouvier, 1993); and Scholdt, "'Ein Geruch von Blut und Schande,'" 23–28.

[120] Ehrke-Rotermund and Rotermund, *Zwischenreiche.*

[121] Zuckmayer, *Geheimreport.*

[122] Dolf Sternberger, "Nachbemerkung," in *Figuren der Fabel: Essays* (Frankfurt am Main: Suhrkamp, 1990), 179. Many would now prefer the more accurate term "verdeckende (concealing) Schreibweise."

[123] Dodd, *"Jedes Wort wandelt die Welt"*; Ehrke-Rotermund and Rotermund, *Zwischenreiche*; Rotermund and Ehrke-Rotermund, "Nachwort," in *Stefan Andres: Wir sind Utopia*, 275–311. See also "The Art of Camouflage" in chapter 2 of this book.

[124] For example, Schmollinger, *"Intra muros et extra"*; Günter Scholdt, "'Den Emigranten nach außen entsprechen die Emigranten im Innern': Kasacks Diktum und die Kritik an einem Begriff," in *Hermann Kasack—Leben und Werk: Symposium 1993 in Potsdam*, ed. Helmut John and Lonny Neumann (Frankfurt am Main: Lang, 1994), 99–109; and Günter Scholdt, "Kein Freispruch zweiter Klasse: Zur Bewertung nichtnazistischer Literatur im 'Dritten Reich,'" *Zuckmayer-Jahrbuch* 5 (2000): 127–77. See also Zimmermann, "'Innere Emigration,'" 45–61.

[125] See Scholdt, "'Ein Geruch von Blut und Schande,'" 24.

[126] Ernst Fischer, "Den Kongreß über Bord?," *Neue Deutsche Blätter* 1, no. 1 (1933): 59, cited in Emmerich, "Die Literatur des antifaschistischen Widerstands," 429.

[127] Otto Flake, "Der Fall Thomas Mann," *Badener Tagblatt*, December 8, 1945, in Grosser, *Die große Kontroverse*, 54.

[128] Dodd, "Dolf Sternberger's *Panorama*," 201.

[129] Scholdt, "'Ein Geruch von Blut und Schande,'" 24.

[130] See Hans Dahlke, *Geschichtsroman und Literaturkritik im Exil* (Berlin: Aufbau, 1976), 91–101.

[131] See, for example, Franz Carl Weiskopf, "Hier spricht die deutsche Literatur!: Zweijahresbilanz der 'Verbrannten,'" in *Zur Tradition der sozialistischen Literatur in Deutschland: Eine Auswahl von Dokumenten*, ed. Deutsche Akademie der Künste (Berlin: Aufbau-Verlag, 1967), 663–68; and Kurt Hiller, "Zwischen den Dogmen," *Die neue Weltbühne* 4, no. 50 (December 12, 1935): 1580–81.

[132] Alfred Döblin, "Historie und kein Ende," *Pariser Tageblatt* 4, no. 754 (January 5, 1936): 3, in *Alfred Döblin: Schriften zu Ästhetik, Poetik und Literatur*, ed. Erich Kleinschmidt (Freiburg im Breisgau: Walter, 1989), 288–291; Ludwig Marcuse, "Die Anklage auf Flucht," *Das neue Tagebuch* 4, no. 6 (1936): 131–33; and Georg Lukács, "Der Kampf zwischen Liberalismus und Demokratie im Spiegel des historischen Romans der deutschen Antifaschisten," in Arnold, *Deutsche Literatur im Exil 1933–1945*, vol. 2, *Dokumente und Materialien*, 173–99.

[133] Richard Löwenthal, "Widerstand im totalen Staat," in Löwenthal and Mühlen, *Widerstand und Verweigerung*, 23.

[134] Philipp, "Distanz und Anpassung," 13.

[135] See Martin Broszat, "Plädoyer für eine Historisierung des Nationalsozialismus,"in Martin Broszat, *Nach Hitler: Der schwierige Umgang mit unserer Geschichte* (Munich: Deutscher Taschenbuch Verlag, 1988), 266–81.

[136] Broszat, "Zur Sozialgeschichte des deutschen Widerstands," 300. Page numbers to this source cited parenthetically in the text for the remainder of the paragraph.

[137] Philipp, "Distanz und Anpassung," 15–16.

[138] Karl Müller and Johann Holzner, "Vorwort," in *Zwischenwelt: Literatur der 'Inneren Emigration' aus Österreich*, Jahrbuch der Theodor-Kramer-Gesellschaft 6, ed. Johann Holzner and Karl Müller (Vienna: Theodor-Kramer-Gesellschaft, 1998), 10.

[139] Frank-Lothar Kroll, "Intellektueller Widerstand im Dritten Reich: Möglichkeiten und Grenzen," in Kroll and von Voss, *Schriftsteller und Widerstand*, 16.

[140] Esther Dür, *Erika Mitterer und das Dritte Reich: Schreiben zwischen Protest, Anpassung und Vergessen* (Vienna: Praesens-Verlag, 2006), 78.

2: The Writers of the Inner Emigration and Their Approaches

INNER EMIGRANTS WERE a relatively small subset of the approximately five thousand writers who in 1941 were members of the Reich Chamber of Literature (RSK).[1] However, if we accept the definition of literary inner emigration that has emerged in recent years, namely, that it is a descriptive rather than an evaluative term for a way of life under National Socialism and that the very act of social and literary withdrawal from the regime constituted dissent from its ideals, then the field is inevitably broader than was suggested in the postwar period. Between the extremes of, on the one hand, illegal dissemination of openly anti-Nazi texts and propagandistic leaflets by the Bund Proletarisch-Revolutionärer Schriftsteller (League of Proletarian Revolutionary Writers) or the oppositional Weiße Rose (White Rose) group, and on the other, the activities of writers who put themselves at the service of the Propaganda Ministry and whose careers flourished thanks to the backing of the NSDAP (National Socialist German Workers' Party), there was a large number of authors whose attitudes, behavior, and literary output after 1933 placed them in an intermediate space somewhere between Grimm's extremes of open action and complete silence.[2]

These writers, who were not assimilated to and did not conform with the regime, were far from a homogeneous group and espoused diverse philosophical, political, and religious views, covering the whole political spectrum from Left to Right.[3] They ranged from archconservatives (for example, Friedrich Reck-Malleczewen), national conservatives (Ernst Wiechert), and liberal conservatives (Rudolf Pechel), to socialists (Jan Petersen, Adam Kuckhoff) and communists (Ernst Niekisch); they included Christian writers of both confessions (Reinhold Schneider, Rudolf Alexander Schröder, Ernst Wiechert, Werner Bergengruen, Theodor Haecker, Elisabeth Langgässer), academics (Victor Klemperer, Werner Krauss), journalists and publicists (Dolf Sternberger, Rudolf Pechel, Carl Linfert), philosophers (Karl Jaspers), military men (Ernst Jünger), temporary or longer-term fellow travelers (Gottfried Benn, Hans Carossa), those in semi-exile in German-occupied territory (Stefan Andres), and those who began writing in Germany under National Socialism, went into exile, and then returned to Germany (Wolfgang Koeppen and Irmgard Keun from Holland, Ernst Glaeser from Switzerland). Inner emigrants came from differing social backgrounds and different parts of Germany, belonged to more than one literary generation, and enjoyed contrasting literary reputations and standings. Some did not write at all, either through choice or because they were banned, and of these some wrote "for the drawer" and later publication; some wrote harmless texts on non-contentious topics, for example, travel or children's literature; whereas others wrote works critical of National Socialism but in a veiled fashion designed to evade censorship. Inner emigrants can also not be defined or grouped by literary style or theme, being active in a wide range of genres including historical or documentary novels, shorter prose texts, and nature poetry. However, the largest number were certainly strongly influenced by Christian beliefs and tended to write in a manner indebted to the unity of form and meaning characteristic of the nineteenth-century tradition in narrative fiction.

Before considering the features and techniques of inner emigrant writing, the first four sections of this chapter demonstrate the breadth of the phenomenon and suggest an approach to how one might differentiate within it. Excluding those writers dealt with at length in chapters 3 to 10, the following categorization is offered largely for the purposes of orientation in a large and complex field; it is not watertight or without overlap, and some of the categorizations may be contestable, but it will help to delineate more clearly the type of writers and literary concerns that are the focus of the greater part of this book.

Oppositional Writers

Among oppositional literary figures, who might, strictly speaking, be classed as "resistance" writers rather than inner emigrants, are Günther Weisenborn, Jan Petersen, Adam Kuckhoff, and Werner Krauss. Weisenborn (1902–69), whose books were banned in the first year of the regime, managed to remain active as a writer through the use of various pseudonyms. He emigrated to the United States in 1936 but returned to Germany in 1937 and thereafter continued to work in theater, film, and radio, while also contributing to the activities of the resistance group Rote Kapelle (Red Orchestra).[4] Arrested for these links in 1942, he escaped execution when his death penalty was commuted, and survived the war in prison. Curiously, his formal exclusion from the RSK did not occur until 1944.

Petersen (1906–69) too left Germany (in 1934) and spent the Nazi years in exile in France, Switzerland, and England. However, he wrote the novel *Unsere Straße* in Germany in 1933–34 (translated into English in 1938 as *Our Street: A Chronicle Written in the Heart of Fascist Germany*), and it was smuggled abroad to be published first in extract form in Paris in 1935, then in full in Bern and Moscow in 1936, before subsequently being smuggled back into Germany and circulated illegally.[5] Focusing on a communist resistance group and its battle with Nazis for control of a street in Berlin-Charlottenburg, the first-person and strongly autobiographical narrative employs documentary techniques, including newspaper articles, speeches, and firsthand accounts, in combination with reports of characters' feelings and impressions, dialogue, and free indirect speech, to interweave personal experience and political events of the period. The further inclusion of a fictive diary allows the reader access to the activities of a resistance fighter.[6]

Kuckhoff (1887–1943) had links to left-wing resistance groups, primarily the circle around Arvid Harnack and later the Rote Kapelle. He was arrested for this involvement in Prague in September 1942 and was killed a year later in Plötzensee Prison in Berlin. In the novel *Der Deutsche von Bayencourt* (1937, translated into English in 2014 as *The German from Bayencourt*), set during the First World War, the actions of Bernhard Sommer, a native German farmer but French citizen and patriot, whose befriending of German soldiers leads to him being tried before a French military court and shot for treason, appear to allow a German nationalist interpretation. Evidence for a very different reading, however, relating to a reconciliation between nations, is to be found both in the pacifist views of Sommer's son, Marcel, and in those of the farmhand, Barnabas, who is inclined toward a more revolutionary response. Indeed, the book later came to be seen by Brekle from an East German perspective as an anti-militarist and anti-imperialist work: Marcel represents the weakness of the liberal bourgeoisie, which recognizes an evil regime but lacks a clear idea of how to change social circumstances; the clarity of Barnabas's revolutionary views, by contrast, suggests the need for civil war, dispossession of the rich, and thus removal of the conflict of interests within the country.[7]

Krauss (1884–1959), a professor of Romance languages, was arrested for his association with the resistance circle of Harro Schulze-Boysen and Arvid Harnack. He wrote his novel *PLN: Die Passionen der halykonischen Seele* (PLN: The passions of the halyconian soul, 1946) in Plötzensee prison under extraordinary conditions: he was facing the death penalty, often had to write with his hands tied, and had to get a fellow inmate to smuggle the manuscript out of prison.[8] The highly cryptic, bitterly satirical work makes for difficult reading, especially owing to its loose structure, but it provides an encoded panorama of life in Nazi Germany in 1944, with readily identifiable figures, including Hitler (Großlenker Muphti), Göring (Luftmarschall Oleander), Goebbels (Koben, "Staatsminister für die Verbreitung von Wahrheit und Optimismus," Minister for the Dissemination of Truth and Optimism!), and an archetypal figure of German inwardness (the postal minister Schnipfmeier). Besides providing a hidden portrait of Schulze-Boysen's oppositional group, Krauss also seeks here to analyze how Germans succumbed to the Nazis without serious resistance and condemns the majority for their unconditional and unquestioning obedience, excepting from his strictures only the "cata-comb" society of postal criminals, who resist the state-backed postcode.[9] Although the greatest sarcasm is reserved for the Nazi Germanic cult, the work is also highly critical of the passivity and inconsequential behavior of those who do their duty regardless, are indecisive and uncommitted, and who pursue an inwardness that leaves the political field to the morally corrupt instead of demanding the practical realization of their professed values of humanity, intellect, and culture.[10]

Nonconformists

This is the largest and most varied grouping of inner emigrants, encom-passing work that lacks the transparency of Petersen's or Kuckhoff's writ-ing but nevertheless reveals an identifiable nonconformist stance, often shrouded in ambiguity, or at the very least a pointed nonengagement with Nazi themes and values.

The poet and novelist Elisabeth Langgässer (1899–1950) was threat-ened with deportation to the camps owing to her paternal Jewish origins but was saved thanks to her "Aryan" husband, Wilhelm Hoffmann. However, her daughter Cordelia, the fruit of an earlier relationship with a Jew, was deported to Auschwitz since she was classed a "full Jew." Langgässer her-self was excluded from the RSK in 1936 and thus banned from publish-ing, although she managed to publish in preannexation Austria the book *Rettung am Rhein* (Salvation on the Rhine, 1938), which contained three stories showing the crisis of modernity, namely, the clash of reason with religious awareness.[11] She worked for the next nine years on the novel *Das unauslöschliche Siegel* (The indelible seal, 1946), which she kept hidden under challenging circumstances. The work is about the victory of good over evil and celebrates the power of faith from a Catholic perspective. It tells the story of the spiritual journey of Lazarus Belfontaine, a Jewish con-vert to Catholicism, during and after the First World War: having led a dis-solute life in France, the inveterate rationalist rediscovers the significance of his baptism (the "indelible seal"), returns to Germany, and submits willingly to Nazi anti-Semitism by way of reparation. This redemptive self-identification with the oppressed has wider, exemplary social significance, and the novel, seen as a classic text of the inner emigration, became one of the most fêted works of the postwar period.

In her postwar pronouncements, Langgässer was surprisingly critical of inner emigrant positions, especially those of writers who had retreated to inwardness and ignored what was going on around them. In an address to the First All German Writers' Congress in 1947, she referred to the characteristic dangers of esotericism, of the "anakreontische Tändeln mit Blumen und Blümchen über den scheußlichen . . . Abgrund der

Massengräber" (anacreontic trifling with pretty little flowers at the dreadful . . . abyss of the mass graves), which she associated with poetry of the period and which she labeled "unverbindlich, wertlos und deshalb verabscheuungswürdig" (noncommittal, worthless, and thus detestable). She also wrote that it was sometimes a blessing to be excluded from the official cultural life of the Third Reich since that meant one never succumbed to the temptation to compromise with the regime.[12] However, at the same time, she hinted that she included her own past in these strictures, perhaps referring to the fact that she had voted for Hitler in the elections of March 1933[13] and, while rejecting the Nazis' racial policies, had welcomed their assumption of power as an opportunity to transform the country for the better. Moreover, it has been argued that although *Das unauslöschliche Siegel* presented National Socialism as a pernicious force, it also tended toward a negative portrayal of its French protagonists as physically and mentally corrupt, which was quite in keeping with elements of Nazi racial ideology.[14] Although she was one of the unequivocal literary victims of National Socialism, even Langgässer's case provides evidence of the ambiguous situation of authors who remained in Germany, examination of whose backgrounds has revealed a far more complex picture of the reality of life within the inner emigration than initially assumed.

Another "victim" of the Third Reich was the theologian, journalist, and writer Jochen Klepper (1903–42), who is particularly remembered for his production of sacred songs and hymns.[15] He was married to a Jew and when, towards the end of 1942, his wife and stepdaughter were threatened with deportation to a camp, the whole family committed suicide. Klepper was best known in Nazi Germany for his historical work *Der Vater: Der Roman des Soldatenkönigs* (The father: Novel of the soldier king, 1937), about the controversial figure of Friedrich Wilhelm I of Prussia, which reveals a characteristic inner emigrant vacillation between affirmation of many aspects of the Nazi regime and criticism of its core ideals. On the one hand, it seems to glorify authoritarian rule, the strong leader, and the role of the military, while also justifying on biblical grounds absolute obedience to the state in all circumstances. And indeed, for these reasons, the novel was welcomed in official reviews[16] and also appealed to the Nazi hierarchy, with reports of ministers ordering copies and giving them as presents and the War Ministry recommending it as suitable reading for the armed forces.[17] On the other hand, the work offers a counterimage to National Socialist rule by supporting religious tolerance and insisting on the primacy of justice, including a clear distinction between just and unjust military action.[18] Friedrich Wilhelm's rule is presented as a patriarchal monarchy that is informed by a sense of duty and places human concerns above political power games. The monarch adheres to the law, exercises tolerance, and listens to others, while his control of state finances, the abolition of serfdom, and the restriction of feudal privileges are held up as exemplars of distinguished statesmanship. At the same time, the novel does not entirely hide negative aspects of Friedrich Wilhelm's reign: his authoritarianism, the close surveillance of and checks on his subjects, and the use of physical punishment. In such negative traits one can see parallels with contemporary Nazi Germany, as indeed one can in references to the Prussian state as a large prison and a galley ship.[19] In general, Klepper's thinking was dominated by the notions of nation and fatherland, of an absolutist monarchy ready to embrace suffering on behalf of its people, but also by such an intense, biblically based sense of loyalty to the state that he resisted approaches from the oppositional Bekennende Kirche (Confessing Church), as he saw in their activities an unacceptable politicization of religion.

Theodor Haecker (1879–1945) was a writer, cultural critic, and translator who made significant contributions to the discussion of Catholic existentialism, being particularly concerned with the work of Søren Kierkegaard and John Henry Newman. In 1923 he began an association with Karl Muth's Catholic journal *Hochland* and in due course became one its major contributors. A convinced opponent of the Nazis, the convert to Catholicism was banned from speaking in public in 1935 and then, in 1938, from publishing independently, although he still worked on translations and published shorter pieces, especially in *Hochland*.[20] Moreover, despite his publication ban he managed in 1944 to have a small volume containing extracts from his works published illegally by the same Alsatia Verlag in Colmar that had published works by Reinhold Schneider.[21] Although outwardly conforming, Haecker mixed with representatives of the White Rose resistance movement and, after the first arrests, came under investigation himself, though the charge of "preparing treason" was eventually dropped.[22] On another occasion, during a search of his flat, extracts from his explicit secret diaries were smuggled out only thanks to his daughter's quick-wittedness.[23] These diaries are Haecker's best-known publication. Not always easy to read, they consist of a mixture of philosophical and religious musings, acerbic, often aphoristic observations on current affairs, and a good deal of self-reflection. Dialogue is prevalent, as Haecker talks to his diary in what Siefken calls a "Socratic mode of discovering the truth."[24] The diaries were clearly not for publication under National Socialism, as they are explicit in their repudiation of the regime and in the vitriol they pour on the Nazis, and Haecker consequently ensured that multiple versions of the manuscript existed at any time so that one copy could always be buried or otherwise kept hidden.[25] The diaries could be published only in 1947 and are considered a seminal inner emigrant text. And indeed the conservative Haecker was himself a classic inner emigrant whose respect for tradition, morality, and hierarchy rendered Nazism's destructive nihilism, moral vacuity, and crude populism completely anathema to him.

A very different opponent of Nazism was the established novelist Ricarda Huch (1864–1947). By 1933 she was almost seventy years old and had already published much of her life's work. However, she was to prove herself one of the bravest writers to remain in Germany.[26] She resigned her membership of the Prussian Academy of the Arts in 1933 and in her resignation letter to the President of the Academy, the composer Max von Schillings, criticized the new regime, saying its national ethos did not correspond with her idea of Germanness and that she considered its use of compulsion and brutality, its persecution of those opposed to its ideas, and its boastful self-importance to be both "un-German" and a disaster for the country.[27] Her writing was informed by her Christianity and a commitment to Europe's humanist inheritance, which was allied to a historian's belief in historical progress. The first volume of her substantial *Deutsche Geschichte* (German history), entitled *Römisches Reich Deutscher Nation* (The Roman Empire of the German nation, 1934), was subjected to a fierce attack in the *Nationalsozialistische Monatshefte* for its allegedly anti-German sentiments.[28] This confirmed her "undesirable" status in the eyes of the regime, but the authorities were still keen to tolerate most of her publications owing to the propaganda capital to be had from allowing an internationally respected figure to continue to publish. Although, apart from her major history, Huch wrote relatively little under National Socialism, significant literary works include her poem "November" (1938), which is a stand against the persecution of the Jews, and the poems collected under the title *Herbstfeuer* (Autumn fire, 1944), which reflect her skepticism of heroic military sacrifice, her desire for peace, and her anguish at the suffering inflicted on Germany and Europe by the war.[29] Huch's opposition to the regime can still be seen in the novella *Weiße Nächte* (White nights, 1943), a positive portrayal of Russians set in June 1915 in a St. Petersburg beset by concerns over war and its consequences. This work, written in a spirit of international understanding at precisely the time when German troops were instigating one of history's most agonizing sieges outside the same city—by then named Leningrad—epitomizes the writer's humanist instincts.

Rarely mentioned in connection with inner emigration is the writer Olaf Saile (1901–52). As editor of the *Rathenower Zeitung*, he was an outspoken opponent of the Nazis and was arrested in June 1933 following the banning of the SPD (the Social Democratic Party of Germany). He was imprisoned in Oranienburg concentration camp and upon release was banned from working as a journalist. His novel *Kepler: Roman einer Zeitwende* (Kepler: A novel of a new era, 1938) is a fictional biography of the seventeenth-century German mathematician, astronomer, and astrologer Johannes Kepler, famous for his laws of planetary motion. The nonconformist aspects of the novel have been largely neglected, although it has been frequently reprinted and in

1940 was even published in New York under the title *Troubadour of the Stars*. Although it lacks any obvious reference to contemporary political relations, its relevance becomes clear when one notes that Kepler is an intellectual who is persecuted for his views under an absolutist regime, and whose work is banned and subsequently burned. Indeed, his situation has echoes of the oppressed academic or scientist in Nazi Germany: "Aber hinter allem stand immer wieder die dunkle Angst vor der Zukunft. Was sollte aus ihm werden, wohin sollte er mit den Seinen ziehen, wo ließ sich noch einmal leben? Denn dieses Österreich ging zugrunde und die Zeichen der Zeit . . . in den Wissenschaften, auf den Universitäten, verkündeten einen jähen Zusammenbruch." (But behind it all there was repeatedly a dark fear of the future. What was to become of him, where were he and his family to move to, where could they settle? For this Austria was heading for ruin and all the signs . . . in science, at the universities, presaged a sudden collapse.)[30]

Kepler is a man of progress, determined to affirm the Copernican view of the solar system as part of the wider sixteenth-century scientific revolution. Against a background of superstition, blind religious dogma, and war, he condemns the powerful in society for allowing hostilities to proliferate and indeed profiting from them, and is frustrated when his mentor, Professor Mästlin, is reluctant to teach publicly Copernican theory, arguing that the time is not yet "ripe" for it. One of the key aspects of this society's obscurantism is its persecution of supposed witches and, in an interesting parallel with Erika Mitterer's allegorical *Der Fürst der Welt* (1940, English translation *The Prince of Darkness*, 2004—see chapter 10), the arrest and trial of Kepler's mother on suspicion of witchcraft conjures up the atmosphere of a police state, where denunciations and torture are the norm. Kepler undertakes to fight the prejudice and "madness" of the witch-hunt mentality, and in an exchange with the lawyer Besold, which encapsulates the contemporary German nonconformist's dilemma, asserts: "Jeder, der hier schweigt, macht sich mitschuldig!" (All who remain silent here share in the guilt!), to which Besold responds: "Und jeder, der zu offen spricht, bringt sich in Gefahr" (And all who speak too openly put themselves in danger, 294–95).

A particularly complex case of distance from and complicity with the regime is that of the author and screenwriter Erich Kästner (1899–1974). In the Weimar period he had attained a reputation as a prominent intellectual, prolific author of poems, articles, and reviews, and a leading figure in the *Neue Sachlichkeit* (New Objectivity) movement in literature, which satirized contemporary society through an objective, distancing style. Owing to these earlier publications, his (lifelong) pacifism, and his rejection of National Socialism, Kästner's books were burned in May 1933. He was furthermore denied membership in the RSK and all his past publications were banned, although this did not constitute a general ban on writing. Moreover, reflecting the confused circumstances in literary policy at the time, his popular novels *Emil und die Zwillinge* (1934, translated into English in 1949 as *Emil and the Three Twins*) and *Drei Männer im Schnee* (1934, translated into English in 1935 as *Three Men in the Snow*) could still be published abroad, and indeed sold in large numbers, while other works published in Germany since the end of 1933, including *Das fliegende Klassenzimmer* (1933, translated into English in 1934 as *The Flying Classroom*), still managed to appear in German shops.[31] Although nevertheless officially deemed "unreliable," Kästner managed to continue to work under different pseudonyms, producing politically uncontentious light novels and children's stories as well as uncontroversial poetry in the collection *Lyrische Hausapotheke* (Lyrical home pharmacy, 1935). He also became an author for the entertainment industry, writing numerous theater texts and screenplays.[32] Such work could in normal circumstances be carried out only by a member of the RSK, but it was commissioned with the full knowledge of Propaganda Minister Goebbels himself, who, in also allowing the likes of Hans Fallada and Alexander Lernet-Holenia to write film scripts (see below), was making a conscious decision to promote through strong writing the increasingly important propaganda medium of film.[33] In 1942, Kästner was even granted a "Sondergenehmigung" (special permission) to work on the screenplay of the high-profile film *Münchhausen* for the anniversary of the UfA film studios. However, he was subsequently denounced by Rosenberg's Reichsstelle and banned from all writing.[34]

Disputes have raged about Kästner's precise role in the Third Reich. Some claim he refused to collaborate with the regime or to compromise his integrity, whereas others question his supposed retreat into silence, his paid employment in the service of the Nazi entertainment industry, and his continuing income from children's writing. There seems little doubt that his work in Nazi Germany was received by many as a type of antidote to Nazi ideas, a form of entertaining consolation (for example, handwritten copies of his poems are said to have circulated in the Warsaw ghetto and some poems appeared in literary compilations produced by resistance publishers in occupied France),[35] but his postwar self-stylization as a "passive" member of Nazi society deliberately downplayed his active role in maintaining contact with the German cultural industry, his acceptance of the restrictive conditions placed on his work in return for employment, and the willing depoliticization of his writing.[36] Kästner's case is a good illustration of the problems facing those who seek to allocate writers in Nazi Germany to fixed categories; indeed he might also be listed under the third or even fourth headings employed here.

Turning attention to Austria, even before annexation in 1938 nationalist writers had made preparations for the takeover and had formed the Bund deutscher Schriftsteller Österreichs (Association of German Writers in Austria), headed by the Catholic author Max Mell.[37] One writer who stands apart from this development was Alexander Lernet-Holenia (1897–1976). He is remarkable for his high profile as a writer in Austria and his substantial oeuvre, but also for being simultaneously little known abroad. He was an aristocratic individualist who has been deemed both naïve with regard to politics but also a shrewd survivalist.[38] Although he held deeply conservative social views, he was one of the few major Austrian writers who did not align themselves with the Nazis, having little time for their proletarian tendencies, though he did seek accommodation with the regime to ensure he could pursue his career as a writer. Thus, following Austrian annexation, he wrote a good deal for the German film industry and even became chief dramaturge of the Heeresfilmstelle (Army Film Center) in Berlin. This work for the Nazi film industry proved lucrative and in 1942 his income reached a very substantial 30,864 Reichsmark.[39]

Elements of nonconformism have been discerned in Lernet-Holenia's novels *Der Mann im Hut* (The man in the hat, 1937), about a search for Attila the Hun's treasure, which serves as a metaphor of German expansionism in pursuit of lands lost through war, and *Ein Traum in Rot* (Dream in red, 1939), a veiled critique of Nazi eastward expansion set in Poland at the end of the First World War.[40] However, his major contribution to inner emigrant writing is the strongly autobiographical work *Mars im Widder* (Mars in Aries, 1940, 1947).[41] It is a novel about the start of the Second World War, in particular the invasion of Poland by the *Wehrmacht*, to which Lernet-Holenia had been called up, and is written in a style that merges the actual events of battle with fantastical elements, making it difficult in places to discern what is reality. It is marked throughout by a distinct lack of militant triumphalism or any championing of the German fighting spirit, seen most graphically in the image of a procession of crabs as a symbol of the great armies of panzers blindly heading toward their destruction, but significantly heading west not east,[42] which Eicher likens to a procession of lemmings and interprets as a "visionary symbol" of the impending destruction of the invading army, the westward direction perhaps hinting at the future revenge of Soviet troops.[43] The depiction of the German aggressor also little resembles the heroic portrayals of official propaganda and, most strikingly, there is clear sympathy for the suffering of the Polish enemy, whose impressive culture and great past as a nation are also highlighted in distinctly "off-message" tones. Furthermore, in its depiction of the aristocratic central character, Wallmoden, and his fellow officers, the work focuses on the continuing prominence of the old Austrian aristocratic order in the "new" Reich, in a way that could only irritate the Nazis. Finally, Lernet-Holenia's characteristic fatalism is seen in the astrological symbolism and the attendant apocalyptic mood, which suggests that fate ultimately holds sway over Nazi ambitions.[44] Lernet-Holenia is, in summary, difficult to categorize:

a writer guilty of accommodation with National Socialism but one whose work also evinces a strong element of inner emigrant distancing from the ideals of the regime.

Lyric Poetry

It has been claimed that poetry is *the* genre of inner emigration, that it served as an ideal medium for expressing opposing values. Although, in terms of sheer volume, prose is the dominant form of nonconformist writing, it is undeniably true that poetry was a significant vehicle for those seeking a means to affirm spiritual values and was a medium well suited to the ambiguity and veiled mode of writing that the times demanded. The prevalence of nonconformist poetry under the Nazis is to be explained not just by the opportunity it afforded writers to lend veiled expression to their rejection of the regime but also by its usually succinct form, which meant poems lent themselves well to being circulated illicitly.[45]

Although the ode was seen as a Germanic form and thus figured most prominently in the Nazi poetic canon,[46] the sonnet became the single most favored poetic genre among nonconformists, possibly because, as a nonnative form, it stood as an expression of opposition to Nazi cultural policies,[47] and, as a classical poetic structure, could further be seen as a means of confronting the chaos of Nazism with ordered form.[48] However, the large number of sonnets produced by *völkisch* and nationalist writers makes it seem unlikely that it could be considered an intrinsically oppositional medium.[49] Several writers, such as Stefan Andres and Marie Luise Kaschnitz, produced individual sonnets as part of larger collections, but Reinhold Schneider was the most prolific exponent of the form, writing over two hundred, few of which could be published before 1945, although it is claimed that several circulated in camps and prisons and were also found among the possessions of soldiers killed in action.[50]

A significant sonnet collection was *Venezianisches Credo* (Venetian Credo, 1945) by Rudolf Hagelstange (1912–84), who was a Wehrmacht soldier in France and Italy during the war and became known as a writer only after 1945. He wrote his collection in Italy in 1944 and managed to have a small number of copies produced on a local hand press in April 1945.[51] The poems were subsequently circulated among fellow soldiers in the final months of the war. They are concerned with the chaos, death, and destruction of military conflict but also promote the cultivation of humane values, a belief in the restoration of justice, and hope for the future. Their idealist analysis of the German present is rooted in a Schiller-like contrast between passion and intellect.[52]

The link between the strict form of the sonnet and a content focused on the humanist virtues of Europe's cultural heritage can be seen in the very different case of the *Moabiter Sonette* (1945, translated into English in 1978 as *Moabit Sonnets*) by Albrecht Haushofer (1903–45). Haushofer was a professor of political geography who also acted as policy adviser in the propaganda department of the Foreign Ministry and helped Rudolf Heß plan his flight to Britain. He was briefly imprisoned as a consequence of the latter escapade, fired from his post in the Foreign Ministry, and placed under close observation by the Gestapo. Only late in the day did he become a conservative, Christian humanist opponent of the regime. He had links to the conspirators of July 20, 1944, was incarcerated in Moabit prison in Berlin in December 1944, and was shot in April 1945 by a group of SS men as Soviet troops closed in on the city. He wrote his eighty sonnets while in prison and his brother found them in the dead man's hand. The works constitute a review of Haushofer's life, in which he reflects on his Bavarian home, his travels, his role under National Socialism, and the nature of power and violence. One of the best-known poems is entitled "Schuld" (Guilt) and ends with the deliberately ambiguous line: "Und heute weiß ich, was ich schuldig war" (And today I know what I was guilty of / what my obligation should have been).[53] Haushofer also wrote three historical dramas—*Scipio* (1934), *Sulla* (1938), and *Augustus* (1939)—which are concerned with maintaining traditional forms of government in the face of revolutionary violence but also with responsible use of power by the state.[54] Written from a humanist standpoint, they contain critical analogies to contemporary Germany as well as counterimages in the shape of ideal historical ruler types.[55]

Religious poetry was especially prominent in the work of inner emigrants. Besides Schneider and Werner Bergengruen (see chapters 7 and 3, respectively), one of the most significant practitioners was the poet and translator Rudolf Alexander Schröder (1878–1962), who had close links to the Confessing Church but was also a conservative nationalist. Schröder's distance from the regime is clearest in his insistent emphasis on Christian values in his essays from the 1930s, most especially in "Dichtungen der Naturvölker" (Literatures of indigenous peoples, 1935), in which he argues against contemporary racial theories and emphasizes that the writings of Africa, Asia, Polynesia, and elsewhere are part of a shared human cultural inheritance and are to be seen as examples of higher-level "Erleuchtung und Offenbarung" (illumination and revelation).[56] The titles of other essays from the period convey the flavor of his intellectual, ethical, and religious inclinations: "In memoriam Hugo von Hofmannsthal" (1929), "Racine und die deutsche Humanität" (Racine and German humanity, 1932), "Thomas Mann zum 60. Geburtstag" (Thomas Mann on his sixtieth birthday, 1935), "Shakespeare als Dichter des Abendlandes" (Shakespeare as poet of the West, 1944),[57] "Kunst und Religion" (Art and religion, 1934), and "Christentum und Humanismus" (Christianity and humanism, 1942).[58] Generally, however, he was someone who avoided engagement with political reality, moving in 1936 from Bremen to rural Bavaria and devoting himself to pastoral work as a Protestant lay preacher.[59] His poetry and sacred songs lend themselves much less obviously than Schneider's or Bergengruen's lyric poetry to a dissident interpretation, focusing as they do on the religious concepts of original sin, suffering, and salvation. Seen now as highly stylized and as neglecting the reality of Nazism, his poetry from the Third Reich, for example *Die Ballade vom Wandersmann* (The ballad of the wanderer, 1937) and the many hymns he composed, have nevertheless been considered an appeal to human conscience, a source of comfort for "the persecuted and the bereaved."[60] In a postwar speech he even referred to consolation as the principal role of the writer, providing what some would see as the classic statement of the inner emigrant mindset: "Das innerste Wesen aller Kunst ist Trost über die Vergänglichkeit des Daseins" (The essential character of all art is consolation for the transience of existence).[61]

Nature poetry was also well represented among inner emigrant poetry. One of the most significant figures here was Oskar Loerke (1884–1941), who had been a leading exponent of the genre in the 1920s. He shunned politics in his work but his life was increasingly constrained by political developments: removed by the Nazis in 1933 from his position as secretary of the literature department of the Prussian Academy of the Arts, he suffered greatly under the compromises he had to make in order to survive in his job as an editor with the Jewish publishers S. Fischer[62] and then, as his employment options narrowed, experienced increasing isolation, bouts of depression, and the ill health that was eventually to cause his death. In his two volumes of poetry published in Nazi Germany, *Der Silberdistelwald* (Silver thistle wood, 1934) and *Der Wald der Welt* (The forest of the world, 1936), Loerke's nature poetry begins to voice his distance from contemporary social and political developments, as it introduces the themes of fear, violence, and persecution, and creates a series of references to and allegories with the present—for example, in the ironically entitled "Genesungsheim" (Convalescent home) in *Der Silberdistelwald*, with its depiction of a skull being shattered by (it is presumed) a concentration camp guard's club.[63] In subsequent isolated poems one comes across examples of some of the most virulent anti-Nazi verse written under the regime; for example, the poem "Leitspruch" (Motto), dated November 1940, just months before his death, which also reveals his continuing attempt to lend meaning to a tortured existence:

Jedwedes blutgefügte Reich
Sinkt ein, dem Maulwurfshügel gleich.
Jedwedes lichtgeborne Wort
Wirkt durch das Dunkel fort und fort. (871)

[Every blood-decreed empire / Collapses like a molehill. / Every light-born word / Shines on and on through the dark.]

Such poems remain in the minority in Loerke's work, but here, and in his nature poetry more generally, he attempts to establish an alternative world to that of the German present, one which at the same time signals a distancing from modern technology in its various manifestations. The poems move between flight from and protest against the regime, between a mood of contemplation and opposition, in which untrammeled nature embodies a basic, elemental, and magical power beyond the reach of man and lends meaning to human existence.[64] His diaries, published after the war by the writer Hermann Kasack, reflect Loerke's depression and the dominant pessimism of his poetry; they further document his conservative views but also his antipathy toward the regime.[65] Here he lays the blame for his feelings of hopelessness, for the loss of his sense of literary self, on the demands of Nazi ideology and institutions. Schnell sees in Loerke's tendency to demonize National Socialism a symptomatic inner emigrant failure or inability to perceive events in a historical context: an emphasis on the demonic nature of historical forces, it is argued, frees the individual from responsibility for events and helps explain Loerke's apolitical view of Nazism.[66] More typically, others have found much to praise in his writing, and Loerke's increasing tendency to see social causes behind human suffering prompts Brekle, for example, to talk about his "bewußt antifaschistische Haltung" (consciously antifascist stance).[67]

Besides Loerke, the most significant figure in nature poetry of the Nazi era was Wilhelm Lehmann (1882–1968). This writer and teacher joined the NSDAP in 1933 against his innermost convictions, he later claimed,[68] but did little to engage with the regime subsequently. His poetry offers only a very loose connection with the Third Reich and he was a naturally unpolitical person who was depressed by the Nazis' attack on culture.[69] His poems, with the characteristic inner emigrant title of *Antwort des Schweigens* (Silent response, 1935), seek solace in the varied splendors of nature, which is again portrayed as "magical." Like the later collection with the equally characteristic title *Der Grüne Gott* (The green god, 1942), *Antwort des Schweigens* only indirectly suggests links to contemporary social or political reality.[70] Indeed, with such titles as "Trost der Blätter" (Consolation of leaves), the poems reveal a tendency to turn away from the world, to subordinate historical or political inclinations to the need for forbearance and endurance, trusting in the timeless, eternal power of magical nature.

Similar examples of *Trostdichtung* (poetry of consolation) with a strong attachment to nature can be found in the work of Karl Krolow (1915–99). Typically considered a poet of postwar Germany, Krolow in fact published poems, lyrical prose, and literary criticism quite extensively between 1940 and 1945. He did so in a variety of publications, including *Das Reich*, the weekly newspaper founded by Goebbels, the right-wing but non-Nazi *Deutsche Allgemeine Zeitung*, and the by now decidedly less liberal *Das Innere Reich*. His early poems, with their focus on the reassuring rhythms of the diurnal and seasonal round, bear such titles as "Ende des Sommers" (End of the summer), "Geist des Abends" (Evening spirit), "Der Wald" (The forest), "Waldmusik" (Music of the forest), "Nußernte" (Nut harvest), "An einen Herbst" (To an autumn), and "November." Such works served, in Neil H. Donahue's words, as "an aesthetic anaesthesia" that divorced human experience from analysis and transported the reader to "an eternal realm of sublimely uncritical reflection," creating a form of complicit "*Blüte-und-Boden* literature" that uncritically drew a veil over contemporary reality.[71] In this sense, Krolow, an established member of both the *Hitlerjugend* (Hitler Youth) and the NSDAP, is a writer who might more properly be categorized under the third, or even the fourth, section of this chapter.

Finally, mention should be made in this context of the poetry of Gertrud Kolmar (1894–1943?), most of which was published posthumously. Born the daughter of a Jewish lawyer (and the cousin of the cultural critic Walter Benjamin), she was transported to Auschwitz in 1943, where she is presumed to have been killed. Among her few publications in Nazi Germany was the collection *Die Frau und die Tiere* (Woman and animals, 1938), which appeared with the *Berlin Jüdischer Buchverlag*, whose activity between 1933 and 1938 in publishing work by Jewish intellectuals is one of the period's most extraordinary stories.[72] The title of the volume neatly encapsulates Kolmar's principal poetical themes, and a number of the poems reveal an understanding of nature as a magical sphere, to be contrasted unfavorably with the sphere of mankind. The book was withdrawn and pulped shortly after its appearance as part of the pogrom associated with the *Reichskristallnacht* (Night of Broken Glass) in November 1938. Kolmar's work has only recently gained the attention it deserves, finally appearing in 2010 in a three-volume critical collection.[73]

The Apolitical and the "Young Generation"

In the early years of exile, Bertolt Brecht wrote in his poem "An die Nachgeborenen" (To those who come after us): "Was sind das für Zeiten, wo / Ein Gespräch über Bäume fast ein Verbrechen ist / Weil es ein Schweigen über so viele Untaten einschließt!" (What are these for times, when a conversation about trees is almost a crime, because it involves silence about so many atrocities).[74] Intended partly as a reprimand to those who maintain a silence about the atrocities of the regime, the poem implies future generations' censure of writers who fail in their duty to respond politically to National Socialism in their writing. In tacitly condemning writers who had remained in Germany, Brecht seems to adopt almost as hard a line as Thomas Mann was to do in 1945. However, the poem can also be read as a lament at the nature of pernicious times, in which literature is rendered impotent and is sullied by involuntary association with oppression.

The latter interpretation is one that fits most readily the lives of a group of largely apolitical writers in Nazi Germany. Following a major study by Hans Dieter Schäfer, this group has come to be known as the "non-Nazi young generation" of writers, who made their literary debut in the Third Reich but who were more noted for their work after the war in either West or East Germany.[75] There are overlaps between this category and "mainstream" inner emigrants but they can be broadly characterized as those born in the early years of the century, for whom National Socialism and its cultural life quickly became normative and who sought to make their way within the Nazi system. They included: Alfred Andersch (1914–80), Johannes Bobrowski (1917–65), Günter Eich (1907–72), Gerd Gaiser (1908–76), Albrecht Goes (1908–2000), Peter Huchel (1903–81), Hermann Kasack (1896–1966), Marie Luise Kaschnitz (1901–74), Wolfgang Koeppen (1906–96), Friedo Lampe (1899–1945), Horst Lange (1904–71), Hermann Lenz (1913–98), Hans-Erich Nossack (1901–77), Ernst Penzoldt (1892–1955), Martin Raschke (1905–43), Hans Werner Richter (1908–93), Luise Rinser (1911–2002), Oda Schaefer (1900–1988), Wolfdietrich Schnurre (1920–89), Edzard Schaper (1908–84), Wolfgang Weyrauch (1904–80), and Eugen Gottlob Winkler (1912–36). The list includes some who were not actually that young in 1933 (Kasack, Lampe, Penzoldt), but what unites them is their response to National Socialism, their use of a politics-free or depoliticized cultural space that the Nazis were happy to tolerate in the interests of ensuring a cohesive society—once, that is, they had ensured the withdrawal or imprisonment of Jewish and left-wing writers. This, of course, was on the condition that writers did nothing to express openly whatever reservations they might have about prevailing social, political, and economic conditions.

With a few exceptions, these writers avoided the longer narrative forms, preferring shorter novels, novellas, short stories, sketches, essays, feuilleton columns, diaries, reports, and, to a lesser extent, plays and poetry. The principal distinguishing feature of their work is that it was devoid of historical and political awareness. Schäfer links this to their reluctance to undertake large-scale narratives in which social context would have to figure more prominently.[76] The group thus included writers who wrote light fiction or *Unterhaltungsliteratur* (entertainment literature), including Heinrich Spoerl, best known for his *Feuerzangenbowle* (Punch bowl, 1933) and various humorous novels and stories. Children's literature also featured here, including selected works by Erich Kästner and Hans Fallada, though overall the literary activities of these two suggest a different categorization. The grouping also encompasses literature produced for literature's sake, such as the poetry of Georg Britting, Peter Huchel, or Friedrich Georg Jünger, and the prose of Kaschnitz—for example her bildungsroman *Elissa* (1937)— and Lange's fatalistic work, for instance the novel *Schwarze Weide* (Black willow, 1937). Furthermore, there were examples of more mainstream inner emigrant religious writing, like that of the Protestant clergyman Goes, who, although he published works after the war that were seen as classics of inner resistance, such as *Unruhige Nacht* (Restless night, 1950, English translation *Arrow to the Heart*, 1952) and *Das Brandopfer* (1954, English translation *The Burnt Offering*, 1956), devoted himself in the Third Reich to writing simple plays for use in the Christian community and occasional poetry, notably the well-received collection *Der Hirte* (The shepherd, 1934). Several of the non-Nazi young generation of writers also sought to escape the reality of the Third Reich by embracing themes from classical antiquity, in particular ancient myths and legends (here revealing affinities with more established nonconformist writers), by undertaking work on film scripts, radio plays, and other broadcasts, and—reflecting both the spread of the car and the increasing popularity of travel in the 1930s—by producing travel writing, which during the war was frequently supplemented by or merged with reports on military campaigns.[77]

The literary lives of these writers under National Socialism were often complex and have in some cases proved difficult to pin down, especially as the individuals concerned were often later in denial about their past. The figure of Günter Eich provides an interesting and in many ways representative case study. In 1932, Eich had given up his degree in Chinese Studies to become an independent writer and, encouraged by early successes with radio plays, used the income from these to finance work on his main interest, lyric poetry. He subsequently managed to forge a career as a writer under National Socialism and wrote 19 radio plays up to 1940, published 35 poems between 1933 and 1938, and in total wrote or coauthored about 160 radio broadcasts, especially for the popular programs *Deutscher Kalender: Monatsbilder vom Königswusterhäuser Landboten* (German calendar: Monthly views from the Königs Wusterhausen Country Herald) and *Märkischer Kalendermann* (Mark Brandenburg calendar man).[78] It is worth noting that each episode of *Deutscher Kalender* ended with the verse:

Verachtet, liebe Freunde, nicht,
des Bauern Herz und Hand!
Er nährt, was euer Stolz auch spricht,
euch und das ganze Land.[79]

[Dear friends, do not despise the peasant's heart and hand! Whatever your pride may say, he feeds you and the whole country.]

It might be thought this is evidence of the role of such broadcasts in promoting and supporting Nazi society in line with official propaganda directives. Although Eich later claimed his productions were little noticed at the time (thus implying they played no part in sustaining the regime), Cuomo has determined that "the multiple accolades his radio plays received in the Nazi press between 1933 and 1940 place him amongst the most prolific and respected authors who worked for Goebbels's broadcasting system."[80] For instance, Eich's play *Tod an den Händen* (Death on their hands) was selected as one of the most popular plays of 1938–39.[81] There is also ample evidence to suggest that, uneasy about his past under National Socialism, Eich sought to downplay the political compromises he made at the time, in particular the way he accommodated Nazi policy and broadcasting guidelines within his radio work.[82]

However, while Cuomo's verdict of compromise is supported by Vieregg, whose argument is essentially that in accepting radio work under National Socialism, Eich "sold" himself to the regime, Storck argues that much of the evidence has been exaggerated or even distorted; he claims that Eich's radio work was exclusively motivated by financial concerns, and suggests the writer withdrew as much as possible from public life during the 1930s, spending a good deal of time at his modest hut on the Baltic coast. Moreover, Eich did not join the Nazi Party (unlike Lehmann and Fussenegger), is not known to have made any public commitment of loyalty to Hitler or the regime (compare Benn, Loerke, Flake, Seidel, and von Molo), is not listed in the majority of literary reference works from the period (unlike Andres, Goes, Lange, Schaper, and Weyrauch), did not contribute to the publication dedicated to Hitler's fifty-second birthday in 1941 (unlike Britting, Carossa, Jünger, and Schröder), and did not participate in any of the Nazi writers' congresses (unlike Carossa, von Molo, or Wiechert).[83] Hermann Kasack's reference for Eich, delivered to the Nachrichtenkontrollamt (Intelligence Control Board) in Regensburg after the war, is instructive: after affirming that Eich was no supporter of Nazi ideology, it noted that he was by nature someone who was naïve and disinterested when it came to questions of politics, and that "Es handelt sich bei ihm um reine Dichtung" (with him it is a case of pure literature).[84]

Eich is not alone in having his past scrutinized, for in the postwar period several of the writers in this category (e.g., Andersch, Huchel, Koeppen, Richter, Weyrauch) either evinced differing degrees of disingenuousness regarding their publishing activity in the Third Reich, tended to gloss over their role between 1933 and 1945, or exaggerated the extent to which they or their works had not been welcome to the authorities. Indeed Kasack's verdict on Eich could apply to many of the "young generation" who, in seeking their way as writers under National Socialism, found solace in nature, escaped to ancient poetic forms, or composed words of consolation that were "wie auf Kissen gestickte Spruchbänder" (like banderoles sewn on cushions).[85] In contrast to Schäfer's rather benign verdict that these writers were impotent spectators under National Socialism, other critics have been more damning in their assessment of attempts to retreat to a neutral, noncontentious space. Blanket judgments, however, do little to help understand the true situation. Rather, individual writers' status and the value of their works both need to be evaluated through scrutiny of personal circumstances, as scholars have started to do over the past thirty years or so.[86] Insofar as any generalizations are permitted, however, the key difference between this group and those I have labeled "mainstream nonconformists" is the presence among the latter of Grimm's recognizable posture of opposition.[87]

The Compromised and the Conformist

Finally, we turn to the most problematic and contentious grouping of writers associated with inner emigration. As with the whole spectrum, one is dealing here with a continuum and can discern nuanced shades from reluctant partial fellow traveler through to unashamed conformist. These were writers who, for at least some of the period under National Socialism, were close to the regime and acquiesced in its basic literary-political assumptions and policies, even though they may not all have been explicit or open in their support. In turn, they were accepted and, in some cases, actively promoted by the regime. Keen to sustain their literary career through the Nazi era, they may have allowed themselves to be used by the system, indeed in some cases to be persuaded to pay public tribute to Hitler and his domestic and foreign policy initiatives. Insofar as they evinced an oppositional mindset, this was inconsistent or debatable. At the more extreme and questionable end of the spectrum are to be found figures who have either been portrayed or who sought to portray themselves as belonging to the broad inner emigrant church, but whose work, actions, or pronouncements mark them out as essentially conforming to Nazi ideology and policy and willingly doing the regime's bidding.

A particularly complex figure in this category is the Expressionist poet Gottfried Benn (1886–1956). Influenced by Nietzsche, he saw in the liberal intellectual a sign of decadence but perceived in the brutal aesthetics of National Socialism the beginnings of a new "heroic nihilism," which through strictly regimented authoritarian states could free politics from the sphere of morality. Thus in 1933 he welcomed the creation of a totalitarian state under a Führer seen as "höchstes geistiges Prinzip" (ultimate spiritual principle).[88] Within a month of the Nazis' assumption of power, he wrote to a friend: "Die Revolution ist da und die Geschichte spricht" (the revolution has arrived and history speaks), saying anyone who failed to see the dawn of this new epoch was "schwachsinning" (insane).[89] He swore his loyalty to the Nazi state and was for a while the Nazi-endorsed replacement of Heinrich Mann as head of the literature section of the Prussian Academy of the Arts.[90] His forceful response to criticisms of his position by literary emigrants also seemed to reflect his closeness to the new regime.[91]

However, in the essay "Bekenntnis zum Expressionismus" (Commitment to expressionism) of November 1933, Benn sought to defend modernist developments in literature against Nazi attacks, and in due course, as the regime's lawlessness and despotism became clearer (the Röhm putsch in June 1934 was a turning point), and perhaps particularly as the effects of cultural *Gleichschaltung* made themselves felt, he lost his illusions about the regime. His association with literary modernism duly led to his rejection by the Nazis, and in 1934 he was banned from broadcasting and condemned for his alleged Jewish ancestry, prompting desperate and embarrassing attempts by Benn to deny this and to prove his non-Jewish identity through reference to official genealogical documentation. Over the next few years his poetry also came in for criticism, although he still managed to publish his *Ausgewählte Gedichte 1911–1936* (Selected poems, 1936), a collection notable for the absence of recent Expressionist poems that had prompted attacks in the Nazi press.[92] In 1934 he began his inward retreat to a life of art, to a "two kingdoms" theory of the separation of intellect and spirit, on the one hand, and power and history, on the other.[93] His decision to join the army as a surgeon in 1935 was "die aristokratische Form der Emigrierung" (the aristocratic form of emigration),[94] and he saw his existence in the military as a "double life"[95] of outward conformity and inner self-preservation. The year 1938 was a watershed for Benn's writing: though finally expelled from the RSK in March of this year, he continued to write in private and distribute his work to friends, his former aristocratic disdain now giving way to harsh criticism of the regime in poems such as "General" (1938) and "Monolog" (c. 1941) and the essays "Kunst und Drittes Reich" (Art and the Third Reich, 1941) and "Zum Thema Geschichte" (The theme of history, c. 1943). In general, however, the bulk of his poems and essays from the period illustrate a withdrawal to the world of art and the spirit.[96] After the war, the publication of his poems from the years of inner emigration helped him to a period of belated fame as a writer, albeit one that was contested and controversial.[97]

Like Benn, Ina Seidel (1885–1974) was a supporter of the Nazis from the early days of the regime and, along with eighty-seven other writers, signed the declaration of loyalty to Hitler in October 1933. Unlike Benn, however, she made several further public declarations of support for Hitler and his policies, including the annexation of Austria, none more sycophantic than her greetings to him on his fiftieth birthday on April 20, 1939. Her work, which is dominated by themes relating to childhood and womanhood, for example in the novels *Das Wunschkind* (Wish child, 1930) and *Der Weg ohne Wahl* (The path with no choice, 1933), is characterized by a belief in fate, a deep-seated religiosity with Protestant and theosophist tendencies, and a pervading nationalist sentiment. Seidel's books sold in large numbers and were positively reviewed in such publications as *Bücherkunde*, *Die Neue Literatur*, and the feuilletons of various daily newspapers. They belonged very much to the literary canon of the Nazi period, were widely translated and publicized abroad, and Seidel herself was regularly promoted by the regime for the purpose of talks and readings.[98] The visionary writer saw in Hitler an almost mythical figure, calling him the "Auserwählten" (chosen one), who united the various "cosmic strands" of German fate.[99] However, in contrast to the tendency toward self-justification and whitewashing of the past to be found in similar works by other authors, Seidel's postwar diaries acknowledge wrongdoing and personal failings under Nazism.[100]

Hans Carossa (1878–1956) is often unquestioningly labeled an inner emigrant. Yet for all his principled inwardness and self-distancing from the Nazis, he was actually a writer who came to an arrangement with the regime, made use of the Nazi machine for his own purposes, and partly allowed himself to be used by them. Thus he gave readings to National Socialist audiences, signed the loyalty agreement to Hitler, put his name to birthday greetings to the Führer, attended the Weimar writers' meetings, and accepted literary prizes. In 1941 he even agreed to be nominated by Goebbels for election as president of the European Writers Association, a grouping sympathetic to fascism, which, however, never got off the ground. Carossa's autobiography constitutes a classic attempt at retrospective self-justification and is an egregious example of the apologism that brought inner emigration in general into disrepute in subsequent years.[101] The work also has a tendency throughout to insist on a naïve division between literature and politics, consistent with Carossa's 1938 Goethe speech in Weimar, which had argued for the separation of all cultural matters from historical and social reality and had posited culture as an autonomous realm beyond politics.[102] His relatively sparse literary work, consisting of both lyric poetry and prose, is, however, infused with a humanism much influenced by Goethe, which offered encouragement to an educated readership to hold firm to their ideals. Furthermore, he is known to have intervened on behalf of other authors threatened with persecution, such as the Jewish Alfred Mombert, who was deported from Baden to an internment camp in Gurs in France in 1941 as part of the so-called Wagner-Bürckel-Aktion, which involved the removal of some 6,500 Jews from southwestern areas of Germany.[103]

Another ambiguous figure, whose reputation was tainted particularly by his role in the postwar controversy, is Walter von Molo (1880–1958), who from 1928 to 1930 had been president of the literature section

76 ♦ THE WRITERS OF THE INNER EMIGRATION

of the Prussian Academy of the Arts. Despite his national conservative leanings, he was viewed with suspicion by the Nazis for his supposed liberalism and pacifism, and was consequently deemed "undesirable" by Rosenberg's Reichsstelle, although he was still able to publish freely. Concerned about attacks on him, von Molo made direct approaches to Goebbels and Philipp Bouhler, head of the PPK,[104] to seek their protection, drawing attention to his earlier work and the recently published historical novel *Eugenio von Savoy* (Eugenio of Savoy, 1936), which glorified "German blood," the idea of the German Reich, and the role of the military leader.[105] Such efforts seem to have paid dividends, as he continued to be regularly invited to the Weimar writers' meetings and none of his books were ever blacklisted.

A very different, more complex case is that of Hans Fallada (1893–1947), a pseudonym for Rudolf Ditzen, who had been an established journalist and novelist in the Weimar Republic. Described by one biographer as "among other things an alcoholic, drug addict, womanizer, jailbird and thief,"[106] his early years also included a period in a psychiatric hospital after killing a friend in a duel and prison sentences for embezzlement. However, he attained a first major publishing success with the novel *Kleiner Mann—was nun?* (1932, published in English in 1933 as *Little Man, What Now?*), whose realistic description of life at the end of the Weimar Republic—in particular the effects of war and economic downturn—and whose at times penetrating social criticism helped it to become a best-seller in the United States and the United Kingdom and to be made into a Hollywood film in 1934. Fallada's work was criticized by Nazi commentators, and in September 1935 he was declared "undesirable," which led to bans on his translated work and overseas publications. He was still a member of the RSK, however, and sought to survive as a writer by embracing nonpolitical genres such as children's literature and fairy tales, but also light novels that could be serialized and film studio commissions.[107] An exception to this, his critique of Weimar, the novel *Wolf unter Wölfen* (1937, English translation *Wolf Among Wolves*, 2010), met with official approval, in particular that of Goebbels. It also resulted in compromising commissions from the Minister of Propaganda, most notably the request that Fallada rewrite the ending of his next and more socially critical work, the substantial novel *Der eiserne Gustav* (1938, English translation *Iron Gustav*, 1940), about a Berlin cabdriver and the suffering caused by the First World War; Fallada eventually did this by having Gustav's positively depicted son join the SA, the Nazi storm troopers.[108] A lifetime user of drugs and alcohol, Fallada became increasingly addicted to them and died prematurely before his final novel could be published. The posthumous *Jeder stirbt für sich allein* (1947), a thriller about a real-life protest against the Nazi regime staged by a working-class couple killed in 1943, was translated into English in 2009 as *Every Man*

Dies Alone / Alone in Berlin and became a major publishing success. This latter-day response throws a fascinating light on the lasting influence of works exploring opposition and courage in the face of tyranny, even if it does little to change Fallada's place in the cultural history of the Third Reich. Though not a willing collaborator, he did nonetheless allow himself to be used by the regime, and although some of his work is informed by an insistent humanity in the face of hardship and suffering, he stands out as a weak and compromised writer.

The journalist and literary critic Friedrich Sieburg (1893–1964) enjoyed some notoriety after the war as a controversial and deeply conservative literary critic for the *Frankfurter Allgemeine Zeitung*. From 1925 he worked as the France correspondent for the *Frankfurter Zeitung*, but by around 1930 his political views meant he became a supporter of Kurt von Schleicher, the Weimar Republic's last chancellor, and he remained throughout the Third Reich a contradictory figure. Thus his book of strongly nationalistic political observations, *Es werde Deutschland* (Let there be Germany, 1933), also contains criticism of anti-Semitism and for this reason it was subsequently banned by the Nazis in 1936.[109] He continued to work for the *Frankfurter Zeitung* until 1939 and his book *Robespierre* (1935) was seen by some as a subversive parable of Nazi Germany.[110] Nevertheless, he was able to publish freely throughout the 1930s and his books on authoritarian leadership in Poland, Portugal, and Japan were in keeping with Nazi propaganda.[111] In 1939 he agreed to be used for propaganda purposes in France by the German Foreign Office and in 1941 applied for Nazi Party membership. From 1940 to 1942, he was a counselor at the German embassy in Paris and later a companion to Marshal Pétain, although Ribbentrop seems to have lost faith in him.[112] In summary, Sieburg was a self-centered aesthete and an opportunist who, for personal advancement, was prepared to put his abilities at the services of the Nazi regime, and although one might accept that he was not an adherent of National Socialism, given his involvement in diplomatic affairs it is difficult to attach to him in any meaningful sense the labels "nonconformist" or even more generally "inner emigrant."

The situation of Ernst Glaeser (1902–63) under National Socialism is especially intriguing. Head of literature at the radio station Südwestdeutscher Rundfunk and subsequently an editor with the publisher Propyläen Verlag, Glaeser was a supporter of the German Communist Party (KPD) in the later years of the Weimar Republic. Together with the communist writer Franz Carl Weiskopf he wrote a book on the Soviet Union (*Der Staat ohne Arbeitslose*, The state without unemployed, 1931), and from 1931 to 1933 was a member of the literary committee of the Moscow-based journal *Literatur der Weltrevolution*.[113] His first novel, *Jahrgang 1902* (Born in 1902), published in 1928, was a critique of Wilhelmine society, seen as politically, morally, and sexually corrupted;

the book enjoyed considerable international success.[114] However, it was rejected in right-wing circles for its pacifism, social criticism, and open sexuality. It was thus no surprise that Glaeser's work fell victim to the Nazi book burnings in May 1933, his name being specifically mentioned, along with those of Heinrich Mann and Erich Kästner, in the second of nine standard incantations spoken over the flames.[115] Glaeser was forced to emigrate, first to Czechoslovakia and then to Switzerland. Over the next few years, however, he came to miss Germany greatly, steadily distancing himself from the antifascism of German emigrants and developing increasingly conservative views. His move toward an inner emigrant position is witnessed by his reworked story "Der Pächter" (The tenant farmer, 1936) with its description of an emigrant returning to his homeland in Rhine-Hesse to stay with an old acquaintance, an educated Huguenot farmer, who is seen as a representative of "another Germany," a "Deutschland des Maßes und der Humanität" (Germany of moderation and humanity).[116] The stay on the island on the Rhine, symbolically cut off from the social and political turmoil of contemporary German reality, allows the narrator to rediscover the world he has lost and that he vows will never be taken from him again.[117] To the astonishment of many and the anger of fellow emigrants, in 1938 Glaeser returned to Germany. There he was used for propaganda purposes, was able to publish again (mostly under the name Ernst Töpfer), became an editor with two Luftwaffe front newspapers, and contributed occasional pieces to the *Krakauer Zeitung*. Though he continued to publish after the war, his repeated attempts to portray his political about-turn in the positive light of a shift to an inner emigrant position, including occasional camouflaged writing, meant he forfeited all artistic credibility.[118]

A particularly difficult case of disputed nonconformism is Frank Thiess (1890–1977). He was a writer of historical fiction during the Third Reich and, as seen in chapter 1, was to become one of the principal public faces of "inner emigration" in the postwar controversy over the term. However, in 1933, in a newspaper interview with the *Hannoversches Tageblatt*, Thiess had expressly welcomed the Nazi assumption of power.[119] Two of his pre-1933 works were eventually, in 1935, placed on a list of "undesirable literature,"[120] but none of his other writing in the Third Reich was ever banned. Moreover, although Rosenberg's Reichsstelle had tried to suppress Thiess's work, the writer enjoyed the protection of Hans Hinkel, a former editor of the *Völkischer Beobachter* in Berlin and an assistant manager of the RSK, and he was never excluded from the RSK.[121] Among his post-1933 works perhaps the most significant is the novel *Tsushima* (1936, translated into English in 1937 as *The Voyage of Forgotten Men*), about the Russian-Japanese sea war of 1904–5, which praised the heroic soldier and emphasized the preeminent role of the nation in human history. The novel was well received in the press, had sold one hundred thousand copies by 1944 (in contrast to Thiess's later claim that it had sold badly),[122] and was reportedly read with enthusiasm by Hitler, who also gave it to others as a present.[123]

However, Thiess is probably best known for the 1941 novel *Das Reich der Dämonen* (The kingdom of demons), a historical-metaphysical work about intellectual and cultural history from ancient Greece through to the decline of Rome, focusing on military conflict, religious disputes, and the rise of the Byzantine Empire. The work addressed, in part, a major feature of Nazi ideology, the glorification of Sparta and the attempt of Nazi race theorists, such as Hans F. K. Günther, to portray ancient Greeks and Romans in general as being originally of Nordic origin.[124] However, Thiess's very different view of Spartan life was bound to appear out of step with such thinking: Sparta's isolation here is shown to have a negative effect on its cultural development, and the total control exerted by the military state is seen to harm individual spiritual development; Sparta is a "sozial-human[es] Gefängnis" (a social and human prison, 49) with a "Kasernenkultur" (barracks culture, 51). The book also passed the censors without any problem, was published in the "aryanized" Paul Zsolnay Verlag, and sold over thirty-five thousand copies in two print-runs,[125] although Thiess later stated it had been immediately banned after publication.[126] He also claimed the work had clear anti-Nazi tendencies, pointing to the subtitle "Der Roman eines Jahrtausends" (The novel of a millennium), to the ban on reviews imposed by the Nazis, and to certain key critical passages, although most of the latter seem to have appeared for the first time in the almost one-hundred-page longer 1946 edition.[127]

Archival research on the genesis of the work does suggest that several topical references were removed by Thiess or his editor prior to publication.[128] However, Thiess's nonconformism in *Das Reich der Dämonen* is to be found less in camouflaged references to the Nazi present than in his adoption of an essentially humanist position in which the values of classical civilization and Christian love and ethics are held up against Spartan militarism and Germanic barbarism and are seen as the foundation of western civilization—for example, in the final two chapters, significantly entitled "Das Recht" (Law) and "Menschlichkeit" (Humanity). Here, in the depths of inhumanity, he sees "untrügerische Zeichen des Menschlichen" (unmistakable signs of the humane, 693) and affirms the power of the rule of law, religion, and the civilizing force of education—evidence perhaps of Thiess's claim to belong to the inner emigration, his desire to emphasize the transience of Nazism and to offer consolation and sustenance to the like-minded reader. Ultimately, Thiess was a writer who was tolerated by the regime and, these occasional passages in *Das Reich der Dämonen* apart, his claim to belong to the ranks of those opposing Nazism is based on thin evidence.

With regard to Austrian authors, mention ought to be made of the controversial Catholic writer Gertrud Fussenegger (1912–2009), who produced a substantial oeuvre of more than sixty works. After the war she was condemned in sections of the Austrian press for her past, being seen as politically compromised through her membership of the Austrian NSDAP from 1933 and her later decision to join the German NSDAP. Denk, however, has made a lengthy defense of her, arguing that this political dalliance has led to her work being misrepresented.[129] His, at first sight, questionable argument for including her under the heading "literature critical of the regime" rests particularly on the work *Mohrenlegende* (The legend of the moor, 1937), a historical novella depicting a young black boy captured by Christian Crusaders in the Holy Land and brought back to Austria, where he is treated as a racial inferior.[130] The story's implied philo-Semitism (the boy's Jewish heritage is suggested by his biblical name Gideon) and the negative portrayal of racist Crusaders point to a failure of Christianity at home and abroad, and it prompted a reviewer in *Die Weltliteratur* to reject what he saw as religiously inspired support for racial equality and thus a contravention of the spirit of Nazi race laws.[131] Like all the writers in this section, Fussenegger's behavior under totalitarian rule is questionable and might be considered opportunistic, but elements of her work do suggest something more than unthinking conformism.

A number of other Austrian authors who had belonged to the NSDAP sought at the end of the war to contest legally their potential punishment under the denazification process. Among these were Maria Grengg, Paul Anton Keller, Franz Resl, Franz Spunda, Erwin Rainalter, Friedrich Schreyvogl, and Franz Tumler.[132] A surprising proportion successfully argued through reference to their published work that they were in reality Austrian patriots and effectively inner emigrants under Nazism. The writer and theater critic Mirko Jelusich (1886–1969) is a particularly remarkable case and takes this overview of writers closer to the conformist end of the spectrum. Jelusich was an early member of the Nazi Party and wrote historical novels that focused on the principle of the Führer and glorified strong leaders such as Caesar, Cromwell, and Hannibal. He welcomed the annexation of Austria and, in 1939, established the Wiener Dichterkreis (Viennese Writers' Group), whose members included the anti-Semitic, Nazi-friendly Bruno Brehm, the nationalist writer and president of the Nazi-leaning Bund deutscher Schriftsteller Österreichs (League of German Writers in Austria) Max Mell, and the poet, essayist, and Nazi Party member Josef Weinheber. After the war, Jelusich sought to downplay his past and even present himself as an inner emigrant concerned with promoting the "true" Austria in the face of the "Prussian" (that is, Nazi) enemy, arguing that his historical novel *Der Traum vom Reich* (Dream of empire, 1941) about Emperor Joseph II and Prince Eugen von Oranien was merely pressing Austria's leadership claims within Germany.[133] In fact, the work's Nazi credentials have been well established: in line with Nazi propaganda on the eve of war, it depicts the historical struggle for a German *Reich*, displays anti-French and anti-Semitic tendencies, and brands as traitors all opponents of the idea of the *Reich*.[134]

The reputation of genuinely nonconformist writers has suffered partly from the activities of such compromised writers as those listed in this section, whose proximity to and even collaboration with the regime were at best ambiguous and convenient, at worst complicit and deeply conformist, and whose later attempt to deploy the "inner emigrant" label to cover up or whitewash a culpable past has had long-lasting consequences.

The Options Facing Writers

Writers who stayed in Germany faced the fundamental question: To publish or not to publish?

Publication

Among those who decided to continue to seek a public audience for their work, we can distinguish three distinct categories:

"Nonpolitical" Genres and Topics

This type of noncommittal writing encompasses literature that did not seek to address contemporary social or political reality in any way and restricted itself to "safe" or unproblematic areas such as travel writing, children's books, feature films, radio plays, other radio broadcasts, and general interest pieces for newspapers, particularly literary supplements or illustrated magazines. Numerous writers, including many inner emigrants whose other outputs display distinct nonconformist tendencies published such work but, as indicated, this was a particular preserve of the "younger generation."

Anonymous Publication

Anonymous or pseudonymous publication was also occasionally possible in Nazi Germany. Kästner was a particularly frequent writer under pseudonym, publishing under the names Berthold Bürger, Melchior Kurtz, and Robert Neuner. Similarly, Weisenborn's works were published under such pseudonyms as Christian Munk—for example, the volume of stories *Traum und Tarantel* (Dreams and tarantulas, 1938)—and Eberhard Förster. One of the most interesting examples of anonymous publication

is Bergengruen's unattributed poem collection *Der ewige Kaiser* (The
eternal emperor, 1937), whose critical content came to the attention of
the authorities and prompted official but ultimately fruitless inquiries into
the identity of the author.[135]

A variant on this form of publication was the dissemination of cyclo-
styled manuscripts and leaflets. The most famous example of the latter
was the oppositional leaflets illegally distributed by the students in the
White Rose group.[136] As the war developed and restrictions on all writers increased, most notably through the strict rationing of paper, and it
became extremely difficult to publish books and even articles in newspapers and journals,[137] the age-old practice of secret copying and illicit
circulation of essays, stories, and poems became common once more.
As Bergengruen later claimed: "Das war schon fast, als habe Gutenberg
umsonst gelebt. Jeder schrieb ab, was ihm gefiel, mit der Hand oder mit
der Schreibmaschine, und machte es seinen Freunden zugänglich. . . ."
(It was almost as if Gutenberg's life had been in vain. Everyone copied
out the things they liked—either by hand or on the typewriter—and made
it available to their friends.)[138]

Camouflaged Publication

This is the broadest of the publishing categories, denoting the techniques writers employed to veil their dissent or nonconformist messages
so that a sensitized audience could still recognize the disguised message. The approach is explored in detail below in the section "The Art
of Camouflage." A major feature of it, however, is the use of history as
topos. Reflecting the veritable explosion of historical works among both
conformist writers (such as Hans Friedrich Blunck, Werner Beumelburg,
and Erwin Guido Kolbenheyer) and those who sought exile (for example, Bruno Frank, Gustav Regler, Lion Feuchtwanger, Joseph Roth, and
Hermann Kesten), the historical genre was strongly represented among
inner emigrant writers. The latter's particular use of the genre involved
exploiting historical settings to convey indirectly distinct types of criticism of the present, depicting violent rulers, oppression, and injustice
from across the ages and leaving readers to draw their own lessons and
conclusions from the fiction.[139] The vast majority of these texts were
novels and novellas, although they also included factual works by creative writers such as Reinhold Schneider. A classic example in the latter
category is Huch's aforementioned *Römisches Reich Deutscher Nation*,
the first part of her three-volume *Deutsche Geschichte*, which contains a
remarkable chapter on Jews. Huch here ignores Nazi historical orthodoxy entirely to draw a positive picture of German Jews generally, but
particularly of those in the fourteenth century, whose persecution is said
to have resulted from "bestialischen Trieben" (bestial impulses) within

Germans and who are labeled "heroic."[140] Six of the works discussed in detail in part 2 of this book provide opportunities to explore this turn to history in greater detail.

Nonpublication

Those who answered the publish or not publish question in the negative, and indeed those who were forced into public silence, were essentially writing either for posterity or for their own sanity, as a personal intellectual survival strategy. Among the best-known works here are Theodor Haecker's *Tag- und Nachtbücher 1939–1945* (1947, English translation *Journal in the Night*, 1950) and Victor Klemperer's *Ich will Zeugnis ablegen bis zum letzten: Tagebücher 1933–1945* (I will bear witness to the last: Diaries, 1995).[141] Of course, for those writers excluded from the RSK— also for some others producing what the regime might consider ideologically suspect individual works—there was no choice but to commit their work "to the drawer," since formal exclusion from their profession inevitably meant they had no hope of immediate publication. The prime example here is Langgässer's novel *Das unauslöschliche Siegel*, which became a postwar publishing success. It is also important to recognize that even those authors who freely and simultaneously published imaginative fiction and poetry withheld certain texts owing to their content. Such works that could not appear under the regime include Ernst Wiechert's novel *Die Jeromin-Kinder* (The Jeromin children, 1945), Reck-Malleczewens's diary *Tagebuch eines Verzweifelten* (1947, translated into English in 1970 as *Diary of a Man in Despair*), Stefan Andres's trilogy *Die Sintflut* (The flood, 1949–59), and Jochen Klepper's diaries from 1932 to 1942, *Unter dem Schatten deiner Flügel* (Beneath the shadow of your wings, 1955). And, finally, writing produced while in camps or prisons also comes under this heading, including such diverse documents as Haushofer's sonnets, Krauss's novel *PLN*, and Wiechert's report on life in Buchenwald, *Der Totenwald: Ein Bericht* (1945, translated into English as *Forest of the Dead*, 1947).

The Art of Camouflage: Reading and Writing in the Inner Emigration

Inner emigrant authors who rejected literary silence and sought to publish work with oppositional content had to overcome or circumvent the censorship barrier. An important prerequisite in this was self-censorship.[142] Besides the "precensorship" of textual camouflage, all writers recognized the need for pragmatic compromise and frequently agreed to changes to content, wording, or title suggested by a favorably disposed publisher, often one versed in publishing nonconformist material. Behind the decision to acquiesce in the latter changes was a consideration of the potential futility and the danger to a publisher's livelihood and personal safety should a planned publication fall foul of censors even before it had reached the reading public.

However, publication also meant that writers' texts had to be hybrid in nature, open at one and the same time to both a conformist and a nonconformist reading. The desire to facilitate the latter and appeal to a like-minded reader's private disposition, while simultaneously offering other readers the possibility of a conformist reading, meant that the message had to be skillfully encoded and a delicate balance struck between dissent from and apparent acquiescence in Nazi values.

In the postwar period Werner Bergengruen became one of the most prominent apologists of this approach. He writes in his memoirs that both Nazis and their opponents were "monomanisch" (obsessive) in relating every conversation and everything they read to the contemporary political situation, that every piece of writing was inevitably shaped by the times.[143] In his diary he says this mass fixation is difficult to appreciate in retrospect and talks of "die Technik der stichworthaften Anspielung, die Technik der indirekten und doch unmißverständlichen Aussage . . . die immer mehr sich verfeinernde Kunst des Schreibens—aber auch des Lesens—zwischen den Zeilen" (the technique of using key word allusions, the technique of indirect and yet unambiguous messages . . ., the ever more refined art of writing—but also reading—between the lines). He concludes: "Damals . . . regierte eine unglaubliche Hellhörigkeit; die leiseste Andeutung wurde nicht nur verstanden, sondern sie hatte auch ihr Gewicht" (There was an incredible sensitivity among readers in those days; the merest intimation was not only understood but also carried weight).[144] No claim is made for the regime-changing possibilities of such activity; rather it is argued that the art of camouflaged writing contained the potential to reassure non-Nazis, to counteract the regime's lies, to offer courage to those living in fear, to provide reassurance that the regime would not last, and to reiterate the value and durability of humane values, which were currently being threatened. By thus opening people's eyes to the truth, the aim was to cause those intoxicated by the achievements and superficial splendor of the "new Germany" to pause and reflect: "Es galt, zu klären und aufzurütteln, Mut und Trost zu kräftigen und das Bild des Menschen ungeschändet zu bewahren" (It was a question of providing clarity and rousing people, of fortifying and consoling, and of preserving the image of man unsullied).[145]

From 1935 onward, a virtual manifesto for oppositional writers from the pen of Bertolt Brecht, entitled "Fünf Schwierigkeiten beim Schreiben der Wahrheit" (Five difficulties in writing the truth), began to be secretly circulated. Written in Danish exile in 1934, it suggested ways in which authors, particularly those still in Germany, could make readers aware of the truth about the Nazi regime and its practices:

> Wer heute die Lüge und Unwissenheit bekämpfen und die Wahrheit schreiben will, hat zumindest fünf Schwierigkeiten zu überwinden. Er muss den *Mut* haben, die Wahrheit zu schreiben, obwohl sie allenthalben unterdrückt wird; die *Klugheit*, sie zu erkennen, obwohl sie allenthalben verhüllt wird; die *Kunst*, sie handhabbar zu machen als eine Waffe; das *Urteil*, jene auszuwählen, in deren Händen sie wirksam wird; die *List*, sie unter diesen zu verbreiten.[146]

> [Nowadays, anyone who wishes to combat lies and ignorance and to write the truth must overcome at least five difficulties. He must have the *courage* to write the truth, even though truth is opposed everywhere; the *shrewdness* to recognize it, even though it is concealed everywhere; the *skill* to manipulate it as a weapon; the *judgment* to select those in whose hands it will be effective; and the *cunning* to spread the truth among such people.]

The fifth of these relates to techniques of writing and is the one Brecht devotes most attention to in his article. He mentions examples of how a writer might undermine a ruling regime and thereby alert readers to his or her true intent by replacing emotionally charged or propagandistic terms typical of the prevailing discourse with more sober or neutral equivalents; thus *Volk* might be replaced with *Bevölkerung* (population), *Boden* (soil) with *Landbesitz* (privately owned land), *Disziplin* (discipline) with *Gehorsam* (obedience), and *Ehre* (honor) with *Menschenwürde* (human dignity). And he goes on to list examples from Thomas More, Voltaire, Shakespeare, and Swift on the use of style, parable, and irony to disguise true literary intent, drawing particular attention to the potential for subversion in praising a hated individual or describing something negative in excessively positive and thus transparently ironic terms (81–82).

As this makes clear, the idea of writers employing methods of camouflage in their published writing under repressive regimes was not new. A common descriptor of camouflaged nonconformist writing is the Aesopic style or method. This refers back to the ancient art of fable and fairy tale, which made use of myths and folklore to demonstrate through veiled means a particular moral. The term "Aesopic" has come to be applied more broadly to all camouflage and allegory in art, including "the description of a critical intellectual attitude and its artistic and academic expression."[147] A good example of it at work, which also acts in this instance as self-commentary, is provided by Dolf Sternberger's analysis of Aesop's fable "The Wolf and the Lamb," published in 1941 in the *Frankfurter Zeitung* as part of the essay "Figuren der Fabel," in which the rhetoric of the wolf (here standing for the Nazi) in his exchange with the lamb (here the Jew) reveals the regime's abuse of language as it attempts to shroud its violence in a deceitful veil of legitimacy.[148]

Brecht's article discusses two aspects of such camouflage that are especially pertinent to inner emigrants. First, the use of a high literary style to lend a statement protection applies, in the German literary context, to the demanding style of Reck-Malleczewen or, in journalism, Sternberger's articles and editorials, and the art history articles of Carl Linfert (see below). Second, the claim that ruling powers have an aversion to change, to disharmony or internal contradiction, and a desire for the permanence of, for example, a thousand-year *Reich*, suggests that writers should seek to subvert this by focusing on a regime's temporary existence and the potential for it to change, and thereby offer consolation to those suffering under it: "Eine Betrachtungsweise, die das Vergängliche besonders hervorhebt, ist ein gutes Mittel, die Unterdrückten zu ermutigen" (An approach that stresses the ephemeral nature of things is a good way to encourage the oppressed, 87). The emphasis repeatedly placed, particularly by Christian nonconformist writers, on the transitory nature of human affairs, the finiteness of political regimes, and the nugatory nature of earthly power in general, provides ample illustration of how this principle was realized—most notably in the work of Schröder, Schneider, and le Fort.

Further interesting interpretative guidelines on the production of literature under oppressive regimes are provided in the article "Persecution and the Art of Writing" by Leo Strauss, a German Jewish exile, who established himself in America as a political philosopher and classicist. Originally published in—significantly—1941, in the journal *Social Research*, the article deals with the possibility of writers expressing, in public, truths that are at odds with the prevailing political orthodoxy and the need for caution and artifice. Quite independently, it seems, of the inner emigrant discourse within Germany, he deploys the phrase "writing between the lines" to denote writers' method of disguising the true meaning of their texts and introduces the terms "exoteric" and "esoteric" to distinguish ostensible contributions to a dominant orthodox discourse from a writer's actual desire to address a select "insider" audience:

> Persecution . . . gives rise to a peculiar technique of writing, and therewith to a peculiar type of literature, in which the truth about all crucial things is presented exclusively between the lines. That literature is addressed, not to all readers, but to trustworthy and intelligent readers only. It has all the advantages of private communication without having its greatest disadvantage—that it reaches only the writer's acquaintances. It has all the advantages of public communication without having its greatest disadvantage—capital

punishment for the author. . . . The fact which makes this literature possible can be expressed in the axiom that thoughtless men are careless readers, and only thoughtful men are careful readers. Therefore an author who wishes to address only thoughtful men has but to write in such a way that only a very careful reader can detect the meaning of his book.[149]

In such circumstances, and depending on the writer's skill and degree of caution, the censor faces a difficult task in proving that stylistic blemishes or ambiguities in the particular text are deliberately contrary to the political philosophy of the regime.

Strauss talks about a writer's esoteric audience being guided to the truth by obtrusive enigmatic elements of the text, including: "obscurity of the plan, contradictions, pseudonyms, inexact repetitions of earlier statements, strange expressions, etc.," and says these act as "awakening stumbling blocks" for those capable of distinguishing popular views from the truth (36). These ideas characterize with remarkable accuracy the type of deliberate shortcomings, obscurities, and apparent irrelevancies to be found, for example, in the complex historical asides in Friedrich Reck-Malleczewen's *Bockelson: Geschichte eines Massenwahns* (1937, translated into English in 2008 as *A History of the Münster Anabaptists:*), in the aforementioned talk of crabs in Lernet-Holenia's *Mars im Widder*, or in the extended botanical descriptions in Ernst Jünger's *Auf den Marmorklippen* (1939, English translation *On the Marble Cliffs*, 1947). The function of such features, often relating to complex, obscure, or recondite aspects of history, mythology, philosophy, and theology, was to alert an attentive readership to unorthodox messages. This often presented readers with significant challenges, assumed a certain level of education among the esoteric audience, and is what Strauss has in mind when he talks about "the beauty of those hidden treasures which disclose themselves only after very long, never easy, but always pleasant work" (37).

Heidrun Ehrke-Rotermund and Erwin Rotermund, in their major study of the phenomenon, provide a significant step forward in the understanding of camouflaged approaches to writing under National Socialism, one that further develops and explicates some of Strauss's ideas.[150] The challenge for nonconformist or oppositional writers in the Third Reich was to communicate critical statements to a select group of like-minded readers, while at the same time withholding the "actual" meaning of such utterances from censors and publishers' readers and editors. In general, writers did this by deploying oppositional or dissenting messages with "affirmative, conformist, or neutral statements" in order to disguise the critical content (16). This mixture of messages can be understood in terms of the categories of classical rhetoric derived from Quintilian: *adiectio* (addition), *detractio* (subtraction), *transmutatio* (reordering), and *immutatio* (substitution). The use of one or more of these techniques can transform an oppositional text into a camouflaged one. Thus, starting from an unambiguously critical text (a "Klartext"), disguised content can be produced by adding an affirmative element, by removing an oppositional element, by reordering oppositional elements, or by substituting an affirmative or neutral element. An analogous process can be applied when starting from an affirmative or neutral text (17).

The tropes and figures of speech used in traditional rhetoric can also help us to understand camouflage techniques. Under the heading "Addition," one might include forms of contrast, contradiction, or comparison, of bathos, commonplace statement, or antithesis. For example, in le Fort's *Die Magdeburgische Hochzeit* (The wedding of Magdeburg, 1938), the military commander Graf von Tilly's sensitivity to the moral consequences of his actions contrasts strongly with his generals' disregard for suffering and their ambition to achieve victory at all costs. Similarly, in Bergengruen's *Der Großtyrann und das Gericht* (The great tyrant and the court, 1935), the protagonist's enlightened absolutism, especially his genuine human concern for his subjects, makes him, in fact, the near antithesis of his presumed historical referent, and he thus serves as a positive counterimage to contemporary Nazi despotism. "Subtraction," or omission of critical elements, was a common strategy. The danger here was that the reader might not detect the intended reference and so the use of ellipsis or the premature ending of a sentence was common. Classic examples of such omission are provided by Reck-Malleczewen's *Bockelson* with its satirical portrayal of the Münster Anabaptists' violence and corruption, in which the author repeatedly lists comparator evil regimes and acts from history, most notably from Napoleonic France and the Soviet Union, and leaves the reader to complete the list for themselves with examples from life in the Third Reich. Under "Reordering," the most common feature is a camouflaged rearrangement of textual elements: critical sections could be moved to a "more protected" position in the text, whereby the beginning and end were particularly precarious owing to the reading habits of censors.[151] For example, in Mitterer's *Der Fürst der Welt*, the first two hundred pages contain virtually nothing that any censor could object to and similarly the ending focuses on largely unimpeachable spiritual reflections and the burning of a supposed witch by the Catholic Inquisition (see chapter 10 of this book). In Andres's *El Greco malt den Großinquisitor* (1936, English translation *El Greco Paints the Grand Inquisitor*, 1989), the reordering undertaken by the author in bringing forward the rule of the Grand Inquisitor Niño de Guevara to coincide with the death of King Philip II does not correspond to historical fact but serves to concentrate political and religious power in the hands of the cardinal and allows implied criticism of Nazi tyranny behind a veil of apparent criticism of the Catholic Church (see chapter 4). "Substitution" techniques are by far the most important for nonconformist literature. Among these are mean-ings whose relationship to the expression replaced is one of similarity (metaphor, allegory, fable), of opposition (irony, litotes), and adjacency (metonymy, synecdoche), as well as the use of synonym, homonym, allu-sion, quotation, polysemy, and hyperbole.[152] For example, in Wiechert's *Der weiße Büffel oder Von der großen Gerechtigkeit* (The white buffalo, or concerning great justice, 1946), the fable-like narrative of Vasudeva's championing of justice and his challenging of the authority of the oppres-sive ruler Murduk (see chapter 9) is a fairly transparent reference to the structures of oppression in Nazi Germany. Or, in Schneider's *Las Casas vor Karl V.: Szenen aus der Konquistadorenzeit* (Las Casas before Charles V: Scenes from the time of the Conquistadors, 1938, English translation *Imperial Mission*, 1948), the depiction of the fate of the native Indians in sixteenth-century Middle and South America at the hands of Spanish colonialists stands as an extended metaphor for the fate of Europe's Jews (see chapter 7).

As indicated, Brecht's article had drawn attention to some of these substitution techniques, and he provides a particularly clear illustration of the practice through an example taken from recent Russian history:

> Lenin, von der Polizei des Zaren bedroht, wollte die Ausbeutung und Unterdrückung der Insel Sachalin durch die russische Bourgeoisie schildern. Er setzte Japan statt Rußland und Korea statt Sachalin. Die Methoden der japanischen Bourgeoisie erinnerten alle Leser an die der russischen in Sachalin, aber die Schrift wurde nicht verboten, da Japan mit Rußland verfeindet war. Vieles was in Deutschland über Deutschland nicht gesagt werden darf, darf über Österreich gesagt werden.[153]

> [Lenin, threatened by the czarist police, wanted to describe the Russian bourgeoisie's exploitation and oppression of Sakhalin Island. To do this, he put Japan in place of Russia, and Korea in place of Sakhalin. The methods of the Japanese bourgeoisie reminded all his readers of the Russian bourgeoisie on Sakhalin, but the document was not banned since Russia and Japan were enemies. Many things that cannot be said in Germany about Germany can be said about Austria.]

The Rotermunds also refer to four conversational principles, follow-ing the philosopher of language Paul Grice's ideas on conversational implicatures.[154] According to these, an effective contribution to dis-course needs to be: as informative as is necessary (principle of quantity), as truthful as possible (principle of quality), as relevant as is neces-sary (principle of relevance), and as clear as possible (principle of clar-ity). Contraventions of these principles by a person who is in all other respects observing the rules of discourse signals meanings not explicitly present in the text and encourages readers to form assumptions about these meanings ("Mitzuverstehendes" or implicatures).[155] Breaching of the principles of quantity and relevance are well illustrated in Herbert Küsel's article on the seventy-fifth anniversary of the birth of the Nazi hero Dietrich Eckart, which was published on March 23, 1943 and led to the *Frankfurter Zeitung* being closed down.[156] Nazi propaganda praised Eckart's achievements as a writer and deemed him a prophet and martyr of the Nazi movement, whereas Küsel avoids such tributes and provides almost no information on Eckart's literary production, preferring instead to introduce several digressions on banal, philistine, and contentious facts about his life. In omitting expected information and focusing on peripheral biographical detail, Küsel aims to bring the reader to a subversive view of Eckart as a scurrilous, petit bourgeois bohemian and failed writer.[157]

However, although writers could count on the "hermeneutische Sensibiliserung" (interpretative sensitization) of critical readers in the Third Reich,[158] this by no means guaranteed the latter's ability to decipher critical messages. Intensive use of camouflage techniques could make texts overcomplicated, with the result that critical readers could sometimes recognize the signal that an esoteric meaning was being advanced but not be sure precisely what that meaning was, with the result that communication of the intended message was obscured for both oppositional and conformist readers. The essays on art and art history by Carl Linfert in the *Frankfurter Zeitung, Die Neue Rundschau,* and Goebbels's weekly paper *Das Reich* provide good examples of this, revealing a complex style based on "eigenwilligem Metaphern- und ausgiebigem Periphrasengebrauch sowie auf einer komplizierten Syntax" (idiosyncratic use of metaphor and extensive paraphrase, and a complicated syntax, 22).

Where writers chose not to adopt such overelaborate camouflage, believing it could hinder communication with readers, and sought a less-than-perfect disguise for their text, they of course increased the risk of detection. In such circumstances authors needed to pursue the "Absicherung" (safeguarding) of their writing by adopting additional strategies to leave potentially nonconformist texts open to a "safe," conformist reading. One can therefore see camouflage and safeguarding as developing in inverse proportion to each other: the less well concealed a critical statement was, the greater the safeguarding needed to be.[159] A classic example of this safeguarding technique can be found in the article "Siberia" by Rudolf Pechel, published in 1937 in the journal *Deutsche Rundschau,* which purports to review the book of the same title by the exiled Russian writer Ivan Solonevich but draws instead a negative picture of repression and harsh living conditions in the Soviet Union to exercise a veiled critique of life in Nazi Germany.[160]

Esotericism and Its Challenges

The ability of the esoteric audience to know what to look for in their reading was, of course, crucial to the whole enterprise of inner emigrant writing, and, in support of Bergengruen's claims about the monomania of readers in the Third Reich, there are numerous testimonies to people's sensitivity to nuances, to deviations from the expected, and to the ability to read an apparently neutral text against the background of Nazi reality. Most notably, Jochen Klepper writes to Reinhold Schneider in connection with *Las Casas vor Karl V.*: "Wie hat die Gegenwart uns gelehrt, Quellen zu lesen!" (How the present has taught us to read sources!)[161]

Support for such esoteric readers was provided by publishers of non-conformist works. Given the impossibility of publishing anything that could be perceived as unambiguously oppositional, the publisher needed to find a way nevertheless to allow the reading public to recognize a disguised nonconformist work. It is reported that book dealers employed a form of code to alert retailers via the *Börsenblatt* to the types of text being referred to: on the one hand, standard formulations such as the author possessing an "unbeirrbaren Gemeinschaftswillen" (unwavering communal will) or a book constituting "für unsere Gegenwart . . . eine wesentliche Bereicherung" (a real enrichment for our present) signaled books that conformed to Nazi orthodoxy, while on the other, the mere absence of such terms alerted retailers to the type of audience a book might be targeted at, most likely a Christian, conservative, educated readership.[162] In the same way, in the *Frankfurter Zeitung*, journalists' avoidance of "approved" expressions from in-house guidelines signaled distance from the "inhuman" language of official announcements.[163]

However, things were made more complex for nonconformist writers and publishers by the awareness among some far-from-naïve censors of the sort of techniques writers were employing. Thus, in an article published in September 1936 in the SS weekly *Das Schwarze Korps*, the *Frankfurter Zeitung* is warned that authorities have seen through its use of "Verdecktes Schreiben" (veiled writing) and its related "Methoden der Hinterlist und der getarnten Angriffe" (methods of cunning and disguised attacks), adding, "Als ob wir nicht ebenfalls zwischen den Zeilen lesen könnten" (as if we couldn't read between the lines as well).[164] In a similar vein, a year earlier, in an attack on the journalist and essayist Joachim Günther, the same journal had warned of the "dangerous dialectic" of writers who employ a "verdeckte Schreibweise" (veiled method of writing), the "softness" of which is a mere cover for attacking the new *Reich*.[165] Similarly, the prominent Nazi literary historian Hellmuth Langenbucher showed that he was on the trail of the many authors who sought alternative battlefields in historical narrative: "Vielfach zeigt sich, daß historische Stoffe lediglich als Tarnung gewählt werden für Versuche, rein private oder gesellschaftliche Angelegenheiten, wie sie heute nicht mehr gefragt sind, auf dem Umweg über historische Zustände zur Darstellung zu bringen" (In many works one sees historical subject matter being chosen merely as a disguise for attempts to portray, via historical conditions, purely private or social affairs that are today no longer in demand). He praises instead some young writers who show the role of the historical novel to lie in providing "ein Bild vom ewigen Wesen und Schicksal unseres Volkes" (an image of the eternal being and fate of our people),[166] and calls on publishers to be more careful with this genre in future, promising the regime will be merciless in combating all attempts to disguise material through historical writing ("historisch zu tarnen," 145).

As has been shown,[167] the tolerance of "free space" in the coordinated cultural landscape was a deliberate policy, and the above examples show that the authorities were alert to authors' tactics. Although occasionally inner emigrant writers might have been able to benefit from and exploit the porous nature of state-controlled publishing, and although many aspects of stories, including references to little-known chapters of history, abstruse theological ideas, or obscure mythological imagery may have by-passed individual censors, the evidence strongly suggests that authorities were alive to what writers were doing, and one therefore has to be cautious not to overestimate the deficiencies of Nazi censorship or to caricature censors as largely incompetent.[168] One should also treat circumspectly authors' retrospective claims that censors were not up to grasping what they were reading. This was, for example, Bergengruen's interpretation of investigating officers' failure to arrest him when his illicitly published poems, *Der ewige Kaiser*, had been discovered.[169] Elsewhere, his talk of censors' "Dummheit und Unbildung" (stupidity and lack of education) and "An- oder doch Halb-Alphabetismus" (semi- or complete illiteracy) may be wide of the mark.[170]

The recondite nature of much oppositional writing was, in fact, likely to have been a significant problem for the *reader*. Veiled oppositional messages could only be effectively communicated when author and reader had access to the same broad field of reference and shared similar values. And yet the historical, mythological, philosophical, biblical, and sometimes theological content of several narratives, allied to the complex written style of many camouflaged texts, presupposed such a high level of education and cultural capital that the sphere of potential influence was inevitably restricted. Indeed, in some cases (Reck-Malleczewen's texts are a prime example), the sheer breadth and richness of cultural-historical analogy would have made it well-nigh impossible for most contemporary readers to identify the material's nonconformism with any certainty, however sensitized they had become to the subtle tones of dissenting literary voices.

The more writers were forced in this way to hide the meaning of texts written in the "Sklavensprache" (language of subjugation),[171] the greater the danger was of the camouflage proving *too* effective, of their writing appearing to the reader to be ambiguous, pointless, misguided, or even escapist. This led to the possibility of some texts being open to multiple interpretations. Jünger's *Auf den Marmorklippen* provides perhaps the best example of this, his esotericism here coming close to arrogant or snobbish withdrawal. In this case, however, owing to the author's considerable public standing and the potential fallout, should it be admitted that the work of one of the Nazi movement's early ideological beacons was to be considered anti-Nazi, the official press was required—on Hitler's orders, it seems—to simply ignore the book.[172] Another example is Gertrud von le Fort's historical narratives, most of which are so firmly rooted in the particular setting and engage primarily with issues of the time—whether this be the fate of the Carolingian Empire or twelfth-century papal succession—that contemporary relevance is difficult to discern; it is no surprise therefore that a work such as *Das Reich des Kindes* (The kingdom of the child, 1934) was seen as little more than a tasteful treatment of antiquity[173] rather than offering parallels with illegitimate claims to authority and the formation of a German *Reich*.

However, even with texts containing distinctly nonconformist messages, the necessary openness to interpretation led in several cases to the works being read overall as conformist. Examples include: the neglect of dissident aspects of Andres's *El Greco malt den Großinquisitor*—for example, the Inquisition's funeral pyre with its invocation of Nazi book burnings—in favor of its apparently conformist anti-Catholic elements; the praise lavished on Bergengruen's *Der Großtyrann und das Gericht* in the Nazi press for its portrayal of a "strong leader"; and Jochen Klepper's *Der Vater*, which was spoken of in equally warm terms for its apparent championing of Prussian militarism and was made official reading for the *Wehrmacht*. There was also the danger of the *willful* misinterpretation of texts as a way of subverting what was recognized to be a potentially awkward or inconvenient nonconformist message. For example, this occurred with le Fort's collection of patriotic verse *Hymnen an Deutschland* (Hymns to Germany, 1932) about the guilt and suffering of a people that mistakenly sees itself heading for triumph while actually facing doom as it has distanced itself from Christ: a judicious selection of these poems published in *Die Deutsche Frau*, the weekly supplement of the *Völkischer Beobachter*, was designed to claim the whole work for the Nazi cause.[174] Similarly, Kuckhoff's *Der Deutsche von Bayencourt*, in which the principal character is portrayed as a German victim of French chauvinism, readily lent itself to a distorting German nationalist interpretation, most notably in an article in the *Völkischer Beobachter*, which reduces the novel to Bernhard Sommer's "Germanness" and his victimization,[175] but also in

Hellmuth Langenbucher's review, which sees in it a portrayal of the irresistible ties of blood and the submission of personal will to the *Volk*.[176]

Conversely, there was the danger of an obsessive focus on esoteric messages, causing highly sensitized readers to see hidden criticism of the regime in every piece of writing, which was bound to lead to misinterpretation in some cases. This inclination to read into certain texts improbable nonconformist elements was a particular danger in postwar interpretations, among both apologist critics and some authors themselves, who sought to claim retrospectively a form of protest for their work that in reality is difficult to justify.

A particular challenge facing nonassimilated writers in Nazi Germany was that, as Victor Klemperer later amply illustrated in his linguistic treatise on the Third Reich,[177] language was increasingly being corrupted and that in using this same language in their work (in order to secure publication) writers ran the risk of being misunderstood. This was why, as part of their esoteric enterprise, many employed a particularly "stylized language" to distance themselves from the "polluted" language of National Socialism.[178] In fact, it was not one but a range of distancing styles, including: the deliberately unsophisticated writing of Ernst Wiechert's *Das einfache Leben* (1939, English translation *The Simple Life*, 1954) with its conscious avoidance of all rhetoric and its suspicion of contemporary jargon; the elevated prose of Erika Mitterer's expansive portrait of life in a sixteenth-century southern German town; the slightly archaic language of historical novels by Bergengruen; the chronicle-like style of le Fort's historical novels; the deeply symbolic language of many sonnets; the pastoral tones and images of nature poetry; and the biblical language, Christian humanist tenor, and heavy spiritual tone of much narrative prose and essayistic work. The use of such linguistic styles to underpin a network of veiled references, images, analogies, and parallels from the historical, biblical, and classical realms is nowadays perceived as alien and, with regard to the common understanding of opposition, as ineffectual and even escapist. Indeed it was perceived as such immediately after the war. As the journalist and writer Gustav René Hocke noted in his essay "Deutsche Kalligraphie," referring to an Italian debate at around the turn of the nineteenth century on the pure aestheticism of literary form, the characteristic style of writing under the Hitler dictatorship was what he calls (in less-than-straightforward prose of his own): "aesthetisierende Prosa . . . in ihrer symbolistischen, pastoral-idyllischen, elegisch-egozentrischen oder maniriert-essayistischen Form" (aestheticizing prose with its symbolist, pastoral-idyllic, egocentrically elegiac, or mannered essayistic form). Such "merkwürdige stilistische Esoterik" (remarkable stylistic esotericism) was motivated by the need for caution in expressing oneself but, Hocke claims, the content increasingly gave way to and disappeared behind the form of expression.[179] Yet these various styles, this "calligraphic" approach, need to be seen and interpreted in the context of and as a reaction against the dominant discourse of the time, the swollen and bombastic language of National Socialist newspaper reports, bureaucratic language, and public speaking, with their clichés, false pathos, and military metaphors.[180] Quite in contrast to the present-day reader's perception of this calligraphic style as rebarbative, for the contemporary reader in Nazi Germany it was precisely its alien and difficult nature that served to mark it out as an expression of nonconformity and dissent from the prevailing orthodox discourse.

This chapter has established a number of basic principles with regard to literary nonconformism in Nazi Germany. First, it has demonstrated the heterogeneity of nonassimilated writers who remained active under the regime, in particular their varied political, philosophical, and religious standpoints, and has proposed a tentative categorization. However, it has also shown the importance of recognizing that nonconformist writing does not lend itself to generalized or blanket judgments, and that a full appreciation of writers' oppositionality is dependent on detailed biographical and textual exploration. Second, it has outlined the equally varied techniques of camouflaged writing and has illustrated how their deployment and reception were fraught with difficulties; they depended for their effect on a particularly sensitized educated readership and were seldom free from ambiguity, misinterpretation, or controversy. These principles underpin the individual author case studies in part 2 of this book, which provide a representative cross-section of inner emigrant activity in Nazi Germany and Austria.

Notes

[1] Strothmann, *Nationalsozialistische Literaturpolitik*, 29.

[2] Grimm, "Innere Emigration als Lebensform." And see "Critical Reception" in chapter 1 of this book.

[3] However, the presence of most inner emigrant communists or socialists was short-lived since, by the summer of 1933, the vast majority of such opponents of the regime were already in prison or had fled abroad.

[4] See Barbian, "Zwischen Anpassung und Widerstand," 75–76.

[5] Jan Petersen, *Unsere Straße: Eine Chronik. Geschrieben im Herzen des faschistischen Deutschlands 1933/34* (Berlin: Dietz, 1947), 11.

[6] See Sigrid Bock, "Arbeiterkorrespondenten und -schriftsteller bewähren sich: Jan Petersen: *Unsere Straße*," in *Erfahrung Nazideutschland: Romane in Deutschland 1933–1945*, ed. Sigrid Bock and Manfred Hahn (Berlin: Aufbau, 1987), 44–98; also Brekle, *Schriftsteller im antifaschistischen Widerstand*, 61–67.

[7] Brekle, *Schriftsteller im antifaschistischen Widerstand*, 100–101.

[8] "Vorwort," in Werner Krauss, *PLN: Die Passionen der halykonischen Seele* (Potsdam: Rütten & Loening, 1946), 5.

[9] See Brekle, *Schriftsteller im antifaschistischen Widerstand*, 108–21.

[10] See Elisabeth Fillmann, "*PLN*-Dechiffrierungen: Verarbeitung konkreter Zeit-realität und Kritik der 'Innerlichkeit' in Werner Krauss' satirischem Roman," in Krohn, Rotermund, Winkler, and Koepke, *Aspekte der künstlerischen Inneren Emigration 1933–1945*, 64–65.

[11] Daniel Hoffmann, "An den Grenzen des aufgeklärten Selbstbewusstseins: Elisabeth Langgässers Auseinandersetzung mit den Bedingungen menschlicher Existenz," in *Eigensinn und Bindung: Katholische deutsche Intellektuelle im 20. Jahrhundert*, ed. Hans-Rüdiger Schwab (Kevelaer: Butzon & Bercker, 2009), 292, 296.

[12] Langgässer, "Schriftsteller unter der Hitler-Diktatur," 283, 284–85.

[13] Scholdt, *Autoren über Hitler*, 477.

[14] Cathy S. Gelbin, "Elisabeth Langgässer and the Question of 'Inner Emigration,'" in Donahue and Kirchner, *Flight of Fantasy*, 270, 274.

[15] Jochen Klepper, *Kyrie: Geistliche Lieder* (Witten: Eckart, 1957). See Holger Sonntag, "'The Night Will Soon Be Ending'. Jochen Klepper: A Luther Hymn-writer in Dark Times," *Logia: A Journal of Lutheran Theology* 18, no. 2 (2009): 31–40. These songs lack any real criticism of the Nazi regime, although a posthumously published collection of poems is more closely concerned with the present, especially the portrayal of the ideal Christian ruler. See Jochen Klepper, *Gedichte: Olympische Sonette/Der König* (Berlin-Dahlem: Der Christliche Zeitschriftenverlag, 1947).

[16] Günther Wirth, "Geschichte in metaphorischer Gestalt: Jochen Klepper: 'Der Vater,'" in Bock and Hahn, *Erfahrung Nazideutschland*, 196–97.

[17] See letter to Juliane and Kurt Meschke of June 20, 1937, in *Jochen Klepper: Gast und Fremdling: Briefe an Freunde*, ed. Eva-Juliane Meschke (Berlin: Eckart, 1960), 82.

[18] See the epigraph to the novel's first chapter: "Den Königen ist Unrecht tun ein Greuel; denn durch Gerechtigkeit wird der Thron befestigt" (Kings cannot bear to commit an injustice; for thrones become stronger through justice). Jochen Klepper, *Der Vater: Roman eines Soldatenkönigs* (Stuttgart: Deutsche Verlags-Anstalt, 1937), 1:11.

[19] Klepper, *Der Vater*, 2:197–98.

[20] Hinrich Siefken, "Totalitäre Erfahrungen aus der Sicht eines christlichen Essayisten: Theodor Haecker im Dritten Reich," in Kroll, *Die totalitäre Erfahrung*, 124. On publication in *Hochland*, see Hinrich Siefken, ed., *Theodor Haecker 1879–1945*, Marbacher Magazin 49 (Marbach am Neckar: Deutsche Schillergesellschaft, 1989): 89–92 passim.

[21] The volume was entitled *Über den abendländischen Menschen* (On western man, c. 1944). See Hinrich Siefken, "The Diarist Theodor Haecker: *Tag- und Nachtbücher 1939–1945*," *Oxford German Studies* 17 (1988): 125.

[22] Hildegard K. Vieregg, "Theodor Haecker: Christliche Existenz im totalitären Staat," in Schwab, *Eigensinn und Bindung*, 117–35.

[23] Theodor Haecker, *Tag- und Nachtbücher 1939–1945*, ed. Heinrich Wild (Munich: Kösel, 1947), 9–10. Wild's introduction dates this incident, based on a

later recollection of Haecker's daughter, to 1943, although Reck-Malleczewen's diary refers to a very similar incident reported to him by his friend Haecker as early as 1937. See entry for September 9, 1937, in Friedrich Reck-Malleczewen, *Tagebuch eines Verzweifelten* (Lorch: Bürger, 1947), 41–42.

[24] Siefken, "Diarist Theodor Haecker," 126.

[25] On the editorial history, see "Bermerkung des Herausgebers," in Haecker, *Tag- und Nachtbücher 1939–1945*, 245–47.

[26] For a detailed study, see Cordula Koepcke, *Ricarda Huch: Ihr Leben und ihr Werk* (Frankfurt am Main: Insel, 1996).

[27] Ricarda Huch, *Briefe an die Freunde*, ed. Marie Baum (Berlin: Deutsche Buch-Gemeinschaft, 1960), 161.

[28] Gisela Berglund, *Der Kampf um den Leser im Dritten Reich: Die Literatur-politik der "Neuen Literatur" (Will Vesper) und der "Nationalsozialistischen Monatshefte"* (Worms: Heintz, 1980), 82–83.

[29] Ricarda Huch, *Herbstfeuer* (Leipzig: Insel, 1944). See Brekle, *Schriftsteller im antifaschistischen Widerstand*, 184–85.

[30] Olaf Saile, *Kepler: Roman einer Zeitwende* (Stuttgart: Behrendt, 1949), 325.

[31] Jan-Pieter Barbian, "'Nur passiv geblieben'?: Zur Rolle von Erich Kästner im Dritten Reich," in *Die vollendete Ohnmacht?: Schriftsteller, Verleger und Buchhändler im NS-Staat: Ausgewählte Aufsätze* (Essen: Klartext, 2008), 150–61.

[32] See Stefan Neuhaus, *Das verschwiegene Werk: Erich Kästners Mitarbeit an Theaterstücken unter Pseudonym* (Würzburg: Königshausen & Neumann, 2000); and Ingo Tornow, *Erich Kästner und der Film* (Munich: Deutscher Taschenbuch Verlag, 1998).

[33] Barbian, "'Nur passiv geblieben'?," 172–73.

[34] Tornow, *Erich Kästner und der Film*, 19–20.

[35] See, for example, Luiselotte Enderle, *Erich Kästner in Selbstzeugnissen und Bilddokumenten* (Reinbek bei Hamburg: Rowohlt, 1966), 92–93.

[36] Barbian, "'Nur passiv geblieben'?," 180–81.

[37] Karin Gradwohl-Schlacher, "Innere Emigration in der 'Ostmark'?: Versuch einer Standortbestimmung," in Holzner and Müller, *Zwischenwelt*, 77.

[38] Robert von Dassanowsky, *Phantom Empires: The Novels of Alexander Lernet-Holenia and the Question of Postimperial Austrian Identity* (Riverside, CA: Ariadne, 1996).

[39] Gradwohl-Schlacher, "Innere Emigration in der 'Ostmark'?," 84.

[40] Roman Roček, "Zwischen Subversion und Innerer Emigration: Alexander Lernet-Holenia und der Nationalsozialismus," in Holzner and Müller, *Zwischenwelt*, 181–211.

[41] The work was serialized in 1940 in the Berlin illustrated journal *Die Dame* under the title *Die Blaue Stunde* (Blue hour), and the retitled book was planned for publication the following year by S. Fischer Verlag. However, it was refused the requisite publication permit by the Propaganda Ministry, even though fifteen thousand copies had already been printed. It could only be published by Bermann

Fischer in Stockholm in 1947. Robert von Dassanowsky, "Österreich contra Ost-mark: Alexander Lernet-Holenia's 'Mars im Widder' as Resistance Novel," in Holzner and Müller, *Zwischenwelt*, 159.

[42] Alexander Lernet-Holenia, *Mars im Widder: Roman* (Stockholm: Bermann-Fischer, 1947), 152–60.

[43] Thomas Eicher, "Im Zwischenreich des Alexander Lernet-Holenia," in *Im Zwischenreich des Alexander Lernet-Holenia: Lesebuch und "Nachgeholte Kritik,"* ed. Thomas Eicher (Oberhausen: Athena, 2000), 190. See also Otto F. Beer, "Lernet im Mars (Nachwort)," in Alexander Lernet-Holenia, *Mars im Widder* (Vienna: Zsolnay, 1976), 261–68.

[44] Dassanowsky, "Österreich contra Ostmark," 161.

[45] Schoeps, *Literatur im Dritten Reich*, 230.

[46] The work of the conservative poet and essayist Friedrich Georg Jünger—for example, the collection *Der Taurus: Gedichte* (Hamburg: Hanseatische Verlag-sanstalt, 1937)—constitutes an exception here.

[47] Hagelstange noted it became almost a "fashionable" form of resistance. Rudolf Hagelstange, "Die Form als erste Entscheidung," in *Mein Gedicht ist mein Messer: Lyriker zu ihren Gedichten*, ed. Hans Bender (Munich: List, 1964), 38.

[48] Ziolkowski, "Form als Protest," 165.

[49] Rotermund and Ehrke-Rotermund, "Literatur im 'Dritten Reich,'" 378.

[50] Ingo Zimmerman, *Reinhold Schneider: Weg eines Schriftstellers* (Berlin: Union, 1982), 136. See also "Schneider and National Socialism" in chapter 7 of this book.

[51] Rudolf Hagelstange, "Nachwort," in *Venezianisches Credo* (Munich: Insel, 1946).

[52] See Hoffmann, *Opposition Poetry in Nazi Germany*, 45. Hoffmann's book discusses the poetry of, inter alia, Bergengruen, Hagelstange, Haushofer, and Schneider.

[53] Albrecht Haushofer, *Moabiter Sonette: Die letzten Gedichte Albrecht Haushofers* (Berlin: Privatdruck, 1945).

[54] Albrecht Haushofer, *Gesammelte Werke*, Teil 1, *Dramen I*, ed. Hans-Edwin Friedrich and Wilhelm Haefs (Frankfurt am Main: Lang, 2014).

[55] See Thomas Dupke and Petra Treiber, "Gedichte aus dem Widerstand: Albrecht Haushofer und die 'Moabiter Sonette,'" Radioessay, August 5, 1993 (Cologne: DLF, 1993), Typescript, Deutsches Literaturarchiv, Marbach, Biblio-thek. Also: Ursula Laack-Michel, *Albrecht Haushofer und der Nationalsozialismus: Ein Beitrag zur Zeitgeschichte* (Stuttgart: Klett, 1974), 275–76.

[56] Rudolf Alexander Schröder, "Dichtungen der Naturvölker," in *Gesammelte Werke* (1952–65), 2:1143.

[57] All these are contained in Schröder, *Gesammelte Werke*, vol. 2.

[58] Both in Schröder, *Gesammelte Werke*, vol. 3.

[59] Rudolf Alexander Schröder, *Abendstunde: Ein Selbstbildnis in Gesprächen*, ed. Lutz Besch (Zurich: Die Arche, 1960), 28. Also Hans-Albrecht Koch, ed., *Rudolf Alexander Schröder (1878–1962)* (Frankfurt am Main: Lang, 2013).

[60] H. R. Klieneberger, *The Christian Writers of the Inner Emigration* (The Hague: Mouton, 1968), 29.

[61] Rudolf Alexander Schröder, "Vom Beruf des Dichters in der Zeit: Rede bei einer Tagung junger Dichter 1947," in *Gesammelte Werke*, 3:43.

[62] For example, Samuel Fischer encouraged him to sign an oath of loyalty to Hitler in October 1933 in order not to bring the firm into greater difficulties. Oskar Loerke, entry for November 1, 1933, in *Tagebücher*, 349–50. It was, however, a step he regretted and never fully came to terms with.

[63] Oskar Loerke, "Genesungsheim," in Oskar Loerke, *Sämtliche Gedichte*, vol. 2, ed. Uwe Pörksen, Wolfgang Menzel, and Lutz Seiler (Göttingen: Wallstein, 2010), 615. Page numbers to the poems are hereafter cited parenthetically in the text.

[64] The works of Loerke and Lehmann were singled out for praise after the war by Elisabeth Langgässer, who called them the "two great lyrical poets of these barbaric years" ("Schriftsteller unter der Hitler-Diktatur," 284). Kasack even designated Loerke's work a form of "resistance" to the regime. Hermann Kasack, "Oskar Loerke," in Kasack, *Mosaiksteine: Beiträge zur Literatur und Kunst* (Frankfurt am Main: Suhrkamp, 1956), 148.

[65] For example, the entry for May 17, 1939, which records his "Lebensekel in dieser Umwelt" (disgust with life in this environment), in Loerke, *Tagebücher*, 339.

[66] Schnell, *Literarische innere Emigration*, 41–42.

[67] Brekle, *Schriftsteller im antifaschistischen Widerstand*, 193.

[68] "Nachwort," in *Werner Kraft—Wilhelm Lehmann: Briefwechsel 1931–1968*, ed. Ricarda Dick (Göttingen: Wallstein, 2008), 2:677. He felt compelled to do it in order to preserve his civil service status and thus his career.

[69] Hans Dieter Schäfer, *Wilhelm Lehmann: Studien zu seinem Leben und Werk* (Bonn: Bouvier, 1969), 56.

[70] Both collections are contained in Wilhelm Lehmann, *Sämtliche Werke in drei Bänden* (Gütersloh: Mohn, 1962).

[71] Donahue, *Karl Krolow and the Poetics of Amnesia*, 31, 33.

[72] Anatol Schenker, *Der Jüdische Verlag 1902–1938: Zwischen Aufbruch, Blüte und Vernichtung* (Tübingen: Niemeyer, 2003).

[73] Gertrud Kolmar, *Das lyrische Werk*, ed. Regina Nörtemann (Göttingen: Wallstein, 2010). See also Ilse Nagelschmidt, Almut Constanze Nickel, and Jochanan Trilse-Finkelstein, *Dichten wider die Unzeit: Textkritische Beiträge zu Gertrud Kolmar* (Frankfurt am Main: Lang, 2013).

[74] Bertolt Brecht, "An die Nachgeborenen," in Bertolt Brecht, *Svendborger Gedichte* (London: Malik, 1939), 84.

[75] See Hans Dieter Schäfer, "Die nichtfaschistische Literatur der 'jungen Generation' im nationalsozialistischen Deutschland," in Denkler and Prümm, *Die deutsche Literatur im Dritten Reich*, 459–503.

[76] See Schäfer, *Das gespaltene Bewußtsein*, 24.

[77] Johannes Graf, *"Die notwendige Reise": Reisen und Reiseliteratur junger Autoren während des Nationalsozialismus* (Stuttgart: M & P, 1995).

[78] Glenn R. Cuomo, "Günter Eichs Rundfunkbeiträge in den Jahren 1933–1940: Eine kommentierte Neuaufstellung," in *Rundfunk und Fernsehen: Wissenschaftliche Vierteljahresschrift* 32, no. 1 (1984): 83–96.

[79] Gerd Eckert, "Deutscher Kalender," *Die Literatur* 41, no. 9 (1938–39): 561.

[80] Glenn Cuomo, "Opposition or Opportunism?: Günter Eich's Status as 'Inner Emigrant,'" in Donahue and Kircner, *Flight of Fantasy*, 177–78.

[81] See Gerd Eckert, "Hörspielmanie und Hörspielpflege," *Die Literatur* 41, no. 8 (1938–39): 495.

[82] See Cuomo, *Career at the Cost of Compromise*, 26–28. One should also note, however, that in 1947 Eich himself told Willi Fehse, who was preparing an essay on figures belonging to "Das heimliche Deutschland" (the secret Germany), that he did not think he belonged in such company: "Ich habe dem Nationalsozialismus keinen aktiven Widerstand entgegengesetzt. Jetzt so zu tun, als ob, liegt mir nicht." (I offered no active resistance to National Socialism. To pretend now, as if I had, is not for me.) "An Willi Fehse, 1 November 1947," in Axel Vieregg, *Der eigenen Fehlbarkeit begegnet: Günter Eichs Realitäten* (Eggingen: Edition Isele, 1993), 10.

[83] Joachim W. Storck, "Anatomie einer Denunziation: Der 'Fall' Günter Eich," in *Widersprüche im Widersprechen: Historische und aktuelle Ansichten der Verneinung*, ed. Peter Rau (Frankfurt am Main: Lang, 1996), 164–65 and 172–73.

[84] Cited in Gerhard Hay, Hartmut Rambaldo, and Joachim W. Storck, eds., *"Als der Krieg zu Ende war": Literarisch-politische Publizistik 1945–1950: Eine Ausstellung des Deutschen Literaturarchivs im Schiller-Nationalmuseum Marbach a.N.* (Munich: Kösel, 1973), 143.

[85] Schäfer, *Das gespaltene Bewußtsein*, 54.

[86] Besides the Eich studies referenced, one could mention the lengthy controversy over Peter Huchel: Stephen Parker, "Collected—Recollected—Uncollected?: Peter Huchel's *Gesammelte Werke*," *German Life and Letters* 40, no. 1 (1986/87): 49–70; Axel Vieregg, "The Truth about Peter Huchel?," *German Life and Letters* 41, no. 2 (1987/88): 159–83; Hub Nijssen, *Der heimliche König: Leben und Werk von Peter Huchel* (Würzburg: Königshausen & Neumann, 1998); and Jan-Pieter Barbian, "'. . . im Augenblick restlos aufgeworfen': Peter Huchel als Autor im Dritten Reich," in Barbian, *Die vollendete Ohnmacht?*, 185–203. Also: David Basker, "'I Mounted Resistance, Though I Hid the Fact': Versions of Wolfgang Koeppen's Early Biography," in Donahue and Kirchner, *Flight of Fantasy*, 258–68; Gerald Funk, "Between Apocalypse and Arcadia: Horst Lange's Visionary Imagination during the Third Reich," in Donahue and Kirchner, *Flight of Fantasy*, 248–57; Diana Orendi, "Luise Rinser's Escape into 'Inner Emigration,'" in Donahue and Kirchner, *Flight of Fantasy*, 199–210; Stefan Reinhardt, *Alfred Andersch: Eine Biographie* (Zurich: Diogenes, 1990), 43–126; and Donahue, *Karl Krolow and the Poetics of Amnesia*.

[87] Grimm, "Innere Emigration als Lebensform," 48.

[88] Gottfried Benn, "Züchtung," in Gottfried Benn, *Sämtliche Werke*, ed. Gerhard Schuster and Holger Hof (Stuttgart: Klett-Cotta, 1986–2003), 4:33.

[89] Gottfried Benn, letter to Egmont Seyerlen, February 27, 1933, in *Gottfried Benn–Egmont Seyerlen, Briefwechsel 1914–1956*, ed. Gerhard Schuster (Stuttgart: Klett-Cotta, 1993), 14.

[90] Joachim Dyck, *Gottfried Benn: Einführung in Leben und Werk* (Berlin: de Gruyter, 2009). Dyck's biography is, compared with some, a notably sympathetic portrayal of Benn's early dalliance with the regime, and he clearly establishes the absence of anti-Semitism in Benn's writing and pronouncements.

[91] See Gottfried Benn, *Der neue Staat und die Intellektuellen* (Stuttgart: Deutsche Verlags-Anstalt, 1933).

[92] Dyck, *Gottfried Benn*, 110–14.

[93] Jürgen Schröder, "Benn in den dreißiger Jahren," in *Intellektuelle im Bann des Nationalsozialismus*, ed. Karl Corino (Hamburg: Hoffmann and Campe, 1980), 49–50, 56.

[94] Gottfried Benn, letter to Oelze, November 18, 1934, in *Briefe an F. W. Oelze 1932–1945*, ed. Harald Steinhagen and Jürgen Schröder (Frankfurt am Main: Fischer-Taschenbuch-Verlag, 1979), 1:39.

[95] This was the title of Benn's later autobiography *Doppelleben: 2 Selbstdarstellungen* (Wiesbaden: Limes, 1950).

[96] Jürgen Schröder, "Gottfried Benn als Emigrant nach Innen," in *Literatur in der Diktatur: Schreiben im Nationalsozialismus und DDR-Sozialismus*, ed. Günther Rüther (Paderborn: Schöningh, 1997), 139–40.

[97] Gottfied Benn, *Statische Gedichte* (Wiesbaden: Limes, 1948).

[98] Jan-Pieter Barbian, "'Ich gehörte zu diesen Idioten': Ina Seidel im Dritten Reich," in Barbian, *Die vollendete Ohnmacht?*, 130–32.

[99] Ina Seidel, in *Der Deutsche Schriftsteller* 7, no. 4 (1942): 37, cited in Barbian, *Die vollendete Ohnmacht?*, 133–34.

[100] Ina Seidel, *Aus den schwarzen Wachstuchheften: Monologe, Notizen, Fragmente*, ed. Christian Ferber (Stuttgart: Deutsche Verlags-Anstalt, 1980).

[101] Carossa, *Ungleiche Welten*.

[102] Hans Carossa, *Wirkungen Goethes in der Gegenwart* (Leipzig: Insel, 1938); see also Schnell, *Literarische innere Emigration*, 65–66. Carossa conveniently omits to mention in his autobiography that he delivered this speech.

[103] Philipp, "Distanz und Anpassung," 19.

[104] See "Party Inspection Commission" in chapter 1 of this book.

[105] See entry for January 19, 1938, in Joseph Goebbels, *Die Tagebücher von Joseph Goebbels: Sämtliche Fragmente*, part 1, vol. 5, ed. Elke Fröhlich (Munich: K. G. Saur, 1993–2008), 106.

[106] Jenny Williams, *More Lives Than One: A Biography of Hans Fallada* (London: Libris, 1998), xi.

[107] See, for example, Michael Töteberg, "'Beim Film weiß man nie': Ein Autor scheitert an der Filmindustrie," in *Hans Fallada*, ed. Gustav Frank and Stefan Scherer (Munich: text + kritik, 2013), 40–50.

[108] Williams, *More Lives Than One*, 186, 194.

[109] Franz Schonauer, "Der Schöngeist als Kollaborateur oder Wer war Friedrich Sieburg?," in Corino, *Intellektuelle im Bann des Nationalsozialismus,* 113–15.

[110] Tilman Krause, *Mit Frankreich gegen das deutsche Sonderbewußtsein: Friedrich Sieburgs Wege und Wandlungen in diesem Jahrhundert* (Berlin: Akademie, 1993), 126–33.

[111] Gregor Streim, "Junge Völker und neue Technik: Zur Reisereportage im Dritten Reich, am Beispiel von Friedrich Sieburg, Heinrich Hauser und Margret Boveri," *Zeitschrift für Germanistik* 2 (1999): 349.

[112] It is not clear if he ever became a member of the Nazi party. See Gunther Nickel, "Die Schwierigkeiten politischer Hermeneutik am Beispiel Friedrich Sieburgs," in Braun, Guntermann, and Gandner, *"Gerettet und zugleich von Scham verschlungen,"* 45, 56–57.

[113] Erwin Rotermund, *Zwischen Exildichtung und innerer Emigration: Ernst Glaesers Erzählung "Der Pächter"* (Munich: Fink, 1980), 11.

[114] See Christian Klein, "Nachwort," in Ernst Glaeser, *Jahrgang 1902: Roman,* ed. Christian Klein (Göttingen: Wallstein, 2013), 321–89.

[115] See Joseph Wulf, *Literatur und Dichtung im Dritten Reich: Eine Dokumentation* (Frankfurt am Main: Ullstein, 1989), 49.

[116] Ernst Glaeser, *Das Unvergängliche: Erzählungen* (Amsterdam: Querido, 1936), 112 and 106, respectively.

[117] For a detailed discussion of the story, see Rotermund, *Zwischen Exildichtung und innerer Emigration.* Rotermund attributes Glaeser's volte-face, in part, to the fact that he had become distanced from his political allies in emigration following harsh Communist Party criticism of his two antifascist works *Das Gut im Elsass* (The Alsace estate, 1932) and *Der letzte Zivilist* (The last civilian, 1935), according to which the works revealed "social fascist," that is, social democratic traits (12–13). Rotermund also sees *Der Pächter* as a preparation of the ground for Glaeser's eventual return to Germany and as an apologist justification of the way he had turned his back on his former ideological allies (32).

[118] Klein, "Nachwort."

[119] Frank Thiess, "Hitlers Werk—eine erlösende Tat," reprinted in *Neuer Hannoverscher Kurier,* June 21, 1946, cited in: Thomas Mann, *Tagebücher 1944–1.4.1946,* ed. Peter de Mendelssohn and Inge Jens (Frankfurt am Main: Fischer, 1986), 704.

[120] Ulrike Knes, "Frank Thiess: Ein Autor zwischen Realität und Selbststilisierung," in Holzner and Müller, *Zwischenwelt,* 54–55.

[121] Knes cites a letter from Thiess to Hinkel, in which he seeks to avoid a writing ban by pointing to the aspects of his past work that can be seen as having "prepared the way intellectually for the new Germany" and mentions he has drawn the "hatred" of Jewish writers and the Jewish press for this (Knes, "Frank Thiess," 56–57).

[122] Frank Thiess, *Jahre des Unheils: Fragmente erlebter Geschichte* (Vienna: Zsolnay, 1972), 197.

[123] Knes, "Frank Thiess," 60–61, 63–64.

[124] See Yvonne Wolf, *Frank Thiess und der Nationalsozialismus: Ein konservativer Revolutionär als Dissident* (Tübingen: Niemeyer, 2003), 227–35. Quotations from Thiess's text are taken from Frank Thiess, *Das Reich der Dämonen: Der Roman eines Jahrtausends* (Berlin: Zsolnay, 1941).

[125] Wolf, *Frank Thiess*, 186.

[126] Thiess, *Jahre des Unheils*, 133. This can only relate to the Propaganda Ministry's request in July 1941 that he rewrite parts of the book relating to ancient Germanic history. See Gerhard Renner, "Frank Thiess: Ein 'freier Schriftsteller' im Nationalsozialismus," in *Buchhandelsgeschichte* 2, no. 51, Beilage zum Börsenblatt für den deutschen Buchhandel (June 26, 1990): 41. Also Murray G. Hall, *Der Paul Zsolnay Verlag: Von der Gründung bis zur Rückkehr aus dem Exil* (Tübingen: Niemeyer, 1994). This request may have been prompted by the sections "Die Tyrannen" (The Tyrants) and "Sparta, Die Verwirklichung einer Utopie" (Sparta, Realization of a Utopia), in which Thiess had depicted an absence of the rule of law, which had clear parallels with contemporary Nazi Germany. For example: "[Man] suchte gelegentlich die Emigration dadurch zu verhindern, daß man alle 'die nicht dazugehörten' ganz gleich ob sie 'schuldig' oder 'nicht schuldig' waren, ausrottete" (Attempts were occasionally made to prevent emigration by exterminating all those who "did not belong," regardless of whether they were "guilty" or "not guilty," 48).

[127] Frank Thiess, *Das Reich der Dämonen* (Hamburg: Krüger, 1946). This applies particularly to the new chapter "Rauborganismen" (Predatory Organisms). See Grimm, "Innere Emigration als Lebensform," 43; Wolf, *Frank Thiess*, 186; and cf. Wiesner, "'Innere Emigration,'" 396.

[128] Wolf, *Frank Thiess*, 189–90.

[129] Denk, *Die Zensur der Nachgeborenen*, 13–138.

[130] See Rainer Hackel, *Gertrud Fussenegger: Das erzählerische Werk* (Vienna: Böhlau, 2009), 39–46.

[131] See Friedrich Denk, "Regimekritische Literatur im Dritten Reich: Eine Problemskizze," in *Wort und Dichtung als Zufluchtsstätte in schwerer Zeit*, ed. Frank-Lothar Kroll (Berlin: Gebr. Mann, 1996), 26.

[132] Murray G. Hall, "'Ich bitte um Nachsicht. . . .': Innere Emigration privat," in Holzner and Müller, *Zwischenwelt*, 393–416.

[133] Ibid., 401.

[134] Jürgen Hillesheim and Elisabeth Michael, *Lexikon nationalsozialistischer Dichter: Biographien, Analysen, Bibliographien* (Würzburg: Königshausen & Neumann, 1993), 257–60.

[135] In this volume, see chapter 3, note 12, for Bergengruen's description of the confiscation and banning of *Der ewige Kaiser*.

[136] See Hinrich Siefken, ed., *Die Weiße Rose und ihre Flugblätter: Dokumente, Texte, Lebensbilder, Erläuterungen* (Manchester: Manchester University Press, 1994).

[137] It has often been assumed subsequently that such denial of paper for publication was a form of censorship or sanction against a particular writer. Rather, it was usually a case of genuine paper shortages resulting in the need for selectivity and

the authorities prioritizing those publications they deemed most important (see Schäfer, *Das gespaltene Bewußtsein*, 22).

[138] Werner Bergengruen, *Dichtergehäuse: Aus den autobiographischen Aufzeichnungen* (Zurich: Verlag der Arche, 1966), 150–51.

[139] See John Klapper, "Categories of the Nonconformist: The Historical Fiction of Inner Emigration," *German Life and Letters* 67, no. 2 (2014): 158–81.

[140] Ricarda Huch, *Deutsche Geschichte*, vol. 1, *Römisches Reich Deutscher Nation* (Zurich: Manesse, 1987), 321.

[141] Translated into English as: *I Shall Bear Witness: The Diaries of Victor Klemperer 1933–41*, translated by Martin Chalmers (London: Weidenfeld & Nicolson, 1998–99).

[142] Magdalena Michalak-Etzold, "Zusammenspiel von Innerer Emigration und Innerer Zensur," in Holzner and Müller, *Zwischenwelt*, 111–25.

[143] Werner Bergengruen, *Schreibtischerinnerungen* (Munich: Nymphenburger Verlagshandlung, 1961), 176.

[144] Bergengruen, entry no. 948, in *Schriftstellerexistenz*, 172. Elsewhere he refers to "die Feinhörigkeit der Unterjochten" (the sensitive hearing of the subjugated) and the extra senses they inevitably developed (*Schreibtischerinnerungen*, 199).

[145] Bergengruen, *Schreibtischerinnerungen*, 205.

[146] Bertolt Brecht, "Fünf Schwierigkeiten beim Schreiben der Wahrheit," in *Bertolt Brecht Gesammelte Werke*, vol. 22, *Große kommentierte Berliner und Frankfurter Ausgabe*, ed. Werner Hecht et al. (Berlin: Suhrkamp, 1993), 74. Page numbers cited parenthetically in the text in the following paragraphs.

[147] Gert Reifarth and Philip Morrissey, "Aesopic Voices: A Foreword," in *Aesopic Voices: Re-framing Truth through Concealed Ways of Presentation in the 20th and 21st Centuries*, ed. Gert Reifarth and Philip Morrissey (Newcastle upon Tyne: Cambridge Scholars Publishing, 2011), 2.

[148] Dolf Sternberger, "Lektionen vom Wolf und Lamm," the first subsection of "Figuren der Fabel," *Frankfurter Zeitung*, December 25, 1941, in *Dolf Sternberger: Schriften*, vol. 9 (Frankfurt am Main: Insel, 1988), 14–18. See also Dodd, *Jedes Wort wandelt die Welt*, 158–59.

[149] Leo Strauss, "Persecution and the Art of Writing," in *Persecution and the Art of Writing* (Chicago, London: University of Chicago Press, 1952), 25. Page numbers cited parenthetically in the text in the next paragraph.

[150] The following summary is based on Ehrke-Rotermund and Rotermund, *Zwischenreiche*. Page numbers cited parenthetically in this paragraph.

[151] Cf. Strauss, who says that "between the lines" statements "do not usually occur in the preface or other very conspicuous place" (Strauss, "Persecution and the Art of Writing," 32).

[152] Ehrke-Rotermund and Rotermund, *Zwischenreiche*, 17–18.

[153] Brecht, "Fünf Schwierigkeiten," 82.

[154] Paul Grice, "Logic and Conversation," in Grice, *Studies in the Way of Words* (Cambridge, MA: Harvard University Press, 1989), 22–40.

155 Ehrke-Rotermund and Rotermund, *Zwischenreiche*, 19.

156 Herbert Küsel, "Dietrich Eckart: Geboren am 23. März 1868," *Frankfurter Zeitung*, Erstes Morgenblatt, March 23, 1943, in Küsel, *Zeitungs-Artikel* (Heidelberg: Schneider, 1973), 26–34.

157 See Erwin Rotermund, "Herbert Küsels 'Dietrich Eckart'-Artikel vom 23. März 1943," in Rotermund, *Artistik und Engagement: Aufsätze zur deutschen Literatur* (Würzburg: Koenigshausen & Neumann, 1994), 242–43.

158 Ehrke-Rotermund and Rotermund, *Zwischenreiche*, 18. Page numbers cited parenthetically in this paragraph.

159 Ibid., 24.

160 Rudolf Pechel, "Sibirien," *Deutsche Rundschau* 252 (1937): 172–75. For an analysis, see Erwin Rotermund, "Tarnung und Absicherung in Rudolf Pechels Aufsatz 'Sibirien' (1937): Eine Studie zur 'verdeckten Schreibweise' im 'Dritten Reich,'" in Rotermund, *Artistik und Engagement*, 225–38.

161 Letter from Jochen Klepper, November 29, 1938, in *Jochen Klepper: Briefwechsel 1925–1942*, ed. Ernst G. Riemschneider (Stuttgart: Deutsche Verlags-Anstalt, 1973), 116.

162 Siegfried Lokatis, *Hanseatische Verlagsanstalt: Politisches Buchmarketing im "Dritten Reich"* (Frankfurt am Main: Buchhändler-Vereinigung, 1992), 95.

163 Dodd, *"Der Mensch hat das Wort,"* 13.

164 "Hinterlist mit Methode: Der Fall M.," *Das Schwarze Korps*, September 24, 1936, cited in Erwin Rotermund, "Zu Joachim Günthers Publizistik im 'Dritten Reich,'" *Zeitschrift für Germanistik*, Neue Folge 9, no. 2 (1999): 331.

165 *Das Schwarze Korps*, June 12, 1935, cited in ibid., 330–31.

166 Hellmuth Langenbucher, "Sinn und Unsinn der Buchproduktion," in *Bücherkunde der Reichsstelle zur Förderung des Deutschen Schrifttums* 4, no. 3 (March 1937): 138.

167 See "The Muddy Waters of Opposition and Conformism" in chapter 1 of this book.

168 See, for example, Eberhard Lämmert's suggestion that censors "mangels hinreichender gründlicher Bildung die allegorische Bedeutung des Textes schwer oder nicht erfassen würden" (lacking a thorough education, would only with difficulty, if at all, comprehend the allegorical meaning of the text). Lämmert, "Beherrschte Prosa: Poetische Lizenzen in Deutschland zwischen 1933 und 1945," *Neue Rundschau* 86 (1975): 408.

169 See Bergengruen, *Schriftstellerexistenz*, entry no. 794, 70–77.

170 Werner Bergengruen, "Zum Geleit," in Rudolf Pechel, *Zwischen den Zeilen: Der Kampf einer Zeitschrift für Freiheit und Recht 1932–1942* (Wiesentheid: Droemer, 1948), 8.

171 The term "Sklavensprache" (language of slaves) was much in circulation at the end of the war and was given prominence in Karl Paetel's collection of essays, *Deutsche innere Emigration*. However, it came to be disputed by Sternberger on the grounds that it failed to do justice to the use of the "free word," which many

had been courageous enough to use under the regime. Sternberger, "War das Sklavensprache?," *Frankfurter Allgemeine Zeitung*, July 8, 1961.

[172] See "The Muddy Waters of Opposition and Conformism" and "Genesis and Publication of *Auf den Marmorklippen* (1939)" in chapters 1 and 8 of this book, respectively.

[173] Bernt von Heiseler, "Nachwort," in Gertrud von le Fort, *Die Krone der Frau* (Zurich: Arche, 1952), 143.

[174] Gertrud von le Fort, "Hymnen an Deutschland," *Völkischer Beobachter*, August 23, 1933. See also "From Catholic Spirituality to the Christian Reich" in chapter 6 of this book.

[175] Bernhard Payr, "Deutsch-französische Begegnungen im deutschen Roman 1937," *Völkischer Beobachter* (Norddeutsche Ausgabe), February 2, 1938. See also Brekle, "Die antifaschistische Literatur," 92–93. See also the section "Oppositional Writers" in this chapter.

[176] Hellmuth Langenbucher, "Neuerscheinungen 1937," in *Nationalsozialistische Monatshefte* 8, no. 93 (December 1937): 1144.

[177] Victor Klemperer, *LTI: Notizbuch eines Philologen* (Berlin: Aufbau, 1947).

[178] Schmollinger, *"Intra muros et extra,"* 80.

[179] Gustav René Hocke, "Deutsche Kalligraphie oder Glanz und Elend der modernen Literatur," *Der Ruf* 1 (1946): 9.

[180] See Eugen Seidel and Ingeborg Seidel-Slotty, *Sprachwandel im Dritten Reich: Eine kritische Untersuchung faschistischer Einflüsse* (Halle: Verlag Sprache und Literatur, 1961).

Part II

Fig. 3.1. Werner Bergengruen. Photo by Maria Diedenhof,
courtesy of Deutsches Literaturarchiv Marbach.

3: Werner Bergengruen: "*The* Führer Novel"?

A Baltic German Loner and Outsider

WERNER BERGENGRUEN WAS born in 1892 in Riga. Throughout his life he retained a keen awareness of his ethnic origins in the eastern Baltic region, and the mature writer's internationalism has its roots in his inherited dual identity: the Baltic Germans were citizens of Russia and owed allegiance to the tsar and the empire, but at the same time they saw themselves culturally and linguistically very much as ethnic Germans, and indeed several of Bergengruen's relations fought on different sides in the First World War.[1]

Bergengruen's parents left Riga in 1909 to move to Marburg an der Lahn, and from 1911 to 1914 he studied history, German, theology, and art history in Marburg, Berlin, and Munich. During the First World War, he fought as a volunteer in the German Army and later served as an officer in a German-Baltic unit of the White Army fighting to free the Baltic region from the Bolsheviks. However, the revolutionary events of 1917 put an end to the German dominance of the Baltic region, and Bergengruen was subsequently cut off from his native land. From 1920 he worked as an editor and translator for different journals focused on eastern Europe and lived variously in Berlin, Munich, Tirol, Zurich, and Rome[2] before becoming an independent writer in 1924 and settling in Berlin, where he lived until 1936. Although he had contacts with many leading writers, he generally kept his distance from the intellectual and cultural life of the capital, showing himself from the start to be an independent-minded nonconformist for whom alignment with any particular literary school was quite alien.[3]

In 1935, Bergengruen and his wife, Charlotte (a granddaughter of Fanny Mendelssohn-Bartholdy, the sister of the composer Felix Mendelssohn), whom he had married in 1919, converted to Catholicism. Bergengruen's early ties to the Russian Orthodox faith no doubt played a role here, and, after the family's move in 1936 from Berlin to Solln near Munich, he was increasingly attracted to Catholic resistance circles. In Solln he was a neighbor of Karl Muth, the founder and editor of the journal *Hochland*, and through Muth developed links to such figures as the writer Theodor Haecker, the philosopher Alois Dempf, the writer Max

Stefl, and the student Hans Scholl.[4] Indeed, Bergengruen and his wife were later to be involved in copying the leaflets of the Weiße Rose (White Rose) resistance group and sending them to carefully chosen addressees.[5]

The years 1933 to 1945 proved difficult for Bergengruen in a number of ways. He was originally classed as an "auslandsdeutscher Schriftsteller" (expatriate German writer). Income from his writing was limited and the need to feed a family of five was a challenge, a situation not helped by the banning in 1934 of the novel *Das große Alkahest* (Great alkahest, 1926)—see below—and the stories *Des Knaben Plunderhorn* (The boy's junk horn, 1934).[6] Owing to her Jewish origins, Charlotte was unable to produce the required *Ariernachweis* (proof of Aryan origins) and Bergengruen was under official pressure to divorce her. This was never an option for him, but, equally, emigration seemed to be out of the question.

After the Nazi takeover, Bergengruen showed some short-lived signs of accommodating himself to the regime. Thus, on May 4, 1933, he attended the annual gathering of the Schutzverband deutscher Schriftsteller (Association of German Writers) and was elected to the board of the organization.[7] However, there is scant further evidence of this sort of alignment with Nazi cultural authorities. Indeed, in an "assessment" produced by the local branch of the NSDAP (Nazi Party) of Munich-Solln in 1940, it is clear that the Nazis considered Bergengruen suspect.[8] He is here described as not being a member of the party and never having held an office within the party or any groups or associations affiliated to it; his wife is recorded as not belonging to the Nazi Women's League, his children as not being members of the Hitler Youth or the League of German Girls. It is conceded that he displays the swastika flag on special occasions and contributes to collections, but his behavior otherwise warrants the description "unzuverlässig" (unreliable) and, with unintended humor, the report adds that he does not use the "German greeting" ("Heil Hitler") "auch wenn er ab und zu die Hand ein wenig erhebt" (even though he now and again raises his hand a little).[9] The report goes on to say that it is suspected that Bergengruen's wife is Jewish, a claim based on the fact that Bergengruen often visits an acquaintance whose wife is "Volljüdin" (a full Jew), that his daughter visited a school in Munich attended by mostly "Juden-Mischlinge" (Jewish crossbreeds), and that paperwork relating to Bergengruen's son suggests one of the grandparents is of Jewish descent. Such a characterization of his "unreliable" status would no doubt also have been reinforced by the writer's repeated failure to respond to annual requests to contribute poems for anthologies published in honor of the Führer on his birthday (*S*, 130).

On March 10, 1937, Bergengruen was expelled from the Chamber of Literature (RSK) and banned from all public writing (*GV*, 154). This meant that, like other inner emigrants such as Stefan Andres or Jochen Klepper, he was forbidden from speaking in public, was placed under observation, and could from now on only publish by receiving a "Sondergenehmigung" (special permit) through his publisher, the Hanseatische Verlagsanstalt, Hamburg. It seems he had Heinz Wismann—until July 1937 the head of the Propaganda Ministry's literary section (Schrifttumsabteilung)—to thank for this concession, who had argued for the literary quality of Bergengruen's work.[10] He managed to survive as a writer in these circumstances reasonably successfully, steering a course between the Ministry of Propaganda, the Gestapo, and Rosenberg's Reichsstelle,[11] and benefiting from both the rivalry that existed between such bodies and, on one occasion at least, the censors' pride and incompetence.[12] Despite the RSK expulsion, Bergengruen managed to publish a total of twenty-eight titles under National Socialism.[13] However, this period was characterized by bouts of deep depression and for months on end he found himself incapable of writing anything at all.[14]

In 1942, following severe bomb damage to his house in Solln, Bergengruen and his family moved to Achenkirch in the west Austrian state of Tyrol. The following four years of rural seclusion, though characterized by continuing concerns for his wife's safety, proved to be a productive period. Although he had now ceased even to try to publish his work and regularly declined invitations from publishers and journalists alike, he produced a considerable number of novellas and poems for later publication "für die Schreibtischschublade" (for the desk drawer), as he put it (*D*, 149). Caution required that manuscripts be hidden under a large pile of logs in a wood store. Nevertheless, and despite the fact that he was not allowed to speak in public, Bergengruen still found means to address like-minded groups, reading from such works as the poems in *Dies irae* (1945) at informal gatherings in churches and private houses.[15] He notes that some gatherings in churches attracted as many as seven hundred people, that after many readings of his work in private circles he was asked for copies of the poems or other works he had read from, and that these typed copies were then further copied by hand and passed on, often to soldiers in the field (*D*, 153–54). Furthermore, he recalls nights when he and his wife themselves worked on copying out political fliers or speeches by Graf von Galen, the Bishop of Münster, which they distributed by bike all over the Munich area (*D*, 151).[16]

Bergengruen finally managed to leave Austria in May 1946 and settled in Zurich, where he lived until the move back to Baden-Baden in 1958. He was one of the few inner emigrants whose reputation survived intact in postwar Germany, becoming one of the most widely read writers of the 1950s and receiving numerous awards, both in Germany and abroad. However, although involved in postwar literary life, he remained until his death in 1964 in many ways the loner he had always been, one who mourned the passing of, as he saw it, the more humane pre-1914 world of the old Europe embodied by his Baltic homeland.

The Political and Literary Conservative

Bergengruen was a prolific writer and produced a vast oeuvre of more than one hundred books, encompassing eleven novels, more than two hundred stories, and around five hundred poems. Over many years he reissued novels under new titles, some of them revised and edited, others with only minimal changes. He also republished or reprinted short stories many times for new collections, including differing amounts of new material. In this sense his work is a major challenge for the bibliographer.

He remained, throughout his career, deeply conservative in his choice of both subject matter and traditional, almost classical linguistic forms. He was opposed to all forms of collective political or economic endeavor, spurned mass culture, and, in the face of a hostile, totalitarian world, championed freedom, justice, and human dignity from an essentially Christian standpoint. The main themes of his work can be summed up as follows: human imperfection, the ubiquity of guilt, and the need for reconciliation; insecurity, transience, and man's instinctive search for permanence; fear and the conquest of fear through the assertion of trust and confidence in the divinely inspired and sustained world; the sense of a purpose and order beyond all wordly chaos and destruction; power and its abuses, and the conflict between power and the rule of law; and the search for a just resolution of the tension between the individual and the community.

His first novel, *Das große Alkahest* (Great alkahest, 1926), subsequently published under the title *Der Starost* (The lord of the manor, 1938), is set in eighteenth-century Courland, modern-day western Latvia. Its principal theme is that knowledge and scientific pursuits offer no lasting solution to the inherent insecurity and uncertainty of existence. Przegorski is a nobleman of Polish descent and an alchemist who is trying to find the alkahest, a hypothetical universal solvent that can dissolve every other substance. But he also becomes embroiled in politics and through intrigue seeks to gain power in Courland, which leads to criminal acts and to partial responsibility for human tragedy. Nevertheless, before he dies, Przegorski shows contrition and rediscovers the uncomplicated faith of his fellow Polish countrymen. As Bergengruen was subsequently to reflect in the motto to a later book:

Das Unendliche mindert sich nicht,
wenn das Endliche wächst.
Und das Geheimnis bleibt. (*GV*, 5)

[The infinite does not diminish / if the finite grows. / And the mystery remains.]

It is futile to pursue single-mindedly an understanding of human existence or to try to make that existence more certain through the exclusive pursuit of knowledge of nature or human history. Man's aim should not be to improve the world but to respect it as it is, in a spirit of humility and hope. It is here that one finds Bergengruen's true conservatism, a theologically inspired worldview, which has little place for rebels, social engineers, proselytizers, or writers of tendentious literature (*GV*, 127), but which affirms "Maß, Bestand und Dauer" (moderation, continuance, and permanence, *D*, 70), the existing order, human frailty, and man's tenuous hold on existence, and considers them to be essential prerequisites for the realization of human goodness.

Existence is characterized by transience, an inherent uncertainty, and insecurity, and many of Bergengruen's works show how characters' lives are suddenly turned upside down as their hitherto stable and ordered way of life and their material well-being are threatened. Besides *Der Großtyrann und das Gericht* (The great tyrant and the court, 1935), the best example is Bergengruen's major historical novel of inner emigration, *Am Himmel wie auf Erden* (In heaven as on earth, 1940), where the onset of an all-encompassing fear of flood waters leads to social turmoil in the city of Berlin and eventually to rebellion. Less dramatically, in *Das Feuerzeichen* (The beacon, 1949) a well-meaning act leads to the arrest and banishment of a popular innkeeper, who has devoted his life to helping the community.

Bergengruen was a literary traditionalist, believing the task of the writer was to establish a coherent and comprehensive epic world, against which an omniscient narrator develops a largely linear plot. This approach to narrative fiction is closely linked to his religious worldview and the belief that literature should serve the purpose of revealing the "eternal order" of existence in the ordered nature of the cosmos, and that the writer's work should, in effect, constitute a microcosm of the latter.[17] Like a medieval painter seeking to capture the cosmos on a single canvas, he says he was always tempted to try "im Gedicht oder in der Erzählung die Gesamtheit des Weltalls, visibilia omnia et invisibilia, wenigstens in Abbreviaturen aufscheinen zu lassen" (to allow the totality of the universe, the whole of the visible and the invisible world, to appear in a poem or a story, at least in abbreviated form, *D*, 213). The inevitable symbolism of his writing means identifying in the particular a reference to more general circumstances, and in the temporal a reference to timeless phenomena.

Although the two major novels produced in Nazi Germany are among Bergengruen's best-known works, he was, as he acknowledges in his memoirs, more at home in the short prose form, in which action frequently takes precedence over characterization. For him a narrative always proceeds from an extraordinary event or action, and character and milieu follow on from that event—hence his strong inclination toward the novella (*S*, 164–65). The individual case, the depiction and interpretation of "the unique," however unusual or isolated in nature, demonstrates the eternally valid laws of existence, and the point of all narrative art is to reveal those laws.[18] *Der Großtyrann und das Gericht* in fact started life as a novella but as the material developed and became more complex, so a different format appeared to be needed, and it is no coincidence that the plot and its development dominate here, rather than the detailed portrayal of characters.[19]

For all that Bergengruen's work also demonstrated in full measure human contradictions, shortcomings, and weaknesses, it is his absolute trust in the "rightness" and the "order" of the world, allied to a strict adherence to traditional Christian moral values, that was largely responsible for the fading interest in his work amid the postwar, in particular the post-1968, reassessment of literary form and function. The anachronism of his convictions concerning the essential correctness of the world and the certainty of salvation was bound to alienate a new generation of writers and readers with their postmodern relativities and uncertainties.

Bergengruen's political sympathies lay with a predemocratic conservative social order and a key aspect of this conservatism is his nationalist outlook, which is strongly shaped by the values he associates with the Holy Roman Empire. He rejects the post-1871 "kleindeutsches," or lesser German, *Reich* and the "fateful" turn taken by German history under Bismarck, with both of which he associates a narrow-minded nationalism, blind to the virtues of other nations. For the old conservative Bergengruen, the nationalism of the "Reichsdeutschen" (Germans of the 1871–1945 empires) was to be regarded as a degenerate form of a healthy patriotic pride in the nation, a sentiment he particularly harbored for the beloved Baltic homeland, which he had irrevocably lost.[20] The traditional influences of his upbringing, in particular the deep respect for the notion of "empire" embodied in the reign of Augustus, the first Roman emperor, and renewed in the Charlemagne empire, led him to glorify the distant Holy German Empire. For Bergengruen, the "Holy Alliance" was part of a historical continuity that guaranteed man a fixed point amid the vicissitudes of existence (*D*, 412), and this almost mystical dream of a lasting union of Germans under the imperial banner was designed to guarantee justice and the rule of law.[21] His vision of empire was essentially metaphysical in nature, with the Holy Roman Empire being seen as "das irdische Reich als Vorform des Gottesreiches" (the earthly kingdom as a preform of the Kingdom of God);[22] elsewhere he saw in the subsequent "Holy Roman Empire of the German nation," for all its shortcomings, traces of the "Friedensreich Christi" (Christ's Kingdom of Peace).[23]

Bergengruen retrospectively ascribed a quasi-political status to the cycle of poems *Der ewige Kaiser*, which he had worked on from summer 1935 to spring 1936 and which could only be circulated illegally in Germany. The poem "Das Dauernde" (The lasting) particularly stands out in the collection, owing to its powerful first stanza and its denunciation of the "tyrants":

Erblosen Todes sterben die Tyrannen.
Tribunen zeugen nicht.
Und die der Tausenden Gehör gewannen,
gewannen sich Gericht.[24]

[Tyrants die an heirless death. / Tribunes bear them no witness. / And those who once gained the ear of thousands, / Have now gained judgment on themselves.]

In these poems, the Christian legal and moral order associated with western empire are championed against state despotism and tyranny, whereas the hated Third Reich, a "travesty" of the conception of empire, and a caricatured image of the Führer are contrasted with the ideal of the Holy Roman Empire of the German nation and the elected emperor. This empire is seen as the key formative influence on the west, capable of imposing the "yoke" of a higher spiritual order on "dem Zerstörungsdrang der Barbaren, den zügellosen Egoismen der Stämme und ihrer Nachfolger, der Nationalstaaten" (the destructive urges of the barbarians, the boundless egoism of the tribes and their successors, the national states).[25] Deeply influenced both by the ideas of a Christian *Reich* and by fascist conceptions of a political *Reich*, which had been circulating in the late Weimar years among members of the Conservative Revolution, Bergengruen now sought in this volume to use the notion of a "spiritual kingdom" as a means to distance himself from the Nazi state.

The proximity of Bergengruen's religious faith to his particular brand of nationalism is revealed repeatedly in his writing. On occasions he ventures into dangerous territory, for example, in his article on the relationship between Germanness ("Deutschtum") and Christianity, where he answers the Nazi author Richard Euringer's[26] suggestion that Christianity has falsified or adulterated Germanness by countering that the two are inseparable, that they stand in the same relationship to each other as Teutonism ("Germanentum") and heathenism, and that Christianity is what has helped make Germanness a reality. Clearly any such suggestion, especially the contradiction of one of Goebbels's favored writers, would have been unwelcome to Nazi ideologues in 1937, but Bergengruen goes further and turns the question around by asking whether, conversely, Germanness could ever falsify Christianity, answering his own question by insisting that to deny the Christian origins of German culture and art would be to return the nation to the ranks of the "primitive."[27] The implied snub to Nazi notions of the purity and essentially secular nature of German culture, and the tying of art to Christian moral precepts, is typical of Bergengruen's understated but insistent form of conservative opposition.

One of his best-known novellas, *Die drei Falken* (1937, English translation *The Three Falcons*, c. 1950), provides a good illustration of this. The main figure is a cripple, Cecco, who is due to inherit money through the auction of a valuable falcon bequeathed by a deceased falcon master. However, he is repulsed by the jealousy and wrangling that the process has unleashed and, before the auction can take place, he lets his falcon fly free. In so doing he renounces worldly claims and material ties, affirming man's God-given freedom; thanks to his humane and charitable disposition he is duly celebrated as a true heir to the honorable brotherhood of falconers and receives their chained necklace as a reward. The novella reveals nothing that one could consider in any way overtly critical of contemporary Germany but it is significant that such a work appeared at the very time when the foundations were being laid in Nazi Germany for the systematic persecution and murder of the mentally and physically handicapped, and it has to be seen as a bold move to place a disabled individual in such an "exposed" position as hero of the story. It reveals a writer decisively opposed to Nazi notions of racial purity and the survival of the fittest, or, as Bergengruen was to write later, it presented "ein Bild der Großmut, der Hochherzigkeit" (an image of magnanimity, of generousness), of spiritual elements that had disappeared without trace from German reality (*S*, 176–77).

Further evidence of Bergengruen's unabashed but cautious dismissal of ideological purity can be found in the proclamation of his unorthodox background. In an invited biographical sketch for *Die Neue Literatur* in 1939, he establishes quite clearly his Swedish origins (hence the unGerman spelling of his surname) and his ancestors' roots in Livonia, Estonia, and Courland. Indeed, his needlessly protracted enumeration of the mixed origins of Baltic families, encompassing eleven nationalities and including even the racially suspect Russian Tartars, seems almost an implicit statement against the folly of policies of racial purity.[28]

Bergengruen's view of the cataclysmic events of the twentieth century was that they constituted a fundamental shift in epochs, a unique period in human history of greater significance than even such momentous historical occurrences as the French Revolution.[29] National Socialism had broken the continuity of German history and opened up a chasm between itself and the past. These ideas fed into the deep cultural pessimism that informs many of the author's autobiographical writings after 1945, a preoccupation with mankind's increasing loss of freedom, the normative pressures of modern existence, rationalization, bureaucratization, the automatization of man and society, and the threat of nuclear catastrophe.[30] In his concern about totalitarian control over all aspects of human existence, Bergengruen has much in common with fellow inner emigrant Stefan Andres,[31] while the pervasive cultural and, to a certain extent, historical pessimism of his later years, and his ideas on the irrevocable loss of a traditional and essentially Christian value order, suggest comparisons with the position of Ernst Wiechert in *Das einfache Leben* (1939, English translation *The Simple Life*, 1954) and *Die Jeromin-Kinder* (The Jeromin children, 1945)—see chapter 9.

Bergengruen's poems give a further indication of his opposition to the regime.[32] From 1933 to 1939 he produced a number of "Schüttelreimgedichte" (spoonerist couplets), which circulated anonymously and were reportedly among the clearest anti-Nazi statements of the author.[33] The relevance of *Der ewige Kaiser* in this regard has been touched on above. The later *Dies irae* (1945) suggests an equally critical stance. The seventeen poems, written in the summer of 1944, were read to small groups of like-minded oppositional acquaintances in the writer's home in Achenkirch in the Tirol and were subsequently passed from hand to hand; they were not published until after the war.[34] Strongly biblical in tone, they are concerned with the themes of guilt and atonement, with the moral damage caused by Nazism, the need for spiritual forbearance in the face of hardship, and the notion of the Nazi years as suffering endured by the Germans on behalf of the whole world.

In the grand ode "An die Völker der Welt" (To the peoples of the world), which concludes the collection and, unlike the other poems in it, was written in 1945 after the cessation of hostilities, he blames the peoples of the earth for having done nothing when it was clear the world would be bound to "go up in flames," and he calls on them not to forget this failure on their part. Coming close to the deeply contentious sentiments expressed by von Molo and Thiess after the war in connection with exiled writers (see chapter 1), he tells the "peoples of the world" that, since they themselves had never been tempted in the way Germans had, they are in no position to pass judgment:

Völker der Erde, ihr haltet euer Gericht.
Völker der Erde, vergeßt dieses Eine nicht:
Immer am lautesten hat sich der Unversuchte entrüstet,
immer der Ungeprüfte mit seiner Stärke gebrüstet. (*DI*, 43)

[Peoples of the earth, you pronounce your judgment. / Peoples of the earth, do not forget this one thing: / It is always those never tempted who are most outraged, / always those untested who boast about their strength.]

The religious emphasis becomes clear in the conclusion to the poem with its message that judgment is for all mankind, not a single nation, that all need to respond to the divine imperative to repent.

In the same collection, the poem "Wer will die Reinen von den Schuldigen scheiden?" (Who can separate the pure from the guilty?) echoes this notion of shared responsibility (*DI*, 33), and in their barely veiled references to the hardship of life under the Nazi regime, other poems, such as "In dieser Zeit" (At this time), reflect that archetypal inner emigrant note of consolation and encouragement:

> Inmitten eurer eignen Wände
> Seid ihr Verfolgte und verhöhnt.
> Wer aber ausharrt bis ans Ende,
> wird überwesentlich gekrönt. (*DI*, 21)

> [Within your walls / You are persecuted and ridiculed. / But whoever forbears to the end, / will be most substantially crowned.]

In a poem such as "Die Sühne" (Expiation), the transitory nature of contemporary Germany is emphasized, whereas God's timescale is seen to overshadow Nazi pretensions to a thousand-year *Reich*:

> Aber ihm und seinen Scharen
> Ist die Zeit ein Flügelschlag,
> ist ein Tag gleich tausend Jahren,
> tausend Jahre sind ein Tag. (DI, 39)

> [But for him and his heav'nly hosts / Time is a mere flap of the wings, / a day is like a thousand years, / a thousand years just like a day.]

Dies irae was one of the first books published in Germany after the collapse of the Third Reich and its positing of the notion of a "collective" guilt became a major point of public debate. The collection's embodiment of a Christian view of resistance to Nazism, and its reflection of a more widespread tendency to promote tolerance, passivity, and atonement, incurred the displeasure of Max Frisch, who objected, in particular, to the tendency to allow personal and specific guilt for National Socialism to be merged into an amorphous general guilt that is to be shared by all humans.[35] The postwar view of Bergengruen is further summed up by Wolfgang Brekle's objection to the writer's "mythologization of the war."[36] The new Germany was not minded to neglect the social and economic roots of fascism and the Second World War, in the way most former inner emigrants seemed inclined to do.

Der Großtyrann und das Gericht (1935): Genesis and Publication

In his "Rückblick auf einen Roman," Bergengruen says *Der Großtyrann* was prompted by an oriental fairy tale he came across in the autumn of 1926, in which a sultan orders his wesir to clear up a mysterious murder within three days, otherwise he will be executed. He notes that the real starting point of the book was a merging of the basic action with a thematic complex of justice and conscience, the relationship between power and the law, human vulnerability and susceptibility to temptation, and the process of atonement, representative sacrifice, and love.[37] The theme developed over a period of three years. Bergengruen wrote the "Preamble" and the first three chapters to the novel during a journey in autumn 1929, returning periodically to the work in the following few years. The main exchanges between the Great Tyrant and Diomede were partly composed in summer 1931 in the Riesengebirge. The bulk of the book, however, was written in 1933 and 1934, with much of the latter year being devoted to it exclusively. It was completed in October 1934 (*S*, 173–74).

With the Nazi takeover of power, Bergengruen notes, the developing plot of the novel suddenly took on a frightening reality and the country increasingly found itself confronted with the questions faced by the novel's characters; quoting partially from his "Preamble," he writes: "Allenthalben erwies sich die Leichtverführbarkeit der Unmächtigen und Bedrohten. Alle menschliche Freiheit war aufgehoben, über jedem hing die Drohung." (Everywhere it was evident how easily the powerless and the threatened could be led astray. All human freedom was removed, everyone was under threat, *S*, 174–75.) As he worked further on the text after the start of 1933, the original "Fürst" (prince) became a "Großtyrann" (great tyrant), who insisted on the use of the title "Herrlichkeit" (magnificence), asserted his godlike status, and created a sense of awe by allowing himself to appear unannounced in any of the citizens' houses. It was now that the author knew his work was not just to be concerned with eternal questions of human existence but that it had to address specific issues of the German present, a realization that altered and sharpened the focus of many aspects of the draft, making him see that it required only a few shifts of emphasis in order to take on a political dimension (*S*, 175). He says the embracing of this new opportunity became a duty toward fate understood as a Nietzschean "amor fati," and he felt driven to complete the newly meaningful project, regardless of whether he would ever be able to publish it (*S*, 175–76).

The date and setting were crucial. He states he was not motivated by any historical interest, although it became clear that the events and the theme could be located only in the past, in an entirely prescientific world (*S*, 168). However, he was careful to avoid any specific historical period for the setting of the novel, saying it was set in an age of still unbroken religious trust, suggesting "fifteenth century at the latest" (*S*, 172–73), which elsewhere he extends to the thirteenth, fourteenth, or fifteenth centuries.[38] The geographical setting is also left deliberately vague, though he acknowledges that his long-standing interest in Italy and Italian culture had a decisive influence on the final novel.

The question of how the novel could be published in Nazi Germany is to be explained in part by its reception and misinterpretation by Nazi censors (see below) but also by the fact that it appeared in a publishing house, the Hanseatische Verlagsanstalt (HAVA) in Hamburg, that, as a publisher of works of unambiguously Nazi writers, was considered to be above suspicion and had been integrated into the Deutsche Arbeitsfront. HAVA's fiction section, under the influence of its editor in chief Benno Ziegler, was largely responsible for the publisher's reputation among the educated readership of Nazi Germany, and yet it is clear that the section had an unusually free rein (or "Narrenfreiheit") to publish material by conservative writers of a distinctly nonconformist hue, such as Ernst Jünger, Rudolf Fischer, Gustav Hillard, and August Winnig.[39] Bergengruen had become one of HAVA's authors because he detected in it a residual conservative anti-Nazi stance (*S*, 181). He ascribes the decision to publish the novel to the bravery of Ziegler, who was opposed to Nazism, and claims that the message of the book was clear to all but convinced Nazis. HAVA was particularly forceful in its marketing of the work. Far from being concerned about using the term "great tyrant" in its publicity, it advertised the novel in the weekly magazine of the German book trade, promising book retailers an exciting read and referring in a surprisingly bold résumé to the mortal danger encountered by the "Leiter der Sicherheitsbehörde" (head of the security services).[40]

By contrast, Karl Silex, editor of the large circulation daily *Deutsche Allgemeine Zeitung* in Berlin, to which Bergengruen had offered the novel for serialization, had serious reservations about it.[41] He had immediately seen the danger of publishing the text as it stood and had demanded that parallels with Hitler, such as his lack of children or his love of architecture, be changed or downplayed, that the description "Großtyrann" should be avoided completely, that the title should be changed to "Die Versuchung" (The temptation), and that Bergengruen should cut all references to politics, power, and the dispensing of justice (*S*, 183–84). Astonishingly, Bergengruen complied with this in order to get the book serialized, and in his memoirs one detects an author downplaying the significance of this far from trivial compromise. Notwithstanding this murky episode, subsequent serializations and the published novel itself were not subject to such restrictions.

Unlike several other texts by inner emigrant writers, both Bergengruen's major novels of the Third Reich sold in large numbers. *Der Großtyrann*, for example, had sold sixty thousand copies by 1941 alone,[42] and despite calls for it too to be banned following the suppression of *Am Himmel wie auf Erden*, it could still appear in 1943 in a *Wehrmacht* edition published by HAVA.[43]

Summary

The novel is set in Cassano, a fictional Italian city-state, but one clearly located in northern Italy (it is a day's ride from Bologna), at the time of the Renaissance. It is based around a murder and is narrated in some respects like a detective story, albeit one told in an archaic and formal style. The monk Fra Agostino, a diplomat and "skillful negotiator" of the Great Tyrant and head of state, has been murdered in the garden of the tyrant's palace. Massimo Nespoli, the latter's chief of police, is given three days to find the murderer. The ensuing search creates widespread mutual suspicion, and a range of suspects is identified. Among others, Nespoli lays the blame for the murder on a pregnant girl who has recently taken her own life, but the Great Tyrant readily rejects this, as there is evidence the girl was seen alive at the time far from the crime scene. Nespoli's deadline for finding the killer is extended but he is left in no doubt that further failure will cause him to lose his job, and he is even threatened with execution.

Vittoria Confini tries to save her lover Nespoli by forging a letter from her dying husband, Pandolfo, in which he confesses to the murder. Following the latter's death, his son, the law student Diomede Confini, seeks to protect his father's honor by getting a prostitute to say Pandolfo had been with her during the night of the murder and so could not be the culprit. The Great Tyrant obtains the forged letter fragment and has its authenticity tested by a writing expert. He refuses to release the body for burial until the matter is clarified, since, if Pandolfo is the murderer, all his wealth will go to the state. Mafalda, Confini's feisty elderly sister, meanwhile seeks to protect her brother's reputation by using bribery to get the prostitute to revoke her statement and thus disprove the claim. Before reporting to the Great Tyrant, the writing expert seeks to bribe Vittoria with a test result that would allow her to inherit Pandolfo's fortune; however, she is not to be bribed. Similarly, the old priest Don Luca, who has heard Pandolfo's final confession, refuses to break the secrecy of the confessional despite the Tyrant's threat of torture. In order to put an end to the pressure that the whole town finds itself under, the pious clothes dyer Sperone, who seeks to live his life in imitation of Christ and is viewed with reverence by the people as a holy fool possessed of extraordinary powers of healing, confesses to the crime. However, this is subsequently revealed to be a vain and self-indulgent attempt to seek a Christ-like death.

Finally, the Great Tyrant presides over a court and, in front of all the main characters, summarizes what has happened in the city, showing how everyone was tempted and incurred guilt. He solves the murder mystery by admitting that he himself had killed the monk, since he feared that pending court proceedings against Fra Agostino would have led to the release of state secrets and would have endangered Cassano. However, he also says he had thereby wanted to test his subjects' views, their loyalty, and fallibility. Don Luca reproaches the Great Tyrant for playing at being God: his guilt lies as much in manipulating the lives of his subjects and acting as their judge and jury as it does in the act of murder itself. The Great Tyrant recognizes his wrongdoing and guilt, burns all documents relating to the case, and seeks his subjects' forgiveness. Ultimately, the focus of the novel is not on the wrongdoing of the Great Tyrant but rather on the way the vacillating people allow themselves to be so readily duped and seduced by an authoritarian ruler.

Reception

Contemporary responses to the novel demonstrate better than perhaps any other work produced under National Socialism the inherent ambiguity of inner emigrant writing. For Benno von Wiese the resonance was clear: "Meine Generation . . . hat das Buch durchaus als eine getarnt kritische, für uns jedoch unmißverständliche Auseinandersetzung mit dem herrschenden Regime gelesen" (My generation certainly read the book as a veiled critical examination of the ruling regime, but one that for us was unambiguous). And he notes that the book was passed excitedly from one person to the next.[44] This is a view reiterated more forcefully by Werner Wilk, who recalls reading the book, amazed that it could have been published and freely marketed in Nazi Germany, and convinced censors must either have been blind or have forgotten how to read critically.[45] Bergengruen himself reports on the many personal communications, including some from former inmates of prisons, concentration camps, and prisoner-of-war camps, that he had received affirming the support, the "Rückgratstärkung" (moral encouragement), and the courage to resist that the book had provided during the Third Reich (*S*, 208–9).

Whereas many may have thus read and understood the book as a comment on authoritarianism and the fickleness of human nature, it was equally the case that others perceived in it a hymn of praise to the strong leader. Elsewhere Bergengruen notes that many read and praised the book without realizing the judgment it was passing on what they themselves embodied (*S*, 181). The author's claim that the *Völkischer Beobachter* wrote about the book: "Das ist *der* Führerroman der Renaissancezeit!"

(That is *the* Führer novel of the Renaissance period! *S*, 182) has often been repeated but it has not been possible to track down the source. Furthermore, Bergengruen reports that in 1936, a year after the novel's publication, Alfred Rosenberg spoke "überaus anerkennend" (most appreciatively) of the work (*S*, 185); but again it is difficult to pin this down to a specific source. It may be that, in one or another of these cases, Bergengruen is referring to the description in the *Völkischer Beobachter* of the Great Tyrant as "eine der Herrengestalten der Renaissance" (one of the master figures of the Renaissance), a review that says the whole novel is well written and "exciting."[46] In any case, this seal of official approval was decisive in the novel being published in a number of newspapers and being translated during the Third Reich into Dutch, French, and Swedish. Indeed Bergengruen even reports receiving an offer to dramatize the novel, which he declined fearing distortions might occur in the process (*S*, 182).

The protection of the *Völkischer Beobachter* review further proved decisive whenever the Gestapo raised questions with the publishers. Indeed it was not until 1941, when Rosenberg's office began to criticize the novel (prompted no doubt primarily by concerns about the already prohibited *Am Himmel wie auf Erden*) and to demand it be banned, that the work came to be seen in official circles as problematic. However, the earlier novel benefited from the antagonism and rivalry between the Reichsstelle and the Propaganda Ministry, as the latter seems to have ignored the concerns of the former, and the book was never proscribed in Germany (*S*, 188–92).

Other contemporary reviews found little to object to. Most notable was one in the *Bücherkunde*, which stated the work had a lot to offer the reader, particularly because of the artistic strengths of the writing and the mix of philosophical, ethical, legal, political, religious, and ideological problems discussed.[47] Another, in *Die Literatur*, called it "a deeply moral detective story," and identified its principal themes as guilt, temptation, and responsibility.[48] A discussion in *Hochland* saw the Great Tyrant as "das Urbild des Machtmenschen" (the archetype of the man of power) and considered the novel to be deeply moral, a "great and poignant book."[49] Hans Franke in *Die Neue Literatur* saw it as an important work about power and service but also the principles of egotism, sacrifice, and love.[50] Meanwhile, as part of a more general discussion of Bergengruen's work, Loesch detected unease and despair behind the "geisterleuchtete Männlichkeit" (manliness enlightened by intellect) of the Great Tyrant, and interpreted the novel as a dialogic work about might and right, causality and freedom, sin and mercy.[51] Finally, in an article published in the *Völkischer Beobachter* in honor of Bergengruen's fiftieth birthday—an indication, of course, that he was not seen as a major "problem" for the state even at this time—the novel was seen as a huge success and as preeminent among the author's historical novels.[52]

More recently, some critics have bemoaned the work's failure to engage politically with National Socialism and have denied its status as a supposed criticism of the regime.[53] Hanimann is concerned that the contemporary reader would most likely have seen the figure of the Great Tyrant as a positive führer figure and that this would have served to support the popular perception of Hitler in 1935.[54] Emmerich also notes Bergengruen's frequently "archaisierende, priesterliche, schwulstige Sprache" (archaic, priestly, pompous language) and doubts whether a tyrannous regime in Renaissance Italy is the most suitable sociohistorical model for a camouflaged attack on fascist rule.[55] He further sees what he considers the essentially Catholic structure of the novel reflected in the pattern of the plot (temptation—guilt—sacrifice—remorse—mercy—divine punishment), which by its very nature excludes any notion of active resistance.

On the other hand, it is fair to say the work remains to this day Bergengruen's most famous book and is still regarded as one of the more significant literary products of the Nazi period, prompting Kroll's verdict on it as "das wohl wichtigste Buch der 'Inneren Emigration' überhaupt" (probably the most important book of the whole inner emigration).[56]

"Ne Nos Inducas in Tentationem"

As noted, the novel has its origins in the late 1920s and was not conceived or written, at least initially, as a response to or a parallel with Germany under National Socialism. The principal motivation was the desire to address certain themes of universal and timeless significance, such as human imperfection, guilt, justice, and atonement.

In keeping with the orthodox Christian notion of "original sin," Bergengruen posited imperfection as an essential and inevitable characteristic of human existence, but considered acknowledgement of imperfection to be the prerequisite of recognizing and achieving goodness.[57] *Der Großtyrann* explores particular forms of this imperfection: human hubris, temptation, and the easily manipulated fear of the weak and powerless in society.[58] In keeping with its motto, "Ne nos inducas in tentationem" (And lead us not into temptation),[59] the novel shows how all strata of society buckle under the threat of terror and how all standards of normal behavior are corrupted, as each individual in his or her own way, including the Great Tyrant, is subjected to and succumbs to temptation, and how mutual suspicion and intrigue lead to guilt through betrayal, denunciation, violence, and even further death.

As Bergengruen writes in the "Preamble":

Es ist in diesem Buche zu berichten von den Versuchungen der Mächtigen und von der Leichtverführbarkeit der Unmächtigen und Bedrohten. Es ist zu berichten von unterschiedlichen Geschehnissen in der Stadt Cassano, nämlich von der Tötung eines und von der Schuld aller Menschen. Und es soll davon auf eine solche Art berichtet werden, daß unser Glaube an die menschliche Vollkommenheit eine Einbuße erfahre. Vielleicht, daß an seine Stelle ein Glaube an des Menschen Unvollkommenheit tritt; denn in nichts anderem kann ja unsere Vollkommenheit bestehen als in eben diesem Glauben. (7)

[This book will tell how those with power are tempted and how those without power and those under threat are easily led astray. It will report the various events that happened in the town of Cassano, that is, the killing of one person and the guilt of all. And this will be reported in such a way as to cause us to lose our faith in human perfection. Perhaps the latter will be replaced by faith in man's imperfection, for our perfection can consist in nothing other than this same faith.]

The "temptation" facing the Great Tyrant is to exploit his position of power to assume the role of judge over the hearts and minds of his subjects, to test their moral resolve and their consciences. He thus observes his citizens with a cold, superior, and merciless impassivity as they become entangled in various webs of temptation and guilt, and he later confesses to having wanted to see at close quarters the extent of his subjects' weakness as their morality was put to the test. In succumbing to the temptation to conduct this human experiment, the Great Tyrant reveals his own weakness and how easily he too can be "led astray."

However, the novel also illustrates the weakness and susceptibility to temptation of the various other characters.[60] Thus, in the case of Nespoli, the hitherto assured chief of police in Cassano, who embodies rationality in all he undertakes but whose clarity of thought and morality desert him in the unsolved and unsolvable murder case and put him in fear of his life, the temptation consists in resorting to dubious tactics (81), illogical patterns of thought and behavior that he knows are wrong, and to shaping the facts to fit his immediate need—seen most obviously in the attempt to pin blame for the murder on the innocent pregnant girl who had committed suicide. Nespoli's development through the novel shows the shortcomings of an exclusive reliance on rationality and the extent to which fear can drive a rational being to desperate measures.

Vittoria's fate, on the other hand, suggests that human love for another can also be susceptible to weakness of resolve and temptation. Her temptation lies in compromising herself for the sake of her lover, Nespoli, and willfully neglecting her sick husband: she provides the chief of police with an alibi by falsifying a confession by her deceased husband, thus sacrificing the latter's honor for the sake of the former. Her love is at one and the same time self-sacrificing and acquisitive (102), for, in defending Nespoli, she seeks to tie him to her. Yet the precarious nature of her would-be selflessness becomes clear later when, faced with the threatened loss of her wealth, she abandons her lover.

In the character of Diomede Confini, Bergengruen shows the futility of striving for perfect justice on earth. The young law student argues that the legal affairs of state must in all circumstances be governed by the principles of absolute justice, and yet he betrays this principle in his own life by bribing and threatening members of the lower classes to lie on oath in order to save his father's reputation, and thus shows the inevitability of guilt in human affairs. He finally acknowledges the truth of the Great Tyrant's claim that in this world "strong hands" cannot remain pure (232), that power and justice can never be fully reconciled with each other, and that earthly justice is only ever imperfect and conditional.

The illustration of fallibility and the inevitability of guilt in human affairs extends to a whole range of other characters, including the priest Don Luca, Mafalda, Rettichkopf, and Perlhühnchen. On the one hand, this theme is a theological assertion of essential human imperfection and of the world's need for redemption, and thus constitutes an attack on humanist faith in man's perfectibility. On the other, the novel's exploration of the fate of the powerless and the weak in society and their ready descent into lies and denunciation offers a veiled portrait of contemporary Nazi society. Sperone's diagnosis of the ills of Cassano are ambiguous and potentially provocative in the context of mid-1930s Germany: "Ist [die Stadt] nicht vergiftet bis auf den Tod? . . . Da ist Versuchung, Verdacht und Verrat. Lüge und Meineid gehen um zwischen Brüdern und Ehegatten. Gewalttaten werden geübt, Leiber verderben und Seelen verderben" (Isn't the town fatally poisoned? We see temptation, suspicion, and betrayal. Lies and perjury are common between brothers and married couples. Acts of violence are being committed, bodies are being corrupted, and souls are being corrupted, 279.)

The antidote to this web of fear, deceit, and lies is Sperone's selfless act of love in confessing to the crime and being prepared to make a Christ-like self-sacrifice in order to put an end to the town's suffering and wrongdoing. In explaining his motives for his supposed murderous act, he tells the Great Tyrant that the events unfolding in Cassano are more than the conscience of the person originally responsible for this chain of misery can cope with (279–80). Both this and Sperone's would-be heroic act—which enacts a key leitmotif of the novel, namely, the many forms that human love can assume—have a decisive effect on the Great Tyrant and influence his decision to reveal all and bring the city's suffering to an end (314).

However, Sperone too is shown to be at fault in succumbing to the temptation and hubris involved in seeking to become Christ-like (302). In his self-sacrifice he sees a way of atoning vicariously for the city's multiple offences against the principle of justice (277), and yet, as the Great Tyrant points out, Sperone has sought to avoid the laborious, life-long vocation of the religious life by giving in to the lure of a one-off, heroic act that would secure him eternal life through self-sacrifice for others (303).

A Novel of and for Its Time?

This focus on the restoration of the disturbed divine order and the emphasis on the universality of the temptation/guilt theme chime with much of Bergengruen's other writings. What distinguishes this novel is that, as he himself noted, under the influence of developments in the early 1930s and especially after 1933 it began to assume features directly relevant to the lives of contemporary readers. How much of this entered the narrative in 1934, which was when a good deal of the final text was written, is not recorded. And one must acknowledge the possibility that Bergengruen's memoirs and comments on the novel featured a certain amount of "self-reconstruction." Nevertheless, even a cursory reading of the text at a remove of some eighty years reveals numerous aspects of life in Cassano, which in 1936 and the following few years can only have been understood as veiled references to circumstances under National Socialism. Thus, the preface quoted above is in a very prominent position in the novel and, in referring to the powerful, to the seduction of the disenfranchised, and to threats, killing, and guilt, it uses terms that in Nazi Germany were highly charged and significant.

The most obvious references to contemporary Germany are the numerous parallels between, on the one hand, the Great Tyrant and his reign, and on the other, Hitler and elements of Nazi rule. The very title of the novel evokes associations with dictatorship, cruelty, and oppression. The Great Tyrant is a childless, solitary individual who has a tendency to withdraw to rural isolation in the mountains (119); he is obsessed with town planning, with architecture, and building projects; and he aspires to construct a monument to himself (227). He infiltrates both public life and the minds of his subjects by creating an aura of omnipresence (60), taking people by surprise by appearing without warning. Owing to his lower-class origins (269), the Great Tyrant is viewed as something of an outsider, an impertinent upstart in the world of the old patrician families that used to rule the city-state; on the other hand, he enjoys popular support for having solved the earlier party conflict between opposing aristocratic factions, for forcing aside old, established families (60, 77) and dealing harshly and decisively with all remaining opposition.[61] He is besotted with power (230), suppresses oppositional voices, and undermines democratic processes and institutions (17, 234–37). In discussion with Diomede he calls himself the "hidden will of the people" and, in a veiled reference to the Weimar Republic, says he could never have achieved his aims if he had respected the will of the people as allowed for in the old constitution of Cassano with its provision for the role of parties (234). In an echo of the origins of the SA and SS, he surrounds himself with a brave young "brotherhood" (67), and through Nespoli's sophisticated system of spies and informers he ensures all potential enemies within the city are held in check. He repeatedly refers to "Providence" (122, 227), echoing perhaps Hitler's claim to have been chosen by Providence, and, in a possible reference to Hitler's concordat with the Catholic Church, seeks an accommodation with the bishop (24–25).

These similarities notwithstanding, Bergengruen was unequivocal in rejecting any direct parallel, seeing clear differences between his fictional character and Hitler. The former was a thoughtful type, ambiguous and complex, a gifted man but also a decent one, and "ein großer Herr" (a great lord), and he goes on to affirm that the dangers and temptations of power could never be demonstrated through "a criminal fool" but had to be shown through a man of intellect and statesmanlike rank: "Wie hätte ich denn auf den Gedanken kommen sollen, ein Hitler könnte eine seelische Umkehr erfahren und erschüttert sich selber vor das Gericht des eigenen Gewissens stellen?" (How would I have ever thought that a figure like Hitler could undergo a spiritual change and, deeply shaken, put himself on trial before the court of his own conscience? *S*, 180).

And indeed it is clear that the Great Tyrant is not a simple cipher for Hitler. Despite his absolute power in Cassano he is shown to be an honest and in many ways enlightened individual, who is self-critical and acutely aware of his own fallibility. He has an interest in history, philosophy, and jurisprudence, and his behavior is dictated by a respect for God (26–27) and for the practices of the church (147–49). Furthermore, toward the end of the novel, in his response to Don Luca's charges, he shows himself to be a man possessed of insight, sensitivity, and a magnanimous spirit (316). He willingly accepts the criticism leveled at him, encourages mutual forgiveness, and resolves to help his citizens embrace change (318–19). These are not the characteristics of a Hitler figure but might even be thought to constitute an idealized *Gegenbild* (counterimage) to the contemporary despot. Indeed, in the central conversations with Diomede, the Grand Tyrant makes clear the advantages of absolutist rule over other forms of government and, as the novel progresses and he is depicted more and more as a reasonable ruler concerned for his subjects' well-being, this absolutism comes across as a form of enlightened despotism.[62]

As shown by the generally positive official reception of the novel, this portrait of an enlightened despot served, whether intentionally or not, as an effective form of camouflage. However, behind the ambiguous picture of the strong leader figure there are several aspects of the novel that would not have escaped the attention of the sensitized German reader of the late 1930s. Thus, when Diomede and the Great Tyrant are discussing the exercising of power, the latter echoes Hitler's oft-repeated claim to be destined to assume power, to be "der verborgene Wille des Volkes" (the hidden will of the people), a ruler who recognizes the will of the governed more clearly than they do (231–32). This notion of embodying the will of the people is linked to the image of the Tyrant as a self-appointed divine authority over his subjects. The source of many of Cassano's ills is seen to lie in the Great Tyrant's hubris, in his desire to assume God-like traits. The theological overlay here serves as further security for Bergengruen's text. Although the Great Tyrant is not threatened, like others in Cassano, and thus is not guilty of the same fear-induced temptations, he succumbs to the lure of absolute power, the temptation to play, in God-like fashion, with the lives of his subjects and to sit in judgment over them. In a key exchange, Diomede asks whether an absolute ruler is not comparable to God, and the Great Tyrant replies that such a ruler inevitably contains an element of God in himself (236) and must therefore act according to the principles of his own existence rather than being bound by external measures or standards, prompting Diomede to detect in the Great Tyrant an "immense arrogance" almost bordering on the insane (237).

The arrogance is underlined (and thus the camouflage reinforced) by biblical echoes; for example, when he tells Nespoli, in the words of Exodus (20:3) "Du sollst keine anderen Götter haben neben mir" (Thou shalt have no other gods than me, 41). Furthermore, various Christ-like traits are attributed to him; he tells Diomede that he dreams of gathering around him a group of faithful and devoted apostle-like supporters (67) and is reported as adapting Christ's words in telling his security officials he wishes to make them "fishers of men" (18). It is only toward the end of the novel that the Great Tyrant finally acknowledges his presumptuousness. Don Luca tells him straight that he has given in to the worst of all temptations, namely, the desire to be godlike (310), linking his accusation to a parallel with the serpent in the Garden of Eden and the fateful discovery of good and evil. Unlike all the others involved, the Great Tyrant was not under any external compulsion but was driven merely by his aspiration to act as God's equal in influencing humans' fate and passing judgment on them (311). All subsequent confusion and torment of conscience are seen to be rooted in this basic temptation.

Central to the depiction of life in Cassano, and providing a significant parallel with Nazi Germany, is the sense of a society paralyzed by fear. It is the fear of their own destruction that undermines the moral principles of the people, and fear is the fertile ground on which wrongdoing and sin are shown to thrive. The very first chapter, with the Great Tyrant's unannounced visit to the chief of police's home, his instructions concerning the mysterious murder of Fra Angelo, and Nespoli's unease in the presence of the Great Tyrant—even after being in his service for fourteen years (9)— sets the tone of mistrust, suspicion, and threat, the sense of needing to be on one's guard at all times in this world. The depiction of a tyrant feared by all constitutes an almost overt parallel with Hitler's Germany: "So gewaltig war der Schatten, welchen der Großtyrann über alle Lebensverhältnisse in Cassano warf, daß kaum die vertrautesten Menschen unter vier Augen abschätzig oder auch nur urteilerisch von ihm zu reden wagten" (The shadow that the Great Tyrant cast over all relations in Cassano was so powerful that even those most intimately acquainted dared not speak disparagingly or even judgmentally of him in private, 60).

Fear infects the lives of all layers of Cassano's society. Apart from Nespoli, who is terrified of losing his job, the Great Tyrant himself is terrified of death (272), Vittoria fears for the fate of her lover, Mafalda for the reputation of her brother, while Diomede fears the ruin of his family and the loss of their fortune. Fear is further reflected in the behavior of Rettichkopf, who engages in blackmail, and in Perlhühnchen's susceptibility to repeated bribery. Even the would-be Christ-like Sperone displays fear, although he overcomes it through his religious faith and his display of selfless love. It is his simplicity, purity, and self-sacrifice that serve as the antidote to the mix of deceit, lies, and ever-present threat of violence that poison the city.

The general sense of mutual suspicion and mistrust, of petty intrigue and false witness engendered by this pervasive fear offers further parallels with life under the Nazis. This is a society of spies and vengeful denunciations: "In alles Leben hatte eine wechselseitige Belauerung Einlaß gefunden" (A tendency to eye one another suspiciously had found its way into all aspects of life, 247), and the slightest dispute or petty desire for revenge on an enemy prompts anonymous reports to the police. Similarly, no contemporary reader could have failed to relate to the following depiction of the atmosphere of suspicion and rumor: "Wie in allen Gemeinwesen, in welchen keine vollkommene Freiheit öffentlichen Meinungsaustausches gewährt wird, gab es in Cassano eine rasch, ja eine unbegreiflich rasch wirkende Art gerüchtweiser Verständigung" (As in all communities in which there was no guarantee of complete freedom to exchange opinions in public, there was in Cassano a form of rapid communication through rumors, which spread through the town with incredible speed, 201). In this connection, in his testimony to the powerful effect of the novel on the contemporary reader in Germany, Benno von Wiese talks of the schizophrenic public/private existence led by the average German, with private cursing of the regime going hand in hand with public compromise in an atmosphere of mistrust, fear, and lies.[63]

This same atmosphere is linked in the novel with the oppressive wind, which accompanies the unfolding action like a doom-laden leitmotif. Under its influence people suffer, are tempted, and sin (248); it is "giftig" (poisonous, 306) and "tückisch" (malicious, 313). The wind is a symbol of the uncontrollable forces of nature, impeding rational thinking and clear judgment, prompting extremes of behavior, and leading to the various fevered attempts at self-exoneration and the complex network of lies, counterlies, and corruption (84–85).

The Challenge of Justice

This major theme had a clear signaling effect for readers under an authoritarian regime and moved its author into dangerous waters. Bergengruen notes in his memoirs that he had always been fascinated by the task of clarifying complex points of law, especially where the consequences proved fateful for those concerned and where they were linked to that most elemental of human experiences, guilt. He talks of his long-standing concern with the tension between law and power, between basing decisions on the principle of justice and reasons of state, but also his exploration of the simultaneous indissoluble bond and irreconcilable conflict between divine and human justice (*S*, 162–63).

The essence of the justice debate is contained in the intense exchange between the Great Tyrant and Diomede just over halfway through the novel. Diomede, we are told, is a young "Trachter nach dem Unbedingten" (striver after the absolute), who had yet to learn from experience that legal matters and affairs of state were concerned with the conditional (189). He insists on the validity of a universal and eternal law, and his fundamental belief is expressed in the maxim "Fiat justitia, pereat mundus," the idea that the world may come to an end but justice must take its course (190–91).

In contrast to the rigid idealism of Diomede, the Great Tyrant is a thoroughgoing pragmatist who believes that the most mankind can hope to discern in this life is a mere trace of divine principles, and that consequently justice needs to focus on worldly concerns and the well-being of mankind. Accordingly, he propounds the view that justice should serve the interest of the community and that any legal judgment passed to secure the welfare of that community automatically also serves the divine justice invoked by Diomede, regardless of whether in the process an individual's minor rights are occasionally infringed (190). For him, where necessary or expedient, the state should be governed by a different law from that of the individual. On this Machiavellian view of the state, politics and morality are quite separate, and religion and the law are to be seen essentially as aids to the political process.[64]

Diomede, however, will not countenance any compromise with the principle of the indivisibility and universality of justice. In a veiled warning to the Great Tyrant, he says that any ruler who fails to dispense justice objectively and disinterestedly will suffer the torment of a conscience at odds with itself. More significantly, Diomede points to the danger of compromising with the universal principle and "divine epitome" of justice, of subordinating legal judgments to concerns of state, and thus knowingly dispensing injustice: "denn es kann unter Umständen mit einem ungerechten Spruch einem Staatswesen mehr gedient sein als mit einem gerechten . . ." (for under certain circumstances a state might be better served by an unjust judgment than a just one . . ., 190). Such statements had a distinct resonance for the Germany of 1933–35, as the Nazi state sought to legislate to secure its power and neutralize its internal enemies.

Yet the tenor of this debate and the plot of the novel do not constitute an unambiguous condemnation of the Great Tyrant for his stance. It is problematic that in the concluding section of the novel scant attention is paid to the Fra Agostino's murder and that the strong impression created is that his guilt lies not in the murder itself but in the way the Great Tyrant turns his subjects into virtual playthings in his ethical and moral game; indeed the murder seems solely to serve the purpose of misleading the citizens of Cassano and putting their integrity to the test. A reader might be forgiven for thinking that, given the scale of his crime and cruel deception, the Great Tyrant thus gets off lightly and is inadequately punished.

Moreover, although the Great Tyrant is indirectly criticized at the end in the words of the priest Don Luca and acknowledges his own temptation and power, the criticism is directed merely at the Great Tyrant's actions, not at the system of tyranny that allows him to exercise such power and to expose his subjects to their various forms of temptation. No alternative response to the dictator is offered, as it is made clear the latter is solely responsible to God for his actions, whereas the other characters are shown, even at the end, to be still wholly dependent on the Great Tyrant. Thus, even when he seeks their forgiveness, his stunned, silent citizens confirm their subjugation: "'Vergebt mir,' sagte er in die Stille hinein. 'Denn ich bin der Schuldige.' Alle fühlten, daß es ungeziemend gewesen wäre, eine Antwort zu geben; denn in dieser Bitte des Herrschers lag ihre Gewährung durch die Untertanen beschlossen." ("Forgive me," he said into the silence. "For I am the guilty one." All felt that it would have been unseemly to respond to this; for contained in the ruler's request was an assumption that it would be granted by his subjects, 315.)

This failure to go beyond criticism of the individual provides ammunition for those who see in Bergengruen's work an aversion to Nazi ideology and society but a failure to subject these to any real criticism. Thus Nyssen sees the portrayal of the Great Tyrant's rule as "apologetic" since tyranny is not radically questioned but ultimately confirmed.[65] Limited though this verdict may be in its assessment of the novel as a whole, it is indeed significant that the Great Tyrant's insight into his own short-comings does not extend to any fundamental criticism of the hierarchical social order he presides over or of autocratic rule in general. Rather, there is an affirmation of the historical role of rulers to carry out God's will, which, it is implied, is the ultimate and immutable determining factor in human history. The type of society the tyrant rules over and the values he subscribes to are thus not susceptible to change, and his authority is of divine origin.[66] Bergengruen objected to any unduly simplistic parallels with Hitler because he wished to emphasize the virtues and talents of his central figure, in whose role and office he saw the earthly representative of the supposed divine power that shapes human history.

Though on this view both the denouement and the novel's basic premise appear flawed, a different reading is also tenable. Central to Bergengruen's fictional strategy is the way the narrative serves to unsettle both his characters and the reader. As the plot develops, the reader's expectations (that the crime will be investigated by the chief of police, that suspects will be brought forward and questioned, and that one of these will be revealed to be the culprit, whereupon appropriate justice will be dispensed) are confounded: instead of gaining gradual clarity, the characters, and the reader too, are disoriented by the turn of events.[67] First, Nespoli, the man entrusted with solving the mystery, becomes constrained by fear, doubt, and a sense of confusion, starts to lose his grasp on reality (47–48), and experiences a crisis of identity (59); as things develop, his continuing failure to make any sense of events causes him to question the very basis of his existence. Second, as Vittoria interferes with the treatment of her husband (104–6), thereby, it is suggested, hastening his death, she too starts to experience confusion and a sense of personal crisis (105). Third, as Diomede resorts to desperate and illegitimate means to save his inheritance (185), he finds that events spiral out of his control, that the witness he has bribed succumbs to counterbribes; in this situation the student's ethical rigor is compromised, he feels he has abandoned and denied the principle of divine justice when faced with the realities of his family crisis (230), and he acknowledges he has acted against his conscience and betrayed his whole being (255). The same sense of confusion spreads throughout those sections of the wider population affected by the affair, as one deceit follows another, as injustice leads to further injustice, and as more and more people are sucked, self-protectively, into the tangled web of deceit and lies, and various individuals queue up to perjure themselves according to whatever story is required of them (246). And finally, it transpires that it was the murderer himself who had requested the investigation of the crime. In this situation, rational norms and moral values, hitherto unquestioningly accepted by those involved, are undermined and abandoned out of fear for self and loved ones.

Nespoli, the ultimate rationalist, utterly devoted to the reasoned resolution of mysteries and unexplained crimes, develops into a representative of the way rational thought in Cassano falls victim to the uneasy course of events. The loss of bearings he experiences is shared by the reader, and this is an important part of Bergengruen's narrative method. For when the Great Tyrant, who has in the eyes of the reader assumed the role of investigator himself (for example, interviewing suspects and repeatedly quizzing Nespoli), and who promises to restore some sanity and logic to this world, is revealed to be the murderer, the reader's sense of disorientation is complete: "Die Personalunion von Detektiv und Verbrecher zeigt deutlich die Perversion aller moralischer Vorstellungen" (The merging of detective and criminal in a single person shows clearly the perversion of all moral ideas).[68] The lack of the expected development of the plot alerts the reader to the fact that it is something other than the murder mystery that counts in this novel: what matters is not the crime of a tyrant, it is the consequential chain of wrongdoing and guilt, which serves to point up the universality and inevitability of human imperfection.

The reader's experience of this distortion of traditional norms and values is significant in the context of Nazi Germany. The unexpected development of the plot, the sense of not understanding or being in control of events, the weakened grasp on reality, and the apparent undermining and even inversion of accepted moral values, all reflect the reality of what had happened to Germany in 1933–34. Yet that is not how things are left: the example of Sperone acts as the catalyst for the conciliatory ending, the restoration of the natural order that underpins much of Bergengruen's thinking and writing. Some might choose to interpret this as the oppositional writer's skillful disguise of the novel's real import, whereas others will see it as the inevitably theological response of a writer who, skeptical of purely rational solutions to the problems of the world, saw in Christianity the only fixed moral point in the face of the threat posed to human integrity by the Nazi dictatorship.

Conclusion

Der Großtyrann und das Gericht is an exploration of human imperfection and weakness. The guilt of the Great Tyrant, resulting from the "temptation of the powerful" referred to in the preface to the novel, is seen to lie not just in the act of murder that he commits for reasons of state but in the desire to test his subjects by placing temptation in their way and in his interpretation of justice as something subject to the exigencies of daily politics.

The value of the novel as a coded commentary on Nazi Germany, camouflaged by a highly stylized, archaic language, does not lie in mere parallels with Hitler or his regime; indeed the Great Tyrant is seen to be a very different figure, more magnanimous, reflective, and philosophical. Rather it lies, as with *Am Himmel wie auf Erden*, in its emphasis on the need to resist and renounce fear, in its encouragement to readers to hold firm in the face of barbaric tyranny, to recognize that ultimately the latter's power was limited and unsustainable, and to retain their own integrity by clinging to a resistance mentality (*S*, 204). The judgment of the court in the novel is directed at those who fail in this endeavor.

Although fêted as one of the most important products of the inner emigration, *Der Großtyrann* remains a problematic work. For all the sustenance it provides to inner oppositional resolve, at no point does it reject the fascist state or the notion of an inspiring leader, and nowhere does it suggest that people should themselves exercise greater power. Rather it is primarily intent on establishing the principle that any ruler should be subject to a divine law that is never elucidated but remains a vague abstraction. Furthermore, the ending of the novel, with its all-too-easy forgiveness of cold-blooded, calculating murder and its infectious spirit of reconciliation, constitutes a weak response to the tyranny portrayed. The depiction of Nespoli's secret police as "Menschenfischer" (fishers of men) almost trivializes the reality of the police state, and the fundamental adherence to the ideal of the strong ruler undermines the general ethical and humane tenor of the work and its attempt to posit an enlightened *Gegenbild* to Nazi rule.

Bergengruen illustrates with great skill how people are easily manipulated, all too readily abandoning under external threat what were formerly held to be inalienable principles, and how their weakness and selfishness result in widespread intrigue and denunciation, which destabilize the city. For Schnell,[69] this theme is not tied to a specific historical period or to the internal dynamics of the novel but is central to Bergengruen's desire to illustrate a basic and exemplary pattern of human conflict. Although the attempt to specify certain immutable features of human behavior can be applied to the situation of people in Nazi Germany, the author's ahistorical approach to time and setting, the representativeness of his characters, and the exemplary nature of events reveal his essential historical irrationalism, which consists in both a belief in certain immutable constants in human existence and an equally fundamental rejection of social change dependent on specific historical circumstance.

This tendency to posit the timelessness of human conflict, the almost mythical and inevitable nature of tyranny, and the eternal frailty of human responses to it, but also the abiding nature of immutable truth and moral certainties, can be detected among other writers of historical fiction in the inner emigration too, including Friedrich Reck-Malleczewen in *Bockelson* (1937), Stefan Andres in *El Greco malt den Großinquisitor* (1936, English translation *El Greco Paints the Grand*

Inquisitor, 1989), and Jochen Klepper in *Der Vater* (The father, 1937).
And while such an irrational approach to history might be thought to
imply rejection of any role for social, political, or economic change, this
is not to deny the potential contribution of such works to encourage
others, to communicate to readers suffering under National Socialism
that history (however fictionalized) offered powerful examples of fortitude and endurance, but also that there were like-minded individuals similarly opposed to the regime: "Verzweifelte merken auf. Es wird
ihnen zugerufen: Du bist nicht allein, nicht verlassen, es sind viele, die
deine Gesinnung teilen, und dir zur Seite stehen, lasse den Mut nicht
sterben, auch dieser Winter wird einmal Vergangenheit sein. . . ." (The
desperate sit up and take notice. They hear someone calling to them:
You are not alone, not abandoned, there are plenty who share your convictions and are standing with you, don't lose heart, this winter too will
eventually belong to the past, *S,* 200–201).

Indeed the novel's appeal to individual conscience, its message about
human fallibility and guilt, and its depiction of an all-pervading atmosphere of fear, suspicion, betrayal, lies, and broken oaths, spoke directly to
those similarly entangled in the contemporary mesh of National Socialism.
As von Wiese notes from the perspective of the contemporary reader:

> Die Herrschenden konnte Bergengruen in seinem Roman nicht
> erreichen. Aber er erreichte die Ohnmächtigen, die Unsicheren,
> die der Lüge Preisgegebenen; er weckte die Instinkte des *inneren*
> Widerstandes; er zerstörte Illusionen; er bekämpfte den Hitler in uns
> selbst, und das bedeutete zu dieser Zeit schon sehr, sehr viel.[70]

> [Bergengruen could not reach the ruling classes through his novel.
> But he did reach the powerless, the insecure, those exposed to lies;
> he awakened in them the instincts of *inner* resistance; he battled
> against the Hitler in ourselves and in those days that truly meant a
> great deal.]

Notes

[1] Werner Bergengruen, *Das Geheimnis verbleibt* (Munich: Nymphenburger Verlagshandlung, 1952), 103. Subsequent references appear parenthetically as (*GV*,
page number).

[2] Werner Bergengruen, "Bekenntnis zur Höhle," in *Die Welt Werner Bergengruens, mit einem Nachwort des Dichters,* ed. Theoderich Kampmann (Warendorf:
Schnell, 1952), 69–70.

[3] Frank-Lothar Kroll, *Dichtung als Kulturvermittlung: Der Schriftsteller Werner
Bergengruen: Beiträge für Unterricht und Weiterbildung* (Filderstadt: Weinmann,
1997), 14.

[4] Luise N. Hackelsberger, "Werner Bergengruen im Dritten Reich," in *Resistance to National Socialism: Kunst und Widerstand: Forschungsergebnisse und Erfahrungsberichte*, ed. Hinrich Siefken and Hildegard Vieregg (Munich: Iudicium, 1995), 75.

[5] Bergengruen, *Schreibtischerinnerungen*, 210. Subsequent references to this volume of memoirs are cited parenthetically in the text as (*S*, page number).

[6] Bergengruen, *Dichtergehäuse*, 109. Subsequent references are indicated parenthetically in the text as (*D*, page number). The title of the volume of stories plays on the title of Achim von Arnim's and Clemens Brentano's famous collection of German folk songs and poems, *Des Knaben Wunderhorn* (The boy's magic horn, 1805).

[7] Heidrun Ehrke-Rotermund and Erwin Rotermund, "Werner Bergengruen," in Ehrke-Rotermund and Rotermund, *Zwischenreiche*, 267; and Barbian, *Literaturpolitik*, 93.

[8] Bergengruen, *Schriftstellerexistenz*, Dokument I.

[9] Ibid., 252.

[10] See Barbian, *Literaturpolitik*, 373.

[11] See "The Regulation of Literature in Nazi Germany," in chapter 1 of this book for information on these bodies.

[12] See Bergengruen's description of how, in 1938, following the annexation of Austria, the Gestapo investigated the Austrian publisher of his anonymously published poems *Der ewige Kaiser* (The eternal emperor, 1937), banned the book, and confiscated all remaining copies. Ultimately he was saved from arrest only by the alleged inability of the investigating officers to understand the poems and by the fact that, in their hatred of the educated elite of the Propaganda Ministry, they failed to refer the material on (*Schriftstellerexistenz*, entry no. 794, 70–77). Hackelsberger further claims the matter was finally abandoned, as the Propaganda Ministry decided the poems could be seen as presenting Hitler as the legitimate representative of the emperor (see "Werner Bergengruen im Dritten Reich," 74). On *Der ewige Kaiser*, see also the section in this chapter "The Political and Literary Conservative."

[13] Listed in Frank-Lothar Kroll, ed., *Flucht und Vertreibung in der Literatur nach 1945* (Berlin: Gebr. Mann, 1997), 123–24.

[14] Cf. Jochen Klepper's diary entry of November 25, 1938: "Bergengruen arbeitet überhaupt nicht mehr" (Bergengruen is not working at all any more). Klepper, *Unter dem Schatten deiner Flügel*, 685.

[15] Hackelsberger, "Werner Bergengruen im Dritten Reich," 76–77.

[16] Clemens August Graf von Galen (1878–1946) was Catholic Bishop of Münster and a prominent opponent of the Nazi euthanasia program, which involved the killing of those suffering from incurable diseases, physical deformities, and mental illness. His public intervention from the pulpits of his diocese in the summer of 1941 has been seen as part of the most substantial protest movement against any policy in the Third Reich. Richard J. Evans, *The Third Reich at War 1939–1945* (New York: Penguin Press, 2009), 98. Von Galen was made a cardinal by Pope Pius XII in 1946 and was beatified by Pope Benedict XVI in 2005.

[17] Bergengruen, "Bekenntnis zur Höhle," 74–75.

[18] Ibid., 75.

[19] Indeed the work lacks any real development of its surprisingly narrow range of characters; there is no attempt to draw extended psychological portraits and the reader consequently fails to connect consistently with them. This is linked to Bergengruen's general prose style, which is very deliberate, betraying a strong sense of conscious planning, leading a number of critics to label it "dry" and "academic" and to consider his dialogues wooden and artificial. See, for example, Hans Bänziger, "Werner Bergengruen," in *Christliche Dichter der Gegenwart*, ed. Hermann Friedmann and Otto Mann (Heidelberg: Rothe, 1955), 345; Hans Bänziger, *Werner Bergengruen: Weg und Werk* (Thal: Pflugverlag, 1950), 92; and Klieneberger, *Christian Writers of the Inner Emigration*, 127–29.

[20] Frank-Lothar Kroll, "Geschichtserfahrung und Gegenwartsdeutung bei Werner Bergengruen," in Kroll, *Wort und Dichtung als Zufluchtsstätte*, 58. See on this also Bergengruen, *D*, 411–12, e.g.: "Mein Patriotismus [ist] von Natur immer mehr konservativ als national bestimmt gewesen" (My patriotism is by its nature always more conservative than nationalist, 411).

[21] See Ernst Keller, "Der Tag des Gerichts: Werner Bergengruen," in *Nationalismus und Literatur: Langemarck, Weimar, Stalingrad*, ed. Ernst Keller (Bern: Francke, 1970), 159–60.

[22] Werner Bergengruen, *Baedeker des Herzens: Ein Reiseverführer* (Berlin: Tradition, 1932), 252.

[23] Werner Bergengruen, *Römisches Erinnerungsbuch* (Freiburg: Herder, 1949), 96.

[24] Werner Bergengruen, "Das Dauernde," in *Der ewige Kaiser: Ein deutscher Gedichtkreis vom Glauben an das christliche Kaisertum* (Graz: Schmidt-Dengler, 1951), 44.

[25] Werner Bergengruen, "Nachwort," in *Der ewige Kaiser*, 76.

[26] Richard Euringer (1891–1953), a staunchly right-wing writer, was an early member of the NSDAP, from 1931 a cultural correspondent for the *Völkischer Beobachter*, and, from 1935, a "Reichskultursenator." The work Bergengruen is referring to here is Euringer's *Chronik einer deutschen Wandlung: 1925–1935* (Hamburg: Hanseatische Verlagsanstalt, 1936).

[27] Werner Bergengruen, "Die Antwort der Geschichte," in *Die Stunde des Christentums: Eine deutsche Besinnung*, ed. Kurt Ihlenfeld (Berlin-Steglitz: Eckart, 1937), 18.

[28] Werner Bergengruen, "Vorfahren und alte Häuser," *Die Neue Literatur* 49 (1939): 170–72. See similarly Wiechert's autobiographical *Wälder und Menschen* (Forests and people, 1936), where the author defies the convention of providing as long a list as possible of one's German ancestors in order to establish personal racial purity, and instead emphasizes his "dark origin," with its mix of Slavic, Germanic, and Latin blood.

[29] Bergengruen, *Schriftstellerexistenz*, entry number 761, 67.

[30] For a succinct discussion, see Frank-Lothar Kroll, "Das Deutschlandbild Werner Bergengruens im Spiegel seiner Tagebücher," *Zuckmayer-Jahrbuch* 7 (2004): 200–205.

31 See Stefan Andres, "Der Mensch inmitten der Dämonien dieser Zeit," in *Stefan Andres: Ein Reader zu Person und Werk*, ed. Wilhelm Große (Trier: Spee, 1980), 53–62; also Andres, *Der graue Regenbogen* (1959), the third part of *Die Sintflut* trilogy (1949–59, 2007).

32 His poetry often lacks the atmosphere, images, and passion of more typical lyric poetry and can be characterized as a cerebral form of verse in which the techniques of, say, the sonnet or of meter and rhyme more generally are expertly handled, but in which a sense of sober reflection and a dry "prose voice" dominate.

33 The originals were lost, but the rhymes, which are virtually impossible to translate, were partially reconstructed by Bergengruen in his postwar diaries (see *D*, 110–14).

34 Werner Bergengruen, *Dies irae: Eine Dichtung* (Munich: Desch, 1945). Hereafter cited parenthetically in the text as (*DI*, page number.)

35 Max Frisch, "Stimmen eines anderen Deutschland?: Zu den Zeugnissen von Wiechert und Bergengruen," *Neue Schweizer Rundschau* 13 (1945–46): 537–47.

36 Brekle, *Schriftsteller im antifaschistischen Widerstand*, 175.

37 Werner Bergengruen, "Rückblick auf einen Roman," in *Abhandlungen der Klasse der Literatur 1961*, ed. Akademie der Wissenschaften und der Literatur (Wiesbaden: Steiner; Mainz: Akademie der Wissenschaften und der Literatur, 1961), 20–21.

38 Ibid., 22.

39 See Siegfried Lokatis, "Hanseatische Verlagsanstalt: Buchmarketing im 'Dritten Reich,'" *Archiv für Geschichte des Buchwesens* 38 (1992): 91.

40 "*Der Großtyrann und das Gericht* (Voranzeige)," *Börsenblatt*, October 9, 1935, cited in Lokatis, "Hanseatische Verlagsanstalt," 96. For more on techniques employed by publishers to alert readers to nonconformist texts, see "Esotericism and its Challenges" in chapter 2 of this book.

41 Bergengruen, *Schriftstellerexistenz*, entry no. 761, 65. Bergengruen describes Silex here as "charakterlos und feige" (unprincipled and cowardly). He was editor of the paper from 1933 to 1943 and sought to retain its traditional conservative direction but also to preserve a modicum of independence from the Nazi authorities, which led to several clashes and short-lived publication bans. See Heinz-Dietrich Fischer, "Deutsche Allgemeine Zeitung (1861–1945)," in *Deutsche Zeitungen des 17. bis 20. Jahrhunderts*, ed. Heinz-Dietrich Fischer (Pullach: Dokumentation, 1972), 280–81.

42 Lokatis, "Hanseatische Verlagsanstalt," 96.

43 Brekle, *Schriftsteller im antifaschistischen Widerstand*, 167.

44 Wiese, "Gegen den Hitler in uns selbst," 62, 63.

45 Werner Wilk, *Werner Bergengruen* (Berlin: Colloquium, 1968), 37–38.

46 Werner Bergengruen, "Neue Romane für den Weihnachtstisch," *Völkischer Beobachter* 48, no. 341 (Norddeutsche Ausgabe), December 7, 1935: 12. The editors of Bergengruen's diaries seem to imply this is a different source from the alleged "Führerroman" quotation (see *Schriftstellerexistenz*, entry no. 761, 66 n27), whereas the Rotermunds imply confusion on Bergenguen's part and

suggest this is what he had in mind in his original reference (Ehrke-Rotermund and Rotermund, *Zwischenreiche*, 265).

[47] Anon., "Der Großtyrann und das Gericht," *Bücherkunde* 3, no. 3 (1936): 81.

[48] Wilhelm Emanuel Süskind, "Mut zum Unbedingten: Anmerkungen zu sechs neuen Romanen," *Die Literatur* 38 (1935–36): 271.

[49] Eugen Gottlob Winkler, "Erzählende Literatur," *Hochland* 33, no. 2 (1935–36): 264, 265.

[50] Hans Franke, "Bergengruen, Werner: *Der Großtyrann und das Gericht*," *Die Neue Literatur* 37 (1936): 346.

[51] Ronald Loesch, "Werner Bergengruen," *Die Neue Literatur* 40 (1939): 179.

[52] Arnold von Vietinghoff, "Werner Bergengruen 50 Jahre," *Völkischer Beobachter* 55, no. 259 (Münchener Ausgabe), September 16, 1942.

[53] For example, Elke Nyssen, *Geschichtsbewußtsein und Emigration: Der historische Roman der deutschen Antifaschisten 1933–1945* (Munich: Fink, 1974), 104.

[54] Willy A. Hanimann, *Studien zum historischen Roman (1933–1945)* (Bern: Lang, 1981), 181.

[55] Emmerich, "Die Literatur des antifaschistischen Widerstands," 449–50.

[56] Kroll, "Das Deutschlandbild Werner Bergengruens," 191.

[57] As he was to write in a later novel: "Unsere irdische Welt ist unvollkommen oder, um es in der Sprache der Theologen auszudrücken: durch den Sündenfall verderbt. . . . Aber die ursprüngliche Richtigkeit schimmert noch überall durch." (Our earthly world is imperfect or, to put it in the language of theologians: corrupted by the Fall. . . . But the original rightness of things still shimmers through to us everywhere.) Werner Bergengruen, *Das Feuerzeichen* (Munich: Nymphenburger Verlagshandlung, 1949), 55–56.

[58] Bergengruen, "Rückblick auf einen Roman," 19.

[59] Werner Bergengruen, *Der Großtyrann und das Gericht: Roman* (Munich: Deutscher Taschenbuch Verlag, 2002), 7. Subsequent page references cited parenthetically in the text are to this edition.

[60] See Peter Meier, *Die Romane Werner Bergengruens* (Bern: Francke, 1967), 7–9.

[61] A good part of the novel was written at the time when Hitler was liquidating the remaining political parties in Germany and "dealing" with the SA. Early in the novel we read about: "jene furchtbaren Verschwörungen . . ., die in den ersten Jahren vielfach des Großtyrannen Herrschaft bedrohten" (those terrible conspiracies . . ., which in the first years frequently threatened the rule of the Great Tyrant, 21).

[62] See Colin Riordan, "Depictions of the State in Works of the *Inner Emigration*," in Donahue and Kirchner, *Flight of Fantasy*, 155–57. See also "*Las Casas vor Karl V.* and Nazi Germany" in chapter 7 of this book for the parallel situation with Schneider's story.

[63] Wiese, "Gegen den Hitler in uns selbst," 65.

[64] Hans-Jürgen Wipfelder, *Die Rechts- und Staatsauffassung im Werke Werner Bergengruens* (Zell am Main: Schmitt-Meyer, 1966), 74–75.

[65] Nyssen, *Geschichtsbewußtsein und Emigration*, 104.

[66] See Schnell, *Literarische innere Emigration*, 131.

[67] For a discussion of the way Bergengruen deliberately undermines the norms and expectations of the detective novel genre, see Schmollinger, "*Intra muros et extra,*" 120–38.

[68] Schmollinger, "*Intra muros et extra,*" 127.

[69] Schnell, *Literarische innere Emigration*, 123–24.

[70] Wiese, "Gegen den Hitler in uns selbst," 66.

Fig. 4.1. Stefan Andres. Photo courtesy of Frau Irene Maria
Röhrscheid-Andres and Dr. Freimund Röhrscheid.

4:   Stefan Andres: The Christian
        Humanist Response to Tyranny

O<small>NE OF THE YOUNGEST</small> of nonconformist writers, Stefan Andres was
an exceptional inner emigrant in the sense that he spent the greater
part of the Nazi period abroad, in what might be termed "semi-exile" in
occupied southern Italy, though like other writers discussed here he could
continue to publish with relative ease in Germany. He gained a reputation over the years as an able prose writer in the conservative narrative
tradition of the nineteenth century but is probably best known for his
two so-called master novellas, *El Greco malt den Großinquisitor* (1936,
English translation *El Greco Paints the Grand Inquisitor*, 1989) and *Wir
sind Utopia* (1942, English translation *We Are God's Utopia*, 1950),
which became staple reading in German schools and many universities
after the war. In recent years there has been a degree of renewed interest in Andres, with the discovery of a number of camouflaged short stories, legends, and anecdotes published under National Socialism and the
appearance of a ten-volume works edition published by Wallstein.[1]

Religion, Flight, Commitment, and Withdrawal

The crucial formative influences on the young Andres were, on the one
hand, his father's rich, colorful, but undogmatic Catholic faith, and on
the other the decision to dedicate him, even before he was born, to the
Catholic priesthood. His boyhood and youth were consequently marked
by a protracted spiritual and physical itinerancy: first, as a pupil in a strict
Redemptorist college in Vaals, Holland, which he endured for just over
two years;[2] subsequently, at the age of fifteen, as assistant in a charitable
institution for the mentally sick and terminally ill in Trier;[3] then, from
1923 to 1926, at a Franciscan school near Vaals and later in Neuss, where
he trained to be a teacher (33). Still believing he had a vocation, he later
became a novice in the Capuchin order in Krefeld but was released, as he
was deemed unsuited to the religious life.[4]

Deciding on a role as a "lay priest," from 1928 to 1929 he edited
the Franciscan monthly journal *Marienborn* in Leipzig, where he published his first literary works, including poems, religious tales for children,
his first novel *Das heilige Heimweh* (Sacred longing, 1928/29), and his
first drawings. Keen to study theology at university and explore his ideas

for reform of Catholic dogma, Andres abruptly changed his mind following a negative encounter with church orthodoxy and bureaucracy (34).
The resulting disillusionment with ecclesiastical dogma and the church's
claims to exclusivity were to be key factors in the development of his subsequent heterodox religious thinking and were to find expression in a
range of works from the 1930s to the 1960s.

From 1929 until 1932 he studied German, drama, philosophy, and
art history in Cologne, Jena, and Berlin, before taking up writing full
time in the summer of 1932 and marrying the half-Jewish Dorothee
Freudiger. After accepting a position with the radio station in Cologne,
he experienced an early taste of problems to come when he annoyed a
former fellow student, who reported him for his "non-Aryan" marriage.
This led to an interview with the student's father, a senior SA official, who
warned him that his published writings would henceforth be closely scrutinized (38). The years 1933–37 were spent in different parts of Germany
and the family became increasingly aware of the difficulties they would
face if they were to stay in Germany. This was made all the clearer in 1935
when Andres lost his post at the radio station because he was unable to
produce the now compulsory proof of Aryan descent (40). The family
subsequently moved to a small flat in Munich, where he worked for the
feuilleton of the newspaper *Münchner Neueste Nachrichten* and wrote a
large number of short prose works for the press.

Although Andres's membership of the Reichsschrifttumskammer
(RSK) was questioned, he was not excluded from it at this stage. In spring
1940 he was still referring to himself as a member of the Chamber and it
was only in November of that year that he was finally excluded—for being
resident abroad for too long.[5] This situation is to be explained in part
by the fact that he had secured himself a reputation as a *Heimatdichter*
(regional writer) through his work, including the semiautobiographi-
cal novels *Bruder Lucifer* (Brother Lucifer, 1933) and *Eberhard im
Kontrapunkt* (Eberhard in counterpoint, 1933), but especially the novel
Die unsichtbare Mauer (The invisible wall, 1934), the novella *Utz, der
Nachfahr* (Utz the descendant, 1936), and the collection *Moselländische
Novellen* (Mosel novellas, 1937), all set in and around the writer's native
Mosel area. Though some critics detected "individualistic" tendencies in
his writing and one criticized an "Abkehr vom Politischen" (a rejection of
the political) and eschewal of the collective,[6] Nazi officials did not generally consider him "problematic"; thus the NSDAP (Nazi Party) organization in Munich was able to inform the RSK in August 1937 that nothing
negative was known about the writer from either a criminal or political point of view.[7] Such a verdict may have been reinforced by Andres's
naïve brief involvement in the so-called Bamberg Writers' Circle, a group
that organized meetings of writers and journalists and reading tours
around Germany designed to support Nazi propaganda. It included such

Nazi-friendly writers as Heinrich Zerkaulen, Ernst Ludwig Schellenberg, and Hans Christoph Kaergel, from whom Andres kept his distance and who in turn seem not to have trusted the young author.[8]

After a period of much uncertainty and unease, exacerbated by concern for his wife's safety in an increasingly Jewish-hostile environment, the dispossession of her parents in Lomnitz, and friends' repeated reports of the horrors of the concentration camps (39), Andres finally managed in September 1937 to secure an exit visa to travel to the impoverished southern Italian coastal village of Positano, near Salerno. This was a compromise solution, as the original plan to seek exile in Greece had failed when the RSK refused the necessary foreign currency and travel permits. Andres and his wife had first visited Positano in 1933 and had discovered a thriving artistic colony of assorted ex-patriot, mostly German and Scandinavian writers, sculptors, and painters.[9] It was to become the family's principal home for the next twelve years. Although initially a relatively benign environment for foreigners, including foreign Jews, things changed in 1938 with Mussolini's racial decree of September 7, which gave all post-1918 Jewish immigrants six months to leave the country.[10] Even though this legislation was not rigorously enforced, Andres still felt the need to seek alternatives. However, subsequent short visits to Paris and Berlin, where he experienced *Reichskristallnacht* (Night of Broken Glass), confirmed him in his choice of the—for the moment—more Jewish-friendly southern Italy (42).

Life was, however, hard, as the minimal income, frequent food shortages, and constant uncertainty were compounded by tragedy when in November 1942 the Andreses' oldest daughter, Mechthild, died from typhus. Fascist Italy was also not without its dangers, of course, including repeated denunciations for Andres's numerous injudicious anti-Nazi outbursts, often made under the influence of alcohol (44), and a rising tide of anti-Semitism. Following Italy's entry into the war alongside Germany, the family was reported by a young fascist in Positano, which meant Dorothee Andres and the children were forced in May 1940 to return to Germany, while Andres himself fled to Rome. Through contacts in the Italian Embassy in Berlin, however, the family remarkably managed to return four months later to Rome and eventually, a year later, after the fascist had left the village, to Positano.

After the war, despite initial difficulties in securing a visa to return to Germany, Andres found a publisher (Piper Verlag) for his many works written in Italy, negotiated republication of several texts from the 1930s, and in the course of the 1950s duly became a best-selling author. Political and social developments now gradually turned the withdrawn inner emigrant into a morally, socially, and eventually politically engaged writer, most notably in his leading role in the antinuclear movement, which alienated several fellow writers and representatives of the church and exposed him to considerable public vilification.[11] However, disillusioned with the society of the economic miracle, its burgeoning consumerism, and its reluctance to face up to the Nazi past, he returned to Rome in 1962, where he threw himself into intensive fictional work, especially on religious themes, and became closely engaged in the discussions about ecclesiastical reform surrounding the Second Vatican Council.

Between Inner Emigration and Exile: Andres and National Socialism

Although the move to Italy meant that Andres's work came to be largely ignored by critics, until 1943 he still had numerous opportunities to publish, including with Ulrich Riemerschmidt in Berlin the novels *Der Mann von Asteri* (The man from Asteri, 1939), *Das Grab des Neides* (The grave of envy, 1940), and *Der gefrorene Dionysos* (Frozen Dionysus, 1942); with Paul List in Leipzig the novellas *Moselländische Novellen*; and in a range of newspapers and magazines (see below). Such ongoing publication was possible only because he was able to secure for each individual work a Ministry of Propaganda "Sondergenehmigung" (special permission).

There has been relatively little discussion of Andres's exact status in Italy and the extent to which the term "inner emigrant" can be applied to him.[12] In works on inner emigration he is either almost completely ignored or only fleetingly mentioned.[13] In one study he is even designated a Christian writer of "the outer emigration."[14] His position abroad and his continuing publication activity in Germany do indeed make precise categorization difficult. The nature of his many publications in Germany during the Nazi period place him firmly in the inner emigrant camp. However, he shared with many other writers who had left Germany the privations of exile and, in the immediate postwar years, the fate of those whose return to the country was rendered difficult by Allied occupation policy. And the particular danger for exiled writers in countries bordering Germany is clearly illustrated by the arrest of figures such as Paul Kornfeld in Prague or Georg Hermann in Holland.[15] Even in neutral countries such as Switzerland,[16] or in Allied countries,[17] writers were not always safe. Andres's description of the danger of his situation in his "selbstgewählten Halbexil"[18] is therefore not without justification: "Jeder wußte, wo ich saß, und jeden Tag konnte man mich packen und verfrachten, wohin man wollte" (Everyone knew where I was and any day they could grab me and ship me off to wherever they wanted).[19]

Wir sind Utopia

Yet life in Italy also proved productive, including the writing of Andres's best-known work, which was first published in serial form in February

1942 in the feuilleton of the *Frankfurter Zeitung* and then in 1943 by Ulrich Riemerschmidt. Hadley's research into the context of publication reveals that the text was initially accepted by sympathetic junior censors on the pretext that it represented an attack on communism, leading to a permit to publish and a print-run of ten thousand.[20] The further claim, however, that later, after a suspicious senior official had examined the work, it was withdrawn from sale and the publisher closed down, is questionable.[21] Be that as it may, it seems the novella circulated widely, with extracts from the *Frankfurter Zeitung* serialization reported to have reached as far as Stalingrad.[22] After the war, Wilhelm Hausenstein wrote that it was unrivaled among works written in exile,[23] and while allowing for the characteristic apologist hyperbole of this letter, the novella did prove to be a phenomenal postwar success: it appeared in numerous editions, was dramatized for the stage by Gustaf Gründgens, and repeatedly adapted for television.[24]

Set in the Spanish Civil War, the work describes the ex-monk Paco Hernandes's return as a prisoner of war to the monastery where he had served his novitiate. Back in his old cell, he remembers the island of Utopia to which he used to escape in his dreams, a fantasy eventually destroyed by his confessor Padre Damiano, whose pragmatic words had driven the young monk out into the world. Forced back into the role of priest by his captor, the Republican commander Pedro Gutierrez, Paco learns of the latter's intention to shoot all the prisoners before the arrival of Franco's troops and is faced with the dilemma of using the knife he has acquired to kill Pedro and thereby saving his fellow prisoners, or of respecting one human life at the expense of two hundred others. When Pedro discovers the knife, however, Paco appears to interpret this as a divine verdict on his situation, willingly surrenders his weapon, and agrees to dispense absolution to the collected prisoners in the certain knowledge that he and they are subsequently to be gunned down. By renouncing violence for the sake of his fellow man and making his final act one of love, as Damiano had insisted he should, Paco realizes utopia in himself, defiantly asserting his individuality in the face of Pedro, the embodiment of violent oppression.

This ending clearly allows the novella to be read as an endorsement of quiescence, of nonresistance to evil, and therefore as a classic example of the ineffectual inwardness that characterized a good deal of inner emigrant writing. It might also be seen as promoting a degree of fatalism about life under National Socialism that encourages post hoc rationalization of and self-exoneration from complicity with the regime. However, the ending makes clear that Paco is not to be seen here as a hero, nor is his fate to be considered that of a martyr. For, crucially, he feels a deep-seated sense of guilt about what has happened. Faced by the condemned prisoners, he reflects on his failure to act and help them to escape

("Was hatte er aus dem Messer und den vielen Gelegenheiten zur Flucht gemacht?" What use had he made of the knife and the many opportunities to flee?, 89), and on his near complicity with the enemy.[25] Then, in his address to the prisoners while giving them final absolution, he says: "All unsere Gewaltsamkeit ist zusammengekommen, und jetzt tobt sie sich aus . . . aber auch all unsere Unentschiedenheit, unsere Schwäche und Furcht. . . . Denn ja, hätte einer von uns zur rechten Zeit das Messer gebraucht." (All our violence has come together and now it's raging itself out . . . but also our indecision, our weakness, and our fear. . . . If only one of us had used the knife at the right time, 90.) The work thus moves beyond a simple and—in view of the prisoners who die—potentially grotesque Christian moral parable to become a poignant depiction of the dilemma facing all those under National Socialism who felt alienated by the regime and who had the chance to act against it but failed to do so, an analysis of the dilemma of the "men with the knives," their failure to resist, and their subsequent fate.[26] This establishes links with the activities of the army officers, some of them associated with the Kreisauer Kreis (Kreisau Circle),[27] who, all too late, took action against the regime and whose bravery and tragic failure is commemorated in Andres's powerful Frankfurt speech of 1966.[28]

The rejection of Utopia, as expressed by Padre Damiano's words ("Gott geht nicht nach Utopia!," God does not go to Utopia, 57), relates primarily to the theological exchange with his confessor about the imagined island of perfection and harmony that plagues the young novice, but beyond this it also strongly implies rejection of all utopian political philosophies, a recurrent theme in Andres's writing, one lent emphatic expression in the substantial trilogy Die Sintflut (The flood, 1949–59), which he was working on at the same time.

Die Sintflut

This monumental work, totaling two thousand pages in the original edition, could not be published before 1945 owing to its explicit critique of and satire on National Socialism. Its eventual publication was a factor in Andres's growing reputation in the 1950s, and the importance of the material to him is reflected in his intense efforts from the late 1950s up until his death in 1970 to create an abridged, one-volume edition of the work.[29]

The trilogy represents a bold, if seriously flawed attempt to locate the origins of totalitarianism, chart its development, and explore the possibilities of its aftermath. The first volume—originally Das Tier aus der Tiefe (The beast from the depths, 1949), in the revised version "Abwässer" (Waste water)—describes the rise to absolute power in a socially divided and democratically unstable Germany of the "Norm," a messianic social movement and political party, and the latter's charismatic and domineering leader Alois Moosthaler. The main opponents of the Norm are also introduced here, in particular the blind goldsmith and humanist Emil Clemens, along with the uncertain theology student and implacable enemy of the Norm, Lorenz Gutmann. By the start of the second volume, *Die Arche* (The ark, 1951), Germany and almost the whole of Europe have been subjected to the dictatorship of the authoritarian regime. The narrative focus here moves to the oppositional forces surrounding Emil and Lorenz, who either exercise inner resistance, emigrate, or resort to violent measures to try to overthrow the dictatorship. However, humanist and Christian forces can only look on from afar as Germany is embroiled in a world war. By the third volume, *Der graue Regenbogen* (The gray rainbow, 1959), the country has been defeated and in place of the Norm the victorious Allies have established a provisional government. Opponents of the Norm return from exile and witness the rehabilitation of leaders and supporters of the totalitarian regime. Bitterly disappointed by such developments and disillusioned with the inwardly divided new government, Emil and Lorenz feel ill at ease in this restorative postwar society and resolve to emigrate once more.[30]

Die Sintflut is an attempt to evaluate different human responses to evil, especially the justification of inner emigration.[31] First, the quietist, passive waiting of the humanist Clemens, who is intent on maintaining intact his human dignity in readiness for involvement in the country's subsequent reconstruction, is contrasted with the engaged activism of his brother Gabriel, the anarchist and socialist, who represents the option of violent resistance. There is then a gradual but clear shift of focus from Clemens's spiritual and Gabriel's physical resistance to Lorenz's passionate and impatient striving for religious certainty and the attempt to realize a practical, this-worldly Christianity. These opposing tendencies in the author himself evidently plagued him during his protracted and isolated exile in southern Italy and he sought to work through them in expansive fashion in the pages of the trilogy. The emerging dominance of Lorenz's position suggests that developments in Germany and the experiences of war had led to a reevaluation of the original premise of the work and to a more critical engagement with the question of passive withdrawal and inner resistance.

Camouflaged Writing in the Nazi Press

El Greco malt den Großinquisitor and *Wir sind Utopia* are the mere tip of an iceberg of camouflaged oppositional narratives published by Andres under National Socialism. These have been the subject of intense research interest in recent times, as ever more published items have come to light.[32] The texts concerned include stories, parables, anecdotes, and articles, and they appeared in such varied publications as *Deutsche Rundschau, Die Neue Rundschau, Münchner Neueste Nachrichten, Berliner Tageblatt, Frankfurter Zeitung, Kölnische Zeitung, Fränkischer Kurier, Deutsche Allgemeine Zeitung, Rheinisch-Westfälische Zeitung,* and *Linzer Tages-Post,* but also in the Nazi press, including most notably the *Völkischer Beobachter* and the *Krakauer Zeitung.*

An especially significant subset of these short prose works are a group of around fifteen historical anecdotes and parables, most of which were based on Andres's reading of the memoirs of Johann Konrad Friederich, a military officer from Frankfurt. The memoirs, published in 1848–49, describe Friederich's service in Napoleon's army, and Andres's reworking of them includes veiled political content designed to arouse the attention of sensitized readers through repeated use of key terms and tropes.[33] Camouflaged critique is achieved, on the one hand, by emphasizing eternal positive and humane values that imply a conscious distancing from the regime and its perverted morality; such loaded terms as freedom, tolerance, justice, truth, obedience, despotism, spying, and oppression had a clear signaling effect in the Third Reich. On the other hand, the works focus attention on variously disguised historical parallels, with references to past dictatorships and rulers prompting associations with the German present and encouraging esoteric readers to apply the inferred criticism to their own circumstances.

A good example of the first approach is the anecdote "Das Trockendock" (The dry dock, 1936), which explains the circumstances that led to the invention of the first dry dock by the engineer Grognard in Toulon at the end of the eighteenth century. Having witnessed the gruesome existing practice whereby convict laborers sentenced to life in prison had to remove the blocks holding the ship on the slipway and, if they managed to avoid the moving ship and thus death, were granted their liberty, Grognard, the enlightened man of progress, determines to find a more humane solution. His new technique of ship construction denies the prisoners their one chance of release and condemns them to a life devoid of hope. He fails to understand that it is the intensity of the moment, the tantalizing prospect of becoming free men again that matters to the prisoners. His attempt to rationalize something essentially irrational is thus presented as misconceived and, ironically, it leads to his own senseless death at the hands of a resentful convict (114).[34] The story affirms the freedom denied readers under National Socialism. At a time when individual room for maneuver was being more and more ruthlessly restricted, such a strong plea for human free will acted as a striking signal to readers. The anecdote also questions a one-dimensional notion of progress that reduces man to little more than a tool and warns against an unquestioning acceptance of technical progress. The sensitized reader of 1943 was bound to be struck by the stark contrast between Andres's ideas and those represented in other, conformist texts of the *Krakauer Zeitung*. At the same time, the more conformist pessimism about the Enlightenment implied by the story doubtless served to safeguard the oppositional message.

In the anecdote "Der König im Gedränge" (The king in the crowd, 1937), the dominant tropes of revolution and freedom are rich in associations and point to the work's political content.[35] Set in 1830, it tells the tale of how during a public carnival the King of Württemberg decides to demonstrate his closeness to the people by dressing as a normal citizen and mixing with the crowds. In comic fashion, the nobility spend too long at table and thus delay the common people's access to the food laid on by the king, which gives rise to revolutionary thoughts. In revised versions of the story in the Nazi press this satire on the relationship between ruler and subjects is furthered by reference to the "Zuchthaus" (jail) that faces dissenters, to "politische Artikelschreiber" (writers of political articles) as suspected propagators of revolutionary ideas, and to the king's perception of his furious citizens' voices as a threatening "flüsternde und raschelnde Zeitungssprache" (whispering, rustling newspaper language).[36] The king's inauthentic and hypocritical relationship with his subjects suggests parallels with the performances of Hitler at state and Nazi Party celebrations, with their deceitful aura of false approachability and closeness to the people.

The anecdote "Klavichord und Schachbrett" (Clavichord and chessboard, 1937) depicts a Prussian officer's attempt in a defeated Paris of 1815 to get to the bottom of a theft committed nine years earlier in Berlin.[37] He finds the stolen instrument in the home of an absent French officer and in an act of selflessness renounces the valuable article and refrains from exacting revenge. In "gewalttätigen Zeiten" (violent times) characterized by "Ungeschmack eines Tyrannen" (a tyrant's lack of refinement), this act is seen to be an exemplary sacrifice, the very opposite of the more commonly prevailing "Gesetz der Vergeltung" (law of retribution, 161).[38] The word *Gerechtigkeit* (justice) is mentioned at the very start of the story and significantly occurs three times in the first nine lines, followed shortly by *gerecht* (just). Against this background, the reference to the "miracle" of justice prevailing (161), the promotion of Christian love of one's enemy, and the rejection of nationalist enemy stereotypes all offer the nonconformist message that might is not necessarily right and that the defeated deserve to be treated humanely.

"Die Instruktion" (The instruction, 1936), set against the backdrop of the French Revolution, describes the Jacobite siege of the royalist city of Toulon and the bold actions of a Captain Muiron, who leads his troops through fierce defenses to capture a strategically important fort, thus paving the way for the capture of the town.[39] Yet, inexplicably, at the very moment when victory seems guaranteed, Muiron's commanding officer,

General Doppet, sounds the retreat and Muiron and his men are forced to fall back. It transpires the cowardly Doppet had got cold feet upon seeing his adjutant killed by canon fire. Muiron, devastated by the decision, subsequently commands his men to turn their guns on him and leaves a note, in which he holds up the incident as an example to his superior of how to follow orders.

Andres's anecdote criticizes the culture of blind obedience to military dictates: Doppet's order to retreat, when victory is within the grasp of Muiron's men, is senseless and illogical, and yet it is one Muiron feels obliged to follow. In the same way, his own men unquestioningly obey the command to shoot their much-respected officer. Muiron's suicide note presents his death as a lesson in the "tadellose Mechanik der Maschine" (faultless operation of the machine, 131). The implied reference to the Nazi military machine and its championing of duty at all costs and the reference to soldiers being at the mercy of "unzuverlässigen und schwankenden Befehlen" (unreliable and vacillating orders, 129) had a potential resonance specifically for readers whose soldier offspring were suffering the vagaries of a Nazi-inspired war. Similarly, a sensitized readership could not have failed to see in Muiron's note to "dem Pariser Gesindel" (Paris riff-raff, 131), and in his bitter accusation of cowardice, veiled and ironic references to the contemporary "riff-raff" in Berlin, their immoral deployment of soldiers, and the obsession with duty even in the most meaningless of circumstances.

"Der geheime Auftrag" (Secret mission, 1937) concerns Napoleonic occupation policy in Italy in 1808 and the culture of denunciation, spying, suspicion, and intrigue.[40] The story of the failure of a young German Captain Grün serving with the French Army to conduct an incognito check on Napoleon's network of spies is used by Andres to point to the injustices of foreign occupation. The prevalence in the narrative of terms with obvious relevance to contemporary German society, such as "Spion" (spy), "Späherdienst" (spy service), "Verdächtigungen" (suspicions), "soldatische Rechtlichkeit" (soldierly rectitude), and "politische Erschütterungen" (political tremors), serves to create a familiar atmosphere for readers. This is intensified by the eightfold recurrence of the word "geheim" (secret), with its evocation of the Nazi "Geheimpolizei" (secret police),[41] and the justification offered for the checking of the spy network—namely, that "der geheime Widerstand in offene Empörung überzugehen drohte" (secret resistance was threatening to descend into open revolt, 38)—is another sentence with clear contemporary implications for the finely attuned German reader.

In an article that appeared in the *Kölnische Zeitung* in 1941 and subsequently in the *Krakauer Zeitung* in 1943, Andres provides what almost amounts to a commentary on his activity in publishing these camouflaged historical narratives.[42] The piece talks of "vor den Zeitgeschehnissen ratlos gewordene[n] Köpfe[n]" (individuals hopelessly perplexed by contemporary events), who reach for the "Ersatzmittel des historischen Romans" (the replacement form of the historical novel) to better understand the situation, and it labels both reader and author in such situations a "Janus" figure, who when looking to the past is thinking of the present and worrying about the future (197). This might serve as an effective epigraph to Andres's story about El Greco.

Background and Genesis of *El Greco malt den Großinquisitor* (1936)

The decision of Cologne Radio in January 1935 to end Andres's contract threatened his livelihood and plunged his whole existence into uncertainty. An official communication mistakenly attached to a letter from the Chamber of Literature indicated the reason: "Der Andres hat noch immer nicht den rassischen Nachweis für sich und seine Frau erbracht" (Andres has still not produced the proof of racial purity for himself and his wife).[43] Dorothee Andres had a Jewish mother and, following the writer's dismissal, the family went to stay with her parents in Lomnitz in the Riesengebirge for a few months. It was here that Andres found in a magazine, which he had borrowed from the local priest, El Greco's painting of the Grand Inquisitor dating from 1600. This discovery, allied to growing unease, a sense of being under threat, and having to watch his every word, proved a fertile mix for the writing of the novella, which was completed in a short period of time in spring 1935.[44]

The central figure is Doménikos Theotokópoulos (1541–1614), a painter, sculptor, and architect of the Spanish Renaissance, who was born near Iraklion in Crete and was commonly known as "el Greco" (the Greek).[45] It is believed he received artistic training in Greece before moving to Venice some time before 1567, where he worked in Titian's studio and came under the influence of paintings by Tintoretto and Veronese.[46] After moving for a number of years to Rome, where he was unable to establish a career for himself in the Vatican, in 1577 he traveled with his assistant Francisco Preboste to Toledo, via Madrid, after being commissioned to paint the convent church of Santo Domingo el Antiguo.[47] In 1580 he received a commission from King Philip II to paint *The Martyrdom of St. Maurice and the Theban Legion*, which on its completion in 1584 met with the king's displeasure. Although primarily a painter of religious subjects, especially altars, for which he received a large number of royal commissions, El Greco is also known for his portraits.

El Greco's style, commonly labeled "mannerist," featured elongated figures, a limited range of strong, expressive colors, and the dramatic use of light and atmospheric features. It was a reaction to the harmonious classicism and the naturalistic ideal of High Renaissance art and was viewed with some consternation by contemporaries.[48] The portrait of Grand Inquisitor Niño de Guevara is considered particularly significant by modern-day critics because Niño had himself painted in the sort of full-figure image that in those days was reserved by Titian and Raphael for papal portraits—a way of asserting his authority and that of his position over contemporary secular power interests.[49] For Andres, by contrast, the focus of interest in the painting and the principal motivation for writing the story was the penetrating look of the cardinal, exaggerated by his prominent black-rimmed glasses, and the parallels to be drawn between Spain under Philip II and Nazi Germany.

The novella is set in the *Siglo de Oro* (Golden Age or Century), that period of much more than a century that saw a flourishing of art and literature but also many dark chapters in the political and religious history of Spain—as amply demonstrated by Reinhold Schneider's story set in the early sixteenth century (see chapter 7). Interestingly, however, it includes no dates and, with the exception of the death of King Philip II (1598), few fixed points of reference to contemporary events. The implication is that the narrative is to be seen as timeless, of relevance beyond the immediate historical setting.

Summary

The novella is a reconstruction of the creation of El Greco's portrait of Spanish Grand Inquisitor Cardinal Fernando Niño de Guevara, seen from the point of view of the artist. It is an attempt to establish the appropriate intellectual and artistic response to despotic totalitarian rule, and El Greco's painting represents not just the figurehead of the Catholic Inquisition, whose brutality is infamous throughout the land, but through him the church itself and the state that sustains it. The commission is a potentially dangerous undertaking and presents the painter with a dilemma, which he discusses with his doctor friend Cazalla, whose own brother, Agostino, an outspoken theologian, has been one of the cardinal's victims. El Greco at first struggles to find a way to approach his subject, but a conversation with the probing Inquisitor about the incremental path of fear, the start of true wisdom, helps him find the right theme for his painting. Faced by the cold, dark, and unmoving eyes of the Inquisitor, El Greco decides he wants to preserve for future generations the fear that emanates from this figure. People are to find the image frightening and both Niño and the world are to see what the Grand Inquisitor looks like on the inside. A dramatic storm in Toledo symbolizes the fear experienced by all those who come into contact with the dreaded Inquisition.

The painting is delayed owing to the Grand Inquisitor's illness. On El Greco's recommendation the cleric calls on Dr. Cazalla to treat him. The medic is reluctant to respond to this call in view of his brother's fate, but overcomes his fear and hatred, accepts his ethical duty, treats the Grand Inquisitor, who places his fate entirely in the doctor's hands, and restores him to health. In a narrative parallel, El Greco comes to realize the artist's lofty mission is at all times to overcome fear and maintain his freedom to stand up for the truth. He resumes his painting and completes a blood-red portrait of the cardinal against a dark background, including an ominous viper motif in the eyes. The artist's sharp observant eye begins to detect in the deathly face of his subject a cold, stony melancholy. Having at first felt only enmity toward the Grand Inquisitor but now wanting to capture the fear he inspired, Niño comes to paint a human being, a figure in which the Grand Inquisitor can recognize himself. The dramatic clash between the artist, who remains true to his calling to paint as dictated "by truth," and the cleric, whose life and actions are governed entirely by his vocation and the perceived interests of the church, appears to culminate in an affirmation of human dignity and some sort of reconciliation of the two worlds. Outwardly, however, little has changed: the Grand Inquisitor will remain a fanatical adherent of his faith and, undaunted, El Greco will continue to commit his work to truthfulness.

The work adopts the form of the classical novella, most notably in its focus on a single problem or conflict and a restricted number of characters, the paring down of the narrative to the essential, and the condensing of the action into a two-month period. It is tightly structured: a lengthy exposition set in Toledo establishes the basic conflict facing El Greco; the main section of the narrative consists of six scenes, all set in Seville (the two portrait sittings—in early Advent and a week after the Feast of the Epiphany—are interspersed with four scenes that serve to heighten the tension of the dramatic portrait scenes); and a final scene, in which the portrait is viewed and commented on. It further follows the traditional novella in its use of key leitmotifs (fear and illness) and of recurrent symbols denoting deeper meanings (the snake, the eyes, and the slicing of fruit). The slightly archaic use of language, entirely in keeping with the historical subject matter, is further reminiscent of the nineteenth-century novella, especially the historical novellas of the Swiss writer Conrad Ferdinand Meyer, which reveal a shared interest in the sixteenth century, including cruel and fanatical figures of the Spanish Inquisition and a concern for strict, classical narrative form.[50]

Reception

Andres's reputation as a *Heimatdichter* is reinforced in promotional literature produced by his first publisher, Eugen Diederich, which says the writer evinces "die urwüchsige Natürlichkeit bäuerlichen Wesens" (the untouched naturalness of rural being), and his novel *Die unsichtbare Mauer* is described as "bodenständig" (rooted in the soil).[51] The *Moselländische Novellen* seemed to confirm the view that this was an author who could be deployed to promote *völkisch* ideals, and the authoritative trade journal *Der Buchhändler im neuen Reich*, published by the NSDAP's central publisher, the Eher-Verlag, described the stories as "valuable" narrative works.[52]

In view of this solid reputation as a writer largely beyond suspicion of modernist or otherwise "subversive" tendencies, it is no surprise that reviews of *El Greco malt den Großinquisitor* were in turn largely positive or noncommittal in their interpretation. Most discussions indicate an essentially descriptive and factual reception of the text and emphasize Andres's "mature" narrative art.[53] The twenty-eight contemporary reviews available in the Andres archive in Schweich betray little sense of the work being considered as anything more than a dramatic and intense exchange between the feared executor of the inflexible will of the Catholic Church and the free, spirited artist. In certain articles, however, one is tempted to see veiled indications of contemporary relevance. Thus, in a review of the *Volksbildungsstätte Breslau*, a publication of the *Deutsches Volksbildungswerk*, the nationalist training organization aligned with the NSDAP, readers might have detected a certain unintended irony in the comment that the novella's setting is "eine Zeit der Unterdrückung, des Mißtrauens, der Todesfurcht . . ., wie wir sie uns heute gar nicht mehr vorstellen können" (a time of oppression, mistrust, and mortal fear, the like of which we can no longer imagine today).[54] Meanwhile, publicity for the novella produced by Paul List Verlag seems to hint at implied hidden depth and meaning: "Von diesem Buche könnte man sagen, daß viel mehr darin stehe als gedruckt ist" (You could say there is a lot more to this book than appears on the printed page).[55] In a positive, if largely neutral review in *Hochland*, the novella is described as "glänzend und geistvoll" (brilliant and intellectual) and the open ending as enigmatic. Although due attention is also drawn to criticism of the Inquisition for perverting the true mission of the church, the reviewer implicitly seeks to defend the church, saying no one has the right to judge and even suggesting the ending presents the Inquisitor as morally superior to the artist and Cazalla.[56] And in a sign that the initiated understood the novella's contribution to spiritual resistance, Ernst Jünger wrote to Andres in August 1937 to say he had enjoyed reading the text and that it seemed in keeping with the times since it discussed questions "die . . . den Geist bewegen" (that stir the spirit).[57]

The Nazi press found little to criticize in *El Greco malt den Großinquisitor*, praising its depiction of the historical setting, its tense psychological drama, and its closely structured narrative. It appeared as recommended Christmas reading in an overview list of new publications in Will Vesper's *Die Neue Literatur*.[58] In a general review article in the *Völkischer Beobachter*, Heinz Grothe endorses Andres as an anti-intellectual whose abandonment of the priesthood is a sign of his commitment to "true humanity," and he describes his work as being based in the experience of the countryside and originating from the "Kreis heimatlicher Wirklichkeiten" (sphere of rural realities). Specifically with regard to *El Greco malt den Großinquisitor*, the review talks in equally positive tones of the artist as an example of the racially approved "Vollblutmensch" (thoroughbred) and emphasizes the criticism of the Catholic Church. However, it also suggests Andres's writing occasionally lacks folk tradition (it is "unvolkstümlich"), that it has a tendency toward the "literary"; and the reviewer notes, in cryptic but clearly deprecatory manner, the author's attempt to introduce a forced meaningfulness ("eine besondere Bedeutsamkeit") to his narratives.[59] By 1940 the official view of Andres had changed as, in a damning review by the literary section of Rosenberg's Reichsstelle, the now nonresident author was associated with the authors of a so-called intermediate realm of suspect writers, whose false claims to intellectual rule and control had not only not been exposed by reviewers but had also been praised—even in National Socialist publications.[60]

El Greco malt den Großinquisitor proved to be a considerable publishing success. The novella sold widely both before and during the war, reaching its thirty-sixth edition in 1944 as a *Feldpostausgabe*.[61] Critics' view of the work as anticlerical is not surprising, as the writer who had turned his back on the religious life was coming to be regarded in official circles as a proponent of German vitality. Consequently, a story championing the vivid, blood-red portrayal of a sly clergyman, the archrepresentative of National Socialism's intellectual enemy, the Catholic Church, could only find approval.

Evil: An Inner Emigrant Response

El Greco faces the challenge to paint Niño de Guevara true to his external appearance, as is expected of him, or to reflect the inner reality of the man, as demanded by his artistic integrity; in other words, fail as an artist or follow his conscience. Whereas the first would mean compromising his integrity and would make him almost a fellow traveler of the cruel Inquisition, the latter option could risk punishment for heresy and perceived criticism of the church. Potential solutions to this dilemma, with its echoes of the challenge facing all artists and writers in the Third Reich, are discussed by El Greco and Cazalla. First, the painter could consider a form of inner exile, for example by embracing the religious life and joining a monastic order. Second, he could betray his artistic principles, conform, point to his many religious paintings by way of self-defense, and compose religious verse (15–16).[62] Third, he could seek exile and flee abroad with his family and associates, returning to the artistic freedom he had enjoyed in Italy ("Warum bleiben wir in diesem Bann, wenn es ein freies Venetien gibt?" Why do we stay under this spell when there is a free Venice we could go to? 16). Fourth, he could opt for active opposition, as reflected in Cazalla's agonizing over the opportunity he has been given to hasten the cardinal's demise.

The question of how one can justify living a lie is the theme of an exchange with Cazalla, who is convinced that dissembling is essential for survival in a totalitarian state: "Aller Träume sind erfüllt vom Tanz der Flammen. Wenn wir leben wollen, lernen wir die Lüge!" (Every dream is filled with the dance of the flames. If we want to live, we must learn to lie!, 16). For El Greco, on the other hand, the artist is committed to truth at all times and must follow his conscience, regardless of the demonic powers that threaten his existence. Cazalla is skeptical about this since it was precisely such moral rigor that led to his brother's death. However, El Greco has no sympathy with obsequious conformity to church or state, which he sees as pious self-deception. This is why he responds to the Grand Inquisitor's surprise at the choice of bright red paint for the portrait with the message that he chooses colors as commanded by God, "by truth" (21), and boldly likens the church to a "Feuer in der Nacht" (fire in the night, 22), telling the cardinal it has become "ein blutiges Feuer" (a bloody fire, 22).

The notion of active, violent opposition appears in an earlier exchange, when Cazalla announces the death of King Philip. El Greco's instinctive exclamation about what would now become of the world prompts the reflection:

> Mein Ausruf beweist, wie sehr wir alle, trotz inneren Widerstrebens, von der Notwendigkeit der Despoten überzeugt sind. Wir sprechen schon mit ihren anmaßenden Worten ihre Unersetzlichkeit aus! Es wird Zeit, daß alle, die im geheimen wissen, daß die Erde nicht Mitte der Welt ist, auch keinem Menschen mehr einräumen, Mitte der Menschen zu sein. Wir haben eine andere Mitte. (13)

> [My outburst proves how much we all, in spite of our inner resistance, are convinced of the need for despots. We even use their own presumptuous words to suggest they are irreplaceable! It is time that all those who secretly know that the earth is not the center of the world stop allowing any one person to claim to be the center of humankind. We have another center.]

For Wagener this provides a clear reference to the world of 1935, a condemnation of the modern personality cult surrounding Hitler, Mussolini, and Stalin, of the way the despot has supplanted God in people's lives.[63] El Greco's words stand for a rejection of Nazi despotism, which encourages the sort of allegiance to a person that is more properly addressed to God. Faith in transcendence, he believes, ensures that man does not descend into tyranny and does not seek to deify another human being.

At the same time, of course, there is reference here to the emerging scientific revolution that threatened to shake the foundations of church and religious state through its confirmation of Copernican heliocentrism (Copernicus himself had died more than fifty years before the narrative present). The relevance of this becomes evident when one considers particularly the observational astronomical work of Galileo, whose championing of the Copernican worldview was to lead to his investigation by the Inquisition in 1615, and the far-reaching heterodox views of the philosopher Giordano Bruno, whose support for Copernicanism, his proposition of a multiplicity of life-supporting planetary systems, and his pantheistic belief in an immanent God, caused him to be put on trial by the Inquisition and burnt at the stake in Rome in 1600.[64] This is what lies behind El Greco's warning to his friend Cazalla about the danger of the latter's "neue Weisheit über die Sonne und den nur in Naturgesetzen sich erfüllenden Willen Gottes" (new wisdom about the sun and about the will of God, which is only realized through the laws of nature, 14).

El Greco's struggle with the appropriate response to evil is elaborated through a review of some of his major paintings. These include *The Martyrdom of St. Maurice* (1580–82), based on the story of the saint's Theban Legion, who were executed by the soldiers of Emperor Diocletian for refusing to relinquish their Christian faith and worship the heathen gods. The artist recalls being quizzed by the Grand Inquisitor about the significance of a snake motif in this painting. The snake is clearly associated in El Greco's mind with the sly and dangerous world of the inquisitorial church and with the threat it poses for him; indeed he will later discern it in the eyes of the cardinal himself. His explanation here (he claims it serves as a barrier to evil entering the picture) is evidently an evasive one in a dangerous game of intellectual cat and mouse with both the cardinal and Philip. As he subsequently reflects: "Die Viper soll den Namen El Grecos nicht entziffern! Und wenn Niño de Guevara gemalt im Bild steht, braucht keine Schlange mehr unter mein Namensschild." (The viper shall not decipher El Greco's name! And when Niño de Guevara stands painted in the picture, there will be no more need for a snake beneath my nameplate, 13.)

This absence of the snake in the portrait is to be explained by the fact that Niño de Guevara is the embodiment of evil but El Greco can banish evil by fearlessly painting the cardinal as he perceives him and thus, as it were, holding up a mirror to the man so he can recognize his true self. As he tells the Inquisitor concerning the "absent" snake in the finished work:

"Zwar fehlt sie nicht, Ihr seht es, doch ist sie nicht so aufgerichtet wie jetzt in Euren Augen, Eminenz!" (It is not missing, you can see it, but it is not as prominent as it is in your eyes at present, Your Eminence!, 34). Evil is now not banished from the painting by the snake motif but rather captured in the eyes of the painted subject and thus rendered less terrifying and harmful. Niño does not like the end product but he accepts what El Greco has done: he understands the significance of the snake in his eyes and of evil in the portrait. He responds with biblical reference: "Gleich wie Moses die Schlange in der Wüste aufgerichtet hat—auch die Schlange bildet Christus vor, alles kann ihn vorbilden! Die von Schlangen gebissen sind, sollen durch das Bild von Schlangen geheilt werden!" (Just as Moses lifted up the snake in the wilderness—the snake can also represent Christ, everything can represent Him! Those who are bitten by snakes shall be healed by the image of snakes!, 34).[65] The snake represents evil but it also contains within it the seeds of salvation.

The Inquisitor's belief in the need to fight evil in the world, and the cruelty that is inevitably associated with the high office he holds, make him sad, and he thus becomes both a saint in the service of the church and an executioner in the eyes of his victims: "Er ist ein Heiliger um seiner Schwermut willen, ein trauriger Heiliger, ein heiliger Henker!" (He is a saint because of his melancholy, a sad saint, a holy hangman!, 35), which is why El Greco includes the portrait among his pictures of saints. This paradox and the novella's emphasis on the inevitability of evil in the world are linked to the Inquisitor's role as a healer. He is the representative of the church and, as such, he represents a vengeful God: he has to kill heretics to stamp out evil in the world and to heal sinful man. Those who repent can be saved—a message aimed at El Greco and Cazalla too. Hence the cardinal's curious question at the end of the novella after he has been cured of his illness; he asks El Greco and Cazalla: "Seid ihr geheilt?" (Are you healed? 34). The roles of doctor and patient are now reversed, and it seems El Greco is indeed "healed" or (using the double meaning) "saved" since, through his encounter with evil and through facing up to fear, he has come to understand the Inquisitor's redemptive role, has recognized in the fanatical cleric's cryptlike eyes the deadliest of creatures, the snake, but has also perceived humanity: "Was traurig ist, rückt in das Reich des Menschlichen" (Things that are sad shift to the realm of humanity, 33). It is in this sense that the image of the snake has "healed" El Greco.

This is also the reason the Inquisitor pays El Greco ten times more than a typical royal commission for his work (35): he is grateful to him for having recognized his true nature. Niño has understood the significance of the blood-red color of the painting against the black background, has realized that he has blood on his hands and that in human terms his actions are difficult to justify, that he will go down in history as a butcher.

Hence his sadness as a "holy hangman": he is a human being who suffers with his victims but he knows that if salvation is to be brought to the eternal soul, man's sinful body must be purged, it must die. Since evil is ever present, its representatives are as much unwilling victims as agents, victims of the inevitably corrupt human condition.[66] El Greco's Christian humanist belief in the harmonious relationship between the earthly and the supernatural means he does not condone the cardinal's actions but he does understand him, for, crucially, he recognizes in him that same sense of sacrifice for the sake of a higher ideal that drives himself.[67]

Fear and Oppression

A major element of the novella, with clear resonance for contemporary readers, is the recurrent theme of fear. This is established early on when El Greco receives the request to appear before the Grand Inquisitor, and the very first line describes the visit of the latter's emissary, the chaplain, as "ein kalter Schlag" (a chilling blow, 9) for the painter. His instinct is mentally to check his "inner world," to recall risky friendships with individuals considered undesirable by the Inquisition, to reflect on careless statements he may have made to his assistant, and to review in his mind his many artistic commissions for potential controversy (9). This instinctive desire to insulate himself from the dictatorial powers of the time powerfully evokes the atmosphere of life under an oppressive regime. This is a world in which mistrust rules, in which human communication is distorted, and people are forced to lie and maintain their silence. It is a world in which the cynical view of man and existence expressed by King Philip is seen to dominate: "Der Mensch ist schlecht; wenn er nicht an der Hand Gottes das Laufen lernt, muß er es im Laufställchen von Partisanen lernen" (Man is bad; if he will not learn to walk holding the hand of God, he must learn it in his playpen by being poked with pikestaffs, 14). This is also ultimately the basic belief of the cardinal as the representative of a church that has lost sight of individual human goodness, sees mankind as little more than sinful disembodied "Puppen" (dolls, 24), and has become "blind" to the concept of mercy.

The undercurrent of fear in the exchange with the chaplain becomes more evident when El Greco arrives to paint the cardinal. At the first sitting in the cardinal's library, El Greco is unnerved by the sights and smells that assail him. First, the Inquisitor's ruby ring is compared to a spot of dried blood left on the hand of a stern housewife "die sich die Hände nach dem Hühnerköpfen zu flüchtig wusch" (who, after beheading a chicken, has not washed her hands thoroughly enough, 18). Then the painter smells the camphor in the cardinal's winter cloak and links this musty smell to the dusty odor of the library, to the clergyman's pale, skeletal features and their association with death, and his striking, heavy-framed glasses. Furthermore, there is a stale and sterile aura about the man, who is described as lacking all sweetness, "Bitterholz, hart, trocken" (bitter wood, hard, dry, 19) and whose eyes are seen as cold, dark, and motionless. The Grand Inquisitor and his ordered, ascetic existence thus evoke the cool, clinical intellectual who is engaged in a process of ruthless purification, as hinted at in the indirect reference to bloody violence. His whole existence is predicated on mortification of the flesh, ruthless policing of the faith, and merciless killing of transgressors.

This threatening atmosphere sets the tone for the discussions the artist becomes involved in. They touch on the themes of life and death, as the cardinal quizzes him about the significance and content of his previous paintings, reflecting the ambiguous situation El Greco finds himself in: on the one hand, the favored artist chosen to preserve for posterity the image of the distinguished cleric, but on the other, just another member of the faithful, at risk of falling foul of the Inquisition for perceived heretical views. El Greco's treading of this thin line between trusted artist and potential victim is what lends the novella its acute psychological tension. He repeatedly responds to the Inquisitor's tricky and potentially incriminating questions with a mixture of nods and shakes of the head, veiled, even cryptic utterances, and silent use of his brush, as he applies a new feature to the portrait in a process that turns the painting into an intense intellectual duel with his subject.[68] As he counters the cardinal's questions with aggressive brush strokes, he metaphorically turns the screws on his interrogator: "El Greco erhob sich, hob messend Daumen und Zeigefinger wie eine Zange, als hätte er den Kopf des Kardinals bohnengroß dazwischen" (El Greco stood up and lifted by way of measurement his thumb and index finger like a pair of tongs, as if he were holding the bean-sized head of the cardinal between them, 21). But all the time, in true inner emigrant fashion, he secures his position by leaving his behavior and utterances open to an entirely conformist interpretation.

In a digression on El Greco's painting *The Burial of the Count of Orgaz*,[69] the Inquisitor mentions the legend's reference to people's "fromme Bestürzung" (devout confusion) and "heiligen Schrecken" (holy terror, 20), and criticizes El Greco's painting for lacking these qualities. However, the artist is not to be intimidated and initially, instead of a verbal reply, responds with a bold stroke on the canvas; then, reflecting the championing of his own fear, counters the Inquisitor's dry authoritarian concept of fear with the challenging but hopeful message of the Gospel not to be afraid: man should fear nothing but God. Fear is merely the starting point on the path to wisdom via freedom, joy, and love (21), and only these constitute true humanity.

A key leitmotif of the novella is the eyes of the cardinal, which are referred to repeatedly and are central to El Greco's portrait. They are associated with cold intellectualism and administrative zeal, and—reminiscent of Dostoyevsky's story of the Grand Inquisitor in *The Brothers Karamazov* (1880)—their penetrating appearance seems to suggest the omnipresence of the Inquisition's sharp, judgmental gaze as it seeks out the slightest hint of heresy.[70] The glasses shielding the eyes render them less open and accessible, and they are likened to bars at a window or a grille over the wells of the artist's childhood in Crete. He recalls his mother's warnings not to lift the grille (19), but the artist determines to raise this barrier protecting the cardinal, to penetrate to the inner man and lay him bare. The eye imagery recurs when El Greco hears from his cell in the Dominican monastery the passing procession of the Inquisition, leading the condemned to their death on the ceremonial pyre.[71] He refers to the words on the Inquisition's flag, "misericordia et justitia," which are seen as two glistening eyes (23), and it is implied the church remains blind in at least one of these, knowing no mercy and dispensing inhuman justice.[72] This metaphor is further extended in El Greco's subsequent dream, in which he sees a barred rectangular window, which becomes round and takes the form of the frame of a pair of glasses, across which doll-like figures in tall caps proceed, and he recites their names as numbers, expecting to hear his own "name" at any moment. The dream as a reflection of his fear, focused as it is on the figure of the Inquisitor, in whose eyes barely a trace of mercy is to be found, is clear, but equally significant is the absence of his own name in the dream: the indication that he is overcoming his fear and is ready to complete the painting.

In the course of his discussion with Cazalla, El Greco comes to recognize that it is God that is to be feared, not the Grand Inquisitor and his henchmen. This is the relevance of the highly contrived storm scene in Toledo, where the artist steps out fearlessly onto the streets to witness the city illuminated by lightning. In the same way, he resolves, he will face up to the cardinal's commission and paint him according to the dictates of truth. The portrait of the Inquisitor will reveal the terror the man embodies, in accordance with the artist's God-given imperative. As Cazalla later observes, looking back on the Toledo storm scene: "Der gemalte Blitz hat Dauer und verewigt den Schrecken" (The painted lightning will endure and fix the terror for ever, 31). Painting is here conceived not as a faithful recording of physical appearance but as a process of probing beneath the surface and recognizing the true nature of the subject.

The word for fear used by El Greco is *Furcht*, which is to be distinguished from the vague and more general fear of life conveyed by *Angst*. The latter is an unproductive phase of experience that renders man powerless, leads to passive suffering, and promotes neither knowledge nor insight, whereas *Furcht* is both more specific and productive: this is what equips him with the ability to paint, it is a step on the way to a higher form of being, lending individuals courage and allowing them to penetrate to the heart of existence. This is linked to the recurrent

leitmotif of peeling and cutting into fruit, a metaphor for the attempt
to penetrate a person's outer defenses to discover the true inner person. Thus the Grand Inquisitor's chaplain peels an orange with his pale,
bony hands and pointed fingers, and proceeds to probe El Greco's
beliefs. Similarly, Cazalla later recalls a conversation with the artist in
which El Greco says that before eating an orange he first takes the pre-
caution of cutting open the fruit to avoid the risk of getting a worm and
its excrement in his mouth. As the painter extrapolates from this, fear is
a positive human response that serves to pierce the world: "Die Furcht
zerschneidet die Welt, die Furcht dringt bis ins Kerngehäuse vor" (Fear
cuts the world into pieces, fear penetrates to the core, 32); it lends man
courage, security, and joy. He notes this is what he has done with the
cardinal: fear and the desire to overcome it had been the motivation for
undertaking the painting and had helped him reveal the truth, the real
man behind the mask of the despot.

A Work of Opposition?

The use of historical guise without precise dates to portray the timeless
difficulties for artists under totalitarian regimes is an example of customary inner emigrant camouflage and protection.[73] Yet, beyond the safeguarding of the text, one can readily see in the events depicted in the
novella parallels with life under National Socialism. Thus, reference to
the "bloody fire" of the church (22) and to the Inquisition's ceremonial funeral pyres for heretics suggests parallels with Nazi book-burning
ceremonies. The flag-bearing procession of the Dominicans, an inte-
gral part of this process, evokes images of standard-bearing formations
of Nazi paratroopers. The royal residence of the Escorial near Madrid is
described with almost chilling prescience as having the shape of a gridiron
("Dächerrost") on which the world is roasted, "und gebranntes Fleisch
stinkt" (and burned flesh stinks, 12). And in the pointed discussion of
the purpose and effect of El Greco's choice of colors for the painting, it
is not difficult to associate the mixture of red and black with the swastika
flag.[74] In general, the elaboration of different responses to life under a
dictatorial regime (exile, violent resistance, conformity, inner exile) was
likely to strike a chord with many persons facing similar dilemmas in Nazi
Germany. More specifically, the artistic situation of El Greco and his
response to the challenge he faces offer striking parallels with the type of
debates on art and the power of the state conducted in Germany in the
first year or two of the Hitler regime—including among Nazi functionaries themselves.[75]

This reflection on the role of art and the artist is a significant element
in the work's oppositional content. Andres's lofty conception of art is as
a temple in which the only "mission" of the artist-priest is to help make

visible to the average person transcendental connections, to reveal "die Verborgene Ordnung der Dinge" (the hidden order of things),[76] and, crucially: "Zeugnis abzulegen für die Wahrheit und mitzuhelfen am geistigen Gesundungsprozeß des Volkes, ja der Zeit!" (to bear witness to the truth and to help the spiritual healing of the people and the times!, 65–66). It eschews advocacy or championing of any political or religious philosophy, any "mit Kunst getarnte Apologetik" (apologetics dressed up as art, 67), in an uncompromising commitment to the rigorous pursuit of truth. This places great demands on the artist, including the writer. It brooks no accommodation with tyranny or oppression, insists that the artist must never allow art to serve any external authority or purpose, and requires him or her at all times to remain independent of church and state.

In this spirit, El Greco sees his prime duty to lie in faithful and truthful representation of his subjects. The commitment to these principles in his dealings with the state is prefigured in the flashback to the painting of St. Maurice and the potentially threatening encounter with king and cardinal. For El Greco, truth means deploying shapes and colors to reveal hidden qualities: colors do not denote merely the external elements of a painting but go to its very heart, are capable of capturing the essence of things. In this sense, artistic creation is compared to divine revelation; as he later tells Niño in explaining how he has chosen the colors: "Nach jener Wahrhaftigkeit, die der Herr aussprach, als er sich in das Bild des Blitzes begab, der leuchtet von seinem Anfang bis zu seinem Niedergang und alles enthüllt, was im Verborgenen ist" (According to the truth that the Lord pronounced when He assumed the shape of the lightning that burns from His beginning until His descent and reveals all that is hidden, 21). His insistence on going out to experience the storm in Toldeo is symbolic of the need for the artist to face up to danger in the interests of truth. This is why he cannot accept any suggestion that he live a lie and conform: his art is a profession of his faith, and he believes his duty lies in producing a work of art in which later generations will see their own suffering objectified and thus rendered more bearable. This demand that art be free from political ties can be seen as a response to Nazi *Gleichschaltung* in the field of culture, a stand against enforced, state-approved uniformity at a time when all non-*völkisch* art was being designated "degenerate," and approved artists were being tied to the yoke of the Nazi state and would soon be celebrated in public exhibitions.[77]

Of further significance in this context is Andres's championing of an artist whose work bears unmistakable Expressionist elements. Such a positive depiction of both artist and painting, at precisely the time when Nazism was abandoning its early flirtation with modernism and turning decisively against, in particular, expressionism in all its forms, lends greater contemporary relevance to the novella's exploration of the relationship between art, artists, and power.

The novella's avoidance of historical specificity allows El Greco's bold stance and (admittedly ambiguous) opposition to the totalitarian state he inhabits to be applied to despotic rule in any analogous historical setting, including Germany under National Socialism. Andres performs a historical sleight of hand by pre-dating the office of Niño de Guevara as Grand Inquisitor to allow the narrative to convey the impression of both political and religious power being concentrated in the hands of this one individual: fear in this society infiltrates all aspects of public and private life.[78] The distortion of historical fact is supported by the clear parallel drawn between the king and the Grand Inquisitor: both are ruthless in carrying out what they see as their respective duties (the king's last act, we are told, is to issue a death sentence on a heretic), but both also display genuine humanity (when the king's servant inadvertently hurts him, Philip consoles the young man and prays for him) and both suffer the loneliness of high office. Similarly, both suffer physically—the king from gout, the Inquisitor from gall—a parallel that aligns the authoritarian church with the despotic state and provides further evidence of the characteristic inner emigrant trope of illness and disease.[79] On the one hand, all this avoids any possible suspicion on the part of censors that the work might constitute a criticism of the Nazi regime and seems to promote a largely conformist attack on the church. On the other, the association of the dreaded cleric with the stern secular ruler and the pervasive atmosphere of fear and suspicion, of the all-encompassing totalitarian oppression of the individual, could not help but evoke contemporary parallels among German readers in 1936.[80]

However, there are also reasons why it is difficult to see the novella as in any real sense oppositional. First, it has been argued that in light of the work's reflections on the appropriate response to evil and the omnipresence of fear, the writing of *El Greco malt den Großinquisitor* can be considered an attempt by Andres to come to terms with his own situation in 1935, after he had retreated to the Riesengebirge and was wrestling with the options of embracing active resistance, escaping abroad, or retreating to his native village on the Mosel to live the sort of "lie" proposed by Cazalla.[81] Seen in this way, the process of writing the novella helped Andres to "solve" the ethical dilemma of the appropriate artistic response to oppression, causing him to abandon his self-isolation, follow his artistic conscience, and settle in Munich. In fact, things were more complicated than this: far from being a clear statement of the artist's duty to stand up for ethical and artistic truth, the move to Munich was undertaken not only with an eye to the likeliest escape route out of Germany but also partly out of a desire for readier access to the world of publishing, for the company of other intellectuals, and a basic human need for social intercourse.

Second, although the paradoxical ending, with its contradictory interpretation of the Grand Inquisitor and its surprising, ambiguous reversal of roles, may well have served to alert the sensitive reader to the potentially hidden significance of the text, the exchange between El Greco, Cazalla, and the cardinal seems to offer a legitimization of evil: only through the existence of evil in the world can man lend expression to his free will and prove himself as a free being before God. However, the two characters that embody evil, the cardinal and the king, suffer under its burden and are in need of redemption, making them sad saints or holy hangmen. The ambiguous portrayal of the Inquisitor, in particular, distinguishes between the man and the office, suggesting an essentially just man who comes to appreciate the full horror of his activity only through the artist's perceptive intervention, and whose brutality almost seems to be excused by his essentially human sadness. This twist renders the discussion of possible forms of resistance to tyranny less explicit, thus undermining the text's expressive power as a work of opposition.

Third, one of the most telling exchanges in the novella is between El Greco and Cazalla, when the artist tells the doctor to go and heal the sick cardinal so that he can complete the painting. El Greco says here: "Wißt, es ist umsonst, die Inquisitoren zu töten. Was wir können, ist— das Antlitz dieser Ächter Christi festzuhalten!" (You know it is useless killing inquisitors. What we can do is capture and record the visage of these men who outlaw things in the name of Christ!, 27). Murdering despots is pointless because they are merely the incarnation of evil, a sempiternal phenomenon, firmly rooted in and coterminous with human existence. The artist's commitment to truth, to unveiling the "hidden order of things," means revealing this fact of existence through the concrete expression of evil. Niño de Guevara, who is merely one example of evil, is to be cured so the painting can be completed. This conception of art and despotism can certainly be read as oppositional in the contemporary German context, but it provides a good example of the particularly acute insight and sensitivity required of the esoteric reader under National Socialism, and it is a message that many might be forgiven for missing or misconstruing.

Conclusion

A striking aspect of the reception of *El Greco malt den Großinquisitor* is the contrast between the largely neutral or positive reviews from the 1930s and subsequent interpretations of it as camouflaged oppositional writing. The question facing us is how it could be so widely distributed and read in the Third Reich. Was it because it served to offer conformist criticism of the church and thus met with official approval? Was it because its author, with his established reputation as a *Heimatdichter*, seemed to be avoiding political comment? Or was it because it conveyed to readers a subversive message about tyrannous regimes and both a warning and consolatory message about the dangers of an anthropocentric view of the world, which failed to be picked up by naïve Nazi censors? There is no simple answer and all three explanations are likely to have been factors in the novella's extraordinary publication history.

The work is essentially ambiguous: its depiction of the confrontation of two opposing worlds cannot be reduced to a simple struggle between good and evil, for the portrayal of both Philip and the Grand Inquisitor reveals human traits. Equally, it does not offer any manifesto for action or even a solution to the dilemma of the artist under oppressive regimes, for it promotes a contemplative understanding of artistic activity, which subordinates direct action to a higher calling.[82] In essence it belongs to the quietist German tradition of *Innerlichkeit*; this rejects the use of force as something alien and inferior to the world of the spirit, the purity of which is to be preserved at all costs. Primarily, Andres reflects here on his own situation of helplessness, the sense of being denied a voice, and of a partly enforced, partly self-imposed passivity. El Greco thus stands as a representative of inner emigration, and in ultimately renouncing active resistance, the novella appears to reduce the artist's potential opposition to the role of depicting evil as an inevitable component of existence. Notwithstanding the work's implied rejection of totalitarian rule, this admission of powerlessness runs the risk of confirming contemporary readers in their own impotence and thus rendering them defenseless victims—in much the same way as the later *Wir sind Utopia* reflects the fate of the "men with the knives," who fail to act in timely fashion against oppression.

The work certainly does nothing to promote *active* resistance; indeed, the emphasis on the artist's role in reflecting rather than changing specific contemporary manifestations of evil might even be seen as a flight from responsibility, serving to confirm the legitimacy of passivity. Nevertheless, it is difficult to overlook the stress placed on the freedom of the artist, and by extension on political liberty, on religious faith as precluding support of barbaric regimes, and the insistent rejection of the type of anthropocentric worldview promoted by Nazi ideology. Mindful, furthermore, of the thinly veiled allegory on despotism, the analysis of the inhumanity of totalitarian rule, and the appeal to the reader and fellow artists not to allow themselves to be corrupted by the chimerical values of the present, it is doubtful whether the popularity of a work that reached thirty-six editions in the Third Reich really is to be ascribed solely to readers' inclination toward individualistic, contemplative, and passive assimilation processes. The reading public under National Socialism was necessarily a more skillful, sensitive, and perceptive body than is often appreciated, and there is much to support the view that *El Greco malt den Großinquisitor* contributed to and sustained an oppositional mindset.

Notes

[1] *Stefan Andres: Werke in Einzelausgaben*, 10 vols., ed. Christopher Andres, Michael Braun, Georg Guntermann, Birgit Lermen, and Erwin Rotermund (Göttingen: Wallstein, 2007–). Eight volumes have appeared to date.

[2] Günther Nicolin, "Stefan Andres als Internatsschüler am Collegium Josephinum (1918–1920)," *Mitteilungen der Stefan-Andres-Gesellschaft* 16 (1995): 47–62.

[3] Stefan Andres, "Jahrgang 1906: Ein Junge vom Lande," in Große, *Stefan Andres*, 32. Subsequent in-text references in this section are to this essay.

[4] See Stefan Andres, "Aquaedukte der Erinnerung," *Welt und Wort* 5 (1950): 506; also the partly autobiographical novel *Bruder Lucifer* (Brother Lucifer, 1933).

[5] See Andres's letter of April 10, 1940 to Werner von der Schulenberg at the German Embassy in Rome, in Konvolut "Briefe 1931–1947," Archiv der Stefan-Andres-Gesellschaft, Schweich, Germany (hereafter ASAG). Also letter to Andres, November 18, 1940, in Konvolut "Korrespondenz mit Ämtern," ASAG.

[6] Hermann Pongs, "Rheinische Stammesseele in der Dichtung der Gegenwart," *Dichtung und Volkstum* 39 (1938): 123.

[7] Communication to RSK of August 6, 1937, Berlin Document Center, cited in Barbian, *Literaturpolitik*, 388.

[8] See Otto Landspersky, "Stefan Andres," in *Der Bamberger Dichterkreis 1936–1943*, ed. Wulf Segebrecht (Bamberg: Staatsbibliothek, 1985), 86.

[9] Dorothee Andres, "Vortrag an der Gedenkfeier für Stefan Andres aus Anlaß seines 25. Todestages am 29. Juni 1995 in Trier," *Mitteilungen der Stefan-Andres-Gesellschaft* 16 (1995): 66. See also Klaus Voigt, *Zuflucht auf Widerruf: Exil in Italien 1933–1945*, vol. 1 (Stuttgart: Klett-Cotta, 1989).

[10] Voigt, *Zuflucht auf Widerruf*, 474.

[11] See Stefan Andres, "Gegen die Atomaufrüstung," in Stefan Andres, *Stefan Andres: Der Dichter in dieser Zeit: Reden und Essays*, ed. Christopher Andres and Michael Braun (Göttingen: Wallstein, 2013), 140–48; also Hermann Erschens, "Stefan Andres und die Anti-Atom-Bewegung Ende der 50er und Anfang der 60er Jahre," in *Mein Thema ist der Mensch: Texte von und über Stefan Andres*, ed. Wissenschaftlicher Beirat der Stefan-Andres-Gesellschaft (Munich: Piper, 1990), 262–82.

[12] The notable exception is Michael Braun, "'Ein kläglicher Prophet in seinem Fisch': Stefan Andres und die Probleme der inneren Emigration," *Zeitschrift für Deutsche Philologie* 115 (1996): 262–78.

[13] See, in the first case, Schnell, *Literarische innere Emigration*; and, as examples of the second, Schäfer, *Das gespaltene Bewußtsein*; and Donahue and Kirchner, *Flight of Fantasy*.

[14] Klieneberger, *Christian Writers of the Inner Emigration*, 13.

[15] Karl Otten, *Das leere Haus: Prosa jüdischer Dichter* (Stuttgart: Cotta, 1959), 614–16 and 643–44; and Cornelis Geeraard van Liere, *Georg Hermann: Materialien zur Kenntnis seines Lebens und seines Werkes* (Amsterdam: Rodopi, 1974).

[16] Werner Mittenzwei, *Exil in der Schweiz: Kunst und Literatur im antifaschistischen Exil 1933–1945*, vol. 2 (Frankfurt am Main: Röderberg, 1981).

[17] David Pike, *German Writers in Soviet Exile 1933–1945* (Chapel Hill: University of North Carolina Press, 1982), 354–55.

[18] Hans Wagener, "Stefan Andres: Widerstand gegen die Sintflut," in Große, *Stefan Andres*, 99.

[19] Stefan Andres, "Innere Emigration," in Andres, *Stefan Andres: Der Dichter in dieser Zeit*, 58.

[20] Hadley, "Resistance in Exile," 166. See also Rotermund and Ehrke-Rotermund, "Nachwort," 291.

[21] It is unlikely, for example, that a banned work could have been reviewed in the conformist *Krakauer Zeitung*, as the novella was in January 1944, or in the *Kölnische Zeitung*, as happened in June 1944. See Manfred Moßmann, "Wir sind 'Verboten'?: Zu einer Rezension von 'Wir sind Utopia' aus dem Jahr 1944," *Mitteilungen der Stefan-Andres-Gesellschaft* 31 (2010): 76–77; and Manfred Moßmann, "Verboten?: Eine Ergänzung," MdSAG 33 (2012): 65–66.

[22] Karl O. Nordstrand, "Stefan Andres und die 'innere Emigration,'" *Moderna Språk* 63, no. 3 (1969): 249 and 251.

[23] Wilhelm Hausenstein, "Bücher—frei von Blut und Schande: Ein Wort an Thomas Mann," *Süddeutsche Zeitung*, December 24, 1945, cited in Grosser, *Die große Kontroverse*, 69.

[24] See Hermann Erschens, "Anmerkungen zu 'Gottes Utopia' von Stefan Andres," *Mitteilungen der Stefan-Andres-Gesellschaft* 24 (2003): 5–6.

[25] Page references in brackets are to Andres, *Stefan Andres: Wir sind Utopia*, 36–90.

[26] See Karl Eibl, "Selbstbewahrung im Reiche Luzifers?," in Wissenschaftlicher Beirat der Stefan-Andres-Gesellschaft, *Mein Thema ist der Mensch*, 229–31.

[27] The Kreisau Circle was one of the main dissident groupings in Nazi Germany, a gathering of largely aristocratic and conservative landowners, diplomats, and clergy focused on the estate of Helmuth James Graf von Moltke in Kreisau, Silesia (modern-day Poland). The group planned for a post-Nazi Germany based on Christian values, with some envisaging a restoration of the monarchy. With time, several members began to consider a more active political response to the regime and took part in the failed assassination attempt on Hitler by Claus Schenk Graf von Stauffenberg on July 20, 1944 (Evans, *Third Reich at War*, 632–34).

[28] Stefan Andres, *Der 20. Juli, Tat und Testament: Rede* (Frankfurt am Main: Klostermann, 1966).

[29] He engaged in particularly intensive editing of the volumes from 1964 to 1966 and 1968 to 1969, but publisher concerns repeatedly prevented the plans being realized. After his death, Andres's widow undertook further editing herself, most notably cutting the fifteen Noah legends that were interwoven with the original text. The "new" *Sintflut* was only published in 2007 as part of the collected edition of the writer's works: *Stefan Andres: Die Sintflut: Roman*, ed. John Klapper (Göttingen: Wallstein, 2007).

[30] In the original version the protagonists had retreated to an idyllic life of rural self-sufficiency, a simplistic solution that attracted much criticism from reviewers.

[31] The topic remained a key one well into later years, featuring in his novel about Jonah, *Der Mann im Fisch* (The man in the fish, 1963), who seeks to flee his calling, in the inner emigration/exile novel par excellence, *Der Taubenturm* (The dovecot, 1966), based on Andres's time in Positano, and in the posthumous *Die Versuchung des Synesios* (The tempting of Synesius, 1971), where he attempts to achieve a synthesis of these long-standing opposing tendencies.

[32] For up-to-date bibliographical information, see "Stefan Andres-Bibliographie," http://stefan-andres-gesellschaft.de/?page_id=25 (accessed December 17, 2014). For relevant studies, see Erwin Rotermund and Heidrun Ehrke-Rotermund, "Getarnte Regimekritik in Stefan Andres' Kurzprosa der frühen Vierziger Jahre," in *Stefan Andres: Zeitzeuge des 20. Jahrhunderts*, ed. Michael Braun, Georg Guntermann, and Birgit Lermen (Frankfurt am Main: Lang, 1999), 105–21; John Klapper, "Encouragement for the 'Other Germany?': Stefan Andres' Publications in the *Krakauer Zeitung* 1940–1943," in *The Text and Its Context: Studies in Modern German Literature and Society*, ed. Nigel Harris and Joanne Sayner (Frankfurt am Main: Lang, 2008), 121–32; Gerhard Ringshausen, "Regimekritik in der Erzählung *Der Palast des Marquis* von Stefan Andres," *Mitteilungen der Stefan-Andres-Gesellschaft* 35 (2014): 68–74; Rotermund and Ehrke-Rotermund, "Nachwort," 275–314; Wolfgang Keil, ed., *Poetischer Einfall—politische Zensur: Kurzprosa von Stefan Andres aus den Jahren 1933 bis 1945* (Schweich: Stefan-Andres-Gesellschaft, 2011); Manfred Moßmann, "Andres zwischen LTI und nationalem Wahn: Zu den Publikationen 'Sphinxe, Köpfe und Fische' und 'Der Tod als Instrukteur' in der Krakauer Zeitung," *Mitteilungen der Stefan-Andres-Gesellschaft* 33 (2012): 59–65.

[33] See Ehrke-Rotermund, "Anekdoten aus den Napoleonischen Kriegen," 26–51; and John Klapper, "'[. . .] um aus dem Vergangenen Gesetz und Maß des Gegenwärtigen herüberholen': Zur Einordnung von Stefan Andres' geschichtlicher Prosa im Dritten Reich," in *Mimesis, Mimikry, Simulatio: Tarnung und Aufdeckung in den Künsten vom 16. bis zum 21. Jahrhundert: Festschrift für Erwin Rotermund*, ed. Hanns-Werner Heister and Bernhard Spies (Berlin: Weidler, 2013), 61–73.

[34] "Das Trockendock: Anekdote," *Berliner Tageblatt*, April 29 1936; republished in *Münchner Neueste Nachrichten*, no. 133 (May 14, 1936), and in *Krakauer Zeitung*, July 4, 1943. Page numbers in the text refer to the version published in Andres, *Stefan Andres: Wir sind Utopia*, 111–14.

[35] "Der König im Gedränge: Anekdote," *Münchner Neueste Nachrichten*, no. 3 (January 3, 1937), republished in slightly amended form in *Völkischer Beobachter* 51, no. 240 (Münchener Ausgabe), August 28, 1938, and in *Krakauer Zeitung*, no. 88 (April 11, 1943).

[36] All these formulations were added to the more "political" versions in the *Völkischer Beobachter* and the *Krakauer Zeitung*, the latter bearing the evocative subtitle "Der Horcher an der Wand" (The eavesdropper at the wall). See "Kommentar," in Andres, *Stefan Andres: Wir sind Utopia*, 252.

[37] "Klavichord und Schachbrett: Anekdote," *Münchner Neueste Nachrichten*, no. 221 (August 16, 1937), republished in *Fränkischer Kurier*, September 16, 1937, and in *Krakauer Zeitung* 5, no. 243 (October 10, 1943).

[38] In the pillaging of art during the Napoleonic wars, Richter also sees a reference to Hans Frank, Governor-General of Poland, and the abduction of art works from occupied territories in eastern Europe. "Nachwort," in *Stefan Andres: Terrassen im Licht: Italienische Erzählungen*, ed. Dieter Richter (Göttingen: Wallstein, 2009), 306.

[39] "Die Instruktion: Anekdote," in *Fränkischer Kurier*, September 24, 1936, 4, in *Münchner Neueste Nachrichten*, no. 92 (April 4, 1937), and in *Luxemburger Wort*, January 6, 1938; republished under the title "Der Tod als Instrukteur: Anekdote," in *Krakauer Zeitung*, no. 147 (June 23–24, 1940).

[40] "Der geheime Auftrag: Eine Anekdote in Politik und Liebe versponnen," *Völkischer Beobachter* 50, no. 220 (Münchener Ausgabe), August 8, 1937, republished in *Kölnische Zeitung*, no. 319 (June 28, 1938). Reference is to the original version as it appears in Andres, *Stefan Andres: Terrassen im Licht*, 38–42.

[41] Ehrke-Rotermund, "Anekdoten aus den Napoleonischen Kriegen," 39.

[42] Stefan Andres, "Zwischen zwei Stühlen: Ein Streitgespräch," *Kölnische Zeitung*, no. 138, March 16, 1941, 8; under the title "Zwischen zwei Stühlen: Gedanken zum historischen Roman," *Krakauer Zeitung* 5, no. 1 (January 1, 1943): 10.

[43] Andres, "Jahrgang 1906," 40.

[44] See Stefan Andres, letter to Pierre Elcheroth, April 23, 1935, where he refers to being engaged in the writing of an "Inquisitionsnovelle." "Briefe an einen Theologen," *Nouvelle Revue Luxembourgeoise* 1, no. 3 (1970): 269.

[45] Quotations from Andres's text will henceforth retain his forms "Theodokopulos" and "El Greco."

[46] "El Greco, Spanish Artist: Middle Years," *Encyclopedia Britannica*, http://www.britannica.com/EBchecked/topic/244100/El-Greco/2824/Middle-years (accessed September 2, 2014).

[47] Ibid.

[48] "Mannerism," *Encyclopedia Britannica*, http://www.britannica.com/EBchecked/topic/362538/Mannerism (accessed September 2, 2014).

[49] Wilhelm Große, "Nachwort," in *Stefan Andres: El Greco malt den Großinquisitor: Erzählung*, ed. Wilhelm Große (Stuttgart: Reclam, 1994), 49.

[50] See Hans Hennecke, "Stefan Andres," in *Stefan Andres: Eine Einführung in sein Werk* (Munich: Piper, 1962), 11. Also Klaus Jeziorkowski, "El Greco malt den Großinquisitor," in *Interpretationen zu Stefan Andres*, ed. Ruppert Hirschenauer and Albrecht Weber (Munich: Oldenbourg, 1969), 86–88.

[51] Publicity sheet of Eugen Diederichs Verlag, Jena, in Deutsches Literaturarchiv Marbach, Nachlass: Andres, Stefan, Mappe "Rezensionen."

[52] Anon., "Stefan Andres," *Der Buchhändler im neuen Reich*, nos. 11–12, Ausgabe A (November–December 1937): 360.

[53] For example, Anon., "El Greco," *Nürnberger Zeitung*, May 30, 1936, Archiv-Box "El Greco malt den Großinquisitor," ASAG.

54 Anon., Extract from review, *Volksbildunggsstätte Breslau*, May 25, 1936, Archiv-Box "El Greco malt den Großinquisitor," ASAG.

55 Anon., Publicity material of Paul List Verlag," Archiv-Box "El Greco malt den Großinquisitor," ASAG.

56 Adolf Fleckenstein, "Erzählende Literatur," *Hochland* 34, no. 7 (1936–37): 70–71.

57 "Ernst Jünger an Stefan Andres," August 28, 1937, in *Ernst Jünger–Stefan Andres: Briefe 1937–1970*, ed. Günther Nicolin (Stuttgart: Klett-Cotta, 2007), 8.

58 Anon., List of recent publications, *Die Neue Literatur* 37, no. 12 (1936): 700–701.

59 Heinz Grothe, "Wege der Dichtung: Zu den Arbeiten des jungen Schriftstellers Stefan Paul Andres," *Völkischer Beobachter* 51, no. 19, Süddeutsche Ausgabe (January 19, 1938): 12.

60 Hauptlektorat Schöngeistiges Schrifttum, "Jahresbericht 1940," 7. And see "A Watertight System of Control?" in chapter 1 of this book.

61 Nordstrand, "Stefan Andres und die 'innere Emigration,'" 251.

62 Page references in brackets are to "El Greco malt den Großinquisitor," in Andres, *Stefan Andres: Wir sind Utopia*, 9–35.

63 Hans Wagener, "Stefan Andres: El Greco malt den Großinquisitor," in *Interpretationen: Erzählungen des 20. Jahrhunderts*, vol. 1 (Stuttgart: Reclam, 1996), 226–27.

64 See John L. Heilbron, *Galileo* (New York: Oxford University Press, 2010); Paul Richard Blum, *Giordano Bruno: An Introduction* (Amsterdam: Rodopi 2012). The significance of Bruno's vision of God as the "Unity," which holds together an infinite number of solar systems, was to be given prominence in the epigraph to Andres's *Die Arche* (1951, 6), the second part of the *Sintflut* trilogy, and, in truncated form, in the revised edition *Die Sintflut* (2007), 386.

65 Cf. "Just as Moses lifted up the snake in the wilderness, so the Son of Man must be lifted up." John 3:14, *The Bible: New International Version*, https://new.bible gateway.com/passage/?search=john+3%2C+14&version=NIV (accessed June 28, 2014).

66 A parallel to this view of the Grand Inquisitor as an object of pity is Cazalla's response to the death of King Philip: "Ich habe Philipp gehaßt wie Ihr, aber wer einen Gehaßten wie einen König sterben sieht, vergißt ihm alles!" (I hated Philip as you do, but when you see a hated man die like a king, you forgive him everything!, 14).

67 See Fernand Hoffmann, "Zeitlose Ästhetik als Vorwand und Politik als Zweck—und etwas mehr: Zu der Novelle 'El Greco malt den Großinquisitor' von Stefan Andres," *Mitteilungen der Stefan-Andres-Gesellschaft* 8 (1987): 41.

68 Jeziorkowski, "El Greco," 68–69.

69 The painting is based on the legend of St. Stephen and St. Augustine descending from heaven to perform the burial to the consternation of the attendant mourners.

70 Jeziorkowski, "El Greco," 53 and 75.

[71] There is, of course, an ironic association between the painter's first name, Domenikos, and this billeting of him with the Dominican order, closely associated as it was with the Inquisition.

[72] This view of the church is consistent with Andres's criticism of the behavior of the Catholic Church throughout history but especially under National Socialism. See Lena Burm, "Stefan Andres' kritische Stellungnahme gegenüber der römisch-katholischen Kirche," in Große, *Stefan Andres: Ein Reader*, 180–92. He points to the silence of the church hierarchy despite the overwhelming evidence of the Nazis' racial policies and politics of hate: "Im Jahre 1932 hätte die feierliche Exkommunikation aller Anhänger dieser Irrlehre Deutschland und der Welt zumindest die Augen geöffnet; statt dessen bescherte man uns ein Konkordat. . . ." (In 1932 the formal excommunication of all supporters of this heresy would at least have opened the eyes of Germany and the world; instead we were presented with a concordat. . . .). Andres, "Jahrgang 1906[: Ein Junge vom Lande]," in Große, *Stefan Andres: Ein Reader*, 32.

[73] See chapter 2, particularly the section "The Options Facing Writers" and its subsections "Publication" and "Camouflaged Publication," and the section "The Art of Camouflage."

[74] Michael Braun, "Stefan Andres: El Greco malt den Großinquisitor," *Mitteilungen der Stefan-Andres-Gesellschaft* 33 (2012): 24.

[75] It almost seems superfluous to record the author's own response to the question of whether Nazi book burnings and cultural politics in the early years of the Third Reich in general had played a role in his conception of the novella: "Aber selbstverständlich! Wie wäre ich sonst auf die Idee gekommen!" (Of course! How else would I have got the idea!) Interview, quoted in Karl O. Nordstrand, "El Greco malt den Großinquisitor," in *Utopia und Welterfahrung: Stefan Andres und sein Werk im Gedächtnis seiner Freunde* (Munich: Piper, 1972), 131.

[76] See Stefan Andres, "Über die Sendung des Dichters," in Große, *Stefan Andres: Ein Reader*, 72.

[77] See Nordstrand, "Stefan Andres und die 'innere Emigration,'" 258–59.

[78] The painting of the Grand Inquisitor is carried out in Seville and coincides with the death of Philip II (1598), yet in reality the portrait was made in about 1600, when Niño de Guevara was Archbishop of Toledo; in 1598 he had not yet become Grand Inquisitor (this occurred in August 1599) and had thus not moved to Seville (1601). Jeziorkowski, "El Greco," 54.

[79] El Greco reflects at one point that, like the king, the whole of Spain is suffering from gout: "die Gelenke des Staates sind steif und geschwollen, unbewegsam geworden" (the joints of the state are stiff and swollen, and cannot move, 13). See, on this topic, the writing of Reck-Malleczewen (especially the section "The Role of History"in chapter 5 of this book) and Wiechert (especially the section "Ambiguous Cultural Pessimism" in chapter 9 of this book). See also Uwe Klein, *Stefan Andres: Innere Emigration in Deutschland und im Exil*, PhD diss., University of Mainz, 1991.

[80] It is, however, important not to equate the Inquisition too closely with National Socialism. The notion of man having "eine andere Mitte" (another center) points

to the essential difference between the two: the focus of human existence on God. Though the church has gone "blind in one eye," El Greco insists man's other-worldly orientation should remain unaffected.

81 Nordstrand, "Stefan Andres und die 'innere Emigration,'" 130.

82 Eibl, "Selbstbewahrung im Reiche Luzifers?," 223–24.

Fig. 5.1. Friedrich Reck-Malleczewen. Courtesy of
Frau Andrea Clemen and Frau Viktoria Reck-Malleczewen.

5: Friedrich Reck-Malleczewen: The Snobbish Dissenter and His Tale of Mass Insanity

Fact and Fantasy of the Would-Be Aristocrat

ESTABLISHING A RELIABLE biographical portrait of Reck has proved a significant challenge, and autobiographical sources, in particular, have to be treated with the greatest caution and skepticism.[1] Despite his undoubted, if modest, literary success, Reck felt an abiding need for public recognition and he repeatedly fabricated elements of his biography as a form of compensation. Until Kappeler's detailed biographical researches in the 1950s and 1960s, the accepted version of Reck's life, one propagated and perpetuated by various uncritical commentators, was based on the writer's own claim to an aristocratic heritage and a whole host of adventurous experiences and colorful episodes.[2]

So who was the self-styled aristocrat Friedrich Percyval Reck-Malleczewen?[3] He was born on August 11, 1884 as the youngest of four children on the family's Malleczewen estate in Kreis Lyck in East Prussia, close to the Russian border. His father, Hermann Reck, was a successful farmer, a Protestant monarchist and a Conservative member of the Prussian parliament and subsequently the Reichstag, where he represented the interests of Prussian landowners. His mother Emma, by contrast, was an Austrian national, a Catholic descended of a family of industrialists. Following his *Abitur* at the Royal Prussian Grammar School in Lyck in 1904, Reck was encouraged by his father to volunteer for the Fifth Thuringian Infantry regiment in Jena but abandoned his officer training after just six months and, contrary to his own fanciful imaginings, never returned to the military.

Declining to study law, as expected by the family, in the autumn of 1904 Reck opted for medicine and subsequently pursued his studies in Königsberg, Innsbruck, Rostock, and Jena, completing them in 1911. This too was not to be his vocation, however, as, following short periods of locum work in the country, the by now married Reck decided to pursue his literary ambitions and desire to travel. Although he had fallen out with his father and failed to receive the inheritance he had expected, his wife's parents were prepared to subsidize his ambitions. Following his trips to England, Belgium, and the Americas, he and his family relocated to Pasing in Munich. Reck found outlets for his writing in various newspapers, most notably up until 1914 in the newly reestablished *Süddeutsche Zeitung*. He did not participate in the war, having been declared unfit for military duty.[4] Following a period as a trainee in the office of the Director of the Königliches Hof- und National-Theater (Royal Court and National Theater) in Munich, from 1915 he became a freelance writer and journalist, first in Munich and later in Poing, near Truchtlaching in the Chiemgau, an estate he acquired in 1925. Throughout the war he published regularly in such newspapers as the *Berliner Tageblatt* and the *Frankfurter Zeitung*, but also tried his hand at literature, writing his first stories, three books for young readers, and a drama.

Reck experienced the end of the First World War in Munich, and amid the revolutionary confusion of the years 1918–19 remained a resolute royalist. Despite his deeply held objections to the new republic, he never shared the reactionary antisocialism of many on the right and remained wedded to the conservative principles of honor, chivalry, and humanity. After the war, he turned to light fiction and proved to have a gift for the genre, producing in rapid succession a number of commercially successful works, including the novel *Frau Übersee* (Mrs. Overseas, 1918), which became a best-seller, and *Die Dame aus New York* (The lady from New York, 1921). In 1921, he became an author with the publisher August Scherl, part of the Hugenberg concern, with whom he published nine novels over the subsequent twenty years. Having suffered financially in the inflation of 1923, he came to depend on income from this writing to support an extravagant lifestyle and, in the late 1920s, a second household as his wife and four children moved out of the family home.[5] There followed the novels *Sif: Das Weib, das den Mord beging* (Sif: The woman who committed murder, 1926) and *Sven entdeckt das Paradies* (1928, English translation *Sven Discovers Paradise*, 1929). These light novels were reprinted a number of times, sometimes under new titles.[6] Indeed Reck was always very effective in marketing his writing, selling his literary works for prepublication serialization in newspapers and often publishing the same articles in different journals and newspapers. He also enjoyed some limited success with the more serious collection of stories *Phrygische Mützen* (Phrygian caps, 1922) and with a futuristic novel *Die Siedlung Unitrusttown* (The village of unitrusttown, 1925) about an American industrial concern, which lent expression to his fear of the threat to mankind from a degrading technocratic society dominated by powerful captains of industry. The lighter comedy novel *Bomben auf Monte Carlo* (Bombs on Monte Carlo, 1930) proved to have wider appeal and sold in large numbers; it was filmed in 1931 under the title *Monte Carlo Madness*, starring Hans Albers, and in the same year appeared in a separate French-language version and as a stage comedy.

In view of his pressing need to write to earn money, as if on some sort of literary production line, it is perhaps not surprising that Reck was little commended in reviews and his name seldom appears in literary histories of the time. Indeed, up to this point he was seen by critics as almost exclusively a writer of light fiction, adventure, and detective novels. Today, all of his works from this period, with perhaps the sole exception of *Bomben auf Monte Carlo*, are unknown and are subsumed under the heading of kitsch and "station literature."[7]

Throughout the 1920s, Reck pursued the creation of an extravagant self-image, which, though primarily intended for external consumption, was one he himself seemed increasingly to believe in. He sought to portray himself as a member of the social elite, pretending at various times to be a well-to-do traveler, a former cavalry officer, a rich Prussian army officer, or a descendant of Prussian landowning Junkers. He also enjoyed having people address him as "Herr Baron," having long since assumed the affected, grandiose name of Friedrich Percyval Reck-Malleczewen. Such behavior, the need to avoid real life, the compulsion always to be something different and to play a different role depending on whom he was with, cannot solely be explained as a nostalgic response to financial loss or a need for social admiration or affirmation. As Zeile claims, it was far more likely to be part of his wider notion of the dangers posed to the individual by the "massification" of contemporary culture and the compulsive need to assert his individuality, his superiority over the undistinguished masses, and to lend expression to what he saw as his exceptional aesthetic and moral qualities.[8]

During the Third Reich, Reck continued to write moderately successful novels, such as *Ein Mannsbild namens Prack* (A fellow called Prack, 1935), which was also filmed in the same year under the title *Henker, Frauen und Soldaten* (Hangmen, women, and soldiers). Like almost all his work from the 1930s, this novel received official approval, being positively reviewed in Rosenberg's annual *Jahres-Gutachtenanzeiger*[9] and formally recommended by the weekly *Gutachtenanzeiger*.[10] Indeed, although occasional reviewers objected to Reck's monarchist and feudalist thinking, and although the local Gestapo regularly collected evidence on him,[11] his literary work rarely prompted official concern.

There were, however, two significant exceptions to this. First, in a highly critical review of the communist Ernst Nickisch's journal *Widerstand* in the *Bücherkunde*,[12] Reck's essay "Ewige Gironde" (Eternal gironde)[13] is praised for the clarity with which it unveils the supposed aim of the French Revolution as an attempt by an alternative elite of self-seeking moneymen and "hysterical literati" to use the workers to help replace the ruling nobility. But he is also criticized for allowing the essay to appear in the journal and for failing to refer to Hitler's achievements. However, judgment is ultimately reserved: "Fritz Reck-Malleczewen könnte unseres Geistes sein" (Fritz Reck-Malleczewen could be a kindred spirit).[14] Second, Reck is taken to task in a review of his *Acht Kapitel für die Deutschen* (Eight chapters for the Germans, 1934).[15] This classic conservative manifesto, begun as early as 1928, contains reflections on the role of Germany in the world and the threat from the east but also criticism of megalomania and a rejection of the Nazi regime's anti-Semitism. The reviewer acknowledges there is a lot in the book he can agree with but takes Reck to task for asserting that Germany is wrong to pass all the blame for its problems onto the Jews and to overlook the fact that many distinctly Aryan "parasites" have plagued the country. Reck, it says, is an outsider who should refrain from philosophizing and from "prophecies" but stick to harmless lightweight adventure novels.[16]

The veritable explosion in the growth of German-language historical novels and monographs around the mid-1930s[17] is to be ascribed in part to conscious attempts to develop "Gegenbilder" (counterimages) and parallels and in part to the frustrations of novelists deprived of alternative means of expression. Reck's three historical works of the period, *Sophie Dorothee* (1936), *Bockelson: Geschichte eines Massenwahns* (1937, English translation *A History of the Münster Anabaptists*, 2008), and *Charlotte Corday: Geschichte eines Attentates* (Charlotte Corday: The story of an assassination, 1938), all managed to distinguish themselves in this crowded market. The first of these, a biography of Frederick the Great's mother, was bound to find favor with the Nazis for its glorification of Frederick and its apparent conformity with "Blut und Boden" (blood and soil) thinking. Although it was criticized by professional historians for its lack of accuracy and its exaggeration of the influence of Stuart blood on German royal families from the seventeenth century onward, the work received positive reviews in a range of literary journals.[18] Similarly, despite the earlier *Bücherkunde* criticisms, the historical fiction *Bockelson* (the focus of the second half of this chapter) and *Charlotte Corday* prompted no negative reaction.[19] The latter was actually praised in a report for publishers for its portrait of the French "anarchist and psychopath" Marat and was formally recommended by Bernhard Payr, head of the editorial office (Lektorat) of the Reichsstelle zur Förderung des deutschen Schrifttums, for its psychological analysis of mass hysteria and for constituting a symbol of *völkisch* honor and national tradition.[20] It was only after the war that it came to be considered an oppositional text and a work of intellectual resistance.[21] The sympathetic portrayal of the French murderer of a criminal, shown to share several characteristics with Hitler, constitutes a less overt commentary on contemporary Germany than *Bockelson*, but, as shown in a review written by Reck's friend and confidant Erich Müller, the parallels are nevertheless clearly there, especially for someone familiar with the techniques employed in the recently published *Bockelson*. Müller refers knowingly to the "Wahnsinnsreigen entfesselter Bosheit, Niedrigkeit und

Schlechtigkeit" (mad dance of unbridled malice, baseness, and turpitude) of the French Revolution and to Marat as a "false idol," a godless individual driven by a burning "Geltungsbedürfnis" (need for admiration), and talks of Marat's "hysterical" public appearances.[22] After these two historical works, however, Reck did not venture into print with anything that might be considered vaguely risky, publishing, for example, harmless annotated anthologies and the decidedly "safe," because anti-Soviet, novel *Diana Pontecorvo* (1944).

The end for Reck came surprisingly quickly and in unexpected fashion. On August 9, 1944, he finally received a comprehensive publication ban from the Propaganda Ministry.[23] Then, on October 13, he was arrested for not responding to a call-up to the German territorial army in Seebruck and was locked up in military barracks for approximately a week (*T*, 233–34). Worse was to come, however, when he was maliciously denounced by Alfred Salat, head of the Knorr & Hirth publishing house in Munich, and arrested on the orders of the Gestapo on December 29, 1944 for denigrating the German currency and making statements detrimental to the state, charges related, it seems, to Reck's outspoken contesting of proposed payments from the publisher for a serialization of one of his works.[24] He died of typhus fever in Dachau concentration camp on February 16.[25]

Reck never belonged to any active resistance groups (for example, he kept well away from the July 20 circle of would-be assassins, with whom one might have thought he could find common ground), even though he was well informed about their activities and was sufficiently well connected to them to have joined, had he so wished.[26] Nevertheless, he stands out among his social class in rejecting the deceit and delusion practiced in the later years of the Weimar Republic by many sections of the German social and political elite, who helped to install Hitler as chancellor in order to serve their own purposes, in the belief they could in time easily rein in the "drummer boy." For all his arrogant, snobbish, and at times obnoxious attitudes, Reck comes across in his writings as a decided opponent of such greed, lust for power, and self-seeking opportunism. From 1934 onward he became a particularly fierce opponent of the Nazi regime, developing a venomous hatred of its practices and its leading figures. He never shared the anti-Semitism of many like-minded conservatives[27] and expressed both concern for the victims of Kristallnacht (Night of Broken Glass) (*T*, 80–83) and horror at the massacre of "thirty thousand" Jews in Kiev (*T*, 192). In general, his pronouncements suggest a strict, uncompromising, and at times intemperate arbiter of moral right and wrong.

The Role of History

Reck's understanding of history is crucial to an appreciation of *Bockelson*. He was a cultural pessimist deeply disturbed by the modern age, one of many right-wing intellectuals, like Friedrich Georg Jünger, Ernst Jünger, Oswald Spengler, and Hugo von Hofmannsthal, who in their desire to turn the clock back and to effect a "conservative revolution," rejected all aspects of modernity, including democracy, liberalism, nationalism, rationalism, progress, technology, modern art, and experimentation in literature.[28] Reck's diary and the posthumously published *Das Ende der Termiten* (The end of the termites, 1946)[29] show that he had an abhorrence of the nineteenth century and all it stood for, that he espoused a form of "counterenlightenment" based in a belief in the immutable laws of the earth and medieval irrationalism. The Renaissance constituted a great historical caesura, the replacement of *homo religiosus* by material man, who was the product of a new technical and mechanistic age focused exclusively on progress and the improvement of material circumstances. The roots of all modern ills were to be traced to this secularizing, "alien" Renaissance and the birth of capitalism, which supplanted the magical worldview of the Middle Ages with its affirmation of God and gothic influences in art and architecture.

The growing sense in Reck's writings of decline, pending doom, and the end of an era is part of a pessimism that is not just religiously based but is primarily historical. On the one hand, he sees the process of "Entgötterung" (removing the gods) as a consequence of the French Revolution (*T*, 49), and on the other suggests the Nazi regime is not the product of chance political circumstances but is to be blamed on Bismarck and his "artificial" construction of a nation, on the smothering of small German states by Greater Prussia, and on the subsequent Wilhelmine "arrivistes" and their Weimar successors.[30]

In the essay "Vom Reich der Deutschen" (On the Germans' empire), published in 1932, he talks about his "undemocratic heart" and further decries the *Reich* of 1871 for pretending to be conservative and yet being "polluted" by liberalism, saying that for this reason it contained within it the seeds of its own downfall.[31] In the spirit of the Conservative Revolution, he says Germany is witnessing the decline of liberalism, the possible fading of technical thinking, and he angrily denounces the wretched, "God-forsaken" nineteenth century (*RD*, 57). He rejects contemporary calls for a return to the Germany of Bismarck, noting that you cannot rebuild on rotten foundations. The Iron Chancellor, though acknowledged as a great man, is considered responsible for giving modern Germany its mad obsession with industrialization and causing it to be overrun by the power-hungry masses (*T*, 96). Instead, Reck affirms as a self-evident truth the superiority of the "first" German Empire, the Holy Roman Empire of the German nation, and goes on to claim that the old *Reich* was the birthplace of the "great architects of the mind" (*RD*, 53). This *Reich* was firmly tied to the German countryside, which is now threatened by industrial "pirates" (*T*, 70), and he favorably contrasts the

German farmer, countryside, and forest with the mass-man of the city, factories, and asphalt streets. *Das Ende der Termiten* links this critique to Nazism's deceitful attitude to nature: the regime's supposed embracing of nature and championing of the native soil stands in stark contrast to its glorification of technological progress and its enhancement of the role played by industry during the Weimar Republic.

Another key element of Reck's historical understanding was his monarchist upbringing and convictions: "die Existenz des Königtums gehört zu meinem physischen Wohlbefinden" (the existence of the monarchy is essential to my physical well-being, *T*, 223). As a Wittelsbach loyalist, he rejected both Prussia — at whose door he unjustly laid most of the blame for National Socialism — and the Hohenzollern dynasty, seeing in Wilhelmine Germany hated modernist tendencies. Nevertheless, he condemns as a mark of disgrace the way the Kaiser was treated at the end of the First World War, objecting to the cynical manner in which the idol of just four years earlier was vilified and unceremoniously dropped, and bemoans the Germans' failure to examine more honestly their own shortcomings, reproaching in particular the country's generals, the north German "oligarchy," and the Prussian nobility for their undignified and disloyal behavior (*T*, 154–57).

In his nonfictional writing, especially his diary, the sense of hopelessness and despair at the present colors the gloomy picture he draws of recent history. He attacks the supposed glorious Prussian tradition for its aridity, meanness, and lack of imagination. Prussia's embracing of industrialization comes in for particular criticism, while in the Prussian senior military he sees the vulgarity of an unscrupulous class, which compromised itself as long as it sensed personal gain—for example, von Papen is accused of having the sense of honor and conscience of "a butcher's dog" (*T*, 18).

The vituperative comments about Prussia are part of a broader diagnosis of the decay of western culture at the hands of the "Massenmensch" (mass-man, *T*, 52–57). This mass-man, or mass-produced man, as Reck sometimes referred to the phenomenon, is a concept he picked up particularly from José Ortega y Gasset's book *La rebelión de las masas* (1930, English translation *The Revolt of the Masses*, 1932). It denotes persons who fail to ascribe particular significance to themselves and are quite at ease with the notion of simply being "average." In contrast to mass-man, the elite in society place demands on themselves and strive to achieve higher goals. The absence of such aspirations threatens the very existence of human culture, and the spreading influence of mass-man is responsible for the violence, the lack of intellectualism ("Ungeistigkeit"), and the virulent immorality threatening the whole of human culture.[32] However, though the rise to prominence of mass-man and the associated "Massendenken" (mass thinking, *T*, 52) are clear symptoms of this insidious illness and though they celebrate their ultimate triumph in the figure of Hitler and his regime, mass-man is not to be considered synonymous with the proletarian. Rather, the "rot" started in the upper echelons of modern society, and mass-man is to be found especially in management circles and in the "gilded youth" of the industrial class (*T*, 171).[33]

Besides his ideas on the massification of mankind, with the associated decline of human culture and the dissolution of traditional social ties and social rank, Reck shared conservative concerns about the modern state, in which economics took precedence over politics and professional politicians and party functionaries of questionable motivation determined the fate of a country. The state under Weimar democracy had allegedly become a make-do management and economic construct, whose role in wealth distribution reduced it to the status of a mere industrial or commercial firm and undermined its historical authority. It is no coincidence that he spent much time reading and reflecting on Oswald Spengler's *Der Untergang des Abendlandes* (1918–22, English translation *The Decline of the West*, 1926–28), for these ideas on mass-man, cultural decay, and the demise of the state have many similarities with Spengler's prophecies of the end of Western history, even though Reck was reluctant to acknowledge too much of an affinity with Spengler (*T*, 9).

Despite initial hopes that National Socialism could address this state of affairs, it soon became clear that the Nazis' aggressive mass nationalist movement had little at all in common with the monarchical state up to the eighteenth century, which Reck looked back on so fondly, a state in which clear structures, social rank, and strong leadership prevailed,[34] and, along with the likes of Spengler, Ernst Jünger, and the right-wing professor of law Carl Schmitt, Reck quickly became disillusioned with the Nazi regime. However, to an extent unprecedented among all like-minded cultural and political conservatives who had originally placed their hopes in the Nazi state, Reck's disillusionment rapidly developed into a pathological hatred of and revulsion at what was happening. His secret diary provides the most explicit expression of this antipathy.

Tagebuch eines Verzweifelten

From May 1936 to October 1944, Reck recorded in this diary an array of observations, documenting his clear and outspoken opposition to National Socialism. The explosive potential of such a document meant it could only be published posthumously in 1947.[35] From the start, he set it up as a literary undertaking, a contribution to "the cultural history of Nazism" (*T*, 47), the essayistic testament of a desperate observer of unfolding events. The manuscript was necessarily hidden in different locations in his house in Poing: the completed sections were kept in a tin box, which was buried in one of the fields, while ongoing work was stored in a barn.[36] The intermittent entries address all manner of themes, including the most contentious and dangerous. For example, there are references to reports of mass murder taking place in the east, and assorted legal infractions in his local area are faithfully recorded. They are written as immediate responses to current events, which have not been subject to considered reflection. For this reason they do not seek to be fair, do not aspire to balance or objectivity. They include anecdotes, rumor, gossip, and clear examples of prejudice and resentment. Exaggeration vies with arrogant claims, one-sided argument with wild generalizations.

The diary is filled with a sense of a steady demise, of an impending end, as Germany moves inexorably toward military conflict. Indeed Reck shows a certain prophetic sense, writing in September 1937 about the complete certainty of an approaching Second World War (*T*, 57). The text starts, symbolically, with the announcement of the death of Reck's ideological soul mate, Spengler. The air Reck has to breath is oppressive and he is obsessed by a passage from Dostoyevsky predicting the end of the world (*T*, 58–59). He sees death lurking everywhere: in the country-side, in the bomb-damaged cities, and in his own home.

The style is striking, evincing in places a classical grandeur and haughtiness, a powerful rhetoric that is forceful to the point of violence in places, and a rich, vibrant vocabulary accompanied by colorful imagery and witty but also sometimes crude turns of phrase. The reader is at once bemused, shocked, and offended by Reck's views, for example, when he talks arrogantly of "little people" in society, describes disparagingly German military recruits as "diese weißen Nigger" (these white niggers, *T*, 71) and ordinary Germans as "Negermassen" (negro masses, *T*, 106), and refers hatefully to "die Verniggerung" of the world and of German culture in particular (literally "niggerization" or demoralization, *T*, 52). Both here and in *Bockelson* one discerns the arrogant aristocrat repeatedly decrying the demise of his cherished premodern world.

Throughout, the reader is presented with an unrestrained hostility toward Hitler and all he stands for. Hitler is a "failure" (*T*, 19), a "starv-ing stray dog," and a "psychotic" (*T*, 25); he is compared with, variously, Genghis Khan, Napoleon (*T*, 29), Satan (*T*, 87), and Pericles (*T*, 117); and he has the voice of a power-drunk schizophrenic (*T*, 97). Indeed, the dominant mood of the diary is an undisguised hatred, summed up by an entry from August 1936 that simultaneously captures his abiding pes-simism, the recurrent sense of an approaching demise, and his contempt for the Nazis. He says he is entering his fifth year living in this "Pfuhl" (foul hole) and notes that his every act is suffused with intense hatred (*T*, 23). He sees the hatred engendered by the Hitler regime to be one of its most baleful consequences but also ultimately a form of deadly poison for the Nazis (*T*, 142), since it prompts action (*T*, 97). Besides Hitler, the diary's anger is directed at all manner of other developments in Nazi

Germany, including the new business German spoken by the masses in Berlin and the bureaucracy spawned by party and state, with its petty-minded functionaries, office managers, and jobsworths.

Notwithstanding the, at times, extreme views expressed and the intemperate language used in the diary, Engelmann notes that it serves to document the more positive features of the anti-Nazi political right: "Recks Tagebuch ist ein Zeugnis dafür, daß es auch im reaktionären Lager . . . anständige, ehrenhafte, ihren Grundsätzen bis in den Tod treue Menschen gegeben hat" (Reck's diary is a testament to the fact that the reactionary camp . . . also contained decent, honorable people, who to their very end remained true to their principles).[37] It is also invaluable as background and as an interpretative aid to the story *Bockelson*.

Bockelson: Geschichte eines Massenwahns (1937): Genesis and Publication

The work was first published in Berlin by Schützen-Verlag in 1937. Subsequent editions were produced in 1946 by the Droemersche Verlagsanstalt and in 1968 by Henry Goverts. The introduction to the 1946 edition notes that, owing in part to the restrictions he was subjected to when writing the story, Reck saw *Bockelson* as merely a prelude to *Das Ende der Termiten* on the collapse of values in the age of mass formations, unbridled technology, and arrogant nationalism and fanaticism.[38]

Reck first had his attention drawn to the Münster Anabaptist theme, probably in 1936, by Erwein von Aretin, a close friend, whose own opposition to Nazism led him into difficulties.[39] By August 1936 Reck was deep in research on the topic (*T*, 19–21) and, reflecting the speed with which the book was written, by November he could already announce it was completed and with the publisher.[40] It was duly published in March 1937. The historical sources Reck drew on were many and varied but one of the most important was Kerssenbroch's original Latin work, which had been translated into German in both the eighteenth and nineteenth centuries.[41] Significantly, in view of Reck's historical bias in the book, Kerssenbroch's history, for all its authoritative historical detail, is not a direct, personal account, as he had been banned from Münster for refusing to accept Anabaptist practices, and his work is duly colored by both anti-Anabaptist and anti-Bockelson rhetoric. Indeed, Reck acknowledges in a few places Kerssenbroch's addition of fanciful details and notes that he always writes "aus der Perspektive der beleidigten patrizischen Wohlanständigkeit" (from the perspective of offended patrician correctness—my translation, JK).[42]

Of all the works with oppositional content that managed to pass Nazi censors, Reck's story is perhaps the most surprising. The suggestion that the material was so abstruse that the authorities could not possibly have entertained the thought that it might be conceived as a parallel with the present is partly contradicted by Scholdt's clear demonstration of contemporary writers employing Hitler-Bockelson and Münster-Germany parallels both within Germany before 1933 and in exile thereafter.[43] So how could the book be published? Clearly, the author's conservative credentials, his reputation as a writer of largely apolitical light fiction, and the anti-Bolshevist fervor of his story were all critical and may have desensitized those charged with vetting the book. Furthermore, it is likely that—as in other cases, most notably Stefan Andres's *Wir sind Utopia* (1942, English translation *We Are God's Utopia*, 1950)—publication resulted from a combination of chance circumstance and of deficiencies, rivalry, and conflicting opportunism in the network of state control over literature.[44]

Summary

Given the proximity of narrative and history, we start with a historical overview of Reck's raw material.[45] In 1533, the city of Münster in Westphalia was still reeling from the effects of the Reformation as both Catholics and Lutherans vied for control of the city. The official recognition of the Reformation in the Treaty of Dülmen (February 1533) secured for the Lutherans a firmer base in the city under the leadership of Bernhard Rothmann. Rothmann, however, sought to take Luther's reforms further, disputing teaching on communion (favoring a more symbolic interpretation of the host) and baptism (opposing child baptism), and he soon abandoned Lutheranism altogether to become an Anabaptist. Conflict with the Münster city council ensued, but the Anabaptists eventually gained a majority in council elections on February 23, 1534. They held power until June 25, 1535, when they were overcome by the emperor's forces. Anabaptism was a force to be reckoned with across Europe, and one of its early prophets was Jan Matthys (or Matthijs), a baker from Leiden, who arrived in Münster in 1534. Matthys died just two months later, as he sought to defend the city from imperial forces, and the twenty-seven-year-old former tailor's apprentice, actor, and tavern-keeper Jan van Leiden, also named Bockelson after his father Bockel, became the self-appointed leader of the radical sect. Bockelson was a gifted orator and managed to draw large numbers to the cause. In accordance with Anabaptist millenarian beliefs, he taught that Christ had established his kingdom in Münster in readiness for his Coming, and Bockelson duly presented himself to the people as the "King of the New Zion," who was paving the way for Christ's thousand-year reign.

With key allies, such as the propagandist Johann Dusentschuer ("Dusentschnuer" in Reck's text), Bockelson sought to spread the

Anabaptist word far and wide, sending emissaries to neighboring cities to convert their citizens. In Münster, he set up a ruthless religious dictatorship based around a council of twelve elders, which oversaw the destruction of all Catholic icons and books. The Bible was the only book allowed and its teachings were established as the sole authoritative guide for the people. Non-Anabaptists were either killed or forced to flee. The military forces of Bishop Count Franz von Waldeck soon laid siege to the city and forced the Anabaptists to requisition all precious metals to be used in forging weaponry and to level church spires to facilitate the construction of defensive positions. Under Bockelson's police chief, the former merchant and early convert Bernhard Knipperdolling, the people of Münster were subjected to the harshest of punishments for any act thought to be against biblical teaching or deemed to undermine the defense of the city. Increasingly, the siege took its toll, inflicting starvation on the people and causing many to resort to desperate measures. Promises of support from Anabaptist forces in the Netherlands and other parts of Europe never materialized and, in a final bloody battle, the city was taken and reclaimed for Catholicism. Bockelson and Knipperdolling were tortured and killed, and their bodies were left to rot in cages suspended from the Lamberti church tower.

The beliefs of the Anabaptists were founded on the central notion that they offered a "restoration" of Christian faith in several areas. As Reck presents it in his story, their faith involved new revelations about the Old Testament and emphasized the central importance of Christ's incarnation (114–16). They preached a God-fearing way of life, thus correcting what was seen as the errors of the Old Believers (Catholics), whose lifestyle was considered dissolute, and they rejected the Lutheran adoption of Catholic practices. This applied particularly to the areas of baptism, which they "restored" as an act for fully aware adults, communion, and marriage, within which they justified polygamy on the basis of alleged scriptural authority. In a revolt against the practices of early capitalism, they promoted communal property and rejected buying and selling, working for money, pensions, and usury (115). Furthermore, jewelry and fine clothing were frowned on and people were encouraged to wear black, while mirrors and all decorations, both considered frivolous, were banned.

Reck's narrative broadly follows the historical facts. However, he shapes the historical in many different ways to fit his allegorical purpose, seeking, via an overarching pseudo-academic camouflage, to attribute authenticity to his story by regularly quoting from historical sources, referring to these in seemingly scholarly footnotes, and listing all his sources at the end of the text. His interpretation of the Münster Anabaptist revolt is manipulated in such a way as to suggest that a historical aberration, explainable by a mass popular psychosis, has its parallel in contemporary events in Nazi Germany. Yet, as historians have indicated, it is inadequate to define the "kingdom of Zion" under Bockelson as a form of mass hysteria and an example of arbitrary terror comparable to modern totalitarianism.[46] And indeed Reck's portrait of the Anabaptists is largely one-sided and almost exclusively negative, showing them to be deluded, violent, and vindictive aggressors, and ignoring the way in which they too were victims of sectarian wrongdoing. In this, Reck consciously allows his narrative to be colored by the bias that characterizes Kerssenbroch's contemporary account.

Reck reserves particular vitriol for Rothmann, ironically referred to throughout as "Dear Rothmann" and depicted as a fashionable pastor and womanizer, who comes to be the intellectual force behind the movement and thus bears considerable blame for its crimes. But the supposed mass psychosis in Münster is supported by a number of other key figures, presented in an equally critical light, including second-in-command Bernd Knipperdolling, who is both head of the city police and Bockelson's chief executioner, the preacher Bernhard Krechting, and the propagandist Dusentschnuer, an ill-disguised caricature of Goebbels.

The one-sided portrayal of the Anabaptists focuses particularly on their indulgence in wild celebrations and presents the permissive approach to polygamy in negative terms, with no attempt to explain the phenomenon as the reasoned demographic response to the historically attested preponderance of women over men in Münster. Similarly, their iconoclasm and policing of religious practice is depicted as a self-serving and self-enriching reign of terror with summary justice, including executions and the desecration of churches and monasteries, with no suggestion that the confiscations served primarily a military purpose.

The story moves quickly and repeatedly from one narrative perspective to another and is interrupted time and again by authorial asides and direct, often heavily ironic commentary, featuring prophecies of doom, warnings, and strongly, sometimes violently worded condemnation. The use of a present-tense narrative and a fictive "we" have the effect of rendering the historical material much more immediate to the reader.[47]

Reception

With the negative review of Reck's *Acht Kapitel für die Deutschen* still fresh in the memory, the *Gutachtenanzeiger* and the *Bücherkunde* refrained from any comment on *Bockelson*, although the regional press did comment positively, if briefly.[48] The story was reviewed several times and at greater length in the more liberal sections of the press, and almost without exception was praised for its distinctive narrative tone and its linking of the Münster uprising to key events in Western history. Perhaps the most striking review is the one that appeared above the anonymous pen name "–per" in the *Frankfurter Zeitung*.[49] This review itself reads like an example of camouflaged writing, full of bold, ambiguous references to the narrative, which have clear applicability to contemporary Nazi Germany but are also firmly safeguarded against any such charge. The very first paragraph offers an overwhelming set of characteristics that can be readily applied to the Nazi takeover and securing of power, including references to "den Bann chiliastisch-kommunistischer Ideen" (the spell of chiliastic-communist ideas), to "a regime of terror," to increasing numbers of arbitrary executions, and to an attack on the legal basis of the *Reich*. Mention of the split among the Anabaptists between those wishing to pursue their ends via preaching and conversion, and those favoring the use of violence, mirrors the Nazi turn to physical brutality in the late 1920s and early 1930s, while the description of the bloody response to resistance reflects the wave of suppression of oppositional groups between 1933 and 1935. In a clever reversal, the reviewer concludes by praising the book for its sharp and telling observations and its suspense, but laments the very point the review has been seeking to highlight: "Im ganzen aber ist hier die aberwitzige Vergangenheit der Jahre 1534 und 35 doch wohl zu sehr aus der Gegenwart heraus gesehen" (On the whole, however, the mad past of the years 1534 and 1535 is seen too much from the perspective of the present)—a means of drawing attention to the subversiveness of the text being discussed while simultaneously distancing oneself from it.

A similar game seems to be played in a review, signed simply "E. A.," in the journal *Hochland*, where Reck's work is described as a masterpiece and a "fascinating" book.[50] This review is a classic example of the use of Bolshevism to denote Nazism, in keeping with replacement techniques described by Brecht in his landmark article.[51] Von Aretin here reflects Reck's own tendency to draw parallels between his narrative and events in revolutionary France or Russia. However, he brings it even closer to home by employing language redolent of contemporary German propaganda: "nicht anders, als es . . . 1917 der Bolschewist in Rußland und in unseren Tagen jener in Spanien mit den chiliastischen Ideen eines tausendjährigen Zukunftsreiches taten" (no differently from the Bolshevists in Russia in 1917 and the present-day ones in Spain with their chiliastic ideas of a kingdom of the future lasting a thousand years, 161). The further use of 1936 without specific mention of Spain makes the point even more clearly for the esoteric readership of *Hochland*: "Es ist . . . ein unbestreitbares Verdienst, die Vorgänge im wiedertäuferischen Münster einmal wieder der *verständnisvoller* gewordenen Leserwelt vor Augen zu führen und die geradezu aufdringliche Parallele mit den Erscheinungen von 1789, 1917–18 und 1936 mit kundiger Hand zu deuten" (The author unquestionably makes a significant contribution . . . by drawing the events in Anabaptist Münster to the attention of a now *more knowing* reading public and by interpreting so knowledgeably the positively insistent parallel with 1789,

1917–18, and 1936. Emphasis mine, 162). It is also significant that von Aretin draws attention to the use of propaganda, describing it as a real "danger" for Münster and its inhabitants, and refers to the mendacity of the language used by these "Unterweltler" (denizens of the underworld, 163). He concludes with the boldly ambiguous sentence: "Vor zwanzig Jahren hätte [das Buch] kein deutscher Mensch schreiben können" (No German could have written this book twenty years ago, 163).

Other reviews were less striking but generally positive. Ernst Samhaber, who wrote camouflaged articles for the journal *Deutsche Rundschau*,[52] offers in the weekly magazine *Deutsche Zukunft* a generally positive review but suggests that the desire to seek parallels with other epochs and the narrow focus on exploring the "mad doctor" Bockelson tends to push key religious and political issues into the background, and he regrets the failure to point to the major influence of the German Peasants' War, which linked religious questions with political and social ones.[53] However, he positively encourages the reader to seek links with the present by stating that Reck equates Münster with Germany and by employing parallels with the Spanish Civil War, that favorite alternative referential setting of oppositional writers in Nazi Germany. A review in the monarchist *Weiße Blätter* describes the book as "brilliantly successful" and calls Reck a spirited writer who is attracted to the turbulent periods of history.[54] The story also came to the attention of German emigrants, and one curious detail of its reception is the reported plan of Otto Strasser, brother of the murdered SA figure Gregor, in Czech exile, to make a film of *Bockelson*, a sort of dark forerunner of Chaplin's *The Great Dictator* (1940), as well as to arrange a translation of the work in Paris.[55]

Although, for reasons that remain unclear, Reck was unable to secure publication of a new edition of the story in the period 1941–42, at no point was there any question of the work being banned (despite the repeated propagation of this rumor after the war, right up to the 1970s),[56] of negative reviews appearing in the press, or of Reck experiencing any difficulty publishing subsequent work. Furthermore, no document has been found in Nazi official records, such as Reck's Gestapo files, of any criticism linked to the story.[57] Indeed, Reck's work continued, on the whole, to be reviewed positively, his ideological standpoint apparently assured.

The first postwar edition of *Bockelson* was published in 1946, and in a review in the *Süddeutsche Zeitung*, Johannes Tralow, who knew Reck personally, describes the work as a "spine-chilling dress rehearsal" for Germany, elucidates the Bockelson-Hitler / Münster-Nazi Germany parallels, and suggests that, during the Nazi years, Reck's story circulated widely among readers who were "in the know," but also suggests, misleadingly, that the book could not be mentioned in public.[58]

In 1964 Peter Härtling was one of the first commentators to reexamine Reck's work,[59] and this initiated a revival of interest in the writer, leading two years later to the reissuing of Reck's diary and, in 1968, to a third edition of *Bockelson*. This edition of the story drew a good deal of critical attention; for example, Manfred Müller called the story a "Schlüsselroman" (roman à clef), considering it to be typical of the way inner emigrant writers sought to document their resistance to National Socialism but also noting that it proved the "illusory" nature of such literary resistance.[60] On the hundredth anniversary of the author's birth, however, the book was still being praised as a brilliantly written "historiographically camouflaged criticism of National Socialism."[61]

Parallels with Hitler's Germany

The full title indicates the dual focus of the story. The prominence given first to Bockelson's name suggests Reck's prime concern is to explore the character of the leader of the Münster uprising, but the subtitle, *A Tale of Mass Insanity*, points to his concern also with the history of ideas, the religious and psychological roots of the terror. Meanwhile the blurb that accompanied the first edition of the work can actually be seen as drawing the reader's attention to contemporary relevance: it refers to the story's vivid portrayal of a geographically restricted uprising, which nevertheless shines "durch die Leuchtkraft der Flammen der Zerstörung und Vernichtung wie eine Brandfackel in alle Lande . . . —bis hinüber in unsere Zeit" (through the brightness of the flames of destruction and extermination like a firebrand across all lands—right into the present day).[62]

The parallels with events in contemporary Germany that Reck was seeking to establish are made clear in his contemporaneous diary, in *Das Ende der Termiten*, and in assorted private correspondence.[63] An explicit commentary is provided by the early entries in the diary:

> Wie bei uns, so ist auch dort ein Mißratener, ein sozusagen im Rinnstein gezeugter Bastard der große Prophet, wie bei uns kapituliert vor ihm, unbegreiflich für die staunende Umwelt, jeder Widerstand. . . . Ein Mäntelchen von Ideologie verhüllt in Münster just wie bei uns einen Kern von Geilheit, Habgier, Sadismus und bodenlosem Geltungsbedürfnis. (*T*, 19–20)

> [As in our case, a failure, a bastard conceived, so to speak, in the gutter, becomes the great prophet, and all opposition simply capitulates before him, while the world looks on in incomprehension and astonishment. . . . In Münster, too, a thin veneer of ideology covers lewdness, greed, sadism, and an incredible lust for power.]

Similarly, in *Das Ende der Termiten*, he refers to the way Münster acts as a "model" of contemporary Germany, sharing with the latter an extreme autocracy based on the support of "mass-man" as well as "die allen gemeinsame Hysterie, das lethargische Verstummen der Opposition, die auch inmitten des Paradoxen ihre Stimme nicht wiederfindet, und vor allem—den Führer" (the universal hysteria, the lethargic silencing of oppositional voices, in spite of the paradoxes encountered, and, above all, the Führer).[64]

The links with Nazi Germany are at their clearest in the figures of Bockelson and Hitler. Here Reck seems to have mined the historical sources in order to extract precisely those biographical features that point unmistakably to a parallel. Thus, his aristocratic disdain for Hitler's lowly origins is reflected in the comparison he draws between the Führer and the "King of Zion." Bockelson's origins are unclear but he appears to have been born out of wedlock and is said to have the features of a "bastard born in a roadside ditch" (39), while the parentage of Hitler's father was also uncertain and Hitler was born to his father's much younger third wife.[65] Like Hitler, Bockelson has had a restless, unstable youth, and like Hitler the would-be artist, Bockelson is a frustrated actor and playwright. Furthermore, just like his modern-day counterpart, Bockelson is possessed of rhetorical ability with a tendency toward theatricality and, in a parallel with Hitler's early oratory in beer halls, he first discovers his public-speaking abilities in a tavern and ultimately sees the chance to realize his restless ambition in a movement looking for a charismatic leader. Finally, like Hitler, Bockelson comes from another country to assume power.

There are numerous parallels to be found between the Anabaptists' rise to power in Münster and the early days of the Nazi regime. Thus, in its desire to avoid bloodshed, the council of the city decides not to take further action following the failure of its attempt to have Rothmann removed from the city, choosing instead to negotiate with the rebels and to seek to live in "peaceful coexistence" (43). The echoes of the appeasement of Hitler by the German political establishment prior to 1933 are clear. Similarly, as the Anabaptists seek to assert themselves in Münster, there is talk of emigration and flight (44), while elections to the city council are held under the threat of terror (54) and feature the promotion of disreputable, criminal delegates, prompting parallels with Nazi election success between 1930 and 1932 and the use of heavy-handed, intimidatory tactics by the SA. Just as in Nazi Germany, the old democratic order is dissolved with little opposition, its signs and symbols are erased, streets are renamed, and dissenters liquidated.

The parallels even seem to indicate remarkable prescience on Reck's part as the defeat of the Anabaptists bears a close resemblance to the later stages of the Nazi regime. He describes a regime engaged in the promotion of all-out war in an already broken city, the pointless demands for citizens to hold out further against overwhelming odds regardless of the human cost, the deceitful prospect of last-minute intervention by Dutch or Friesian allies to save the city, a leader who desperately promotes his henchmen and allots them lands that are yet to be taken, and finally the tendency for the defeated to deny their views and disown their actions.[66]

A recurrent feature of the story are parallels between Münster in 1534 and other periods of European history. For instance, in discussing the Anabaptists' construct of an "external enemy" in its propaganda offensive, the author notes: "Es ist das alte Spiel, mit dem in allen revoltierenden Staaten und Städten die Machthaber die Aufmerksamkeit der Masse von ihren eigentlichen Plänen ablenken—es war 1792 in Paris, es war 1917 in Moskau so, und es konnte in Münster kaum anders sein" (It's the same old game that all rulers of rebellious states and cities employ to divert the attention of the masses from their real plans—so it was in Paris in 1792 and in Moscow in 1917, and it could hardly be different in Münster, 44). The implied comparison with Nazi propagandist uses of the hated Versailles Treaty is not difficult to discern and is conveyed without the need for any direct reference to the present. Moreover, as seen in the above passage, Reck repeatedly uses such phrases as "it is always the same," "it is always so," "as usual," "as ever," and so on, which, besides betraying his essentially conservative view of history, serves to emphasize the exemplary nature of many of the events he is describing and thus to signal to the reader their applicability to the German present.

Reck refers in his diary to the pervasive practice of informing and denunciation that was poisoning life in Nazi Germany: "Und Kinder denunzieren ihre Eltern, und der Bruder, wenn ein kleiner Gewinst dabei herausspringt, liefert die eigene Schwester ans Messer, und überhaupt ist Recht das, was Deutschland nützt" (And children denounce their parents, and brothers, if they think there's something to be gained from it, deliver up their sisters, and all in all, what is right is what is useful for Germany, *T*, 104).[67] This reiterates the message of *Bockelson*, which presents the same poisonous atmosphere but distances the obvious parallel with Nazi Germany through a deliberate comparison with hated Soviet Russia: "Und es verrät das Weib den Mann, und es verrät, wenn nur ein bescheidener Vorteil winkt, die Tochter an die Tscheka von Münster den eigenen Vater" (And wife shall betray husband, and daughter—for only modest gain—shall betray her own father to the Cheka of Münster, 102; my translation).

Such repeated links between events in Münster in 1534–35 and, variously, the French Revolution, the Soviet October Revolution, and the revolutionary stirrings in Germany following the First World War, along with parallels between Bockelson or other characters and such historical figures as Calvin, Cromwell, and Robespierre, are intended as interpretative aids and pointers to the text's contemporary relevance, but at the same time they mitigate the risk to the author by creating deliberate ambiguity and blurring the applicability to Nazi Germany. Reck's insistence on not viewing the events described in the story independently of similar phenomena in human history is, however, necessarily partial, and readers have to supplement the process for themselves by developing the historical parallels or inferring the association with the present day. The inferred link between the Nazi thousand-year Reich and the Anabaptists' millenarian beliefs is a good example of this.

In the Anabaptists' public burning of all texts except the Bible (72), one sees a particularly thinly veiled reference to the book burnings initiated by Goebbels in spring 1933. Less pointed but equally relevant is the description of draconian punishments, including the death penalty, for minor infringements, especially "blasphemy" (73) or contravention of the laws on polygamy (112), which have their parallel in the summary justice dispensed by the Nazi Volksgerichtshof (People's Court) and its issuing of thousands of death penalties between 1934 and 1944 for the slightest act of disloyalty.[68]

There are several further parallels that a reader can start to see in the text, once attuned to the communication of esoteric messages. Thus, Bockelson's personal involvement in such events as public beheadings (102) reflects rumors of Hitler personally killing opponents in the wake of the 1934 Röhm putsch. Indeed, Reck talks openly about this in his diary: "Wie bei uns im Röhm-Putsch Herr Hitler getan, so spielt in Münster dieser Bockelson den Staatshenker" (Bockelson in Münster played the same role of chief executioner as that played by Hitler in the Röhm putsch, *T*, 20). It has also been claimed that in the demise of Jan Matthys and the immediate assumption by Bockelson of the title "First Prophet" and subsequently "King," Reck was hinting at Hitler's assumption in August 1934 of the combined offices of Reich President and Reich Chancellor upon the death of President Hindenburg, soon to be followed by the more widespread use of the term "Führer."[69] In the Anabaptists' propaganda, which is designed to suggest that life in the city is not as barbaric as has been made out, one might further find parallels with Nazi attempts to display liberal leanings to the outside world via the cultural thaw that attended the Olympics in 1936 and via the continued existence of liberal journals and newspapers such as the *Frankfurter Zeitung*. In Bockelson's harem of sixteen wives and his elevation of one, Divara, to "Queen" (111), there are parallels with Hitler's alleged multiple superficial liaisons with young women and his favoring of Eva Braun;[70] and in Bockelson's difficulty producing an heir one might see a reference to Hitler's childlessness. In the exhortation that the people of Münster testify to their faith using a new credo, the words "Ich glaube an das Neue Reich und an den Grund meiner Taufe" (I believe in the New Kingdom and the basis of my baptism, 142; my translation) could be understood as a reference to the way in which in mid-1930s Germany the ideas, rites, and language of Nazi ideology were increasingly being used to displace traditional religious practice. Furthermore, in the description of the population swearing loyalty to the bitter end, the reader has no difficulty recognizing a parallel with the Hitler salute: "die Menge [hat] nach altem deutschem Schwurzeremoniell stumm und feierlich über sich die Hand gehoben" (the masses silently raised their hand, as was the old German custom when swearing an oath, 165).

Camouflage and "Securing" the Text

In the very first paragraph of the Prologue, Reck presents an introduction to his treatment of sixteenth-century Münster, which contains clear parallels with Hitler and the rise of National Socialism but at the same time deploys sufficient references to the specific historical period and events to "anchor" the text and safeguard it from all-too-ready deciphering:

> Wenn aber eine ganze Stadt sich für volle achtzehn Monate absperrt gegen die Außenwelt, wenn sie, nicht nur unter dem Geschrei des Mobs, sondern unter lebhafter Zustimmung auch von Handwerkern, Großbürgern, Patriziern und sogar von diesem und jenem in die Stadt gelaufenen Edelmann einen landfremden Schneidergesellen von anrüchiger Vergangenheit zum König von Zion wählt, wenn endlich dieser König, wiederum unter Zustimmung von hoch und gering, alle gewohnten Begriffe auf den Kopf stellt, alle bürgerlichen Bindungen des Mittelalters zerreißt . . .: Dann ist es doch am Ende wohl am Platze, von einem Massenwahn, von einer rätselhaften, auf ein ganzes Gemeinwesen gefallenen Psychose zu sprechen. (29)

> [Yet when an entire city closes itself off from the outside world for a full eighteen months; when it elects a foreign tailor's apprentice with a checkered past as King of Zion and does so not only amid the cheers of the rabble but also with the enthusiastic consent of craftsmen, the prosperous upper middle class, patricians, and even a few noblemen; and when finally this king—again, with the approval of great and small alike—turns all traditional values upside down, tears apart the moral fabric of the medieval bourgeoisie . . .: then one might legitimately speak of mass insanity, of a mysterious psychosis overwhelming an entire community.]

Reck makes it clear early on in the work that, in focusing on the figure of Bockelson, he is less interested in him as a historical figure than in his broader significance: his real importance and that of the "mass insanity" associated with him lie in their representativeness beyond the sixteenth century. This representativeness is emphasized but simultaneously camouflaged by frequent mention of the French and Russian revolutions, and of miscellaneous historical figures and events from across the centuries. The exclusively negative references to Bolshevism and Jacobinism could, of course, only serve to enhance the prospects of publication. They draw the reader into making certain key connections with the Nazi present but also serve to provide what have been called "historical red herrings"[71] and to sow a degree of confusion. Thus, the Anabaptist city government is repeatedly labeled "Tschekistenregime" (Cheka regime, 97); and, playing to the Versailles-hostile ideology of the time, Reck refers to the French troops, who up to 1936 had occupied the Rhineland west of the river, as an army "das bis vor kurzem auf unserem Boden stand und so elegant und so geräuschlos alles verdarb, was auf diesem Boden sich den ein wenig schal, ein wenig verstaubt, ein wenig vermottet gewordenen Ideen Rousseaus noch widersetzte" (that until recently stood on our own soil and so elegantly and so silently spoiled everything that still resisted Rousseau's somewhat stale, dusty, moth-eaten ideas, 83; my translation). In the final pages of the story he then exploits this by now well-established context to fire a salvo at all forms of socialism, perhaps especially National Socialism, saying the roots of the movement should be sought in "anticapitalist problems" of the time and in the communism manifest in Anabaptist rule, or this first "soviet republic," as he calls it (203). The rejection of anticapitalism and the dismantling of class structures were targeted at contemporary Germany as much as they applied to Münster, but the inclusion of the reference to the soviets was sufficient to ward off any potential criticism from a sharp-witted censor.

The task of the reader in search of esoteric messages in *Bockelson* is, in general, never an easy one, owing to Reck's very wide field of historical reference, allied to his challenging, syntactically involved, and lexically rich prose style. On occasions, just as a potentially clear link to the Nazi present is emerging, one finds the author engaging in a deliberately complex obfuscation intended to throw a censor off the trail, and as a result the true meaning eludes the reader too, perhaps leading both to gloss over the point in some puzzlement. For example, in the description of Bockelson's rise to prominence, Reck vents his disdain for Hitler: "Denn die Geschichte . . . erlaubt sich wohl manchmal den grausamen Scherz, den Jämmerling, den Schwätzer und Hysteriker für kurze Zeit auf ihre Podeste zu heben, das Nichts für kurze Zeit zum Mittelpunkt der großen Dinge . . . zu machen" (For history . . . permits itself on occasion the cruel joke of lifting a miserable wretch, a windbag, an hysteric onto her pedestals for a while, hence turning nothingness for a short time into the center of great affairs, 40). However, he then quickly covers his tracks in a long, rambling paragraph by introducing little-known figures from ancient Greece (Kleon), the French Revolution (Baboeuf), ancient Rome (Gracchus Cornelius), and Neapolitan/Italian theater (Policinelle) to disguise the parallel.

The link between Dusentschnuer and Goebbels is even clearer. The former, made one of the visionaries of the movement and part of Bockelson's inner circle, is described as "ein armer Krüppel" (a poor cripple, 106) and is likened to a "hinkenden Propheten" (limping prophet, 107), as he has a deformity of the foot; he is also a propagandist, who employs his rhetorical talents to persuade the people of the need for sacrifices.[72] At this point, lest the parallel become too clear, Reck employs a characteristic tactic of distraction and camouflage with a frankly rambling two paragraphs of obfuscation and not entirely relevant reflections on "Encyclopedism," the demise of the myth of the divine right of kings, Napoleon, the German Peasants' War, the Staufen dynasty, Karl von Luxemburg, Maximilian I, and the crowning of the King of Hungary. Only then does he return to his main theme with a bold and direct statement: "Hier aber geschieht es, daß ein sozusagen im Straßengraben geborener nach der Krone greift" (But here fate would have it that someone born in a gutter grabs for the crown, 108). Yet, at the same time, he distances himself from the description of Bockelson/Hitler as "Theaterkönig und Hurenoberst" (a theater king and commander of whores, 108) by attributing these words to the historian Kerssenbroch.

Finally, a further example is found in the description of the newly minted coins in Münster, which bear the inscription: "Ein König aufrecht über alles. Ein Gott, ein Glaube, eine Taufe" (One king upright above all. One God, one faith, one baptism, 112) with its unmistakable echo of "Ein Volk, ein Reich, ein Führer." Here Reck again secures his text by employing one of his favored historical references: "Und so wären wir ja wohl, in der historischen Parallele zur Französischen Revolution. . . ." (And so we would appear to have come to a parallel with the French Revolution, 112).

Bockelson and History

A distinctive feature of Reck's historical approach is his tendency to compare the Anabaptist uprising with, variously, meteorological and geological extremes, cosmic excesses, and medical disorders. Thus events in Münster are repeatedly described as being part of a "storm" (203) that has descended on the city. Such meteorological and cosmic comparisons are employed, both in *Bockelson* and the diary, to emphasize the almost apocalyptic vision of the decline of Germany and the civilized Western world as a whole, to suggest that "Hitlerism" is merely the symptom of a deeper cosmic disturbance of the world.[73]

An essentially irrational historical underpinning of this stance is provided early in *Bockelson* where, with reference to the fateful loss of gothic religious values, he talks about the baleful influence of the Renaissance, comparing it to the eruption of a volcano. The events in Münster are seen as reverberations emanating from this original event: "Die unsichtbare Hand der Geschichtslenkung rührte die Gewässer der Seelen um so furchtbarer um, je tiefer diese Gewässer waren. . . . Das, was damals in Münster geschah, war ja nur das abgelegene Teilfeld eines kosmischen Bebens." (The deeper the waters of the souls, the more terribly they were stirred by the unseen hand guiding history. . . . What happened in Münster back then was but the remote subfield of a cosmic tremor, 30–31, my translation.) History is a fate imposed on human beings, one which they have no power to influence, and traumatic events such as the Münster uprising are merely ripples emanating from larger-scale "cosmic" eruptions.[74]

Closely linked to this is the abiding sense of a past order superior to that of the present. Human history is to be considered a steady move away from this supposed former ideal state, and it is from this that the conservative draws his conviction of a moral right to resist the ills of his time. Regret for the loss of an idealized past makes the conservative immune to the reason and rationalism underlying revolutionary aspirations to change society in pursuit of a better future. The antipathy, the abusive and violent language, and the powerful emotions stirred up by Reck in his diary, in *Bockelson*, and in *Das Ende der Termiten* reflect, on the one hand, his sense of powerlessness and, on the other, his fundamental fatalistic belief that the Third Reich and the Anabaptist kingdom constitute two examples of inevitable periodic seismic shifts in human history:

Und immer vergaßen die rückwärts schauenden Betrachter, daß Revolutionen in der Geschichte die gleiche Rolle spielen wie in der Geologie die Vulkane: daß diese für den Überdruck der Lavamassen, jene aber für den Innendruck des angestauten sozialen und seelischen Eiters die Sicherheitsventile bilden und daß ihre Ausbrüche brechbar sind erst nach Wiederherstellung des inneren Gleichgewichts. (97)

[In looking back the observer always forgot that revolutions play the same role in history as do volcanoes in geology: both are safety valves—the latter for the excess pressure of lava, the former for built-up social and spiritual pus, and their eruptions can only be controlled after inner balance has been reestablished.]

At the end of *Bockelson* Reck employs a favored medical image in comparing history's periodic "mass psychoses" to hallucination-inducing fevers that pass through periods of crisis; in the case of medieval Germany the virus of the Renaissance is linked to the two "Fieberkrisen" (fever crises, 203) of the German Peasants' War and the Anabaptist uprising in Münster. He also refers to such periods as "pus-filled abscesses" with fatal consequences (203), and the rise of "mass-man," to which he attributes many of the ills of modern Germany, is likened time and again to the growth of these boils or to malicious tumors.[75]

He rejects the notion that the roots of such "catastrophes" as those besetting Münster and, by implication, contemporary Germany can be found exclusively in an analysis of rational human actions, insisting that the associated moral and ethical degeneration have their roots in the irrational and the pathological (*T*, 215). However, he is clear that this is not a specifically or solely German phenomenon but one that could easily overtake any other country and its people. Seen in these various ways, the "mass insanities" of the Nazis and the Anabaptists are merely instances of a global cleansing process, of the sort that characterizes much inner emigrant writing and is evidenced most notably in the use of the myth of the Flood, for example, in Stefan Andres's *Die Sintflut* trilogy (The flood, 1949–59).

This view is reinforced by the parallels between the Anabaptist revolt and the French and Russian revolutions, through which Reck frequently makes disparaging references to the lowly social origins of the Anabaptists, thereby betraying his value system and essentially class-ridden thinking. In connection with this and on the basis of a review of historical texts on the Münster Anabaptists, Schnell argues that in *Bockelson* Reck is trying to target the social origins of the Anabaptist movement and its positing of a communist-like utopia amid revolutionary stirrings in early capitalist society; but, he claims, Reck pays no attention to the socioeconomic factors behind the emancipatory and anticapitalist tendencies within the lower classes that found expression in the chiliastic ideas of the time. He further points to the historical origins of such phenomena as the community of property and the constitutional separation of spiritual and worldly power, and notes that the introduction of polygamy and the social terror within Münster were not, as Reck's narrative describes them, part of some sort of spiritual "abscess," the constituent elements of the eponymous social-psychological mass hysteria, but rather deliberate social and defense measures taken out of necessity by a government faced with an imbalanced population and under the extreme pressures of a siege.[76]

The treatment of these phenomena in the story certainly reflects Reck's deeply conservative suspicion of revolutionary and democratic movements. Yet, while one can acknowledge that his inclination toward a simplistic tendency to equate fascism and communism, and his attempt to draw parallels between a proletarian millenarian movement and a fascist one, were entirely in keeping with this conservative worldview, it is going too far to see in the parallels between sixteenth-century Münster and Nazi Germany an "historical agnosticism" that places Reck "objectively on the side of the fascists."[77]

Reck's political and historical philosophy and his hatred of the Nazi regime inevitably introduced a degree of distortion into the portrayal of events in Münster. In the character of Bockelson there is far more of both Hitler's physical features and of the contemporary conception of a dictator figure than historical facts would permit. And the poisonous portrait of Bockelson stands in stark contrast to that drawn by both historians and other commentators. Leopold von Ranke, for example, whose major history of the Reformation[78] Reck lists in his bibliography (214), is generally considered a far more objective chronicler of the period and his picture of Bockelson is seen as a more balanced one, free of Reck's wild-eyed vitriol.[79] Similarly, Reck could never have shared the view of Bockelson as socially progressive and an early "freedom fighter."[80]

In this sense, Schnell is right that Reck underestimates the significance of social issues, refuses to see the socioeconomic basis of events in Münster and of the Anabaptist movement more generally. Instead, in his portrayal and analysis of the phenomenon he employs explanations relating to the baseness of human motives, evil instincts, illegitimacy, or, most frequently, fevered madness or disease. The legitimate motives of want, need, and social exclusion rarely get a mention and, where they do, they are adduced as evidence of mere envy or resentment. In the suppression of Anabaptist uprisings, especially in Münster, Reck saw the end of any prospect for utopian thinking on Germanic territory. He refused to see in Anabaptism any form of social or religious renewal and could not possibly acknowledge the role of the movement in influencing utopian developments in other countries, even though English Puritanism, the French Revolution, and Russian Bolshevism could all trace their roots in part to the influence of Baptist thinking. In his deliberately one-eyed take on events in Münster, Reck fails to recognize that though the lower classes commanded the streets, power and senior positions remained in the hands of a bourgeois elite, who exploited the Anabaptist ideology to press their own interests.[81]

On the other hand, it is clear from the start that, despite the historical, chronicle-like approach and the references to historians of the period, Reck had no intention of aspiring to historical objectivity. His was a creative work, with a clear and conscious tendentiousness dictating which features of the period, which aspects of the narrated events, and which elements in the character of Bockelson he should highlight and, at times, distort. Consequently the historiographical façade is penetrated repeatedly by passages of essayistic prose and colorful, personal, and, at times, aggressive comment, suffused throughout with a light but unrelenting irony.

Conclusion

Reck was a well-traveled, humanistically educated conservative and monarchist, an upper-class snob, with a broad field of historical reference. He was also a fantasist, a player of roles who was not averse to distorting the truth when it suited his self-stylization. His initial dislike of the Nazis was as much aesthetic as anything else, but after 1933 it soon developed into a deep-seated antipathy, fueled by his rejection of the masses, who were facilitating the "madness" of the immoral regime. He rejected unequivocally the regime's violent ways, its flouting of legality, and its anti-Semitism. However, one needs to be clear about the motives for his antipathy. National Socialism exacerbated his preexisting unease, alienation, and isolation from the modern world, and it is significant that his revulsion was most often centered on a rejection of the regime's technocratic approach, its promotion of industry and technology, its urbanization, and concreting-over of nature. Having little sympathy with democracy, he was not at all concerned with Nazism's authoritarianism, rather he saw in it the inevitable consequence of the hated nineteenth century and, beyond that, of the fulfillment of the protracted but steady decline of human civilization, the origins of which he traced back to the Renaissance.

Despite the commercial success that Reck's adventure novels enjoyed, he was not an accomplished novelist and was more at home in the format and language of the essay. *Bockelson* has enjoyed nothing like the popularity (or notoriety) of, say, Ernst Jünger's *Auf den Marmorklippen* (1939, English translation *On the Marble Cliffs*, 1947—82,000 copies sold by 1942) and did not sell in anything like the numbers of Werner Bergengruen's *Der Großtyrann und das Gericht* (The great tyrant and the court, 1935—60,000 copies by 1941).[82] The style of the work, its hybrid genre, and the absence of any whiff of controversy surrounding its publication in Nazi Germany have doubtless all contributed to this neglect. Beyond this, however, the contentious nature of his views on history, the Renaissance, rationalism, the Enlightenment, and technology, on the one hand, and his association with the discredited Conservative Revolution, on the other, have done nothing to endear him to subsequent readers.

His various critiques of the ills of Western civilization, part cultural historical reflection and part inflammatory reactionary polemic, often repeat themselves and do not make for easy reading. *Bockelson*, however, a work that straddles the fictional/historical divide, stands out for its authenticity, based as it largely is on historical facts; for its lively, not to say fiery, style and colorful language; for its passion and, above all perhaps, for its skillful camouflaging of an oppositional message. The failure of the authorities, even such watchful organs as the *Bücherkunde*, to object to the work is a testament to the success with which Reck managed to veil his criticism of the regime and its leading figures, and to disguise what now appear as striking parallels behind a screen of anticommunist rhetoric, convoluted historical references, red herrings, and plain obfuscation.

The process of narrating the historical events surrounding the Münster uprising served for Reck to keep alive his bitterness at contemporary

Germany, to stoke the fires of his seething anger with National Socialism. But this was not an entirely negative or destructive process since the rage of this "man in despair" was intended to act as a means of sustaining his hopes for the future. There are two aspects to this. On the one hand, Scholdt is right to emphasize the role of *Bockelson* in "de-demonizing" the Nazi regime, of showing that, despite National Socialism's manifold horrors, there was, for the enlightened reader, ultimately something ridiculous, grotesque, and anachronistically medieval about the contemporary regime's bizarre mixture of terror, sectarian idealism, bombastic propaganda, and slapstick farce.[83] More important, on the other hand, is the role played by the story's emphatic prediction of the demise of the reign of terror. Indeed, in the literature of the inner emigration it is difficult to find a more pronounced form of consolation and moral sustenance than Reck's repeated emphasis on the short-lived nature of the Münster dictatorship, on the impending doom of the regime, which he depicts with conspicuous delight, and the gruesome end that awaits the dictator himself. As the final lines of the story suggest, cast inevitably in Reck's customary "decline of the West" terms, this bitter tale of social psychosis, violence, and murder contains the seeds of change and holds the promise of a potentially brighter future: "An den feinsten Barometern der Zeit heute ihr [der Renaissance] mähliches Abebben ablesen zu dürfen, bedeutet jene große Hoffnung, die die Hoffnung einer leidensbereiten und genesenden Generation sein mag" (To be able today to read [the Renaissance's] gradual decline on the most sensitive of barometers of the time offers great hope, possibly the hope of a generation that is ready to suffer and is already starting on its convalescence, 204; my translation). Such a message had the potential to inspire hope, to reassure, and even to act as a call to nonconformity.

Notes

[1] For the sake of brevity, the original form of the author's name is used throughout this chapter.

[2] Alphons Kappeler, *Ein Fall von "Pseudologia phantastica" in der deutschen Literatur: Fritz Reck-Malleczewen: Mit Totalbibliographie*, 2 vols. (Göppingen: Kümmerle, 1975).

[3] The following two paragraphs draw on Kappeler's authoritative overview, *Ein Fall.*, 1:5–12.

[4] Ibid., 1:118–20.

[5] Christine Zeile, "Friedrich Reck: Ein biographischer Essay," in Friedrich Reck, *Tagebuch eines Verzweifelten* (Frankfurt am Main: Eichborn, 1994), 260–61. All subsequent references to this volume are indicated parenthetically in the text as (*T*, page numbers).

[6] Kappeler, *Ein Fall*, 2:502–9.

[7] See, for example, Erich Müller-Gangloff, "Ein Dichter und Deuter der Zeit," *Berliner Hefte für geistiges Leben* 4 (1949): 198–201; and Gérard Imhoff, "Friedrich Reck-Malleczewen," in *Christen im Widerstand gegen das Dritte Reich*, ed. Joël Pottier (Stuttgart: Burg, 1988), 359.

[8] Zeile, "Friedrich Reck," 264.

[9] "Ein Mannsbild namens Prack," *Jahres-Gutachtenanzeiger*, no. 2054 (1936): 91.

[10] "Ein Mannsbild namens Prack," *Gutachtenanzeiger* 2, no. 6 (1936): 2.

[11] Paul Zöckler, "In Memoriam Friedrich Reck-Malleczewen," in Friedrich Reck-Malleczewen, *Bockelson: Geschichte eines Massenwahns* (Wiesentheid: Droemer, 1946), xi–xii.

[12] Anon., "Statt eines besonderen Vorwortes!," *Bücherkunde* 1, nos. 11–12 (1934): 201–3.

[13] The essay appeared in *Widerstand: Zeitschrift für nationalrevolutionäre Politik* 9, no. 9 (1934): 289–95, and was included in Reck's essay collection *Ablauf der Renaissance: Ein Versuch über eine Zeitwende* (1934), which seems not to have made it beyond the manuscript stage (Kappeler, *Ein Fall*, 2:511).

[14] Anon., "Statt eines besonderen Vorwortes!," 203.

[15] Fritz Reck-Malleczewen, *Acht Kapitel für die Deutschen* (Großschönau/Sachsen: Kaiser Verlag, 1934).

[16] Anon., "Acht Kapitel für die Deutschen," *Bücherkunde* 2, no. 2 (1935): 47.

[17] See Günter Mühlberger and Kurt Habitzel, "The German Historical Novel from 1780 to 1945: Utilising the Innsbruck Database," in *Travellers in Space and Time: The German Historical Novel*, ed. Osman Durrani and Julian Preece (Amsterdam: Rodopi, 2001), 5–23.

[18] For a summary see Kappeler, *Ein Fall*, 2:403–4.

[19] Reck designated the two works "Geschichte" (story), using the convenient ambiguity of the German term to suggest both fiction and history. Although historians would certainly not accept their status as historical works, a purely fictional genre descriptor such as "Roman" (novel), as used on the title page of the 1968 Henry Goverts edition of *Bockelson*, is also problematic. Franz A. Hoyer, "Die Wiedertäufer als Modell?: Friedrich Percyval Reck-Malleczewen, *Bockselson: Geschichte eines Massenwahns.* Stuttgart 1968," *Frankfurter Hefte* 24 (1969): 525, refers to *Bockelson* as "ein romanhafter Bericht" (a novel-like report), which captures the essence of Reck's historical fiction and is to be preferred to Kappeler's "Studie" (study), despite the latter's attribution of the term to Reck himself (Kappeler, *Ein Fall*, 2:421). As will become clear, there is considerable artifice at work in Reck's historical writings and, despite his reliance on historical sources, there is at least as much fictional shaping as there is historical inquiry. Where necessary in this chapter, the term "story" will thus be employed to refer to *Bockelson*.

[20] Bernhard Payr, "Gutachten für Verleger: Fritz Reck-Malleczewen: Charlotte Corday," *Börsenblatt für den deutschen Buchhandel* 105, no. 67 (March 21, 1938): 1540.

21 Kappeler, *Ein Fall*, 2:441–42. And also, most recently, Günter Scholdt, "Geschichte als Ausweg?: Zum Widerstandspotential literarischer Geschichtsdeutung in der 'Inneren Emigration,'" in Kroll and von Voss, *Schriftsteller und Widerstand*, 106–7.

22 Erich Müller, "Die Revolution und ihr Racheengel," *Deutsches Adelsblatt* 56, no. 9 (February 26, 1938): 264–65, as cited in Kappeler, *Ein Fall*, 2:445–46.

23 Kappeler, *Ein Fall*, 2:449.

24 Kappeler, *Ein Fall*, 1:8–9.

25 There has been considerable speculation about how precisely he died, including stories of him being shot, but two later testimonies confirm the true circumstances: Max von Riccabona, "F. Reck-Malleczewen," *Der Monat* 18, no. 216 (1966): 94; and Nico Rost, *Goethe in Dachau* (Frankfurt am Main: Fischer Taschenbuch Verlag, 1983), 218–20.

26 Indeed he is highly critical of the group of officers around von Stauffenberg for their betrayal of the monarchy and "the republic" and their all-too-cosy relations with the "industrial oligarchy." See his diary entry for July 21, 1944 (*T*, 222–23).

27 Reck's stance was linked in part to his relationship with his Jewish secretary (and possible mistress), Irma Glaser, who subsequently committed suicide in his flat. It is also claimed by his widow (see Kappeler, 2:452) that Reck was asked by Goebbels to write the screenplay for the film *Jud Süss* (The Jew Süss) but courageously refused, saying his gratitude to Jewish friends made such an undertaking impossible. On the other hand, the novel *Diana Pontecorvo* (1944) contains several derogatory references to Jews among the hated Bolsheviks. See Walter Wenzel, "Widerstandskämpfer des Geistes?," *Geist und Zeit* 1, no. 4 (1956): 137–38.

28 See Mohler and Weißmann, *Die Konservative Revolution*. See also "The Intellectual Background" in chapter 1 of this book.

29 This substantial fragment of a planned critique of human history and contemporary culture, work on which was cut short by Reck's arrest, provides insights into various aspects of the writer's philosophical-historical thinking.

30 See Friedrich Percyval Reck-Malleczewen, *Das Ende der Termiten: Ein Versuch über die Biologie des Massenwahns*, Fragment (Lorch: Bürger, 1946), 87–88; also *T*, 212–13.

31 Friedrich Percyval Reck-Malleczewen, "Vom Reich der Deutschen," in *Was ist das Reich? Eine Aussprache unter Deutschen*, ed. Fritz Buechner (Oldenburg: Stalling, 1932), 51. Hereafter cited parenthetically in the text as "*RD*, page number."

32 Reck-Malleczewen, *Das Ende der Termiten*, 85–86.

33 Cf. ibid., 29, where Reck-Malleczewen asserts the "Massenmensch" is more likely to be found among the state's worthless "card index administrators" and "questionnaire dispatchers" than among the genuinely productive working classes.

34 For a more detailed discussion, see Zeile, "Friedrich Reck," 274–76. Whereas Reck's ideal state was one of sacrifice and an expression of a country's national character, the nation and the nation-state, as understood by contemporary

nationalism, were for him hated products of the French Revolution and ill-suited to form the basis of any state (see *RD*, 57), showing why the Nazis might find him a distinctly uncomfortable bedfellow.

[35] Reck-Malleczewen, *Tagebuch eines Verzweifelten* (1947), subsequently republished in 1966, 1971, 1981, and, incorporating a small amount of newly discovered material, 1994.

[36] The attention of mice seriously damaged the manuscript and made the task of deciphering it particularly challenging for his postwar editor (see Kappeler, *Ein Fall*, 2:465).

[37] Bernt Engelmann, "Vorwort," in Reck-Malleczewen, *Tagebuch eines Verzweifelten* (1981), 10.

[38] Zöckler, "In Memoriam Friedrich Reck-Malleczewen," xxi–xxii.

[39] Kappeler, *Ein Fall*, 2:407. Erwein Freiherr von Aretin was a monarchist and home affairs editor of the *Münchner Neueste Nachrichten*. He was twice arrested during the Third Reich, spending time in Dachau concentration camp in 1933 and later receiving a publication ban.

[40] Letter to Erich Müller of November 15, 1936, cited in Kappeler, *Ein Fall*, 2:413.

[41] Hermann von Kerssenbroch, *Hermanni a Kerssenbroch Anabaptistici furoris: Monasterium inclitam Westphaliae Metropolim Evertentis: Historica narratio*. It was written in the 1550s, published in 1730, and first translated into German in 1771. A revised Latin version, edited in German by H. Detmer, appeared in 1899. This latter version is the one cited by Reck in his bibliography at the end of *Bockelson* and is available online, http://www.archive.org/details/herman niakersse00westgoog (accessed July 10, 2014). The most recent German version is *Geschichte der Wiedertäufer zu Münster in Westfalen*, trans. Simon Peter Widmann (Münster: Verlag der Aschendorffschen Verlagsbuchhandlung, 1929). http://www.google.co.uk/search?tbo=p&tbm=bks&q=bibliogroup:%22Herma nni+a+Kerssenbroch+Anabaptistici+furoris:+monasterium+inclitam+Westphaliae +Metropolim+Evertentis+:+historica+narratio+:+im+Auftrage+des+Vereins+f%C 3%BCr+Vaterl%C3%A4ndische+Geschichte+und+Altertumskunde%22&source= gbs_metadata_r&cad=3

[42] Friedrich Reck-Malleczewen, *Bockelson: Geschichte eines Massenwahns* (Stuttgart: Henry Goverts, 1968), 92. All further references to this edition are indicated by page numbers in the text. English translations are taken from: *A History of the Münster Anabaptists: Inner Emigration and the Third Reich: A Critical Edition of Friedrich Reck-Malleczewen's 'Bockelson: A Tale of Mass Insanity'*, translated and edited by George B. von der Lippe and Viktoria M. Reck-Malleczewen (New York: Palgrave Macmillan, 2008); in a few places I have substituted my own translations and have indicated where this is the case.

[43] Günter Scholdt, "Wiedertäufer und Drittes Reich: Zu einer Verschlüsselung im literarischen Widerstand," in *Literatur und Sprache im historischen Prozess: Vorträge des Deutschen Germanistentages in Aachen 1982*, vol. 1, ed. Thomas Cramer (Tübingen: Niemeyer, 1983), 356–63.

44 See Karl Heinz Schoeps, "Conservative Opposition: Friedrich Reck-Malleczewen's Antifascist Novel *Bockelson: A History of Mass Hysteria*," in Donahue and Kirchner, *Flight of Fantasy*, 196.

45 The following is based on Hans-Jürgen Goertz, *The Anabaptists* (London: Routledge, 1996).

46 Richard van Dülmen, *Reformation als Revolution: Soziale Bewegung und religiöser Radikalismus in der deutschen Reformation* (Munich: dtv, 1995), 364, cited by Schoeps, "Conservative Opposition," 195.

47 Scholdt, "Wiedertäufer und Drittes Reich," 351.

48 Ehrke-Rotermund and Rotermund, *Zwischenreiche*, 540–42.

49 per, "Die Wiedertäufer zu Münster," *Frankfurter Zeitung* 81, no. 269 (May 30, 1937): 6.

50 E. A., "Die Wiedertäufer in Münster," *Hochland* 35, no. 2 (1937): 162. Kappeler's research later revealed the author to be Erwein von Aretin (see note 39 above). See Kappeler, *Ein Fall*, 2:416.

51 Brecht, "Fünf Schwierigkeiten," 82. See also "The Art of Camouflage: Reading and Writing in the Inner Emigration," in chapter 2 of this book on Rudolf Pechel's review of Ivan Solonevich's *Die Verlorenen*: Pechel, "Sibirien," 172–75.

52 See Rudolf Pechel, *Deutscher Widerstand* (Zurich: Rentsch, 1947), 288.

53 Ernst Samhaber, "Massenwahn," *Deutsche Zukunft* 6, no. 2 (January 9, 1938): 10–11.

54 Erich Müller, "Bockelson—eine deutsche Utopie," *Weiße Blätter* 6 (July 1937): 209–10.

55 See Kappeler, *Ein Fall*, 2:428–29. Also Peter Hughes, "Dichtung, Wahrheit, Lüge: Fritz Recks 'Tagebuch eines Verzweifelten,'" *Variations: Literaturzeitschrift der Universität Zürich* 5: *Fälschungen/Faux/Fakes* (2000): 72.

56 See, for example, in 1946, Curt Thesing's note on the back of the title page of *Das Ende der Termiten*, according to which the book was banned immediately after its publication. Also Hoyer, "Die Wiedertäufer als Modell?," 525; and Manfred Müller, "Eine Flucht in Haß und Verzweiflung: Friedrich Reck-Malleczewen, ein Konservativer in der Inneren Emigration," *Frankfurter Rundschau* 26, no. 56 (March 7, 1970): 4.

57 See Kappeler, *Ein Fall*, 2:423, 430–32, and 434.

58 Johannes Tralow, "Die Geschichte eines Massenwahns," *Süddeutsche Zeitung* (Munich) 2, no. 17 (September 26, 1946): 5.

59 Peter Härtling, "Friedrich Percyval Reck-Malleczewen: *Tagebuch eines Verzweifelten*," in *Vergessene Bücher: Hinweise und Beispiele* (Stuttgart: Goverts, 1966), 133–42.

60 Müller, "Eine Flucht in Haß und Verzweiflung," 4. See also the pieces by Joachim Fest, "Wider einen Widerstand: Über Friedrich Reck-Malleczewen: 'Tagebuch eines Verzweifelten,'" in *Literatur im "Spiegel,"* ed. Rolf Becker (Reinbek bei Hamburg, 1969), 188–93; and "In Münster und anderswo: Zu Friedrich Reck-Malleczewens 'Bockelson,'" in *Aufgehobene Vergangenheit: Portraits und*

Betrachtungen, ed. Joachim Fest (Stuttgart: Deutsche Verlags-Anstalt, 1981), 96–114.

[61] Erich Mayser, "Die Leidenschaft verzweifelter Verachtung," *Frankfurter Allgemeine Zeitung*, no. 177 (August 11, 1984).

[62] Friedrich Reck-Malleczewen, *Bockelson: Geschichte eines Massenwahns* (Berlin: Schützen, 1937).

[63] See, for example, letter to Giese of January 2, 1942: "Es ist eine Exegese des Münsterer Wiedertäuferreiches und Sie werden manche seltsame, höchst aktuelle Parallele darin finden. . . ." (It is an exegesis of the Münster Anabaptist Kingdom and you will find some strange and highly contemporary parallels in it. . . .), cited in Kappeler, *Ein Fall*, 2:411–12.

[64] Reck-Malleczewen, *Das Ende der Termiten*, 58.

[65] Ian Kershaw, *Hitler: 1889–1936: Hubris* (London: Allen Lane, 1998), 3–10.

[66] See Joachim Fest, "Vorwort," in Friedrich Reck-Malleczewen, *Bockelson: Geschichte eines Massenwahns*, ed. Joachim Fest (Stuttgart: Goverts, 1968), 14–15.

[67] Cf. Reck's reflection in an earlier diary entry of August 11, 1936, during the composition of *Bockelson*: "[Ich habe] es mehrfach erlebt, daß Kinder ihre Eltern politisch denunzierten und damit ans Messer lieferten" (I have experienced several cases of children denouncing their parents politically, and thereby delivering them to the executioner, *T*, 22).

[68] See Reck's diary entry for March 1943: "Die Schnellgerichte . . . arbeiten prompt, sie fällen Todesurteile auf Grund von fünfminutigen Verhandlungen. . . . Man köpft für Bagatellen, man köpft für Zweifel am guten Ausgang dieses für jeden Einsichtigen längst verlorenen Krieges . . . und man köpft natürlich besonders gern wegen jeder Beleidigung des größten Feldherrn aller Zeiten." (The Summary Courts . . . work quickly, sentencing people to death after no more than a five-minute trial. . . . Heads roll for a bagatelle: they roll for expressing doubts about the outcome of a war that anyone with any sense knew was lost long ago . . . and, of course, they roll especially if anyone insults the Greatest General of All Time, *T*, 203.)

[69] Lippe and Reck-Malleczewen, *A History of the Münster Anabaptists*, 66 n2.

[70] Kershaw, *Hitler*, 351–52. See also Reck's Diary: "Nota bene gibt es auf dem Obersalzberg einen kompletten Harem von jungen Mädchen, die ganz nach dem Muster des Bockelsonschen [. . .] vor dem großen Manitu tanzen" (Nota bene: there is a whole harem of young girls on the Obersalzberg who dance before the Great Spirit exactly as the women did for Bockelson, *T*, 116–17).

[71] George B. von der Lippe, "Translator's Preface," in Lippe and Reck-Malleczewen, *A History of the Münster Anabaptists*, xvi.

[72] Reck is again more explicit about the parallel in a diary entry written around the time he was completing *Bockelson*: "Just wie Nazideutschland, so schickt auch Münster seine fünften Kolonnen und Propheten zur Unterminierung der umliegenden Staaten aus, und daß der Münstersche Propagandaminister Dusentschnur [*sic*], just wie sein großer Kollege Goebbels, *gehinkt* hat, ist ein Witz, den die Weltgeschichte sich vierhundert Jahre vorweg nahm." (Exactly as Nazi Germany has done, Münster dispatched its fifth columns and prophets to

undermine neighboring states. The fact that the Münster propaganda minister, Dusentschnur, *limped* like Goebbels is a joke that history preempted by four hundred years, *T*, 20.)

[73] E.g., see *T*, 51.

[74] Reck's irrational concept of "history" is heavily influenced by a metaphysics of fate, which has much in common with that of Ernst Wiechert's ideas on "discontinuity" in Western civilization; see "Ambiguous Cultural Pessimism" in chapter 9 of this book; also John Klapper, "Cultural 'Diskontinuität' and Thematic Continuity: Ernst Wiechert after 1945," *German Life and Letters* 62, no. 4 (2009): 442–44.

[75] Cf. Reck-Malleczewen, *Das Ende der Termiten*, where he draws a parallel between the sociological "Vermassung der Völker" (loss of individual identity for whole peoples) and the physical "Verkrebsung des Einzelmenschen" (contracting of cancer by the individual, 26), both of which are considered to lead inevitably to the death of the respective organism.

[76] Schnell, *Literarische innere Emigration*, 126.

[77] Ibid., 127.

[78] Leopold von Ranke, *Deutsche Geschichte im Zeitalter der Reformation*, vol. 3 (Berlin: Duncker und Humblot, 1840). Reck refers at one point to von Ranke's allegedly sympathetic, indeed positive image of Bockelson (129).

[79] See Lippe and Reck-Malleczewen, *A History of the Münster Anabaptists*, 131.

[80] E.g., see Georg Lukács, *Deutsche Literatur im Zeitalter des Imperialismus: Eine Übersicht ihrer Hauptströmungen* (Berlin: Aufbau-Verlag, 1950), 39.

[81] Fest, "Vorwort," 16.

[82] Lokatis, "Hanseatische Verlagsanstalt,'" 91 and 96.

[83] Scholdt, "Wiedertäufer und Drittes Reich," 368.

Fig. 6.1. Gertrud von le Fort. Photo by Eduard Lasow,
courtesy of Deutsches Literaturarchiv Marbach.

6: Gertrud von le Fort: Religious Wars and the Nazi Present

A LONG WITH SUCH figures as Georges Bernanos, Graham Greene, and Werner Bergengruen, Gertrud von le Fort was one of the foremost Catholic writers of the twentieth century. Since her death in 1971, a small number of her works have remained popular and been widely translated, although there is still no critical or complete edition available, nor even an authoritative biography. Discussion of her writing has for several years been hampered by a tendency toward the "hagiographic,"[1] and the substantial religious content of her work has attracted several interpretations by theologians, which usually feature a narrow focus on the spirituality underlying character and plot. This has resulted in less attention being paid than one might expect to the nature of her particular form of inner emigration.

The Prussian Aristocrat in Search of Religious Meaning

Compared with the many inner emigrants who were ready to share their recollections of the period 1933–45, le Fort was decidedly reserved. All her autobiographical material was published after 1950, and a grand total of 180 pages for someone who, in 1965, was almost ninety represents thin pickings, suggesting extreme selectivity and close editing of her reminiscences.[2] This makes things difficult for the biographer but also renders more complex the job of exploring le Fort as an inner emigrant writer.

Her father was a major in the Prussian army and her religious mother, a descendant of an old Huguenot family, came from landed gentry in the Mark Brandenburg.[3] Le Fort had a privileged upbringing but a deficient informal education. However, under the influence of her father's fascination with both military and general European history, the intellectually gifted youth was, by the age of sixteen, already reading Ranke and Kant.[4] A key experience for the adult le Fort in the period 1904–7, and a possible factor in the later development of her notion of representative sacrifice, was her secret love for a Catholic priest, a love she was forced to renounce.[5] At the age of thirty-two she began to attend university in Heidelberg, studying theology, religion, and history, and it was during her six-year period at the university that she fell under the influence of the cultural historian and theologian Ernst Troeltsch, who was to become her mentor and whose posthumous *Glaubenslehre* (Dogmatics, 1925) she was later to edit.[6] During the First World War, le Fort was a fervent nationalist, convinced of Germany having a just cause and being a morally superior people.[7] She spent the war in relative comfort on the family estate in Boek on the Müritzsee in Mecklenburg, although she also worked for the Red Cross for a time. After the war she suffered, first, the death of her mother in 1918, then the takeover of the family estate by Spartacists, and subsequently its confiscation by the government of Mecklenburg.

In 1922 she moved with her sister to a house in Baierbrunn near Munich, where she was to live for the next seventeen years. It was here that she entered the final stages of her conversion to Catholicism (in 1926), which had begun twenty years earlier, when trips to Rome had first drawn her to both the art and faith of Catholicism. This did not represent a break with the Protestant faith of her upbringing but was rather the logical conclusion of the path she had been following since her youth, under the influence of what she calls her "der Einheit der Kirche zugewandte Innerlichkeit" (inwardness, which was devoted to the unity of the church).[8] Such thoughts foreshadow the ecumenism that informs *Die Magdeburgische Hochzeit* (The wedding of Magdeburg, 1938), a lifelong conviction that later motivated her to bequeath part of her royalties in equal measure to the Protestant theology faculty of Munich University and the Catholic theology faculty at Heidelberg University.[9] For her conversion she received instruction from the well-known Jesuit theologian Erich Przywara, who was to exert a lasting influence by introducing her to the notion of vicarious sacrifice as an element in the process of divine salvation.[10] Her writing career proper began in the early 1920s, and over the next few years she produced the major narratives that were to bring her international fame.

Le Fort was not a member of the Prussian Academy of Arts, and so in 1933 was not in the position of many writers who had to face either expulsion or the prospect of swearing a loyalty oath. She did join the Reichsverband Deutscher Schriftsteller in December 1933, just before it was subsumed under the new Chamber of Literature (RSK), and was able to remain a member of the RSK until 1945. Following the introduction of universal conscription, she was quoted in a newspaper interview as welcoming the new German Army and the "idea of the new *Reich*."[11] One can, like Hornung-Berk, interpret this charitably as an example of her political naïveté, but it is the sort of statement that ensured the regime's approval of her as a potential nationalist fellow traveler. And indeed there is no evidence of the regime ever taking steps against her or even of serious criticism of her work in official quarters. It is not true that her work was suppressed after 1938, as has been claimed.[12] In fact, a report produced by the Wolfratshausen NSDAP (Nazi Party) in 1939 stated that it was not possible to say anything definite about her political views but that it could be assumed she was not opposed to National Socialism.[13] Furthermore, the Nazis publicly celebrated her birthday in 1941,[14] and all her individual works sold freely. Her book sales were considerable and she became in due course one of the best-selling authors under National Socialism: by 1940 her publications had sold 159,000 copies, and during the period 1935–39 eleven individual translations of her work appeared in seven countries.[15] Of particular note were the nonfictional *Die Ewige Frau* (The eternal woman, 1934), which by 1940 had sold 47,000 copies, and the novella *Die Letzte am Schafott* (1931, translated into English in 1953 as *The Song at the Scaffold*), which had sold 25,000 by the same date. These were among the best-selling books in the whole of Germany at the time.[16] Although, as the war progressed, le Fort experienced difficulties in obtaining paper for her publications, this should not necessarily be interpreted as evidence of official censorship.[17] In 1942 she did decline to write the poem requested of her for the army paper *Münchner Feldpost* on the occasion of Hitler's birthday, saying she could only write about themes that came from within herself and could not respond to externally imposed commissions. However, she subsequently supplied a poem for the same publication, praising the sacrifice of the soldier at the front in strongly patriotic language, a poem that, in the context of a publication that included a contribution from Hitler, was clearly used to appear as support for the regime and its actions.[18]

Shortly after the start of the war, le Fort moved to Oberstdorf in the Allgäu, where, with the exception of a lengthy stay in Switzerland, she spent the rest of her life. The next twenty years saw the writer receive numerous prizes and distinctions, and even in her seventies and eighties she remained productive, writing essays and stories in which she expressed sympathy for the victims of war, including those who died at German hands,[19] Germans killed as a result of allied bombings,[20] and those forced from their homeland.[21] Although by and large a theological traditionalist, she followed with close interest the reformist moves of the Second Vatican Council and was especially encouraged by what she saw as a thaw in relations between Christian sects,[22] a theme to which she devoted her final work, the story *Der Dom* (The cathedral, 1968), where Magdeburg Cathedral stands as a symbol for the healing of the divisions within Christianity.

From Catholic Spirituality to the Christian *Reich*

Le Fort's work is dominated by what she sees as the commonality of literature and Christianity. She compares theologians' talk of the naturally occurring human soul (*anima naturaliter christiana*) with the essence of literature and asserts that literature inevitably contains an element of the Christian. This is because great literature is less concerned with the successful and the contented than with the unfortunate, those who have lost

214 ◆ Gertrud von le Fort: Religious Wars and the Nazi Present

their way, and the guilty.[23] Biser duly asserts that le Fort's historical fictional portraits and descriptions are all merely different reflections of the soul's "dramatic path to God."[24] This points to the problematic nature of Christian literature: the simply structured and inevitably optimistic message of Christianity sits awkwardly with the demands of literary tension, which, alongside the prospect of salvation, requires the existence of genuinely tragic possibilities. Lessing argues that good Christian tragedy is inconceivable,[25] for regardless of the outcome (martyrdom or reconciliation) the very awareness of divine mercy and salvation deflates dramatic tension. As Elisabeth Langgässer further explains:

> Die Fabel der christlichen Heilsgeschichte und damit auch die Fabel des christlichen Romans ist von bestürzender Monotonie, von erschütternder Einfachheit. Ihre Elemente heißen Sünde, Gnade und Erlösung, und wenn diese Elemente auch in jeder einzelnen menschlichen Seele andere Farben annehmen . . ., so ist doch die Grundstruktur des Erlösungsgeschehens einfach und unabänderlich wie das Mysterium selbst; sie ist von der Eintönigkeit einer Fuge, der Eintönigkeit des Ewigen.[26]

> [The plot of the Christian story of salvation and thus the plot of the Christian novel is one of startling monotony, of shocking simplicity. Its elements are sin, mercy, and redemption, and though these elements take on different colors in each individual human soul . . ., the basic structure of redemptive action is simple and immutable like the mystery itself; it has the uniformity of a fugue, the uniformity of the eternal.]

The closed dramatic nature of le Fort's work is no doubt part of the reason why her narratives have not found much resonance beyond a Christian (and largely but by no means exclusively Catholic) readership. Although there is no questioning her literary craft and linguistic power, the nonreligious reader might be forgiven for thinking that if you have followed the spiritual journey of one le Fort protagonist, you are not going to be surprised by that of others. However, it is precisely the way this consistent religious view of existence, in particular its emphasis on the centrality of Christian morality and ethics, is held up against the perverse ideals of National Socialism and is affirmed as a core and inalienable element of German culture that makes le Fort a significant nonconformist writer.

Another striking feature of her writing is that her figures are often less than fully rounded, as she has a tendency to present them as *types*, as representatives of certain principles or ideals, whether that be the young religious person who assumes the role of vicarious sufferer or the convert who emerges triumphant from a battle with the opposing external forces of atheism and religious neurosis. Although her fictional characters from the twelfth, sixteenth, or eighteenth centuries are drawn with convincing period detail and an (albeit limited) degree of psychological motivation, one is always aware of them appearing *sub specie aeternitatis*, as figures standing for beliefs or a philosophy applicable to all periods of history.[27] Here again, however, a potential literary weakness represents a nonconformist strength, as her work largely falls into that category of inner emigrant historical writing that uses the fictional past to assert the universal significance of values, the suprahistorical relevance and timeless nature of key issues and phenomena, and that invites the esoteric reader to apply these values to the contemporary German situation under National Socialism.

Le Fort became established as a writer only at the age of forty-seven with her volume of thirty-seven psalm-like poems, *Hymnen an die Kirche* (1924, English translation *Hymns to the Church*, 1938), which exemplify the intense religiosity of her writing. They were an expression of the life-changing spiritual turmoil she underwent in the early 1920s and represented a significant milestone in her religious conversion, indeed she viewed them as the "foundation" of all her work.[28] Taking the form of a dialogue between the author and the church, these mystical songs, whose imagery reflects the romantic influences of, in particular, Joseph Eichendorff, lack any reference to the social, psychological, or political, being exclusively concerned with spiritual searching and, increasingly, the identity and universal role of the church.

The two novels that have been given the umbrella title of *Das Schweißtuch der Veronika* (English translation *The Veil of Veronica*, 1970), namely, *Der römische Brunnen* (The Roman fountain, 1928) and *Der Kranz der Engel* (The wreath of angels, 1946), record the story of le Fort's own faith and conversion. The first volume, part bildungsroman, is the first-person story of the young German Veronika in Rome and her life there with her grandmother, and her aunt and guardian, the neurotically religious Edelgart. A key element is the burgeoning relationship between Veronika and Enzio, a wild nihilistic poet and Nietzschean intellectual who has little time for religious faith. Caught between conflicting powerful forces—modern Roman Christianity, Enzio's wild Dionysian impulsiveness, her grandmother's ordered Apollonian concern with the heathen classical ideals of ancient Rome, Edelgart's troubled faith, and her own love for Enzio—Veronika is drawn increasingly to the Catholic faith and the novel ends with her conversion.

The historical novel *Der Papst aus dem Ghetto: Die Legende des Geschlechtes Pier Leone* (The pope from the ghetto: The legend of the lineage of Pier Leone, 1930) adopts the narrative form of old chronicles. Set in eleventh- and twelfth-century Rome, it concerns Pier Leone, son of a wealthy Jew, his false election to the papacy as Antipope Anacletus II, and his subsequent flight and replacement by Innocent II. Le Fort focuses on the contentious role of Jews in the Christian scheme of redemption, and the novel, her response to the rising tide of anti-Semitism in contemporary Weimar Germany, offers a powerful picture of Jewish humanity and religious belief. She downplays theological differences and emphasizes the common ground of Judaism and Christianity. Although at one point she, prophetically, provides a chilling vision of the Rhine as "rot und brausend . . . vom Blut der deutschen Juden" (red and foaming . . . with the blood of German Jews, 2, 58) and presents anti-Semitism as an unchristian impulse, her interest here is not in ethnic or racial issues but in religious and ethical ones.[29] The novel makes clear that spirit always takes precedence over blood, and the objections of the "blond capitane" (2, 18) to Pier Leone's election are countered in the novel by the words of the Cardinal Chancellor Heimericus: "Auch der heilige Petrus war ein Sohn Israels!" (St. Peter was a son of Israel too, 2, 187).

Set at the time of the French Revolution and based on an actual historical event that le Fort had studied in the archives of Munich University,[30] the classical novella *Die Letzte am Schafott* represents one of her finest, most convincing psychological portraits. It enjoyed commercial success in the Third Reich and after the war, and over the years it has been translated into fifteen languages and adapted for both screen and stage.[31] Narrated in the form of a letter written in Paris in 1794 by a French nobleman, Herr von Villeroi, it relates the events he witnessed during the final days of the revolution, specifically the execution of sixteen Carmelite nuns and the death of the young noblewoman Blanche de la Force. When the nuns are led, singing, to the gallows to be executed, the latter leaves the safety of the jeering crowd in order to share their fate; she sings their hymn to its conclusion but, before reaching the scaffold, is murdered by the angry mob. It is a story of moral frailty and trust in God, of standing up for one's beliefs by acknowledging and staying faithful to Christ's example on the cross. It contains little apparent contemporary reference, although the terror and oppression are presented as universal, and occasional statements can readily be applied to the increasing extremist violence on German streets.

The collection of poems *Hymnen an Deutschland* (Hymns to Germany, 1932) had its origins in the period after the First World War and they reflect, on the one hand, le Fort's sense of disorientation and disillusionment with the Versailles settlement, and on the other, her views on German nationalism as they had developed amid Catholic deliberations on the notion of the *Reich*. The poems mix notions of guilt, the cross, and divine mercy with Germany's supposed fate and calling, and feature nationalist, even chauvinistic sentiments and images. For example, in the first section of the cycle, "Das Schicksal" (Fate), the wings of the imperial eagle are seen to beat for the world as a whole, and in the second section, "Die Sendung" (Mission), one finds descriptions of Germany as

a "colossus" among peoples and as "Kaiservolk der Erde, berufen zur
Krone" (imperial people of the earth summoned to the crown).[32] What
le Fort is doing here is pursuing thoughts of a monarchist restoration
and presenting the old idea of Christendom as an alternative to contemporary distortions of the *Reich*: Germany is endowed with Christ-like
features and dubbed a "redeemer," while Germans are a chosen people
who bear suffering on behalf of other peoples.[33] However, since it was
not difficult to adapt to a *völkisch* national agenda the recurrent idea of a
German empire divinely ordained to exercise power over Christianity, the
collection was appropriated by the Nazi regime,[34] most notably in a carefully chosen selection of four hymns featuring references to the *Reich*.[35]
Yet there was also official recognition that the religious notion of empire
being promoted by such Christians as le Fort was a dissident one that
threatened to undermine the Nazi concept of the *Reich*.[36]

Religious Continuity and the Challenge of Nazism

The year 1933 did not mark any sort of caesura in le Fort's work as she
continued to write unhindered, publishing seven books up until 1945.
Thematically, too, continuity was in evidence as she further pursued the
notion of Christian empire in the legend *Das Reich des Kindes* (The kingdom of the child, 1934), about the birth of the religious idea of the *Reich*
amid the ruins of the Carolingian empire. At the same time, she was working on a series of three nonfictional texts on the idea of womanhood and
femininity. In the resultant book, *Die Ewige Frau*, she distances herself
from the feminist movement and modern science in order to promote a
symbolic religious understanding. Women are naturally directed toward
the religious[37] and, thanks to the special status of Mary, have a symbolic
role as *sponsa* (bride of Christ), as virgin, and as mother in the divine plan.
Besides expressing deeply conservative views on marriage and family life
(83–87) and on the supposed "tragedy" of childlessness (45), she identifies
the essence of the metaphysical role of the feminine as "Stellvertretung"
(representative or vicarious suffering),[38] an idea much influenced by the
work of Edith Stein, with whom le Fort had close links.[39] The reception
of *Die Ewige Frau* by the Nazi press was mixed, with extracts appearing
in magazines that supported a Nazi view of motherhood but criticism also
being made of the book's positive portrayal of female celibacy and "spiritual
motherhood," which were seen as incompatible with Nazi encouragement
for women's procreative role.[40] However alienated today's reader might
be by this book, and whatever similarities there are between le Fort's ideas
and Nazi ideals of motherhood and sacrifice, the work does point to the
author's increasing distance from National Socialism and shows the idea of
representative suffering starting to inform her particular brand of spiritual
inner emigration from the regime.

The novella *Die Abberufung der Jungfrau von Barby* (The maiden of Barby is called away, 1940) is one of a number of short prose works written under National Socialism that reveal le Fort's credentials as an inner emigrant writer. It is set during the days of Reformation iconoclasm in 1524 and shows how even the destruction of the outward symbols of religion, here seen in a physical attack on the blessed sacrament, cannot stop the efficacy of the sacraments and of divine grace. The work is a statement of the church's resilience in the face of persecution and highlights the power of individual sacrifice in the shape of the young mystic nun, the maiden of Barby, who is "called away" from her true self when she has ecstatic visions of the destruction of all the images of Christ and the saints, and envisions Mechthild of Magdeburg urging her to realize the idea of vicarious atonement. Although the abbess considers the maiden's ecstasies to be the spiritual counterpart of the iconoclasts' "Godless" behavior and an act of disobedience, in due course the maiden suffers for the sake of the abbess, being killed in her cell when the mob storms the convent, a sacrifice in imitation of Christ, it is suggested. By seeing contemporary equivalents in the iconoclastic "Schwarmgeister" (or zealots, 3, 95), one can interpret the work as a response to Nazi attacks on "degenerate" art and literature deemed hostile to the regime.[41] At the same time, one might be inclined to see in the attacks on the convent a more general parallel with Nazi aggression toward the church.

The theme of vicarious suffering can be further found in what is perhaps le Fort's most powerful short prose work from the Third Reich, the novella *Die Consolata* (1947), which, though written in about 1943, could not be published until after the war owing to its strong contemporary allegory. It depicts the final days of the tyrannical rule of Ansedio in medieval Padua, the point at which the city is about to be freed by papal soldiers. The stipulation of the liberating forces is that the citizens themselves overthrow the dictator, but their inability or reluctance to do so reflects the extent to which evil infects people under an oppressive dictatorship and undermines their capacity for resistance. Ansedio has committed all manner of atrocities in oppressing the people and they have consequently lost the ability to distinguish right from wrong, truth from lie. This is just one of several implied parallels with Nazi Germany in the story. Others include: the portrayal of the extent to which evil regimes depend on the compliance of the many; the question of the fellow traveler, guilt and responsibility (3, 224); the large numbers of citizens who have gone into exile or been banished (3, 226); and the opponents who have stayed and are killed without trial (3, 228–29). A group of local Franciscan lay brothers, the "Consolata," support the suffering population, comfort the sick and oppressed, and help others to flee into exile. The prayers and sacrifice of the aptly named brotherhood, along with the mercy they show the tyrant, stand as testimony to the power of the spirit in resisting oppression. A further theme is the nature of evil as mere appearance, founded on the "powerlessness of the good" (3, 234). There is consolation here but also a reminder that evil can only flourish when the good through their own omission allow it to. The ending, where the lay brothers tend to the soul of the despot and the papal legate ensures a fair trial for Ansedio's adherents rather than allowing the angry masses to exact their revenge, represents a powerful reinforcement of this central message of reconciliation and justice.

A third significant inner emigrant short prose work from the Nazi era is the story *Das Gericht des Meeres* (The court of the sea, 1943) about Anne de Vitré, a thirteenth-century Breton woman who is captured by the troops of the English King John and subsequently killed by a Breton patriot for failing—out of maternal compassion—to take the opportunity to kill the sovereign's son and avenge her people's suffering. She is thus another le Fort female protagonist who affirms her role as sustainer of life and, through self-sacrifice, bears witness to the truth. It is claimed le Fort wrote this story after learning for the first time about children being killed in the gas chambers, although the publication history makes this questionable.[42] Perhaps more credible is the claim that it refers to Nazi euthanasia practices, as condemned by August Graf von Galen on August 3, 1941.[43] Be that as it may, the following words certainly carry significance for contemporary German crimes and guilt more generally:

> Es gibt nichts Ruchloseres auf Erden, als ein Kind zu ermorden. . . . Wenn man zu einem Verbrechen schweigt, so willigt man in dasselbe ein, und ich habe doch dazu geschwiegen—jeder einzelne von uns . . . wir haben geschwiegen, daß es zum Himmel schrie. Wir haben gegessen und getrunken, als ob nichts geschehen wäre . . . die Richter schliefen auch—sie mußten ja schlafen—man befahl ihnen doch. (3, 209)

> [There is nothing more infamous than to kill a child. . . . If one is silent in the face of a crime, one acquiesces in it, and I was silent about it—each of us was . . . we were so silent that our silence cried to heaven. We ate and drank as if nothing had happened. . . . The judges also slept, they had to sleep for they were ordered to.]

Throughout the war, le Fort worked on the novel *Der Kranz der Engel*, the sequel to *Der römische Brunnen*. In the new, secularized setting of Heidelberg, Veronika's relationship with the atheist Enzio proves problematic as he develops nationalist beliefs stoked by resentment at the Versailles settlement, threatening Veronika's religiously informed ideas of the German nation. Enzio is depicted as a "blond German type" (1, 347), a typical indignant product of the disenfranchised post-1918 generation and a representative figure of National Socialism. He is consequently seen by Veronika's professor and guardian as a threat to essentially Christian German culture (1, 546). In the problematic ending to the novel, Enzio, when faced with Veronika's serious illness, decides to call for a priest, leading to a precipitate reconciliation. His action is a "Bußgang" (act of penitence, 1, 656) and he is now prepared to accept the sacramental marriage he had earlier rejected. The work's claim to nonconformism resides in its characteristically heavy religiosity, in the hope it offers of overcoming National Socialism through faith and devotion to one's fellow man, and in its positing of religious spirituality as a positive "counterpole" to the nihilist ideals of the time.

After the war, the by now seventy-year-old le Fort attracted considerable international attention with her talk "Unser Weg durch die Nacht" (Our way through the night, 1947), a look into the "abyss" of the contemporary world, which included a statement that the author was grateful for having experienced her country's dark trauma and the deeply controversial claim that the shattering events of the recent past had produced fruitful insights, had enriched humanity through a renewed religious awareness and need.[44] She makes a plea for the reality of Christian love, which consists in recognizing the full horrors of the depths to which mankind can sink and yet still seeking to understand and forgive,[45] and concludes with a plea for such love to be shown to Germans. The speech's humanitarian spirit of compassion and Christian forgiveness, along with the inevitable theme of representative suffering, inform much of le Fort's subsequent literary work, most of which features historical subject matter; for example, the highly regarded story "Am Tor des Himmels" (At the gates of heaven, 1954, 3, 459–522), concerning Galileo Galilei's trial before the Inquisition for promoting heliocentrism. Le Fort also applies her critical spirituality to contemporary issues, as in the essay "Der Christ im Atomzeitalter" (Christians in the nuclear age, 1958), which raises concerns about the destructive potential of technology. Similarly, in the partly autobiographical story Das fremde Kind (The alien child, 1961) and the legend "Die Tochter Jephtas" (Jephta's daughter, 1964), prompted by the Eichmann trial in 1961,[46] she touches on the persecution of Jews under National Socialism and German guilt.

The Uses of History

In her consistent deployment of historical material and settings, le Fort is not concerned primarily with faithful portrayal and does not place royalty or religious leaders at the center of her fiction, but rather focuses on key turning points that allow her to explore issues of universal significance, in particular fear, temptation, hatred, violence, and evil, and to develop ideas on a Christian Reich. Ever since the early Middle Ages, Christianity has held dear the notion of a Christian social order as embodied in the ninth-century rule of Charlemagne, the first Holy Roman Emperor, and in the success of the Western European Carolingian empire more generally. This focus on medieval Christendom was a feature of the thinking of the *renouveau catholique*, associated in France with the writers Georges Bernanos, Léon Bloy, Paul Claudel, and the philosopher Jacques Maritain. In Germany, it played a considerable role as an imagined ideal of the *Reich* among such Catholic intellectuals as Theodor Haecker, Karl Muth, Alois Dempf, Peter Wust, and others, like le Fort, more loosely associated with the journal *Hochland*.[47] Although, as seen with *Hymnen an Deutschland*, the general notion of a German Christian empire brought its adherents into dangerous ideological proximity to the Nazis, the specific conception of a state informed by religious ideas allowed the circle around Muth to develop a position opposed to Nazi historiographical emphasis on the national state and *völkisch* racist ideology.[48]

In mining the past for the raw material of her narratives, le Fort rejected the idea that to use history was to turn away from the present. Reflecting on the origins of *Die Letzte am Schafott*, for example, she calls it an example of her tendency to "reflect back into the past" contemporary issues and figures in order to be able to shape them more purely and calmly from a distance.[49] Elsewhere she develops this notion of "distance" to defend her choice of historical settings, affirming that the historical is never a form of flight from one's own time but a means of gaining perspective on present-day human problems by taking a step back, just as the shape of mountains becomes clearer from a distance.[50] Quite apart from not constituting avoidance of contemporary issues, historical narrative was a means of facing up to and engaging with them at those periods when they manifested themselves most prominently and directly. Indeed, as far back as 1935, in a reading she openly stated that history was merely a "cloak" for topical problems.[51]

Although such thoughts seem to bring le Fort into line with other writers of nonconformist historical fiction employing camouflage techniques, she saw her work going beyond this, in not just using the past to illuminate the present but also in dealing with a past that people had failed to come to terms with at the time.[52] This is a telling qualification, as it reveals an essential difference from the approach to history of, for example, Reinhold Schneider, Fritz Reck-Malleczewen, or Stefan Andres. In the latter's work the dissenting message may at times be veiled and encourage an esoteric reading, but the authorities frequently recognized the nonconformist reference to the present—notwithstanding occasional initial "misjudgments," as in the case of Jochen Klepper's or Werner Bergengruen's novels. In le Fort's writing, by contrast, the primary focus on tackling the issues of the past is dominant and, notwithstanding her theoretical reflections above, the link to the present can prove quite tenuous, with the result that readers might be forgiven for failing to apprehend whatever significance for contemporary Germany the work contains. The occasional startling sentence, which in other nonconformist writers' work might stop the reader in his or her tracks, is largely absent here, and le Fort's works' rootedness in and apparently exclusive focus on self-contained chapters of history not surprisingly meant the authorities—even after 1938 when she became "unerwünscht" (undesirable)—had no problem allowing a writer with, as they saw it, proven nationalist credentials to continue to publish, hold public readings, and travel with relative freedom.

Le Fort's historical analysis of Germany's National Socialist past, as reflected in her postwar Zurich lecture and her essays, is colored by an omnipresent and invasive sense of German guilt, which prevents her attempting even the sort of, albeit flawed and skewed, analysis of historical and political causes that we find in Reck-Malleczewen's writing. Remarkably, she talks about the First World War in terms of the "Wehmut deutungslosen Geschehens" (melancholy of meaningless events),[53] betraying thereby her essential apoliticism, her reluctance to seek empirical reasons for the events of her times, and her insistent, almost inevitable, it seems, metaphysical approach to both the key questions of existence and the central events of history. For Pottier, one of the keenest commentators of her work, her naïveté in political matters caused her often to lose sight of the broader context. However, he suggests her metaphysical standpoint, her look into the darkest reaches of human nature, along with the rich imagery and symbolism of her writing, were ample and eloquent compensation.[54] Nowhere are both these strengths and weaknesses as a writer of historical fiction more clearly illustrated than the novel *Die Magdeburgische Hochzeit*.

Genesis and Publication of *Die Magdeburgische Hochzeit* (1938)

The novel distinguishes itself from the other works discussed in this book in that it offers fewer parallels with or references to the reality of Nazi Germany. Its significance lies rather in its championing of a humanist standpoint as a "Gegenbild" (counterimage) to the values of National Socialism and in its enactment of and reflection on the issue of inner emigration. It also demonstrates with particular clarity le Fort's tendency to seek the origins of historical phenomena in the realm of the metaphysical.

The idea for the novel came during a visit to Magdeburg in 1934. Allowed into the cathedral for a personal viewing, le Fort was inadvertently locked in for several hours and, reflecting in the increasing darkness on the inscription to a Protestant vicar named Bake, who during the Thirty Years War had taken several hundred citizens into the church to seek refuge while the city burned, she felt the past come alive; by the time she was let out, the idea for the narrative had formed in her mind.[55]

Originally conceived as a novella, the work was written during a period of recuperation from severe bronchial problems in Arosa, Switzerland, where le Fort spent fourteen months during 1937 and 1938. It was to be the final novel she wrote. The original plan inspired by the Bake story had been for a narrative about religious conflict set against the background of war, but it is clear that the final product, possibly under the influence of the emigration atmosphere of Arosa, became a more complex work, including an enactment of the exile–inner emigration debate and the elaboration of appropriate responses to tyranny. The title derives from fliers common in 1630–31, which labeled the Catholics' conquest of the city "the wedding of Magdeburg." The work reveals le Fort's characteristically thorough research of historical background, and the frequent references to specific figures and events of the time show that the narrative is largely based on historical fact.[56]

Summary

Set in 1630–31 in the middle of the religious strife and complications of the Thirty Years War and written in a slightly archaic language that recalls the chronicle-like style of le Fort's *Der Papst aus dem Ghetto*, the novel focuses on the fate of the city of Magdeburg, which has been Lutheran for more than a century and lies between the warring fronts of the Protestant Swedes and the Papists. The emperor's Edict of Restitution of 1629 has decreed that the Protestants return all the property of the Catholic Church that it acquired over the past century, the aim being to marginalize Protestants and to make the German *Reich* a Catholic entity. In the novel, this unreasonable and intolerant stance of the emperor and the Jesuits has led Magdeburg to consider switching its allegiance to the Swedes. The restitution forces, led by the military general and Jesuit scholar Graf von Tilly, reach the city under orders to enforce the imperial edict there too.

Strategically, Magdeburg is important for the imperial troops since by besieging the city it is hoped they can draw the forces of Swedish King Gustav Adolf away from Silesia to come to the aid of Magdeburg. From the Swedish point of view, however, it is important that the city rejects a peace accord with the imperial troops and holds out against the emperor so that his forces remain tied up there and the Swedes can retain their hold over Silesia.

The invading Swedish general and near-dictator Falkenberg thus seeks to persuade the city council to ally itself with Sweden, to reject attempts to return Magdeburg to the control of the emperor, and to repel any attack by the imperial forces. The key issue facing the councilors is whether the city should remain true to its Protestant faith and thus accept Swedish control, thereby surrendering its privileged position as a free state of the Catholic

Reich, or whether it should give in to considerable pressure from the emperor and his military commanders, accept the return of Catholicism, and play the role expected of it in defending the *Reich* against Sweden.

The relationship between Willigis Ahlemann, a Protestant town councilor, and the young maiden Erdmuth Plögen provides a parallel with the political and military action of the novel. At the profession of their vows in the cathedral, the minister, Bake, links the young couple's fate to that of the city by preaching a sermon that calls for resistance to the imperial Catholic forces; he holds out the prospect of help from the advancing Swedish king and urges alignment with Sweden in order to defend the Protestant faith. The sermon causes Willigis to leave the cathedral and to abandon his bride-to-be. Willigis goes to meet with other members of the city council and is sent by them as a negotiator to his uncle, a former council member loyal to the emperor. Erdmuth waits for Willigis to return for her on her "Jungfrauenabend" (maiden evening), but when he fails to appear she doubts his love for her and subsequently, out of wounded pride and a desire for spiteful revenge, succumbs to the advances of Falkenberg, who deceives her about his intention to marry her in order to persuade the city to embrace Swedish rule.

Willigis remains opposed to the Swedes and is exiled from the city when the council decides to side with Falkenberg. Tilly's generals advise storming Magdeburg immediately but Tilly, the convinced Catholic Christian, wants to avoid the destruction of the city on humanitarian grounds. He therefore tries, unsuccessfully, to get the emperor to agree to a temporary suspension of the edict and a reprieve for Magdeburg. Meanwhile Willigis has joined the imperial army and pleads with Tilly, who is now under a direct imperial command to attack the city, to delay his advance. The latter agrees to a stay of execution and a tight ultimatum for the city to sign a surrender, and Willigis returns there incognito to persuade the council to reconsider. However, he discovers that Falkenberg, who is already in the city, has got the council on his side and is about to marry Erdmuth. In this way she is shown to symbolize the Protestant city of Magdeburg's proud, defiant attitude toward the Catholic imperial forces.

The ultimatum runs out and Tilly has no choice but to order the attack. The city is devastated, fire spreads rapidly, and virtually the only building that is not reduced to ashes is the cathedral, where Bake and a small number of citizens have managed to find refuge. Falkenberg is killed during the onslaught and Erdmuth is raped by a Croatian soldier of the imperial army. However, she and Willigis are finally reconciled and are married in the cathedral. Following the battle, a mass is celebrated there for the victorious forces; although the Catholic liturgy is alien to the Protestant Bake, who is forced to flee the now officially Catholic city, he is moved by the common creed shared by the confessions and the novel ends with his recognition of the unity of the Christian faith.

Reception

Although critical attention was limited, the work was generally positively reviewed by those papers and journals that did choose to discuss it. Thus, in a review in the *Kölnische Zeitung*, Dettmar Heinrich Sarnetzki calls it a work "of the highest order" but also notes it has significance beyond its historical setting and considers the exiled Willigis to be "der typische Deutsche jener und auch so mancher andern unglückseligen Zeit unsrer deutschen Vergangenheit" (the typical German of that and so many other hapless periods of German history).[57]

Bernt von Heiseler too sees relevance beyond the seventeenth-century setting: "Hier ist an einer historischen Begebenheit etwas immer Geltendes, Gegenwärtiges gefühlt: eine Tragik und Notwendigkeit, welche die unsere ist" (Here in a historical event there is a sense of something always valid and current: a tragedy and a necessity that is our own). Identifying the central theme as the indissoluble link between faith and *Reich*, he calls le Fort the writer for those who carry within themselves both the Christian and the German "als ein untrennbares Licht" (as an indivisible light).[58]

Hans Pflug-Franken in *Die Literatur* describes the novel as a work that is equally strong in its command of history and its poetic exploration of the theme. He concludes, perhaps pointedly, by saying that the book is: "ein dichterisches und reifes Werk, in dem das Unausgesprochene webt und wirkt" (a mature literary work that is interwoven and knitted together by the unspoken).[59] The likelihood of this constituting a coded message that there is more to this book than meets the eye is supported by the fact that the author, a former feuilleton editor with the Magdeburg paper *Der Mitteldeutsche*, had resigned his post and distanced himself from the Nazi publishing machine.

Reinhold Schneider's review in *Eckart* provides a classic inner emigrant interpretation. He says the novel depicts a world that has lost its sense of order, and he sees the focal point of the historical narrative to be the conflict between the inseparable vital forces of faith and the *Reich*; but behind these lies divine justice, which is to be achieved not by the power of the sword but through suffering. He thus considers the novel a "tröstliches Buch" (a consoling book); the order of the world has been shaken, but beyond the devastation one can discern "die Ordnung der Liebe, der Geduld und Demut, auf die diese zerrüttete Welt angewiesen ist, wenn sie genesen soll" (the order of love, patience, and humility, which this shattered world has to rely on if it is to recover).[60]

One slightly critical review in *Hochland* objects to the overworked metaphor of the maiden of Magdeburg and to the obtrusive impression of a "rational allegorical interpretation," which denies characters a life of their own; the heartless and domineering Falkenberg, in particular, is seen as lacking the intellectual and spiritual standing to make him a credible

figure. In light of the contrived ending, designed to reflect the wider reconciliation of Christian faiths in the personal fates of Erdmuth, Willigis,
and Bake, the reviewer concludes: "Alle Figuren sind mit der Aura einer
gedanklich konzipierten Ideologie umgeben" (All the characters are surrounded by an aura of a theoretically conceived ideology).[61]

Although it did not attain the high sales figures of *Die Letzte am
Schafott* or of Bergengruen's *Der Großtyrann und das Gericht* (The great
tyrant and the court), *Die Magdeburgische Hochzeit* sold well, and indeed
continued to do so for several years, reaching the fifty thousand mark by
1950.[62] Later scholars have tended to pay greater attention to le Fort's
Das Schweißtuch der Veronika novels and *Die Letzte am Schafott* than to
Die Magdeburgische Hochzeit but have noted with approval the superior
blend of thought and action in the latter.[63]

Forbearance and Moral Example

The novel depicts through the city of Magdeburg a world that has lost its
connection with the supposed divine order. As he witnesses the devastation wrought by the war throughout northern Germany, Willigis reflects
on the causes of the city's plight:

> Denn, wenn alles was erschaffen ist zur Geduld und zur Sanftmut und
> zum Gehorsam, aus der Ordnung springt, wenn keiner mehr warten
> und demütig sein und auch einmal Unrecht dulden will, dann bleiben
> eben nur Stolze und Trotzige und Herrschsüchtige übrig—also muß
> ja diese Welt zerbrechen, und wahrlich, es geschieht ihr recht! (2, 403)

> [For when everything that is created to be patient, meek, and obedi-
> ent loses its sense of order, when no one is prepared any longer to
> wait and to be humble and even to tolerate injustice, then all that
> remains are the proud, the defiant, and the tyrannical—and this
> world is therefore bound to collapse and, truly, it serves it right!]

The strong message of forbearance, tolerance of wrongdoing, and subor-
dination to a higher order is a classic statement of inner emigrant quietism
and points to the central conflict of faith and conscience that assailed both
seventeenth-century Magdeburg and inner emigrants under National
Socialism: whether the injunction to show unflinching loyalty and obedience to the state extends to obeying even an unjust ruler (2, 342–43).
This linking of religion and politics is adumbrated at the start of the novel
in Dr. Gilbert's reaction to Bake's sermon, which he interprets as a call
for a popular revolt. Bake is horrified at this, saying he thought he was
merely reiterating the council's view and that Luther himself would be
appalled by the idea (2, 305). In affirming that man was created by God

to obey and that any move away from such a stance threatened to unleash a "demon" on society, he refers indirectly to *Romans,* chapter 13 (1–2):[64] "Es stehe doch auch in der Heiligen Schrift, daß alle Obrigkeit von Gott verordnet und daß man nicht nur den gütigen und gerechten, sondern auch den ungerechten Herren gehorsamen solle, solche gehörten eben mit zum Kreuz des Christenmenschen" (After all, Holy Scripture also stated that all authority comes from God and that one should obey not only benevolent and just but also unjust masters, for the latter were part of the cross to be borne by Christians, 2, 305).

It is only toward the end of the novel, amid the devastation of the city, that a definitive position is taken on this conflict, when Willigis, who has suffered the dilemma of obeying the emperor and his faith or acting in the interests of his native city, concludes: "Die Stadt muß dem Kaiser geben, was des Kaisers ist,—denn sonst geht der Glaube unter; aber der Kaiser wird Gott geben müssen, was Gottes ist,—denn sonst geht das Reich unter" (The city must give the emperor what is the emperor's, for otherwise faith will be destroyed; but the emperor will have to give God what is God's, for otherwise the *Reich* will be destroyed, 2, 488). On the one hand, this is a reaffirmation of the scriptural teaching of submission to "lawful superiors" and the belief that all authority comes ultimately from God; on the other, it argues that the emperor has no power over religious faith and that faith can only be saved through God. This neatly encapsulates not only the archetypal inner emigrant inwardness of le Fort's position with its clear links to Jochen Klepper and Ernst Wiechert but also her religious conception of the *Reich* with its similarity to Schneider's and Bergengruen's ideas on the Kingdom of God. Alongside the sympathetic depiction of the inner emigrant dilemma in the figures of Guericke and Willigis, and the deeply negative allegorical portrayal of the despotic Falkenberg, it is the novel's insistence on the primacy and indivisibility of faith that ultimately constitutes its nonconformist response to National Socialism.

The moral focus of the novel is General Graf von Tilly, described as a "great, intrepid soldier," whom le Fort sees as embodying exemplary humanity and compassion, without which a soldier becomes an agent of barbarism.[65] Tilly's military resolve is shaken by Willigis's intervention on behalf of the city and his request that he delay implementing the edict. Willigis, a Protestant, who also represents and argues for the integrity of the *Reich*, realizes the Lutheran archbishopric of Magdeburg cannot continue under a Catholic archbishop but nevertheless reasons that the city can remain "imperial": "Ich meine, wenn der Glaube nicht angetastet wird, so können wir allesamt gemeinsam den Schweden aus dem Reich schlagen!" (It is my view that if faith is not encroached on, then together we can all of us drive the Swedish out of the *Reich*!, 2, 354). Tilly's Jesuit confessor, on the other hand, represents the triumphalism of the church and advises him against allowing an earthly power to establish itself and drive a wedge between worldly authority and the authority of the church. Tilly, however, is deeply troubled by the divide that seems to be opening between the demands of *Reich* and church. He does not want the destruction of Magdeburg (2, 458–59), but is under pressure from the fanatics at the imperial court in Vienna and indeed his own generals to be merciless. Yet he believes there can be no such thing as a justifiable religious war, that any military conflict offends against the principles of religion and against the teachings of Christ. He sees the sword, or military might, as the last resort and the sole source of mercy (2, 462–63). In this sense, he is portrayed as the conscience of the novel, for he recognizes, first, that the attack on the largely helpless citizens of Magdeburg is immoral, and that second, the *Reich* can only be saved if the emperor reverses the edict and draws back from his determination to spread Catholicism by force of arms, for the attack on the city will only serve to alienate the Protestant subjects of the empire. He therefore dispatches his confessor to Vienna to request that the emperor agree to a delay of forty years in implementing the edict (2, 368–69), although the priest deliberately undermines the plan and ensures the request never reaches the emperor.

While Tilly's forces may be victorious in the storming of the city, he himself, it is suggested, is in the wrong in ordering such action against a Christian city, in causing the death of twenty thousand people, and this outcome is shown to represent the defeat of both empire and church. Tilly himself knows the capture of Magdeburg has not been a victory; it has not closed the gap between the confessions but simply widened it, indeed threatens to cement it ("niemals wird die heilige Kirche wieder einig werden," never will the holy church be one again, 2, 509), for the devastation of the city will simply drive more Protestants into the arms of the Swedish and French enemies of the *Reich*. The rift can only grow wider, he suggests, as long as one fights for Christ using the weapons of this world; the latter merely serve to secure earthly victories, however, "die Welt überwinden kann man nur, wenn man die Welt überwindet!" (we can only overcome the world by overcoming the world!, 2, 509). The young priest, in whom Tilly confides, explains this perspective when he argues that religion itself is innocent of what has happened in the city; what those involved have not realized is that: "Christus siegt nicht im Kampf gegen das Kreuz, sondern am Kreuz—Christus kann das Kreuz der Glaubensspaltung nur am Kreuz der Glaubensspaltung besiegen—Christus siegt nur im Mysterium seiner Liebe!" (Christ triumphs not in the fight against the cross but on the cross—Christ can only defeat the cross of divided faith on the cross of divided faith itself—Christ triumphs only through the mystery of his love!, 2, 510). Division in the Christian church can only be removed through the by now all-too-familiar le Fort theme of vicarious sacrifice: the cross (or burden) of schismatic faith can only be overcome through the sacrifice represented by the crucified Christ. For the priest, this message is religion's riposte to all the forces of division and revolt, and it represents a victory over them (2, 510). This is also the essence of le Fort's inner emigrant response to National Socialism. In keeping with the novel's virtual leitmotif of "Die Liebe vermag alles" (Love can do all things, 2, 516),[66] the response to the tyranny of the present is the quiescent one of self-sacrifice as an expression of the mystery of divine love, a love that paradoxically is at its most triumphant precisely when it is defeated by worldly powers. In this spirit, those who at the start of the work faced each other as enemies experience in the final chapter an ecumenical encounter that points to the common core of a shared Christian faith, a reading confirmed by the very last words of the novel taken from the common Nicene Creed, dating back to the First Ecumenical Council of the church in the year 325: "Confiteor unum baptisma in remissionem peccatorum" (I confess one baptism for the remission of sins, 2, 522).

Tilly's ethical stance on religious war is closely bound up with his attachment to his military standard, a flag bearing the image of the Virgin Mary, signifying mercy and forgiveness. He is in the habit of regularly consulting with this standard to determine his *ratio belli*, or military strategy, and these mystical consultations reveal the division within him. What counts, what helps "to overcome the world," is ultimately not military might or the brutality of fighting but the power of the cross: "Denn Maria siegte nicht mit dem Schwert in der Hand, Maria siegte mit dem Schwert im Herzen, sie siegte durch die leidende Liebe ihres göttlichen Sohnes!" (For Mary did not win with the sword in her hand, Mary won with the sword in her heart, she won through the suffering love of her divine son!, 2, 364). Though he feels duty bound by his professionalism as a soldier and his loyalty to the emperor to carry out his orders faithfully, when he conquers the city and takes possession of little more than a pile of rubble, he realizes he has only succeeded in prolonging and exacerbating the religious war, that the attack on the city has been an unjust and cruel act. It is in part because of this that he seeks to bring a swift end to the three-day plundering of Magdeburg, does all he can to limit its destruction by deploying teams of firefighters (2, 498), orders soldiers to protect women (2, 498–99), and allows bread to be distributed to the survivors (2, 506). This impression of sensitivity to the moral consequences of one's actions is heightened by the contrast with Tilly's two generals, Pappenheim and Mansfeld, who represent overweening ambition and display a callous disregard for the human suffering caused by military conflict.

While Willigis presents key arguments that serve to fuel Tilly's moral dilemma, Tilly in turn plays an important role in Willigis's development by subjecting him to a trial by fire. He sends him back to Magdeburg, not, as Willigis had intended, in the role of strict and merciless judge on his fellow citizens and as avenger of the wrong Falkenberg has done him

230 + ♦ GERTRUD VON LE FORT: RELIGIOUS WARS AND THE NAZI PRESENT

in stealing his bride, but as an emissary bringing the city Tilly's final offer of clemency. Willigis consequently sets out on a bitter path of self-renunciation as a representative of the compassion and mercy symbolized by Tilly's standard. Having read out the general's ultimatum to the council, he catches sight of the flag and his anger recedes, he renounces revenge and becomes a representative of a love that speaks with "the sword in the heart" rather than in the hand. Although the offer of mercy comes too late to change events, Willigis's new-found love ensures he is there in the city's hour of need—in accordance with Guericke's earlier plea that he remain favorably disposed to his native city in spite of everything (2, 402). Tilly has diverted him from the way of proud vengeance and helped him find an authentic Christian path.

Magdeburg and Nazi Germany

Though relatively few in number, the novel's parallels with Germany under National Socialism are significant. At a general level, the work is an accomplished depiction of the conflict of right and wrong in one and the same cause. Just as Tilly's motives in protecting the integrity of the *Reich* are seen as noble but his destruction of the near defenseless city immoral, and just as the right of Magdeburg's citizens to their faith is upheld but their pride and their undermining of the *Reich* is condemned, so German patriotism and the performance of military duty in Nazi Germany conflicted with support for a base and inhuman regime. And it is further not difficult to see in Tilly's inner struggle a working through of some aspects of the dilemma of the Christian conservative military figures associated with the later July 20 plot against Hitler.

More specifically, Falkenberg is conceived as a Hitler figure, a totalitarian ruler, a strong leader with persuasive powers, a great public performer and dissembler, who deceives the people and leads them astray. He also has a violent streak: "Er sagte schneidend . . ., er werde jeden hängen lassen, der auch nur von Akkord rede, aber auch jeden, der an dem königlichen Sukkurs zweifle" (He said sharply that he would have anyone hanged who even dared talk about a peace agreement, as well as anyone who doubted the succor of the Swedish king, 2, 424). He is, furthermore, an alien in the city, a fanatic, a "Besessener" (a man possessed, 2, 435), who seeks to harness a mass and increasingly angry anti-Catholicism. And he ferments war, death, and destruction. At the same time, extending the parallel, the citizens of Magdeburg show a complete lack of ethical judgment and backbone and blindly follow their new authoritarian leader.

This moral blindness applies particularly to Erdmuth, the petit bourgeois representative of the city, who in her pride and self-centeredness is indifferent to the great religious and ideological conflict unfolding around her. In connection with her longing for the arrival of the Swedish king, Falkenberg observes: "sie dachte doch gar nicht an das Schicksal der Stadt, gerade das kam ihm immer so ärmlich und kleinlich an ihr vor, daß sie beständig nur mit ihrer eigenen Person beschäftigt war" (she gave absolutely no thought to the fate of the city; he found it particularly shabby and petty that she was constantly only ever concerned with her own person, 2, 414). Obsessed with her domestic duties and with the increased social status afforded her by the liaison with Falkenberg, she is criticized as an archetypal, apolitical fellow traveler.

The decision of "die eigenwilligen und ungestümen Männer" (the willful and impetuous men, 2, 290) of the new council to oust the former city council, led by Willigis's uncle, Johann Ahlemann, because it had not resisted the edict forcefully enough, might be linked to the fateful political maneuvering of the dying days of the Weimar Republic or even to the 1918 rejection of the old monarchical German order. Either way, as Otto Guericke, Willigis's fellow councilor, notes, echoing Bake's earlier words, it seems that as a result of the popular uprising a "demon" has been unleashed "im Vaterlande deutscher Nation" (in the homeland of the German nation, 2, 342). This demon denotes the increasingly fanatical atmosphere encouraged and harnessed by Falkenberg and evokes the rise of Nazism. As in 1930s Germany, large numbers of Magdeburg's citizens readily align themselves with the would-be despot's xenophobic rhetoric, and in due course many adapt and conform. As in the Third Reich, some fellow travelers prove even more zealous than the zealots themselves:

Es gebe noch genau so viele Kaiserliche wie vordem, allein eben diese gebärdeten sich jetzt aus Angst am allerschwedischsten und verfolgten die, welche eigentlich derselben Meinung seien wie sie; also müsse man sich vor ihnen noch viel mehr in acht nehmen als vor den wirklich schwedisch Gesinnten. (2, 387–88)

[There were still just as many imperialists as before but these were the people who now out of fear were behaving most like the Swedes and persecuting those whose views they actually shared. One therefore had to beware of them much more than of those who genuinely thought like the Swedes.]

As a free city of the *Reich*, Magdeburg claims the right to the principle of *cuius regio, eius religio* (that is, the person who governs the territory decides its religion), which underpinned the Augsburg religious peace of 1555. As a Catholic, le Fort was opposed to this disputed principle and in her novel she seeks to show the dangers of suppressing religious faith, linking the failure to respect human conscience with the norms of a totalitarian state. In Falkenberg's cynical statement: "Das begrüße ich, wenn die Herren Pastoren sich nach ihrem Gewissen verhalten; denn das

Gewissen der Herren Pastoren bestimme jetzt ich" (I welcome it when pastors behave according to their conscience; for I now determine the conscience of pastors, 2, 436) Schröter sees a parody of Göring's "Wer Jude ist, bestimme ich" (I determine who is a Jew).[67] The underlying message is that when a state suppresses belief and neglects the principles of tolerance and mercy, it is doomed to endless conflict.

Willigis, who is loyal to the *Reich* and fiercely opposed to Swedish rule, and Guericke, who remains in the town and is prepared to work with Falkenberg, represent the positions of exile and inner emigration, respectively. Their exchange when Willigis secretly returns to the city is pivotal to the novel's elaboration of this theme, constituting an early attempt to mediate between the two camps and to establish the sort of message that might have enriched the infamous postwar debate. While Willigis here argues from the perspective of the angry and self-righteous exile, Guericke, the only level-headed individual among the naïve and gullible citizens of the city, who alone sees through the pretence of Falkenberg's motives, offers an impassioned defense of his own position, a plea for understanding of the dilemma of the inner emigrant:

> Denn es sei ja gewiß schwer, wenn man, wie Willigis, aus seiner lieben Vaterstadt verbannt werde, aber viel schwerer sei es doch, innerhalb seiner lieben Vaterstadt ein Verbannter zu sein, allen Unverstand, der hier geschehe, schweigend mit ansehen zu müssen, so als ob man überhaupt nicht mehr da sei! Und er selbst—Guericke—verstehe sehr wohl, wenn Willigis über einen schwachen Rat den Stab breche, aber Willigis verstehe noch nicht, was es heiße, selber dieser schwache Rat zu sein und ausharren zu müssen, als ob man ein starker Rat wäre, wiederum schweigend, alles Unrecht und allen Unverstand auf sich nehmend, mittragend und mitverantwortend (obwohl man sie doch nie verantworten könne), nur damit man hernach im allerletzten Augenblick noch zur Stelle sei und helfen könne, wenn der Unfug der Pastoren und des Volkes hier einmal zu Ende gehe. Aber ob das nun schwer oder leicht falle, ob man damit Ehre einlege oder den Verrätertitel gewinne, darauf komme nichts mehr an—es komme nur noch darauf an, die liebe Heimat vor dem Allerschlimmsten zu bewahren, und in dieser Sorge sei doch Willigis noch immer mit ihm einig. (2, 401–2)

> [For it was certainly difficult to be banished, like Willigis, from your beloved native city, but it was a good deal more difficult to be an exile within your beloved native city, to have to look on in silence at all the foolishness occurring here, as if you were no longer here at all! And he, Guericke, understood very well if Willigis were to condemn the weak council, but Willigis did not yet understand what it was like to be this weak council oneself and to have to endure as if one were a strong council, silently accepting, endorsing, and

sharing responsibility for all the injustice and all the folly (although of course you could never really justify them), just so that at the very last moment you could be on hand to help when the mischief of the pastors and the people came to an end. But it no longer mattered whether that proved difficult or easy, whether you thereby gained glory or were called a traitor—all that mattered was saving your beloved native land from the very worst and, in their concern for this, Willigis and he were still of one mind.]

Guericke implores Willigis to remain true to his city, not to condemn it outright but to be patient, to await the moment when all exiles would return and take their rightful place in the city. Though he is troubled by his situation, which he realizes makes him complicit in the Swedish take-over, he believes he has a duty not to abandon Magdeburg in its hour of need and to contribute to the recovery of the city. The exchange shows le Fort's desire to understand the reality of an inner emigrant mentality, the psychological burden that those who remain have to live with, but also the nature of their inner resistance and spiritual conviction. However, for all her sympathy with many of Guericke's ideas, she also presents in Willigis's reaction to them the alternative view, that of the combative exile prepared to fight against his native land. Willigis has no sympathy for Guericke's inclination to prioritize survival and to await the post-Falkenberg world. He has been so alienated from Magdeburg that he has no sense of *Heimat* any longer (2, 402). He is made to feel like a criminal despite his best intentions: "Was ist denn das für ein Regiment, das seiner Untertanen gute Meinung nicht mehr von der bösen Meinung unterscheiden kann!" (What sort of regime is it that can longer distinguish the well-intentioned opinions of its subjects from evil ones!, 2, 389). He sees his sole aim in life to be the defeat of Falkenberg, even at the cost of reducing the city to ruins, and is thus determined to join the imperial forces to help bring this about.

Finally, depictions of totalitarian collapse are a striking feature of some of le Fort's narratives from 1938 on. Although *Die Consolata* is the clearest example of this, in its portrayal of the conflagration that is sweeping through German lands *Die Magdeburgische Hochzeit* can be seen as foreshadowing the fate of Germany just a few years later. It is not difficult to see in Willigis's apocalyptic vision a prescient warning to contemporary Nazi Germany; in a hearth fire in the council room he sees the sacrificial flame of war: "[Er] erblickte durch sie entzündet alles Vaterland deutscher Nation von der Oder bis zum Rhein, von der Ostsee bis nach Bayern lichterloh brennend—erblickte das ganze Reich als einen zukünftigen Schutthaufen" (He saw lit up by it all the native lands of the German nation from the Oder to the Rhine, from the Baltic to Bavaria burning brightly—saw the whole *Reich* as a future heap of rubble, 2, 482).

The Religious Response to National Socialism

Notwithstanding these echoes of life in Nazi Germany, the contemporary applicability of the novel is far less pronounced than many other inner emigrant works. Le Fort's narrative focus is on a broad-based and extended theological metaphor linking Erdmuth Plögen and the city of Magdeburg, itself closely associated with the figure of the Virgin Mary. The ironic and ambiguous allegorical title refers, on the one hand, to Erdmuth and Willigis, who are engaged to be married but are driven apart by the conflict. On the other, it denotes the capture of the city and the forced marriage between the "maiden" of Magdeburg (depicted as such on its coat of arms) and the emperor. Falkenberg's declared intention to marry Erdmuth is insincere, in the same way that his "seduction" of the citizens of Magdeburg merely serves the cause of war. In the novel, the city is closely associated with the medieval Emperor Otto I (or "the Great"), who established the first archbishopric in Magdeburg, who is seen as the groom of the "maiden city," and whose burial in the city ties him irrevocably to his "bride." In this sense Magdeburg has to be an obedient bride to Otto's successors on the imperial throne (2, 327).[68] In the same way that Erdmuth comes to desire another man, however, Magdeburg turns away from the emperor and seeks a new master; both "maidens" are seen to be unfaithful to their respective suitors. The allegory is made explicit by the frustrated Willigis when he says: "Die Braut will nicht mehr auf den Bräutigam warten, die Stadt will nicht mehr auf Kaiserliche Majestät warten" (The bride is no longer prepared to wait for her groom and the city is no longer prepared to wait for his imperial majesty, 2, 403). The parallel is carried through to the end of the novel when the city is devastated and pillaged by the imperial troops and Erdmuth is raped. Moreover, just as Tilly tries to mitigate the suffering of defeated citizens, Willigis shows mercy and forgiveness toward his betrothed.

The religious resolution to human conflict, which lies at the heart of the allegory, is most clearly seen in the figure of the Protestant Bake. At the start of the novel, as he prepares to preach defense of the Lutheran faith and allegiance to the Swedish invaders, he compares the fate hanging over the city with the Day of Judgment (2, 289). At the end, after he and a few others have escaped the attack on the city and fled to the cathedral, he prostrates himself before the huge crucifix, puts himself at the mercy of the judgment of Christ on the cross, and acknowledges his personal guilt in having been blinded by the Swedes, in failing to demonstrate true Christian love and having thereby contributed to the destruction of the city. He is forgiven, is allowed to live, to continue to serve the faithful, and to help his wife give birth to their new child. He subsequently counters Guericke's dire prediction (that the bloody conflict will inevitably spread to all the German lands) with the imperative of Christian love and unity. He is now ready and able to accept the transformatory power of love, to put his trust in God, in accordance with the idea he had articulated at the start of the novel but had not been able to embrace at that time: "Es kann ja gar nichts geben, was die christliche Seele nicht von ihrem himmlischen Bräutigam und Herrn anzunehmen vermöchte, und wenn es wirklich das irdische Ende all unserer Dinge, ja selbst unsres Glaubens wäre" (There can be nothing that the Christian soul could not accept from its heavenly groom and master, even if it were the earthly end of all our affairs, indeed of our faith itself, 2, 289). Filled with this awareness of the insignificance of earthly strife and inspired by the creed, which he hears coming from the cathedral, he finds hope in the example of Christ's love for mankind and perceives in the destroyed city the opportunity for religious renewal free of confessional strife. But more than this, he sees in the city's transformation a reflection of national unity and harmony; the homeland of the German nation had found peace "durch die brüderliche Besinnung aller seiner Glieder auf das gemeinsame Bekenntnis der Väter und, so Gott wollte, der Kinder und der Kindeskinder bis ans Ende der Zeiten" (as a result of all its different parts contemplating in a fraternal spirit the common profession of faith of their fathers and, God willing, of their children and their children's children, to the very end of time, 2, 520.) The triumphant rise from the ruins, which he envisages for Magdeburg, will make it "the heavenly Jerusalem" (2, 521). We see here once more the influence on le Fort's thinking of conservative-nationalist ideas of the German *Reich* as the realization of God's kingdom on earth and the clear links to Schneider's two-kingdoms theology.[69]

Le Fort's novel thus evinces a conciliatory approach to what she sees as the tragedy of the split of Christianity, and the portrayal of Bake reveals just how much of her original Protestant faith fed into her Catholicism to create ecumenical views that were ahead of their time. The pastor feels the inherent unity of the two Christian churches when, with his wife and children, he is forced to leave his native city following the Catholic take-over. He passes the cathedral where Tilly's troops are holding a service and hears the Catholic troops reciting the same "great Christian creed" that he himself had repeated in his own Protestant services. He sees in it a strong bond linking his predecessors and his descendants, one that transcends sectarian division, which is likened to an artificial and ultimately meaningless human creation:

> Es war Bake, als werde mit jedem dieser kurzen majestätischen Sätze ein zeitlos-gewaltiges Fundament freigelegt, auf dem die im hohen Dom Versammelten und er selbst, der Ausgeschlossene, . . . gleicherweise standen—nur durch die Mauer des hohen Domes, nur durch eine einzige Mauer, von Menschenhand errichtet, getrennt! Und um dieser Mauer willen war ganz Magdeburg in Schutt und Asche gesunken! (2, 519)

[It seemed to Bake that with each of these short majestic sentences an everlasting and powerful foundation was laid bare, on which both those gathered in the cathedral and he himself, shut out . . ., stood in like manner, separated only by the wall of the lofty cathedral, by just a single wall that human hands had raised! And for the sake of this wall, the whole of Magdeburg had been reduced to dust and ashes!]

He acknowledges the common commitment of all Christian faiths. In the destroyed city, where the love of Christ "had been crucified" through confessional strife, he suddenly sees a new resurrection, a new "Golgotha," on which the whole of Christianity has been united (2, 520). It seems to him as if the love of Christ, which has been buried along with the twenty thousand dead in the ruins of the city, is about to explode forth from its "crypt." This climax to the novel is significant insofar as its appeal to all Christians across confessional boundaries to embrace common prayer and common action had the potential to act as a signaling effect for Germans under National Socialism, conveying the reassuring and consoling message that Christianity had the inner resilience to withstand the challenges posed by the regime.

Conclusion

Le Fort was a consistent chronicler of history in her narratives with fictional settings ranging across the centuries right back to the Middle Ages. And like other inner emigrant writers, most notably Reck-Malleczewen, she readily shaped and distorted history to suit her literary needs. However, the key and consistent message of her work from the 1920s to the 1960s is the central one of Carmelite spirituality that evil is to be overcome only through vicarious sacrifice, embodied in the example of Edith Stein, or St. Teresa Benedicta of the Cross, and exemplified in a range of heroines such as Blanche de la Force, the maiden of Barby, and Anne de Vitré. Carmelite teaching also places emphasis on the role of love in human relations but le Fort's recurrent reference to the power of universal and unconditional love for one's fellow man, including one's enemy, shares elements of a Franciscan understanding of concern for the world and all its inhabitants. The strongest example of this can be seen in *Die Consolata* and the conciliatory response to Ansedio's rule of terror but it also informs the endings of *Die Magdeburgische Hochzeit* and *Das Gericht des Meeres*.

Although it is difficult to claim that le Fort's work after 1933 was marked by a significant change in style or content, it is certainly true that there is a move throughout her career from the internalized religiosity of the early work to the focus in her middle period on the church (*Hymnen an die Kirche*) and ideas of a Christian empire (*Hymnen an Deutschland* and *Das Reich des Kindes*), and to a greater engagement in later works with the affairs of the world. In the course of this development, a narrow concern with Catholic piety and ecclesiasticism gives way to a broader conception of Christianity, to a focus on universal truths, in which the church is but one element and the human plays an increasingly significant role.[70]

Le Fort shows little interest in or allegiance to democratic rule, and her utopian image of a Christian kingdom reflects her essentially national conservative standpoint. She clearly distances herself from any notion of a state based exclusively on worldly power: the state that ignores the need for Christian tolerance, mercy, and divinely inspired justice is one that is doomed. Nevertheless, in its response to the tyrannous state, her work displays a fundamental problem shared with other inner emigrants. As with Jochen Klepper's adherence to blind trust in divine Providence, which promotes a sense of human resignation in the face of despotism and makes active resistance impossible, and with Schneider's notion of representative suffering and endurance through prayer, le Fort's portrayal of passive suffering as a form of redemptive, Christ-like self-sacrifice might be considered to promote passivity, inaction, and a sense of impotence.

A further consistent problem with her writing is its troubled relationship to reality. The fiction consistently lacks reference to aspects of characters' psychological, social, and economic reality and, instead, narrative resources are largely focused on ideological questions, on symbolical portrayal and allegories of redemption. Rarely are le Fort's explorations of spiritual and intellectual reality rooted in a convincing physical reality. As Knapp comments in connection with *Der Kranz der Engel*, although it applies to all her writing, the novel's validity is called into question by it never moving beyond "schwerelose Ideendichtung, Epik ohne die breite Unterlage . . . psychologisch-soziologischer Wirklichkeitsergründung" (a lightweight literature of ideas, epic narrative without the broad base of psychological and sociological exploration of reality).[71] The recurrent theme of self-sacrifice and martyrdom as a response to conflict and persecution, and the chronicle-style narrative approach, which result in often distinctly awkward dialogue, might help to explain why le Fort's work has not attained a wider readership. Of course, within this "monotonous" literary representation of Christian salvation—to refer back to Langgässer's definition—what counts, le Fort would argue, is not the verisimilitude of individual sacrifice as a means to resolve often deep-rooted problems (religious warfare, revolutionary upheaval, internecine rivalry), but the mystery of faith involved in linking vicarious suffering to Christ's crucifixion and redemption of mankind.

Ironically it is this, in literary terms, fatal flaw at the heart of le Fort's writing, this repetitive spiritual redemptive scheme with its absence of empirical detail that, in the context of Nazi Germany, constitutes the nonconformist strength of her work. In their intense focus on religious questions, works such as *Die Magdeburgische Hochzeit* may provide less obvious (and therefore one could argue less effectual) examples of inner opposition to the Nazi regime, but its focus on Tilly's moral honesty, the sympathy for those suffering the consequences of war, the consolatory aspects of Christian faith, the persistent ecumenism, the stylized championing of powerful examples of selfless commitment and martyrdom, and above all the insistent theme of the ephemeral and thus nugatory nature of earthly despotism and terror, all combine to establish a clear distance from and to offer a powerful religious and moral alternative to Nazi ideology.

Notes

[1] Joël Pottier, "'Ich habe das Historische nie als eine Flucht aus der eigenen Zeit empfunden': Wahrnehmung und Deutung der Geschichte bei Gertrud von le Fort (1876–1971)," in *Freie Anerkennung übergeschichtlicher Bindungen: Katholische Geschichtswahrnehmung im deutschsprachigen Raum des 20. Jahrhunderts*, ed. Thomas Pittrof and Walter Schmitz (Freiburg im Breisgau: Rombach, 2010), 380.

[2] See Gertrud von le Fort, *Aufzeichnungen und Erinnerungen* (Einsiedeln: Benzinger, 1951) and *Hälfte des Lebens: Erinnerungen* (Munich: Ehrenwirth, 1965).

[3] An ancestor was made a Baron of the *Reich* by Emperor Franz I in 1759, since when the family surname had been spelled with a small "l," and the author herself inherited the title "Freiin" (Baroness). Nicolas Heinen, *Gertrud von le Fort: Einführung in Leben, Kunst und Gedankenwelt der Dichterin*, 2nd ed. (Luxembourg: Editions du Centre, 1960), 53.

[4] Gertrud von le Fort, "Vermächtnisse," in *Mein Elternhaus: Bekenntnisse, Dank und Vermächtnis*, ed. Martin Warneck (Berlin: Warneck, 1937), 145; also le Fort, *Hälfte des Lebens*, 32.

[5] Joël Pottier, "Zwischen Ernst Troeltsch und Edith Stein: Gertrud von le Forts einsamer Weg," *Wiener Jahrbuch für Philosophie* 34, no. 2002 (2003): 189–90.

[6] Nicholas J. Meyerhofer, *Gertrud von le Fort* (Berlin: Morgenbuch, 1993), 26–28.

[7] Gertrud von le Fort, letter of August 8, 1914, cited in Joël Pottier, "Gertrud von le Fort: Eine biographische Skizze," in *Deutsche christliche Dichterinnen des 20. Jahrhunderts: Gertrud von le Fort, Ruth Schaumann, Elisabeth Langgässer*, ed. Lothar Bossle and Joël Pottier (Würzburg: Creator, 1990), 32.

[8] Le Fort, *Hälfte des Lebens*, 84.

[9] Meyerhofer, *Gertrud von le Fort*, 39.

[10] See Helena M. Saward, "A Literature of Substitution: Vicarious Sacrifice in the Writings of Gertrud von le Fort," *German Life and Letters* 53 (2000): 181.

[11] Gerda Hornung-Berk, "Die schaffende Frau: Gertrud von le Fort," *Münchner Neueste Nachrichten* 203 (July 26, 1936): 28, cited in Joël Pottier, "Der Widerstand der deutschen christlichen Dichter gegen den Nationalsozialismus am Beispiel Gertrud von le Forts und Werner Bergengruens," in *". . . aus einer chaotischen Gegenwart hinaus . . .," Gedenkschrift für Hermann Kunisch*, ed. Lothar Bossle and Joël Pottier (Paderborn: Bonifatius, 1996), 175.

[12] Gisbert Kranz, *Gertrud von le Fort: Leben und Werk in Daten, Bildern und Zeugnissen*, 3rd ed. (Frankfurt am Main: Insel, 1995), 203.

[13] Report of Kreisleitung Wolfratshausen, March 27, 1939, Bundesarchiv, Berlin, cited in Pottier, "Zwischen Ernst Troeltsch und Edith Stein," 199.

[14] In the *Völkischer Beobachter*, October 11, 1941.

[15] Strothmann, *Nationalsozialistische Literaturpolitik*, 379 and 458, respectively.

[16] Donald Ray Richards, *The German Bestseller in the Twentieth Century: A Complete Bibliography and Analysis, 1915–1940* (Bern: Lang, 1968), 176.

[17] Cf. the situation of Reinhold Schneider in "From Despair to Christian Utopia and Renewed Disillusionment," chapter 7 of this book.

[18] See Pottier, "Zwischen Ernst Troeltsch und Edith Stein," 203–4.

[19] Gertrud von le Fort, "Die Unschuldigen: Dem Andenken der toten Kinder des Weltkrieges" (1954), in *Erzählende Schriften*, vol. 3 (Munich: Ehrenwirth; Wiesbaden: Insel, 1956), 413–57. Subsequent references to this partial collection of her works appear parenthetically as (volume, page number).

[20] Gertrud von le Fort, "Am Tor des Himmels," in *Erzählende Schriften*, 3:459–522.

[21] See Gertrud von le Fort, *Den Heimatlosen: Drei Gedichte* (Munich: Ehrenwirth, 1950).

[22] Le Fort, *Hälfte des Lebens*, 84.

[23] Gertrud von le Fort, "Vom Paradox des Christentums: Vorwort zu dem gleichnamigen Buch von Graham Greene," in le Fort, *Die Krone der Frau*, 42–43.

[24] Eugen Biser, *Überredung zur Liebe: Die dichterische Daseinsdeutung Gertrud von le Forts* (Regensburg: Habbel, 1980), 142.

[25] Gotthold Ephraim Lessing, *Hamburgische Dramaturgie*, 2. Stück, in *Lessings Werke*, vol. 2, *SchriftenI*, ed. Kurt Wölfel (Frankfurt am Main: Insel, 1967), 129.

[26] Elisabeth Langgässer, *Das Christliche der christlichen Dichtung: Vorträge und Briefe* (Freiburg im Breisgau: Walter, 1961), 35–36.

[27] "Es handelt sich bei den Gestalten meiner Dichtung nicht um Portraits, sondern um Typen" (The characters in my writing are not portraits but types). Gertrud von le Fort, "Behütete Quellen," in *Gertrud von le Fort: Werk und Bedeutung: "Der Kranz der Engel" im Widerstreit der Meinungen* (Munich: Ehrenwirth, 1950), 6.

[28] See Eleonore von La Chevallerie, ed., *Gertrud von le Fort: Wirken und Wirkung: Ausstellungskatalog* (Heidelberg: Universitätsbibliothek, 1983), 187.

[29] See Helena M. Tomko's discussion of the novel in *Sacramental Realism: Gertrud von le Fort and German Catholic Literature in the Weimar Republic and Third Reich (1924–1946)* (London: Maney Publishing, 2007), 105–14.

[30] Ita O'Boyle, "Gertrud von le Fort's *Die Letzte am Schafott*," *German Life and Letters* 16 (1963): 98.

[31] For example, it inspired George Bernanos's posthumously published play *Dialogues des Carmélites* (1949), made famous by Francis Poulenc's opera of the same name, which was completed in 1955 and premiered in 1957.

[32] Gertrud von le Fort, *Hymnen an Deutschland* (Munich: Kösel & Pustet, 1932), 19 and 24, respectively.

[33] See Klaus Breuning, *Die Vision des Reiches: Deutscher Katholizismus zwischen Demokratie und Diktatur 1929–34* (Munich: Max Hueber, 1969), 121.

[34] See, for example, Kurt Matthies, "Hymnen an Deutschland," *Deutsches Volkstum* 15 (1933): 613–21; and Bruno Markowski, "Hymnen an Deutschland," *Zeitschrift für Deutschland* 48 (1934): 198–206.

[35] In *Die Deutsche Frau*, weekly supplement of the *Völkischer Beobachter* of August 23, 1933, cited in Pottier, "Der Widerstand der deutschen christlichen Dichter," 163.

[36] *Berichte des SD und der Gestapo über Kirchen und Kirchenvolk in Deutschland 1934–1944*, ed. Heinz Boberach (Mainz: Matthias-Grünewald-Verlag, 1971), 9–10, cited in Pottier, "Zwischen Ernst Troeltsch und Edith Stein," 204.

[37] Gertrud von le Fort, *Die Ewige Frau* (Munich: Kösel & Pustet, 1934), 6. Subsequent references to this volume are cited parenthetically in the text by page numbers.

[38] See Saward, "A Literature of Substitution." The idea is also prominent in Schneider's work. See the sections "Schneider and National Socialism" and "A Christian Story of Conscience" in chapter 7 of this book.

[39] Born into a Jewish family, Stein joined the Carmelite order in Cologne in 1933 and later died in Auschwitz, providing, in le Fort's eyes, a lived example of the concept of "representative suffering." She was subsequently canonized by the Catholic Church.

[40] See Werner Volke, ed., *Gertrud von le Fort*, Marbacher Magazin 3 (Marbach: Deutsche Schillergesellschaft, 1976), 22–23.

[41] Biser, *Überredung zur Liebe*, 44–45.

[42] The story was written as early as 1941: "Das Gericht des Meeres: Erzählung," *Das Inselschiff* 22 (1941): 86–107. Le Fort may have somehow heard about the secret experimentation with gas during 1940 and 1941, but it seems doubtful the story refers specifically to this. See Eva C. Wunderlich, "Gertrud von le Fort's Fight for the Living Spirit," *Germanic Review* 27, no. 4 (1952): 308.

[43] Gerhard Ringshausen, "Der christliche Protest: Konfessionelle Dichtung und nonkonformes Schreiben im Dritten Reich," in Kroll and von Voss, *Schriftsteller und Widerstand*, 286. On von Galen, see chapter 3, note 16 in this volume.

[44] Gertrud le Fort, *Unser Weg durch die Nacht: Worte an meine Schweizer Freunde* (Wiesbaden: Insel, 1949), 11.

[45] Ibid., 18.

[46] Meyerhofer, *Gertrud von le Fort*, 89.

[47] Breuning, *Die Vision des Reiches*. See also Joël Pottier, "Ein Anti-Claudel?: Gertrud von le Fort und der französische Renouveau catholique," in *Moderne und Antimoderne: Der "Renouveau catholique" und die deutsche Literatur*, ed. Wilhelm Kühlmann and Roman Luckscheiter (Freiburg im Breisgau: Rombach, 2008), 489–509.

[48] See on this, Tomko, *Sacramental Realism*, 86–94.

[49] Le Fort, *Aufzeichnungen und Erinnerungen*, 83.

[50] Gertrud von le Fort, "Über den historischen Roman," in le Fort, *Die Frau und die Technik*, 47.

[51] See Eleonore von La Chevallerie, ed., *Ausstellung im Juni 1981, veranstaltet von der Universität Würzburg aus Anlaß des 10. Todestages der Dichterin* (Würzburg: Fränkische Gesellschaftsdruckerei, 1981), 23.

[52] Le Fort, "Über den historischen Roman," 48.

[53] Le Fort, *Hälfte des Lebens*, 149.

[54] Joël Pottier, "Erlebte und gedeutete Geschichte: Gertrud von le Forts 'Weg durch die Nacht' im Dritten Reich," in Kroll, *Die totalitäre Erfahrung*, 169.

[55] Gertrud von le Fort, letter of July 6, 1960 to Dr. Hajo Jappe, cited in Kranz, *Gertrud von le Fort*, 140.

[56] See Reinhard Göllner, *Der Beitrag des Romanwerks Gertrud von le Forts zum ökumenischen Gespräch* (Paderborn: Bonifacius, 1973), 58–64.

[57] H. D. Sarnetzki, "Gertrud von le Fort: Die Magdeburgische Hochzeit," *Das Inselschiff* 19 (1937–39): 188.

[58] Bernt von Heiseler, "Gertrud von le Fort," in Heiseler, *Ahnung und Aussage* (Munich: Kösel & Pustet, 1939), 169.

[59] Hans Pflug-Franken, "Gertrud von Le Fort: Die Magdeburgische Hochzeit. Roman," *Die Literatur* 40 (1937–38): 752.

[60] Reinhold Schneider, "Die Magdeburgische Hochzeit," *Eckart* 14 (1938): 277.

[61] Adolf Fleckenstein, "Erzählende Literatur," *Hochland* 36, no. 1 (1938–39): 157.

[62] Gisbert Kranz, *Gertrud von le Fort: Leben und Werk in Daten, Bildern und Zeugnissen* (Frankfurt am Main: Insel, 1976), 32.

[63] E.g., Ian Hilton, "Gertrud von Le Fort," in *German Men of Letters*, vol. 2, ed. Alex Natan (London: Wolff, 1966), 289.

[64] See "Inwardness" in chapter 1 of this book.

[65] Gertrud von le Fort, "Autobiographische Skizze," in le Fort, *Die Frau und die Technik*, 42.

[66] In contrast to the oft-repeated counterleitmotif associated with Erdmuth and the city of Magdeburg: "Der Stolz vermag alles" (Pride can do all things).

[67] Klaus Schröter, "Der historische Roman: Zur Kritik einer spätbürgerlichen Erscheinung," in Grimm and Hermand, *Exil und innere Emigration*, 140–41.

[68] The bride-and-groom imagery extends to the chapter titles: "Der Jungfrauenabend" (Maiden's Evening), "Der Ehrentanz" (First Dance), and "Das Brautgemach" (The Bridal Chamber).

[69] See "Schneider and National Socialism" in chapter 7 of this book.

[70] See Aleksandra Chylewska-Tölle, *Literarische Entwürfe und Formen der Wandlung im Werk Gertrud von le Forts* (Frankfurt am Main: Lang, 2007), 47–49, who talks about an ultimate "Verschmelzung von Christentum und Humanismus" (fusion of Christianity and humanism, 47).

[71] Friedrich Knapp, "*Der Kranz der Engel* und die Menschen," *Frankfurter Hefte* 2 (1947): 972.

Fig. 7.1. Reinhold Schneider. Photo courtesy of
Deutsches Literaturarchiv Marbach.

7: Reinhold Schneider: Indios, Jews, and Persecution

WITH A SUBSTANTIAL oeuvre consisting of almost 1,200 books and articles, the Catholic writer, poet, and historian Reinhold Schneider
was a significant nonconformist figure under National Socialism. He was
also one of the few former inner emigrants to play a major public role
after 1945 when, owing to his antinuclear stance and his peace-related
work, he became an object of hate for sections of the West German establishment. More than any other nonconformist writer, with the possible
exception of Ernst Wiechert, Schneider's thinking and work developed
considerably over the period from 1928 to the late 1930s and the discussion in the first part of this chapter necessarily concentrates on his writing
prior to the appearance in 1938 of his landmark story *Las Casas vor Karl
V.: Szenen aus der Konquistadorenzeit* (Las Casas before Charles V: Scenes
from the time of the conquistadors, 1938, English translation *Imperial
Mission*, 1948).[1]

From Despair to Christian Utopia
and Renewed Disillusionment

Schneider was born in Baden-Baden in 1903. His childhood in his parents' international hotel lacked security and a sense of belonging, while his
youth was characterized by melancholy and depression.[2] His father was a
Protestant, his mother a Catholic; he too was brought up as a Catholic
but soon lost his faith. Following his *Abitur* in 1921, instead of going to
university, the young Schneider embarked on a short-lived agricultural
training course before taking up a post in a printing works in Dresden.
In April 1922 his father committed suicide after the family's business and
wealth had been destroyed by inflation. Following his own personal crisis and suicide attempt a few days later, Schneider was helped through
this period by his burgeoning relationship with the forty-one-year-old
Anna-Maria Baumgarten. This was to become a long-lasting liaison, with
Schneider entrusting over the years many of his innermost thoughts to
the older woman. The years in Dresden from 1921 to 1928 were a period
in which, alongside his unrewarding office work in a printing firm, he
devoted himself to language learning, philosophy, and literature, and

developed a strong interest in history, especially of the Iberian peninsula. In 1928 he resigned his post and embarked on a nearly eight-month trip to Spain and Portugal, after which he returned to Dresden and sought to establish himself as a writer.

After three peripatetic years, during which he repeatedly relocated within Germany, he finally settled in Potsdam in 1932 (*VT*, 65–73). This was a period of renewed uncertainty in both his personal and professional life, with continuing doubts about the relationship with Anna-Maria and disappointing book sales, causing him to turn to essay writing in such journals as *Der Tag*, *Eckart*, and *Hochland*. His only formal link to the new Nazi state was a part-time job in 1934 as reviewer for the monthly catalogue of the Schulungsamt der Reichskulturkammer (Training Office of the Reich Chamber of Culture). A job working for Berlin Radio led to the start of a period of intensive intellectual exchange and friendship with the writer Jochen Klepper, the painter and member of the Berlin Secession artists' group Leo von König, the writer Harald von Königswald, and the Bavarian monarchist Karl Ludwig von Guttenberg. For several years Schneider also collaborated on the conservative journal *Monarchie* (renamed *Weiße Blätter* in 1935), edited by von Guttenberg and Kurt Jagow. Beginning in the mid-1930s Schneider returned to an intensive involvement with Catholicism, a development reflected in his religiously colored poetry.

After 1941 he was denied paper for further publications, which effectively constituted a publication ban, although thanks to the commitment of Joseph Rossé, head of the publishing house Alsatia in Colmar, a few works could still appear, including, semilegally, the devotional meditations *Das Vaterunser* (The "Our Father," 1941) and, illegally, hectographed collections of sonnets (*VT*, 122–27). In 1944 an army chaplain in Cracow arranged for five thousand copies of Schneider's sonnets to be copied illicitly on an army printing press,[3] an action that a year later almost got the writer into serious trouble: he avoided arrest for high treason only because he was ill in hospital when the Gestapo came for him; the end of the war prevented the matter being taken further (*VT*, 156–57).

After the war, Schneider was prominent on the German cultural scene, receiving numerous honors and prizes, including in 1952, when President of the Federal Republic Theodor Heuss recommended him for the order *Pour le mérite*. He developed into a highly active public speaker and essay writer focused far more than hitherto on social commitment, in particular the theme of peace, a rejection of both German rearmament and the stationing of nuclear weapons on European soil. The bitterness of the resultant public backlash against him proved painful and demoralizing.[4] His publications after 1950 were initially dominated by political essays, pamphlets, and autobiographical prose, although he also turned his hand to several dramas. As his health steadily deteriorated, he mused pessimistically in a range of autobiographical works on the contradictions between the Christian message of salvation and modern science's vision of natural destruction. He died in 1958, shortly before his fifty-fifth birthday.

Schneider's Development as a Historical Writer

A large part of Schneider's prose work sits somewhere between traditional literature and historical-philosophical essay. His early work, in particular, is shaped by that sense of the post-1918 period as a major historical caesura that encouraged a reflection on history, historiography, and historical philosophy, most notably among such figures as Oswald Spengler and Theodor Lessing. Schneider considered his writing at this time to be an attempt to reflect the contemporary world through a combined focus on individual historical figures and philosophical ideas, though he did not see himself as a historian as such.[5] And, indeed, although his early work is assumed to be exclusively historical, from 1927 to 1931 he was simultaneously working on several autobiographical novellas and stories, in which he sought to come to terms with his personal and professional lack of direction in the early 1920s and worked through his troubled early adulthood, in particular his suicidal tendencies.[6]

In overcoming his personal identity problems, he drew on nineteenth-century thinking, particularly Schopenhauer and Nietzsche. Ideas on the loss of the metaphysical and a lack of direction in the modern world helped shape the tragic interpretation of history and existence that underpin much of his early work. Freed from the transcendent realm in a post-Enlightenment world, man experiences a "loss of the I," and the longing for permanence and experience of an Absolute collides with a seemingly chaotic world in which the individual is left on his own and which lacks any overarching meaning or coherence.[7] In particular, from Schopenhauer's division of the world as will and representation, and the notion of will and existence as suffering, Schneider learned to root individual experience in a broader intellectual context and to free himself from his own subjectivity (*VT*, 47–48). In Nietzsche, whose thinking he admired and was repulsed by in almost equal measure, he discovered a provocative catalyst, found similarities with his nihilism at the time, and was drawn to the notion of absolute loneliness as a heroic form of free existence committed only to itself, even flirting with the idea of the superman and rejection of the commonplace and mediocre.[8]

A significant influence was Miguel de Unamuno. The Spanish writer and philosopher's ideas on the "tragic sense of life," as expressed in his main philosophical work, the essay collection *Del sentimiento trágico de la vida en los hombres y en los pueblos* (1913, English translation *The Tragic Sense of Life in Men and Nations*, 1921), were a particular interest. For Unamuno there is a permanent battle between the heart and the mind, and although consciousness and the intellect are central to our attempt to come to terms with the world, they are incompatible with the longing for immortality. The tragic tension between this longing and the knowledge of the inevitability of death is seen as creative, generating many of mankind's greatest achievements. Passion and suffering are considered more essential to life than reason and intellect, which are rejected as inimical to the human heart and the desire for eternal life.[9] Schneider found in Unamuno's philosophical ideas on existence the courage to live his own life. But the latter's nonphilosophical essays on Spanish and Portuguese history also served to awaken Schneider's interest in cultural and national history as a way of making sense of human existence, and they determined the course of his work for the next decade.

The major product of the visit to Spain and Portugal in 1928–29 was a historical work, *Das Leiden des Camões: Oder Untergang und Vollendung der portugiesischen Macht* (The suffering of Camões: Or decline and fulfillment of Portuguese power, 1930), about the experiences of the sixteenth-century writer in Portugal's Far Eastern and Asian colonies. The "fulfillment" of the subtitle refers to Schneider's notion of the historian as someone who does more than convey or evaluate facts; he is also a "Geschichtsdichter" (poet of history), in whose artistic work the meaning of historical events only belatedly becomes fully clear and is completed. In this and subsequent works is to be found Schneider's belief in the operation of the tragic principle in history, as national powers and ideologies became embroiled in apparently unavoidable and inevitably doomed conflicts. Schneider's historical pessimism here, the belief in the tragic futility of human action, would appear to preclude any attempt to deal with contemporary issues or to comment on the present.

Schneider shared with many fellow writers in the 1920s a disillusionment prompted by the experience of war, inflation, and a seemingly "alien" democracy. He saw the only antidote to nihilism in the aesthetic notion of "form," a phenomenon or idea in art or history that is an expression of human creative power championed by whole peoples or heroic individuals in the face of a world perceived to be both chaotic and meaningless. Unamuno's influence and the notion of "form" are both evident in the substantial biographical work *Philipp II oder Religion und Macht* (Philip II, or religion and power, 1931), written in 1930 from the experience of two visits to Spain.[10] The key insight of the work is that life becomes meaningful only to the extent that it finds its fulfillment in form. The latter is partly exemplified in the interpretation of landscape portraits;

in the case of Montserrat near Barcelona, for example, the mountain and the abbey of Santa Maria de Montserrat provide evidence of "new form" shaping earlier ruins and providing a symbolic representation of how form can counter chaos. As in so much of Schneider's historical writing, geographical space forms the basis of historical imagination and provides a way into reading the past and its significance; fundamental ideas and historical figures arise from a metaphorical description of the physical landscape or architecture.[11] The perfection of form is thus also seen in Philip's castle, the Escorial, which was to exert a lasting influence on Schneider (*VT*, 74). It is further seen in poetry, such as that of Camões, lending shape to diffuse and meaningless events. And it is seen both in the life of King Philip, especially his radical, unworldly Christian approach to affairs, and in his death. Philip, the lonely heir to responsibilities and duties of state, appears as the traditionalist who has been shaped by past form, not just in his architectural endeavor but also in his respect for his predecessors and their legacy. The fateful deployment of the Armada shows him ultimately to be a tragic hero who pursues a hopeless ideal—reestablishing the dominion of Catholicism in Europe—but does not allow its hopelessness to deter him, as he sees it as his sacred duty.[12] The controversial aspect of the idea that life is only lent meaning through form is the tendency to compulsion and the denial of freedom, and Schneider's positive evaluation of the Inquisition, for example, leads to utterances quite incompatible with his later Christian ethics.[13]

With his next major works, *Innozenz der Dritte* (Innocent the Third),[14] *Fichte: Der Weg zur Nation* (Fichte: The path to nationhood, 1932), and *Die Hohenzollern: Tragik und Königtum* (The Hohenzollerns: Tragedy and kingship, 1933), Schneider turned his attention to German history, and these works are marked by a stronger ideological content. His publisher noted that Schneider seemed here to be moving away from his earlier sensuous portrayal of places, people, and events, and to be pursuing rather "desperate" nationalist ideas.[15] And, indeed, the decision in *Fichte* to write about a thinker, whose *Reden an die deutsche Nation* (Addresses to the German nation, 1808) delivered under French occupation made him one of the fathers of German nationalism, could not help but align Schneider in the eyes of many in 1932 with contemporary German nationalist forces. The book depicts the nation as the fertile ground on which the utopian notion of form grows, an elemental principle inaccessible to rational thinking, as a result of which a country can insist on complete independence from the dictates of any treaty and assert "der Wille zum Ich" (the will to I).[16] Meier considers this a reference to the hated Versailles Treaty and a justification for totalitarian policies.[17] In light of Schneider's later disavowal of nationalism and his reluctance to countenance a restoration of the monarchy (despite remaining a monarchist),[18] his faith at this time in the bond between nationalism and monarchism is striking, while his (and others') belief that Hitler might restore the monarchy is a spectacular misjudgment.

In *Die Hohenzollern* the focus is on Friedrich Wilhelm I and Frederick the Great, in whose example we see the renewed emphasis on form and order. The thrust of the work is that a sense of unswerving duty should be embodied in and modeled by a country's leader; this particularly strict sense of duty takes precedence over personal happiness, wealth, and human relations, and has its theoretical basis in Kant's categorical imperative. The book also enacts in the guise of Prussian history the "tragic" divergence between *Geist/Macht* (intellect/power) and culture/nation in contemporary Germany—expressed here via the formulaic Weimar versus Potsdam—, and further rejects race and blood as decisive factors in the pursuit of form in preference for ethical considerations and, above all, the "Wille zur Form" (will to form).[19] The denial of the Nazis' supposed renewal of German history could only irritate the new regime; it was perhaps therefore no surprise that the work was subsequently suppressed.[20] However, while *Die Hohenzollern* affords less potential for exploitation in the Nazi cause, it is also true that the concept of Prussian duty, the praise of the strong leader, and the enthusiasm for the creation of a new German state readily lent themselves to being misinterpreted and abused in the year 1933, in precisely the way this was later to happen with Klepper's depiction of Friedrich Wilhelm I in *Der Vater* (The Father, 1937).

Schneider and National Socialism

What of Schneider's pronouncements on politics at this time? These are contradictory and fail to clarify how he viewed National Socialism. For example, following Nazi election successes on September 16, 1930, he notes he might sympathize with their protests were their ideology not so brutishly stupid and crude, and also indicates a not untypical national conservative underestimation of their potential threat.[21] In a letter to a friend in January 1931, he writes that Germany is facing its greatest disappointment in Hitler and his Third Reich,[22] while in his diary he calls Hitler a "demagogue" and describes the thinking in *Mein Kampf* (*My Struggle*) as foolish and primitive.[23]

Elsewhere, on the other hand, especially in letters to Anna-Maria Baumgarten, he is more ambiguous. For example, while bemoaning Nazi proximity to socialism, he acknowledges that Hitler has once again brought the country to national awareness;[24] and in a description of the events of the "Tag der erwachenden Nation" (Day of the Awakening Nation), the eve of the March 5, 1933 elections, he notes he had the feeling of a people finally "returning to its history" and that this caused him to forget his reservations about the means being employed.[25]

This equivocation about National Socialism rested on two principles: the fateful conservative illusion that a country in the process of rediscovering its "true past" would soon reject Hitler but that for the moment the supposed "puppet" was serving a useful purpose, and the commitment to monarchical rule (see *VT*, 79). In his most open support for the new regime, an article in the nationalist newspaper *Der Tag*, he draws a parallel between the assumption of power by Friedrich Wilhelm I in 1713 and the creation of the Hitler state, suggesting the latter constitutes the rebirth of the notion of Prussian "form," and welcomes the well-formed military columns in Potsdam for bringing about the disappearance of communist flags and demonstrations.[26]

Schneider's discovery in January 1934 of the realities of Dachau, as reported to him by Rudolf Pechel (*VT*, 73), confirmed him in his rejection of Nazism. Quite apart from the concentration camps, the regime's violence, corruption, and flouting of the law led him to champion universal moral principles against an increasingly eschatological background— albeit through veiled literary means. In "Der Tröster" (The comforter, 1934), for example, a story based on the figure of Friedrich von Spee (1591–1635), the Jesuit priest and opponent of witchcraft trials, he expresses his reaction to the new regime in a tale set against the background of the Thirty Years War. Here a cleric, who is prepared to take on the sin of a young woman wrongfully accused of being a witch and to protest against the flawed justice system of the time, is portrayed as a model of representative suffering, in imitation of Christ.[27]

The realization that his hope of finding historical form in the new German state was misplaced, indeed that form alone was inadequate as a means of investing historical phenomena with meaning, presented a new challenge. Following the artistically less satisfying forays into German history, Schneider's remaining works during the Third Reich constitute by and large a return to foreign subject matter. On this "safer" ground, he was able to lend expression to his rejection of National Socialism to varying degrees in such works as the historical *Das Inselreich: Gesetz und Größe der britischen Macht* (The island empire: Law and greatness of British power, 1936) and *Las Casas vor Karl V.*, as well as his poetry. Although he retained here his fundamental historical notion of the tragic sense of life, he sought to move beyond the problems he had had with monarchy and nationalism by embracing as a point of historical identification Catholic heritage (*VT*, 58) instead of the nation, which at the time seemed necessarily also to imply identification with the Nazi state.

The extensive correspondence from 1934 onward with such committed Catholic figures as the religious philosopher Leopold Ziegler,

Leo von König, Werner Bergengruen, and in particular Jochen Klepper, were a significant influence on Schneider's rediscovery of his religious faith,[28] though he was only to embrace the Catholic faith fully beginning in 1937 (*VT* 102). Primarily a history of England from Roman times to the Industrial Revolution, *Das Inselreich* provides evidence of the development of a more specific religious content in his writing as he seeks to engage with history from a Christian standpoint. Although initially well received by such journals as *Hochland* and *Die Neue Rundschau*, it was subjected to "massive" attacks in the Nazi press (*VT*, 111) and eventually banned in 1937.[29] The key theme is the ethical and moral aspects of the guilt of particular powerful historical figures and leaders, and in this new, religiously imbued approach to history, the king remains responsible to God and the commandments for the exercise of his power.[30] Pointedly, in the Afterword to the original edition, Schneider asked the reader to see the work as referring to the law "das über aller Geschichte waltet" (that presides over all history), offering a hint of its relevance to Nazi Germany.[31] The attempt to view history from the perspective of religious faith leads to an emphasis on conscience in human affairs, a refusal to recognize national greatness outside of the ethical realm, something that could not fail to alienate official critics.[32] Schneider was duly listed as one of the "undesirable" authors of the Third Reich and *Das Inselreich* was among the total of eleven of his works included in official listings of undesirable literature for the period 1933–44, six appearing for 1939–41 alone.[33]

Another significant work from this period is the story *Kaiser Lothars Krone* (Emperor Lothair's crown, 1937) about the twelfth-century life and rule of Lothair III of Supplinburg, Duke of Saxony and subsequently Holy Roman Emperor. After his late appointment to the throne, the former rebel undergoes a remarkable transformation, becoming a peacemaker and assuming what for Schneider is a sacred role, the realization of God's kingdom on earth. His principal weapon in imposing order is justice. This representation of a state based on Christian morality met with official disapproval in the *Völkischer Beobachter* review of March 5, 1938, which takes Schneider to task for encroaching on the inviolable realm of "our historical myth," and in response to the author's assertion that Christ's appearance on earth and his teaching constituted the only valid point of historical orientation, it advises him not to use religious revelation to measure "the greatness" of German history and German rulers and artists.[34]

From the late 1930s, Schneider's work is dominated by Christian themes, in particular by the challenge posed by the symbol of the cross and the succession to Christ as a process of suffering, sacrifice, and witness. Just as important, he devotes considerable attention to an eschatology in which the "Weltreich" (the earthly realm or the kingdom of man, associated with Babylon and focused on the human self, the will, and earthly power) is confronted by the "Gottesreich" (the Kingdom of God, associated with Jerusalem and focused on God and a life shaped by love of God). The very different conception of history that this entails is reflected in the essay "Das Gottesreich in der Zeit" (The Kingdom of God in time, 1942), where it is seen as the history of salvation, as a struggle to establish the Kingdom of God in man and the world. The Christian insistence on personal responsibility contrasts with the totalitarian demand for blind obedience and suppression of the individual: the Kingdom of God is realized wherever someone seizes his or her inalienable rights and responds to the "call of love."[35] Though Schneider was criticized for it in a Propaganda Ministry report from 1940, this strongly religious tone served as a form of camouflage and was, along with his reputation abroad, a factor in him being allowed to continue to publish for so long.[36] The importance of this message for Christians in the Third Reich was that the Kingdom of God would triumph at the end of time but that this did not justify passivity: the certainty of salvation did not mean waiting to be saved but involved an active process in which the individual must ensure that all are aware of this salvation, even the enemies of Christ.[37]

Schneider was particularly concerned with the implications of this two-kingdoms theology for those in positions of power. Worldly power is not considered to be of itself evil: it is lent to man by God and it is the duty of Christian statesmen to use it responsibly according to the dictates of conscience. However, power can also be a temptation to do wrong and those who abuse it are seen as succumbing to the forces of evil.[38] For those entrusted with inherited power and the responsibility of administering it, the clash of the two kingdoms is an especial source of anguish.[39] For this reason the role of the monarch (for example, Friedrich Wilhelm I) is seen as a form of Christ-like suffering and passion. Schneider illustrates the comparison in historical figures such as Pope Innocent III, Cardinal Newman, and Charles V, but especially in his major essay on the rule of Philip II of Spain.[40]

In the Second World War Schneider saw a thinly veiled enactment of the clash of the two realms and considered its horrors to be a necessary prerequisite for the reestablishment of divine authority. This idea underpins a range of almost hagiographic stories and legends from the period 1939–45 featuring Christian saint and martyr figures. A good example is the story "Vor dem Grauen" (Before the horror), written in 1939 but not published until 1943. St. Benedikt Labre is speaking just before the outbreak of the French Revolution to a young nobleman, and in response to the latter's question whether he senses impending doom, the saintly beggar replies: "Niemand weiß es mit Sicherheit, niemand weiß die Stunde, aber das müssen Sie doch fühlen, daß das Falsche sich der Menschen bemächtigt hat und daß auch die Kirche ihm nicht standhält. Die Herausforderung geschieht einen jeden Tag. . . . Gehen Sie mitten hinein! . . . Werden Sie zum Zeugen, mitten im Feuer!" (No one knows for certain, no one knows the hour but you must surely sense that something false has taken hold of man and that even the church cannot withstand it. The challenge occurs every single day. . . . Go to the very center of things! . . . Become a witness, in the midst of the fire!)[41] The parallels with the situation in Germany on the eve of war are not difficult to discern, including the swipe at the failure of the Catholic Church to stem the drift toward the false gods of National Socialism. The passage encapsulates Schneider's ideas on the role of conscience and on self-sacrifice as a form of Christ-like witness. The problematic aspects of this submissive stance as a form of opposition are discussed below in connection with *Las Casas vor Karl V.*

Despite his views, Schneider never seriously considered fleeing abroad. Careful to distance himself from the postwar anti-exile sentiment, he later noted he had nevertheless felt the need to show solidarity with fellow Germans (*VT*, 76). However, he was also honest enough to note his personal failings: after bemoaning the Christian churches' failure to take a stand against anti-Semitic violence, he writes: "Aber was tat ich selbst? Als ich von den Bränden, Plünderungen, Greueln hörte, verschloß ich mich in meinem Arbeitszimmer, zu feige, um mich dem Geschehenden zu stellen und etwas zu sagen. . . . Dankbar folgte ich im Dezember einer Einladung nach Paris. Das war schmähliche Flucht." (But what did I myself do? When I heard about the fires, lootings, and atrocities, I locked myself away in my study, too much of a coward to face up to what was happening and to say something. It was with gratitude that I accepted an invitation to go to Paris. That was shameful flight, *VT*, 117–18.)

Schneider was in sympathy with the aim of the Kreisau Circle to bring about a moral renewal of Germany predicated on a future political order involving the intellectual elite of the country. Indeed he participated in an early meeting in December 1941 at the invitation of the painter Heinrich Graf Luckner.[42] However, he does not seem to have been involved in any subsequent gatherings, and indeed his pacifist views made it impossible for him to work with those who planned the assassination attempt of July 20, 1944, though he later paid fulsome tribute to their sacrifice.[43]

Of all the nonconformist writers who stayed in Germany, Schneider boasts the highest number of works distributed, both legally and otherwise, during the war. Five hundred thousand copies of the devotional text *Das Vaterunser* alone were published and widely distributed among soldiers.[44] Just as significant in this connection were his sonnets. He wrote a large number of these between 1933 and 1945, and relatively few of them were legally published. As early as 1937, Schneider's friend Heinz Ludewig produced a typewritten, mimeographed volume of the sonnets, which the author distributed to friends.[45] The first legally published collection, *Sonette*, appeared in 1939 and was reprinted twice. Schneider produced five further volumes,[46] but four of these were private and only semilegal publications, being copied and passed from hand to hand, while the fifth was produced illegally by Joseph Rossé in Colmar (*VT*, 156–57). This repeated illicit reproduction and dissemination meant Schneider's poems reached a large readership, and they have consequently been deemed to constitute a "counterliterature" seeking a secret "counterpublic."[47] A striking example of their resonance is provided in the statements of former inmates of Nazi prisons and concentration camps, describing the effect that Schneider's consolatory and exhortative writings had on them.[48] Further evidence of his influence can be found in the "hidden" side of Schneider's wartime work, his extensive correspondence with soldiers: the Reinhold Schneider Archive in the Badische Landesbibliothek in Karlsruhe contains an astonishing thirty thousand or so letters to Schneider from soldiers (some dating from after the war), most of which he replied to, and this pastoral work or spiritual welfare is perhaps the most underestimated and underresearched aspect of inner emigrant activity.[49]

The reason for the popularity of the poems is, besides their content, no doubt related to the strict form of the sonnet, its rhyme scheme and meter, which facilitated memorization. Many of them have a rather breathless tone and, as Klieneberger notes, are of variable quality, with powerful and inventive formulations alternating with banal phrases.[50] Some read like rather stiff professions of faith or declarations of ethical stances set in verse, while others betray their origins as immediate responses to political events of the day, and it is the intense rhetoric of the message that counts here rather than stylistic polish.

Although in their call for humility, sacrifice, and the restoration of the example of Christ to the center of man's worldview the sonnets repeatedly encourage inwardness, they nevertheless constitute a form of semipublic spiritual resistance to Nazism. They share with Schneider's prose work a concern for Christian morality, and the theologically colored eternal truths that they affirm stand in opposition to the immorality and empty pathos of the regime. Several insist the time has come for a change, encourage Germans to turn away from the criminal and false powers they have been serving, and seek to warn, console, and lend courage to endure. Thus, as early as 1937 Schneider employed the typical inner emigrant trope of madness to issue a warning about the unsound edifice of the Nazi regime and about the dangers of people's judgment being clouded by grandiose public displays:

Nun baut der Wahn die tönernen Paläste
Und läßt sein Zeichen in die Straßen rammen;
Er treibt das blind verwirrte Volk zusammen
Vom Lärm zum Lärm und vom Fest zum Feste.[51]

[Madness now builds palaces of clay / And has its mark imprinted on the streets; / It drives together the blind and confused people / From noise to noise and celebration to celebration.]

One of the best examples of Schneider's use of the language of biblical prophecy and ideas of Christian salvation to make links with the German present is the poem "Der Antichrist." Though camouflaged by a subtitle that refers to the frescoes of the Renaissance painter Luca Signorelli,[52] and though apparently describing Christ's adversary, the poem contains unmistakable references to Hitler's arrogance and presumption, his usurpation of power, the way people allow themselves to be seduced by him, and his obsessive building, as well as a prophecy of his demise:

Er wird sich kleiden in des Herrn Gestalt,
Und Seine heilige Sprache wird er sprechen
Und Seines Richteramtes sich erfrechen
Und übers Volk erlangen die Gewalt.

[He will clothe himself in the form of the Lord / And will speak His sacred language / And will have the audacity to assume His judicial office / And attain power over the people.]

Und Priester werden, wenn sein Ruf erschallt,
Zu seinen Füßen ihr Gerät zerbrechen,
Die Künstler und die Weisen mit ihm zechen,
Um den sein Lob aus Künstlermunde hallt.

[And when his call rings out priests will / Smash their tools at his feet, / Artists and wise men will carouse with him, / Praise of whom resounds from artists' lips.]

Und niemand ahnt, daß Satan aus ihm spricht
Und seines Tempels Wunderbau zum Preis
Die Seelen fordert, die er eingefangen;
Erst wenn er aufwärts fahren will ins Licht,
Wird ihn der Blitzstrahl aus dem höchsten Kreis
Ins Dunkel schleudern, wo er ausgegangen.[53]

[And no one suspects that Satan speaks through him / And that the price he demands for the wondrous edifice of his temple / Are the

souls he has captured. / Only when he desires to rise to the light, /
Will a flash of lightning from the highest circles / Hurl him into the
darkness whence he came.]

As always in Schneider's writing, it is the role of Christianity to stand
in opposition to the powers that be, following the example of Christ and
the early church (see *VT*, 131).

Genesis and Publication of *Las Casas vor Karl V.: Szenen aus der Konquistadorenzeit* (1938)

Schneider was reflecting on the figure of las Casas as early as 1934, as
revealed in his diary and an essay on "Die Rechtfertigung der Macht"
(The justification of power).[54] He produced a ten-page résumé of the
planned story in 1937,[55] before moving in the autumn of that year from
Potsdam to Hinterzarten in the Black Forest, where he worked on the
text proper until March 1938. The story was published in September
1938. It developed at the same time as the first part of Alfred Döblin's
Amazonas (Amazon) trilogy, *Die Fahrt ins Land ohne Tod* (Journey to
the land without death, 1937), in the third chapter of which las Casas
appears as a tragic Christian figure, and although Schneider did know
Döblin and the latter had sent him a copy of his novel, there is no evidence of any influence.[56]

The accurate use of source materials was a feature of Schneider's
historical work, and *Las Casas vor Karl V.* was no exception. Here he
employed extensive extracts of the historical literature, most notably the
Brevísima relación de la destrucción de las Indias Occidentales (A short
account of the destruction of the Indies) by the Spanish Dominican monk
Bartolomé de las Casas (1484–1566), which was written in 1542 but not
published until 1552. Besides this, he used various reports on a public
disputation on the theme in 1550 between las Casas and Juan Ginés de
Sepúlveda (1489–1573), the Spanish humanist, philosopher, and theologian. He also drew on the *Apologías y discursos de las conquistas occidentales* (*Defense and discourse of the western conquests*) by Bernardo de Vargas
Machuca, governor of the island of Margarita; this work was published
in 1612 as a form of rebuttal of las Casas's charges, part of the backlash
against the Dominican that took place under Charles's successor, Philip
II, who was to oversee an even more ruthless exploitation of the New
World colonies.[57]

Don Bartolomé de las Casas's father, Don Francisco, was among the
early conquistadors who followed Columbus to the Americas in 1492.[58]
Don Bartolomé traveled there shortly after him (he is known to have
been in Hispaniola in 1502) and for almost fifteen years was indistin-
guishable from many other colonialists, being involved with Velásquez

in the subjugation of Cuba in 1512 and running a plantation with slave labor. The turning point in his thinking can be dated as 1514, when he renounced his estates and slaves and became involved in the administration of conquistador business. His attempts to free the native Indians from slavery led eventually to an audience with Charles V, which resulted in a judgment that the conquistadors' activities in the New Indies were unlawful and that the new plantations should be ruled without use of weapons. The promised legislation, however, was slow to be realized and little changed. Las Casas subsequently spent time documenting in great detail the history of the conquistadors and traveled extensively throughout America and Peru to promote his campaign. He spent the years 1540 to 1543 in Spain, during which he wrote his report, was made a bishop, and finally secured the passing of "Las nuevas leyes de las Indias" (The new laws of the Indies), which banned slavery and required that Indians be treated like any other citizens of the Spanish empire. The new laws met with determined and organized resistance in the colonies and were undermined by the legal authorities there, causing Charles to revoke them in 1545. Las Casas continued to pursue his aims as Bishop of Chiapa in Mexico. The highlight of his final years in Spain was the successful disputation with Sepúlveda in 1550, which, however, also ultimately failed to achieve any significant change in the colonies.

Ever since it first appeared in 1552, the accusation in las Casas's report of genocide (close to twenty million people died in just a few decades) has fired the emotions. Indeed its uncompromising approach and its championing of the oppressed meant no one in Spain or South America dared republish it in its original form until the late nineteenth century. From contemporary (sixteenth-century) calls for the "dangerous" document to be banned and condemnations of the author as fanatical, evil, and inspired by the devil, through its role in inspiring leaders in the wars of independence against Spanish colonial authorities, to twentieth-century historians' characterizations of las Casas as "sick," a preacher of Marxism, and a dangerous demagogue, the work has never failed to be a source of controversy.

Schneider's text was originally conceived as a biography,[59] but, as the dramatic potential of the material became ever clearer, a more fictional approach took over, influencing both chronology and focus.[60] Thus, the new laws are presented as one of the outcomes of the disputation, whereas the latter did not take place until five years after the laws had been revoked and las Casas had already been appointed Bishop of Chiapa—chronological shifts made in the interests of narrative coherence but also contributing to a distinctly positive ending to the fiction. This approach was in marked contrast to Schneider's principle of faithfulness to historical sources in earlier works.

The question of how the work could be published in the Third Reich is perhaps more readily answered than in the case of, say, Friedrich Reck-Malleczewen's *Bockelson* (see chapter 5). The historical camouflage here was strong, as the focus was very specifically sixteenth-century Spain; as with Stefan Andres's *El Greco malt den Großinquisitor* (1936, English translation *El Greco Paints the Grand Inquisitor*, 1989), one could argue the work presented the church in a poor light; and, above all, the author had already long established himself as a knowledgeable and (in the eyes of the authorities) inoffensive expert on the Iberian area, such that a further work in this field was unlikely to arouse undue suspicion.

Summary

In Schneider's reworking of the source material there are four chapters, the first two of which are devoted to historical background and the life of the conquistadors in the West Indies, the second two to the public disputation between the fictional Las Casas and Sepúlveda and its aftermath.

In chapter 1, Las Casas is returning to Spain and on the long crossing meets Bernardino de Lares, a Spanish knight, who is troubled by nightmares about his experiences in the new lands, including his own wrongdoing. Bernardino, injured by a poisoned arrow and in mortal danger, seeks to unburden himself by telling Las Casas about his experiences, particularly the atrocities committed by the conquistadors in the name of Christianity and the expansion and enrichment of the Spanish empire. Through Bernardino's lengthy flashbacks we learn about the deeds of Columbus and conquistadors such as Hernán Cortéz, the violent conquests of Alonso de Hojeda and Diego de Nicuesa, and the suffering of the Indians at their hands. These opening sections also describe the work of Las Casas, especially his attempts to support the Indians and his return to Spain to make representations to King Charles V about the inhuman treatment of the natives.

In chapter 2, back in Spain, Las Casas travels to Vallodolid to prepare for the debate with Sepúlveda. Meanwhile Bernardino visits a friend in Toledo and experiences here how greed for material possessions and earthly happiness prompts envy, resentment, and hatred. He subsequently decides to visit his brothers disguised as a beggar in order to test their character. However, he is rejected by them, as they too have succumbed to the temptation of wealth. Chastened by these experiences, he embraces a life of poverty and tries to trace the local girl whom he had left with child when he departed for the New World.

In the debate itself, in chapter 3, Bernardino, though seriously ill, assists Las Casas by appearing as a witness for him. The reader learns about the history of the colonies and the oppression of the natives through a mixture of reports, stories, and witness statements. Sepúlveda seeks to show Las Casas's own past guilt in having mercilessly exploited the natives on his plantation and having even recommended the importing of Negro slaves. He thus undermines Las Casas's moral integrity and, from the point of view of the Spanish state, is seen to have the better arguments. For Sepúlveda, the interests of the state are paramount and the law should serve them rather than stand above them. He quotes from his book *Über die gerechten Gründe des Krieges gegen die Indios* (On the just reasons for the war against the Indians) and adduces evidence from the Old Testament to show that one people has the right to rule over another. Las Casas, on the other hand, thinks Spain should be converting the Indians through faith alone, independently of any interests of state. He criticizes the legal abuses committed in the New World and posits an eternal law that he insists the state too must obey. He reports on the atrocities committed in Spain's name and asks the king to give the Indians their freedom, suggesting that otherwise a terrible vengeance will be wreaked on the country.

In the final chapter, just before Bernardino dies, Las Casas finds the knight's illegitimate son, who, it transpires, has become a priest, and who now determines to make restitution for Bernardino's wrongdoing by accompanying Las Casas to the Indies and using his father's wealth to support their work there. After several days' deliberation, Charles, moved by Las Casas's pleading, decides in his favor and promises to give the Indians their freedom, resolving to send Las Casas back to the conquered lands as a bishop. Las Casas duly returns to Mexico as Bishop of Chiapa to proclaim and disseminate the "new laws," but the ending of the story seems to hold out little prospect of them succeeding.

Of all the historical works produced within the inner emigration, *Las Casas vor Karl V.* reveals perhaps the greatest contemporary relevance. First, it was published at a time of progressive geographical expansion of the Third Reich and the consequent subjugation of whole nations: this was, of course, the time of the annexation of Austria, the Sudetenland crisis, and, less than a year later, the invasion of Poland. Second, publication was soon followed by *Reichskristallnacht* (the Night of Broken Glass), and the fate of native South American Indians was beginning to appear a possibility for Europe's Jews too. And, third, the story appeared at the height of the Spanish Civil War: criticism of the behavior of Spanish state and church in the fifteenth and sixteenth centuries would have had added poignancy when read against the background of a contemporary Spain in which there was a widespread clerical alignment with Franco's Falangists.

Reception

Las Casas vor Karl V. encountered no difficulties with censors, was never banned, and was reprinted three times up until 1941, although the denial of further paper allocations meant it could no longer appear thereafter. Although the tendency was to pass over publication of the story in silence, it is noteworthy that in its brief introduction a key book trade review journal found little to object to, stating the dramatic story provided a rare mix of literary and historical writing.[61]

Many other reviews were neutral or positive, and among these one finds some that appear to make telling points. Thus Walter Kalthoff discusses the story largely as a historical document, although he notes at one point that all the writer's historical works prompt reflection on one's own situation in the present.[62] Similarly, a review in the *Frankfurter Zeitung* talks about "the accusations" of Las Casas's arguments resounding across the centuries and emphasizes that careful consideration should be given particularly to the question of "the meaning of power."[63] In a review with potentially camouflaged content, Hans E. Friedrich, editor of the *Deutsche Allgemeine Zeitung*, focuses on the relationship between power and religion, on the book's insistence on what is right as dictated by individual conscience, regardless of whether this flies in the face of worldly power or Church authority.[64] More strikingly still, a review by Ernst Lucas sees the book as the struggle of justice and Christian faith against the caviling ("Deuteleien") and the claims to power of a nominally Christian state. He goes on to indicate a connection between sixteenth-century Spain and contemporary Germany by referring to the book as a "warning" to the present, saying Las Casas's talk of a divine judgment rendering the "greatest *Reich* on earth" utterly insignificant strikes the reader with the full force of its "uncompromising truth," a truth that has proven itself like no other prophecy.[65]

Numerous correspondents conveyed to Schneider that they had understood the book's hidden message. For example, Leopold Ziegler wrote to him in April 1939 and noted that the latter's recent work displayed an "ungeheuere Aktualität" (tremendous topicality).[66] Similarly, the historian and archivist Ludwig Dehio wrote in October 1938 about the effect the book had had on him: "Hier wird aufgerüttelt, angeredet und unausweichlich zur Stellungnahme aufgefordert" (The reader here is shaken up, spoken to directly, and inevitably challenged to take up a position).[67] Jochen Klepper was also quick to see the critical message in the work, writing in 1938 that in the book's more distressing sections, one could detect an examination of racial tragedies from the 1930s.[68] Werner Bergengruen too saw in the story an "Aufruf zur Ehrfurcht vor allem, was ein menschliches Antlitz trägt" (appeal to respect humanity in all its guises).[69]

Postwar critics consistently commented on the story's oppositional content, and in 1952 the Kulturbund of the GDR proposed Schneider for the National Prize for *Las Casas vor Karl V.* Even the critical Schonauer, while denigrating any attempt to address the horrors of Nazi Germany via historical parallels, sees the work as a form of resistance to "unjust

power."[70] And for Brekle, from the GDR perspective, the story constituted a protest against fascism and military conflict in which, a year before
the Second World War, the author was arguing for peace and equality
between races and peoples.[71]

A Christian Story of Conscience

Las Casas vor Karl V. constitutes a significant development in Schneider's
historical work. In contrast to the earlier focus on the collective will of
peoples, on form in history, and the championing of monarchical rule,
the emphasis here is on the moral decisions and responsibility of the individual and, through Bernardino's confession and his rejection of illegally
acquired possessions, on atonement and expiation of guilt.

But above all, the story is about the role of conscience in human
affairs. Schneider's draft notes on his text state: "Das Gewissen,
die Aufrüttelung des Gewissens ist der eigentliche Gegenstand der
Erzählung" (Conscience, the stirring of conscience is the real subject of
the story).[72] For Schneider, the historical las Casas was the personifica-
tion of Christian conscience who was prepared to stand up to the might
of the state, to papal power, and to conventional imperial thinking in
order to propose a new Christian ethics for the Spanish colonies. This
partly explains the changes to historical chronology in the story: as a
result of developments in Germany in 1937, an appeal to conscience
seemed imperative and the moral issue could be highlighted by allowing
the central exchange to assume the characteristics of a court case rather
than a disputation, with prosecuting and defending counsels making
their cases, calling on witnesses, and hoping for a favorable judgment
from a judge with genuine decision-making powers. What counted
was less the depiction of the specific historical circumstances than the
fictional Las Casas's appeal to the conscience of the king and thus all
other Spaniards (LC, 237),[73] and at the same time Schneider's ability to
alert contemporary readers to the suprahistorical relevance of the ideas
presented. Through a narrative that starts with the awakening of an
individual conscience and the conversion of an unscrupulous conquistador, and ends with legislative changes motivated by a broader-based
acknowledgement of guilt, he offers readers amid their own suffering
a degree of consolation, encourages the individual to choose between
right and wrong, and champions the exercising of nonviolent protest
against abuses of human rights.

The story is unequivocal in its condemnation of the conquest,
oppression, and exploitation of the Indians. The attempt to bring
the natives into the Spanish empire can only proceed via preaching
of the Gospel and baptism; civilization is only possible if their dignity
is respected and they are treated as "brothers in Christ." This is why

their suffering is presented as a parallel to the suffering of Christ. Thus Bernardino recalls the capture of a cacique (Indian tribal leader) who, through his physical and mental torment, stands as the representative of the Indians and of human suffering more generally. The image of the enchained cacique makes a strong impression on the old women of the village, who bring what few ornate possessions they own to secure the release of their "leidenden Herrn" (suffering lord, LC, 139). Meier sees here a reference to Jesus: the cacique is initially the subject of a Judas-like embrace (LC, 136); he is then humiliated and has his arms and legs bound; he is venerated by women and, through his suffering, his soul is "destined for eternity" (LC, 137); like Christ, the cacique is a "prince" and, as he returns in the boat to his people, he carries "like a scepter" the Spaniards' ironic gift of a hoe (LC, 141).[74] Allied to Las Casas's outspoken defense of the Indians' rights, a scene such as this served to convey the message of the sanctity and value of all human life, to admonish but also sustain a (Christian) readership in contemporary Germany that was being bombarded by a very different set of ethics.

A crucial element of the scene is its contribution to Bernardino's gradually awakening conscience, a process accelerated by the example of the native Indian girl Lucaya, whom he buys at a slave market. She is for him the representative of her people's suffering and comes to embody Christian love of one's neighbor and hope for the future. She alerts the unscrupulous Spanish knight to the mystery of suffering ("Wen es zum Leiden zieht, der ist vielleicht noch nicht ganz verloren," A person who can still be moved by suffering may not be entirely lost, LC, 180) and makes him aware of his guilt. She successfully instructs the natives in the ways of Christianity and thus also provides an example of nonviolent conversion. However, it is only after she dies that Bernardino can address the deep contradiction in his life, selling his estates, setting his Indians free, and seeking the encounter with Las Casas. The whole Lucaya subplot serves to underpin Las Casas's view that injustice in the colonies is personal in origin and can be overcome only by personal recognition of wrongdoing and restitution. The knight's conversion from conquistador to repentant humanitarian is therefore a direct parallel to Las Casas's own transformation and reinforces the idea for contemporary readers that radical change is possible for the individual.

The Disputation

The disputation with Sepúlveda forms the core of the story and in it Schneider returns to a theme he had been concerned with in previous historical works, especially *Das Inselreich*: the relationship between the power of the state and the demands of the Gospel. The need for courage in order to change one's ways, to make decisive moral reforms, applies as much to the state as it does to a single human being, as much to the emperor himself as the individual conquistador.[75] In exploring this theme, Schneider presents the clash of the two very different political moralities: Las Casas's endeavor to realize in the political realm the lessons of the Sermon on the Mount and Sepúlveda's philosophy of state, which acknowledges only political exigencies and the realities of power politics.

The debate is opened by the Cardinal of Seville, who not only seeks to guide it but also to set its parameters, raising the question of how much authority the state can cede in accommodating the demands of religion (LC, 201–4). In attempting to restrict Las Casas's potential radicalism, the cardinal also warns of the consequences of upsetting the established order in the New World and of the potential financial losses for the Spanish state. His advocacy of a strict pragmatism constitutes an attempt to manipulate the debate in advance, to the disadvantage of the monk.

At the root of the exchange is the clash of two conflicting models of legitimizing a country's actions: the natural law represented by Las Casas and national law (*Staatsrecht*) as expounded by Sepúlveda (LC, 215). Las Casas affirms a people's natural right to freedom and asserts that the Spanish have no right to claim the Indians' natural resources as their own. He accepts the Spaniards' duty as missionaries to convert the natives to Christianity but rejects any attempt to force them to accept the faith. Whereas for Sepúlveda military measures are required to subjugate and colonize a people in readiness for conversion, Las Casas argues for the power of the Christian message without recourse to violent reinforcement (LC, 202).

He insists that a Christian monarchy, as a theologically based order, must place supernatural considerations above reasons of state, must see its role as acting as an instrument of salvation rather than as serving human needs. In countering Sepúlveda's arguments, and thus indirectly the authoritarian ideology of the Nazis, he rejects the notion of one race being more highly developed than another, arguing that all humans are equal before God. The greatest duty of the state is to treat people humanely, whereas that of Christianity is to convert souls without recourse to violence. Expressed in terms of Schneider's evolving thinking, the state is no longer to be based on the "will to form" but on the imitation of Christ, and this implies the clear demand to repudiate wars of conquest: "Taufen wir, so haben wir kein Recht, die Abgötterei zu strafen; taufen wir nicht, so haben wir kein Recht, nach den Indien zu fahren. Darum erachte ich die Kriege gegen die Indios für unerlaubt, die Sklaverei für unchristlich." (If we baptize people, we have no right to punish their idolatry. If we do not baptize them, then we have no right to travel to the Indies. Therefore

I consider the wars against the Indians to be forbidden by God, and slavery to be unchristian, LC, 205–6.)

The key question is how achievable this is in practice, and Sepúlveda, the hardheaded pragmatist, counters that a state cannot be based solely on faith. Rather it is the role of the state to create the conditions under which a people can practice their religion in the first place; only through an ordered state with solid foundations can faith be promoted (LC, 207). He warns that interpreting Christ's teaching as something absolute, independent of the need for order on earth, can endanger a Christian state and thus damage Christianity itself: "Dagegen seien alle Mittel, die dem christlichen Staate dienen, auch dem Christentum selbst förderlich" (On the other hand, any means that serve the Christian state also help to promote Christianity, LC, 208). He insists that in establishing this order and in securing the power of the emperor, the ruling classes, and the church, the most extreme forms of suppression and cruelty are justified, concluding that the wars against the Indians are therefore not only just but also "holy." This ends-justify-the-means argument went to the heart of the Nazi transformation of German society and specifically the dilemmas of 1937–38.

Whereas such views on order and the justification for forcible subjugation of heathen peoples might not have been wholly inimical to the Schneider of the 1920s, developments under National Socialism had led him to embrace the alternative religious utopian vision of Las Casas based on the ethics of the Sermon on the Mount, which are incompatible with the argument that ends justify means: "wir können mit schlechten Mitteln Gutes nicht erreichen. Und unsere Mittel sind schlecht" (we cannot achieve good by evil means. And our means are evil, LC, 224–25). This moral rigor was to be a decisive influence on Schneider's refusal to become involved in the conspiracy of July 20, 1944 on the grounds that it involved assisting in murder (VT, 142) and was to motivate his involvement in the postwar antinuclear debate.

Las Casas vor Karl V. and Nazi Germany

Looking back from the position of the 1950s, Schneider says he had wanted to use *Las Casas vor Karl V.* to protest against the persecution of Jews in Nazi Germany (VT, 111). However, while links with contemporary German anti-Semitism can indeed be seen in the depiction of the fate of the Indians, by the time the book had been published Germany had invaded Czechoslovakia and the story was thus also interpreted by some as referring to Nazi expansionism, to the suppression and exploitation of occupied peoples,[76] and there are, in fact, as many parallels with the subsequent German invasions of Poland and the Soviet Union and the treatment of "inferior" Slavic peoples. The essence of this aspect to the work can be found in the exchange with Sepúlveda. Las Casas cannot accept the latter's fundamental belief that "ein höher geartetes und höher entwickeltes Volk . . . zum Frommen der Welt ein Recht innehätte über tiefer stehende Völker" (a people of a higher species and higher development, for the good of the world, should have rights over inferior peoples, LC, 215). Sepúlveda accuses the monk of having accepted in his conquistador days the principle that a different law applies to "superior" races (LC, 215). This (anachronistic) use of racial language encourages, indeed almost compels, the reader to make the connection with a Nazi Germany adjusting to the consequences of the Nuremberg Race Laws. In this context, the alternative ideal, formulated by and embodied in the example of Las Casas, is rendered all the more powerful: "Gott [hat] den Menschen frei geschaffen und vor ihm [ist] kein Unterschied zwischen den Menschen" (God created man free, and before Him there is no difference between men, LC, 205).

The camouflaged message is flagged up as early as the Calderón quotation in the epigraph to the story:

Christen, dieser ist der Zeuge
der vor künftigen Geschlechtern
meine Redlichkeit bezeugt. (LC, 119)

[Christians, this is the witness who will testify to my honesty before future generations.]

An absolute principle of moral rectitude is firmly established here as the story's fundamental theme and is associated with the character of Las Casas as the work's key figure. At the same time, the epigraph can be taken to refer to Schneider himself, to his religious (and political) position: it serves to signal to readers that the work is about more than a few "scenes from the time of the conquistadors" and, in implying the importance of being true to one's principles and drawing attention to the work's relevance to future generations, it promotes a sense of wider applicability.

In the first "scene," on the quayside in Veracruz, the reader is immediately directed to the ethical core of the story. A rich Spanish plantation owner is being carried in a hammock by two natives; in order to provoke the hated Las Casas, he gratuitously beats the natives and calls them lazy and useless, adding that those who would set them free are even worse. Las Casas meanwhile treats his native entourage like his family and tells them he will return, promising them justice and protection from the "tyrants" (LC, 125). The depiction of the Spaniard's cruelty and of Las Casas's commitment to justice preempt the story's concern with the moral issues of Spanish brutality and Indian freedom; they align the reader with Las Casas and provide the first hint of the work's relevance to the analogous persecution of Germany's Jews.

In general, the applicability of many passages to the situation in Nazi Germany is striking. Repeatedly one can simply replace the words "spanisch" (Spanish) and "Spanien" (Spain) with "deutsch" (German) and "Deutschland" (Germany) to arrive at texts that might have appeared in the Nazi press.[77] For example: "Denn was könnte den Feinden Spaniens erwünschter sein, als aus spanischem Munde zu hören, daß wir jahraus, jahrein die abscheulichsten Verbrechen auf uns lüden? . . . Die Anklagen des Paters Las Casas sind zum unausdenkbaren Schaden des spanischen Namens und somit des spanischen Staates." (For what could be more pleasing to the enemies of Spain than to hear from Spanish lips that year after year we have been committing the most abominable crimes? Father Las Casas's accusations do unimaginable damage to the name of Spain and thus to the Spanish state, LC, 209.) Similarly, the Dominican suggests that the rule of law is especially crucial at this time "da das spanische Volk in Gefahr sei, seine Seele an irdische Mächte zu verkaufen" (when the Spanish people are in danger of selling their souls to worldly powers, LC, 167). He further prophesies divine judgment for the guilt-ridden country: "Wer den größten Auftrag verfehlt, der verfällt auch der schwersten Schuld. . . . Darum tut Gott recht, wenn er dieses Landes Ansehen vernichtet. Für ungeheure Verbrechen erfolgt nun die ungeheure Strafe." (He who fails to fulfill the weightiest of tasks incurs the greatest guilt. That is why God would be right to destroy this country's standing. Terrible punishment follows terrible crimes, LC, 238–39.) Even a modest degree of *Hellhörigkeit* (sensitivity) allows one to see the contemporary applicability here.

Once sensitized to the interchangeability of Spanish and German, of Indians and Jews, the reader is confronted by repeated parallels. For example, Bernardino's description of his entanglement in the rapacity of the wars of conquest in the New Indies suggests subtle links with the situation of Germans under National Socialism. He notes that he and his fellow conquistadors became "intoxicated" by their deeds to the extent that they no longer knew what was happening to them, did not realize the depths to which formerly noble individuals were sinking. In the scene with the imprisoned cacique, Bernardino does not have the courage to try to free the native chief and subsequently feels a deep shame at being a part of the intimidation and humiliation inflicted on the Indians, at having failed to seize the opportunity to make a stand (LC, 138–39, 142). The theme of personal omission and fearfulness, the failure of the "men with the knives" to act decisively and to stand up for what they believed to be right, which lies at the heart of Andres's *Wir sind Utopia* (*We Are God's Utopia*, see chapter 4), can also be readily discerned here—not in an accusatory fashion but as an invitation to readers to reflect on their own situation. Similarly, during the disputation the witness Captain Vargas[78] reports that the Indians never tell the truth, are vice-ridden, unfaithful, mistreat and abuse their own wives, daughters, and sisters, and are capable of all manner of atrocities (LC, 231), words that echo the rhetoric of the Nazi press in its portrayal of the "Jewish enemy."

However, at the same time, Schneider's selective use of such historical facts is also part of his camouflaged critique. First, he suppresses much of the historically documented atrocities committed by Indians against the conquistadors, particularly the forthright material he had found in Vargas's *Apologías*, giving greater prominence to Las Casas's and Bernardino's lengthier descriptions of Spanish crimes in order to weight the debate in Las Casas's favor but also to make state-sponsored oppression the focus of the narrative. Second, he reduces Vargas to a mere captain rather than the governor he actually was, and ensures that he lacks Las Casas's rhetorical fire and passion. And third, Sepúlveda's case is restricted to deployment of arguments based exclusively on national law and reasons of state, whereas the historical Sepúlveda is known to have used Aristotelian arguments pertaining to natural law in support of his case, which in the fiction are the preserve of Las Casas.[79]

Some have suggested that Sepúlveda is to be seen as the scholar or highly educated lawyer who in the Third Reich allowed himself and his scholarship to be harnessed to the Nazi cause and who completely lost sight of fundamental humane values.[80] Certainly his legalistic defense of the rights of highly developed peoples to exercise power over racially inferior ones would have been a line of argument all too familiar to a reading public that had recently experienced the blanket press propaganda surrounding the promulgation of the Nuremberg Race Laws. However, given that Sepúlveda's arguments are largely based on a sense of Christian mission, he is rather to be seen as the sort of Christian who at first welcomed the social order established by the Nazis and subsequently accommodated his beliefs to racist ideas, perhaps in the manner of members of the "Deutsche Christen" (German Christians).[81]

Besides discerning parallels with Nazi Germany in the story, it is also possible to view it as an example of a *Gegenbild* (counterimage) to the regime. In countering Sepúlveda's political expediency arguments, Las Casas argues that the Spanish cause would be better served by looking after the interests of the Indian natives so that they would convert more willingly, be more loyal, and thus become more manageable colonial subjects, resulting in a more secure empire. His notion of reform inspired by Christian values is not based on political and social thought of the sixteenth century, and does nothing to question the Spanish state's right to colonize and convert, but draws more on the principles of a later enlightened absolutism typified by eighteenth-century Prussia under Frederick the Great.[82] The depiction of a humane, enlightened Charles V and the exaggerated promise behind his new laws shows Schneider shaping historical material for the purpose of advocating to contemporary readers an alternative system of values.

It is not easy to assess precisely the boldness involved in what Schneider was doing in this work, but it is clear that having his two principal characters discuss the legitimacy of one people's right to exercise power over another that it condemns as inferior took the work beyond its colonial context and an examination of the Christian past and raised issues with immediate relevance to the German present. It is difficult to avoid the conclusion that the presentation of Spanish assumptions of racial superiority spoke through only the thinnest of camouflages to readers in a country where such perverted beliefs had become an unchallengeable state ideology.

Imitation of Christ and the Tragic Sense of Existence

From the point of view of Schneider's personal and literary development *Las Casas vor Karl V.* was significant, as it served to elaborate and, in a way, to justify his new relationship to Christianity and history. He now believed that the figure of Christ embodied a deep contradiction with the world, that a life lived in the succession of Christ brought man unavoidably into conflict with the representatives of worldly power, and that Christianity was to be seen as a force focused on social change.

More particularly, the story illustrates Schneider's notion of the Kingdom of God, which is informed by his ideas on monarchy and stands as an alternative to the Third Reich. This kingdom is to be realized not just by the individual but also the state. As Las Casas tells Charles: "wenn du lauschen willst, Herr, so vernimmst du vielleicht die Stimme des Lenkers der Geschichte, der dich und deine Krone und dein Land in diesem Augenblick als Werkzeug gebrauchen und sein Reich ausbreiten will durch dich" (If you listen, Sire, you may hear the voice of the guide of history who wishes to use you and your crown and your country as his instruments and to expand his kingdom through you, LC, 237). Unlike in Schneider's earlier, nationalist reflections on the *Reich*, this state of affairs is not to be achieved through the violence of the "will to form" (here, territorial conquest and the suppression of other peoples) but through nonviolence, the following of Christ's example, and an unswerving belief in the inviolability of right and the law.

The imitation of Christ is closely linked to the image of the cross. The story of Bernardino's troubled conscience illustrates the inevitability and omnipresence of guilt. The highly contrived conclusion, involving the saintlike priest who is revealed to be his son, is presented, on the one hand, as a utopian counterimage to an inhuman, cruel world, with the image of the dying knight, crucifix in hand, substantiating this cross symbolism; on the other hand, Bernardino's reluctant renunciation of his worldly goods and his only very gradual acceptance of the need to subordinate earthly endeavor to the dictates of the "das ewige Gesetz" (the eternal law, LC, 167) serve to illustrate the tragic nature of human existence.

And indeed, besides symbolizing Christian faith, the cross also represents this unavoidable tragedy at the heart of life. As they embark on the voyage back to the Indies, Las Casas comments to his companions: "Daran liegt es ja nicht . . ., daß wir die Welt mit dem Kreuze durchdringen; sondern es liegt alles daran, daß wir über unserer Mühe von ihm durchdrungen werden" (It is not so important that we suffuse the world with the cross; rather, what really matters is that in the process we ourselves are suffused with it, LC, 260). Enforced conversion is rejected; all human efforts to effect change need to be suffused with the spirit of Christian teaching and a sense of divine justice. Yet this cannot resolve the tragic hopelessness of existence, as illustrated by the predicament of Charles, who is unable to fulfill his role of spreading the faith in the way he would like and has to accept the persecution of the Indians as a burden on him and on his successors: it is the cross they have to bear (LC, 249–51). This sense of resignation expresses the essence of Schneider's tragic sense of life.

Las Casas too is faced with the apparently insurmountable task of championing the Christian message in the face of, on the one hand, the inimical and firmly embedded power structures of both church and state, and, on the other, pervasive human greed and self-interest. The final lines of the story present in symbolic form the hopelessness of this situation as, alone among the fleet, Las Casas's ship is becalmed in the exit to the harbor and almost capsizes (LC, 260): the scene, with its description of the rising and falling of the ship on the waves, denoting man's inevitable exposure to the vicissitudes of existence, underlines the new bishop's hesitant return to the colonies, a hesitancy that results from the knowledge that the prospects for his mission are poor.

In the increasing awareness of their ultimate impotence and likely tragic failure, both Charles and Las Casas can only find hope in the fifteenth-century mystic Thomas à Kempis's *De Imitatione Christi*. In their final discussion, Charles suggests that his decision to pass the laws is influenced by the human need to act in imitation of Christ and to accept suffering and sacrifice as part of this, in the belief that the latter are transient. He quotes the mystic:

Deine Arbeit hier wird nicht mehr lange währen, und die Schmerzen, die dich jetzt zu Boden drücken, werden bald ausgeschmerzt haben.

Harre noch eine kurze Weile, und du wirst das Ende aller Plage
schnell kommen sehn. . . . Klein ist doch alles und von kurzer Dauer,
was zeitlich ist und deshalb mit der Zeit vorübergeht." (LC, 255)

[You will not have to labor here long, and the sorrows that burden
you now will soon pass. Hold out for a little while longer and you
will soon see the end of all life's trials. All that is temporal and thus
passes away with time is trivial and of short duration.]

In seeking to do what he judges to be right, the king inevitably suffers
because the world is imperfect, and through his suffering he comes closer
to the figure of Christ.

In the context of Nazi Germany, the implication is that the individual may espouse absolute values and pursue humanist or Christian
ideals, but this will not change the basic tragic facts of life, the repressive
measures of the regime will persist, the persecution of minorities will
continue unabated.[83] As Schneider noted in connection with Anna von
König's silent protest of placing a wreath in front of an Ernst Barlach
work in the "Entartete Kunst" (Degenerate Art) exhibition: "Wir stan-
den längst in der Zeit, da im vergeblichen Protest der einzig erreichbare
Wert war" (We had long been living in a time when the only achievable
value was to be found in vain protest, VT, 106). The political impotence
implied by this and by Charles's and Las Casas's respective situations in
the story inevitably means the only solution is to turn to the transcendental for reassurance that all will be well beyond the tragic sphere of
human existence. This is very much the spirit of the sonnets and it is
no coincidence that Schneider's poetry became more prominent in his
output after this story.

However, this emphasis on other-worldly salvation and Christ-like
self-sacrifice raises questions about the status of Schneider's new-found,
nonconformist ethical position in *Las Casas vor Karl V*. Whereas the
stance taken against the "racially inferior" is unequivocal, the basis for
opposing the regime is less clear. For Schnell, the reference to a super-
ordinate power, the search for solace in the transcendental, serves to
belittle or undermine the struggle for change contained in Schneider's
stand against "genocide."[84] Once again, we face the central dilemma of
inner emigrant literary activity, but, in this case, just as important as the
usual game of hide and seek with censors is Schneider's innate tendency
toward a tragic conception of existence, one confirmed by his focus in the
Christian story on the theology of the cross rather than the role of the
joyous resurrection. More than with other Christian inner emigrants, the
philosophical underpinning of Schneider's work militates against positive
action in the earthly realm. Nevertheless, testimonies to the impact of his
work on readers show it met with by far the greatest resonance of any

inner emigrant text, especially during the war, and this must be factored into any evaluation of influence.[85]

Conclusion

The traditional view of Schneider as an orthodox Catholic, firmly rooted in his religious faith, dispensing spiritual consolation to Germans under Hitler, is not helpful, mainly because it does not register the extent to which he was a questioner and doubter, a searcher warning against precipitate responses to life's dilemmas,[86] but also because it fails to capture the development of his ideas.

His early writing, predicated on the belief that man's existential guilt makes the course of history inevitably tragic, lacked any sense of a transcendental order or Christian ethics. Although his subsequent old-style nationalism, with its emphasis on a strong state and the central role of the monarchy, brought him close to reactionary thinking, his championing of monarchic rule in Prussian history, in fact, denied the Nazi state as its legitimate heir and, more generally, rejected totalitarianism as a perversion. His gradually evolving Christian metaphysics led to a problematic political theology, combining the imitation of Christ with deeply antidemocratic ideas. At the center of his utopian vision was the idea of the *Reich* that henceforth came to be associated with the "Weltreich," seen as a staging post on the way to the return of the Kingdom of God at the end of time. Since exile offered no prospect of influencing developments, he chose instead a necessarily circumscribed form of inner resistance, which allowed him to reach an extensive readership. Although the demise of cherished values seemed to suggest helplessness in the face of political violence, much of Schneider's wartime work implies that a life focused on God can provide the strength to resist an inhumane regime.

In terms of aesthetic qualities, *Las Casas vor Karl V.* is certainly not the strongest fictional product of the inner emigration and it betrays its author's literary roots as a historiographer. Characters and events are introduced to serve Schneider's moral and ethical purpose, and there is little character development and minimal psychological motivation. The entirely fictional figure of Bernardino suffers from its functional role as vehicle and didactic ethical model: the knight's confession of past transgressions serves as a parallel to or reflection of Las Casas's own life but also as a minor-key representation of the bitter history of colonial conquest itself. There are further problems with Las Casas's character: although his role as proclaimer of moral and ethical truths served Schneider's camouflaged message well, the monk's tendency repeatedly to talk about the ideas he serves to embody creates the impression of tendentious characterization. The description of the Indians meanwhile reveals an idyllic image of the "noble savage," a primitive but essentially good people that falls victim to an evil civilization; this is something that is both historically dubious and superfluous to the basic theme of the story.[87]

Notwithstanding these weaknesses, the story is a significant milestone both in Schneider's development and in nonconformist writing under National Socialism more generally. The concern in his earlier work with the tragic confrontation of great cultures and the depiction of protagonists who are part of a collective will are replaced by a focus on moral decisions, for which individuals are held personally responsible. The work conveys the inevitability of suffering yet also emphasizes the centrality of conscience and the need to make moral choices amid the vicissitudes of life; the possibility of failure and guilt make life a tragic undertaking, but accepting the dictates of conscience and embracing the imitation of Christ can make sense of existence. In the context of Nazi Germany such a message surely did little to encourage active resistance to the regime. It did, however, have the potential to underline the transient nature of people's suffering, in keeping with one of Brecht's functions of camouflaged writing.[88] It also served to console and reaffirm fundamental principles and beliefs. Furthermore, the emphasis on the values of enlightened absolutism and their potential for improving people's lives provided a distinct *Gegenbild*, contrasting starkly with the values of Nazi Germany. In this sense, the story displays many of the characteristics of other inner emigrant texts that offered camouflaged messages of support to readers alienated by the regime. The difference here is the way Schneider in addition tackles Nazi racial policy and expansionism, making it probably the boldest of nonconformist works published under the regime.

Notes

[1] Schneider designated his text an "Erzählung" (story) and, although some narrative aspects more resemble those of a novel, the original designation is retained here.

[2] Reinhold Schneider, *Verhüllter Tag* (1954), in *Reinhold Schneider: Gesammelte Werke*, ed. Edwin Maria Landau, vol. 10 (Frankfurt am Main: Insel, 1978), 16–17. Subsequent references to *Verhüllter Tag* are cited parenthetically as (*VT*, page number) and references to Schneider's collected works are cited as (*GW*, volume:page number).

[3] See Johannes Kessels, "Reinhold Schneider und die Herausgabe der Sammlung 'Das Gottesreich in der Zeit,'" in *Caritas '83: Jahrbuch des Deutschen Caritasverbandes*, Sonderdruck, ed. Deutscher Caritasverband (Freiburg im Breisgau: Deutscher Caritasverband, 1983), 305–42.

[4] Reinhold Schneider, *Winter in Wien: Aus meinen Notizbüchern 1957/58* (Freiburg im Breisgau: Herder, 1958).

[5] Diary entry for April 9, 1934, reproduced in the documentary collection *Reinhold Schneider: Leben und Werk in Dokumenten,* ed. Franz Anselm Schmitt and Bruno Scherer, 2nd ed. (Karlsruhe: Badenia, 1973), 82.

[6] Hans Getzeny, *Reinhold Schneider: Seine geistige und künstlerische Entwicklung am Beispiel der erzählenden Prosa* (Frankfurt am Main: Lang, 1987), 7–12.

[7] See Claus Ensberg, *Die Orientierungsproblematik der Moderne im Spiegel abendländischer Geschichte: Das literarische Werk Reinhold Schneiders* (Tübingen: Narr, 1995), 128.

[8] For Schneider's reception of Nietzsche, see *Reinhold Schneider: Tagebuch 1930–1935,* ed. Josef Rast (Frankfurt am Main: Insel, 1983), 153–67 and 298–99. For a fuller discussion of the influence of Schopenhauer and Nietzsche, see Getzeny, *Reinhold Schneider,* 13–17.

[9] Friedrich Schürr, *Miguel de Unamuno: Der Dichterphilosoph des tragischen Lebensgefühls* (Bern: Francke, 1962).

[10] Schneider's "Nachwort," in Reinhold Schneider, *Philipp II oder Religion und Macht* (Leipzig: Hegner, 1931), 338.

[11] See Pirmin A. Meier, *Form und Dissonanz: Reinhold Schneider als historiographischer Schriftsteller* (Frankfurt am Main: Lang, 1978), 75–91.

[12] The so-called Spanish Armada was a large fleet of ships under the command of the Duke of Medina Sidonia, which, in 1588, attempted an unsuccessful invasion of England designed to defeat Protestantism there and halt English interference in the Spanish Netherlands.

[13] See, for example, Schneider, *Philipp II,* 83–84.

[14] Although written in 1931, it was published posthumously only in 1960. The theme is the medieval struggle between emperor and pope, between secular and ecclesiastical power.

[15] Letter from Jakob Hegner to Reinhold Schneider, May 3, 1932, in Schmitt and Scherer, *Reinhold Schneider,* 86.

[16] Reinhold Schneider, *Fichte: Der Weg zur Nation* (Munich: Langen, 1932), 93.

[17] Meier, *Form und Dissonanz,* 120–21.

[18] Reinhold Schneider, "Vorwort," in Reinhold Schneider, *Die Hohenzollern: Tragik und Königtum,* 2nd ed. (Cologne: Hegner, 1953), 14, where the monarchy is seen as desirable but impossible ("das nicht Mögliche") and unrealizable ("unerfüllbar").

[19] Reinhold Schneider, *Die Hohenzollern: Tragik und Königtum* (Leipzig: Hegner, 1933), 111 and 84, respectively.

[20] Schmitt and Scherer, *Reinhold Schneider,* 91.

[21] Reinhold Schneider, entry for September 16, 1930, *Tagebuch,* 148.

[22] Reinhold Schneider, letter of January 13, 1931 to his Dresden friend Hans Rösel, cited in Schmitt and Scherer, *Reinhold Schneider,* 71.

[23] Reinhold Schneider, entry for February 5, 1934, *Tagebuch,* 754–55.

[24] Unpublished letter to Anna-Maria Baumgarten, July 28, 1932, in Reinhold-Schneider-Archive, cited in Getzeny, *Reinhold Schneider,* 60.

[25] Unpublished letter to Anna-Maria Baumgarten, March 7, 1933, in Reinhold-Schneider-Archive, cited in Karl Wilhelm Reddemann, *Der Christ vor einer zertrümmerten Welt: Reinhold Schneider—ein Dichter antwortet der Zeit* (Freiburg im Breisgau: Herder, 1978), 78.

[26] Reinhold Schneider, "Der Wiedereintrittt in die Geschichte," *Der Tag*, December 31, 1933, cited in Bruno Scherer, *Tragik vor dem Kreuz: Leben und Geisteswelt Reinhold Schneiders* (Freiburg im Breisgau: Herder, 1966), 50–51. Although this and the other article in *Der Tag* were not published until the end of 1933, it seems they had been written a lot earlier and that Schneider's rejection of National Socialism dates from as early as the summer of 1933. See also Reddemann, *Der Christ vor einer zertrümmerten Welt*, 76–77; Jürgen Steinle, *Reinhold Schneider (1903–1958): Konservatives Denken zwischen Kulturkrise, Gewaltherrschaft und Restauration* (Aachen: Müller, 1992), 66–83; and Ralf Schuster, *Antwort in der Geschichte: Zu den Übergängen zwischen den Werkphasen bei Reinhold Schneider* (Tübingen: Narr, 2001), 81–85.

[27] Reinhold Schneider, "Der Tröster," *Hochland* 31, no. 2 (1933–34): 143–59. Looking back on the story after the war, Schneider writes: "In ihr ['Der Tröster'] war die christliche Wahrheit von der Stellvertretung als Nachfolge unvermittelt da. Das Leiden in den Lagern und Gefängnissen ging mir nun nicht mehr von der Seele." (In "Der Tröster" the Christian truth about vicarious suffering as the imitation of Christ was all of a sudden there. From now on the image of suffering in the camps and prisons weighed heavily on my heart, *VT*, 100.)

[28] See Reinhold Schneider, "Aus dem Briefwechsel von Reinhold Schneider und Leopold Ziegler," *Hochland* 53 (1960/61): 28–34; Reinhold Schneider, ed., *Gestalt und Seele: Das Werk des Malers Leo von König* (Leipzig: Insel, 1936); Hans Jürgen Baden, "Extreme Existenzen—Jochen Klepper und Reinhold Schneider," in *Über Reinhold Schneider*, ed. Carsten Peter Thiede (Frankfurt am Main: Suhrkamp, 1980), 183–201; N. Luise Hackelsberger-Bergengruen, ed., *Werner Bergengruen (1892–1964)—Reinhold Schneider (1903–1958): Briefwechsel* (Freiburg im Breisgau: Herder, 1966); and Meier, *Form und Dissonanz*, 135–36.

[29] Meier, *Form und Dissonanz*, 138.

[30] Reinhold Schneider, *Das Inselreich: Gesetz und Grösse der britischen Macht* (Leipzig: Insel, 1936), 64–66.

[31] Reinhold Schneider, "Nachwort," *Das Inselreich*, 554.

[32] See below the *Völkischer Beobachter* review of *Kaiser Lothars Krone* (1937), which also refers back to the rejection of *Das Inselreich* by the *Bücherkunde* as an attempt to declare the *völkisch* vitality of a nation to be dangerous "demonism" (Anon., "Ist die Geschichte eine Konfession?," *Völkischer Beobachter*, March 5, 1938, in Schmitt and Scherer, *Reinhold Schneider*, 109).

[33] Cf. for the same period: Andres (thirteen), Bergengruen (twelve), le Fort (eight), Jünger (four), Klepper (five), Wiechert (eight); Mitterer and Reck-Malleczewen are not listed at all. Strothmann, *Nationalsozialistische Literaturpolitik*, 444–46.

[34] Anon., "Ist die Geschichte eine Konfession?," 109.

[35] "Das Gottesreich in der Zeit," in *GW*, 9:118.

[36] Letter of May 28, 1940 from the Ministry of Propaganda to the President of the Reichsschrifttumskammer, cited in Steinle, *Reinhold Schneider*, 155.

[37] See also Schneider's talk "Der Bildungsauftrag des christlichen Dichters" (1953), in Reinhold Schneider, *Der christliche Protest* (Zurich: Verlag der Arche, 1954), 65–66.

[38] "Die Verwaltung der Macht," in *GW*, 8:47–48.

[39] Schneider, "Vorwort," in Reinhold Schneider, *Weltreich und Gottesreich: Drei Vorträge* (Munich: Schnell & Steiner, 1946), 8.

[40] Schneider, "Persönlichkeit und Schicksal Philipps II von Spanien," in *Weltreich und Gottesreich*, 41–108.

[41] Schneider, "Vor dem Grauen," in *GW*, 4:477–78.

[42] As reported by Helmuth von Moltke and Heinrich Graf Luckner. See Ger van Roon, *Neuordnung im Widerstand: Der Kreisauer Kreis innerhalb der deutschen Widerstandsbewegung* (Munich: Oldenbourg, 1967), 252. On the Kreisau Circle, see "*Wir sind Utopia*" in chapter 4 of this book.

[43] Reinhold Schneider, *Die innere Befreiung: Gedenkwort zum 20. Juli* (Stuttgart: Hatje, 1947), 18–19.

[44] Reinhold Schneider, "Nachwort," in Schneider, *Das Vaterunser* (Freiburg im Breisgau: Herder, 1960).

[45] Schmitt and Scherer, *Reinhold Schneider*, 111.

[46] *Sonette* (Sonnets, Leipzig: Insel, 1939); *Dreißig Sonette* (Thirty sonnets, Halle: Werkstätten der Stadt Halle, 1941, private printing); *Das Gottesreich in der Zeit: Sonette und Aufsätze* (The kingdom of God in time: Sonnets and essays, Reichshof: Druckerei Udzialowa, 1942); *Sonette—Auswahl* (Sonnets: A selection, Freiburg: Kirchliche Kriegshilfestelle, 1942, typecopy reproduction); *Jetzt ist der Heiligen Zeit* (Now is the time of saints, Kolmar: Alsatia, 1943); *Die Waffen des Lichts* (The weapons of light, Kolmar: Alsatia, 1944). See Kessels, "Reinhold Schneider," 323.

[47] Christoph Perels, "Nachwort," in *GW*, 5:408. On the issue of dissemination, see Ingo Zimmermann, *Reinhold Schneider: Weg eines Schriftstellers* (Berlin: Union, 1982), 136.

[48] See Konrad Hofmann, Reinhold Schneider, and Erik Wolf, eds, *Sieger in Fesseln: Christuszeugnisse aus Lagern und Gefängnissen* (Freiburg im Breisgau: Herder, 1947). For additional testimonies to the poems' impact, see Schmitt and Scherer, *Reinhold Schneider*, 128–33.

[49] See Hans Dieter Zimmermann, "Reinhold Schneider—ein Dichter der Inneren Emigration?," in Kroll and von Voss, *Schriftsteller und Widerstand*, 364.

[50] Klieneberger, "Reinhold Schneider," in Klieneberger, *Christian Writers of the Inner Emigration*, 62–63.

[51] "Nun baut der Wahn" (1937), in *GW*, 5:109.

[52] See Ekkehard Blattmann, *Reinhold Schneider linguistisch interpretiert* (Heidelberg: Stiehm, 1979), 65–68.

[53] Reinhold Schneider, "Der Antichrist" (1938), in *GW*, 5:26.

[54] See entry for September 14, 1934, in Schneider, *Tagebuch*, 795; and "Die Rechtfertigung der Macht" (1935), in *GW*, 8:19–20.

[55] See Barbara Hoth-Blattmann and Ekkehard Blattmann, "Grauen und Passion: Quellenstudien zu Reinhold Schneiders 'Las Casas vor Karl V.,'" in *Reinhold Schneider—Ich, Tod, Gott*, Reinhold Schneider-Jahrbuch 1, ed. Ekkehard Blattmann and Barbara Hoth-Blattmann (Frankfurt am Main: Lang, 1985), 268.

[56] Werner Stauffacher, "Zwischen äußerer und innerer Emigration: Las Casas als Figur des Widerstandes bei Alfred Döblin und Reinhold Schneider," in *Christliches Exil und christlicher Widerstand: Ein Symposion an der Katholischen Universität Eichstätt 1985*, ed. Wolfgang Frühwald and Heinz Hürten (Regensburg: Pustet, 1987), 397–98.

[57] As part of his research Schneider had copied substantial extracts from this document detailing the arguments deployed against Las Casas, especially such Indian practices as cannibalism, murdering missionaries, human sacrifice, debauchery, sodomy, and polygamy (see Hoth-Blattmann and Blattmann, "Grauen und Passion," 273–96 and 327–32).

[58] The following sketch of the historical las Casas's life and the reception of his report are based on Hans Magnus Enzensberger's essay in the German version of the report, entitled "Las Casas oder ein Rückblick in die Zukunft," in *Bartolomé de las Casas: Kurzgefaßter Bericht von der Verwüstung der Westindischen Länder*, ed. H. M. Enzensberger (Frankfurt am Main: Insel, 1981), 124–50, especially 124–28 and 139–46.

[59] Eckart Schäfer, "Die Indianer und der Humanismus: Die spanische Conquista in lateinischer Literatur," in Blattmann and Hoth-Blattmann, *Reinhold Schneider*, 231; see also *VT*, 111.

[60] There were several stage versions produced after the war. See, for example, Schmitt and Scherer, *Reinhold Schneider*, 181; and Schäfer, "Die Indianer und der Humanismus," 236, 240, and 248–52.

[61] Anon., "Las Casas vor Karl V.," in *Der Buchhändler im neuen Reich* 3, nos. 10–11, Ausgabe A (1938): 397.

[62] W. Kalthoff, "Las Casas vor Karl V.," *Deutsche Allgemeine Zeitung* (1938), reproduced in *Das Inselschiff* 20 (1938/39): 92.

[63] Werner Uhde, "Las Casas," *Frankfurter Zeitung*, October 23, 1938, 8.

[64] Hans E. Friedrich, "Reinhold Schneider: Las Casas vor Karl V.: Szenen aus der Konquistadorenzeit," *Die Literatur* 41, no. 1 (1938/39): 185–86.

[65] E. H. Lucas, "Reinhold Schneider: Las Casas vor Karl V.," *Information: Monatsblätter des Deutschen Buch-Clubs Hamburg* 11 (September/October 1938): 9, cited in Ehrke-Rotermund and Rotermund, *Zwischenreiche*, 311.

[66] Letter from Leopold Ziegler, April 29, 1939, in Reinhold Schneider, *Reinhold Schneider und Leopold Ziegler: Briefwechsel* (Munich: Kösel, 1960), 50.

[67] Letter from Ludwig Dehio, October 31, 1938, cited in Steinle, *Reinhold Schneider*, 166.

[68] Letter from Jochen Klepper, November 29, 1938, in Riemschneider, *Jochen Klepper*, 116. For his actual words, see chapter 2 of this book, the first paragraph of the section "Esotericism and Its Challenges."

[69] Cited in Schmitt and Scherer, *Reinhold Schneider*, 114.

[70] Schonauer, *Deutsche Literatur im Dritten Reich*, 152.

[71] Brekle, *Schriftsteller im antifaschistischen Widerstand*, 165.

[72] Typescript dated November 10, 1937, in Reinhold-Schneider-Archive, cited by Schäfer, "Die Indianer und der Humanismus," 234.

[73] All references are to Reinhold Schneider, *Las Casas vor Karl V.: Szenen aus der Konquistadorenzeit*, in *GW*, vol. 3.

[74] Meier, *Form und Dissonanz*, 163–64.

[75] Peter Berglar, "Staatsräson und Christus-Nachfolge: Gedanken zu Reinhold Schneiders Las Casas Dichtung," *Mitteilungen der Reinhold-Schneider-Gesellschaft*, July 4, 1972, 57.

[76] Letter to Frau Heynemann, June 28, 1947, cited in Schmitt and Scherer, *Reinhold Schneider*, 116.

[77] See Brekle, *Schriftsteller im antifaschistischen Widerstand*, 163.

[78] The character is based on the historical Vargas Machuca, who is, however, brought forward in history by a hundred years to allow him to contribute to the debate.

[79] Schäfer, "Die Indianer und der Humanismus," 235.

[80] See Ingo Zimmermann, *Der späte Reinhold Schneider: Eine Studie* (Freiburg im Breisgau: Herder, 1973), 142–43; also Günter Wirth, "Eine Stimme für die Gleichberechtigung der Völker: Reinhold Schneider: 'Las Casas vor Karl V.: Szenen aus der Konquistadorenzeit,'" in Bock and Hahn, *Erfahrung Nazideutschland*, 319, who even sees Sepúlveda as an intellectual "Schreibtischtäter" (desktop criminal).

[81] The "Deutsche Christen" was a racist strand of the German Protestant Church that sought to align the latter with National Socialism. Their increasing infiltration of church leadership led to a schism within the church and the establishment in 1934 of the opposed Bekennende Kirche (Confessing Church), which claimed to defend true Protestant principles.

[82] See Riordan, "Depictions of the State," 152–67, especially 165–66.

[83] See also Ensberg, *Die Orientierungsproblematik der Moderne*, 210–11.

[84] Schnell, *Literarische innere Emigration*, 150.

[85] Contrary to the view that Charles and Las Casas (and Schneider himself) reconcile themselves too easily to their political impotence, it has been argued (see, for example, Schäfer, "Die Indianer und der Humanismus," 237) that the consolation contained in the words of *The Imitation of Christ* are not to be seen as an invitation to indulge in quietism but that they demand an active emulation of Christ to the point of accepting a martyr's death and that it is this that releases renewed strength to pass the new laws and to spread the word of the Gospel in the colonies.

[86] Georg Langenhorst, "Reinhard Schneider heute lesen?: Theologisch-literarische Annäherungen," in *Wege zu Reinhold Schneider: Zum 50. Todestag des Dichters,* ed. Friedrich Emde and Ralf Schuster (Passau: Schuster, 2008), 30.

[87] Meier, *Form und Dissonanz,* 162.

[88] Brecht, "Fünf Schwierigkeiten," 87. See "The Art of Camouflage: Reading and Writing in the Inner Emigration" in chapter 2 of this book.

Fig. 8.1. Ernst Jünger. Photo courtesy of
Deutsches Literaturarchiv Marbach.

8: Ernst Jünger: Spiritual Opposition as Resistance?

F EW GERMAN WRITERS have prompted such conflicting views among commentators as Ernst Jünger. Often the controversies surrounding him were linked to differing political and ideological stances, although it speaks volumes for the contradictory nature of a good deal of his work that support was not always from conservative quarters and opposition not always from the political Left. For his critics, he was a cold, unfeeling fascist who gloried in violence, had limited sympathy for human suffering, "cleared the way" for National Socialism, and was an embarrassment to postwar Germany as it sought to come to terms with the Nazi past. For his supporters and apologists, he was more an apolitical, at times humanitarian visionary, a modernist steeped in classical mythology, whose writings of the 1920s were a reflection and measure of the forces that shook and ultimately destroyed the Weimar Republic. Of all the writers discussed in part 2 of this book, Jünger's status as a nonconformist is thus the most disputed. Despite his withdrawal to an apolitical standpoint and the embracing of an intellectual and aesthetic elitism, he did not regard himself as an inner emigrant, believing his publications, especially the novel *Auf den Marmorklippen* (1939, English translation *On the Marble Cliffs*, 1947),[1] were not a reflection of passivity or withdrawal but rather evidenced a clear anti-Nazi stance. However, his writings and associations up to 1933 had marked him out as a significant right-wing voice in Germany and he was certainly seen in Nazi circles as an important writer favorably disposed to the principles of the movement. His diverse writings stretched over more than seventy years and the complete works run to twenty-two volumes plus a substantial supplementary collection of political publicist contributions. The body of secondary literature is correspondingly large; the Marbach catalogue, for example, records 1,036 items on the writer and his work.

The Defiant Nationalist

More than a quarter of the collected works consist of diaries, and several essays in other volumes are based on sketches and extracts from diaries. There is thus no shortage of autobiographical material, but a lot of the information Jünger provides serves to build a certain image of himself, is highly selective, and lacks personal details. In view of this material's partly controversial nature and the writer's literary longevity, the existence of so many biographies is no surprise.[2]

Born in 1895 in Heidelberg, Ernst Jünger spent most of his childhood in the area around Hanover in Lower Saxony. He was the eldest of five children, and his affluent middle-class parents ensured the children were well educated. However, although Ernst was a voracious reader from an early age, he did not take to school life at all; after several changes of school, the eighteen-year-old, who regularly escaped to the fantasies of Karl May, Daniel Defoe, and James Fenimore Cooper, ran away for a short-lived adventure in the French Foreign Legion. He was a volunteer in the First World War, became a "Stoßtruppführer" (shock troop leader), was wounded several times, and received both the *Ritterkreuz* and the *Pour le mérite*. He remained an officer in the army until August 1923. In that year he met Gretha von Jeinsen, whom he was to marry two years later and with whom he was to have two children, Ernst and Alexander. He took up the study of zoology and philosophy in Leipzig but, as erratic and unfocused a student as he had been a pupil, in May 1926 he abandoned these studies, which had only ever been at best intermittent, and became an independent writer. In 1927 the family moved to Berlin, where they lived until 1933, a period during which Jünger became involved in editing volumes of war photography and enjoyed the cultural life of the capital to the full.

Jünger became a prolific political publicist and evidently enjoyed his status at this time as a leading figure in the "new nationalism" and as spokesman for the war generation. He moved in diverse intellectual circles, with contacts across the political spectrum but predominantly with key figures on the nationalist right. His collaborators included the national revolutionary and later Nazi opponent Friedrich Wilhelm Heinz, the National Bolshevist Ernst Niekisch, the journalist and nationalist youth leader Werner Lass, the National Conservative and later founder of the non-Christian *Unabhängige Freikirche* (Independent Free Church) Friedrich Hielscher, as well as individuals who sought to align themselves with the Nazis, including the playwright and director Arnolt Bronnen, the writer and former *Freikorps* member and putschist Ernst von Salomon, and the writer and fellow "new nationalist" Franz Schauwecker.[3]

After his flat had been searched by the Gestapo in 1933 for evidence of correspondence with his friend Erich Mühsam, an early victim of the SA, Jünger destroyed his notes on recent political events along with his diaries since 1919 and a large part of his correspondence (3:516–19).[4] In December of that year, he moved with his family from Berlin to Goslar in the Harz Mountains, a move that marked the beginning of a physical and intellectual self-distancing from the affairs of state, restriction of communication to a small circle of trusted friends, and a life partly devoted to nature, especially entomology. He began his serious study of the latter in the early 1930s, publishing several articles in specialist journals.[5] Between 1935 to 1938 he undertook a number of trips abroad, including to Norway, Brazil, Morocco, and Rhodes—a measure both of his increasing financial security and of the regime's trust in and indulgence of him. At the end of 1936 a move south to Überlingen on Lake Constance saw Jünger withdraw still further from the world. The years here, shared with his brother Friedrich Georg, were in due course to form the basis of the life of the narrator and his brother Otho in *Auf den Marmorklippen*. In January 1939, however, the family moved back north to Kirchhorst, near Hanover, close to his old military unit.

He signed up once more at the start of hostilities and until May 1940 commanded an infantry company on the upper Rhine, prior to the march into Paris in summer 1940. From 1941 to summer 1944 he lived in the Hotel Raphael in Paris and his desk-bound post involved, among other things, letter censorship. Protected by two cultured superiors, Colonel Hans Speidel, his chief of staff, and General Carl-Heinrich von Stülpnagel, head of the occupying forces in France, Jünger seems to have enjoyed a privileged existence in Paris, allowed to pursue his intellectual, cultural, and romantic interests: he collected antiquarian books; he mixed with literary figures and intellectuals such as Jean Cocteau, André Malraux, Jean Giraudoux, and Paul Léautard, with the painters Pablo Picasso and Georges Braque, and with the newspaper correspondent and writer Friedrich Sieburg; he received visits from the political philosopher Carl Schmitt;[6] he made full use of the active French nightlife; and he had several affairs with French women.[7] The common depiction of him during this period as a sort of dandy[8] is consistent with his earlier self-image.

Owing to a dispute over the inclusion of a controversial reference in Jünger's published diaries *Gärten und Straßen* (Gardens and streets, 1942),[9] paper was denied for new editions of his works, although thanks to the support of senior officers in France, *Wehrmacht* editions of the diaries and *Auf den Marmorklippen* were still published (2:406). He was dismissed from the army in August 1944 in the wake of the July 20 bomb plot against Hitler, in which he was not directly involved, and served in the *Volkssturm* (home guard) in his hometown until the end of the war. The changed view of Jünger among Nazi officials by this time is reflected in the ban imposed on any public recognition of him on the occasion of his fiftieth birthday (3:370).

After the war he received a publication ban from the Allies, which lasted until 1949, and he found himself subject to accusations of having supported the rise of Nazism. His response to such criticisms was consistent with his elitist view of the writer's role, his distance from politics, and his intellectual arrogance: "Nach dem Erdbeben schlägt man auf die Seismographen ein. Man kann jedoch die Barometer nicht für die Taifune büßen lassen, falls man nicht zu den Primitiven zählen will." (After the earthquake people hammer the seismographer. You cannot, however, let the barometer take the blame for typhoons, unless you want to be thought one of the primitives, 2:13.) Jünger spent the remaining forty-eight years of his life still very much as the outsider, the lone and otherworldly aesthete of eccentric style, cultivating an image as the grand man of letters. He published further substantial diaries, three novels, and numerous essays but at no time did he criticize or apologize for his earlier views. In due course he became a popular figure with political conservatives, and his ecological interests even found him followers among environmental activists and in New Age circles.[10] He was repeatedly publicly fêted in the Federal Republic, albeit amid continuing controversy: the award of the prestigious Goethe Prize of the city of Frankfurt in 1982 was contentious, as was the joint visit he received in Wilfingen in 1993 from French President François Mitterand and Federal Chancellor Helmut Kohl on, of all days, July 20,[11] and many objected to the quasi-state funeral he received in 1998.

Literary Development: The Long Shadow of War

Taken as a whole, Jünger's nonfictional writings up to 1932, a mixture of war diaries, aesthetic-metaphysical reflections, and political-philosophical essays, constitute a discussion of the fascist history of ideas. His abstract intellectualism and his aesthetic ideals provide an original, national revolutionary variant on fascist thinking, but they have many links to what was to happen after 1933 and it would be wrong to disassociate them from the rise of Nazism. These writings, however, also provide a basis for understanding better his subsequent fictional work.

The First World War had a decisive influence on Jünger. His writing up to 1925 is marked by the ability to capture and bring to life in just a few lines the full shattering experience of military conflict and its impact on the individual. His texts also faithfully and convincingly record the repeated everyday situations and sensations of trench warfare: the hardship, boredom, fear, tension, sadness, comradeship, and snatched moments of pleasure. *In Stahlgewittern* (1920, In storms of steel, English translation *Storm of Steel*, 1929) proved to be a significant publishing success, reaching by 1943 its twenty-fifth reprinting and total sales of 230,000.[12] The focus of the book, part diary record, part narrated events, is necessarily restricted to the immediate physical reality of war. However, he is not horrified by the enormous suffering and loss of life caused by the first war to be fought with technologically advanced weaponry, but provides detailed descriptions of battles, their violence, and cruelty, and becomes in effect an apologist of war and fighting. He sings the praises of those ordinary soldiers who were used as cannon fodder, escaped death, but returned to an ungrateful country and economic hardship. In the process he turns their military defeat into a form of romanticized nationalist victory, while evincing a deep-seated resentment toward civilians and an intense hatred of democracy and the new republic.

A notable feature of his approach is the transformation of the abhorrent and ugly to something beautiful as he perceives events with a cool and dispassionate eye. The war has the function of transforming our experience of reality: the conventional aesthetic and moral view is considered inadequate and is replaced by a new aesthetics and a new nihilistic morality.[13] For example, soldiers become almost like performers: "Der Handgranatenwechsel erinnert an das Florettfechten; man muß dabei Sprünge machen wie beim Ballett" (Hand grenade exchanges are reminiscent of foil-fencing, in which you need to make ballet-like leaps, 1:224). This extends to descriptions of the new technologies used; thus time bombs are referred to as "Teufelseier" (devil's eggs, 1:137) and grenades as "Eisenvögel" (iron birds, 1:84). Here one sees the cheerful indifference evident in the battle-hardened soldier's mode of expressing himself, which is linked to Jünger's prized pose of *Désinvolture*, a glib insouciance or serene self-assuredness that is a recurrent theme in his work.

The book-length essay *Der Kampf als inneres Erlebnis* (Battle as inner experience, 1922) goes further than *In Stahlgewittern* in outlining an ideological stance. The war's release of long-dormant primitive instincts in man (7:15) gave rise to a new type, a storm trooper who was as hard as steel, whose view of existence was dominated by an instinct to fight in accordance with the dictates of "blood," and who rejected pacifism since he recognized war as a "natural law" (7:40). Jünger uses the essay to have a swipe at the hated Philistine bourgeoisie of the postwar period, who are separated by a gulf from the simple patriotic soldier; he also apostrophizes parliamentary democracy as gatherings of ideologues exchanging slogans and attacks the press for standardizing and "proletarianizing" thinking (7:82).

Weimar and Political Publicist Activity

Up to this point Jünger's publications show him struggling to come to terms with postwar reality and establishing himself as the spokesperson for a whole generation that had committed itself fully to war and endured enormous sacrifice and suffering. These works echo in some ways the resentment-laden outpourings of the early Nazis, reveal nationalist ideas on Germany's supposed role in the world, and target invective at political opponents and democracy in general. From 1926 to 1933 Jünger channeled his energies into political engagement with the hated Weimar Republic. He sought through his writing to support the national revolutionary movement, which wanted to replace the Weimar Republic with an authoritarian, militaristic, national state, and he became its most credible intellectual representative.[14]

He took up the editorship of the renamed and newly independent *Die Standarte*, the nationalist weekly journal of the *Stahlhelm* veterans' organization, in which he increasingly turned his attention away from the war and toward politics. He also published essays and numerous reviews under the pseudonym Hans Sturm in the self-styled polemical nationalist journal *Arminius*. He further edited for short periods the youth journals *Der Vormarsch* and *Die Kommenden*. More than 140 contributions appeared under his name in these various journals, and his growing reputation meant that other organs politically distant from his stance were also keen to have him write for them, including: the NSDAP's *Völkischer Beobachter*; the left-wing weekly *Die Weltbühne*; the monthly journal *Deutsches Volkstum*, edited by the anti-Semitic but also anti-Nazi Wilhelm Stapel; the conservative religious *Eckart*; and the left-of-center weekly journal *Das Tage-Buch*, edited by the Jewish liberal Leopold Schwarzschild. The most significant element of this publicist activity, however, was Jünger's collaboration with Ernst Niekisch's journal for national revolutionary politics, *Widerstand*, which lasted from 1927 to 1933, although most of Jünger's contributions appeared in the first half of the period.[15] Through this journal he associated with proponents of a "national bolshevism," which aimed for a *rapprochement* with the Soviet Union, rejected communism's international mission, and aspired to an elite of workers and soldiers usurping power to create a hierarchic military state.

Jünger's relationship with National Socialism is complex and controversial; accusations of his supposed intellectual support for them continued to the day he died. He had come to the attention of the Nazis in the early 1920s, especially in September 1923 when he had published in the *Völkischer Beobachter* the essay "Revolution und Idee" (Revolution and idea), which expounded the idea of a future revolution whose basic *völkisch* idea was to aspire to dictatorship under the swastika.[16] Again in 1927, he seemed to indicate admiration for the Nazi focus on national integration rather than class warfare and envisaged the need for a strong nationalist leader or leadership group.[17] In general, the aggression and extremism of much of his political publicist work helped shape the political climate in a way that was favorable to the evolving Nazi movement.

However, in spite of such apparent affinities, Jünger's association with the NSDAP was a cool and largely distant one. He met Goebbels socially but remained unimpressed by him other than as an orator (3:427–29). He and Hitler exchanged books,[18] but Jünger's essay in *Arminius* in 1927, "Nationalismus und Nationalsozialismus," with its suggestion that the nationalist idea was greater, more far-reaching than the Nazi organization, made clear his differences with the movement (*PP*, 317–20). Although Hitler offered the writer an NSDAP seat in the *Reichstag* in 1927, Jünger is reported to have dismissed it, saying he thought there was more merit in writing a single verse than in representing sixty thousand "idiots,"[19] providing an early sign of his desire to cultivate an elitist existence above the grubbiness of day-to-day politics. The reasons for this distance were varied: his anarchic thinking and air of isolationist hauteur caused him to reject the Nazis' emphasis on the leading role of the masses; he had no time for the NSDAP's public displays of strength and its violent street tactics; he was alienated by Hitler's obsessive hatred of Russian communism, finding more in common with the National Bolshevists and their desire for a more radical social revolution; and he could never subscribe to any single party program and indeed opposed the decision to go down the electoral route and engage in parliamentary democracy.[20] Jünger's sarcastic caricature of the latter and of the Nazis' anti-Semitism in an article on "'Nationalismus' und Nationalismus" in *Das Tage-Buch* in September 1929, where he alludes to Nazis eating three Jews for breakfast, makes it clear there was little hope of an alliance (*PP*, 504).

With regard to anti-Semitism, he was unequivocal in his rejection of Nazi notions of Aryan purity, making clear in the extended essay *Der Arbeiter: Herrschaft und Gestalt* (The worker: Rule and archetype, 1932) that his understanding of "blood" was not biological but historical and metaphysical (8:156). He did, however, repeatedly publish in the anti-Semitic *Deutsches Volkstum* and elaborated a distinct cultural anti-Semitism,[21] as seen particularly in a 1930 article in *Süddeutsche Monatshefte*, where he accuses Jews of liberalism and of lacking national sentiment (*PP*, 591). Though he believed in the possibility of Jewish assimilation, his idea that Jews might readily become Germans by denying their personal Jewish history was naïve, as the Nazis' pursuit of Jewish ancestry was soon to demonstrate. Whatever the status of his theoretical views, Jünger's direct experience of anti-Semitism was a sobering one: on June 7, 1942, when he first sees Jews wearing the now obligatory yellow Star of David, he feels embarrassed to be in uniform (2:336).

Jünger's unwillingness to follow the Nazi lead in compromising and engaging with Weimar parliamentary politics in order to exploit its weaknesses more effectively gradually led him away from politics and political publicism toward an increasing concern with metaphysical reflection, which was to influence much of his subsequent work. First evident in the collection of twenty-five impressionistic essays and notes, *Das abenteuerliche Herz* (The adventurous heart, 1928), it is most clearly exemplified in the essay "Sizilischer Brief an den Mann im Mond" (Sicilian letter to the man in the moon, 1930). In imagining he sees the man in the moon as it slowly disappears behind the hills, the author senses a split in his perception of reality: the visible and transient world alerts him to the invisible, spiritual, and eternal realm; the lunar landscape is a place of both rational science and the mythical and the wondrous (9:22). A central role in this is the "stereoscopic view," which features frequently in his essays from 1929 onward. In stereoscopy, two offset images appear separately to the left and right eye of the viewer and "merge" to create the impression of three-dimensional depth. Jünger's metaphorical application of this relates to seeing things in a new light by adopting two modes of viewing simultaneously, the optical rational perception of things and the reflective metaphysical view (*Das abenteuerliche Herz*, 9:83; 9:196–97). The detail of concrete objects can thereby be seen to reveal hidden meanings, lending new depth to understanding. The position of the "man in the moon" thus stands as a symbol for the compatibility of the scientific and the wondrous but it also denotes the external observer viewpoint that lends distance and provides both depth and a sense of pattern to what is being observed—a viewpoint Jünger was increasingly adopting for himself.

Der Arbeiter: Herrschaft und Gestalt is the summation of Jünger's thinking of the previous five years and did most to contribute to the image of him as a fascist.[22] It is a dense work, the result of its lack of cohesive and reasoned thinking, its partly aphoristic style, and the attempt to provide a panoramic view of the modern age, while adopting the "man in the moon" position of distanced observer (8:69). He argues here for a radical new beginning for society on a "planetary" scale, the start of a process that he anticipates will overcome nihilism and in which he expects Germany to play a leading role (8:31). Under the influence of Nietzsche's *Übermensch* (superman), he posits a new type of man standing beyond all parties and prejudices (8:13), the "worker" or soldier-worker, a metaphysical archetype and agent of life's essential vital energy, which expresses itself periodically in devastating conflict and conflagration. The worker willingly embraces a global civil war that will lead to the replacement of nation-states by a worldwide empire. In this new hierarchic order each society will consist of an elite of workers energized by Nietzsche's idea of "will to power" and characterized by "total mobilization," which denotes a readiness to allow the spirit of work to take precedence over individual desires and aspirations. Jünger's tendency to think in planetary rather than nationalist terms meant the Nazis themselves had little time for *Der Arbeiter*. Indeed the book contained such a mélange of ideas that it appealed to both the political Left and Right; thus Niekisch was full of praise for its parallels with Marxist ideas, while *völkisch* nationalists objected to its bolshevism and mystification of technology.[23] It acted very much as a "seismograph" of its time (2:13), promoting totalitarian aggression and military action, and it is therefore not surprising it was never subsequently revised.

Jünger under National Socialism

In October 1933 Jünger, along with *völkisch* national writers such as Hans Grimm and Werner Beumelburg, was elected a member of the Sektion für Dichtkunst (literature section) of the Prussian Academy of Arts. However, he promptly declined the invitation to join, saying that his involvement in the German "mobilization" since 1914 did not allow him to be part of the organization, implying that his focus was not on *völkisch* nationalism and that Germany was not to be equated with the Third Reich.[24] This refusal to be part of any attempt at literary or cultural unification provides more evidence of Jünger's determination to adopt the part of the loner and distanced observer. Ideological differences with the Nazis are further evident in revisions to *In Stahlgewittern* in the 1930s, when Jünger removed much of the nationalistic coloring he had added to the fifth edition of 1924.[25] Such public dissent was possible because of the high regard in which he was held by the Nazis, not least in view of his richly decorated military career and still venerated early work, both of which allowed him greater latitude than many other writers. Indeed his writing was still generally positively reviewed in the Nazi press, and the war writings in particular appeared repeatedly in anthologies, were extracted in school textbooks, and became the subject of academic studies.[26]

The significance of "Sizilischer Brief" and other essays from the early 1930s lies in their documentation of Jünger's attempt to make sense of reality by linking the empirical to the mythical, the physical to the metaphysical, an intellectual pursuit that took him steadily further away from daily politics with its need for compromise and opportunism. The increasing concern with aesthetic and psychological issues, including the travel notes, linguistic speculations, and intellectual reflections of the prose collection *Blätter und Steine* (Leaves and stones, 1934),[27] and the introduction of literary elements into the revised editions of *In Stahlgewittern*, were anathema to Nazi commentators. This apolitical tendency is further reflected in the autobiographical novel *Afrikanische Spiele* (African games, 1936), based on his period in the French Foreign Legion, which lacks all reference to contemporary affairs. It is equally evident in *Das abenteuerliche Herz: Figuren und Capriccios* (The adventurous heart: Figures and capriccios, 1938), a radically different second edition of the 1929 book, involving the removal of the more private or personal and tendentious utterances and the inclusion of several new texts.[28]

This collection of over seventy diverse short pieces, influenced by Jünger's naturalist studies and travels, involves mainly detached and quasi-scientific observation and description, either of familiar, everyday items or of dreams, images, and exotic scenes, which are not analyzed and appear to have little connection to everyday life but are linked to experience in an abrupt and peremptory summative conclusion. At times the writing is full of black humor and irony, with an unsettling, dreamlike consciousness that owes much to surrealist influences such as that of the illustrator and author Alfred Kubin.[29] This aspect of the work can be seen in the Kafkaesque piece "Violette Endivien" (Violet endives, 9:183–84). In a gourmet shop, the shopkeeper recommends human flesh to the narrator and takes him down to a cold store, where he sees human bodies hanging on the wall, and hands, feet, and heads with price labels attached. Upon leaving the store, the narrator remarks that he did not realize civilization had already advanced so far in the city (9:184). In this "capriccio,"[30] the dreamlike but realistic narrative creates an aesthetic distance from the gruesome content, almost as a way of covering up the narrator-dreamer's involvement in the practice of cannibalism; Nevin sees this as referring to "modern technological society," which has reduced human worth to butchered flesh.[31] In another short piece, "Der Oberförster" (The Chief Ranger), the narrator is told by the head of a nature reserve that one of his "Adepten" (initiates) is to be killed for having hunted a special blue adder that attracts the best game. Encouraged by the Chief Ranger, the narrator visits the area inhabited by the rare snakes, where he sees an old woman digging a grave and comes to realize that he is the person attracted by the adder, that he himself is to be hunted, and that it is his own grave being dug. He curses his "solitary arrogance" and failure to spot sooner "die Fäden . . ., mit denen [der Oberförster] mich umspann" (the threads . . . with which the Chief Ranger entangled me, 9:215). The narrative reflects Jünger's sense of becoming ensnared by, perhaps even complicit in, the dangerous web of Nazi Germany, despite or precisely because of his solipsistic determination to pursue his own goals and ambitions. In general, *Das abenteuerliche Herz* promotes the world of dreams as a means of enhancing our view of reality, offering additional new perspectives, but, as the two examples show, the dream sequences are not without links to the reality of Nazi Germany.

In his Second World War diaries, Jünger reveals various personae, ranging from the chronicler of political developments and military strategy, the observer of everyday events, the entomologist, the literary commentator, and the bibliophile—all suffused with his characteristically dispassionate gaze. However, these diaries demonstrate a new concern with humanitarian values, particularly, in the second volume, with Christianity, including repeated references to the Bible.[32] The entries are also full of antipathy to leading Nazi figures, who are referred to in coded names, such as "Kniébolo" ("knieender Diabolus," kneeling devil) for Hitler (see 2:286; 2:321). Jünger expresses disquiet at the "immoral" killing of the mentally ill in occupied Russian (2:431) and notes "rumors" of atrocities against Jews (2:470). Such loss of ethics and morality are considered typical of the era and have damaged in his eyes the image of the soldier.

Notwithstanding this apparent compassionate turn, the abiding sense of the diaries is of a cruel contrast between his refined, dandyesque existence and the hunger and terror experienced by the French, especially from 1942, under Nazi occupation. Although in an entry from early in the war he describes towns and villages destroyed and then cleared by the German army as "ein ungeheures Foyer des Todes" (a horrendous foyer of death) and seems to regret his earlier aestheticization of horror, he undermines the ethical point by distancing himself from the scene, as if he were not himself part of the military machine responsible, revealing once more the psychological distancing, lofty reserve, and lack of genuine human warmth of the earlier writings (2:146–47).

And indeed, there is evidence that he still experiences war in perverse aesthetic terms.[33] Three incidents repeatedly cited by commentators include a detailed account of a soldier shot for desertion, in which the faithful, emotionless description of the minutiae of fear and death seem to take priority over any moral aspects or compassion (2:244–47).[34] Another is the secondhand description of a seventeen-year-old Russian girl killed in a skirmish on the eastern front, whose naked corpse is reported as being left out in the snow so the soldiers had repeated opportunity "zu weiden am Anblick der herrlichen Gestalt" (to feast their eyes on the glorious figure, 2:328); again what seems to fascinate the diary writer is the idea of beauty in death rather than the callous behavior of the soldiers. And third, Jünger describes an air raid on the bridges in Paris as he sits comfortably drinking a glass of burgundy filled with strawberries and watches the spectacle; the city's red towers and cupolas and "mighty beauty" are compared to a calyx that is skimmed over "for the purpose of deadly fertilization": "Alles war Schauspiel, war reine, vom Schmerz bejahte und erhöhte Macht" (All was theater, pure power affirmed and exalted by pain, 3:271). One is justified in asking whether the nihilism underlying this description is a pose or Jünger's genuine conviction, a question one finds oneself asking repeatedly in the diaries. Whatever the answer, Jünger's aestheticization of death and suffering, with its apparent cold indifference, remains a constant theme and is important in understanding *Auf den Marmorklippen*.

The diaries strongly suggest that Jünger knew a good deal about both the Holocaust and other atrocities being committed on the eastern front. The latter are first noted in December 1942 (2:470); then, in the entry for October 16, 1943, he records reports of the gassing of Jews and of crematoria near the Jewish ghetto in Lodz (3:175–76). And yet, alongside such passages, there are entries documenting his varied enjoyment of the cultural pleasures of Paris. For example, there is an echo of the escapist botanical pursuits of the brother knights in *Auf den Marmorklippen* as, amid the destruction of war and the misery inflicted on the French, Jünger finds time to pursue his entomological interests (2:463). He did, in fact, see his role in occupied Paris very much in chivalric terms: under Speidel's command, he and his fellow officers were members of a noble *Wehrmacht* seeking to uphold civilized norms of behavior in the face of SD and SS brutality (2:272). This raises the question of Jünger's involvement in the military assassination plot of July 20, 1944. Carl-Heinrich von Stülpnagel was in many ways a kindred spirit in whom Jünger recognized the valued *Désinvolture* (2:318–19), and since the general was a member of the plot to kill Hitler it can be assumed Jünger was aware of what was planned. However, after July 20 he appears to talk down the idea of assassination, revealing once more his reluctance to be involved in praxis and his preference for the world of the intellect (2:17–18).

The ongoing revision of Jünger's ideas is reflected in the extended tract *Der Friede* (The peace, 1945), a philosophical blueprint for a post-Nazi Germany. The text was written in Paris with the knowledge and under the protection of von Stülpnagel but it could not be published in 1945 owing to the Allies' ban on Jünger.[35] It was, however, illegally circulated among *Wehrmacht* officers (3:190–91; 3:305) and finally published in 1948 in Paris. It talks of punishment for Hitler's "henchmen," of spiritual healing and purification, and of territorial reorganization to integrate the countries of Europe into an economic entity, a state run on military lines but with a constitution to guarantee laws, human freedom, and dignity (7:224). Theology should, Jünger says, become once more a primary science, and he envisages a major role for the Christian churches in creating a new spiritual order to counter nihilism and the effects of totalitarianism (7:230). Although he calls the work his contribution to the July plot (2:18), its status as an oppositional manifesto is undermined by the abstraction of wrongdoing, the failure to attribute specific guilt, and the sense of suffering and responsibility as merely part of a wider universal process, which serves to devalue pain and torture and reveals a writer who has still not relinquished fully his philosophical and metaphysical approach to violence and war.

Genesis and Publication of *Auf den Marmorklippen* (1939)

In his "Adnoten," appended to later editions of the novel, Jünger identifies two important stimuli for the book (22:389–91). One was a nighttime visit to the Jünger brothers in Überlingen by Heinrich von Trott zu Solz (not, as Jünger suggests, his brother Adam), who tried to persuade his hosts to join the resistance against Hitler; in a letter to von Trott in 1943 he says that the visit had provided ideas for the novel,[36] most notably Prince Sunmyra's visit to the Rue Hermitage (15:314–20). The second stimulus was a vision Jünger had following a heavy drinking session on October 29, 1938, in which he saw towns being burned to the ground, and which he considered a premonition of bombed-out cities (22:389). However, it is clear that even before this, Jünger had been considering the idea of a fictional representation of Nazi terror, since the central figures of the Chief Ranger and the Mauretanians had already appeared in the revised version of *Das abenteuerliche Herz*.

The novel was written between February and July 1939 in Kirchhorst. Jünger looked over the final draft in September, by which time he had been called up to the army, and it was published in the autumn by the Hanseatische Verlagsanstalt in Hamburg. It sold remarkably well: within a year, twenty-three thousand copies had been printed[37] and Jünger's editor at the time, Paul Weinreich, reported in the aforementioned letter to Augstein in May 1973 that by October 1943 sixty-seven thousand copies had been produced (20:237). In 1942, as paper began to be in short supply, von Stülpnagel arranged for a twenty-thousand-strong *Wehrmacht* edition to be published.[38] The book was never banned and the only limitations on it were these general paper shortages. In 1942 a French translation appeared with the publisher Gallimard, as did an Italian version and an edition on license in Switzerland; the English translation by Stuart Hood was published in 1947.

A recurrent question is how the novel could appear in Nazi Germany at all. According to Weinreich (20:239), the publisher had not even referred the book to the Parteiamtliche Prüfungskommission (Party Inspection Commission) and had published it without the latter's seal of approval, the so-called "Unbedenklichkeitsvermerk" (clearance note). The hope was that the party would not wish the embarrassment of a post publication ban once several thousand copies had already appeared and that it would not dare to act against the recipient of the *Pour le mérite*, who was now once again on active service in the army.[39] Despite attempts by Reichsleiter Philipp Bouhler, head of the Chancellery of the Führer, to move for an official ban, it is reported that Hitler himself intervened to say nothing was to happen to the writer, a decision that Jünger himself later put down to the high opinion Hitler still held of him (20:235–36; 20:573; 3:615).[40]

Summary

The story is recounted by a nameless narrator looking back on past events, and at its center are the narrator himself and his brother Otho, who live in the "Rautenklause" (Rue Hermitage) on the marble cliffs and spend their time systematically recording the region's flora and fauna. The house is run by an old woman, Lampusa, a witchlike figure who lives in the caves under the main house with her grandson, Erio, the product of the narrator's casual relationship with her daughter, Silvia, who had abandoned the boy at birth. The house takes its name from the "silver-gray" bushes surrounding it, which are supposed to ward off evil spirits,[41] and the path leading to it is flanked by nests of lance-headed vipers, which come out to be fed by Lampusa and Erio.

The marble cliffs belong to the civilized, affluent, and peaceful region of the Marina, a fertile strip on the coast of a large lake or inland sea; this is a land of culture where scholars, monks, artisans, and nobles all live together in harmony. To the south of the Marina the "free mountainous country" of Alta Plana can be discerned rising beyond the water. To

the north lies Campagna, a steppe land of large animal herds, free shepherds, and seminomadic native tribes, who are dedicated to the law of
blood vengeance and inhabit a precivilized animist world. Their powerful
chieftain Belovar bravely defends his people's free way of life, and as long
as he and his clan are on the steppe the brothers are safe. Edging into
Campagna from the north is an uninhabited swampland dotted with reed
huts, in which dark and ominous figures find refuge. Further north still,
the swamps give way to the forested region of Mauretania, the domain
of a wild tyrant, the Chief Ranger ("der Oberförster"), who is a threat to
life in the Marina and the whole region.[42] Finally, beyond these forests is
the native land of the narrator and his brother.[43] Both this far northern
homeland and the southern Alta Plana are powerful, independent, and
able to defend themselves and their way of life. Though still strong, thanks
to its resilient herdsmen, Campagna is gradually being undermined by
the Chief Ranger's anarchic forces. The Marina is in an even more fragile
state and can only defend itself by employing mercenary troops headed by
the corrupt Mauretanian police chief, Biedenhorn.

Seven years previously the narrator and his brother Otho, members
of a knightly order, had served with the Purple Riders and fought alongside the Mauretanians in an unlawful war of conquest against "the free
peoples" of Alta Plana, but had subsequently left behind their warlike past
and retreated to the Rue Hermitage to devote themselves to the pursuit
of botanical and philosophical studies. Here they began to perceive the
increasing signs of decline and decay, responsibility for which lies with
the Chief Ranger and his dissolute band of followers, who are guilty of
assorted atrocities in Campagna and the Marina. This tyrant is a charismatic figure known to the brothers from their military past as one of
Mauretania's "große Herren" (great lords); he is surrounded by an air of
"old power," grandeur (15:265), and an innate "Désinvolture" (15:318).
A key figure for the brothers in their new life is Pater Lampros, an enlightened Christian monk at the monastery of Maria Lunaris near the marble
cliffs on the slopes of the Marina. He is a kindred spirit, a distinguished
naturalist, known by the name Phyllobius, who is privy to the esoteric
knowledge of the old Christian religious orders. He advises the brothers
on their botanical work and teaches the practice of contemplation and
appreciation of the regularities of nature.

One day, on a botanical trip in search of a rare flower, the brothers
penetrate beyond Campagna into the forest of the Chief Ranger and, in the
clearing of Köppelsbleek, come across a white building with a skull fixed
above the entrance and human hands pinned to the wall; the surrounding
trees are also covered in human skulls. Inside this "Schinderhütte" (flaying
hut) they discover the horrors of physical torture and butchery perpetrated
by the tyrant on his own people. The next day the brothers are visited by
Braquemart, a power-hungry Mauretanian warrior, who has turned against

his fellow countrymen, and Prince Sunmyra, a young representative of the power of the spirit and a decaying noble heritage. These two lead some men into the high forest in an attempt to kill the Chief Ranger but are defeated and are themselves killed. Having been asked by Pater Lampros to help the prince, the narrator goes to Belovar and heads north with a large contingent of his men accompanied by a pack of fierce bloodhounds. At the ensuing battle of Köppelsbleek the Chief Ranger's battle-hardened mastiffs engage Belovar's dogs and defeat them; Belovar is killed. In the midst of the battle, the narrator comes across the beheaded Braquemart and the prince, and hides the latter's head in his bag. He then returns to the marble cliffs and sees the whole of the Marina in flames, marking its defeat at the hands of the Chief Ranger. The monastery of Pater Lampros is destroyed and the Rue Hermitage too is threatened by the Chief Ranger's men, but Erio saves its occupants by turning the vipers on the attackers and their dogs. The brothers set fire to the Rue Hermitage and flee, escaping across the lake to Alta Plana on a ship provided by Biedenhorn.

Reception

There were no reviews of the novel in Nazi publications, the nearest being a belated discussion in *Die Weltliteratur*—by 1940 in SS hands—that called on Jünger to abandon his foray into a "Traum- und Scheinwelt" (world of dreams and illusions) and to embrace once more the shared reality of the "elementary experience" of war.[44] One of the few sources of information we have on how the book was received in official circles is a letter to Jünger from Werner Best, plenipotentiary of the *Reich* in Denmark, which reveals that the book had its opponents among the Nazi leadership and that several were in favor of action being taken against the author since the novel was "an anti-Nazi *roman à clef*" and a danger to the party (20:233).

Reviews in the liberal press were generally positive; many critics saw in the novel a clash between spirit and the powers of chaos and violence, a few even took the daring extra step of linking events to the German present.[45] An anonymous reviewer in *Das Deutsche Wort* called it a "bold" book full of fervent ideas on the most pressing problems of the present.[46] A year later in the same journal, Herbert Roch states the book is about the threat posed by anarchy to the spirit, embodied by life under the marble cliffs. However, he goes further than many contemporary critics when he talks about "der Prozeß des Aufruhrs und der Zerstörung, des Schreckens, der die Maske der Ordnung annimmt" (the process of revolt and destruction, of terror that assumes the mask of order). He says the book distills the "quintessence" of political and cultural processes of the twentieth century, but also emphasizes its consolatory message, the certainty that the marble cliffs are not lost forever.[47] In one of the most daring reviews, Gerhard Nebel appears repeatedly to invite comparison with conditions in Nazi Germany. Thus he talks about writers, like the bards in the text, debasing literature by allowing it to be used by the powerful, and he refers to the failure of scholarship and art, to a lack of respect for and sympathy with the weak, and to power that is contemptuous of spirit and human dignity.[48] The book is about how to escape and survive destruction, and Nebel talks of the possibility and imminent appearance of "truth and spirit" (613), concluding that Jünger calls on the reader not to give in to despair or to assume the triumph of the "Nichts" (void). The discussion in the *Kölnische Zeitung* cites Nebel's review and, with reference to the novel's "brennende Aktualität" (burning relevance), talks of readers having a sense of "what is in the air" and identifies a "bestürzende Wahrheit" (disconcerting truth) arising from the work's symbolism.[49] The anonymous reviewer in *Hochland* seems, in a description of the central scene at Köppelsbleek, to be alerting readers to the potential for a topical reading, referring to a "geheimnisvolles Gleichnis für jenen dunklen Untergrund, auf dem die anarchische Macht durch Schrecken ihre Herrschaft aufrichtet und sogar 'die Maske der Ordnung annimmt'" (mysterious allegory of that dark substrate on which anarchic power builds its rule through terror and even assumes "the mask of order").[50] A discussion by the editor of the feuilleton of the *Deutsche Allgemeine Zeitung*, Bruno E. Werner, talks about suddenly seeing in the text a "paraphrase" of the present.[51] Similarly, Heinz Flügel in *Der Eckart-Ratgeber* says the book holds up a mirror to the times.[52]

Of the numerous reviews that appeared abroad, those in Switzerland that interpreted the novel as an oppositional allegory caused Jünger greatest concern, as he feared they could lead to reprisals (2:285; 2:293; 3:342). Reviews in other countries were just as clear about the book's anti-Nazi and satirical stance.[53] After 1945, many readers' views were summed up by Heinrich von Trott's verdict that the novel had been "wie einen Regen in der Wüste" (rain in the desert).[54] Responses from fellow writers were more varied. Thus Thomas Mann called the novel the "Renommierbuch der 12 Jahre" (the most renowned book of these twelve years) and said its author was undoubtedly talented but was to be regarded as a "Wegbereiter und eiskalter Genüßling des Barbarismus" (trailblazer and ice-cold bon vivant of barbarism).[55] In English exile, Erich Fried called the book "brave" but insubstantial.[56] Hermann Broch's retrospective verdict was that the novel was courageous and its publication a "heroic deed," but he also noted an element of "sublimated" Nazism in it.[57] More positively, in 1975 Alfred Andersch called it "die Parabel der Notwendigkeit von Widerstand" (the parable on the need for resistance) and said that it was more powerful than anything produced in exile precisely because it had been written and could be bought in Germany.[58] Similarly, Heinrich Böll called its publication a "sensation" and said it was considered the "book of the resistance."[59] Dolf Sternberger's 1980 retrospective offers a particularly interesting account of

the contemporaneous response: he says that people were incredulous that
something like this could be published, that the book acted like a signal
for readers, strengthening them in their beliefs and serving as a means of
understanding among those who were threatened or tempted by tyranny,
and he adds that none of his acquaintances was in any doubt that the book
referred to current circumstances.[60]

After the war, a veritable flood of publications appeared in connection with the so-called case of Jünger: Paetel's bibliography for the period
1945–51 lists almost nine hundred German titles on the writer.[61] Views
in East Germany were consistently negative,[62] whereas in West Germany
they were for a while positive and, particularly in the 1950s, the novel was
commonly read in secondary schools.[63] However, 1968 marked the start
of a backlash against Jünger's writing in general as the younger generation came to see in him a representative figure of Nazi-tainted reaction.[64]
From about the mid-1980s, however, a more even-handed view has set
in, with criticism of the novel's cyclical-mythical stylization of terror balanced by more positive views based on an analysis of the work in its historical and biographical contexts.

Resistance Novel and Roman à Clef?

The debate over the status of *Auf den Marmorklippen* as a work of resistance against Nazi Germany has raged for several years now. Among its
proponents the most decisive and eloquent has been Günter Scholdt,
whose lengthy article argued that what distinguished the novel from
other works of the inner emigration was the fact that Jünger addressed
the question of tyranny *directly*, without seeking the camouflage of fic-
tionalizing actual historical events or resorting to the stylistic esotericism
of a calligraphic approach.[65] Despite the timeless and mythical model presented in the novel (see following section), Scholdt argues that the links
to and parallels with the reality of Nazi Germany are so tangible that readers were almost inevitably going to seek to decipher the text. Moreover,
besides not understating the description of an oppressive regime, offering an ambiguous portrait of the strong leader, or dealing in any other
form of concession typical of inner emigrant writing, Jünger's text contains a clear personal admission of past wrongdoing and a commitment
to change.[66] Support for Scholdt's thesis can be found in Jünger's statements on the book. For example, in September 1939 he wrote to Carl
Schmitt to say his new book contained "eine Geheim-Ansicht unserer
Zeit" (a secret view of our times).[67] When asked in a television interview
in 1977 whether the book was an attempt at resistance, he responded "of
course," that was what he had intended and readers had also perceived
it in this way.[68] And in an interview in 1995, he said the book was his
response to Goebbels's successes after 1933.[69]

Certainly the most cursory reading of the novel reveals numerous potential parallels with Nazi Germany. For example, informed readers will have immediately recognized that the fictional brothers are closely modeled on Jünger and his brother Friedrich Georg, and the Rue Hermitage on the brothers' "Weinberghütte" (vineyard house) in Überlingen. In the narrator's past links with the Mauretanians it is easy to see Jünger's personal contact with leading Nazis and his well-known involvement with nationalist revolutionary circles seeking to undermine the Weimar Republic. The "fearful joviality" (15:335) of the Chief Ranger suggests an analogy with Hermann Göring, who was noted for his grand lifestyle and coarse sociability and held the titles of "Reichsforstmeister" (Reich Master of the Forests) and "Reichsjägermeister" (Reich Master of the Hunt).[70] Göring, of course, was also charged with the development of the Gestapo and the construction of the first concentration camps.[71] Braquemart's description as a small, gaunt figure "not without wit" (15:314) suggests a Goebbels caricature, a possibility confirmed by Jünger, who reports that Goebbels saw himself in the figure (3:435). Jünger says the character was largely based on a naval ensign he once knew who revealed a mixture of atheism, technical intelligence, and "contempt for man" (3:435). Prince Sunmyra seems to be based in part on Adam von Trott zu Solz, who was killed for his part in the July 20 plot.

Beyond these character parallels, the great war of Alta Plana could be taken to represent World War I or indeed the whole of the Weimar period. We are told there has been a noticeable process of decay in the spheres of culture and politics, and the threats to the Marina's civilization and the rule of law from the violent tactics of the "Feuerwürmer" (glow worms, 15:275) strongly reflect events in Weimar Germany, in particular the lawless behavior and intimidation of the SA. Thus the narrator identifies the most threatening aspect of the unruly activity of the Chief Ranger's men as the failure to punish criminal acts, people's fear of even speaking about them, and the law's weakness in the face of anarchy (15:275). There is also a thinly veiled reference to Germany's fatal shortcomings in allowing the Nazis to attain power through the legitimacy of the ballot box, when the narrator talks about the weak failing to appreciate the law and blindly releasing the "door bolts" closed for their protection (15:287). The analogy can further be seen in the infiltration of institutions and the exploitation of confusion to undermine existing structures, while Hitler's dependency on terror tactics, the projection of the image of the strong leader who will defend the law and restore order to a troubled society, comes through particularly clearly in the following passage:

[Der Oberförster] gab die Furcht in kleinen Dosen ein, die er allmählich steigerte und deren Ziel die Lähmung des Widerstandes war. . . . [W]ährend seine niederen Agenten, die in den

Hirtenbünden saßen, den Stoff der Anarchie vermehrten, drangen die Eingeweihten in die Ämter und Magistrate, ja selbst in Klöster ein und wurden dort als starke Geister, die den Pöbel zu Paaren treiben würden, angesehen. Der Oberförster glich einem bösen Arzte, der zunächst das Leiden fördert, um sodann dem Kranken die Schnitte zuzufügen, die er im Sinne hat. (15:280)

[[The Chief Ranger] applied fear in small doses, which he gradually increased with the aim of paralyzing resistance. . . . [W]hile his agents of lower rank, who had established themselves in the clans of the shepherds, promoted anarchy, the initiated penetrated into public office and the magistracy, and even the monasteries, and gained there the reputation of men of strong mind who would put the mob to flight. The Chief Ranger was like an evil doctor who encourages suffering in the patient so that he can make the surgical incisions he has in mind.]

Similarly, after the description of how the Chief Ranger's lawless "agents" mindlessly skin alive beautiful pearl lizards and throw them off the cliffs, the narrator makes a link to what was happening to people as the tyrant set about terrorizing the Marina: "Dann wiederholten sich die Banditen-Streiche . . ., und die Bewohner wurden bei Nacht und Nebel abgeführt. Von dort kam keiner wieder, und was wir im Volk von ihrem Schicksal raunen hörten, erinnerte an die Kadaver der Perlen-Echsen, die wir geschunden an den Klippen fanden, und füllte unser Herz mit Traurigkeit." (Then the cases of banditry . . . were repeated, and the inhabitants were led away under cover of darkness and mist. No one thus taken returned, and the rumors about their fate spread by the people reminded us of the carcasses of the pearl lizards, which we found lying stripped below the cliffs, and filled our hearts with sadness, 15:282.)

A parallel with the Nazis' cultivation of Germanic myth and writers' flirtation with blood and soil ideology appears in the description of the Marina's men of letters starting to imitate the primitive songs of herdsmen (15:276) and embracing heathen rituals of sacrifice (15:277). Similarly, in connection with the corruption of the once sacred celebration of the dead in the Marina, we learn that hatred and the influence of the Campagna blood feuds have reduced the respectful rites to profane "niederen Haß- und Rachejamben" (base iambs of hate and vengeance, 15:280).

The description of the flaying hut stands out as a scene with allegorical significance. It was readily identified with Nazi concentration camps and torture, and "Köppelsbleek" was understood by contemporary readers—against the author's intention—as "Göbbelsbleek" (2:311; 3:435; 20:299).[72] The depiction of the hut's awful secrets and the following sentence are among the novel's most powerful passages with contemporary reference: "Das sind die Keller, darauf die stolzen Schlösser der Tyrannis sich erheben und über denen man die Wohlgerüche ihrer Feste sich kräuseln sieht: Stankhöhle grauenhafter Sorte, darinnen auf alle Ewigkeit verworfenes Gelichter sich an der Schändung der Menschenwürde und Menschenfreiheit schauerlich ergötzt." (These are the dungeons on which the proud castles of tyrants are built, and above them is to be seen rising the curling fragrant smoke of their banquets. They are the most hideous stinking pits, in which an eternally damned rabble takes gruesome delight in the violation of human dignity and human freedom, 15:310–11.)

It seems difficult therefore to refute at least part of Scholdt's assertion, namely, the deliberate use of parallels. On the other hand, the claim for the novel as a work of resistance is undermined by Jünger's unequivocal rejection of assassination, his belief that murdering Hitler would prove ineffectual. This was something that occupied him in his diaries repeatedly over the years, as he pondered the wisdom of his original decision in 1938 not to become involved in the resistance.[73] However, he remained convinced that revolts only made sense if the public were no longer behind a regime and that in Germany this could only be brought about by military defeat; otherwise: "Wenn Kniébolo fällt, wird die Hydra einen neuen Kopf bilden" (If Kniébolo is killed, the Hydra will simply grow a new head, 3:243). Then, in the entry for the day after the most famous attempt on Hitler's life, he calmly reiterates his belief that the acts of individuals cannot influence the necessary and inevitable course of history, that assassinations never improve situations, adding: "Ich deutete das schon in der Schilderung Sunmyras in den 'Marmorklippen' an" (I suggested this in the portrayal of Sunmyra in the "Marble Cliffs," 3:288): nothing would be gained by killing the violent Chief Ranger since the equally tyrannous Braquemart would simply take his place. Rather, one must await the purifying effect of an internecine conflict, which will sweep away the decay responsible for the original decline. This is evidence of an oppositional mindset but hardly the stuff of resistance.

Timelessness: Setting, Characterization, and Style

Jünger's postwar reluctance to identify the novel as a precise allegory (3:446 and 3:615) and to acknowledge *Auf den Marmorklippen* as a work of resistance is partly to be explained by his characteristic proud defiance and independence and by the "overcompensating" sense of elitism behind his distaste for post hoc resistance talk.[74] It is, however, also related to his claim of multiple interpretations, which in turn is linked to the basic conception of the novel as a timeless comment on existence, applicable to different historical contexts. While writing it, he referred to his portrayal of the nihilism of Mauretania and observed it must "ganz ohne zeitliche Beziehung, aus Eigenem leben können" (live out of itself, completely without reference to time, 2:29). The demise of a just and ordered civilization and its submersion in terror and despotism were to be presented in mythical terms, its events to be seen as applicable to all systems of terror, part of a metaphysical-historical cycle of being. Accordingly, the fictional world of atrocities is repeatedly related to the situation in German-occupied Russia (2:431; 2:486; 3:99; 3:284), and elsewhere he records with a degree of satisfaction that after the war there was talk of illegal copies of the work circulating in the Ukraine and Lithuania (22:390).

In this sense, the process of moral decadence and increasing lawlessness threatening the Marina reflects a broader decline in the face of anarchic forces, part of an inevitable cycle of decay and rebirth affecting all life on earth. Jünger aspires to this higher-level, mythical view by creating a symbolic world through which he can illustrate the operation of supposedly universal and natural laws. Thus there is repeated reference to the regularity or periodic recurrence of events (for example, we live in one of the "Epochen des Niederganges," periods of decline, 15:265–66). And, amid the final cataclysm, in the reference to the rebuilding of the cathedral and to the brothers' escape and preservation of the world of the spirit, there is the promise of a new beginning (15:348).

The timeless, higher-level mythical view is reinforced by Jünger's choice of setting. He deliberately telescopes cultural history, presenting juxtaposed forms of civilization and religious belief at different stages of development: a primitive and wild forest people; a seminomadic steppe culture with pagan religious customs; an old Christian civilization, revealing Roman and medieval influences; and a free peasant-warrior culture. He also consciously mixes historical periods. Thus the characters' customs, clothes, and weapons, along with the description of castles and monasteries, suggest approximately the end of the Middle Ages, yet the cavalry battles of the Purple Riders indicate the nineteenth century,[75] and the brothers venerate the work of the eighteenth-century Swedish botanist and zoologist Carl von Linné. At one point there is a reference to the fifteenth-century French poet and criminal François Villon (15:287) but at another we hear about machines suppressing a rebellion in Iberia, a possible reference to Guernica and the infamous role of the German Legion Condor in the Spanish Civil War (15:267). Similarly, with regard to physical setting, besides the strong partial resemblance to the area around Lake Constance, there are references to numerous historical and contemporary locations, including Burgundy, the Iberian provinces, Britain, the Netherlands, Rhodes, and Upsala, as well as to a diversity of names, some of French origin, some German, some Greek, and some invented. All of this makes it impossible to place the text geographically with any reliability.

A further aspect of the timeless approach is the association of the different regions of the novel with character archetypes. The forest of the north, inhabited by the Chief Ranger, is associated with evil, darkness, nightmares, obscurantism, and melancholy; the southern Marina is linked to goodness, light, dreams, culture, and brightness. Gutmann identifies here what he calls a "psychic diagram" in which the action moves between the two poles of, on the one hand, the irrational (the forest/ the Chief Ranger) and the chaotic/anarchic (the Chief Ranger's rabble as representatives of suppressed impulses and instincts), and on the other, the spirit and rationality (the highly cultured Marina and the enlightened Pater Lampros). This archetypal span is further reflected in the description of the Rue Hermitage with its contrast between the spiritual, intellectual realm upstairs and the sensual, earthy realm of Lampusa's cave kitchen below. The brothers have links to both psychological poles: to the subconscious and instinctive through their friendship with Belovar, their proximity to Lampusa's world, and the past they share with the Chief Ranger; and to the spiritual through their studies of nature and their association with the monastery.[76]

The consequence of this archetype approach is that the novel boasts no realistic, rounded individuals, there is no psychologization of characters (the most egregious example being the narrator passing over in matter-of-fact fashion the abandonment of his own son). Similarly, no explanation is offered for the decaying culture of the Marina or for the Chief Ranger's attack on it: decadence is part of the natural cycle and, since he is the embodiment of the principle of evil, the question of motive is irrelevant.[77] Characters are allocated to symbolic groupings—the "Hohe" (lofty) and "Edle" (noble) or the "Niedrige" (humble), "Verächtliche" (contemptible), and "Gemeine" (common)—according to the author's personal order of values.[78] Jünger's characters are essentially representatives of metaphysical forces. Thus the Chief Ranger represents anarchic power, rejects political order, and lacks all ethical values, although his character is lent at least a modicum of depth by his charisma and "joviality." The Mauretanians represent above all the new type of man who, driven by the will to power, obeys only the dictates of a nihilism that knows no moral constraints. The monk Pater Lampros, "the radiant, illuminating one," serves, through his sacrificial death in the flames, as a symbol of the survival of the spirit, of cyclical demise and rebirth. The natural, unaffected shepherd Belovar is a typical son of the *Heimat*, who embodies bravery and loyalty. The boy Erio represents a natural, childish innocence, whereas his grandmother Lampusa stands for chthonic forces and subterranean spirits. Linked symbolically to these two are the snakes, traditionally seen as guardians and representing in mythology, on the one hand, fertility, rebirth, and healing, and on the other, vengeance, poison, and death: in defending the Rue Hermitage, they effectively become allies of the brothers' spiritual resistance and thus precursors of the rebirth of the Marina.[79]

Prince Sunmyra and Braquemart are the most significant representative characters in the novel. Besides his other possible functions as part

Goebbels and Heydrich caricature, part autobiographical portrait,[80] Braquemart represents the Mauretanian mindset: he is a cunning and dangerous individual with a nihilistic intelligence, as great a threat to the order of things as the Chief Ranger and indeed a rival to him. Unlike the latter, however, who seeks to populate a conquered Marina with wild animals, he wishes to create a primeval division of "races" into master and slave (15:314). Braquemart is an intellectual and a disciple of Nietzsche (whose explosive ideas are denoted by the sobriquet of old "Pulverkopf," powder head). He is "der reine Techniker der Macht" (the pure technician of power, 15:321–22), cold, calculating, and unfeeling. He has the positive human feature of someone who endures pain, but he is beyond salvation; this has made him bitter and desirous of revenge, causing him to enter "with cool courage" the domain of the Chief Ranger (15:318). Prince Sunmyra, by contrast, is one of the guardians of the spirit in the novel. He is portrayed as being young but prematurely aged, burdened by a weakened and decaying noble heritage (15:315–16). His attempt to resist and make a stand against the evil of the Chief Ranger is from the start doomed to failure, but in the process he displays a noble capacity for suffering (15:318) and through his almost sacrificial death he assumes the image of a Christian martyr: rather than take his own life, he is prepared, like Braquemart, to suffer and thereby attains a moral victory over tyranny. The Christian interpretation is reinforced by the narrator's actions in preserving the head of Prince Sunmyra and the decision to place it in the cornerstone of the new cathedral. Sunmyra stands for those conservative and aristocratic German resistance circles whose endeavors were apparently doomed to failure. Together, Braquemart and Sunmyra represent the separation of spirit and power that has undermined the civilization of the region, and the analogy with the fateful passivity of spirit that allowed the rise of National Socialism is difficult to ignore.

Jünger's conscious use of stylistic devices serves to underline the mythological and timeless aspects of his work. Thus the novel reveals a distinct linguistic eclecticism, with a wealth of Latin and Greek terms, Latinized and scholarly sounding name forms such as "Nigromantus," "Phyllobius," and "Linnaeus," antiquated Germanic turns of phrase and spelling, unusual compounds and collocations, and archaic name forms such as "Otho." Furthermore, the narrator engages in a form of dialogue with an imaginary readership, aimed at establishing a basis of understanding or agreement about universal values and attitudes; the use of the "so" (thus/so) particle is important here—for example, "So kommt es, daß Kriegesmut auf dieser Welt im zweiten Treffen steht" (So it comes about that, in this world, a soldier's courage takes second place, 15:311). On occasions he addresses the reader directly and draws him or her into his way of thinking through the use of "wir," as in the very first sentence of the novel: "Ihr alle kennt die wilde Schwermut, die uns bei der Erinnerung an Zeiten des Glückes ergreift" (You all know the fierce melancholy that takes hold of us when we remember times of happiness, 2:249). Moreover, he uses the present tense throughout, which, especially when prefaced by the summative "so" or the contextualizing "auch" (also/even), serves to stress the link between exemplary narrated events and time-attested regularities in human affairs or universal laws.[81] The use of the passive voice furthers the sense of events being at the mercy of ordained historical structures, while frequent aphorisms and generalizing expressions contribute to a knowing sense of phenomena conforming to an entirely familiar pattern. Charges of mannerism and affectation have been leveled at Jünger's text for such stylistic techniques, but their real function and significance would seem to be to distance the reader from the material, while simultaneously underlining its mythical nature and wider applicability.

Finally, the work's dreamlike qualities enhance the impression of timelessness. Its many surrealist features lend expression to Jünger's belief that the way to access reality is via dreams, the subconscious, and the irrational. Several episodes have a nightmarish quality, including most notably the Köppelsbleek scene, the fight between the two sets of dogs, and the final conflagration, a sense enhanced by the anachronisms and sudden absurdities. It is significant in this connection that Jünger refers to the novel as a "capriccio" (2:37), one of those playful nocturnal excesses of the mind that had featured so prominently in his recently published revised edition of *Das abenteuerliche Herz*.[82]

Jünger's insistence that *Auf den Marmorklippen* be considered a timeless statement on human existence, a stand against the drift into meaninglessness and all forms of nihilism, is thus reflected in the work's setting, characterization, and style. The narrator says that he and his brother were driven by the Linnaean model that order prevails in the elements, that "measure and rule" are firmly embedded in the chance and chaos of the world (15:264). This belief, along with Jünger's rejection of a narrow political interpretation of the novel, are consistent with his denial of any special status for history, his repudiation of the uniqueness of events and human experience, and his endeavor, under the influence of Nietzsche's eternal recurrence, to identify the archetypes of existence, the patterns underlying the surface phenomena of life. Such catastrophes as that depicted in the fiction are subject to timeless natural laws and their recurrence cannot be averted—a fatalism seen in other inner emigrants but nowhere else expressed in such unremittingly apocalyptic terms.

Spiritual Opposition and the Aesthetics of Violence

A major theme of the novel is the question of the legitimacy of spiritual versus more active opposition. When circumstances worsen in the Marina, the brothers consider taking up arms again alongside Belovar but resolve instead "allein durch reine Geistesmacht zu widerstehen" (to resist with spiritual forces alone), seeing in this a stronger weapon (15:296–97). Their distance from the affairs of the world and devotion to the observation and recording of nature is presented as a form of resistance against chaos. The beauty of the plants they tend may be short-lived, but their unchanging forms allow an insight into the true nature of existence (15:262). Though the pending catastrophe is inevitable, it is only through the brothers' collecting and systematization that the spirit can affirm itself in the face of barbarism. Having discovered the horrors of the flaying hut, they thus still return to their original purpose in visiting Köppelsbleek and record the beauty of the rare forest flower; their scientific contemplation of order helps them overcome their fear, lends them a sense of integrity, and the indestructibility and beauty of the natural order provide the strength to withstand the smell of decay (15:312). At the end, the brothers can calmly burn their work because they believe it is destined for a new order.

A symbol of their confidence in the natural order, in the promise of rebirth following destruction, is the plantain shrub in the monastery garden. This humblest of plants symbolizes both life and death; amid the transience of its leaves and shoots is revealed an eternal pattern, an unchanging form that persists through all growth and decay (15:294). In the same way, before their meeting with Braquemart and the prince, Otho shows his brother the recently opened gold-striped lily from Zipangu with its pollen-coated stamens awaiting pollination by insects. The delicate flower, with its "flame-shaped streak of gold," pregnant with pollen, symbolizes in a reassuring way the richness and potential of life but also, as a classic Christian symbol of purity and innocence, its vulnerability,[83] and when, after the visit, the narrator revisits the flower, he sees that moths have disturbed the stamens and, as if in a life-generating consummation, have spread the pollen in their "nuptial flight." He comments: "So fließen aus jeder Stunde Süße und Bitterkeit. Und während ich mich über die betauten Blütenkelche beugte, ertönte aus fernen Vorgehölzen der erste Kuckucksruf" (Thus flows from each hour mixed joy and bitterness. And as I bent over the bedewed calyxes, from the distant fringe of the forests the first cuckoo call sounded, 15:320). Linking in this way the creative act of pollination to the threat symbolized by the cuckoo—the traditional harbinger of evil, associated with the Chief Ranger's forces by the reference to the forest—Jünger suggests that beyond the "flames" there is the consoling prospect of new life and new beauty.[84] Only in such spiritual resistance does the inner emigrant in Jünger see the opportunity to counter oppression and nihilism: "Das Leben der Pflanzen und sein Kreislauf sichern die Realität, die durch Dämonenkräfte aufgelöst zu werden droht" (The life of plants and its cycle ensure the reality that demonic forces threaten to dissolve, 3:314).

Besides the natural world, the brothers' concern is with "the word"; the study of language too is a form of resistance to tyranny:

"Wir erkannten im Wort die Zauberklinge, vor deren Strahle die Tyrannenmacht erblaßt. Dreieinig sind das Wort, die Freiheit und der Geist." (In the word we recognized the gleaming magic blade before which tyrants pale. The word, liberty, and spirit form a holy trinity, 15:297). In this creation of a sphere inaccessible to the powers of destruction, one might be tempted to see in microcosm the significance of Jünger's undertaking in writing *Auf den Marmorklippen*.

Important elements of the brothers' spiritual life are the mirror and lamp of Nigromontan. The mirror has the ability to focus the sun's rays into a high-intensity fire with the power to burn down to its bare essence whatever it touches. The brothers believe in the need for a cleansing, indeed purifying conflagration to allow a new order to arise (15:288), and the use of the mysterious object at the right time means that that which is best in man remains inaccessible to the "base powers" of existence, that the results of the brothers' spiritual labors will be preserved in a higher, immortal realm (15:302). This well-established literary trope is linked to biblical and other ancient variations on the myth of the Flood and particularly that of the phoenix rising from the ashes in a process of cyclical regeneration (15:302). The terrifying fire in the Marina is thus a productive one, an inevitable destruction, a mere phase in a natural cycle, to be greeted as the first step on the way to a new world. Similarly, in the burning of the Rue Hermitage the narrator can discern "joy" and consolation at the thought of a new dawn (15:347).

The crisis of civilization is linked to religion. It is the loss of faith that has allowed nihilism to spread and dominate, but amid the smoking ruins of the Marina a song calling for God's help is heard from one of the surviving chapels (15:350), and the thrust of the narrative is that these prayers will be answered, that from the symbolic seed of Sunmyra under the new cathedral will grow the fruit of a new civilization. The Chief Ranger's triumph is a mere episode. Ultimately the conclusion to the novel thus owes more to a longing for death as a prelude to rebirth than to a nihilistic erasing of all values. Whether or not one can see in this rebirth a Christian position, it is certainly a pronounced humanist linking of earthly forces and the power of the spirit.

The strong impression conveyed by the novel is the sense of bitterness with which the narrator now approaches fame and power. Early on we read what is tantamount to a confession of past wrongdoing as he says he and his brother had once enjoyed the company of the Chief Ranger but then quotes his brother, saying "daß ein Irrtum erst dann zum Fehler würde, wenn man in ihm beharrt" (that mistakes become errors only when persisted in, 15:265). He talks of wandering aimlessly in the past or in "distant utopias" (15:266) and, in explaining their departure from the Mauretanians, says they would certainly have had the courage and judgment to attain high office in the order but that they lacked the ability to look down high-handedly on the suffering of "the weak and the anonymous" (15:287). This sense of a new ethical departure is further seen in the response to Sunmyra's death. Though the prince represents the fatally weak nobility, he is not merely a tragic figure; when the narrator retrieves the severed head, he discerns in it a noble man, a martyr who has proven himself worthy of his forebears, and he swears in future to align himself with the free rather than "mit den Knechten im Triumph zu gehen" (walk in triumph with the slaves, 15:337–38). Gone are the militant elitism and the uncompromising will to power of Jünger's early writing, to be replaced by not only an unequivocal rejection of the aberrations of National Socialism but also a powerful statement of moral courage and a commitment to a decisive ethical example.

Nevertheless, aspects of the novel still recall the emphasis in Jünger's First World War diaries on the role of fate in human existence and the aestheticization of battle, violence, and cruelty. For example, in one of the most controversial passages, the narrator focuses on the beauty of the destruction of the towns bordering the Marina:

> Sie funkelten im Feuer gleich einer Kette von Rubinen. . . . Die Flammen ragten wie goldene Palmen rauchlos in die unbewegte Luft, indes aus ihren Kronen ein Feuerregen fiel. Hoch über diesem Funkenwirbel schwebten rot angestrahlte Taubenschwärme und Reiher, die aus dem Schilfe aufgestiegen waren, in der Nacht. Sie kreisten bis ihr Gefieder sich in Flammen hüllte, dann sanken sie wie brennende Lampione in die Feuersbrunst hinab. . . . Von allen Schrecken der Vernichtung stieg zu den Marmorklippen einzig der goldene Schimmer empor. So flammen ferne Welten zur Lust der Augen in der Schönheit des Untergangs auf. (15:342)

> [They sparkled in fire like a chain of rubies. . . . The flames rose free of smoke like golden palms into the still air, while from their crowns there fell a golden rain of fire. High above this whirl of sparks, red-tinged flocks of doves and herons, which had risen from the reeds, floated in the night. They circled until their plumage was engulfed by flames; then they sank like Chinese lanterns into the blaze. . . . Of all the terrors of destruction, only the shimmering golden light rose up to the marble cliffs. So in the beauty of their downfall do distant worlds flare up to delight our eyes.]

All that counts here is the aesthetic effect. The symbolic birds become attractive lanterns,[85] and death and human suffering are ignored, since the main sensation felt by the detached observer is one of pleasure. The passage is reminiscent of others cited above in which Jünger's cool, dispassionate distancing from scenes and acts of destruction serves to focus on the beauty of the moment. The almost telescopic view is attended by a "terrible silence" from which are excluded the anguished cries of those suffering in the fire; all feeling is suppressed, allowing emotion-free contemplation of the spectacle of destruction.

A further example is the scene at Köppelsbleek, where the narrator records the experience of the moment in shockingly aesthetic terms: at the entrance there are "flame-red berries" (15:308) and the narrator notes swarms of "steel-colored and golden flies" (15:310); the brothers detect a "sweet breath of decay" and feel how "die Lebensmelodie auf ihre dunkelste, auf ihre tiefste Saite übergriff" (the melody of life touched its darkest and deepest chord, 15:310). Moreover, the small figure in the flaying hut is possessed of an almost mythical or fairy-tale quality as he goes about his gruesome business while whistling a tune (15:310).

The controversial issue in these scenes is that not only is beauty discerned in what are actually horrific tableaux but that the narrator can take pleasure in it. At such moments it seems that scenes of death and destruction can exercise a compulsive fascination, pain can almost become pleasure, contemplation of the beautiful experience can override moral sensibility, and one is left with the impression of an author who sees himself occupying some elevated position above mere political and moral considerations. For the cool, impassive look, or "Kälte," was something that Jünger had identified as early as the essay *Über den Schmerz* (On pain) as a central asset of the age (7:146, 187); and, although by the late 1930s it had become a problematic issue for him, as shown by both the fictional brothers' inability to continue to look down on the "weak and anonymous" and in the increased compassion evident in his Second World War diaries, the above scenes demonstrate the extent to which it still very much informed his view of existence.

Jünger's aestheticization of violence and destruction prompts a number of questions. Does it draw attention to a phenomenon that most people would care not to acknowledge: that one can indeed find beauty in the spectacle of death and suffering, that "evil" can become "beautiful"?[86] Or is this a critical comment on the way Nazi terror and the harsh realities of totalitarian rule have numbed moral sensibilities, have disengaged the natural moral compass? Or are such scenes evidence of the author's own abiding amorality, evidence that even now, on the eve of war, there is still in his work an essential disconnect between the aesthetic and the ethical?[87] The majority critical opinion tends toward the final proposition but Bohrer's important monograph suggests a more positive view, arguing that the novel's "reception of cruelty" constitutes a new development in Jünger's writing, offering for the first time a moral evaluation of suffering, illustrated above all in the aforementioned negative portrayal of the mindless cruelty inflicted on the lizards by the Chief Ranger's rabble; the subsequent linking of these cruel escapades to attempts to restrict personal liberty is seen as a sign of moral and political judgment beginning to inform the aesthetic.[88] Notwithstanding this qualification and the novel's suggestion of a new beginning built on Christian foundations, there is a real danger that the stylized and rather romanticized portrayal of the Chief Ranger's death camp might appear to trivialize Nazi atrocities. Here, as elsewhere, the reader is left with the impression that the old amoral Jünger is never far from the surface of the text.

Conclusion

Jünger's relationship with the Third Reich is deeply ambiguous. On the one hand, he was tainted by association with it, profiting as he did from the considerable royalties that accrued from his writings. Moreover, although he rejected Nazi political tactics and contended that his writing in the years preceding the Third Reich merely mirrored or offered a "seismographic" reading of reality, his words helped shape totalitarian thinking at the time. On the other hand, he resisted all attempts to draw him into the NSDAP, and by the mid-1930s had become a very different writer from the earlier irrational thinker and prolific publicist who aggressively affirmed the First World War and espoused a radical revanchist national revolutionary ideology.

Jünger was the only thoroughly modernist writer among the major inner emigrant writers, evincing a clear grasp of the avant-garde, the surreal, and a broad field of comparative cultural and literary reference. He was first and foremost an essayist and, in the long run, is likely to be remembered for his many reflective prose pieces with their rich and penetrating imagery, and for his diaries. His writing, like the best literature, challenges our conception of reality, questions accepted perceptions and understandings, makes the reader view things in ways he or she may feel uncomfortable about. However, his aristocratic intellectual stance and elitist distance, his self-assured and grandly delivered conclusions, and his fundamentally antidemocratic mindset, along with the failure to engage the reader in any sort of dialogue or shared exploration, make him, for all his philosophic, aesthetic, and cultural breadth, a problematic writer. Compared with the essayistic brilliance, the narrative work is less distinguished, suffering above all from inadequately developed characterization.

In acknowledging criticisms of *Auf den Marmorklippen* from a twenty-first-century perspective, namely, that the work is misogynistic, takes pleasure in suffering, aestheticizes destruction, and reveals a philosophy of history that is almost contemptuous of life, Kiesel is right to suggest we should see the novel in the context of the author's intellectual development and the influence on this of the specific historical circumstances of the time.[89] One might add to that the context of camouflaged writing and the exigencies of publishing nonconformist work in the Third Reich: a more explicit depiction of tyranny would have meant the novel simply could not have been published in Nazi Germany. In fact, its effectiveness as a critique of National Socialism is seen in the perception of the many who read it at the time as a striking statement against the regime.

Nevertheless, it is difficult to argue that the work is mainly or specifically a camouflaged attack on National Socialism. Although it was possible for contemporary readers to see the text in this light, and many who did so were encouraged in their opposition to the regime and consoled by the work's message, Jünger was primarily concerned to show the timeless and unchanging features of all comparable historical upheavals. Life under a dictatorship employing terror tactics is placed in a broader context: in the greater scheme of the cyclical and ineluctable rise and fall of cultures and political systems, and in accordance with natural laws, it is depicted as a phase of decline and destruction to be followed, with reassuring inevitability, by rebirth and renewed growth.

Parts of this historical-mythical narrative of decline, the romanticizing aesthetics of violence, and the cult of sacrifice and death as prerequisites for renewal, have much in common with and draw on similar ideological sources as those of National Socialism. Such supposed proximity to Nazi ideas has led some to see the novel as trivializing or downplaying the regime's terror. However, its consistent rejection of totalitarianism and its distinctly Christian humanist elements make it a strikingly nonconformist work, even though the debate surrounding Jünger's ethical stance inevitably means it remains as controversial today as when it first appeared.

Notes

[1] The work appeared without a generic designation and although Deutsche Verlags-Anstalt advertised it as an "Erzählung" (story) in *Börsenblatt für den deutschen Buchhandel*, it is most commonly referred to as a novel. See Dolf Sternberger, "Eine Muse konnte nicht schweigen: 'Auf den Marmorklippen' wiedergelesen," in *Dolf Sternberger: Schriften*, vol. 8 (Frankfurt am Main: Insel, 1987), 306. The form "Marmor-Klippen" was used in the first edition; the composite form superseded it in subsequent versions.

[2] The major ones are: Helmuth Kiesel, *Ernst Jünger: Die Biographie* (Munich: Siedler, 2007); Jörg Magenau, *Brüder unterm Sternenzelt: Friedrich Georg und Ernst Jünger: Eine Biographie* (Stuttgart: Klett-Cotta, 2012); Paul Noack, *Ernst Jünger: Eine Biographie* (Berlin: Fest, 1998); and Heimo Schwilk, *Ernst Jünger: Leben und Werk in Bildern und Texten*, 2nd ed. (Stuttgart: Klett-Cotta, 2010). A good deal of biographical material can also be found in Neaman, *A Dubious Past*. The following brief summary is based on Kiesel and Schwilk.

[3] Steffen Martus, *Ernst Jünger* (Stuttgart, Weimar: Metzler, 2001), 50.

[4] In-text references (volume:page number) are to the twenty-two volume *Ernst Jünger: Sämtliche Werke* (Stuttgart: Klett-Cotta, 1978–2003).

[5] See Horst Mühleisen and Hans Peter Des Coudres, *Bibliographie der Werke Ernst Jüngers* (Stuttgart: Cotta, 1996), 162–64.

[6] He also spent time in the company of fascist intellectuals and collaborators. See Peter de Mendelssohn, "Gegenstrahlungen: Ein Tagebuch zu Ernst Jüngers Tagebuch," *Der Monat* 2, no. 1 (1949): 156.

[7] See Allan Mitchell, *The Devil's Captain: Ernst Jünger in Nazi Paris, 1941–44* (New York: Berghahn, 2011), especially 79–89.

[8] See, for example, Wolfgang Kaempfer, *Ernst Jünger* (Stuttgart: Metzler, 1981), 157–64.

[9] He had been asked to make a change to the entry for March 29, 1940, his forty-fifth birthday, where he had referred to Psalm 73, concerning those who gain wealth through violence and the godless masses who follow them (*Gärten und Straßen* 2:19; 2:118). See Martus, *Ernst Jünger*, 154; also Friedrich Denk, "Ernst Jünger: *Auf den Marmorklippen*," in Denk, *Die Zensur der Nachgeborenen*, 371–72.

[10] Neaman, *A Dubious Past*, 55.

[11] The anniversary of the attempt by the Stauffenberg plotters to assassinate Hitler and seize political control of Germany and its armed forces. See Rudolf von Thadden, "Schiefe Allianzen: Warum trafen sich Mitterand und Kohl gerade am 20. Juli mit Ernst Jünger?," Zeit Online, http://www.zeit.de/1993/32/schiefe-allianzen (accessed August 15, 2014).

[12] Eva Dempewolf, *Blut und Tinte: Eine Interpretation der verschiedenen Fassungen von Ernst Jüngers Kriegstagebüchern vor dem politischen Hintergrund der Jahre 1920 bis 1980* (Würzburg: Königshausen & Neumann, 1992), 263.

[13] See Karl Heinz Bohrer, *Die Ästhetik des Schreckens: Die pessimistische Romantik und Ernst Jüngers Frühwerk* (Munich: Hanser, 1978).

[14] See Hans-Peter Schwarz, *Der konservative Anarchist: Politik und Zeitkritik im Werk Ernst Jüngers* (Freiburg im Breisgau: Rombach, 1962), 97–107; also Roger Woods, *Ernst Jünger and the Nature of Political Commitment* (Stuttgart: Hans-Dieter Heinz, 1982), 191–218.

[15] Schwarz, *Der konservative Anarchist*, 106. Although Jünger did not share Niekisch's Marxist ideas, founded as they were on his belief that Stalinist Russia offered a model for revolutionary socialism based on nationhood rather than class, the two men remained friends and Jünger looked after his family when, in 1937, Niekisch was finally arrested and imprisoned.

[16] Ernst Jünger, "Revolution und Idee," in *Politische Publizistik 1919 bis 1933*, ed. Sven Olaf Berggötz (Stuttgart: Klett-Cotta, 2001), 36. Subsequent references to this volume appear parenthetically as (*PP*, page number).

[17] "Der neue Nationalismus," *Die neue Front*, supplement to *Völkischer Beobachter* 40, nos. 23–24 (January 1927), in *PP*, 285–91.

[18] A copy of *Feuer und Blut* (Fire and blood, 1925) in the Washington, DC, Library of Congress bears the inscription "Dem nationalen Führer Adolf Hitler!" (For the national leader Adolf Hitler). Schwarz, *Der konservative Anarchist*, 117.

[19] Karl O. Paetel, *Ernst Jünger: Weg und Wirkung: Eine Einführung* (Stuttgart: Klett, 1949), 89.

[20] See "Von den Wahlen," *Die Standarte* 1, no. 21 (August 19, 1926): 488, in *PP*, 241–45.

[21] Norbert Staub, *Wagnis ohne Welt: Ernst Jüngers Schrift "Das abenteuerliche Herz" und ihr Kontext* (Würzburg: Königshausen & Neumann, 2000), 252–54.

[22] For a good detailed discussion see Gerhard Loose, *Ernst Jünger: Gestalt und Werk* (Frankfurt am Main: Klostermann 1957), 95–129; for a more succinct discussion in English, see Loose, *Ernst Jünger* (New York: Twayne Publishers, 1974), 31–39.

[23] See Ernst Niekisch, *Widerstand: Ausgewählte Aufsätze aus seinen Blättern für sozialistische und nationalrevolutionäre Politik* (Krefeld: Sinus, 1982), 162; and Karl Prümm, *Die Literatur des Soldatischen Nationalismus der 20er Jahre (1918–1933): Gruppenideologie und Epochenproblematik*, vol. 2 (Kronberg, Tn.: Scriptor, 1974), 438–39.

[24] Ernst Jünger, letter of November 16, 1933 to the "Deutsche Akademie der Dichtung, Berlin," cited in Kiesel, *Ernst Jünger*, 412–13.

[25] See Dempewolf, *Blut und Tinte*, 189–90 and 198–99.

[26] Liane Dornheim, *Vergleichende Rezeptionsgeschichte: Das literarische Frühwerk Ernst Jüngers in Deutschland, England und Frankreich* (Frankfurt am Main: Lang, 1987), 119–20.

[27] The volume also included one hundred aphorisms. Some of these were considered critical of the regime, and it is reported in a letter of May 20, 1973 from Paul Weinreich, Jünger's editor at Hanseatische Verlagsanstalt, to Rudolf Augstein, editor of *Der Spiegel*, that Amt Rosenberg had taken exception to them (*Strahlungen V*, 20:235), but there do not appear to have been any consequences for the author. Twenty-one of the aphorisms were replaced for the second edition in 1941.

[28] Norbert Dietka, *Ernst Jünger—vom Weltkrieg zum Weltfrieden: Biographie und Werkübersicht 1895–1945* (Bad Honnef: Keimer; Zurich: Hebsacker, 1994), 94; and Martus, *Ernst Jünger*, 73–74.

[29] Ernst Jünger, "Rückblick," in Ernst Jünger and Alfred Kubin, *Ernst Jünger und Alfred Kubin, Eine Begegnung: Briefe* (Berlin: Propyläen, 1975), 93–108.

[30] Jünger defines these as "nächtliche Scherze" (playful nocturnal occurrences) that combine danger and enjoyment (*Das abenteuerliche Herz*, 9:181); they are "excesses" of the mind freed, as in dreams, from its usual ties and controls.

[31] Thomas Nevin, *Ernst Jünger and Germany: Into the Abyss, 1914–1945* (London: Constable, 1996), 151.

[32] Although many Christian conservatives hoped these references and other signs of an ethical rejection of nihilism indicated Jünger's embracing of Christianity, his concern with the symbolism of the Bible was just one of several metaphysical influences, and he seems to have moved on from this "interlude" fairly quickly after the war. See Hans-Jürgen Baden, "Ernst Jünger's christliches Zwischenspiel," *Neue Zeitschrift für systematische Theologie* 3, no. 3 (1961): 328–45.

[33] See de Mendelssohn, "Gegenstrahlungen," 166–68.

[34] See Bohrer, *Die Ästhetik des Schreckens*, 328–29; and Kaempfer, *Ernst Jünger*, 111–12.

[35] It was begun in autumn 1941, burned the next year, largely rewritten in 1943, and completed in spring 1944. See Dietka, *Ernst Jünger*, 116.

[36] Letter to Heinrich von Trott zu Solz, August 12, 1943, cited in Schwilk, *Ernst Jünger*, 200.

[37] Richards, *German Bestseller*, 159. Although this did not match the life sales of *In Stahlgewittern*, sixty thousand by the same year (84), it is still a sizeable total for the first war year.

[38] Kiesel, *Ernst Jünger*, 473.

[39] Heinz Gruber, the head of censorship in the Propaganda Ministry, also claimed he had categorized *Auf den Marmorklippen* as "not subject to censorship," and in discussion with Rosenberg's office had defended it against charges of being a contemporary critique (Kiesel, *Ernst Jünger*, 473).

[40] The related and oft-repeated story that Roland Freisler, president of the Volksgerichtshof, had written to Martin Bormann to say Jünger had been indicted but that Hitler had told him to drop the charges is a fiction based on a forged document (Kiesel, *Ernst Jünger*, 530).

[41] In a diary note for April 16, 1939 Jünger says the cliffs on which the house stands represent "die Einheit von Schönheit, Hoheit und Gefahr" (the unity of beauty, majesty, and danger, 2:37) and that this seemed better suited as a title than the original "Die Schlangenkönigin" (The queen of the snakes).

[42] Mauretania was part of ancient Libya, on the Mediterranean coast of modern-day Morocco.

[43] The physical setting of the story appears to have been inspired by a range of places familiar to Jünger, particularly coastal locations encountered on his travels to Sicily, Rhodes, Corfu, Corinth, and Rio de Janeiro (2:34), but it was particularly influenced by the Überlingen landscape around Lake Constance. See Arnold Rothe, "Die *Marmorklippen* ohne Marmor," *Internationales Archiv für Sozialgeschichte der deutschen Literatur* 21, no. 1 (1966): 124–27.

[44] Heinrich Ernst, "Ernst Jünger: Auf den Marmorklippen," *Die Weltliteratur* 15, no. 8 (1940): 153, cited in Ehrke-Rotermund and Rotermund, *Zwischenreiche*, 356.

[45] For a more detailed discussion of reviews, see Ehrke-Rotermund and Rotermund, *Zwischenreiche*, 357–72; also Günter Scholdt, "'Gescheitert an den Marmorklippen': Zur Kritik an Ernst Jüngers Widerstandsroman," *Zeitschrift für deutsche Philologie* 98 (1979): 553–61 (for 1939–45) and 544–48 (for post-1945).

[46] N. N., "Aus der ersten Lese," *Das Deutsche Wort* 15 (1939): 322.

[47] Herbert Roch, "Ernst Jünger, Auf den Marmorklippen," *Das Deutsche Wort* 16 (1940): 28.

[48] Gerhard Nebel, "Ernst Jünger und die Anarchie," *Monatsschrift für das deutsche Geistesleben* 41, no. 11 (1939): 612. Next citation given parenthetically in the text by page number.

[49] Ludwig Cremer, "Ernst Jünger, der Dichter: Zu 'Auf den Marmorklippen,'" *Kölnische Zeitung*, nos. 364–365 (July 19, 1940): 1.

[50] S., "'Auf den Marmorklippen,'" *Hochland* 37, no. 1 (1939–40): 244.

[51] Cited in Sternberger, "Eine Muse konnte nicht schweigen," 308.

[52] Heinz Flügel, "Ernst Jünger, Auf den Marmorklippen," *Der Eckart-Ratgeber*, June 1941, 13.

[53] See the summaries in Scholdt, "Gescheitert an den Marmorklippen," 553–55, and Ehrke-Rotermund and Rotermund, *Zwischenreiche*, 373–77.

[54] Heinrich von Trott zu Solz, "Nicht einmal: 'Der Fall Ernst Jünger,'" *Ausblick: Zeitfragen im Lichte der Weltmeinung* 1, no. 5 (July/August 1945): 123.

[55] Thomas Mann, letter to Agnes E. Meyer, December 14, 1945, in *Thomas Mann: Briefe 1937–1947*, ed. Erika Mann (Frankfurt am Main: Fischer, 1979), 464.

[56] Erich Fried, "Bemerkungen zu einem Kult," *Streit-Zeit-Schrift* 6, no. 2 (1968): 65–66.

[57] Hermann Broch, *Kommentierte Werkausgabe: Briefe 3*, ed. Paul Michael Lützeler (Frankfurt am Main: Suhrkamp, 1986), 123–24.

[58] Alfred Andersch, "Achtzig und Jünger: Ein politischer Diskurs," *Merkur* 29 (1975): 242.

[59] Heinrich Böll, "Das meiste ist mir fremd geblieben: Ernst Jünger zum 80. Geburtstag," *Frankfurter Allgemeine Zeitung*, no. 74 (March 29, 1975); reproduced in Böll, *Spuren der Zeitgenossenschaft: Literarische Schriften* (Munich: Deutscher Taschenbuch Verlag, 1977), 172.

[60] Sternberger, "Eine Muse konnte nicht schweigen," 306.

[61] Karl O. Paetel, *Ernst Jünger: Eine Bibliographie* (Stuttgart: Lutz & Meyer, 1953).

[62] See Scholdt, "Gescheitert an den Marmorklippen," 547–48.

[63] Gerhard Friedrich, "Ernst Jünger: 'Auf den Marmorklippen,'" *Der Deutschunterricht* 16 (1964): 41–52.

[64] For a representative sample of critical views, see Denk, *Die Zensur der Nachgeborenen*, 364–66; also Scholdt, "Gescheitert an den Marmorklippen," 546–47.

[65] Scholdt, "Gescheitert an den Marmorklippen." On calligraphy, see "Esotericism and Its Challenges" in chapter 2 of this book.

[66] See Scholdt, "Gescheitert an den Marmorklippen," 548–49.

[67] Helmuth Kiesel, ed., *Ernst Jünger/Carl Schmitt: Briefe 1930–1983*, 2nd ed. (Stuttgart: Klett-Cotta, 1999), 88.

[68] Interview with Walter Bittermann, Saarländisches Rundfunk, January 6, 1979, cited by Scholdt, "Gescheitert an den Marmorklippen," 567.

[69] See Ernst Jünger, with Antonio Gnoli, and Franco Volpi, *Die kommenden Titanen: Gespräche* (Vienna, Leipzig: Karolinger, 2002), cited by Kiesel, *Ernst Jünger: Die Biographie*, 469.

[70] There is little to support the common assumption of a parallel between the Chief Ranger and Hitler: the former's wild exuberance and joviality, extravagant lifestyle, and heavy drinking (see 15:265, 286) contrast markedly with the latter's petit-bourgeois background, lack of humor, asceticism, and abstinence.

[71] Helmuth Kiesel, "Ernst Jüngers Marmor-Klippen: 'Renommier-' und 'Problem'buch der 12 Jahre," *Internationales Archiv für Sozialgeschichte der deutschen Literatur* 14, no. 1 (1989): 133.

[72] The term "Schinderhütte" was inspired by a visit to an actual flaying shed in Überlingen (see 3:571) and Jünger used it repeatedly in his diaries to denote Nazi concentration camps (e.g., 2:315; 3:139–40; 3:447).

[73] There is also a suggestion in the diary entry from June 17, 1944 that von Trott sought to involve Jünger in that summer's plot (3:280).

[74] Scholdt, "Gescheitert an den Marmorklippen," 568.

[75] Hansjörg Schelle, *Ernst Jüngers "Marmor-Klippen": Eine kritische Interpretation* (Leiden: Brill, 1970), 55–56.

[76] See Helmut J. Gutmann, "Politische Parabel und mythisches Modell: Ernst Jüngers *Auf den Marmorklippen*," *Colloquia Germanica* 20 (1987): 59–60.

[77] Peter Uwe Hohendahl, "The Text as Cipher: Ernst Jünger's Novel 'On the Marble Cliffs,'" *Yearbook of Comparative Criticism* 1 (1968): 143.

[78] For Jünger's almost obsessive use of this "hoch/nieder" value order in connection with characters, weapons, use of the fire metaphor, and spiritual versus worldly powers, see Schelle, *Ernst Jüngers Marmor-Klippen*, 110–17. This is undoubtedly one of the more prominent stylistic weaknesses of the text: through repeated use, the terms lose their actual meaning and become vacuous.

[79] See also Henri Plard, "Ex Ordine Shandytorum: Das Schlangensymbol in Ernst Jüngers Werk," in *Freundschaftliche Begegnungen: Festschrift für Ernst Jünger zum 60. Geburtstag*, ed. Armin Mohler (Frankfurt am Main: Klostermann, 1955), 95–116.

[80] For Kiesel, Braquemart is a figure Jünger had almost become or indeed had once been but had now overcome (Kiesel, *Ernst Jünger*, 465). In the same way, Rey sees in Braquemart authorial self-criticism of the nihilism exemplified in *Der Arbeiter*. W. H. Rey, "Ernst Jünger and the Crisis of Civilization," *German Life and Letters* 5 (1951/52): 251. Significantly, though, Braquemart lacks Jünger's serenity and easy superiority, his *désinvolture*.

[81] Such usage is much reduced in the postwar revision of the novel as Jünger responded to criticisms of affectation. See Loose, *Ernst Jünger* (1957), 173–74.

[82] *Das abenteuerliche Herz: Figuren und Capriccios* (1938). See the section "Jünger under National Socialism" in this chapter and also note 30.

[83] Loose, *Ernst Jünger* (1974), 64. "Cipangu" is the medieval European name for Japan, denoting the "land of the rising sun."

[84] Arthur R. Evans Jr., "Ernst Jünger's *Auf den Marmorklippen*: A Sketch toward an Interpretation," in *Symbolism and Modern Literature: Studies in Honor of Wallace Fowlie*, ed. Marcel Tetel (1978), 38–39.

[85] The dove, of course, symbolizes peace, whereas, significantly, the heron is traditionally associated with the self-regenerating phoenix (see Kiesel, "Ernst Jüngers Marmor-Klippen," 156).

[86] Wolfgang Kaempfer, "Das schöne Böse: Zum ästhetischen Verfahren Ernst Jüngers in den Schriften der 30er Jahre im Hinblick auf Nietzsche, Sade, und Lautremont," *Recherches Germaniques* 14 (1984): 103–17.

[87] Martus, *Ernst Jünger*, 136.

[88] See Bohrer, *Die Ästhetik des Schreckens*, especially 441–43.

[89] Kiesel, *Ernst Jünger*, 477–78.

Fig. 9.1. Ernst Wiechert. Photo courtesy of Bundesarchiv, Koblenz.

9: Ernst Wiechert, the Principled Conservative: From Public Dissent to the "Simple Life"

A LONG WITH JÜNGER, Ernst Wiechert is one of the more controversial writers of the inner emigration. His early ideological proximity to extreme German nationalism and his enduring popularity and success as a published author under National Socialism have caused many to question his supposed oppositional stance from the mid-1930s on. Despite his arrest and brief imprisonment in Buchenwald, the subsequent critical silence on his work, and his virtual ostracization by the regime, Wiechert's writing has been criticized for a romantic, antirational, and conservative mysticism, which focuses on the inner suffering of fictional characters and fails to engage in any analysis of contemporary society or historical events; it has thus been considered a form of solace to fellow travelers and he himself has been accused of complicity with the regime. A key work in understanding the writer is the novel *Das einfache Leben* (1939, English translation *The Simple Life*, 1954), in which principled opposition to the regime is offered through the portrayal of an alternative reality based on a commitment to Christian morality, purity of spirit, and compassion for the oppressed, but which also illustrates the more disputed aspects of his writing and thought.

Examination of Wiechert's work is hampered by the patchy nature of the sources available. Following his death there was no systematic attempt to collate and archive the *Nachlass*, and the manuscript collections in the Wiechert archive in the museum Haus Königsberg in Duisburg are limited. Moreover, the archives of Langen-Müller, his publisher up to 1945, were totally destroyed in the war and the "10- or 12-centimeter thick" Gestapo file, which Wiechert claims existed on him, has never been found.[1] Researchers are consequently heavily reliant on Reiner's major four-part documentation.[2]

A Troubled Early Life

Born in 1887, the son of an East Prussian forester, Wiechert remained wedded throughout his life to the rural charms of his native land, and in many ways his writing conveys the impression of a constant revisiting of the lost paradise of his childhood. His early years were beset by tragedy: his younger brother died of diphtheria at the age of four; his uncle died in mysterious circumstances from a gunshot wound, possibly an act of suicide; and his father suffered a serious accident in 1907, in which he lost a leg and thus his livelihood. These events, together with her husband's excessive drinking, made the life of Wiechert's mother unbearable, causing her in 1912 to take her own life. Following secondary school in Königsberg, Wiechert went into teaching, a decision that represented in part a flight from his own wretched circumstances and spiritual turmoil, and it is not by chance that his first novel, with its distorted dream world, was entitled *Die Flucht* (Flight, 1916) and that it appeared under the pseudonym Ernst Barany Bjell.

In spite of a certified physical weakness, which meant he was initially excluded from military service, Wiechert served on the eastern front during the First World War, eventually being promoted to lieutenant. His experiences repulsed him and he felt he was wasting his life as a soldier. Nevertheless, army life shaped him irrevocably and much of his thinking and writing in the 1920s centered on the war and its consequences. He developed staunch national conservative views, opposing the Versailles settlement, rejecting the democracy of the new republic, and mourning the loss of the old Wilhelminian order and with it the possibility of rule by an aristocratic elite.[3] Even when he later came into conflict with National Socialism, he never lost this idealistic picture of the German aristocracy. The latter's nobility of spirit and desire for the common good are at the heart of his view of the immutable and eternal order of nature. The harsh conditions of the working classes on the nobility's estates are glossed over, also being seen as part of the natural social order. As late as the novel *Das einfache Leben* it is as if the promised land is only to be found in the East Prussian forests and lakes, as if the latter is the only antidote to the poisonous, oppressive, and debilitating life of the big city with its "modern civilization." It is no wonder that, even in the later stages of the regime, Nazi ideologues felt comfortable with Wiechert's worldview.

His writing after the First World War is characterized by the sobering and often traumatic experiences of the soldier returning from war as he seeks to come to terms with the past and reintegrate into society. Suffering from the loss of both their youth and the sense of purpose and duty provided by military life, many characters feel estranged from their native soil in the confused world they encounter after the war. However, although Wiechert rejected the military for the way it reduced human beings to ciphers and inanimate "Material" (*JuZ*, 9:460), in his first two postwar works, *Der Wald* (The forest, 1922) and *Der Totenwolf* (The wolf of death, 1924), he describes the devastation and misery of war in a perversely positive tone, which almost seems to glorify the intoxication of murderous combat.[4] Both works served to align Wiechert with right-wing thinking, but *Der Totenwolf* was to prove especially influential in establishing his reputation with the Nazis as a "reliable" writer. Influenced by Nietzschean ideas, Norse mythology, and the Germanic heroic legends of the *Poetic Edda*, the novel shows how Captain Wolf Wiedensahl and his fellow young "wolves" long for the approaching First World War and the intoxicating slaughter of enemies on the battlefield. This is seen as the first step on the way to creating the future "new German," who is to rid the country of communists and corrupt city dwellers. Besides communism, the work's main targets are Christianity's teaching of love and humility and its message of salvation, which are seen as having destroyed the Germans' relationship with the true heathen gods of Germanic mythology. The novel further rejects any party system of government and condemns parliament as a worthless talking shop. Despite its involved style, the work enjoyed several years of popularity,[5] although its cover design—a swastika in the form of the sun wheel, associated with the book's mythical framework—has been a point of controversy, and it clearly aligned Wiechert at the time with right-wing political tendencies.[6]

In the novel *Der Knecht Gottes Andreas Nyland* (God's servant Andreas Nyland, 1926) there is the first sign of a change in Wiechert's work, as Germanic aggression and rejection of Christianity give way to a message of Christian tolerance. The eponymous hero is a priest, who through a life lived according to Christian principles seeks to realize his true self and to achieve fulfillment and salvation by sharing in the suffering of others. However, he encounters resistance and, owing to his inability to see that he cannot free others from their suffering, ultimately fails in his endeavor. The tone and content of the work contrast sharply with the antipathy and bitterness of the early novels.

Spiritual Transformation

Toward the end of the 1920s Wiechert's outlook underwent a major change occasioned by what, in the autobiographical essay "Lebensabriß," he calls "der Durchbruch der Gnade" (the appearance of grace, 10:712). His writing now ceased to express revolt against his times and contemporaries, and he resolved henceforth to follow what he thought of as the voice of God. Although he thus engaged increasingly with Christian themes, it was not the case that he was entirely convinced of the tenets of Christian faith. Rather he maintained a basic rationalist, scientific conviction, which prevented wholesale acceptance of dogma yet was attracted by the spiritual and moral values represented by Christianity. As Klieneberger comments in connection with Wiechert's writing after the Second World War, he was in this sense "a modern version of Pascal's unresolved conflict between head and heart."[7]

The change coincided with developments in his personal life (*JuZ*, 9:579–609). He had met a married woman, Paula Junker, who was to become the cause of the breakup of his first marriage, and whom he was eventually to marry in 1932. Wiechert left the teaching profession in 1933 to take up writing full time (*JuZ*, 9:641). In the same year he moved to rural surroundings near the Starnberger See reminiscent of his Masurian homeland—evidence of the desire to withdraw into "silence," as he repeatedly described it, and the determination henceforth to shun all groups and associations. Although he kept in touch with the intellectual life of Munich and participated in readings and events organized by the Nazi cultural authorities, he was at this stage already an unwilling public figure.

Many of the stories and novels from the late 1920s onward are still set against the background of military conflict and present war as something awful but grand and suffering as noble. However, there is here none of the former glorification of war for its own sake or of the heroic German soldier. Rather, the rejection of war's catastrophic consequences comes through loud and clear as the focus shifts to the sacrifices and suffering associated with it. *Jedermann* (Everyman, 1932),[8] the first work produced after his transformation, reveals a new lighter style, and the essential humanity of its sympathetic portrayal of a persecuted Jew sets the tone for a range of subsequent works in which, in place of anger and violence, one finds characters motivated by self-sacrifice and a focus on the oppressed and spiritually or physically weak. This story marked the start of his real literary success, with sales of his books increasing rapidly and several becoming best-sellers. His output was regularly reviewed in newspapers and journals, and numerous novellas and other prose pieces appeared in the press.

The novella *Der Hauptmann von Kapernaum* (The captain of Capernaum, 1929) is a good example of the development of his writing. In its rejection of militarism, its suspicion of narrow-minded nationalism, its championing of the power of faith, and its proclamation of a humanity that rejects all forms of killing, this short text confirms Wiechert's change of tone and the move away from extreme nationalist positions. The change is further reflected in *Der brennende Dornbusch* (The burning bush, 1932), where moral law is shown to stand above the law of the state and the teaching of the church. The novella's emphasis on the unacceptability of officially sanctioned murder constitutes a warning to a society increasingly mired in paramilitary excesses and the bellicose outpourings of German nationalism. The theme of justice, which was to become so important in his subsequent work, also makes its first appearance here. Wiechert's new focus on the oppressed appears with particular poignancy in *Die Gebärde* (The gesture), a striking exploration of the roots of fascist anti-Semitism in the story of the persecution of a young Jewish boy,[9] while the rejection of politically motivated violence in the novella *Tobias* (1933)[10] underlines an increasing moral distance from the Nazis. The latter work also provides a further early sign of the importance attached to justice and the rule of law, and emphasizes the need to counter the innate human tendency to transgress with silent expiation and reconciliation.

Critical staging posts in Wiechert's literary development were the highly popular *Die Majorin* (The major's wife, 1934) and *Hirtennovelle* (Pastoral novella, 1934).[11] In the former, the soldier Michael Fahrenholz returns from the First World War a full twenty years after being declared dead, having endured a lengthy imprisonment and a period in the Foreign Legion. He is befriended by the eponymous heroine, an estate owner who is grieving the loss of her military husband and son. The motherly concern of the major's wife helps Fahrenholz reintegrate into postwar village society and she thereby overcomes her own moral and spiritual challenges. On the basis of the positive reviews received by the novel in the Nazi press and of its alleged championing of racial mysticism, Hattwig sees in it an affirmation of Nazi ideals.[12] And it is significant, in this regard, that the work came to be recommended for use in the senior classes of girls' schools: in Nazi eyes, the widow of a major killed in battle was an ethical model for young people, a brave modern woman prepared to renounce worldly concerns, in contrast to her pleasure-seeking son who is portrayed as a typical product of the corrupt city.[13] On the other hand, in the novel's flight from the reality of German nationalism, its debunking of the glory of life at the front, and its failure even to mention National Socialism, one can easily see a precursor of *Das einfache Leben*. Indeed Michael is not the type of returning soldier the Nazis could ever approve of: he has been deeply shaken by his experiences and evinces no nationalist sentiment whatsoever. The negative portrayal of war is enhanced by the depiction of Michael's father and Jonas, his friend, who have both been mentally damaged by the conflict. And the emphasis on the Christian virtues of love, spiritual sustenance, and pacifism all run counter to the mood of the times.

A similar pacifist message is conveyed by *Hirtennovelle*, the story of a heroic young shepherd who protects his village and its livestock but is killed in the process by Russian troops. With its rich Christian "lamb of God" symbolism, the story strongly suggests a rejection of Nazi aggression and militarism. However, in its negative portrayal of the civilization of the degenerate city, its deprecation of knowledge and learning, and its championing of the simple, pure, and noble life of the country, the novella can also be read as conforming to Nazi "blood and soil" orthodoxy.[14]

The emphasis in both these works on the eternal, immutable laws of nature and the universe also prefigures once more the message of *Das einfache Leben* with its rejection of the dissonant, diseased city in favor of the harmonious, life-enhancing countryside, where simple toil serves the spiritual restoration of man. These mythical laws governing human existence are, it is suggested, inaccessible to rational thought: they cannot be analyzed, explained, or interpreted but simply need to be accepted and affirmed. And as in the later novel, there is no attempt to address the social and political realities of the present or to subject Nazi ideals to a proper critique. Rather, the response is a turning inward and backward to a world of feudal structures and conservative religiosity.

Despite the marked change in his writing from the late 1920s, Wiechert initially retained an attachment to nationalist thinking and groupings, including the national conservative Fichte-Gesellschaft, and for several years he was associated with Eckart-Verlag and was a member of the Protestant "Eckart Circle" led by Harald Braun (*JuZ*, 9:619).[15] He also developed a long-lasting relationship with Langen-Müller Verlag, which meant he was henceforth published alongside such *völkisch*-inclined authors as Paul Ernst, Hans Grimm, Erwin Guido Kolbenheyer, Emil Strauß, and Hanns Johst, president of the Reichsschrifttumskammer (RSK) from 1935 to 1945 and an important protective presence for the publisher and its authors.[16] Furthermore, once the National Socialists had assumed power, Wiechert's earlier works ensured that he was seen as essentially a kindred spirit, and his writing repeatedly received favorable reviews in the Nazi press, in particular in Will Vesper's journal *Die Neue Literatur*.[17] The authorities initially thought they could exploit for their own purposes both the writer and such works as *Die Majorin* and *Hirtennovelle*, closely tied as they were to the forest and the German soil. It was a number of years before this view changed.

Critical Engagement with Nazi Germany

Key to Wiechert's development are two public speeches delivered at the University of Munich in 1933 and 1935, in which he began to position himself in opposition to the regime. The first, "Der Dichter und die Jugend" (The writer and young people, 10:349–67), is a hesitant questioning of Nazi tactics surrounding the book-burning ceremonies and of the regime's loudspeaker politics, which are contrasted with the writer's aspiration "die großen und schweren Dinge schweigend zu tun" (to do the big and difficult things in silence, 364), in keeping with the belief that writers preserve the essential and act as "stille Mahner" (quiet reminders, 362) in a clamorous world—a first hint of the retreat to inwardness that was to characterize his position after 1938.

By contrast, the 1935 speech "Der Dichter und die Zeit" (The writer and his times, 10:368–80)—one of a series organized by the Kunstring der NS-Kulturgemeinde that included such speakers as the party ideologist Alfred Rosenberg, the racist Austrian writer Erwin Guido Kolbenheyer, and the Nazi eugenicist Hans F. K. Günther[18]—contains a less ambiguous rejection of the surface phenomena of the Nazi "revolution," including the "loud words" (371), the "Blutgesänge" (bloodthirsty songs, 374), and the "Anarchie der moralischen Welt" (anarchy in the moral world, 376–77); he risks Nazi ire in also suggesting the regime is a mere passing phase and that the "law" of the German people's demise is preordained (378–79). Instead, he champions the cultural inheritance of Goethe and Schiller, truth, justice, freedom, love, and, above all, the sense of a great world order (377). The writer is someone "beyond time" (372); rather than engaging with historical events and seeking to instigate change, he or she is concerned with interpreting human affairs and distilling their eternal significance. Totalitarian abuses are apparently dismissed since they, like all contemporary events, are ultimately of no lasting significance. This reveals Wiechert's essentially irrational, ahistorical approach, which causes him to object to particular Nazi tactics, especially in the cultural realm, without questioning their overarching nationalist aims or criticizing more fundamental aspects of the regime.[19] Nevertheless, in a reference to his 1933 speech, he addresses his listeners with an unveiled appeal not to be "seduced" into remaining silent but to have the courage to follow the dictates of conscience (380).

The 1935 speech marked a turning point in the official view of the writer. Henceforth he was seen as untrustworthy,[20] as someone who could not be promoted by the regime.[21] The smuggling abroad of the text of the 1935 speech and its publication in *Das Wort*, the Moscow-based exile literary journal (in an edited version designed to emphasize its antifascist appeal),[22] was duly noted and led to his exclusion from a meeting of German war writers in Berlin in October 1936, since he was to be considered politically unreliable.[23] He thereafter declined to get involved in Nazi-organized events, as his speeches and readings were now being observed by the Gestapo.[24]

Against the background of the infamous 1935 Nuremberg Laws, which banned marriages between Germans and Jews and withdrew citizenship from all Jews and their descendants, Wiechert published *Wälder und Menschen* (Forests and people, 1936), his autobiographical reflection on growing up in the Masurian forests, which, despite its apparently apolitical content, sought to establish a clear distance between his own views and those of the regime. Contrary to customary practice in such works, the author goes out of his way to emphasize his mixed and uncertain racial origins (9:11–12) and holds up as an ethical guide for contemporary society the innate morality nurtured by a childhood spent close to nature and imbued with an enduring concern for one's fellow man.[25] The book's repeated commitment to tolerance and humanist traditions sounded a distinctly discordant note from a Nazi perspective, and the critical response, depicting Wiechert as a "sick" writer, duly followed,[26] as did a demonstrative official silence on the occasion of his fiftieth birthday on May 18, 1937.

Wiechert was indignant in almost equal measure at his literary isolation and Nazi abuses of power, and in autumn 1937 he organized a series of readings in the Rhineland. At each of four venues he read from a selection of his work including, most daringly, extracts of the new novella *Der weiße Büffel oder Von der großen Gerechtigkeit* (1946, English translation *The White Buffalo: Or, Concerning Great Justice*, 1986), a classic example of the inner emigrant Aesopian method,[27] which through the simple tale of a young warrior in pre-Christian India provides a veiled portrayal of humanist and religious responses to totalitarianism. As a result of this action the authorities blocked all future promotion of the writer and his work,[28] he was forbidden by the RSK from undertaking readings from his work in Austria, Italy, and Switzerland,[29] and he was taken to task in a number of reviews, such as one published in *Der Buchhändler im neuen Reich*, which criticized his escapism, his perverted sense of community, and his virtual "Selbstkult" (cult of the self).[30]

Frustration about the limited outlet for his deeply held convictions about the rule of law came to a climax in the protest against the unlawful imprisonment of Pastor Martin Niemöller.[31] Wiechert, who had never met Niemöller and was not a member of any church, saw the arrest as an affront, an act that showed contempt for the basic principles of justice.[32] In a letter of March 21, 1938 to the local Nationalsozialistische Volkswohlfahrt or NSV (National Socialist Welfare Organization), he refused to pay his NSV and Winterhilfswerk (winter relief) contributions in protest at Niemöller's renewed arrest; quoting the slogan recently employed by Hitler in a speech justifying the annexation of Austria, he said he would send the money to Niemöller's family "bis Pfarrer Niemöller aus dem Lager entlassen wird und das Wort der letzten Reichstagsrede auch für ihn Anwendung gefunden haben wird: 'Recht muß Recht sein auch für Deutsche!'" (until Pastor Niemöller is released from the camp and the words of the recent speech in the *Reichstag* are applied to his case too: justice must be the right of Germans too!).[33] On May 6, 1938, Wiechert's house was searched by Gestapo officials, who confiscated diaries, manuscripts, and correspondence. He was arrested and subsequently transported to the concentration camp in Buchenwald, where he was kept for seven weeks until August 26, 1938.

After his release, Wiechert was called to a personal meeting with Goebbels in Berlin and was left in no doubt that any future offence would have fatal consequences.[34] His expulsion from the RSK, effective from his arrest, was reversed and he was able to continue publishing.[35] However, all his new writing was subjected to prepublication censorship and the authorities closely monitored and managed the reception of his works, issuing, for example, negative "expert reports" and recommendations on *Das einfache Leben*.[36] He remained under the watchful eye of the Gestapo until 1945. A Propaganda Ministry report from 1940 notes that he was banned from speaking in other countries and, interestingly, that this had given rise to sharp criticism from abroad of Nazi policy, a sign of the regime's sensitivity to international opinion and an explanation perhaps of why Wiechert's punishment did not come sooner or last longer than it did.[37]

His own portrayal of the authorities' surveillance and restrictions on his movements (*JuZ*, 9:686–87) seems exaggerated, however, in view of the fact that in 1943 he was allowed a visit to Switzerland[38] and that he regularly traveled to Berlin, meeting on more than one occasion the former fellow Buchenwald inmate and communist Walter Husemann (683, 699). In general, Wiechert's desire to portray himself as "unerwünscht" (undesirable)[39] does not stand up to examination. Thus Langen-Müller's list of available books for 1940 included not only the recently published *Das einfache Leben* but also eight other previous best-sellers,[40] and his name does not appear on any of the "Listen des schädlichen und unerwünschten Schrifttums" (Lists of harmful and undesirable writings) and other lists for the period 1935–42 prepared under the aegis of the RSK.[41] Book sales from 1935 to 1942 are also revealing, as he enjoyed consistently high sales of both his previous and new works[42] and, throughout the period following his incarceration, continued to receive a remarkable income both from publication and from translations of his work in German-occupied countries.[43] In summary, it is clear that even after Buchenwald Wiechert belonged to the authors who were tolerated, but not promoted, by the regime.

His response to the death threat hanging over him was to maintain a strict public silence, declining almost all invitations to read in public or to contribute to journals.[44] This public silence later attracted the criticism of some exiled writers, most notably Erika Mann, who, in an article in the *New York Herald Tribune*, spoke of him in derogatory terms as a "gehorsamer Junge" (obedient boy—see *JuZ*, 9:687–88). It was not until a year after his release from Buchenwald that he was able to begin his account of life in the camp, although it was clear *Der Totenwald* could only be published after the war and it was duly buried in the garden. The same fate befell the first volume of *Die Jeromin-Kinder* (The Jeromin Children, 1945).[45] In connection with the attempt to publish the latter, he was forced in November 1941 to attend an interview with Hauptamt Rosenberg to be informed of the book's deficiencies (*JuZ*, 9:698–99), a meeting that once again prompted the feelings of impotence that had caused him to express in a letter of June 13, 1941 to fellow writer Walter Bauer a withdrawal to an extreme inner emigrant position: "Meine Laufbahn ist nun zu Ende, und ich werde ein stiller Gärtner werden, arm wie am Anfang. Höchstens daß ich wieder Ms. für die Schreibtischschublade schreiben werde" (My career is now at an end and I will become a quiet gardener, poor like I was at the start. At most I will once again write manuscripts for the desk drawer).[46]

After the war, Wiechert was seen by many as a champion of opposition to Nazism and there were considerable expectations on the part of the US occupation forces and many Germans that he would play a key role in helping the country come to terms with the past and in building a more humane society. However, his enduring conservatism, in particular his lingering suspicion of democracy and his abiding aristocratic conception of a hierarchical society, meant he soon found himself out of step with postwar political developments.[47] In particular, he incurred the wrath of the Americans for his semipublic criticism of their allegedly exaggerated victor mentality and at times arbitrary actions as occupiers, for which he was reprimanded and forced to make an embarrassing public retraction.[48] He subsequently emigrated in 1948 to Switzerland, where, shortly before his death from cancer in August 1950, he completed his final novel *Missa sine nomine* (1950), with its message that evil can be overcome by love and altruism. His books were for a while published in large numbers in both parts of the divided Germany, though especially in the west, where many of the shorter pieces became for several years the staple fare of school readers. However, from the 1960s his work came to be neglected and it is little known today.

Genesis and Publication of
Das einfache Leben (1939)

In *Jahre und Zeiten*, Wiechert talks about the idea for *Das einfache Leben* being developed during his time in the camp and says that he wrote it both as an escape from the grim reality of the present and as a way of purging the horrors he had endured (*JuZ*, 9:688–89). It was written with remarkable speed in an intensive two-month period between November and January 1938,[49] and Wiechert claimed that it was published in error after a reader in the Propaganda Ministry had evaluated it as "positive"; when Rosenberg's Hauptamt Schrifttumspflege had discovered the error it was too late (690). It may seem difficult to believe this version of events, in view of the strict and special conditions that had been attached to the author's further publication following his arrest. However, a report for publishers from Rosenberg's Reichsstelle did indeed recommend the novel should not be published. The fact that it still made it into print and that a different censor was able to find no objection to publication can perhaps be explained by the fact that Rosenberg's office had by this time lost a lot of its influence and been eclipsed by the Propaganda Ministry. Other possible factors, however, are that the novel is inherently ambiguous, its oppositional content veiled, and most of the views espoused by the main character not entirely inimical to Nazi thinking. Moreover, knowing what we do of Goebbels's fear of disparate oppositional groupings merging to form a religious front against the regime, which had prompted him to release Wiechert early from Buchenwald and to lift the ban on his RSK membership,[50] it is tempting to see in the publication of the book less a hole in the censorship net than a deliberate political calculation, the creation of a semblance of freedom for the purposes of propaganda abroad.[51]

Regardless of the reasons for it passing the censors, what is clear is that the book proved popular with the reading public. In the first eight months after its publication in April 1939 it sold almost 130,000 copies, and by the end of 1942 it had sold 267,234, allowing its author to earn a substantial RM 107,400 from his combined book sales in 1939.[52] Far from damaging his reputation and career, it appears from this that Wiechert's imprisonment and the official silence observed in connection with his work had served to enhance the public's interest in him and his writing. Indeed, just a few months after his open protest and his Buchenwald experiences, the appearance of a new novel could not fail to arouse the curiosity of readers, especially those familiar with his earlier work. After all, it was highly unusual, if not unique, for a writer to be allowed to continue to publish in Germany after spending time in a concentration camp. A favorably disposed and faithful readership was eager to discover what the writer had to say to them in these circumstances.

Summary

The former corvette captain, Thomas von Orla, lives in Berlin after the First World War. The novel mentions no specific dates but it becomes clear that it begins in 1922–23 and depicts a Germany that is only just getting over the lost war and the November Revolution. In all, it covers a period of about seven years and the conclusion appears to coincide with the end of the decade and the increasing political influence of the Nazis.

Orla is a brooding individual, alienated both from the life of the city and from his drug addict wife, Gloria, with whom he has nothing in common. She is an ambitious socialite who loves parties and gambling and has a lively circle of friends, including some naval officers, whom Orla has no time for. The latter seem determined to rebuild the German fleet destroyed in the war as a way of compensating for the perceived disgrace of the Versailles Treaty and the infamous mutiny of the German fleet at Jutland, during which Orla's own ship had been commandeered. His rediscovery of a line from the ninetieth Psalm—"Wir bringen unsere Jahre zu wie ein Geschwätz" (literally: We spend our years as in idle gossip, 4:362)[53]—confirms for him the futility of life in this society.

Despite the prospect of leaving behind his son, Joachim, who dreams of becoming a naval commander himself, Orla decides to abandon the city and his wife and to enter service as a fisherman and hunter. He inhabits a small island amid the East Prussian forests and lakes on the estate of the elderly General Christian von Platen, who lives in a nearby country house with his granddaughter Marianne and talks in the clipped tones and half sentences of the caricature Prussian military leader. Here, together with Bildermann, a seaman of the ranks who had saved his life during the mutiny and who acts as a sort of Man Friday to Orla's Robinson, Orla hopes to discover the all-encompassing law of nature through a life consisting of hard physical work, seclusion from the world, purity of spirit, and renunciation of all but the most basic material possessions. The mutual understanding and support engendered by the two men's island community serves to overcome class division and to champion the nobility of a life devoted to honest endeavor and humility. It transpires that in the fleet's mutiny during the Battle of Jutland, Orla had been thrown over the side of his ship because he had hesitated to shoot his attacker. He has kept the torn fragment of the imperial ensign he had tried to save, a symbol of his past failure but also of his adherence to German nationalist ideals.

Through discussions with the General, with Marianne, for whom Orla is an inspirational teacher, and with the Junker Graf Natango Pernein, the aesthete, botanist, and melancholy scion of an old aristocratic family, Orla develops a deep-seated nature-based mysticism. Gloria is dying of her drug addiction but Orla selflessly takes her in and nurses her through her final days. The relationship between Marianne and Orla becomes closer but toward the end of the novel he renounces his love for her because of their considerable age difference—in acceptance of the "eternal law" and the natural order of things. Orla almost becomes a part of the aristocratic, near feudal rural community when Graf Pernein allows him to use the Pernein estate and house for the rest of his lifetime. Significantly, however, the title and estate are to revert to Pernein's heir upon Orla's death: the patriarchal society honors worthy toil but the prevailing social boundaries are not to be crossed.

Reception

The aforementioned official report on *Das einfache Leben* by Bernhard Payr of the Zentrallektorat in Rosenberg's Hauptamt Schrifttumspflege appeared in June 1939 in the *Lektorenbrief*.[54] By reprinting it in the *Bücherkunde* later the same year, the authorities ensured it reached a wide audience.[55] Despite praise for Wiechert's search for a new "Welt- und Lebensschau" (way of looking at life and the world) and for the work's portrayal of the Prussian countryside, the novel is described as subjective and of no importance for the present day; the characters are also considered unhealthily pensive, brooding, and weighed down by suffering.[56] Furthermore, the reviewer rejects the emphasis on Christian values and the all too frequent quotation of biblical material, and says the world depicted in the novel is not one of healthy inward- ness but rather "eine Welt mit so vielen direkt krankhaft anmuten- den Zügen, daß man sie nur mit Nachdruck ablehnen kann. . . . Der Roman kann nicht empfohlen werden" (a world with so many truly morbid features that it can only be emphatically rejected. . . . The novel is not to be recommended).[57] Similarly, a review in the journal *Die Frau* refers to the work's isolationist stance and lack of human commitment, creating the impression of egotism.[58] Apart from the above, Chatellier's detailed researches only tracked down two further reviews of the novel, a not unfavorable one in the small-circulation *Eckart* and a neutral one in *Die Literatur*.[59]

The novel's individualistic withdrawal to a position of inwardness, along with its rejection of state authority and community, were bound to incur the displeasure of party ideologues. And indeed in another, more general review of Wiechert's work, the author is criticized for his rejection of the organizational role of the state, for failing to see the necessity of the state's power over the individual,[60] while *Der Buchhändler im neuen Reich* further reinforces the official line, accusing the author of celebrat- ing "ein morbider Epikuräismus" (a morbid Epicureanism), of pursuing self-centered themes, and of encouraging readers to turn away from the Nazi ideal of community.[61]

The immediate postwar apologist position, typified by Karl Paetel's view of Wiechert as a "consolation" for the many, appeared to substanti- ate the writer's role as a major oppositional voice whose work validated a position of inner emigration.[62] Puknat sees in Orla's eschewing of the material world "one of the finest and most convincing examples of the Christian life."[63] Meanwhile, Bergstraesser claims that in its portrayal of the contemporary world's loss of humanity and meaning, the work offered inner resistance to the Nazi regime, that in a state in which the powerful had a claim on every single person and on every possible aspect of their life, the novel was bound to take on a political meaning.[64]

Wiechert himself saw the flight to a better life in the stillness of the forests, amid hope and solidarity, as a form of "Tröstung der Menschenherzen" (consoling human hearts, *JuZ*, 9:690). And although the novel depicts in many ways a rural idyll,[65] at the same time it also warns readers, encourages them to preserve moral values in an essentially inhumane world, and draws attention to the possibilities for inner resistance. The writer claimed that he consequently received countless words of thanks for the book from readers, a positive reception that appears to be confirmed by its large sales. However, critics have interpreted the effect of the novel differently. Called by one "a flaccid, faint-hearted novel, lacking direction and drive"[66] and by another a "Fallstudie deutscher Fehlwege" (case study of the wrong turn taken by Germans),[67] the dominant impression it creates is, in fact, one of resignation, conveying the message that the only alternative left in this world is the turn inward to the stillness and simplicity of the mystic, whose sole attachment is to his or her soul and the struggle with faith. Pleßke therefore concludes that, no matter how praiseworthy the writer's sincere desire to build a bulwark against inhumanity, his programmatic "Verinnerlichung" (internalization) served merely to enhance Germans' sense of disorientation.[68]

For many, the novel is an escapist work offering an unpolitical public a refuge from propaganda, denunciation, and mistrust, a refuge that they secretly craved. Schonauer is especially damning in his verdict, calling the novel's appearance in 1939 "grotesque" and a symptom of "intellectual stultification," in that it caused so many to identify with the protagonist and to be fascinated by an illusory idyllic life lived outside the difficulties of contemporary society.[69] More crucially, Wiesner talks about the work provoking in readers a melancholic and fatalistic attitude, which confirmed middle-class Germans in their political passivity and "blinde Aktionslosigkeit" (blind lack of action).[70]

That the novel was not seen in official circles as oppositional is confirmed in the most dramatic way by the comments of Hans Frank, the governor general of Poland, who wrote personally to Wiechert in June 1943 to invite him to read from his work in Crakow and to visit Frank himself. In a remarkable letter he regrets the writer's recent arrest, refers to Wiechert's literary "masterpiece," and even draws a perverse parallel between his own situation in Poland and Wiechert's novel, saying that for the relatively few Germans in senior leadership positions in a region with fourteen-and-a-half million people of foreign race, the book offered an important "literary parallel."[71] He goes on to say the author of such a novel deserves the respect and protection of the authorities. Wiechert declined the invitation, but the fact that Frank could see some sort of solace in the work, possibly even some means of assuaging his guilt at what he was being asked to do in Poland, illustrates the potential for misinterpretation and misuse. It also helps to explain, on the one hand, why the novel was not banned and, on the other, why many Germans could find in it the reassurance that contemporary suffering and hardship was transitory and would be subsumed under Wiechert's only vaguely defined "eternal law."

An Oppositional Novel?

The status of *Das einfache Leben* as a work of opposition is thus controversial and open to dispute. In view of the publishing restrictions placed on Wiechert and of Goebbels's personal threat, it is clear the writer could not allow his work to contain overt criticism. Rather, what he could aspire to was the creation of an alternative to contemporary reality, a radically different world in which fear, spite, and oppression were alien concepts, and whose simplicity, honest toil, and self-sufficient contentment could be contrasted positively with contemporary political developments and worldly aspirations. In his retrospective comments on the novel, Wiechert said this "other life" represented for him not just a flight from the painful present of Nazi Germany but an attempt to build something new, something more "truthful," and the novel was thus a form of victory over it:

> Es war ein Traumbuch, in dem ich mich mit Flügeln über diese grauenvolle Erde hinaushob. . . . Mit ihm baute ich noch einmal eine Welt auf, nachdem die irdische mir zusammengebrochen oder schrecklich entstellt worden war. Nicht eine wirkliche, aber eine mögliche, und jede mögliche Welt ist auch eine wahre Welt. . . . Es war mir, als müßte ich nicht nur mich, sondern auch das Bild meines Volkes retten. (*JuZ*, 9:688–89)

> [It was a book of dreams in which I raised myself on wings above this terrible earth. . . . With it I constructed a new world, after my earthly one had collapsed or at least been frightfully distorted. Not a real world but a possible one, and every possible world is also a true world. I felt as if I had to save not just myself but also the image of my people.]

These words demonstrate the aim to produce a "Gegenbild" (counterimage), a "Gegenwelt" (alternative world) (689) to the contemporary one in which violence and injustice held sway and in which most traces of humanity had been suppressed. The world depicted in the novel, the simple life of humble service and selfless labor, is so distant from contemporary Nazi Germany and the contrast so obvious that it positively invites comparison with the present. The fundamental humanism conveyed through the character of Orla is intended to provide sustenance to a people suffering under the oppression of totalitarian rule, to hold out hope to readers, the hope that dreams of a different life had not been entirely suppressed, to suggest that as long as books such as this could appear there were still grounds for optimism. For this reason, Wiechert considered his novel a heavily loaded invitation to the reader to choose between the world "dictated" by the Nazi present and the imagined one of the fiction (*JuZ*, 9:690).

This imagined world contrasts markedly with contemporary Nazi Germany in a number of different ways. In place of the nationalism and the glorification of war that typify *Der Wald* and *Der Totenwolf*, one finds a near pacifism, a repudiation of war for disregarding the sanctity of life. Furthermore, the sympathetic portrayal of the noble upper classes and a traditional, feudal society of profound social harmony betrays a significant shift away from *völkisch* ideals, from the Nazis' populism, and their instinctively antiaristocratic stance. From the priest whom he consults in search of guidance Orla learns an important lesson, namely, that people need to recognize and accept personal responsibility and show contrition (4:382), a stance far removed from trenchant Nazi chauvinism. Similarly, on his wanderings through the city, Orla is troubled by major doubts about his own way of life and the country's military past—"Gefecht und Schlacht, Tod und Zerstörung, das konnte nicht alles sein" (fighting and battles, death and destruction, that could not be all there was to life, 371)—and he expresses the desire to find a new meaning in life, to gain a brief glimpse of the supposed "plan" for mankind. The absence in the novel of any notion of a proud nation building a glorious future and the willingness meekly to subordinate one's life to a greater design serve to reinforce the sense of an existence divorced from the brave new world of the Nazi present and to suggest shaken confidence in the consequences of fascist practice.

The novel presents a society dominated by landed aristocracy and inherited wealth, in which the few representatives of the lower classes mentioned (farm workers, forest wardens, housekeepers, and tutors) all occupy serving roles and in which honest toil is shown to be rewarded by munificent patrons, who are portrayed as the ideal guardians of the land and have the interests of their servants at heart; the latter consequently have little or no interest in dissent and revolt. In the idyllic portrait of this patriarchal world, Wiechert, true to his national conservative principles, rejects all class-based politics, promotes a return to past social structures, and upholds privilege and inherited wealth as the guarantors of future social stability. Despite its failure to address the reality of postimperial Germany with its political and economic turmoil, the novel's defense of Prussian tradition and Junker values and its positing of a utopia quite at odds with the Nazi *Volksgemeinschaft* (people's community) could be seen to constitute an oppositional response to the regime.

The criticism most commonly leveled at the novel is that in promoting inwardness Wiechert is fleeing from and encouraging people to turn a blind eye to the horrors of contemporary reality. However, reviews at the time show that official reservations focused on precisely the work's advocacy of a solitary existence divorced from all social responsibility and that such withdrawal from society was seen in Nazi circles as synonymous with *rejection* of that society.[72] As Scholdt has noted: "Zu diesem Zeitpunkt [stellte] der Rückzug aus der Öffentlichkeit eine gewichtige politische Handlung dar, eine Reaktion nämlich auf die totale Politisierung des Lebens im Dritten Reich, ein Signal der Resistenz gegenüber der völligen Vereinnahmung des Autors . . . als Mitglied der Volksgemeinschaft"[73] (Withdrawal from public life constituted at this time a momentous political act, for it was a reaction to the total politicization of life in the Third Reich, a sign that authors . . . were resistant to being wholly co-opted as members of the national community). To reproach Wiechert for portraying inwardness as a form of flight from Nazi Germany and to see this simply as an escapist response is thus not especially meaningful, since such a mode of existence contravened the basic principles of National Socialist society and was therefore likely to be viewed by the authorities as a dissonant, if not an oppositional, statement.

The choice of the navy as Orla's military environment, rather than the army, which had formed the backdrop to several of Wiechert's earlier works, is doubtless significant.[74] The navy in the early years of the twentieth century was seen as "*the* symbol of Wilheminian aspirations," as embodying a unified Germany.[75] However, the navy portrayed in the novel is one shamed by the mutiny of its sailors following the Battle of Jutland, and in the book that Orla writes about his experiences he decries the ethical deficiencies of the navy and the gulf it tolerated between the conditions enjoyed by officers and men. The repeated references to the mutiny, Orla's abiding sense of defeat, and the novel's implicit rejection of the heroic German military all serve to undermine the German nationalist position—the view that the brave, honest, and unflinching soldiers and sailors had been sold down the river by Germany's politicians in the Versailles Treaty and that revolutionary tendencies served to compound this "stab in the back." The failure of the world depicted in the novel to embrace ethical values suggests that the harmonious *Volksgemeinschaft* was not being achieved in the Germany of the late 1930s either.

The portrayal of Orla's son is the most overt anti-Nazi element in the work. Joachim is an arrogant, self-centered naval cadet, full of aggressive intent, who cannot wait to engage in military battle in order to reclaim the national respect he believes his father's generation has forfeited through its failings. He longs to wreak vengeance on those weak political leaders at whose door he lays the blame for the supposed betrayal of the German military in the war, and thereby to rid the country of the detested Weimar Republic. His sober thinking, his lack of illusions, and his purposefulness stand in stark contrast to Orla's mystical inwardness. However, when Joachim spouts militaristic slogans, Orla points out that violence and military might are not the way to bring about a new era. By the end of the novel, in his blind pursuit of the supposed honor of the battlefield, Joachim seems to have learned little from his father's example. In proposing a toast on behalf of his comrades to the glorious veterans of the war, he says: "Dieses Haus sei eine Insel für sie. . . . Draußen aber rauschte schon das Meer, das sie rufe. Sie hätten sich ihm angelobt, und dabei wollten sie bleiben. Auch wenn es keine Insel trüge sondern nur den Tod, so wollten sie auch beim Tode bleiben. Denn vor dem Tod stehe die Ehre." (This house was an island for them. . . . But outside the roaring ocean was calling them. They had betrothed themselves to it and wanted to remain faithful to it. And if the ocean had no island to offer but only death, they would remain faithful to death too. For honor stands before death, 721.) In the face of his son's reactionary views and naïve glorification of German military might, Orla champions an alternative morality of selflessness, love, and tolerance, telling Joachim that his task is to avoid future mutinies by treating the men in his charge more humanely and sympathetically. Viewed in this way, Orla's inwardness is to be seen in a distinctly positive light and it contrasts strongly with the immorality of the cadet's embryonic Nazism.[76]

Graf Finckenstein, Joachim's naval colleague, on the other hand, makes Orla more optimistic about the future. Orla rejects the training methods for naval personnel that had led to the suffering of his generation and has written his own ethical guide with an emphasis on individual responsibility. Finckenstein says he has been influenced by these ideas and that, as an officer, he aspires to serve humanity. Orla tells him that in order to act morally he must always be mindful of the greater law governing existence, however unpalatable it may appear on occasions. In the young man and his willingness to acknowledge this eternal law, Orla sees hope for mankind, talking of: "Die Gewißheit, daß man ruhig sterben könne und immer würden ein paar Menschen da sein, die den Pflug wieder in die Hand nahmen. . . . Es gab so etwas wie einen leitenden Faden, der durch das Gewebe lief. Die Schöpfung sorgte von selbst dafür, daß nichts abriß, was nach ihrem Wesen suchte" (The certainty that one could die in peace in the belief that there would always be a few people who could put their hands to the plough. . . . There was something resembling a guiding thread that ran through the fabric. Creation automatically ensured that nothing that sought its inner meaning was lost, 703–4.) This characteristic natural metaphor of the reliability, durability, and indeed inevitability of traditional values points to the positive message conveyed by the novel's conclusion.

The focus of Wiechert's criticism is principally the moral decline associated with modernity, civilization, democracy, and technological progress. His conservative rejection of the city and its industrialization, loosening of traditional ties, moral laxity, and emancipation goes hand in hand with a romantic glorification of the countryside. In concentrating his Spengler-like critique on these aspects of modernity rather than the rise of National Socialism as represented by the figure of Joachim, Wiechert has been accused by one critic of effectively reaching an implicit agreement with the regime: of downplaying the negative portrayal of the Nazis and thus assuring the regime of his "loyalty" in return for being allowed to pursue his conservative critique of civilization and to distance himself from the Nazis' construction of a new society through the depiction of an alternative "space" untouched by them.[77] There was certainly an element of tactical "Duldung einer politikfreien Sphäre" (tolerance of a politics-free zone)[78] behind Goebbels's decision to free Wiechert and allow him to return to writing and publishing, and in return the latter was forced into a good deal of compromise in writing his novel. However, the portrayal of the distinctly negative Joachim and the markedly more positive Finckenstein convey a strong and clear message to the reader. To expect anything other than restraint in the portrayal of Nazism at this time is unrealistic; an author facing Goebbels's unambiguous threat might be forgiven for being cautious in his approach.

Another consequence of his time in Buchenwald was the loss of Wiechert's faith in a personal, caring God. The notion of God as a distant entity, a form of disinterested heavenly body, informs Orla's worldview too as he seeks to immerse himself in work on his island.[79] Thomas Orla has lost his faith and, unlike his doubting biblical namesake, does not regain it.[80] In such circumstances the only real virtue for mankind is to have the courage to live an exemplary life, that is, a life that can act as a positive force for others. While the withdrawal to the isolation of the forest may seem to be a turning away from the affairs of the world, a closing in on oneself, it can also be seen as the opportunity for the essentially good person, selfless and pure of spirit, to inspire others through example, to console them with the thought that a different, an alternative life is possible. The representativeness of Orla's undertaking is first hinted at by the pastor in chapter 1, who uses the first-person plural to talk about the need to work in order to make restitution for past wrongdoing: it is not just Orla's sickness that needs healing but the whole of society's, indeed mankind's. The image of the globe reinforces this: it symbolizes the autonomous nature of metaphysical laws but also man's earthly limitations; it reminds Orla of his relative insignificance in the greater scheme of things and serves to confirm his renunciation of the wider world. Orla's existence is intended to act as a guide to all who have been affected by conflict, violence, or oppression and who aspire to reconciliation and fulfillment through eschewing the surface pleasures and temptations of life. However, his potential for influencing the affairs of this world is strictly limited. He can at best shape the lives of a handful of people; thus he reflects that "dem Menschen wohl nicht mehr gegeben sei, als in dem kleinen Umkreis seines Lebens das Rechte zu tun und zwei oder drei Menschen, bei der Hand zu nehmen und sie zusehen zu lassen, wie man es tue" (man was probably not granted any more than to do right in the small circle of his own life and to take two or three people by the hand and show them how things were done, 467). Only through his personal example and his teaching (that is, the books he writes) can Orla change things—in however small a way. What counts is the *exemplary* nature of his stance, and through his limited sphere of moral influence (Finckenstein, Gloria, the General, and the Graf) he reengages with society.

This exemplariness is reiterated through the novel's recurrent light imagery. Orla's existence is depicted as a beacon shining in the darkness of the present. Thus, under the influence of the old forester's talk of the north star's power and significance, he provides a symbolic description of the island as he returns to it on Christmas Eve: "Dann stand das Licht auf der Insel plötzlich da wie ein Stern über dem Horizont, unruhig zuerst und wieder verweht, bis es mit ruhiger Flamme leuchtete, immer wachsend, eine Verheißung auch über ihrem grauen Dach" (The light on the island suddenly appeared like a star above the horizon, unsteady at first and then covered over once more, until it shone with a steady flame, growing ever brighter, a promising augury even over their grey roof, 580). This can be linked to the ideas expressed in Wiechert's article "Eine Mauer um uns baue. . . ." (Build a wall around us, 1937) in the *Frankfurter Zeitung*, in which he states the special role of the writer is to illuminate the darkness for readers and not to abandon moral principles (10:695). There can be no doubt that the book's popularity owed a lot to the hope, albeit a chimera, that many detected in it, to the "light" it seemed to provide amid the gloom of their present lives. Escapist or not, ineffectual or not, the exemplary significance of Orla's "simple life," the forceful humanist values that the novel promotes, and the prospect it holds out of "another way" constituted a form of oppositional statement for the sensitized reader.[81]

Ambiguous Cultural Pessimism

While there are aspects of the novel that can thus be advanced to support an interpretation of it as a disguised rejection of Nazi ideals, there are other, more problematic elements that suggest a different reading. Wiechert's portrayal of Berlin at the start of the novel is significant and sets the tone for the remainder of the work. The noisy, garishly lit, and intrusive city, with its drug dealers, prostitutes, murders, strikes, and revolutions (372), is seen by Orla as a "Peststadt" (city stricken by plague, 366), the realm of the dead, devoid of all faith but a prey to ideologues. Its houses are described as being eaten away by leprosy (371) and the faces of its people are careworn and ravaged by their experiences (368). This is a city suffering the devastating consequences of war and loss; from the train he sees mothers lost in grief and countless cripples, the resentful "Blutzeugen der großen Opferung" (bloody witnesses of the great sacrifice, 369). This description of life in the early years of the Weimar Republic suggests a society in decay, in which traditional cultural values are being destroyed and people are leading aimless, meaningless lives.

Wiechert gives free rein here to his criticism of modern civilization, in particular its glorification of technology[82] and its suppression of human individuality. In the later essay "Über Kunst und Künstler" (On art and artists, 1946), he writes that many failed to realize that slumbering beneath German culture lay an ancient, uncontrolled, and untamed beast (10:415). He associates the unleashing of this beast on Germany in the shape of National Socialism with the rise of civilization and technology, particularly the splitting of the atom and the development of the atom bomb. The evil of Nazism is to be ascribed to irresistible natural powers arising from the mystical hidden depths of the human psyche, and consequently any rational analysis of the objective historical reasons for what happened in Germany is to be considered futile. As Hattwig notes, Wiechert's failure or reluctance to understand the political, social, and psychological causes of contemporary events causes him to see demonic natural forces behind the shaping of civilization and to place undue emphasis on the role of the individual, on inwardness, emotions, and thoughts, which are erected as a barrier against the contemporary situation and serve to deflect responsibility for social and political developments.[83] The turn inward, designed to keep one's ideals and values intact, is, in this view, deluded and escapist.

The suspicion of civilization is linked to praise of physical labor. When Orla visits the priest to seek guidance, the clergyman recommends that he should seek to lend meaning to his life through manual work, telling him the work of a street cleaner is more meaningful and rewarding than involvement in politics.[84] The suggestion that the laborer is content with his limited environment indicates Wiechert's apolitical and deeply conservative view of the world, his instinctive harping back to feudal social structures. Work is not primarily a means to secure material benefit but rather serves the spiritual restoration of man, and the simpler the activity he is engaged in the happier he can become. For work serves no other purpose than itself and is the key to the meaning of life: "Wer einmal die Phrase hinter sich gelassen hat, für den ist der Pflug oder das Ruder oder die Büchse oder der Spaten kein Ersatz, glaube ich, sondern die Wahrheit, eine einfache, unverdorbene und große Wahrheit" (For the person who has abandoned meaningless words, the plough, the oar, the shotgun, or the spade is no substitute; rather, they represent the truth, a simple unadorned and great truth, 617). Behind this, one can discern the influence on Wiechert's thinking of the philosopher and cultural critic Max Picard: agrarian activities are seen to be fundamental to mankind's way of life, they lie at the heart of our past development, and, Picard claims, will continue to inform our future. By contrast, the technologically based work of the industrial city is a phenomenon of the present; it is considered pernicious because it encourages the despised egalitarianism, which is associated with change for change's sake and rides roughshod over tradition and human continuity.[85]

Flight from the degenerate and poisoned city to the uncorrupted, healthy, and life-enhancing countryside, and the championing of physical work over the deceitful intellectualism of the metropolis, was quite in keeping with Nazi ideology. As in many of Wiechert's other works, such as *Hirtennovelle* and *Die Majorin*, the rejection of the technological city in favor of the simple, primordial tilling of the soil with its potential for spiritual sustenance and renewal, points to a classic conservative repudiation of modernity. Unsurprisingly, this also encompasses suspicion of all social change. Unlike his negatively portrayed predecessor—the communist Christoph, who questions his role, wants to know who benefits from his toil, and is eventually fired by the General for repeatedly raising the red flag on the island—Orla does not see himself as one of the exploited. In sharply criticizing the "alien" workers' strike on Pernein's estate, which has been incited by activists from the city and leads to the Count's murder, Wiechert condemns socially and economically motivated violence as unlawful and counter to the eternal laws of nature. Renewal is to be sought within the individual, not through mass strikes and revolutions that aim to change social conditions. Hard work, a sense of duty, and acceptance of the "natural" social order are held up as the ingredients of human happiness.

An interesting feature of Wiechert's novel, relevant to this suspicion of social change, is the close relationship between Orla, a captain in the navy who is associated with the *Reich*, and von Platen, a senior figure in the army who is associated with Prussia. Their shared ideals of honor and nationalism suggest a dangerous alliance, the suppression of difference in the interests of the country as a whole, which allowed the Nazis to take control of Germany's military elite.[86] It could be argued that this denigration of democracy, the collaborative code of militaristic honor, and the generally sympathetic portrait of Prussian social and moral values run the risk of providing retrospective confirmation of Nazi ideological positions and open up the novel to charges of indirectly supporting the regime.

A further important element of the novel's conservative worldview is Orla's embracing of nature. The East Prussian countryside, far from the hated "masses," acts as an antidote to the oppressive aspects of civilization and its excrescences. Nature follows its own unerring and eternal laws, it is unspoilt, has no purpose beyond itself, and never changes in its essentials. Although man may seek the historical causes of human existence, may try to critique political developments and economic structures, in reality all is in vain, for the "axis" of man's being is unchanging (680): "nur die Oberfläche kräuselt sich wie bei einem großen Wasser, indes in der Tiefe Fische und Pflanzen und Steine unverändert ruhen und ihre Zeit erwarten" (only the surface ripples as on a large stretch of water, while in the depths fish and plants and stones rest unchanged and await their time, 681–82). Orla's silent and isolated existence is at one with the natural cycle, and by renouncing all material values he is able to experience a hitherto unknown degree of freedom. In this sense, the novel reenacts a common mythical pattern in Wiechert's mature narratives, the idea of man's attempt to close the "circle of existence,"[87] to enter a mode of being that enables him to embrace a life in tune with the soil and the unchanging rhythm of the seasons, and to see the roots of contemporary life in the timeless, recurrent world of his ancestors. This more stable and enduring world, which Orla embraces, is symbolized, on the one hand, by the large clock on the General's estate, "the measure and rule" for life in the area, which strikes throughout the seasons and the years (680), and on the other, by the abiding image of the globe, denoting a world in which events conform to eternal laws and time follows a more measured and regular rhythm. Orla's daily round of activities follows the clock of nature, is in harmony with the regularly ordered universe, and it thus allows him to connect with the pattern of recurrence, the eternal round of birth, death, and renewal.

A key feature of this closeness to nature and of Orla's inwardness is the suppression of the self. With Yen-Hui, in the extract from the fourth-century BCE Chinese philosopher Zhuang-Tse quoted in the preface to the novel, Orla can say: "Ich bin alles losgeworden. . . . Ich habe mich von meinem Körper frei gemacht. . . . Ich habe meine Gedanken ent-lassen. Da ich so Leibes und Geistes ledig wurde, bin ich eins mit dem Alldurchdringenden geworden." (I am free of everything. I have liber-ated myself from my body. I have released my thoughts. And since I have unburdened myself of body and mind, I have become one with the All-Pervading, 359.) It is in this spirit of mystical self-purification that Orla pursues his idea of salvation, which is seen to lie in physical labor and renunciation of possessions, worldly success, and honor (he dispenses with both the aristocratic "von" in his name and his military rank). He lives an ascetic life of restraint and self-denial, subjugating personal grati-fication to the needs of others, for example offering unstinting service to the General, caring for Gloria, and forgoing the potential relationship with Marianne.

Central to Orla's "flight within" is the notion of the "island." In works such as *Die Magd des Jürgen Doskocil* (The maid of Jürgen Doskocil, 1932), *Jedermann*, *Die Majorin*, and *Missa sine nomine*, it acts as a metaphor for physical and psychological isolation,[88] but in *Das einfache Leben*, as in *Die Jeromin-Kinder* novels, it is an actual island that serves as a utopian symbol of flight from reality.[89] And this island image, often linked to the contrastive "ocean" metaphor, runs like a leitmotif through the novel, emphasizing the desire to create an alter-native space. Yet the aim to establish a humanist counterimage to the oppressive reality of Nazi Germany is problematic. Like other Wiechert characters' flight to an internalized nature-affirming existence, Orla's life on the island is an extreme form of romantic anticapitalism, domi-nated, as has been seen, by the rejection of the city, mistrust of science and technology, and a deep-seated irrational mysticism. His uncritical embracing of the values of the old class hierarchy suggests a return to a past patriarchal order that fails to acknowledge the social and political realities of the present, does little to address the spread of Nazi ideals, and, as an alternative, can only posit an inwardness that willingly sub-mits to the eternal laws of nature.

The regularity, uniformity, and immutability of the natural world and the seasons mean man must see himself as the servant of nature rather than as a *homo faber* who shapes and controls it: "An jedem Morgen begann die Welt des Hofes sich von diesem Platz aus zu dre-hen, nach alten Gesetzen, über denen lenkend die Sonne stand. Sie alle waren nur Diener, mit Fleiß und Gehorsam, und jede Wolke war mächtiger als ihr Wille." (Every morning life on the estate began in this place, in accordance with the old laws that were directed by the sun. They were all merely servants, industrious and obedient, and every cloud was more powerful than their will, 521.) One is hard pressed to see here any exhortation to act against oppression and injustice, even in the sense of the spiritual opposition posited in *Der weiße Büffel*. The implied passivity behind these ideas on nature and on the harmony of a life lived close to the soil seems to be confirmed by their inaccessibility to rational thought: the eternal mythical laws that sustain creation and life cannot be analyzed, explained, or interpreted; they simply need to be accepted and affirmed.

The lack of opportunity for man to intervene in these immutable laws results in a fatalistic view of existence. When life is determined by extraneous forces, social engagement and resistance to the inevitable become futile and, like Orla (and Wiechert himself perhaps), one ends in resignation (617). Orla's respect for the eternal laws of the universe borders ultimately on blind acceptance of fate,[90] and the "advice" to seek refuge in a form of inwardness that focuses on individual spiritual integrity and shuns all wider social issues holds out no hope of man being able to *change* the course of human affairs; for everything has its set order: "alles war richtig, wie es war und werden würde" (everything was right just as it was and as it would be, 726). The only consolation available is that all-embracing human love and selflessness can make life bearable, can compensate mankind for its inevitable suffering, but it cannot do anything to counter evil in the world (621). It is clear that such a message could never be a "call to arms" to the large numbers of Germans who read this book in 1939 and 1940. Indeed, Orla's flight from the city to a secluded rural existence might well be seen to justify ordinary Germans' withdrawal from public life to the private sphere and to the passive existence of the fellow traveler. Equally it is not too difficult to gain from the novel, even today, a deeply reassuring message that no matter what dangers or oppression life puts in our way, this is as nothing set against the mystical laws of eternity and that, come what may, we are bound by and can depend on the immutable cycle of nature.[91]

Das einfache Leben is therefore a problematic novel. Unlike many inner emigrant works' "flight into history," its setting in the Weimar Republic was not conceived as a straight parallel with Nazi Germany. Rather, it was intended, at least in part, as a critique of Weimar democracy, of the moral corruption and selfishness that Wiechert associated with modernity, and the reader was invited to link this demise of Germany and the loss of moral focus with what was happening in the country in the late 1930s. The problem is that much of his anti-democratic nationalism and his deeply embedded cultural and historical pessimism chimes rather too closely with the Nazis' own criticism of the Republic and their "mission" to save Germany from decadence and corruption. Moreover, the connection between the world depicted in the novel and the rise of Nazism is, at best, unclear, and the novel's message must therefore inevitably remain ambiguous.

However, criticism of Wiechert for complicity with the regime is wide of the mark. Like many members of the German nobility and the officer classes, he thought there was a middle way between conformism with and resistance to Nazism. This middle way lay in a flight to inwardness, to a position in which one outwardly went along with the regime but inwardly withdrew, distanced oneself from political events, and sought to preserve a purity of spirit. The public response to *Das einfache Leben* suggests many recognized in the novel a classic statement of their own forced flight from reality. Whether its effect was to justify the position of the fellow traveler or to strengthen the spiritual resolve of the oppositionally minded will inevitably remain a moot point.

Conclusion

Wiechert's opposition to National Socialism was never grounded in political philosophy. Insofar as one can discern a political standpoint in his work, it is that of the German national conservative wedded to the social ideal of a traditional patriarchal order in which the upper classes, especially the nobility, took seriously their duty of care for the laboring classes and ensured that social tensions were kept to a minimum. In the two Munich speeches, *Der weiße Büffel*, and the Niemöller affair his brave interventions were driven, above all, by *moral* concerns, by outrage at cultural policy or infringement of the principles of natural justice, and by a desire to present the idea of *humanitas* as an alternative to the regime's brutality. But all this was seen as lying outside and beyond politics: the role of the writer was not to critique reality but to transpose it into some superior spiritual realm, thereby offering the reader comfort and succor.[92] Consequently, the sole response to tyranny of Wiechert's literary figures seems to be to resign, to shut themselves off from reality, and to hide behind the notion of "Trost" (consolation), often expressed in cloyingly sentimental tones.

In this sense, Wiechert's writing under Nazism differs from that of other inner emigrant writers. Whereas the latter's literary practice was a forced response to prevailing conditions and was characterized by inwardness for a purpose (the production of parables, anecdotes, and historical parallels typifying Sternberger's "indirect form of writing" and inviting a degree of "reading between the lines"), Wiechert's philosophy and literary theory in the early 1930s were already firmly rooted in notions of an inward cultivation of eternal moral values, an ahistorical, mythical-irrational conception of life, and a proximity to the supposed natural cycle of existence. And this *instinctive* rather than pragmatic turn inward becomes an overt element of both his public speeches and articles, and is the principal force shaping his fiction, especially *Das einfache Leben*.

In view of Wiechert's early ideological reputation and his subsequent fiction's avoidance of political reality, it is no surprise that National Socialism sought to claim him for its cause. For official Nazi literary ideals seemed to accord perfectly with his closeness to nature, his championing of the German peasant, the uncomplicated patriotic German soldier, and the ideal of the self-sacrificing mother, as well as with his traditional artistry and rejection of linguistic and literary experimentation. Moreover, concerned about the potential propaganda fallout, especially abroad, the authorities never saw any pressing reason to ban his books, seeking at most, after Buchenwald, to limit his public influence through imposed media silence or negative reviews. Mindful of this context, it is all too easy to gloss over and downplay, as many have, the courage that lay behind the public protest at the treatment of Niemöller and the public reading of *Der weiße Büffel*; both acts alone distinguish Wiechert from most other inner emigrants. It is also easy to accuse the author of *Das einfache Leben* of escapism and a fateful inwardness, yet this was a writer who by 1939 had good reason to fear for his life. And though his antirationalism, mysticism, inwardness, and withdrawal from politics could be misinterpreted as tacit complicity, Wiechert's commitment to spiritual values created a shared oppositional space for very substantial numbers of readers of a novel that served to sustain and preserve intact a community of right-minded individuals opposed to the immorality of the regime.

Notes

[1] Wiechert, *Jahre und Zeiten* (1949), in *Sämtliche Werke in zehn Bänden*, vol. 9 (Munich: Desch, 1957), 687. References to these memoirs appear henceforth as (*JuZ*, 9:687). See also Hildegard Chatellier, "Ernst Wiechert im Urteil der deutschen Zeitschriftenpresse (1933–1945): Ein Beitrag zur nationalsozialistischen Literatur- und Pressepolitik," *Recherches Germaniques* 3 (1973): 154.

[2] Guido Reiner, *Ernst-Wiechert Bibliographie 1916–1971*, Teil 1, *Werke, Übersetzungen, Monographien und Dissertationen mit kritisch-analytischen Kurzbesprechungen* (Paris: Reiner, 1972); Teil 2, *Ernst Wiechert im Dritten Reich: Eine Dokumentation: Mit einem Verzeichnis der Ernst-Wiechert-Manuskripte im Haus Königsberg* (Paris: Reiner, 1974); Teil 3, *Ernst Wiechert im Urteil seiner Zeit: Literaturkritische Pressestimmen (1922–1975)* (Paris: Reiner, 1976); and Teil 4, *Ernst Wiechert im Wandel der Zeiten: Literaturkritische Beiträge 1920–1980* (Paris: Reiner, 1984). These sources are cited hereafter as D1, D2, D3, and D4, respectively.

[3] Cf. Ernst Wiechert, letter of April 24, 1922 to Friedrich Tucholski, in Reiner, D2, 37.

[4] He was to claim retrospectively that he somehow wrote these works against his own true nature (*JuZ*, 9:513) and reflected on *Der Totenwolf*, in particular, as "ein krankes Buch, vom Fieber der Zeit durchschüttelt" (a sick book thoroughly shaken by the fever of the time, 9:539).

[5] It was widely read through to the Second World War, with twenty-three thousand copies of a new edition being sold between 1936 and 1940 alone. Richards, *German Bestseller*, 243.

[6] Equally controversial is Wiechert's message to his publisher: "Mit einem gleichzeitigen Abdruck in einer großen Zeitung bin ich durchaus einverstanden, unter der einzigen Bedingung, daß es keine jüdische ist" (I am quite happy to agree to simultaneous publication in a major newspaper, on the sole condition that it is not a Jewish one). Letter of June 20, 1924 to Franz Ludwig Habbel, in Reiner, D2, 40.

[7] Klieneberger, *Christian Writers of the Inner Emigration*, 161.

[8] The story was written in 1929–30 and first published in shortened form in 1931 in *Velhagen und Klasings Monatshefte*), appearing in book form only in 1932. Hans Ebeling, *Ernst Wiechert: Das Werk des Dichters* (Wiesbaden: Limes-Verlag, 1947), 152.

[9] The story is dated in the collected works as 1932 (7:605) but was not published at that time. It was to have been included as the chapter "Eli" in the autobiographical *Wälder und Menschen* (Forests and people, 1936), but in view of the recently passed Nuremberg Race Laws such material could no longer be published. The story did not finally appear in book form until after the war: *Die Gebärde—Der Fremde* (Zurich: Die Arche, 1946).

[10] The collected works version wrongly dates it as 1937–38 (7:725). In fact, it was first published in *Hochland* in 1933 (Ebeling, *Ernst Wiechert*, 158).

[11] By 1942 over 172,000 copies of *Die Majorin* and over a quarter of a million copies of *Hirtennovelle* had been sold (Reiner, D2, 162–63).

[12] Jörg Hattwig, *Das Dritte Reich im Werk Ernst Wiecherts: Geschichtsdenken, Selbstverständnis und literarische Praxis* (Frankfurt am Main: Lang, 1984), 80.

[13] See Hans-Martin Pleßke, *Der die Herzen bewegt: Ernst Wiechert, Dichter und Zeitzeuge aus Ostpreußen* (Hamburg: Landsmannschaft Ostpreußen, 2005), 39.

[14] Walter A. Berendsohn, "Ernst Wiechert *Hirtennovelle*," in Manfred Franke, *Jenseits der Wälder: Der Schriftsteller Ernst Wiechert als politischer Redner und Autor* (Cologne: SH, 2003), 211. Like *Die Majorin* before it, the novella came to be recommended reading in grammar schools and senior classes of the Oberschule, reflecting the way Wiechert's affirmation of humanist ethics and Christian morality frequently left his work open to more than one interpretation (cf. Pleßke, *Der die Herzen bewegt*, 39).

[15] Harald Braun (1901–60), who was an editor of radio plays at Berlin Radio under National Socialism and joined the UFA film production company in 1937, was to become a well-known theater director and film producer after the war. He had initially been head of the Evangelical Press Association (Evangelischer

Pressverband) and from 1924 had edited the literary journal *Eckart* published by Eckart-Verlag in Berlin, one of whose major collaborators was Rudolf Alexander Schröder (see "Lyric Poetry" in chapter 2 of this book).

[16] See Reiner, D2, 15–16.

[17] For a brief overview, see Heidrun Ehrke-Rotermund and Erwin Rotermund, "Ernst Wiechert: Der weiße Büffel oder von der großen Gerechtigkeit (1937)," in Ehrke-Rotermund and Rotermund, *Zwischenreiche*, 125–26; see also Chatellier, "Ernst Wiechert."

[18] In Wiechert's audience were a number of prominent NSDAP members, including allegedly Heinrich Himmler (*JuZ*, 9:656).

[19] On this, see Hattwig, *Das Dritte Reich im Werk Ernst Wiecherts*, 56–59; and Schnell, *Literarische innere Emigration*, 38–40 and 58–59.

[20] Q. E., "Wo steht der Dichter Ernst Wiechert?," *Völkischer Beobachter* 48, nos. 108–109, Münchener Ausgabe (April 18, 1935), in Reiner, D2, 66.

[21] Anonymous "Bericht" held in the Berlin Document Center of the US Foreign Office, cited in Sumner Kirshner, "Some Documents Relating to Ernst Wiechert's 'Inward Emigration,'" *German Quarterly* 38, no. 1 (1965): 40.

[22] Edited version of Wiechert's 1935 speech, *Das Wort* 2, nos. 4–5 (1937): 5–10.

[23] Written response of Kulturpolitisches Archiv to a proposed list of approved German war writers, dated September 10, 1936, in Reiner, D2, 73.

[24] See Wiechert letter of February 15, 1936 to Hans Grimm, A: Grimm, Korrespondenz Grimm/Wiechert, Deutsches Literaturarchiv Marbach (DLA), cited in Franke, *Jenseits der Wälder*, 54.

[25] See Leonore Krenzlin, "Autobiografie als Standortbestimmung: Ernst Wiecherts 'Wälder und Menschen' im Kontext der Entstehungszeit," in *Zuspruch und Tröstung: Beiträge über Ernst Wiechert und sein Werk*, ed. Hans-Martin Pleßke and Klaus Weigelt (Frankfurt am Main: Rita G. Fischer, 1999), 142–44.

[26] Hans Gstettner, "Ernst Wiechert und die Jugend: Das Bekenntnisbuch eines Unzufriedenen," *Völkischer Beobachter* 49, no. 271, Württembergische Ausgabe (1936), in Reiner, D3, 45.

[27] See "The Art of Camouflage" in chapter 2 of this book. The novella could not be published until after the war, first in serial form in the *Neue Zürcher Zeitung* in December 1945, then as a book by Rascher in Zurich and Desch in Munich in 1946.

[28] Cf. "Wichtige Hinweise," *Lektorenbrief* 1, no. 2 (February 1938): 5, in Reiner, D2, 129.

[29] Wiechert letter to Hans Grimm of March 18, 1938, in A: Grimm, Korrespondenz Grimm/Wiechert, DLA, cited in Franke, *Jenseits der Wälder*, 65.

[30] Harald Eschenburg, "Die Jugend und der Dichter Ernst Wiechert," *Der Buchhändler im neuen Reich* 3, no. 2 (1938): 61–63, in Reiner, D4, 41–42.

[31] The Protestant theologian had been arrested on July 1, 1937 and was convicted of activities against the state by a "Special Court" on March 2, 1938. Released, as he had already served a seven-month sentence in Moabit, he was immediately

344 ♦ ERNST WIECHERT, THE PRINCIPLED CONSERVATIVE

rearrested by the Gestapo and subsequently spent seven years in Sachsenhausen and Dachau.

[32] See Wiechert, *Der Totenwald* (9:205).

[33] This was a reference to Hitler's speech justifying the annexation of Austria. As reported in a letter of July 2, 1938 from Heinrich Himmler to Wilhelm Hug, cited in Emil Müller, "Die Motive für die Verhaftung Ernst Wiecherts," *Stuttgarter Zeitung* 27, no. 44/B (February 23, 1971): 21; Wiechert's original letter has been lost. See also Wiechert, *Der Totenwald*, 9:204–8; and Wilhelm Haegert, Propaganda Ministry Report of January 13, 1940, in Reiner, D2, 44–46.

[34] Joseph Goebbels, entry for August 30, 1938, in Goebbels, *Tagebücher*, Band 3, *1935–1939*, ed. Ralf Georg Reuth (Munich: Piper, 2003), 1263.

[35] Haegert, Propaganda Ministry Report, in Reiner, D2, 118.

[36] See Chatellier, "Ernst Wiechert," 181–84.

[37] Haegert, Propaganda Ministry Report, in Reiner, D2, 45.

[38] See Reiner, D2, 131.

[39] He claims, for example, that his publisher was forbidden from mentioning his name in its prospectuses and that book shops were not allowed to display his books (*JuZ*, 9:686).

[40] Reiner, D2, 17.

[41] Compiled in summary form by Reiner, D2, 146–50.

[42] By 1945 his total book sales were 1,165,000. Strothmann, *Nationalsozialistische Literaturpolitik*, 379.

[43] His income rose from RM 44,880 in 1938 to RM 107,400 in 1939 (see Reiner, D2, 162–70). See also D2, 182.

[44] Wiechert letter dated May 1939 to Gerhard Kamin, in Sumner Kirshner, *Ernst Wiechert's "Briefe an einen Werdenden" and "Ein deutsches Weihnachtsspiel,"* Monographic Supplement No. 4, vol. 34, no. 1 (March 1966), Research Studies, Washington State University Press, http://www.ernst-wiechert.de/Sumner_Kirshner_Briefe_von_ Ernst_Wiechert.htm (accessed February 16, 2014).

[45] The novel later appeared in an English translation entitled *The Earth Is Our Heritage* (London: Nevill, 1950). The second volume, *Die Furchen der Armen* (The furrows of the poor), was published in 1947.

[46] See Guido Reiner, "Ernst Wiechert und seine Freunde," in *Ernst Wiechert heute*, ed. Guido Reiner and Klaus Weigelt (Frankfurt am Main: R. G. Fischer, 1993), 28.

[47] See Klapper, "Cultural 'Diskontinuität,'" 430–47.

[48] See Ernst Wiechert, "Der reiche Mann und der arme Lazarus" (10:631–56) and "Vom Wolf und vom Lamm" (10:656–62).

[49] Reiner, D2, 130.

[50] Goebbels, entry for August 30, 1938, in Goebbels, *Tagebücher*, 3:1263.

[51] Walter Delabar, "Zu den Verhaltenskonzepten in den Romanen Ernst Wiecherts," in *Dichtung im Dritten Reich?: Zur Literatur in Deutschland*

1933–1945, ed. Christiane Caemmerer and Walter Delabar (Opladen: Westdeutscher Verlag, 1996), 139.

[52] Reiner, D2, 168, 171–72. It has been claimed that shortly after the war a further 260,000 copies of a new edition of the novel were sold; total sales of the work and its translations are estimated at a million. Horst Krüger, "Ein Denkmal deutscher Innerlichkeit: *Das einfache Leben* (1939)," in *Romane von gestern heute gelesen*, ed. M. Reich-Ranicki (Frankfurt am Main: S. Fischer, 1990), 39.

[53] The authorized King James version translates this as: "We spend our years as a tale that is told" (https://www.biblegateway.com/passage/?search=Psalm+90 &version=AKJV, accessed July 23, 2014); whereas the Knox translation ("Swift as a breath our lives pass away") is preferred in Heynemann's translation: Ernst Wiechert, *The Simple Life* (London: Quartet, 1994).

[54] Bernhard Payr, "Mustergutachten," *Lektorenbrief* 2, no. 6 (1939): 8–10, in Reiner, D2, 153–57.

[55] *Bücherkunde* 6, no. 8 (1939): 419–21.

[56] Payr, "Mustergutachten," in Reiner, D2, 154, 156, and 157, respectively.

[57] Payr, "Mustergutachten," in Reiner, D2, 157.

[58] Lina Hilger, "Ein einfaches Leben?," *Die Frau* 47, no. 7 (1940): 198–201, cited in Chatellier, "Ernst Wiechert," 183.

[59] Siegbert Stehmann, "E. Wiechert, das einfache Leben," *Eckart* 15 (1939): 364–66; and Herbert Schönfeld, "E. Wiechert, das einfache Leben," *Die Literatur* 41 (1939): 693; cited in Chatellier, "Ernst Wiechert," 181–82.

[60] J. Peters, "Das Werk Ernst Wiecherts," *Die Bücherei* 7, nos. 1–2 (1940): 9.

[61] H. K. Krüger, "Zur Literaturgeschichte der Neuzeit," *Der Buchhändler im neuen Reich* 8, no. 3 (1943): 28–34, in Reiner, D4, 129.

[62] Karl O. Paetel, "Eine ketzerische Huldigung," in Paetel, *Bekenntnis zu Ernst Wiechert: Ein Gedenkbuch zum 60. Geburtstag des Dichters* (Munich: Desch, 1947), 172.

[63] Siegfried Puknat, "God, Man, and Society in the Recent Fiction of Ernst Wiechert," *German Life and Letters* 3 (1949–50): 227.

[64] Arnold Bergstraesser, "Das einfache Leben: Zu dem Roman von Ernst Wiechert," *Monatshefte für deutschen Unterricht, deutsche Sprache und Literatur* 38 (1946): 293–97.

[65] See Helmut Neuwinger, "Ernst Wiecherts Roman 'Das einfache Leben'—eine ländliche Idylle?," in Pleßke and Weigelt, *Zuspruch und Tröstung*, 149–73.

[66] Bill Niven, "Ernst Wiechert and His Role between 1933 and 1945," *New German Studies* 16 (1990): 3.

[67] Krüger, "Ein Denkmal deutscher Innerlichkeit," 239.

[68] Hans-Martin Pleßke, "Vom Wort als Macht des Herzens," *Sinn und Form* 40 (1988): here 772.

[69] Schonauer, *Deutsche Literatur im Dritten Reich*, 133.

[70] Wiesner, "'Innere Emigration,'" 403.

[71] Letter of June 11, 1943 from Hans Frank to Ernst Wiechert, cited in Reiner, D2, 183.

[72] Schmollinger, *"Intra muros et extra,"* 191–92.

[73] Scholdt, "'Den Emigranten," 107, cited in Schmollinger, *"Intra muros et extra,"* 192.

[74] Eric Dickins, "'Gegenbild' and 'Schlüsselschrift': Wiechert's *Das einfache Leben* and Bergengruen's *Der Großtyrann und das Gericht* reconsidered," *German Life and Letters* 38, no. 2 (1985): 97–109.

[75] Dickins, "Gegenbild," 100.

[76] It is ironic that Joachim bears a surname derived from a form of the Russian word for eagle, *oryol.* The deliberate association of the emblem of German nationalism with non-Germanic influences and the novel's more general references to border regions of the *Reich* shaped by different linguistic and ethnic influences (e.g., the Baltic roots of Graf Natango Pernein) convey a very different message from Nazi racism.

[77] Delabar, "Zu den Verhaltenskonzepten," 149.

[78] Schäfer, *Das gespaltene Bewußtsein,* 135.

[79] The novel is distinctly less Christian in outlook than many have assumed. The anonymous, inexorable, and immutable laws of the universe appear to leave no place for the Christian God of love or for conventionally understood morality. God is accused of standing by while millions suffer; he is "eisig vor Gleichgültigkeit" (icy in his indifference, 618) and "stumm, taub, blind, ein Götz aus Stein" (deaf, dumb, and blind like a stone idol, 619). The impersonal law that governs the vast empty chasm of the universe knows no conscience and is as indifferent to civilized values and humanist virtues as it is to destruction and death.

[80] Cf. John 20:24–31.

[81] An ironic fact of *Das einfache Leben* is that its much-questioned escapist portrayal of retreat to an unadulterated natural world might be seen quite differently by a postindustrial, posturban age with its ecological concerns and its craving for alternative lifestyles, downsizing, and country living. Whether it be young people opting out of society, rejecting democratic structures, and embracing "green" and grassroots politics, or the (middle-class) desire to lend greater meaning to life and distil its core elements by embracing ecologically sound lifestyles, homegrown produce, and ethical animal husbandry, Wiechert's novel may have much to say even to twenty-first-century readers.

[82] The trains are "diese donnernden Ungetüme" (these thundering monsters, 367), which entrap their passengers like prisoners (368), and a bus is described as "ein feuriger Drache" (a fiery dragon, 368).

[83] Hattwig, *Das Dritte Reich im Werk Ernst Wiecherts,* 142–43. This historical pessimism is linked to Wiechert's tendency to relativize German responsibility for National Socialism: given the demise of modern civilization in the technical age, *all* nations are potential victims of violent dictatorship, of demonic natural powers (see also 130).

84 Dickins ("Gegenbild and Schlüsselschrift," 100) sees in this priest, who lives in a west Berlin suburb, a reference to Niemöller, whose parish was in Dahlem.

85 See Siegfried B. Puknat, "Max Picard and Ernst Wiechert," *Monatshefte* 42 (1950): 375–76; see also Hattwig, *Das Dritte Reich im Werk Ernst Wiecherts*, 193–208.

86 See Elizabeth Boa and Rachel Palfreyman, *Heimat—A German Dream: Regional Loyalties and National Identity in German Culture, 1890–1990* (Oxford: Oxford University Press, 2000), 68.

87 Edson M. Chick, "Ernst Wiechert's Flight to the Circle of Eternity," *The Germanic Review* 30, no. 4 (1955): 282–93.

88 See Marianne R. Jetter, *The "Island Motif" in the Prose Works of Ernst Wiechert* (Vancouver, BC: Continental Book Centre, 1957); also Hugh-Alexander Boag, *Ernst Wiechert: The Prose Works in Relation to His Life and Times* (Stuttgart: Heinz, 1987), 217–24.

89 Cf. Paco's flight to the fictional island of "Utopia" in Andres's *Wir sind Utopia* (see chapter 4 of this book).

90 Hattwig, *Das Dritte Reich im Werk Ernst Wiecherts*, 158.

91 See Kirshner, *Ernst Wiechert's "Briefe an einen Werdenden,"* 8.

92 "Interview mit Ernst Wiechert als Einleitung zu einer Lesung in Radio Stuttgart am 7.12.1945," reproduced in Franke, *Jenseits der Wälder*, 225.

Fig. 10.1. Erika Mitterer. Photo courtesy of
Deutsches Literaturarchiv Marbach.

10: Erika Mitterer: Witch Hunts and the Power of Evil

I N ONE OF her later poems, Erika Mitterer wrote:

Keiner wird sein Hiersein überdauern,
der sich nicht die Treue hält.

[No one will outlast their life on earth / if they do not stay true to themselves.][1]

A remarkable feature of the Austrian writer's work is that over a literary career spanning more than seventy years she consistently engaged in both prose and poetry with wide-ranging aspects of social and political reality while remaining faithful throughout to her (traditional) ideas on form and style and to her rigorous Christian principles. Described as one of Austria's conservative writers, she was one of the few who in her postwar writing confronted her fellow Austrians with the country's Nazi past and was responsible for producing possibly the most striking, subtle, but incisive of inner emigrant oppositional works to have appeared under National Socialism, the novel *Der Fürst der Welt* (1940, English translation *The Prince of Darkness*, 2004).

A Life "Swimming against the Tide": Society, Politics, and Religion

Erika Mitterer was born in Vienna in 1906 into a middle-class family. She describes her parents as unconventional and mildly "nonconformist."[2] Her father, a native of Lower Austria, was an architect and civil servant whose real passion was hunting, skiing, and nature, while her mother, a "half Jew," grew up in Berlin and had been a painter before she married. The young Erika attended a grammar school in Vienna, after which she trained and worked as a social worker and nursery nurse, an experience that considerably broadened her social horizons. After short periods in Paris and Vienna, between 1926 and 1929 she took up posts as a local authority social worker in the Burgenland and North Tyrol regions of Austria.

She started writing poetry in her teens and at the age of eighteen began a remarkable correspondence in verse with Rainer Maria Rilke, during which she received almost fifty poems from the by now seriously ill poet, who recognized in her a kindred spirit, possibly even a younger self.[3] Mitterer visited Rilke in Muzot, Switzerland, and the exchange continued until a few months before his death in 1926.[4] The Rilke correspondence has caused many to neglect the rest of Mitterer's work, especially her later poetry. The latter is very different from her youthful efforts, which were inevitably influenced by Rilke's style. In the late 1920s she came into contact with Stefan Zweig, who was instrumental in helping to get her work published, and, through him, with Felix Braun, Hans Carossa, and Hermann Broch. She became friendly with Ina Seidel (at least for a while) and, through their shared publisher, got to know Theodor Kramer. In her prose work, Mitterer acknowledged the influence on her writing of the "großen sozialen Romane" (great social novels) of Tolstoy and Dostoyevsky,[5] and indeed *Der Fürst der Welt* provides ample evidence of this influence. She showed her first inclination toward the use of historical material in drafting a drama about Charlotte Corday, the Girondist sympathizer executed for the assassination of the Jacobin leader Marat; the French Revolution was a contentious topic in the political atmosphere in Austria at the time and numerous theaters declined the play.[6]

Mitterer contributed individual poems to various anthologies in the 1920s and 1930s but her first poetry collections were *Dank des Lebens* (Thanks to life, 1930) and *Gesang der Wandernden* (Song of the wanderers, 1935), the former being awarded the Julius Reich prize and attracting the praise of Stefan Zweig.[7] Her first published prose work was the story *Höhensonne* (Mountain sun, 1933), about a social worker from the city employed in a village in the Tyrolean Alps, a work that draws significantly on her own professional experience.

After the death of her mother in 1930, Mitterer lived with her father and devoted herself to writing, including stories much influenced by her welfare work. She traveled to Germany a lot in the 1930s, visiting relatives but also occasionally reading from her works, both in public and on the radio; these visits gave her clear insights into the nature of Nazism and its tactics. Following on from the audacity she exhibited in her initial approach to Rilke, she was to demonstrate equal courage in 1933 in writing a lengthy letter of complaint to the well-known and influential Gottfried Benn, who, in his role as temporary chair of the literature section of the Prussian Academy of Arts, oversaw the first stages of the "purification" of the Academy under the Nazis. Mitterer was prompted to write by Benn's polemical comments about emigrant German writers in a speech reproduced in his book *Der neue Staat und die Intellektuellen* (The new state and intellectuals, 1933), particularly his unjust criticism of them for alleged opportunism, his support for ideas of a Germanic master race, and his failure to distinguish between the German people and the German government.[8] This aversion to the ideology of the new regime is reflected further in the cooling of Mitterer's hitherto very close relationship with the writer Ina Seidel as a result of the latter signing a declaration of support for Hitler in autumn 1933; Seidel's subsequent pronouncements in favor of the regime appalled the younger Austrian writer.[9]

Before her marriage in 1937 to a lawyer with socialist sympathies, Mitterer also traveled extensively to Greece and Italy. She gave birth in 1938 to a daughter (and later to two sons), yet this year also contained a number of threatening incidents. In the plebiscite on the German annexation of Austria, Mitterer spoiled her ballot paper, fearing "no" votes were being monitored by the authorities. Shortly after this, the house of Ernst Molden, editor of the *Neue Freie Presse*, was searched and an unsigned version of Mitterer's explosive poem "Klage der deutschen Frauen" (German women's lament) was discovered, but Molden pretended he no longer knew who had sent it to the paper.[10] These and other incidents prompted thoughts of emigration to Brazil, but the plans were rejected when it became clear that her husband would not be able to find work there in his field.[11]

Following the annexation of Austria in March 1938, the German system of monitoring writers and their work was simply transferred to Austrian territory and, in order to continue publishing, all writers had to become members of the Reichsschrifttumskammer (RSK) and to provide documentary evidence of their Aryan origins. This restriction is one of the reasons cited for the relatively thin Austrian tradition of published inner emigrant literature.[12] Mitterer duly submitted her documentation and, despite a literal question mark on the form next to the name of her maternal grandfather, who was of Jewish origin, she was accepted as "Aryan," became a member of the RSK as of July 1939, and was thus free to continue publishing.[13] Thanks almost exclusively to the publishing success of *Der Fürst der Welt*, Mitterer's income from writing went from less than RM 100 to RM 24,271 in 1941, and a still healthy RM 21,445 in 1942, a salary not far short of that of a Gauleiter[14]—an uncomfortable contradiction for a writer opposed to the regime.[15]

After the war, Mitterer's work was recognized through a number of awards and prizes, and the 1950s proved a prolific period with the publication of various poetry collections, including the correspondence in verse with Rilke and four novels, most notably *Kleine Damengröße* (Small ladies size, 1953) and *Tauschzentrale* (Barter center, 1958). These two works were designated "Jugendromane" (youth novels), but the latter particularly aspires to much more, showing the effect of political events— war memories and the 1956 Hungarian Uprising—on the hero's development.[16] Mitterer also devoted a considerable amount of time to work on various plays, including *Arme Teufel* (Poor devils, 1954, first performed in 2005), *Verdunkelung* (Blackout, 1956), *Wähle die Welt!* (Choose the world!, 1959), and *Ein Bogen Seidenpapier* (Sheet of tissue paper, 1960, first performed in 2003). Her productivity reduced markedly around the time of her conversion to Catholicism in 1965, and thereafter religious themes are much in evidence in her poetry, including the volumes *Entsühnung des Kain* (Cain's atonement, 1974) and *Das verhüllte Kreuz* (The veiled cross, 1985),[17] in which the earlier expressive, emotive lyric poetry takes back seat to an engagement with religious questions, with the problem of faith, and with those aspects of modern life that she sees as conflicting with basic Christian values.[18] Human advancements in various fields, increased affluence, and contemporary materialism are here negatively contrasted with the failure to exhibit compassion.

From the 1960s Mitterer also became involved in peace initiatives, both through the interdenominational Internationaler Versöhnungsbund (International Fellowship of Reconciliation) and campaigns within the Catholic Church to seek condemnation of war, recognition of conscientious objection, and the introduction of nonmilitary national service.[19] Notwithstanding this, in matters of faith she remained a conservative with little time for the reforms of the Second Vatican Council. She was also very active in the German Samaritans movement (Telefonseelsorge). She further developed into an avid writer of letters to the Austrian press, in which she took issue with, inter alia, the church, its representatives, and a range of cultural and religious issues. One example of this public engagement was her decision in 1984 to leave International PEN and the Austrian Writers Association in protest at their complaint about the ban imposed on Herbert Achternbusch's allegedly blasphemous film *Das Gespenst* (The ghost), and her insistence that freedom of art should not be abused to impinge on others' legitimate rights.[20]

The Persistent *Zeitkritiker*: Erika Mitterer's Development as a Writer

Mitterer's other key works apart from *Der Fürst der Welt* illustrate an abiding concern with contemporary issues. During the period 1932–34 she worked on her first novel, *Wir sind allein* (We are alone, 1945), which could not be published until after the war owing, in part, to its positive portrayal of a Jewish doctor of the poor, Dr. Isidor Löwenberg, whom the author refused to "aryanize."[21] Here Mitterer provided the first signs of her readiness to critically address current social and political issues. She uses her experiences as a welfare worker to tell the story of a pair of teenage twins, Adelheid and Heinrich Hintermoser, the products of a broken family. Set in Vienna and the Tyrol and starting in 1923, the novel describes in realistic manner, and through extensive use of naturalistic dialogue and frequent dialectal forms, life among the lowest social classes in the 1920s, the oppressive poverty of their circumstances, and the competing feelings and pressures on the two central characters as they grow up. Told primarily from Adelheid's perspective, the novel focuses on her attempt to fulfill her ambition to study and pursue a career in the face of numerous disadvantages, including becoming a single parent, and to make a stand against conventional roles and expectations. She is encouraged in this, first by her middle-class Jewish friend Mirjam, and subsequently by her Jewish mentor and benefactor, Dr. Löwenberg, through whose character the novel also depicts the routine and widespread anti-Semitism of the period. Despite her experience of troubled, exploitative relationships, at the end Adelheid appears as a strong independent woman who has gained from her role as mother and has attained a degree of equilibrium. In its portrayal of a society suffering from mass unemployment, inflation, xenophobia, and specifically anti-Semitism, the novel shows a social mix ripe for exploitation by Nazism and, in that sense, it is indeed a sort of prequel to *Der Fürst der Welt*.[22]

Mitterer's third poetry anthology did not appear until 1946. This was a significant collection written between 1933 and 1945,[23] in which the dating of the twelve individual poems points to their link to contemporary (political) events; for example, "Redet leise" (Speak it softly), dated September 1939, which is clearly associated with the outbreak of war. In certain poems the author sympathizes with those persecuted by the regime, as in "Flucht" (Flight, 1933) or "Der Vertriebene" (The exiled, 1938). In another, "Grabstätte Pilzholz" (The graves at Pilzholz, 1934), she addresses Nazi policy on "impure" racial origins and makes a commitment to her grandparents ("Erbschaft verpflichtet," inheritance is an obligation) with their variously "blond German" and Jewish origins:

Sie hinterließen mir lastendes Erbe:
Enkel, hier stehe ich, zwiespältigen Blutes . . .
Doch ich gelobe: ich will, bis ich sterbe,
Nie sie verleugnen! Sie wirkten nur Gutes! (4)

[They left me a burdensome legacy: / Grandchildren, here I now stand of mixed blood . . . / Yet I do vow: I will until I die, / Never them deny! They only did good!]

In the poem "Klage der deutschen Frauen" (German women's lament, 1934), Mitterer's criticism of National Socialism is at its clearest:

Willkür, ihr ward kein Maß
jemals gesetzt.
Wer das zu lang vergaß,
der seh' es jetzt! (6)

[Despotism, was never / limited in any way. / Who forgot that ever / look and see it here today!]

Following a comment on how difficult patriotism has become—Germany is called "einen mißratenen Sohn," a wayward son (5)—women are encouraged not to have children under this regime: "Selig, die heut keinen Sohn gebären" (Blessed are they who today bear no sons, 5). In places, however, the collection also conveys a sense of metaphysical consolation, as in "An den Turmengel des Freiburger Münsters" (To the angel on the tower of Freiburg Cathedral, 1935):

> Ich künde Gottes Ewige Stunde.
> Was unten tost und tobt, vergeht! (8)

> [I proclaim God's Eternal Hour. / The roar and rage below will pass!]

As well as a certain fatalism, for example, in the significantly entitled "Trost" (Consolation, 1939):

> Immer düngten unsre Erde Leichen
> Baum und Blume sind daraus erwacht. (14)

> [The dead have long fertilized our earth; / Tree and flower have from them grown.]

Or a concern for the future, as in "Gebet um Frieden" (Prayer for peace, 1940). Finally, in the poem "An Österreich" (To Austria), dated June 1945, Mitterer makes a plea for Austrians to search their conscience with regard to the past, to acknowledge their guilt but also to exercise Christian forgiveness:

> Bevor du richtest, forsche in Geduld:
> Wie viele unter uns sind ohne Schuld? (19)

> [Before you judge, patiently search and reflect: / How many of us are without guilt?]

In the next two lines, however, she stirred up controversy with an ill-chosen Shylock image, which made it appear the poem was aimed at the Jewish survivors of the regime:[24]

> Und fühlst du dich im Recht und weißt dich rein,
> zerreiße, Shylock, dennoch deinen Schein! (19)

> [If you see yourself as right and pure, / Still, Shylock, tear up your note of debt!]

This poem, and the general sense of despair and resignation in some of the later items in *Zwölf Gedichte*, have prompted accusations of a conciliatory attitude to the Nazi years,[25] but this position is difficult to reconcile with Mitterer's subsequent challenge to postwar Austria to address its recent past without compromise.

The work *Begegnung im Süden* (Encounter in the south, 1941), completed before *Der Fürst der Welt* had appeared, is a surprising follow-on work. The 122-page story is a formally and thematically much slighter narrative than Mitterer's magnum opus and tells the story of Regine, an Austrian teacher, and Helmuth, a married German doctor, who fall in love and have a short-lived relationship on an island in the south of Italy. Mitterer herself termed the work entirely unpolitical,[26] and for that reason there was no problem getting it published, indeed the perception of it as politically "harmless" seems to be confirmed by the decision to publish it in a special run of five thousand for the German Army, as it was considered edifying reading designed to increase morale among the troops.[27]

Die Seherin (The seer), which was published in 1942 and was Mitterer's last publication under National Socialism, retells the Greek myth of Cassandra, who, to the resentment of the people, foretells the downfall of Troy, is not believed, but is proved right when the city is indeed burnt to the ground. It is a visionary story that provides distinct parallels to the Second World War and the collapse of Germany,[28] showing the violence, destruction, and hunger of war. However, at the same time it touches on the question of the writer and her mission. Aglaia tells Cassandra that she is hated for her prophecies and suggests that, rather than aspiring to be a priestess, she would be better off conforming and accepting in humility the role of a simple wife. In fact, she is close to doing this, as, thinking her prophecy will not come true, she sleeps with Agamemnon. However, at the end of the story she sees ("im brausenden Triumph," in thunderous triumph)[29] that she has been proved right, that Apollo has not spurned her, and she commits herself once more, like the writer under an oppressive regime, to her public role.

The postwar novel *Die nackte Wahrheit* (The naked truth, 1951) is a slowly evolving love story between a young Viennese teacher and a mature writer, set in Vienna and the countryside, which through detailed description of the characters' respective environments offers a portrait of postwar Austria and constitutes Mitterer's first clear statement of the importance of memory and learning from the past. The work touches on aspects of the Nazi period and the war in the spirit of the title but these themes are not well developed. Besides the central characters, Mitterer introduces figures such as an opportunistic fellow traveler, a Nazi zealot, Russian occupation soldiers, and a Jewish refugee. However, the superficial treatment of the latter and the fate of the Jews in general run the risk of trivializing the Holocaust theme.[30]

The most interesting of the plays written in the 1950s is
Verdunkelung (Blackout). Originally a tragedy in verse and first performed in 1958 in the Theater der Courage in Vienna, it was subsequently revised in prose but not performed until 2004.[31] Set in the
years 1933, 1940, and 1941, against the background of the 1935
Nuremberg Race Laws, *Verdunkelung* offers a dramatic portrayal of the
identity problems of those "suffering" from mixed race or part non-
Aryan forebears. Specifically, it deals with the situation, by no means
without precedent in the Third Reich, of a son forcing his mother to
claim before a court that he is not the son of his non-Aryan father,
and charts the disintegration of the family, while further touching on
the questions of euthanasia, war crimes, and the questionable role of
the church under Nazism. The wartime "blackout" of the title reflects
the intellectual darkness that descends on people under the regime. The
play represents, in the view of one writer, no less than an examination of
intellectuals' failure under fascism and an attempt to trace the roots of
that failure.[32] Besides suffering from formal weaknesses, including the
final melodramatic shooting of the mother, the play fell victim to the
general postwar reluctance in Austria to address the country's Nazi past,
in particular the culpable role of publishers, editors, and producers.[33]

Mitterer is still generally viewed in Austria as a conservative writer
owing to the preponderance in her prose of classical narratives in the
nineteenth-century Russian tradition and, in her poetry, an adherence to
conventional forms and motifs as well as a disinclination to follow particular trends or movements—for Holzner, her poetry "steht stets mitten in
und doch meistens quer zu allen zeitgenössischen lyrischen Strömungen,
vom Beginn der Moderne bis zur Postmoderne" (is constantly in the
middle of and yet mostly cuts across all contemporary poetic trends, from
the start of the modern age through to the postmodern).[34] This reputation is fueled by her rejection of postwar experimentation as a legitimate
response to the Nazis' degradation of literature; she especially objected
to the then current "Nullpunkt" (zero hour) mentality, which meant dis-
carding much that was worth saving from the past.[35] The adherence to
traditional, prewar forms made her work appear to belong with the artistic
norms of the First Republic. As she was to affirm in later years: "Es geht
mir wesentlich um Inhalte, freilich in möglichst adäquater Form; aber das
gilt heute schon fast als reaktionär!" (I am essentially concerned with content, in its most suitable literary form of course; but these days that is
considered almost reactionary!)[36] Such views meant after the war many
saw her work as further evidence of the tendency among Austrian writers
to seek to pick up where they had left off in 1938.[37] Notwithstanding her
close engagement with Austrian "Vergangenheitsbewältigung" (coming
to terms with the past), this sense of a writer who essentially belonged to
a bygone era led to her post-1945 publications being neglected to a large

extent. However, although she does studiously avoid experimentation, especially linguistic, her novels in particular engage directly with contemporary political and social issues in a way that consistently challenges Austrian reality and Austrian history, whether on the question of children's welfare, the treatment of social outsiders, or reluctance to address the Nazi past.

This is perhaps most clearly illustrated by the neglected *Alle unsere Spiele* (All our games, 1977).[38] After several years searching for a publisher for this novel, which had been completed as early as 1966, Mitterer received positive reviews for its treatment of the Nazi past. Set in the early 1960s but focusing on the years 1939–45, the narrative takes, in part, the form of a letter from the narrator and central character Helga Wegscheider to her son, Gottfried, in which she explains her initial enthusiasm for National Socialism, her behavior under the regime (BDM leader, fellow traveler, engaged to an SS man), and reveals the circumstances of her son's birth (she was raped by Russian soldiers); she seeks thereby to help Gottfried understand the Nazi past and tries herself to come to terms with its causes and consequences. In its exploration of the role of memory ("Wer vergißt, hat vergebens gelebt," he who forgets has lived in vain),[39] the structurally complex novel interweaves the narrative present of the 1960s with events from the narrated past in Nazi Austria. Mitterer focuses on the psychology of her characters, especially how events can result in people deceiving themselves and only later realizing the full extent of their delusion.[40] As increasing numbers of Jews are arrested, the reader is presented with fellow travelers and varying attempts to rationalize experiences and justify behavior, a process that continues beyond the end of the war. In general, Mitterer's desire to reflect and reject the tendency for Austrians to see themselves as victims rather than perpetrators of fascist rule and to place the blame for what had happened exclusively on Germany results in an uncompromising and, in places, bitter critique. However, for all the hard-hitting themes, one of the novel's strengths is that, as in *Der Fürst der Welt*, there are no black-and-white issues here, no simplistic characterization, no blanket value judgments, and no indiscriminate condemnation.

Genesis and Publication of
Der Fürst der Welt (1940)

The origins of the novel go back as far as the 1920s but the main writing occupied Mitterer for seven years through the 1930s. A preliminary text, first produced in summer 1931, took the form of a drama, entitled initially *Die Verwandlung der Nonne* (The nun's transformation), then *Die Nonne von Lissabon* (The nun of Lisbon), which had a number of themes

in common with the later novel, the most notable being that of stigma-
tization and the psychological motivation for such an act in an otherwise
decent and honest individual.[41] The work was begun without political
intent but, as the material developed under the influence of external
events, the personal and the political became intertwined and her focus
shifted to how people so readily become supporters of evil forces.[42]

Mitterer spent considerable time researching the historical, ecclesiastical, theological, and philosophical background to her work, reading
in particular the early church fathers, the pivotal Thomas Aquinas and
Teresa of Avila, but also works of art and intellectual history,[43] and was
guided in her studies by the Viennese literary historian and cultural philosopher Robert Franz Arnold.[44] In the process she shifted the action of
the original drama from the seventeenth to the early sixteenth century
and from Portugal to southern Germany, being careful to avoid confusion with developments surrounding the Reformation.[45] In an effort to
ensure the realistic portrayal of events, characters, and ideas, she referred
extensively to actual historical documents, building her knowledge of the
occult and magic from the writings of Agrippa von Nettesheim, the scholarly theologian, lawyer, and philosopher, who appears in the text as part
of the Nuremberg humanist circle.[46] There is also reference to the papal
bull on witches, issued by Pope Innocent VIII in 1484, which was aimed
at stamping out superstition and heretical practices in parts of Germany
and led to the appointment of the Dominican monks Jakob Sprenger
and Heinrich Kramer (or Institoris) as Inquisitors.[47] Moreover, there is
repeated reference to the text of the important *Malleus Maleficarum*, or
Hexenhammer (Hammer of the witches), produced by Heinrich Kramer
in 1487, which contained a response to those who denied the reality of
witchcraft, described various forms of witchcraft practice, and provided
guidelines for officials in state and church charged with conducting witch
trials.[48] Similarly, almost all the humanist friends of the central character
of Dr. Fabri are based on actual historical figures and documents. The
whole combines to create a highly realistic treatment of a fictional story
and trial set in an invented town.

The first draft was completed in October 1937 with the title *Die
dreizehnte Kammer* (The thirteenth chamber), referring to the central motif of the novel.[49] The initial prospects for publication appeared
bleak: following completion of the final draft, Mitterer spent two years
trying to place it with thirteen different publishers,[50] before Marion von
Schröder in Hamburg finally accepted it in 1940. Mitterer originally
intended to give the work the potentially transparent subtitle "Roman
von der Machtergreifung des Bösen" (Novel about how evil can seize
power), but in the search for publishers pragmatic considerations prevailed.[51] Within four years the book sold nearly fifty thousand copies
in Germany and Austria. Through the efforts of Max Tau, it was even

published in Norwegian translation under the title *Verdens Fyrste* in 1942 by Aschehoug in occupied Oslo. Tau claims that once a critic had drawn attention to parallels in the text with conditions in Nazi Germany, the book was banned and withdrawn.[52] However, doubt is cast on this version of events, certainly as far as publication in Germany is concerned, by the fact that in December 1943, a full year after the publication of the Norwegian version, the novel was still in production and only ceased to appear after the bombing of the premises of Marion von Schröder Verlag in Leipzig had destroyed all the stocks of the fourth print run, leading eventually to the closure of the publishing house.[53]

Der Fürst der Welt subsequently appeared in abridged versions in 1964 and 1988, edited by the author herself, in which the whole of the Prologue was cut and important references to the background of the two main characters as well as the fairy tale of the Thirteenth Chamber were integrated into the first chapter.[54] These changes and other cuts resulted in a loss of coherence and a less satisfying overall structure, which no doubt contributed to the, at best, indifferent critical response.

Summary

The novel presents a precisely described and keenly differentiated picture of life in an unspecified southern German town around the year 1514.[55] The focus is the effect of economic, social, and religious developments on people's psychology and relationships. Over 707 pages in the complete 2006 edition, Mitterer introduces a vast array of characters and provides convincing portraits from across the social spectrum, ranging from landed nobility, senior clerics, medics, mayors, rich merchants, town councilors, monks, and nuns, to simple traders and shopkeepers, lower council officials, prostitutes, beggars, and lepers. The novel is multilayered and features numerous narrative voices. Rapidly alternating subplots are woven around the central story and tragedy of two noble sisters, Hiltrud and Theres vom Ried. The novel abounds with scenes that seem only vaguely related to the main plot but their relevance gradually becomes clear as Mitterer skillfully deploys a varied range of techniques to piece together a complex narratorial jigsaw. These include: the use of leitmotifs, dreams, myths, legends, popular beliefs, folk sayings, and stories; extensive use of epic foreshadowing and deliberate delays in the development of certain aspects of plot, both designed to heighten narrative tension; and ironic recapitulation of other aspects of plot, which serves to make connections between and highlight the significance of particular events or utterances.

A form of extended prologue entitled "Gelübde" (The vow) covers a period of at least ten years, presents the background to the main action, and introduces characters who are later to become significant figures in the story. Here we learn about the knight Arnold vom Ried, the father of the girls, a harsh feudal landlord and adherent of the chivalric code, who opposes reforms and resists to the last the loss of his patriarchal world. The resulting peasant unrest leads to rebellion, the decline of the estate, and indirectly his own death. The proud, independent Hiltrud was dedicated at birth by her parents to the religious life and, after her father's death, she enters the convent in the local town, taking the name Maria Michaela.

The major section of the novel, entitled "Die Besiegten" (The defeated), is set a few years later and covers a period of about two years. It consists of four chapters, each of which is made up of numerous short sections alternating between the multiple narrative strands. Theres is adopted by vom Ried's cousin, the town councilor Matthias Nothaft and his wife, and moves to the town. She is befriended and educated by Dr. Albertus Fabri, a tenant in the Nothaft household, who is a humanist and has links to enlightened intellectuals and artists in Nuremberg. Fabri becomes a father figure to her, offering trust and security. Meanwhile, wavering in her vocation, Maria Michaela enters into an intimate relationship with her confessor, Father Alexander, a dean attached to the local monastery, the very same unfeeling priest, it transpires, who had been responsible for putting pressure on her mother in childbirth to dedicate the baby to the religious life. This relationship adds to Maria Michaela's confusion and spiritual crisis. Nevertheless she excels in her duties and, encouraged by Father Alexander, who sees here the opportunity to increase his power, she assumes in due course the role of prioress. Troubled by guilt about her sinful relationship, wanting to escape the priest's baleful influence over her, and mindful of the convent's need for income, Maria Michaela fakes stigmata and comes to be venerated in the town as a living saint, bringing considerable wealth to the convent in the process.

Meanwhile the town is shown to be a victim of progress: it is beginning to trade successfully with other towns and cities, but in order to secure itself needs to replace the crumbling town walls. The council seeks the services of an Italian architect and builder, Cesare Taglione, to carry out the work and he insists on using laborers from other regions in shift patterns (188). The traders of the town are pleased at the increased trade resulting from these immigrant workers but it comes at a price, as they bring smallpox with them, which spreads rapidly and leads to multiple deaths and disfigurement. Ultimately, it is suggested, it is both the carelessness and the greed of the town that brings about the disaster of the plague.

Hard on the heels of the plague comes further misfortune in a drought and failed harvest, which result in hunger, increased theft, and mutual suspicion. Furthermore, the Inquisitor, Dr. Jakobus Schuller, arrives in the town to investigate reports of witchcraft. He begins by interrogating Marte Stöckler, whose past debauchery and antisocial behavior have made her enemies in the town, meaning that several people are all too willing to denounce her. Through various intrigues and acts motivated by jealousy and petty spite, Theres also becomes the subject of rumor. Father Alexander learns the convent is to be investigated, as Maria Michaela is suspected of being a fraud, and, fearing his own secret may come to light, he first seeks to bribe the Inquisitor by offering to divert to the Inquisition the wealth that has accrued to the convent from the supposed miracle of the stigmata. After pocketing the money, the Inquisitor asks him to head a delegation to the convent to investigate the goings-on there. Without warning his former lover, Father Alexander descends on the convent at night with three other officials, including the town doctor, who unveils the fraud. Maria Michaela is humiliated in front of her fellow nuns, incarcerated in the convent for several weeks, but eventually allowed to repent her sins, undertaking a pilgrimage to Jerusalem as penance.

Alexander sees the opportunity to use Theres as a scapegoat and has her arrested as a devil's concubine. Despite brutal interrogation and torture she denies all wrongdoing but is finally duped by a friend into making a false confession. Theres and other suspected witches are subsequently all condemned to death and burnt at the stake. The one note of optimism for the future comes at the end of the novel, when Dr. Fabri, now blinded by the plague, takes in his nephews from a village in the mountains, where they have been mistreated, and resolves to help and educate them.

The period depicted in *Der Fürst der Welt* is one of upheaval and crisis, in which magic, superstition, and witchcraft are competing with advances in science, engineering, and education, and in which significant economic and social changes are affecting all spheres of society. Mitterer's detailed and realistic descriptions in this wide-reaching novel reflect, on the one hand, challenges to the church's power and religious norms, the flourishing of secret religious societies, and (as also documented in Reck-Malleczewen's *Bockelson*) religious fanaticism and hysteria. On the other hand, these details also reflect major social change: peasant unrest on the land, the demise of a feudal system and its replacement by the new order of an urban entrepreneurial class, represented by Matthias Nothaft, his selfish and vain son George, an array of merchants and traders, but also council bureaucrats such as Fridolin Ebner. Particular attention is paid to the economic concerns and problems of this new social class, as southern German society moves painfully from the rigidity of late medieval patriarchal structures to a fluid and unstable early capitalism still shackled by superstition and religious fervor. The mass psychosis enveloping the town, along with the fear for self and for personal financial well-being, are shown to undermine the very foundations of a humane society, to bring about the collapse of moral values, and to cause the average citizen to ignore or even connive in denunciations and lies, which they know will lead to persecution, violence, and murder.

Reception

The original novel was, to the surprise of the author herself, positively received. Even reviews in the Nazi press were, at worst, vague and neutral in tone. Most striking is one in the *Völkischer Beobachter*, which talks of "an historically significant plot" and—apparently failing or deliberately choosing not to see the parallels with Nazi rule (there is no mention of the Inquisition, for example)—says the sinuous narrative is filled with elements "des Großen und Unbedingten, aus dem alles Leben wächst und sich erfüllt" (of the great and the absolute, from which all life flows and in which all life finds its fulfillment).[56] The work was also listed among recommended books produced by Nazi authorities, including under the heading "Literature and Entertainment" in the Ministry of Propaganda's Annual Review of German Literature for 1941,[57] as well as in its List for the German Lending Library Trade.[58] A positive review in the journal *Die Literatur*, which hints at why the novel might have been welcome to the Nazi authorities, identifies the work's three key factors as the fading power of the chivalric tradition, the flourishing of the towns, and—most significantly—the crisis brought about by the pernicious power of the Catholic Church, which, it says, was crying out for reform by Luther.[59]

Albrecht Goes's short but generally positive review in the *Frankfurter Zeitung* makes no explicit reference to the text's relevance to the present but does see the various characters as witnessing a painful historical period of terrible alternatives and describes them as being measured by "a great justice."[60] A later discussion of Mitterer's poetry, in the same paper, talks of *Der Fürst der Welt* as "diesem Feuerbrand von einem Roman" (this firebrand of a novel).[61] Will Grohmann's review in the *Deutsche Allgemeine Zeitung* calls the book a tremendous achievement and seems close to drawing parallels with contemporary Germany in its mention of fanaticism, the rage of the masses, and the unleashing of "base passions"; it refers to the failure of the just to stand up against the persecution of the innocent, and says the Inquisition is helped in its torturing and burning by general discontent.[62] Similarly, a review in *Weltstimmen* argues that the real disaster depicted in the novel stems not from plague and poverty, but comes from within, from the human mind and heart; the causes are greed, resentment, and madness as well as: "Verfolgung der Unschuld, Triumph der Lüge und der Verblendung im Gewande des Rechts, das den Aberwitz zum System erhoben hat" (persecution of innocence, the triumph of lies, and blindness dressed up as the law that has turned sheer lunacy into a system).[63] Without making any sort of overt connection, this insight into the human causes of evil leaves it open for readers to make links with their own social situation.

Mitterer affirmed that numerous letters from readers testified that her camouflaged writing was readily decoded by many, including inmates of

Dachau concentration camp, where the book was available in the library.[64] Dür's review of personal correspondence received by Mitterer following the novel's publication does indeed suggest the contemporary link was clearly made and that the work served as a form of moral sustenance during the bleak days of totalitarian rule.[65]

Postwar reception of the abridged versions of the novel was muted and, with the exception of occasional recent positive discussions,[66] the text's length, historicity, and veiled relevance to Nazi Germany have conspired to move it to the margins of literary interest. The publication of the full original text in 2006 has done little to change this.

Characterization and the Psychology of Delusion

A major strength of the novel is its differentiated characterization. Not only does Mitterer provide a Tolstoyan human panorama but she also avoids any hint of simplistic or one-sided description, sketching convincing psychological portraits of human beings whose sometimes noble inclinations fall victim to fear, greed, and suspicion, who are all too easily manipulated (for example, the supposed miracles in the convent), who allow rumor to poison their mind, and who turn a blind eye to wrongdoing, provided they themselves remain beyond threat. The most negatively portrayed figures in the novel, such as Doctor Schuller, Father Alexander, and Fridolin Ebner, are all shown to have certain redeeming features. Thus Schuller, who personally presides over the torture of "suspects" (described by Mitterer in chilling, realistic detail), does not appear to be an inherently evil character but rather someone who genuinely believes that his cruel and bloody mission will save the souls of the victims, and who shuns personal gain, devotes himself to a strict regime, and discounts malicious denunciations. Father Alexander, probably the most negative character in the book, is a ruthless, sly individual who manipulates Maria Michaela for his own ends, primarily to secure power, and then, when himself threatened, willingly serves the Inquisition and ultimately flees the town to pursue his scholarly interests in Rome; but he is nonetheless a man of intellect who does initially show concern for Hiltrud/Maria Michaela and, for a while at least, seeks to protect her from shame. And, finally, Ebner, despite being the archcareerist and opportunist prepared to compromise his principles for personal advancement, had earlier proved to be a talented and dedicated tutor to the young Hiltrud and is now a dutiful, caring husband and a conscientious employee.

Similarly, almost all the positive characters in the novel reveal some sort of weakness or shortcoming. The reader is inclined to identify with figures such as Maria Michaela, Matthias Nothaft, Albertus Fabri, Bishop Ulrich, and the abbot Tilmann, yet each is guilty of behaving in ways that warrant censure and contribute to their failure or demise. Thus, Maria

Michaela fails to face up to the realization that her vocation is a mistake and compounds her guilt through repeated lies and deception; Nothaft lends money to the town for the new walls, primarily so that the council is in his debt and he can thus secure his own position; Fabri lacks commitment to his fellow men, rejecting public office to pursue his scientific experiments, removing himself from the town in its hour of need, and thus also abandoning Theres to her fate; Bishop Ulrich, for all his rejection of the Church's terror tactics and his apparent liberalism, fails to offer leadership and intervene when madness grips the town, retreating instead to his sick bed, too afraid to counter the worst excesses of the Inquisition; and Tilmann, despite his deep learning, open-minded reasonableness, and skepticism about the presence of witches, is seen to be ambiguous about the religious fervor that lies behind the town's descent into madness, succumbs to despair about his life in the religious order, and, in resignation, plans to abandon the monastery for an escapist pilgrimage.

The one unambiguously positive figure is Theres. She is a young, kind, and caring girl who only seeks to do good, yet through chance and circumstance she comes to be perceived as a threat by others. This antipathy is not helped by the fact that she is seen to have some of the assumed characteristics of the typical witch: red hair, a suspicious birthmark, and good looks. Thus, jealous of Theres's confidential correspondence with Georg Nothaft, her closest friend Bärbel is the first to label her a witch (261); another friend, the washerwoman's daughter Gerlinde, envious of Theres's happiness, calls her "die rote Hexe" (the red witch, 272) for causing her supposed injury; while Mathilde Hackschneider blames her for her daughter's lameness (476). Misunderstanding, resentment, and prejudice increasingly combine to make Theres one of the prime scapegoats of the petit bourgeois milieu from which she cannot free herself. The fact that she is depicted as naïve and the embodiment of innocence, that to the very end she fails to understand her supposed guilt (693), serves to heighten the pathos surrounding her tragic death.

Mitterer's psychologically convincing characterization is closely linked to her attempt to explore the way ordinary people fall prey to rumor and fear-induced suspicion, how they can be persuaded not only to tolerate but also condone violence. As her narrator states at one point: "Der zeitliche Ablauf von Ereignissen gerät im Bewusstsein der Menge zuweilen in Vergessenheit: Es ordnet sie nach der Wahrscheinlichkeit auf Kosten der Tatsachen und bildet so aus unmöglichen Voraussetzungen ein glaubwürdiges Gerücht" (In the consciousness of the masses the sequence of events is at times forgotten, and in people's minds events are arranged according to likelihood at the expense of fact, thus creating credible rumor from impossible premise, 197). When the town succumbs to the plague, for example, the people seek scapegoats for their misfortune in a variety of individuals: the Italian architect brought in to reconstruct the town walls;

Marte Stöckler, whose loose sexual morals have made her enemies and who is forced to flee to the forest to escape the accusations; and, above all, Theres. As Fabri notes in connection with this process of blame, when people experience evil, they find it easier to endure if they are able to hate the person who is the source of it (198). Amid prophecies of pending doom for the town and an atmosphere in which people are hypersensitive to the slightest sign of supposed evil or devilry, the ground is prepared for the flourishing of the suspicion, mistrust, and petty betrayal that lead ultimately to ritualized burning of the innocent.

A further nuance in the process of psychological self-deception is the effect of scapegoating in helping to block out personal misdemeanors, which might otherwise be interpreted as having brought down the wrath of God in the plague. The narrator refers to the way the citizens suppress this call of conscience and instead: "Jeder half mit, über den welschen Baumeister, die schamlose Hure, den eitlen Ratsherrn und den unfähigen Quacksalber zu schelten und zählte sich zu den Unschuldigen" (Everyone helped to rail against the Eyetie architect, the shameless whore, the vain councilor, and the incompetent quack, and they all counted themselves amongst the innocent, 199).[67]

In parallel to this, the story of Maria Michaela underpins the creeping mass hysteria, encouraging people to see in the strange goings-on a divine intervention in the life of the town, possibly in response to its aberrant ways. The townsfolk's fearful but respectful reaction (414–15) shows their credulity and gullibility in accepting unquestioningly, on the thinnest of evidence, the supposedly miraculous powers of the nun. In the religious fanaticism surrounding the events in the convent, Mitterer demonstrates how rapidly and easily mass hysteria can take hold, thus providing further psychological reinforcement and explanation of the infectious spread of the suspicion that feeds the witch-hunt mentality.

An Allegory of National Socialism

Looking back on her novel in 1988, Mitterer noted that her aim had been to show through the analogy of inquisitional courts and witch trials how readily evil can seize power in even the most ordered and intact of societies.[68] In a written communication on the occasion of the novel's republication in 1988, she reiterated this, adding that the work was also about how we can all become collaborators without realizing the full extent of our "perfidy."[69] From just after the midpoint of the novel, one repeatedly comes across passages buried in the narrative, which seem to speak suddenly and directly to the situation of 1930s Germany and in particular this theme of insidious complicity.

The first striking example is the description of the dungeon in which the suspected witches are kept, and people's reaction to it. The very name, "Judenkeller" (Jew cellar), alerts the reader to a significant passage and to the analogy between witches and Jews. Camouflage is provided by the historical explanation for the name, but the detail of past scapegoating involving Jews provides clear links to the German present, and the description of their ultimate fate is tragically prescient:

> Seinen Namen hatte er vor zweihundert Jahren bekommen, als die von der Pest verstörte Bevölkerung ihre Zuflucht zur Vertilgung der Brunnenvergifter nahm; stehend hatte man die Männer mit den Schläfenlocken unter den spitzen, gelben Hüten mitsamt ihren Weibern und Kindern in die Verliese gepfercht, bis sie durch freiwillige Geständnisse der teuflischen Taten ihre Seelen erleichtert hatten und der Rauch von den häuserhohen Scheiterhaufen über die Dächer zog, letzte Schlupfwinkel der Seuche heilsam ausräuchernd. (460)[70]

> [It had got its name two hundred years earlier when the population, rendered distraught by the plague, had resorted to exterminating the well poisoners. They had crammed into the dungeon the men with the curls over their temples and the pointed yellow hats, along with their wives and children, and had made them stand until they had eased their souls by freely confessing to their devilish acts. And the smoke from the funeral pyres, which were as tall as the houses, drifted over the rooftops, curatively smoking out the last hiding place of the pestilence.]

In a possible reference to Germans turning a blind eye to concentration camps, it is clear that people deliberately ignore what goes on here; the innkeeper above the dungeon typifies the attitude of the population as he minds his own business and tends to his profits (460).

The complacency, willful conformity, and self-satisfaction of many Germans under Hitler comes through particularly strongly in a damning description of the town's inhabitants as they sit hypocritically in church listening to the words of the priest and almost luxuriating in the supposed security of having surrendered their freedom to the ambiguously titled "Great Founder":

> Man betrachtete den Putz der Nachbarinnen, man überzählte im Stillen den Gewinn der letzten Woche, während die Lippen die geläufigen Formeln murmelten. Tod und Teufel buhlten auf dem wilden Meer der Leidenschaften um die nackten Menschenseelen, aber man selbst saß, Gott sei Dank, auf einer wohlgegründeten Insel inmitten dieses Meeres, hörte nur von weitem den schaurigsüßen Anprall der Wogen und durfte sich sicher fühlen dank Ablass und Erlösertod, geregeltem Eheleben und mäßigem Zinsfuß,

neuer Polizeiordnung und geplanter Stadtmauer, heil überstan-
dener Seuche und deshalb gestifteter Pfründe, dank der frommen
Verehrung köstlicher Reliquien und blutig lebendiger Wunder
und dank dem väterlichen Eifer der Heiligen Inquisition. Alles war
einem abgenommen, das ganze Leben die weise Regel eines großen
Stifters, der man sich anzupassen hatte in blindem Gehorsam. (478)

[They looked at the finery of the women who sat next to them and
went over in their mind the past week's profits, while their lips mut-
tered the familiar phrases. Death and the devil were wooing naked
human souls on a wild sea of passion, but they themselves, thank
God, were sitting on a solid island in the middle of this wild sea, and
they heard only from afar the distant gruesomely sweet crashing of
the waves. They felt themselves secure thanks to indulgences and
the death of the Redeemer, their orderly married lives and moder-
ate interest rates, new police measures and the planned town walls,
a plague safely survived and benefices duly donated, thanks to the
devout veneration of precious holy relics and bleeding, living miracles, and thanks to the paternal zeal of the Holy Inquisition. They
were relieved of all responsibility; all life was the wise rule of the
Great Founder whom they simply had to follow in blind obedience.]

The strong allusion here to Germans' and Austrians' myopia under
National Socialism, motivated in part by self-interest and in part by a
desire for a strong leader, is repeated a little later in Fabri's particularly
powerful reflection on the masses of the undecided and the half-hearted,
who long for nothing so fervently than that finally someone should once
again be dominant enough to make up their minds for them, so that they
could follow him "in der warmen Blindheit" (in warm blindness, 543).
It is in such moral cowardice and self-interest that Mitterer repeatedly
locates the failure to make an unambiguous stand against Nazism.

During his discussions with his humanist circle of friends in
Nuremberg, Fabri is introduced to Conrad Peutinger, the butt of jokes
for his obsession with saving mankind through a worldwide German
empire (539). In a satirical passage that mocks contemporary German
pretensions to world domination, Peutinger mourns the passing of the
"Heinrichs and Ottos" as Holy Roman emperors and claims Germans had
lost their power in the world because they had not been sufficiently cunning or evil, but that, reborn, they could help the earth to attain peace,
and in an only thinly veiled ironic reference to Nazi rhetoric, he expresses
regrets for his contemporaries' stupidity, which was delaying the beginning of the "tausendjährigen Friedensreiches" (thousand-year kingdom
of peace, 540).

In the same section, further veiled satire is contained in the interest
shown by the town councilor Willibald Pirckheimer in the Renaissance

368 ◆ ERIKA MITTERER: WITCH HUNTS AND THE POWER OF EVIL

humanist and poet Conrad Celtis, whose patriotism, we are told, was not satisfied with establishing the long and distinguished existence of German tribes but sought to build "eine Brücke des Blutes" (a bridge based on a blood relationship) linking Germanic culture to the Roman and Greek classical world, and who further championed the theory that the Franks were descended from the Greeks (536). Although entirely conformist in its racist ideology, this passage can also be read as taking the tracing of racial purity to absurd lengths and indicating shared ancestry with the hated French.

Of all the morally flawed characters depicted in the novel, Fridolin Ebner is the one with the clearest counterparts in Nazi Germany. He is the opportunist petit bourgeois who works his way up to a position of modest power and, like Tante Adelheid in Irmgard Keun's *Nach Mitternacht* (After midnight, 1937), feels shame and resentment about his lowly social origins, seeking compensation through abuse of his position. He is the ultimate conformist and fellow traveler of authoritarianism, a willing and unquestioning tool of both council and Inquisition, who exploits the climate of fear and denunciation to avenge perceived past wrongs and enmities. Thus he senses the weakness of Maria Michaela's position and looks for revenge on this woman of noble birth for her youthful tormenting of him when he was her tutor (638). Realizing the town needs a scapegoat for its troubles, he sees the opportunity for further revenge by taking advantage of Theres's difficulties. In the midst of all this, he seems entirely immune to any stirrings of conscience. In line with Gottwald's view of him as embodying Hannah Arendt's concept of the banality of evil,[71] Ebner can almost be seen as a desktop murderer who salves his conscience by claiming he is merely doing his job and passing responsibility higher up the chain: "Wozu sollte Fridolin Ebner sich beunruhigen? Es waren gar nicht seine Entscheidungen, die jetzt durchgeführt wurden. Er stellte bloß seine bescheidene Kraft . . . in den Dienst der Heiligen Inquisition" (Why should Fridolin feel uneasy? The decisions that were about to be carried out were in no way his own. He was merely putting his humble capacities at the disposal of the Holy Inquisition, 576).

As Reck-Malleczewen had done in *Bockelson* three years earlier, Mitterer demonstrates how easily mass insanity can take hold in a formerly placid and relatively harmonious community. She shows, among the lowliest members of society, how fertile the ground is for the rapid growth of cruelty to others, and how a desire to see others suffer one's own misery is combined with a need to offload personal guilt. It is significantly the young sculptor Joachim, with the perceptive eye of the artist, who sees in the spiteful Gerlinde a "purgatory face" with an expression somewhere between guilt, despair, and *schadenfreude* (251). The need to identify a scapegoat for personal unhappiness and perceived social ills leads to the likes of Gerlinde relishing and indeed contributing, through false denunciation, to Theres's downfall. In the same way, people find easy targets for their spite and innu-endo in social outsiders such as Marte Stöckler, who from the very start does not belong to the heart of the community and so, like all marginal groups, can more readily be expelled from it.

This psychology of denunciation is the subject of a lengthy section at the beginning of chapter 4, where the narrator asks what it was that drove people to appear before the Inquisitor and relieve themselves of their accumulated suspicions and mistrust about relatives, neighbors, and strangers alike, some of it built up over years of enmity, some of it prompted by the recent encouragement to inform on suspected witches (631–32). The narrator considers conscience as a motive, or people's fear of incurring guilt themselves by silently condoning evil deeds and thoughts, or some gruesome fascination with the process. But then he turns to the question of the psychological need of the socially downcast for self-validation, for status and power as a form of escape from the harsh realities of everyday life, suggesting it is the urge to escape the monotony and baseness of everyday life and briefly experience for once what it feels like to exercise power oneself (632). This is no speculative aside but is precisely what Mitterer substantiates through the behavior of a range of characters in the novel as the madness of the witch hunt spreads through the town like the plague.

As events hasten to their tragic conclusion in the final section of the novel with the pursuit of personal feuds and the proliferation of petty denunciations, this psychological configuration becomes more evident and is increasingly translated into a herdlike mentality. Though they sus-pect innocent people are to be punished, many of the town's citizens use the news of the impending burning as a lightning rod for their own guilt, seeing in the women's fate expiation and a "preventative measure" against the plague (682). Similarly, at the burnings themselves, the mass psycho-sis and the by now unfettered aggression are reflected in the crowd's furi-ous demands for the fire to begin, and their cries for revenge (692) are followed by repeated wild demands to see the alleged devil's mark on Theres's body.

The Camouflaged Text

This reading of *Der Fürst der Welt* as a veiled allegory on Nazi rule is protected from an exoteric audience in a variety of ways. Above all else, the author's reputation in the 1930s as a writer of lyric poetry who was not in any way considered politically suspect or "problematic" was likely to ensure that censors were favorably predisposed. The work itself was, of course, also camouflaged in different ways, some of which were the result of a conscious effort to avoid a ban on publication and others the by-product, as it were, of the type of work it was.

First of all, the novel's very size, its complicated narrative, and its wealth of characters all constituted a form of protection for its more critical content, rendering the latter less accessible to the casual reader. Second, the novel is written in an elevated literary style, which, as Brecht notes,[72] can serve to protect writers whose message is potentially controversial. Third, Mitterer is very careful in the placement of her most thinly veiled critical passages: it is surely no coincidence that, in common with much camouflaged writing at the time,[73] the utterances with greatest relevance and applicability to Nazi Germany are all located in the second half and especially the final third of the novel, as pressurized censors would be unlikely to be able to process every section of such a lengthy and convoluted work, and the later sections were therefore likely to be the least exposed. Fourth, the novel's substantial mythological content and its elements of magical realism[74] both further shroud the content in what thus appears to the unsuspecting to be a novel firmly rooted in its specific historical context. Fifth, in disguising some of the more critical aspects of the novel, Mitterer ensures that subversive or potentially anti-Nazi statements are countered by opposing or alternative views and, moreover, she distributes critical viewpoints across a range of characters (especially Ulrich, Fabri, and Tilmann) so that no one character is simplistically associated with an oppositional stance; this is seen in the exchanges between Fabri's artistic and scholarly friends in Nuremberg, where enlightened progressive ideas vie with mystical thinking and nationalist sentiment, all of which find ready parallels in Nazi Germany. And, finally, the absence of any tyrant or leader figure (the "Prince of Darkness" denotes the abstract principle of evil) and Fabri's indecisive opposition—that is, his lack of conviction about the ideas proposed by his enlightened friends—both make it possible for the text to be read positively from a Nazi perspective.[75]

The novel is, however, best secured from the censor's gaze by the fact that almost every utterance that is potentially critical of the contemporary Nazi state can be readily interpreted as being targeted at the medieval Catholic Church and its ruthless, violent "defenders of the faith." This is an organization that opposes the great advances of enlightened German thinking with obscurantist, backward-looking, and cruel doctrines and practices. It is shown to be cynically satisfied with the renewed religious zeal resulting from the plague and the iniquities of the witch hunt instigated by its militant arm, the Inquisition (477). Nazi censors would have been convinced of this anti-Catholic tenor just by reading the Prologue, where Hiltrud discusses German nationalist political pamphlets with her tutor, one of which refers to Pope Alexander VI's illegitimate children and ends with the words: "Und um dieses Lumpen willen tun wir unser deutsches Blut vergießen!" (And for the sake of this wretch we shed our German blood!); it also shows German mercenaries "von welschem Dolch

durchbohrt" (stabbed by Eyetie daggers, 70).[76] The remainder of the
novel presents other representatives of the church in an only slightly less
negative light. Thus, the abuse of power in the hands of Father Alexander
puts the spotlight on corrupt elements in the medieval church hierarchy,
but equally his callous treatment of Maria Michaela reveals the church's
belittling and sidelining of women, even those who have committed to
the religious life.[77] He also offers active support to the Inquisitor and,
fearing a loss of face for the order, imprisons the abbot in his cell when
the latter threatens to abandon the monastery. Tilmann himself, one of
the two most influential clergymen in the town, sees a positive aspect to
the merciless witch hunt and the burnings, in that they make the people
aware of the life and death responsibility of their faith (353). The bishop,
portrayed as an aesthete with a possible penchant for young boys,[78] claims
that the power of the church, as God's representative on earth, justifies its
at times harsh methods of rule (221) and, despite his undoubted reservations, he shows cowardice in failing to denounce the rapidly spreading
wave of arrests, sending out the message to the faithful that the church
approves of or condones the action of the Inquisition. All in all, it is no
surprise the novel was welcomed in official Nazi circles as anti-Catholic.

The Novel's Positive Alternatives

In a world characterized by petit bourgeois greed, envy, superstition, and
fear, and filled with variously fallible, weak, or corrupt characters, Mitterer
holds up Dr. Albertus Fabri and his Renaissance contacts in Nuremberg
as models of a more sober, rational, and humane mindset.

Fabri represents the impotence of the intellectual in this world. He
is a man of science, pursues experiments in pursuit of knowledge, believing this can advance the good of mankind, and he makes a stand against
prejudice in treating the sick siblings of the ostracized Marte, in whom,
notwithstanding her life as a prostitute, he recognizes genuine human
concern. In what is a highly charged statement for a 1940 readership,
Bishop Ulrich says to him at one point: "Ihr schaut aus wie ein Mensch.
Selten, heutzutage. Nicht nur in Rom, auch im trutzigen Deutschland!"
(You look like a human being. Rare these days. Not only in Rome but in
defiant Germany too! 256). However, Fabri is forced ultimately to recognize his powerlessness in the face of the spreading mass insanity and is left
to reflect on the seeming futility of his life and his failure to do his duty
by accepting a public role (599). He further regrets his escapist flight to
Nuremberg and harbors a sense of guilt in the case of Theres (600), a
guilt he shares with the rest of the town, it is later suggested (703). It is
one of the novel's deep ironies that it is the healer of bodily ailments and
the man of enlightenment, the one who truly sees through ignorance and

superstition, who is physically blinded and unable to heal the more deep-seated illness of this late medieval world.

There is nevertheless an optimism contained in his exchanges with his nephew at the end of the novel. Initially the arrival of the two boys seems a further source of despair: the idyllic rural existence Fabri had contemplated returning to with them is shown to be a chimera, as the full extent of the economic misery in the countryside is revealed in the flight of people to the town. However, when Heinrich, the elder boy, asks whether he can rename the stars, this notion of seeking to question and overturn traditional thinking and dogma reignites Fabri's belief in progress, his hope in the possibility of restoring harmony; he reflects: "auch er hat an den alten Namen nicht genug" (he too is not satisfied with the old names, 703), and resolves to have the boy educated by his humanist friends.

These include the artist Albrecht Dürer, the lawyer and politician Conrad Peutinger, the town councilor Pirckheimer, the scholar Hartmann Schedel, the lawyer and diplomat Christoph Scheurl, and the mathematician and astronomer Johannes Stöffler. The group constitutes an oasis of enlightened thinking and intellectual renewal (535), in stark contrast with the wave of Inquisition-inspired obscurantism sweeping the country. Besides reflecting their role as representatives of progress, these characters' utterances can also simultaneously be read with an eye to the Nazi present, and once the parallel is established in the reader's mind, ambiguous sentences abound. For example, Pirckheimer shows his progressive colors in his insistence that the city fathers have nothing to fear from the spread of knowledge among the people (541). Scheurl, in arguing for complete openness in public affairs, refers to the city's "lächerlichen Polizeiordnungen" (ridiculous police regulations) and he satirizes the German obsession with prohibition and control over every aspect of life (541). Finally, in criticizing the church for acquiescing in the prevailing conditions, he produces a virtual rallying call for the contemporary reader: "aber es sei Pflicht jedes verständigen Mannes, der Wahrheit zum Sieg zu verhelfen" (but it is the duty of every reasonable man to help the truth to victory, 541).

Apart from Fabri and his friends, Bishop Ulrich, for all his lack of commitment, can also partly be seen as a counterbalance to the forces of darkness. He represents the more liberal and humane views within the church, being open to freedom of thought and exploration in the sciences, evincing a lack of prejudice in discussion with Fabri and Tilmann, and showing genuine concern for the well-being of his pages, Beatus and Anton. He also rejects the witch-hunt mentality, has little time for the operations of the Inquisition, and stays away from the funeral pyres. He sees the Inquisitor as a "greasy ignoramus" (352) and resolves not to help him. In the meeting with Schuller he further defends Fabri's scientific enquiries (492–94) and immediately afterward sends the doctor a note warning the absent medic not to return to the town. On the other hand, Ulrich is shrewd enough to recognize the power of the Inquisition and the need for good relations with its representatives (496). And in taking to his sick bed when the persecution gains momentum and in refusing to involve himself in the Theres affair when Fabri returns, he reveals his ultimate failure to alert the people of the town to the injustice they are complicit in or to place the slightest obstacle in the way of the Inquisition. In this way he is more culpable than Fabri and serves as a microcosm of the failure of the churches under National Socialism.

The novel provides several other examples of right-minded role models. Perhaps the most significant positive figure among the minor characters is the bishop's page, Beatus. Though wrongly detained for arson and tortured for helping the devil, he refuses to betray the secret of his master's warning to Fabri and, once released from the horrors of the torture chamber, displays his abiding faith in the goodness of his fellow man: "'Siehst du, die Menschen sind gut!,' sagte Beatus ernst, 'sie irren nur leicht'" ("You see, people are good!," Beatus said in a serious tone, "they just err easily," 673). True to his saintlike name, he stands as a corrective to the selfish and deceitful townsfolk and, destined for life in a religious order, he is the only unambiguously positive religious figure in the novel. Other goodhearted figures include: the young man Rudolf, who stands by the desperate nun Roswitha when she faces disgrace and ruin; Ambros Kühtreiber, Ebner's father-in-law, who is critical of the ruthless young man's behavior; and Maria Michaela, who demonstrates selfless dedication and courage in nursing the sick during the plague and tending to the leper.

Indeed it is the nun's commitment to love, regardless of motive, that represents one of the novel's key counterimages to the madness overcoming this society. As she lies in the dungeon she imagines herself in conversation with Christ and asks whether he cannot take pleasure in her love, even though it was love for someone else, since Christ does not distinguish between types of love (582). Maria Michaela's belief that there is no such thing as bad love is picked up in her confession, when she says she loved a man too much, and the charitable and caring confessor Father Pius tells her it is impossible to love too much (647). Ives rightly sees here the key to Mitterer's social conscience in the novel, and indeed her later poetry.[79] It is the lack of care for the downtrodden, the uneducated, and the sick, who are all cut adrift by the better-off in this society, that is the source of the town's misfortune: left to languish in poverty beyond the town walls and to spread the disease that lays siege to the town, outcasts demonstrate the consequences of a failure to embrace and care for one's fellow man.

The Question of Evil

This is, of course, the central theme of *Der Fürst der Welt*. The title denotes the biblical figure of Satan, who in the New Testament is repeatedly referred to in terms of worldly dominion: as the "prince of the power of the air"[80] or the "god of this world."[81] The original source of Mitterer's title, though, seems to be John's Gospel, where Satan is "the prince of this world."[82] However, the title does not just refer to the devil, nor to any single individual such as the Inquisitor,[83] but to evil in all its many forms, as an inevitable consequence of mankind's fallen state. The original epigraph for the novel points to this understanding of the ever-changing nature of evil, its manifold guises throughout history, and everyone's susceptibility to it:

> Schau nicht in das Eck, wo er gestern noch stand!
> Er wechselt den Ort und vertauscht das Gewand,
> Und eben noch dort, ist er heute schon—hier.
> Im Gegner? Im Bruder! In Dir . . . und in mir. . . ."[84]

> [Don't look in the corner where yest'day he stood! / He changes position, his cloak and his hood, / He was but just there, but now he is here—see. / In enemies, in brothers, in you . . . in me. . . .]

Dür is presumably correct in surmising that this poem fell victim to the exigencies of publication since the epigraph was too overt a guidance to readers that the novel should be read as a depiction of contemporary events and conditions.[85]

It is particularly the insidious nature of evil that Mitterer focuses on in her slowly evolving, multiperspectival narrative: evil does not operate in some sudden eruption of iniquitous behavior but is made up of myriad small acts of spite, lies, and deceit, as well as innocent or unwitting acts of betrayal that lead fearful individuals to lose all sense of decency and right and to betray or scapegoat their fellow citizen. It is in this sense that we are to understand the sole in-text reference to the title, as the imprisoned Maria Michaela reflects: "Der Fürst der Welt hat es selten eilig, unsere Wünsche zu durchkreuzen; er kommt besser auf seine Rechnung, wenn er sich an ihrer Erfüllung weidet" (The Prince of Darkness is rarely in a hurry to thwart our wishes; he gets his money's worth more when he feasts on their fulfillment, 583).

Here we see the significance too of the recurrent fairy tale "Das Märchen vom Marienkind" (The tale of Mary's child), based on the Grimm tale *Marienkind* (1810) and first told to Hiltrud/Maria Michaela in her childhood.[86] The story refers, on one level, to the temptation to go against social constraints in pursuit of selfish desires and the negative effect this has on people, alienating and isolating them. More specifically, it alludes to the fate of Maria Michaela as she succumbs to the temptation of desire in her relationship with Father Alexander and fakes the stigmata; the burning glow of her love for the priest associates her explicitly with the fairy tale and the link becomes unambiguous in the section in which she dreams of having a golden finger and denying her wrongdoing (610).

The notion of evil events being the result of a gradual accretion of, in themselves, seemingly minor acts of wrongdoing is fixed in a significant metaphor, which refers back to the image of the Inquisitor as the Reaper and is lent prominence in the text by its interruption of the narrative and its apparent lack of relevance to the preceding and following sections:

> Durch Monate reift das Korn und fällt in wenigen Stunden unter dem ausholenden Armschwung des Schnitters. Jahrelang kann Krankheit die Eingeweide zerfressen, und du fühlst keinen Schmerz; aber kurz sind die Stunden der Todesqual. Langsam sickert der Schnee in tausend Flocken durch die nächtigen Himmel . . . aber rasch löst sich endlich die Lawine vom Steinhang, die den Jungwald vernichtet und die Hütten begräbt. . . . Rasch, wie die Sense das Korn mäht, rasch, wie der Sturz der Lawine, entscheidet sich oft unser Schicksal. (533)

> [For months the corn ripens and falls in a few hours under the wide-swinging arm of the reaper. For years sickness can eat away at your insides yet you feel no pain; but short are the hours of mortal agony. Slowly the snow seeps in a thousand flakes through the night skies but the avalanche finally breaks suddenly from the rocky precipice, destroying the young forest and burying the wooden houses. . . . Our fate is often decided as quickly as the scythe mows the corn, as quickly as the crashing avalanche.]

An important light is thrown on the central theme of evil by two exchanges about the power of Satan. In his conversation with the Inquisitor, Ulrich is accused of underestimating Satan, and so he asks whose power is greater, God's or Satan's? The Inquisitor responds: "Die Macht des Satans, so wir nicht mit aller Kraft. . . ." (Satan's power, unless with all our strength we. . . ., 496), at which point a disturbed and despondent Ulrich cuts him off. However, in a deliberate reference back to this, almost two hundred pages later, the bishop asks the same question of Beatus, and receives the reply that if man loves God more than he fears Satan, then God "is stronger in our hearts," but that if man fears Satan more than he loves God, then Satan is stronger (685). That such a response is put into the mouth of the symbolically named page, who has resisted the Inquisitor's torture, stood up for his belief in what is right, and revealed his unflinching faith in the goodness of human nature, makes the point that only a commitment to goodness, truth, and love of one's fellow man can banish evil in this world, serving as the moral anti-dote to Mitterer's picture of fear, superstition, and envy, and the threat they pose to man's more positive inclinations. As a veiled reference to how the evil of Nazism is to be countered, this message, which reiterates Maria Michaela's earlier reflections on the power of love, also constitutes a classic form of Christian inner emigrant consolation.

Conclusion

Mitterer's approach and her view of history are essentially different from Bergengruen's in *Der Großtyrann und das Gericht*, where the focus is on the individual leader who is seen to be the principal agent of events. In Bergengruen—as in Schneider and Klepper—history is emphatically influenced by the deeds of individuals. In *Der Fürst der Welt*, by contrast, the cause of events (in sixteenth-century Germany and, by implication, 1930s Germany and Austria) is not the actions of the individual Inquisitor or any single member of the ruling classes, but a complex of psychological processes and social and economic conditions.[87] Whereas many inner emigrant works depict authoritarian rule or mass hysteria as evils visited on mankind, like some form of natural catastrophe or illness, the real source of the evil and suffering in *Der Fürst der Welt* is seen to lie not in ineluctable fate, supernatural power, or external force but in the human psyche, in people's fear, envy, and suspicion, in their pursuit of personal gain, power, and social ambition, as well as in their prejudice, closed minds, and ignorance. Evil in the novel grows from interlinking social, economic, and psychological factors, within which the Inquisition serves as merely the vehicle of persecution. People have opportunities to avert disaster; the victimization and murder are not preordained by a superior force in the face of which the townsfolk are powerless. The tragedy is not in that sense a Greek tragedy but rather the result of preventable human weakness.[88]

In answering the question of how the persecutions and injustices of witch hunts were possible in a world of an Agrippa and a Pirckheimer, Mitterer's convincing psychological profiles from across the social scale illustrate how human fallibility facilitates the *gradual* process of the disintegration of civilized society, how it allows evil forces to seize power step by step. The novel also offers a range of responses to authoritarian rule with clear counterparts in Nazi Germany and Austria: there are victims, both the innocent (Theres) and the not so innocent (Maria Michaela, Marte); there are fellow travelers and careerists (Ebner), cynical opportunists (Father Alexander), malicious informers (Georg Nothaft), and the naïve and exploited (Matthias Nothaft); and there are opponents in exile (Pirckheimer circle), powerless idealists (Tilmann), inner emigrants who refuse all engagement (Bishop Ulrich), and those who are only half committed and realize their error too late (Fabri).

In the early sections of the novel, in particular, one might be for-given for thinking that Mitterer's detailed and historically faithful social panorama reduces the work's impact as a comment on Nazi Germany and Austria. In fact, its complex and sophisticated analysis of the rise of authoritarianism, and of the human behavior that facilitates it, makes the novel one of the most compelling and psychologically convincing offer-ings of inner emigrant literature. Yet it is also essential to Mitterer's origi-nal conception, and a reflection of her theological outlook, that the work be seen to have a much wider applicability, suggesting evil resides in man and can manifest itself at any time, often in the guise of economic self-interest, following orders, or performing a perceived duty. Indeed, the author's essentially conservative mindset is revealed in the recurrent idea that the appearance of phenomena ("der Schein") is in constant flux and that what counts is the underlying reality ("das Sein"). In a section that might almost be seen as a key to reading the events depicted in the novel and that is lent prominence and significance through its position close to the start of the main section of the text, Tilmann comments: "Denn allein die Erscheinungsformen der Kräfte wechseln, sind von den Sternen bestimmt und somit der Zeit unterworfen. Die Kräfte selber aber wandeln sich nicht und wer sie einmal erkannt hat, wiedererkennt sie in allem!" (For only the surface phenomena of forces change, are determined by the stars, and thus subject to time. The forces themselves, however, do not change, and whoever has recognized them once, recognizes them again in all things! 145) And this focus on the immutable forces underpinning existence reflects, of course, once again the archetypal ahistorical and irra-tional mindset of the inner emigrant, suggesting that the ideological dis-tance between Mitterer and the likes of Reck-Malleczewen and Wiechert may not be that great after all.

Notes

[1] Erika Mitterer, "Treue," in *Das verhüllte Kreuz: Neue Gedichte* (Vienna: Nic-derösterreichisches Pressehaus, 1985), 21.

[2] Erika Mitterer, "Selbstporträt," *Modern Austrian Literature* 21 (1988): 2:77.

[3] Roman Roček, "Anstelle eines Nachworts: Rainer Maria Rilke—Erika Mitterer Briefwechsel in Gedichten," in *Erika Mitterer: Der Fürst der Welt*, ed. Roman Roček (Vienna: Böhlau, 1988), 624.

[4] Mitterer, "Selbstporträt," 78–79. Some of these poems were published in 1950 but the full exchange only appeared in *Erika Mitterer: Das gesamte lyrische Werk*, vol. 1, ed. Martin G. Petrowsky and Petra Sela (Vienna: Doppelpunkt, 2001). For a full discussion, see Jochen Meyer, "'Dank des Lebens': Erika Mitterers Brief-wechsel in Gedichten mit Rainer Maria Rilke," in *Eine Dichterin—ein Jahrhun-dert: Erika Mitterers Lebenswerk*, ed. Martin G. Petrowsky and Österreichische Gesellschaft für Literatur (Vienna: Doppelpunkt, 2002), 83–99; and Joachim W.

Storck, "Erika Mitterers Briefwechsel in Gedichten mit Rainer Maria Rilke und sein literarischer Kontext," in *Dichtung im Schatten der großen Krisen: Erika Mitterers Werk im literaturhistorischen Kontext*, ed. Martin G. Petrowsky and Helga Abret (Vienna: Praesens, 2006), 21–34.

[5] Mitterer, "Selbstporträt," 77.

[6] Helga Abret, "Von der Notwendigkeit und der Fragwürdigkeit des Handelns: Erika Mitterers Drama *Charlotte Corday* (1931)," in Petrowsky and Abret, *Dichtung im Schatten der großen Krisen*, 74. The play has never been performed and appeared in printed form only in a 2003 collection: *Charlotte Corday*, in *Erika Mitterer: Dramen III*, ed. Martin G. Petrowsky and Petra Sela (Vienna: Doppelpunkt, 2003).

[7] Stefan Zweig, "Erika Mitterer: Dank des Lebens," *Berliner Tageblatt*, August 3, 1930.

[8] Manuscript "Erika Mitterer an Gottfried Benn," in Deutsches Literaturarchiv, cited by Dür, *Erika Mitterer*, 25–30. See also on Benn, "The Compromised and the Conformist" in chapter 2 of this book.

[9] See Dür, *Erika Mitterer*, 31–42.

[10] Mitterer, "'Sie gehören doch auch zu uns. . . .'" The poem dates from 1934.

[11] Ibid., 3.

[12] Gradwohl-Schlacher, "Innere Emigration in der 'Ostmark'?," 78.

[13] Dür, *Erika Mitterer*, 76–77.

[14] Gradwohl-Schlacher, "Innere Emigration in der 'Ostmark?,'" 83. A Gauleiter was a leader of a regional branch of the Nazi Party, the head of a Gau or Reichsgau; the position was the second highest NSDAP paramilitary rank and was directly appointed by Hitler.

[15] See "The Muddy Waters of Opposition and Conformism" in chapter 1 of this book.

[16] Márta Gaál-Baróti, "Die kathartische Wirkung der Ungarischen Revolution in der *Tauschzentrale* von Erika Mitterer," in Petrowsky and Abret, *Dichtung im Schatten der großen Krisen*, 231–51.

[17] The subsequent *Bibelgedichte—ein Vermächtnis* (Bible poems—a legacy) (Föhrenau: Stiglmayr, 1994) is merely a compilation of previously published poems.

[18] See Peter Bubenik, "Erika Mitterers religiöse Lyrik der späten Jahre," in Petrowsky and Abret, *Dichtung im Schatten der großen Krisen*, 309–41; and Johannes Holzner, "Dialoge und Kontroversen mit der Moderne: Gedichte von Erika Mitterer," in Petrowsky and Österreichische Gesellschaft für Literatur, *Eine Dichterin*, 111–14.

[19] Mitterer, "Selbstporträt," 82.

[20] See Herwig Gottwald, "Erika Mitterers Romane und die Zeitgeschichte," in Petrowsky and Österreichische Gesellschaft für Literatur, *Eine Dichterin* (2002), 11.

[21] See Mitterer, "Selbstporträt," 80. Zsolnay Verlag considered the book both unduly "philosemitisch und sozialdemokratisch" (philosemitic and social democratic). Dür, *Erika Mitterer*, 48.

[22] Dür, *Erika Mitterer*, 71.

[23] Erika Mitterer, *Zwölf Gedichte 1933–1945* (Vienna: Luckmann, 1946). Hereafter cited parenthetically in the text by page number.

[24] See Dür, *Erika Mitterer*, 194–96.

[25] See, for example, Joseph McVeigh, *Kontinuität und Vergangenheitsbewältigung in der österreichischen Literatur nach 1945* (Vienna: Braumüller, 1988), 197.

[26] Elaine Martin, "*Alle unsere Spiele* und die NS-Jahre: Interview mit Erika Mitterer-Petrowsky—Wien, den 3. und 4. Juni 1986," *Der literarische Zaunkönig*, no. 2 (2003): 34.

[27] Dür, *Erika Mitterer*, 169.

[28] Martin, "*Alle unsere Spiele* und die NS-Jahre," 34; also Mitterer, "Selbstporträt," 82.

[29] Erika Mitterer, *Die Seherin* (Hamburg: Marion von Schröder, 1942), 90.

[30] See Dür, *Erika Mitterer*, 216–17.

[31] Erika Mitterer, *Dramen I (Verdunkelung, Ein Bogen Seidenpapier)*, ed. Martin G. Petrowsky and Petra Sela (Vienna: Doppelpunkt, 2001).

[32] Márta Gaál-Baróti, "Wertverlust als Grundlage des Identitätsverlustes in Erika Mitterers 'Verdunkelung,'" in Petrowsky and Österreichische Gesellschaft für Literatur, *Eine Dichterin*, 51.

[33] See Martin G. Petrowsky, "Das Dritte Reich in der Literatur: Verschwiegen und verdrängt: Welche Rolle spielten die 'Vermittler?,'" *Der literarische Zaunkönig*, no. 2 (2012): 26–33; and Esther Dür, "'Der unerwünschte Zeithintergrund': Erika Mitterers Werk als Spiegel der Zeitgeschichte," *Studia Austriaca* 11 (2003): 152.

[34] Holzner, "Dialoge und Kontroversen mit der Moderne," 102.

[35] See Joseph G. McVeigh, "Continuity as Problem and Promise: Erika Mitterer's Writings after 1945," *Modern Austrian Literature* 12, nos. 3–4 (1979): 122.

[36] Mitterer, "Selbstporträt," 82.

[37] McVeigh, *Kontinuität und Vergangenheitsbewältigung*, 2.

[38] Published in English under the title *All Our Games* (Columbia, SC: Camden House, 1988).

[39] Mitterer, *Alle unsere Spiele*, 15.

[40] See Maria Sass, "Wer vergisst, hat vergebens gelebt: Vergangenheitsbewältigung in Erika Mitterers Roman 'Alle unsere Spiele,'" in Petrowsky and Abret, *Dichtung im Schatten der großen Krisen*, 286–90.

[41] For more on the origins of the novel, see Kurt Johann Auer, *Erika Mitterers Roman "Der Fürst der Welt,"* diss., University of Vienna, 1990, 14–16.

[42] Discussion with Erika Mitterer, reported in Herwig Gottwald, "Erika Mitterer und der historische Roman," in Holzner and Müller, *Zwischenwelt*, 217.

[43] Mitterer, "Selbstporträt," 81. See also Schmidt-Dengler, "Geschichte ohne Historie: Typologisches zum Roman 'Der Fürst der Welt,'" in Petrowsky and Österreichische Gesellschaft für Literatur, *Eine Dichterin*, 71–73.

44 Roman Roček, "Vorwort," in *Erika Mitterer: Der Fürst der Welt* (Vienna: Böhlau, 1988), 6.

45 Auer, *Erika Mitterers Roman*, 16.

46 Gerlinde Möser, "Spiegelbild einer Zeitenwende: Geschichtswissenschaftliche Betrachtung der Milieuschilderung im Roman 'Der Fürst der Welt,'" *Der literarische Zaunkönig*, no. 1 (2010): 43.

47 Erika Mitterer, *Der Fürst der Welt*, first complete revised edition, ed. Martin G. Petrowsky (Vienna: Seifert, 2006), 468. All subsequent references are to this edition and are cited parenthetically in the text.

48 Möser, "Spiegelbild einer Zeitenwende," 40–41.

49 Dür, *Erika Mitterer*, 83.

50 Mitterer, "Selbstporträt," 80. Gottwald mentions as many as seventeen publishers ("Erika Mitterer und der historische Roman," 218).

51 Gottwald, "Erika Mitterer und der historische Roman," 217.

52 Max Tau, "Als Lektor in der Emigration," in Tau, *Jahrbuch 1963: Deutsche Akademie für Sprache und Dichtung*, ed. Hermann Kasack and Fritz Usinger (Darmstadt: Lambert Schneider, 1964), 88–89.

53 Dür, *Erika Mitterer*, 95–96. Dür's examination of Norwegian reviews found nothing to suggest a potential ban and nothing of this nature appears in Mitterer's RSK personal file (98, 105). The novel could be published freely and was not even denied precious paper supplies.

54 Erika Mitterer, *Der Fürst der Welt* (Berlin: Non Stop Bücherei, 1964); *Erika Mitterer: Der Fürst der Welt*, ed. Roman Roček (Vienna: Böhlau, 1988); *Erika Mitterer: Der Fürst der Welt*, ed. Roman Roček (Berlin: Volk und Welt, 1988). The abridged versions were produced under pressure from the publishers, who did not believe the full-length text would be well received commercially.

55 Based on references in the novel to historical figures, texts, and events, Möser posits this year as a possible date for the book's witch trial (see Möser, "Spiegelbild einer Zeitenwende," 41).

56 Josef Michels, "Der Fürst der Welt," *Völkischer Beobachter* 33 (February 2, 1941).

57 *Jahresschau des deutschen Schrifttums 1941*, ed. Werbe- und Beratungsamt für das deutsche Schrifttum beim Reichsministerium für Volksaufklärung und Propaganda (Berlin, 1941), 28, cited in Gottwald, "Erika Mitterer und der historische Roman," 232.

58 "Das Buch—ein Schwert des Geistes: Grundliste für den deutschen Leihbuchhandel," ed. Reichsministerium für Volksaufklärung und Propaganda, Abteilung Schrifttum, no. 2 (Leipzig, 1941), 23, as cited in Gradwohl-Schlacher, "Innere Emigration in der 'Ostmark?,'" 80.

59 Werner Schickert, "Der Fürst der Welt," in *Die Literatur* 43 (1940–41): 611.

60 Albrecht Goes, "Erika Mitterer," *Frankfurter Zeitung*, June 9, 1941. As noted briefly in chapter 2, Goes (1908–2000) himself was an inner emigrant. He is best known today for his story *Das Brandopfer* (The burnt offering, 1954) about the

treatment of Jews in a southern German town, which was also one of the first works about the firebombing of Germany.

[61] Helene Henze, "Erika Mitterer," *Frankfurter Zeitung*, December 22, 1941.

[62] Will Grohmann, "Der Fürst der Welt," *Deutsche Allgemeine Zeitung*, December 1, 1940.

[63] Karl Blanck, "Erika Mitterer: Der Fürst der Welt," in *Weltstimmen* 14, no. 3 (1940): 107–8.

[64] According to a later letter from the Viennese councilor Viktor Matejka, an inmate at Dachau, as reported by Gottwald, "Erika Mitterer und der historische Roman," 218–19.

[65] Dür, *Erika Mitterer*, 106–8.

[66] E.g., Wendelin Schmidt-Dengler, "Geschichte bekommt Konturen," *Der literarische Zaunkönig*, no. 1 (2003): 5.

[67] See note 76 below on the use of the term "welsch" in the novel.

[68] Mitterer, "Selbstporträt," 81.

[69] Cited by Gottwald, "Erika Mitterer und der historische Roman," 217–18.

[70] In 1945 a Soviet censor suspected this passage of being anti-Semitic and wanted on this basis to ban the book but was persuaded otherwise by a friend of the author's (Gottwald, "Erika Mitterer und der historische Roman," 219 and note 36, citing a conversation with Mitterer).

[71] Gottwald, "Erika Mitterer und der historische Roman," 223.

[72] Brecht, "Fünf Schwierigkeiten," 83.

[73] Ehrke-Rotermund and Rotermund, *Zwischenreiche*, 18.

[74] See Maria Sass, "Aspekte des Mythischen und des magischen Realismus in Erika Mitterers Roman 'Fürst der Welt,'" *Der literarische Zaunkönig*, no. 3 (2011): 32–52.

[75] Evelyne Polt-Heinzl, "Ein Fürst und ein Herr der Welt: Zwei historische Romane von Erika Mitterer und Alma Johanna Koenig," in Petrowsky and Abret, *Dichtung im Schatten der großen Krisen*, 179.

[76] The very word "welsch"—an old Germanic term for initially Celtic, then Italian and French peoples, and used in modern Austria as a pejorative ("Eyeties")—chimed with Nazi use of the term to designate "un-German" or alien phenomena. It is used repeatedly in the novel as a derogatory description of the Italian architect and the immigrant workers he hires (e.g., 188), who, in true scapegoat fashion, are seen as a major source of the town's suffering.

[77] See also Margaret Ives, "Erika Mitterer as a Christian writer: A Study of the Novel *Der Fürst der Welt* as a precursor of the later poetry," in *Other Austrians: Post-1945 Austrian Women's Writing*, ed. Allyson Fiddler (Bern: Peter Lang, 1998), 83–90.

[78] Polt-Heinzl particularly detects pederast leanings in the bishop's relationship with the page Beatus. See Polt-Heinzl, "Ein Fürst und ein Herr der Welt," 158.

[79] Ives, "Erika Mitterer as a Christian Writer," 87.

[80] Ephesians 2:2.

[81] 2 Corinthians 4:4.

[82] John 12:31, 14:30, and 16:11. This finite conception of Satan and evil is the one behind Luther's famous "Ein feste Burg ist unser Gott" (A mighty fortress is our God), with its lines: "Der Fürst dieser Welt, / wie sau'r er sich stellt, / tut er uns doch nicht. / Das macht, er ist gericht't. / Ein Wörtlein kann ihn fällen." (The prince of darkness grim—We tremble not for him; / His rage we can endure, For lo! his doom is sure, / One little word shall fell him.) Translation by Frederick Henry Hedge, http://en.wikisource.org/wiki/A_Mighty_Fortress_Is_Our_God_(Hedge) (accessed February 17, 2014).

[83] If anything, the Inquisitor is more aligned with death as the "Grim Reaper" (see 448).

[84] Mitterer, first draft of novel, in Nachlass Erika Mitterer, Romane: "Der Fürst der Welt," DLA.

[85] Dür, *Erika Mitterer*, 128–29.

[86] It tells the story of a girl taken into heaven by Mary, who gives her thirteen keys to the chambers of heaven, twelve of which she is told she can use, but she is forbidden from looking into the thirteenth chamber. Each day the girl visits one of the rooms and enjoys its magnificence and splendor. She cannot resist the temptation to look behind the forbidden door too and discovers there the radiant glow and fire of the Holy Trinity; she touches it and it turns her finger gold. Mary returns, sees what has happened, and, because the girl will not own up to what she has done, strikes her dumb and sends her back to earth, where she is imprisoned between hedges of impenetrable thorns. This is where the tale ends in the novel. In the Grimm version the girl is found by a king out hunting and he eventually marries her. The new queen has three children but Mary takes them away from her as punishment for not confessing to her wrongdoing. The people say the queen has killed and consumed her own children and urge the king to burn her. On the funeral pyre the queen admits her guilt, the rain extinguishes the flames, and Mary returns her children to her and they live happily ever after. Jacob Grimm and Wilhelm Grimm, *Marienkind* (1810), in *Kinder- und Hausmärchen*, Ausgabe letzter Hand mit den Originalanmerkungen der Bruder Grimm, vol. 1, ed. Heinz Rölleke (Stuttgart: Reclam, 1980), 36–41.

[87] See Gottwald, "Erika Mitterer und der historische Roman," 227–28.

[88] See Sass, "Aspekte des Mythischen," 36.

Conclusion

THE WEDGE DRIVEN between inner and outer literary opponents of the National Socialist regime constitutes one of the most aberrant developments of postwar German literary history, muddying the waters of the humane legacy that was bequeathed to the country after the war. Much has rightly been made of the achievements and contributions of exiled writers from Nazi Germany, of the privations of what was in the vast majority of cases a harsh and uncertain existence. Much has also been made of those inner emigrant writers whose pronouncements in the postwar period brought into disrepute the notion of an "inner opposition" or literary nonconformism, inviting accusations of self-exculpation and complicity with the regime. Gradually, however, we are also at last beginning to see a more open, better informed, more balanced, and less prejudiced appraisal of the many writers who remained and published in Germany between 1933 and 1945, and who displayed courage and a commitment to spiritual resistance. At the same time, this "drilling down" into context does not always and necessarily exculpate: today's better-informed picture can also support continuing skepticism, an understanding without approval of the compromises and even occasional acts of cowardice that writers engaged in.

Several critics after 1945, following in the footsteps of Thomas Mann, suggested that in retreating to inwardness and in affirming humane and Christian values and norms, inner emigrant writers merely served to anaesthetize the German reading public under Hitler and ensured that no serious resistance was offered. However, this sits awkwardly with the fact that many of these writers were severely criticized by literary critics at the time for failing to align themselves with Nazi values, that some were arrested, imprisoned, or banned from writing: in the eyes of the authorities their potential influence was clearly considered greater than has been suggested. National Socialism demanded of *all* authors that they positively affirm such ideas as racial purity, German supremacy, and a literature "close to the soil," a viewpoint typified by Hanns Johst's complaint about writers who wanted nothing to do with the NSDAP or the Nazi government: "Wir pfeifen auf den Hochmut von sogenannten Dichtern, die da glauben, auf dem Umweg von Innerlichkeit und den Phrasen von Ewigkeitswerten dem schlichten, anständigen, eindeutigen Bekenntnis zum Nationalsozialismus und der Tatsache des Dritten Reiches aus dem Wege gehen zu können" (We don't give a damn about the arrogance of so-called poetic writers who believe that through inwardness and the clichés of eternal values they can eschew the simple, respectable, and unambiguous acknowledgement of National Socialism and the fact of the Third Reich).[1]

The fact that in such an environment so much potentially subversive literature could still appear owes much to the narrow-mindedness of Nazi cultural officials and their failure to appreciate the true import of the material they were reading. As Wilhelm Hausenstein noted in his open letter to Thomas Mann—a contribution to the ill-fated postwar controversy—although the Gestapo and officials of the Propaganda Ministry were skilled in the business of monitoring and censorship, they were in other respects naïve and failed to grasp the ethical and decent ("anständig") aspects of certain books, causing them to misunderstand such works completely.[2] Being admirers of the beautiful in literature, art, and music, and believing that beauty was in itself essentially unpolitical, they frequently failed to detect subversive messages expressed in less obvious a manner and in less strident tones than those employed in the propagation of their own perverted ideals.

As seen in chapter 2, the literary inner emigration is a broad and diverse grouping, characterized by differing forms of withdrawal from National Socialism. The notion of *Resistenz*, a self-immunization against Nazi ideas and practices, offers the most promising approach to understanding the inner emigrant state of mind or way of life, which, with its fluid boundaries, overlaps, and contradictions, fluctuates between, on the one hand, camouflaged protest and a self-distancing from the regime, and on the other, adaptation to and apparent conformity and cooperation with it. In making sense of the phenomenon, this book has sought to adopt a differentiated approach, to consider individual cases through an analysis of the context, genesis, and reception of key texts. It has also sought to supplement a focus on the political content and oppositional stance of such works with Philipp's notion of writers' "perceptual horizon,"[3] including their biographical circumstances, their intellectual influences, their nationalist consciousness, and their conviction of representing a supposed "other" or better Germany.

The examination of individual writers has revealed the potential for works to display simultaneously conformist and nonconformist traits, which inevitably results in a lack of clarity with regard to political significance and effect. In its positive presentation of Prussian authoritarianism, Klepper's *Der Vater* offers the regime an opportunity to claim the work as a championing of Nazi ideals; similarly, Bergengruen's ambiguous portrayal of his tyrant allows the work to be interpreted as glorifying the strong ruler; in his enactment of responses to tyranny in *El Greco malt den Großinquisitor*, Andres provides a sympathetic portrayal of the dilemmas facing Germans under National Socialism, but at the same time his depiction of the Spanish Inquisition and its representatives is very much in line with Nazi rejection of Catholicism; Wiechert's exclusive focus in *Das einfache Leben* on a retreat to the personal sphere of existence as the only source of human happiness seems to exclude any possibility of countering the regime and can thus be seen to contribute to its normalization; and Mitterer's esoteric criticism of the Nazi state is well camouflaged by the vivid exoteric picture she draws of the ruthless and violent medieval Catholic Church. Although all these works can be read as attacks on National Socialism, it was their inherent ambiguity, along with the existence of a sensitized, educated, esoteric, and "stereoscopic" readership, that allowed them to be published and to achieve substantial sales. In the attempt to camouflage their essential nonconformism, oppositionally minded writers on occasions appeared to affirm the reality of Nazism: rejection and unwitting stabilization of the Nazi state frequently, perhaps inevitably, go hand in hand in the literature of inner emigration.

Beyond such ambiguity, inner emigrant writing can be accused of never unequivocally rejecting the fascist state or the ideal of a strong leader. Furthermore, the tendency of the likes of Andres, Bergengruen, Klepper, and Reck-Malleczewen to emphasize the timeless nature of conflict, the inevitability of tyranny, and the perennially weak human response to it, seems to encourage a historical irrationalism that implies a rejection of social or political change resulting from specific historical circumstances, and might be seen to confirm contemporary readers' sense of impotence in the face of Nazi evil. However— no matter how alien it might seem to a relativist, postmodern world with its questioning of all truth systems—these writers' emphasis on supposedly eternally valid truths constituted an attempt to preserve Christian humanist values, which were under constant attack from the Nazi regime, to safeguard and foster basic moral norms, and to offer a clear vision of man and his inalienable rights to which readers could cling through the dark days of totalitarian rule. They served to communicate a sense of encouragement and reassurance, to present an "insider" readership with models of fortitude and ethical behavior, and thereby to alert readers to the existence of like-minded individuals, to suggest that they were not alone in their spiritual opposition. Their aim was perhaps best summed up by Peter Suhrkamp's retrospective "program" for the journal *Die Neue Rundschau*:

> Trost bieten, Verhaltensweisen mitteilen, auf die innere Person sammeln, die Gegenwärtigkeit von Vergangenem lebendig machen, den wirklichen Verhältnissen die überzeitliche Wirklichkeit entgegenstellen, die persönliche menschliche Wirklichkeit in den Wirkungen unseres Wesens und unseres Tuns für das Gedeihen des Guten in der Welt nachweisen.[4]

[Offer comfort, inform readers about possible ways of behaving, concentrate the individual's attention and powers on the inner person, bring alive the relevance of past events for the present, set timeless reality against the conditions under which we live at present, and demonstrate how the good can be fostered by the personal human reality that is made manifest in the outward effects of our being and actions.]

It would be wrong to consider such a contribution trivial, and any judgment of inner emigrants needs to be informed by the sort of caution counseled by Kästner after the war: "Keiner weiß, ob er aus dem Stoffe gemacht ist, aus dem der entscheidende Augenblick Helden formt" (No one knows whether they are made of the stuff from which in decisive moments heroes are formed).[5] The debate over the moral high ground that raged for many years between proponents of exile and inner emigration has proved so fruitless precisely because these terms have been burdened with too great a weight of expectation, resulting in demands on both sides, which simply could not be fulfilled. In the final analysis, neither form of literary distancing, opposition, or resistance had any practical effect on the regime. Scholdt's American comparison is instructive: he points out that even a fêted book such as Beecher Stowe's *Uncle Tom's Cabin* (1852) failed to dismantle slavery.[6] Yet, one might observe, it did gnaw at the conscience of those responsible for its perpetuation and began to change people's perceptions of the slave trade by allowing readers to experience vicariously the conditions of slavery. Moreover, as Scholdt goes on to say, it served to console and to provide spiritual sustenance to the powerless. In the same way, one should not retrospectively expect the unreasonable from writers under National Socialism: the value of writing that promoted nonconformist positions and ideals lay in its contribution to human well-being under an oppressive regime, in its ability certainly to console, but also to strengthen, invigorate, and reassure readers that the world of the spirit and shared moral values would prevail. Ultimately, its practical benefits are to be seen in a longer perspective than that of 1933–45. As Wolfgang Emmerich notes with reference to all forms of oppositional literature produced under conditions of oppression, anyone who engages with antifascist literature is more likely to prove immune in future to the "fascination" of fascist regimes or their contemporary equivalents.[7] There can be no better justification for exploring the legacy of the literary inner emigration.

Notes

1 Hanns Johst, *Völkischer Beobachter* 300 (September 26, 1936): 7, cited by Klieneberger, *Christian Writers of the Inner Emigration*, 196–97.

2 Hausenstein, "Bücher," 72.

[3] Philipp, "Distanz und Anpassung," 11–30.

[4] Peter Suhrkamp, "Die Neue Rundschau," in *Die Stockholmer Neue Rundschau: Auswahl* (Berlin: Suhrkamp, 1949), 15.

[5] Erich Kästner, "Über das Verbrennen von Büchern (10.5.1958)," in *Erich Kästner: Gesammelte Schriften für Erwachsene*, vol. 8 (Munich: Knaur, 1969), 284.

[6] See Scholdt, "Geschichte als Ausweg?," 123.

[7] Emmerich, "Die Literatur des antifaschistischen Widerstandes," 451.

Bibliography

Abret, Helga. "Von der Notwendigkeit und der Fragwürdigkeit des Handelns: Erika Mitterers Drama *Charlotte Corday* (1931)." In Petrowsky and Abret, *Dichtung im Schatten der großen Krisen*, 51–75.

Ackermann, Konrad. *Der Widerstand der Monatsschrift Hochland gegen den Nationalsozialismus*. Munich: Kösel, 1965.

Andersch, Alfred. "Achtzig und Jünger: Ein politischer Diskurs." *Merkur* 29 (1975): 239–50.

Andres, Christopher, Michael Braun, and Georg Guntermann. "Nachwort." In *Stefan Andres: Wir sind Utopia/El Greco malt den Großinquisitor: Zwei Novellen*, edited by Christopher Andres, Michael Braun, and Georg Guntermann, 127–42. Munich: Piper, 2006.

Andres, Dorothee. "Vortrag an der Gedenkfeier für Stefan Andres aus Anlaß seines 25. Todestages am 29. Juni 1995 in Trier." *Mitteilungen der Stefan-Andres-Gesellschaft* 16 (1995): 64–70.

Andres, Stefan. *Das heilige Heimweh: Roman in 18 Teilen*. Marienborn: Monatsschrift des Marienbund im Dienste der Diaspora. Leipzig: Bohn & Sohn, 1928–29.

———. *Bruder Lucifer: Roman*. Jena: Diederichs, 1933.

———. *Eberhard im Kontrapunkt*. Cologne: Staufen, 1933.

———. *Die unsichtbare Mauer: Roman*. Jena: Diederichs, 1934.

———. *El Greco malt den Großinquisitor*. Leipzig: List, 1936.

———. "Die Instruktion: Anekdote" (1936). In *Stefan Andres: Wir sind Utopia*, 129–31.

———. "Das Trockendock: Anekdote" (1936). In *Stefan Andres: Wir sind Utopia*, 111–14.

———. *Utz, der Nachfahr: Novelle*. Saarlautern: Hausen Verlagsgesellschaft, 1936.

———. "Der geheime Auftrag: Eine Anekdote in Politik und Liebe versponnen" (1937). In *Stefan Andres: Terrassen im Licht*, 38–42.

———. "Klavichord und Schachbrett: Anekdote." (1937). In *Stefan Andres: Wir sind Utopia*, 161–64.

———. "Der König im Gedränge: Anekdote." (1937). In *Stefan Andres: Wir sind Utopia*, 118–20.

———. *Moselländische Novellen*. Leipzig: List, 1937.

———. *Der Mann von Asteri: Roman*. Berlin: Riemerschmidt, 1939.

———. *Das Grab des Neides: Novelle*. Berlin: Riemerschmidt, 1940.

———. "Zwischen zwei Stühlen: Ein Streitgespräch" (1941). In *Stefan Andres: Wir sind Utopia*, 197–203.

——. *Der gefrorene Dionysos.* Berlin: Riemerschmidt, 1942.

——. *Wir sind Utopia: Novelle.* Berlin: Riemerschmidt, 1943.

——. *Das Tier aus der Tiefe.* Munich: Piper, 1949.

——. "Aquaedukte der Erinnerung." *Welt und Wort* 5 (1950): 505–6.

——. *Die Arche.* Munich: Piper, 1951.

——. "Über die Sendung des Dichters" (1953). In Große, *Stefan Andres: Ein Reader*, 63–74.

——. "Der Mensch inmitten der Dämonien dieser Zeit." In Große, *Stefan Andres: Ein Reader*, 53–62.

——. *Der graue Regenbogen.* Munich: Piper, 1959.

——. *Der Mann im Fisch.* Munich: Piper, 1963.

——. "Jahrgang 1906: Ein Junge vom Lande" (1966). In Große, *Stefan Andres: Ein Reader*, 13–47.

——. *20. Juli, Tat und Testament: Rede.* Frankfurt am Main: Klostermann, 1966.

——. *Der Taubenturm.* Munich: Piper, 1966.

——. "Briefe an einen Theologen." *Nouvelle Revue Luxembourgeoise* 1, no. 3 (1970): 267–79.

——. *Die Versuchung des Synesios.* Munich: Piper, 1971.

——. *Stefan Andres: Die Sintflut: Roman.* Edited by John Klapper. Göttingen: Wallstein, 2007.

——. *Stefan Andres: Werke in Einzelausgaben.* 10 vols. Edited by Christopher Andres, Michael Braun, Georg Guntermann, Birgit Lermen, and Erwin Rotermund. Göttingen: Wallstein, 2007–.

——. *Stefan Andres: Terrassen im Licht: Italienische Erzählungen.* Edited by Dieter Richter. Göttingen: Wallstein, 2009.

——. *Stefan Andres: Wir sind Utopia: Prosa aus den Jahren 1933–1945.* Edited by Erwin Rotermund and Heidrun Ehrke-Rotermund, with Thomas Hilsheimer. Göttingen: Wallstein, 2010.

——. "Gegen die Atomaufrüstung." In *Stefan Andres: Der Dichter in dieser Zeit*, 140–48.

——. "Innere Emigration." In *Stefan Andres: Der Dichter in dieser Zeit*, 65–72.

——. *Stefan Andres: Der Dichter in dieser Zeit: Reden und Essays.* Edited by Christopher Andres and Michael Braun. Göttingen: Wallstein, 2013.

——. Konvolut "Briefe 1931–1947." Archiv der Stefan-Andres-Gesellschaft, Schweich.

——. Konvolut "Korrespondenz mit Ämtern." Archiv der Stefan-Andres-Gesellschaft, Schweich.

——. Nachlass: Andres, Stefan, Mappe "Rezensionen." Deutsches Literaturarchiv, Marbach.

Anon. "Statt eines besonderen Vorwortes! Widerstand: Zeitschrift für nationalrevolutionäre Politik." *Bücherkunde* 1, nos. 11–12 (1934): 201–3.

——. "Acht Kapitel für die Deutschen." *Bücherkunde* 2, no. 2 (1935): 47.

——. "Neue Romane für den Weihnachtstisch." *Völkischer Beobachter* 48, no. 341, Norddeutsche Ausgabe (December 7, 1935): 12.

————. "El Greco." *Nürnberger Zeitung*, May 30, 1936. Archiv-Box "El Greco malt den Großinquisitor," Archiv der Stefan-Andres-Gesellschaft, Schweich.

————. "Der Großtyrann und das Gericht." *Bücherkunde* 3, no. 3 (1936): 81.

————. List of recent publications. *Die Neue Literatur* 37, no. 12 (1936): 700–701.

————. Publicity material of the Paul List Verlag" (May 1936?). Archiv-Box "El Greco malt den Großinquisitor," Archiv der Stefan-Andres-Gesellschaft, Schweich.

————. Review. *Gutachtenanzeiger* 2, no. 6 (1936): 2.

————. Review. *Jahres-Gutachtenanzeiger*, no. 2054 (1936): 91.

————. Stellungnahme, Kulturpolitisches Archiv, September 10, 1936. In Reiner, *Ernst Wiechert im Dritten Reich*, 73.

————. Untitled extract from review. In *Volksbildunggsstätte Breslau*, May 25, 1936. In Archiv-Box "El Greco malt den Großinquisitor," Archiv der Stefan-Andres-Gesellschaft, Schweich.

————. "Stefan Andres." *Der Buchhändler im neuen Reich*, nos. 11–12, Ausgabe A (November–December 1937): 360.

————. "Ist die Geschichte eine Konfession?" *Völkischer Beobachter* 51, no. 54 (March 5, 1938): 6.

————. "Las Casas vor Karl V." *Der Buchhändler im neuen Reich* 3, nos. 10–11, Ausgabe A (1938): 397.

————. "Wichtige Hinweise." *Lektorenbrief* 1, no. 2 (February 2, 1938): 5. In Reiner, *Ernst Wiechert im Dritten Reich*, 129.

Arnold, Heinz-Ludwig. *Deutsche Literatur im Exil 1933–1945*. 2 vols. Frankfurt am Main: Athenäum-Fischer-Taschenbuch-Verlag, 1974.

Auer, Kurt Johann. *Erika Mitterers Roman "Der Fürst der Welt."* Diss., University of Vienna, 1990.

Baden, Hans-Jürgen. "Ernst Jüngers christliches Zwischenspiel." *Neue Zeitschrift für systematische Theologie* 3, no. 3 (1961): 328–45.

————. "Extreme Existenzen: Jochen Klepper und Reinhold Schneider." In Thiede, *Über Reinhold Schneider*, 183–201.

Bänziger, Hans. "Werner Bergengruen." In *Christliche Dichter der Gegenwart: Beiträge zur europäischen Literatur*, edited by Hermann Friedmann and Otto Mann, 345–58. Heidelberg: Rothe, 1955.

————. *Werner Bergengruen: Weg und Werk*. Thal: Pflugverlag, 1950. 4th ed.: Bern: Francke, 1983.

Barbian, Jan-Pieter. *Literaturpolitik im "Dritten Reich": Institutionen, Kompetenzen, Betätigungsfelder*. 2nd ed. Munich: Deutscher Taschenbuch Verlag, 1995.

————. "'Ich gehörte zu diesen Idioten': Ina Seidel im Dritten Reich." In Barbian, *Die vollendete Ohnmacht?*, 101–44.

————. "'. . . im Augenblick restlos aufgeworfen': Peter Huchel als Autor im Dritten Reich." In Barbian, *Die vollendete Ohnmacht?*, 185–203.

————. "'Nur passiv geblieben?': Zur Rolle von Erich Kästner im Dritten Reich." In Barbian, *Die vollendete Ohnmacht?*, 145–83.

———. *Die vollendete Ohnmacht?: Schriftsteller, Verleger und Buchhändler im NS-Staat: Ausgewählte Aufsätze.* Essen: Klartext, 2008.

———. "Zwischen Anpassung und Widerstand: Regimekritische Autoren in der Literaturpolitik des Dritten Reiches." In Kroll and von Voss, *Schriftsteller und Widerstand,* 63–98.

Bärsch, Claus-Ekkehard. *Die politische Religion des Nationalsozialismus: Die religiöse Dimension der NS-Ideologie in den Schriften von Dietrich Eckart, Joseph Goebbels, Alfred Rosenberg und Adolf Hitler.* Munich: Fink, 1998.

Basker, David. "'I Mounted Resistance, Though I Hid the Fact': Versions of Wolfgang Koeppen's Early Biography." In Donahue and Kirchner, *Flight of Fantasy,* 258–68.

Beecher Stowe, Harriet. *Uncle Tom's Cabin, or, Negro Life in the Slave States of America.* London: C. H. Clarke, 1852.

Beer, Otto F. "Lernet im Mars (Nachwort)." In *Alexander Lernet-Holenia: Mars im Widder,* 261–68. Vienna: Zsolnay, 1976.

Benn, Gottfried. "Bekenntnis zum Expressionismus." *Deutsche Zukunft,* November 5, 1933. Under "Expressionismus" in *Sämtliche Werke,* vol. 4, Prosa, part 2, 76–90.

———. *Der neue Staat und die Intellektuellen.* Stuttgart: Deutsche Verlags-Anstalt, 1933.

———. *Ausgewählte Gedichte 1911–1936.* Stuttgart: Deutsche Verlags-Anstalt, 1936.

———. *Statische Gedichte.* Wiesbaden: Limes, 1948.

———. *Doppelleben: 2 Selbstdarstellungen.* Wiesbaden: Limes, 1950.

———. *Briefe an F. W. Oelze 1932–1945.* Edited by Harald Steinhagen and Jürgen Schröder. Frankfurt am Main: Fischer-Taschenbuch-Verlag, 1979.

———. *Sämtliche Werke.* 7 vols. Edited by Gerhard Schuster and Holger Hof. Stuttgart: Klett-Cotta, 1986–2003.

———. *Gottfried Benn–Egmont Seyerlen, Briefwechsel 1914–1956.* Edited by Gerhard Schuster. Stuttgart: Klett-Cotta, 1993.

Berendsohn, Walter A. "Emigrantenliteratur." In *Reallexikon der deutschen Literaturgeschichte,* vol. 1, edited by Eckehard Catholy, 336. Berlin: de Gruyter, 1958.

———. "Ernst Wiechert *Hirtennovelle.*" In Franke, *Jenseits der Wälder,* 209–11.

Bergengruen, Werner. *Das große Alkahest: Roman.* Berlin: Wegweiser, 1926. Republished as *Der Starost.* Hamburg: Hanseatische Verlagsanstalt, 1938.

———. *Baedeker des Herzens: Ein Reiseverführer.* Berlin: Tradition, 1932.

———. *Des Knaben Plunderhorn.* Berlin: Vorhut, 1934.

———. "Die Antwort der Geschichte." In *Die Stunde des Christentums: Eine deutsche Besinnung,* edited by Kurt Ihlenfeld, 12–21. Berlin-Steglitz: Eckart, 1937.

———. *Die drei Falken: Novelle.* Dresden: Heyne, 1937.

———. "Vorfahren und alte Häuser." *Die Neue Literatur* 49 (1939): 169–75.

————. *Dies irae: Eine Dichtung.* Munich: Desch, 1945.

————. *Am Himmel wie auf Erden.* Zurich: Nymphenburger Verlagshandlung, 1947.

————. "Zum Geleit." In Pechel, *Zwischen den Zeilen*, 8.

————. *Das Feuerzeichen.* Munich: Nymphenburger Verlagshandlung, 1949.

————. *Römisches Erinnerungsbuch.* Freiburg: Herder, 1949.

————. *Der ewige Kaiser: Ein deutscher Gedichtkreis vom Glauben an das christliche Kaisertum.* Graz: Schmidt-Dengler, 1951.

————. "Bekenntnis zur Höhle." In Kampmann, *Die Welt Werner Bergengruens*, 69–75.

————. *Das Geheimnis verbleibt.* Munich: Nymphenburger Verlagshandlung, 1952.

————. "Rückblick auf einen Roman." In *Abhandlungen der Klasse der Literatur*, no. 2, edited by Akademie der Wissenschaften und der Literatur, 19–34. Wiesbaden: Steiner; Mainz: Akademie der Wissenschaften und der Literatur, 1961.

————. *Schreibtischerinnerungen.* Munich: Nymphenburger Verlagshandlung, 1961.

————. "Zum Tode Thomas Manns." In *Werner Bergengruen: Mündlich gesprochen: Ansprache, Vorträge und Reden*, 158–61. Zurich: Arche; Munich: Nymphenburger Verlags-Buchhandlung, 1963.

————. *Dichtergehäuse: Aus den autobiographischen Aufzeichnungen.* Zurich: Verlag der Arche, 1966.

————. *Der Großtyrann und das Gericht: Roman.* Munich: Deutscher Taschenbuch Verlag, 2002.

————. *Schriftstellerexistenz in der Diktatur: Aufzeichnungen und Reflexionen zu Politik, Geschichte und Kultur 1940–1963.* Edited by Frank-Lothar Kroll, N. Luise Hackelsberger, and Sylvia Taschka. Munich: Oldenbourg, 2005.

Berglar, Peter. "Staatsräson und Christus-Nachfolge: Gedanken zu Reinhold Schneiders 'Las Casas Dichtung.'" *Mitteilungen der Reinhold-Schneider-Gesellschaft* 4 (July 1972): 52–71.

Berglund, Gisela. *Der Kampf um den Leser im Dritten Reich: Die Literaturpolitik der "Neuen Literatur" (Will Vesper) und der "Nationalsozialistischen Monatshefte."* Worms: Heintz, 1980.

Bergstraesser, Arnold. "Das einfache Leben: Zu dem Roman von Ernst Wiechert." *Monatshefte für deutschen Unterricht, deutsche Sprache und Literatur* 38 (1946): 293–97.

The Bible, New International Version. https://www.biblegateway.com/. Accessed June 30, 2014.

Biser, Eugen. *Überredung zur Liebe: Die dichterische Daseinsdeutung Gertrud von le Forts.* Regensburg: Habbel, 1980.

Blanck, Karl. "Erika Mitterer: Der Fürst der Welt." *Weltstimmen* 14, no. 3 (1940): 107–8.

Blattmann, Ekkehard. *Reinhold Schneider linguistisch interpretiert.* Heidelberg: Stiehm, 1979.

Blattmann, Ekkehard, and Barbara Hoth-Blattmann, eds. *Reinhold Schneider—Ich, Tod, Gott.* Reinhold Schneider-Jahrbuch 1. Frankfurt am Main: Lang, 1985.

Blattmann, Ekkehard, and Klaus Mönig, eds. *Über den "Fall Reinhold Schneider."* Munich: Schnell & Steiner, 1990.

Bluhm, Lothar. *Das Tagebuch zum Dritten Reich: Zeugnisse der Inneren Emigration von Jochen Klepper bis Ernst Jünger.* Bonn: Bouvier, 1991.

Blum, Paul Richard. *Giordano Bruno: An Introduction.* Amsterdam: Rodopi, 2012.

Blunck, Hans Friedrich. *Unwegsame Zeiten: Lebensbericht.* vol. 2. Mannheim: Kessler, 1952.

Boa, Elizabeth, and Rachel Palfreyman. *Heimat—A German Dream: Regional Loyalties and National Identity in German Culture, 1890–1990.* Oxford: Oxford University Press, 2000.

Boag, Hugh-Alexander. *Ernst Wiechert: The Prose Works in Relation to His Life and Times.* Stuttgart: Heinz, 1987.

Boberach, Heinz, ed. *Berichte des SD und der Gestapo über Kirchen und Kirchenvolk in Deutschland 1934–1944.* Mainz: Grünewald, 1971.

———. *Meldungen aus dem Reich 1938–1945: Die geheimen Lagerberichte des Sicherheitsdienstes der SS.* Herrsching: Pawlak, 1984.

Bock, Sigrid. "Arbeiterkorrespondenten und -schriftsteller bewähren sich: Jan Petersen: 'Unsere Straße.'" In Bock and Hahn, *Erfahrung Nazideutschland,* 44–98.

Bock, Sigrid, and Manfred Hahn, eds. *Erfahrung Nazideutschland: Romane in Deutschland 1933–1945.* Berlin: Aufbau, 1987.

Bohrer, Karl Heinz. *Die Ästhetik des Schreckens: Die pessimistische Romantik und Ernst Jüngers Frühwerk.* Munich: Hanser, 1978.

Böll, Heinrich. "Das meiste ist mir fremd geblieben: Ernst Jünger zum 80. Geburtstag." *Frankfurter Allgemeine Zeitung,* no. 74 (March 29, 1975). Reproduced in Böll, *Spuren der Zeitgenossenschaft: Literarische Schriften,* 172. Munich: Deutscher Taschenbuch Verlag, 1977.

Bottlenberg-Landsberg, Maria Theodora von dem. "Lautlose Stimmen?: Zeitschriften der 'Inneren Emigration.'" In Kroll and von Voss, *Schriftsteller und Widerstand,* 185–204.

———. *Die Weißen Blätter: Eine konservative Zeitschrift im und gegen den Nationalsozialismus.* Berlin: Lukas, 2012.

Braun, Michael. "'Ein kläglicher Prophet in seinem Fisch': Stefan Andres und die Probleme der inneren Emigration." *Zeitschrift für deutsche Philologie* 115 (1996): 262–78.

———. *Stefan Andres: Leben und Werk in Text und Bildern.* Bonn: Bouvier, 1997.

———. "Stefan Andres: El Greco malt den Großinquisitor." *Mitteilungen der Stefan-Andres-Gesellschaft* 33 (2012): 23–26.

Braun, Michael, Georg Guntermann, and Christiane Gandner, eds. *"Gerettet und zugleich von Scham verschlungen": Neue Annäherungen an die Literatur der "inneren Emigration."* Frankfurt am Main: Lang, 2007.

Brecht, Bertolt. "An die Nachgeborenen." In Bertolt Brecht, *Svendborger Gedichte*, 84–86. London: Malik, 1939.

———. "Fünf Schwierigkeiten beim Schreiben der Wahrheit." In *Bertolt Brecht Gesammelte Werke*. vol. 22, *Große kommentierte Berliner und Frankfurter Ausgabe*, edited by Werner Hecht et al., 74–89. Berlin: Suhrkamp, 1993.

Brekle, Wolfgang. "Die antifaschistische Literatur in Deutschland (1933–1945): Probleme der inneren Emigration am Beispiel deutscher Erzähler (Krauss, Kuckhoff, Petersen, Huch, Barlach, Wiechert u.a.)." *Weimarer Beiträge* 11, no. 6 (1970): 67–128.

———. *Schriftsteller im antifaschistischen Widerstand 1933–1945 in Deutschland*. Berlin: Aufbau, 1985.

Brenner, Hildegard. *Die Kunstpolitik des Nationalsozialismus*. Reinbek bei Hamburg: Rowohlt, 1963.

Breuning, Klaus. *Die Vision des Reiches: Deutscher Katholizismus zwischen Demokratie und Diktatur 1929–34*. Munich: Max Hueber, 1969.

Broch, Hermann. *Kommentierte Werkausgabe: Briefe 3*. Edited by Paul Michael Lützeler. Frankfurt am Main: Suhrkamp, 1986.

Brockmann, Stephen. "Inner Emigration: The Term and Its Origins in Postwar Debates." In Donahue and Kirchner, *Flight of Fantasy*, 11–26.

Broszat, Martin. "Zur Sozialgeschichte des deutschen Widerstands." *Vierteljahreshefte für Zeitgeschichte* 34, no. 3 (1986): 293–309.

———. "Plädoyer für eine Historisierung des Nationalsozialismus." In *Nach Hitler: Der schwierige Umgang mit unserer Geschichte*, edited by Martin Broszat, 266–81. Munich: Deutscher Taschenbuch Verlag, 1988.

Bubenik, Peter. "Erika Mitterers religiöse Lyrik der späten Jahre." In Petrowsky and Abret, *Dichtung im Schatten der großen Krisen*, 309–41.

Buck, Theo, Hans-Peter Franke, Ulrich Staehle, Dietrich Steinbach, and Dietmar Wenzelburger. *Von der Weimarer Republik bis 1945: Geschichte der deutschen Literatur 5*. Stuttgart: Klett, 1985.

Burm, Lena. "Stefan Andres' kritische Stellungnahme gegenüber der römisch-katholischen Kirche." In Große, *Stefan Andres: Ein Reader*, 180–92.

Carossa Hans. *Wirkungen Goethes in der Gegenwart*. Leipzig: Insel, 1938.

———. *Ungleiche Welten*. Wiesbaden: Insel, 1951.

Chamberlain, Houston Stewart. *Die Grundlagen des neunzehnten Jahrhunderts*. Munich: Bruckmann, 1899.

Chatellier, Hildegard. "Ernst Wiechert im Urteil der deutschen Zeitschriftenpresse (1933–1945): Ein Beitrag zur nationalsozialistischen Literatur- und Pressepolitik." *Recherches Germaniques* 3 (1973): 153–95.

Chick, Edson M. "Ernst Wiechert's Flight to the Circle of Eternity." *The Germanic Review* 30, no. 4 (1955): 282–93.

Chylewska-Tölle, Aleksandra. *Literarische Entwürfe und Formen der Wandlung im Werk Gertrud von le Forts*. Frankfurt am Main: Lang, 2007.

Corino, Karl, ed. *Intellektuelle im Bann des Nationalsozialismus*. Hamburg: Hoffmann und Campe, 1980.

Cremer, Ludwig. "Ernst Jünger, der Dichter: Zu 'Auf den Marmorklippen.'" *Kölnische Zeitung* no. 354 (July 19, 1940): 1.

Cuomo, Glenn R. "Günter Eichs Rundfunkbeiträge in den Jahren 1933–1940: Eine kommentierte Neuaufstellung." *Rundfunk und Fernsehen: Wissenschaftliche Vierteljahresschrift* 32, no. 1 (1984): 83–96.

———. *Career at the Cost of Compromise: Günter Eich's Life and Work in the Years 1933–1945.* Amsterdam: Rodopi, 1989.

———. "Opposition or Opportunism? Günter Eich's Status as *Inner Emigrant.*" In Donahue and Kirchner, *Flight of Fantasy,* 176–87.

Dahlke, Hans. *Geschichtsroman und Literaturkritik im Exil.* Berlin: Aufbau, 1976.

Dassanowsky, Robert von. *Phantom Empires: The Novels of Alexander Lernet-Holenia and the Question of Postimperial Austrian Identity.* Riverside, CA: Ariadne, 1996.

———. "Österreich contra Ostmark: Alexander Lernet-Holenia's 'Mars im Widder' as Resistance Novel." In Holzner and Müller, *Zwischenwelt,* 157–79.

Delabar, Walter. "Zu den Verhaltenskonzepten in den Romanen Ernst Wiecherts." In *Dichtung im Dritten Reich?: Zur Literatur in Deutschland 1933–1945,* edited by Christiane Caemmerer and Walter Delabar, 135–50. Opladen: Westdeutscher Verlag, 1996.

Delabar, Walter, Horst Denkler, and Erhard Schütz, eds. *Banalität mit Stil: Zur Widersprüchlichkeit der Literaturproduktion im Nationalsozialismus.* Bern: Lang, 1999.

de Mendelssohn, Peter. "Gegenstrahlungen: Ein Tagebuch zu Ernst Jüngers Tagebuch." *Der Monat* 2, no. 1 (1949): 149–73.

Dempewolf, Eva. *Blut und Tinte: Eine Interpretation der verschiedenen Fassungen von Ernst Jüngers Kriegstagebüchern vor dem politischen Hintergrund der Jahre 1920 bis 1980.* Würzburg: Königshausen & Neumann, 1992.

Denk, Friedrich, *Die Zensur der Nachgeborenen: Zur regimekritischen Literatur im Dritten Reich.* Weilheim i. Ob.: Denk, 1995.

———. "Regimekritische Literatur im Dritten Reich: Eine Problemskizze." In Kroll, *Wort und Dichtung,* 11–33.

Denkler, Horst. *Was war und was bleibt?: Zur deutschen Literatur im Dritten Reich: Neuere Aufsätze.* Frankfurt am Main: Lang, 2004.

Denkler, Horst, and Karl Prümm, eds. *Die deutsche Literatur im Dritten Reich: Themen—Traditionen—Wirkungen.* Stuttgart: Reclam, 1976.

Deutsche Bücherei in Leipzig, ed. *Deutsche Nationalbibliographie:* Ergänzung 1, *Verzeichnis der Schriften, die 1933–1945 nicht angezeigt werden durften.* Leipzig: Verlag des Börsenvereins der deutschen Buchhändler, 1949.

Dick, Ricarda, ed. *Werner Kraft–Wilhelm Lehmann: Briefwechsel 1931–1968.* 2 vols. Göttingen: Wallstein, 2008.

Dickins, Eric. "'Gegenbild' and 'Schlüsselschrift': Wiechert's *Das einfache Leben* and Bergengruen's *Der Großtyrann und das Gericht* Reconsidered." *German Life and Letters* 38, no. 2 (1985): 97–109.

Dietka, Norbert. *Ernst Jünger—vom Weltkrieg zum Weltfrieden: Biographie und Werkübersicht 1895–1945.* Bad Honnef: Keimer; Zurich: Hebsacker, 1994.

Döblin, Alfred. *Berlin Alexanderplatz: Die Geschichte vom Franz Biberkopf.* Berlin: S. Fischer, 1929.

———. "Historie und kein Ende." *Pariser Tageblatt* 4, no. 754 (January 5, 1936): 3. In *Alfred Döblin: Schriften zu Ästhetik, Poetik und Literatur,* edited by Erich Kleinschmidt, 288–91. Freiburg im Breisgau: Walter, 1989.

———. "Der Historische Roman und wir." *Das Wort* 1, no. 4 (1936): 56–71.

———. *Die Fahrt ins Land ohne Tod.* Amsterdam: Querido, 1937.

Dodd, William J. *"Jedes Wort wandelt die Welt": Dolf Sternbergers politische Sprachkritik.* Göttingen: Wallstein, 2007.

———. "Dolf Sternberger's *Panorama*: Approaches to a Work of (Inner) Exile in the National Socialist Period." *Modern Language Review* 198, no. 1 (2013): 180–201.

———. *"Der Mensch hat das Wort": Der Sprachdiskurs in der Frankfurter Zeitung 1933–1943.* Berlin: De Gruyter, 2013.

Donahue, Neil H. *Karl Krolow and the Poetics of Amnesia in Postwar Germany.* Rochester, NY: Camden House, 2002.

Donahue, Neil H., and Doris Kirchner, eds. *Flight of Fantasy: New Perspectives on Inner Emigration in German Literature, 1933–1945.* New York: Berghahn, 2003.

Dornheim, Liane. *Vergleichende Rezeptionsgeschichte: Das literarische Frühwerk Ernst Jüngers in Deutschland, England und Frankreich.* Frankfurt am Main: Lang, 1987.

Drews, Richard, and Alfred Kantorowicz, eds. *verboten und verbrannt: Deutsche Literatur—12 Jahre unterdrückt.* Berlin: Ullstein, 1947.

Dupke Thomas, and Petra Treiber. "Gedichte aus dem Widerstand: Albrecht Haushofer und die 'Moabiter Sonette.'" Radioessay, August 5, 1993. Typescript, Bibliothek, Deutsches Literaturarchiv, Marbach.

Dür, Esther. "'Der unerwünschte Zeithintergrund': Erika Mitterers Werk als Spiegel der Zeitgeschichte." *Studia Austriaca* 11 (2003): 135–58.

———. *Erika Mitterer und das Dritte Reich: Schreiben zwischen Protest, Anpassung und Vergessen.* Vienna: Praesens, 2006.

Dyck, Joachim. *Gottfried Benn: Einführung in Leben und Werk.* Berlin: de Gruyter, 2009.

E. A. "Die Wiedertäufer in Münster." *Hochland* 35, no. 2 (1937): 161–63.

Ebeling, Hans, *Ernst Wiechert: Das Werk des Dichters.* Wiesbaden: Limes, 1947.

Eckert, Gerd. "Deutscher Kalender." *Die Literatur* 41, no. 9 (1938–39): 560–61.

———. "Hörspielmanie und Hörspielpflege." *Die Literatur* 41, no. 8 (1938–39): 495–97.

Ehrke-Rotermund, Heidrun. "Anekdoten aus den Napoleonischen Kriegen: Zu Stefan Andres' Rezeption von Johann Konrad Friederichs

'Hinterlassenen Papieren eines französisch-preußischen Offiziers' (1848/49)." *Mitteilungen der Stefan-Andres-Gesellschaft* 31 (2010): 26–51.

Ehrke-Rotermund, Heidrun, and Erwin Rotermund. "Werner Bergengruen." In Ehrke-Rotermund and Rotermund, *Zwischenreiche*, 258–75.

———. *Zwischenreiche und Gegenwelten: Texte und Vorstudien zur "verdeckten Schreibweise" im "Dritten Reich."* Munich: Fink, 1999.

Eibl, Karl. "Selbstbewahrung im Reiche Luzifers?" In *Mein Thema ist der Mensch: Texte von und über Stefan Andres*, edited by Wissenschaftlicher Beirat der Stefan-Andres-Gesellschaft, 214–38. Munich: Piper, 1990.

Eicher, Thomas. *Im Zwischenreich des Alexander Lernet-Holenia: Lesebuch und "Nachgeholte Kritik."* Oberhausen: Athena, 2000.

———. "Im Zwischenreich des Alexander Lernet-Holenia." In Eicher, *Im Zwischenreich des Alexander Lernet-Holenia*, 181–201.

Emde, Friedrich, and Ralf Schuster, eds. *Wege zu Reinhold Schneider: Zum 50. Todestag des Dichters.* Passau: Schuster, 2008.

Emmerich, Wolfgang. "Die Literatur des antifaschistischen Widerstandes in Deutschland." In Denkler and Prümm, *Die deutsche Literatur im Dritten Reich*, 427–58.

Enderle, Luiselotte. *Erich Kästner in Selbstzeugnissen und Bilddokumenten.* Reinbek bei Hamburg: Rowohlt, 1966.

Engelmann, Bernt. "Vorwort." In *Friedrich Percyval Reck-Malleczewen: Tagebuch eines Verzweifelten*, edited by Bernt Engelmann, 7–10. Berlin, Bonn: Dietz, 1981.

Ensberg, Claus. *Die Orientierungsproblematik der Moderne im Spiegel abendländischer Geschichte: Das literarische Werk Reinhold Schneiders.* Tübingen: Narr, 1995.

Enzensberger, Hans Magnus. "Las Casas oder ein Rückblick in die Zukunft." In *Bartolomé de las Casas: Kurzgefaßter Bericht von der Verwüstung der Westindischen Länder*, edited by H. M. Enzensberger, 124–50. Frankfurt am Main: Insel, 1981.

Erschens, Hermann. "Stefan Andres und die Anti-Atom-Bewegung Ende der 50er und Anfang der 60er Jahre." In *Mein Thema ist der Mensch: Texte von und über Stefan Andres*, edited by Wissenschaftlicher Beirat der Stefan-Andres-Gesellschaft, 262–82. Munich: Piper, 1990.

———. "Stefan Andres: El Greco malt den Großinquisitor." In *Ödön von Horváth: Der jüngste Tag: Stefan Andres: El Greco malt den Großinquisitor*, Lehrpraktische Analysen, Universal-Bibliothek, no. 8957, 16–32. Stuttgart: Reclam, 1994.

———. "Anmerkungen zu 'Gottes Utopia' von Stefan Andres." *Mitteilungen der Stefan-Andres-Gesellschaft* 24 (2003): 3–11.

Eschenburg, Harald. "Die Jugend und der Dichter Ernst Wiechert." *Der Buchhändler im neuen Reich* 3, no. 2 (1938): 61–63. In Reiner, *Ernst Wiechert im Wandel der Zeiten*, 41–42.

Euringer, Richard. *Chronik einer deutschen Wandlung: 1925–1935.* Hamburg: Hanseatische Verlagsanstalt, 1936.

Evans, Arthur R., Jr. "Ernst Jünger's *Auf den Marmorklippen:* A Sketch toward an Interpretation." In *Symbolism and Modern Literature: Studies in Honor of Wallace Fowlie*, edited by Marcel Tetel, 26–43. Durham, NC: Duke University Press, 1978.

Evans, Richard J. *The Third Reich at War, 1939–1945.* New York: Penguin Press, 2009.

Fallada, Hans. *Kleiner Mann—was nun?* Berlin: Rowohlt, 1932.

———. *Wolf unter Wölfen.* Berlin: Rowohlt, 1937.

———. *Der eiserne Gustav.* Berlin: Rowohlt, 1938.

———. *Jeder stirbt für sich allein.* Gütersloh: Bertelsmann, 1947.

———. *Alone in Berlin.* London: Penguin Classics, 2009.

Fest, Joachim. "Vorwort." In Friedrich Reck-Malleczewen, *Bockelson: Geschichte eines Massenwahns*, edited by Joachim Fest, 7–20. Stuttgart: Goverts, 1968.

———. "Wider einen Widerstand: Über Friedrich Reck-Malleczewen: 'Tagebuch eines Verzweifelten.'" In *Literatur im "Spiegel,"* edited by Rolf Becker, 188–93. Reinbek bei Hamburg, 1969.

———. "In Münster und anderswo: Zu Friedrich Reck-Malleczewens 'Bockelson.'" In *Aufgehobene Vergangenheit: Portraits und Betrachtungen*, edited by Joachim Fest, 96–114. Stuttgart: Deutsche Verlags-Anstalt, 1981.

Feuchtwanger, Lion. *Die Geschwister Oppermann.* Frankfurt am Main: Fischer Taschenbuch, 1984.

Fichte, Johann Gottlieb. *Reden an die deutsche Nation.* Berlin: Realschulbuchhandlung, 1808.

Fillmann, Elisabeth. "*PLN*-Dechiffrierungen: Verarbeitung konkreter Zeitrealität und Kritik der 'Innerlichkeit' in Werner Krauss' satirischem Roman." In Krohn, Rotermund, Winkler, and Koepke, *Aspekte der künstlerischen Inneren Emigration 1933–1945*, 53–69.

Fischer, Heinz-Dietrich. "Deutsche Allgemeine Zeitung (1861–1945)." In *Deutsche Zeitungen des 17. bis 20. Jahrhunderts*, edited by Heinz-Dietrich Fischer, 280–81. Pullach: Dokumentation, 1972.

Flake, Otto. "Der Fall Thomas Mann." *Badener Tagblatt*, December 8, 1945. In Grosser, *Die große Kontroverse*, 54.

Fleckenstein, Adolf. "Erzählende Literatur." *Hochland* 34, no. 2 (1936–37): 67–74.

———. "Erzählende Literatur." *Hochland* 36, no. 1 (1938–39): 151–61.

Flügel, Heinz. "Ernst Jünger: Auf den Marmorklippen." *Der Eckart-Ratgeber*, June 1941, 12–13.

Franke, Hans. "Bergengruen, Werner: Der Großtyrann und das Gericht." *Die Neue Literatur* 37, no. 6 (1936): 346.

Franke, Manfred. *Jenseits der Wälder: Der Schriftsteller Ernst Wiechert als politischer Redner und Autor.* Cologne: SH, 2003.

Fried, Erich. "Bemerkungen zu einem Kult." *Streit-Zeit-Schrift* 6, no. 2 (1968): 65–66.

Friedrich, Gerhard. "Ernst Jünger: 'Auf den Marmorklippen.'" *Der Deutschunterricht* 16 (1964): 41–52.

Friedrich, Hans E. "Reinhold Schneider: Las Casas vor Karl V. Szenen aus der Konquistadorenzeit." *Die Literatur* 41, no. 1 (1938/39): 185–86.

Frisch, Max. "Stimmen eines anderen Deutschland?: Zu den Zeugnissen von Wiechert und Bergengruen." *Neue Schweizer Rundschau* 13 (1945–46): 537–47.

Frühwald, Wolfgang, and Heinz Hürten, eds. *Christliches Exil und christlicher Widerstand: Ein Symposion an der Katholischen Universität Eichstätt 1985*. Regensburg: F. Pustet, c. 1987.

Funk, Gerald. "Between Apocalypse and Arcadia: Horst Lange's Visionary Imagination during the Third Reich." In Donahue and Kirchner, *Flight of Fantasy*, 248–57.

Fussenegger, Gertrud. *Mohrenlegende: Eine Weihnachtsgeschichte*. Potsdam: Rutten & Loening, 1937.

Gaál-Baróti, Márta. "Wertverlust als Grundlage des Identitätsverlustes in Erika Mitterers 'Verdunkelung.'" In Petrowsky and Österreichische Gesellschaft für Literatur, *Eine Dichterin*, 51–70.

———. "Die kathartische Wirkung der Ungarischen Revolution in der *Tauschzentrale* von Erika Mitterer." In Petrowsky and Abret, *Dichtung im Schatten der großen Krisent*, 231–51.

Gelbin, Cathy S. "Elisabeth Langgässer and the Question of *Inner Emigration*." In Donahue and Kirchner, *Flight of Fantasy*, 269–76.

Getzeny, Hans. *Reinhold Schneider: Seine geistige und künstlerische Entwicklung am Beispiel der erzählenden Prosa*. Frankfurt am Main: Lang, 1987.

Gillessen, Günther. *Auf verlorenem Posten: Die Frankfurter Zeitung im Dritten Reich*. Berlin: Siedler, 1986.

Glaeser, Ernst. *Jahrgang 1902*. Potsdam: Kiepenheuer, 1928.

———. *Das Gut im Elsass: Ein Roman*. Berlin: Kiepenheuer, 1932.

———. *Der letzte Zivilist: Ein Roman*. Zurich: Humanitas, 1935.

———. "Der Pächter." In Ernst Glaeser, *Das Unvergängliche: Erzählungen*, 118–43. Amsterdam: Querido, 1936.

———. *Jahrgang 1902: Roman*. Edited by Christian Klein. Göttingen: Wallstein, 2013.

Glaeser, Ernst, and Franz Carl Weiskopf. *Der Staat ohne Arbeitslose: Drei Jahre "Fünfjahresplan."* Berlin: Kiepenheuer, 1931.

Gobineau, Joseph Arthur. *Essai sur l'inégalité des races humaines* (1853). http://books.google.co.uk/books?id=ak0BAAAAQAAJ&printsec=frontcover&dq=editions:0QOsqwh7Dly1gxD3&redir_esc=y#v=onepage&q&f=false. Accessed July 5, 2014.

Goebbels, Joseph. *Die Tagebücher von Joseph Goebbels: Sämtliche Fragmente*. 29 vols. Edited by Elke Fröhlich. Munich: K. G. Saur, 1993–2008.

———. *Tagebücher*. Band 3, *1935–1939*. Edited by Ralf Georg Reuth. Munich: Piper, 2003.

Goertz, Hans-Jürgen. *The Anabaptists*. London: Routledge, 1996.

Goes, Albrecht. *Der Hirte: Gedichte*. Berlin: Kulturpolitischer Verlag, 1934.

———. "Erika Mitterer." *Frankfurter Zeitung*, June 9, 1941.

———. *Unruhige Nacht*. Hamburg: Wittig, 1950.

———. *Das Brandopfer: Eine Erzählung.* Frankfurt am Main: S. Fischer, 1954.

Göllner, Reinhard. *Der Beitrag des Romanwerks Gertrud von le Forts zum ökumenischen Gespräch.* Paderborn: Bonifacius, 1973.

Gottwald, Herwig. "Erika Mitterer und der historische Roman." In Holzner and Müller, *Zwischenwelt*, 213–34.

———. "Erika Mitterers Romane und die Zeitgeschichte." In Petrowsky and Österreichische Gesellschaft für Literatur, *Eine Dichterin*, 11–25.

Gradwohl-Schlacher, Karin. "Innere Emigration in der 'Ostmark'?: Versuch einer Standortbestimmung." In Holzner and Müller, *Zwischenwelt*, 73–87.

Graeb-Könneker, Sebastian. *Literatur im Dritten Reich: Dokumente und Texte.* Stuttgart: Reclam, 2001.

Graf, Johannes. *"Die notwendige Reise": Reisen und Reiseliteratur junger Autoren während des Nationalsozialismus.* Stuttgart: M & P, 1995.

Grice, Paul. "Logic and Conversation." In Grice, *Studies in the Way of Words*, 22–40. Cambridge, MA: Harvard University Press, 1989.

Grimm, Jacob, and Wilhelm Grimm. *Marienkind* (1810). In *Kinder- und Hausmärchen*, Ausgabe letzter Hand mit den Originalanmerkungen der Brüder Grimm, vol. 1, edited by Heinz Rölleke, 36–41. Stuttgart: Reclam, 1980.

Grimm, Reinhold. "Innere Emigration als Lebensform." In Grimm and Hermand, *Exil und innere Emigration*, 31–73.

———. "Im Dickicht der inneren Emigration." In Denkler and Prümm, *Die deutsche Literatur im Dritten Reich*, 406–26.

Grimm, Reinhold, and Jost Hermand, eds. *Exil und innere Emigration: Third Wisconsin Workshop.* Frankfurt am Main: Athenäum, 1972.

Grohmann, Will. "Der Fürst der Welt." *Deutsche Allgemeine Zeitung*, December 1, 1940.

Große, Wilhelm, ed. *Stefan Andres: Ein Reader zu Person und Werk.* Trier: Spee, 1980.

———. "Nachwort." In *Stefan Andres: El Greco malt den Großinquisitor: Erzählung*, edited by Wilhelm Große, 45–60. Stuttgart: Reclam, 1994.

Grosser, J. F. G., ed. *Die große Kontroverse: Ein Briefwechsel um Deutschland.* Hamburg: Nagel, 1963.

Grothe, Heinz. "Wege der Dichtung: Zu den Arbeiten des jungen Schriftstellers Stefan Paul Andres." *Völkischer Beobachter* 51, Süddeutsche Ausgabe (January 19, 1938): 18.

Gstettner, Hans. "Ernst Wiechert und die Jugend: Das Bekenntnisbuch eines Unzufriedenen." *Völkischer Beobachter* 49, no. 271, Württemberger Ausgabe (1936). In Reiner, *Ernst Wiechert im Urteil seiner Zeit*, 45.

Guillemin, Anna. "The Conservative Revolution of Philologists and Poets: Repositioning Hugo von Hofmannsthal's Speech 'Das Schrifttum als geistiger Raum der Nation.'" *Modern Language Review* 107, no. 2 (2012): 501–21.

Gutmann, Helmut J. "Politische Parabel und mythisches Modell: Ernst Jüngers *Auf den Marmorklippen*." *Colloquia Germanica* 20 (1987): 53–72.

Hackel, Rainer. *Gertrud Fussenegger: Das erzählerische Werk*. Vienna: Böhlau, 2009.

Hackelsberger, N. Luise. "Werner Bergengruen im Dritten Reich." In *Resistance to National Socialism: Kunst und Widerstand: Forschungsergebnisse und Erfahrungsberichte*, edited by Hinrich Siefken and Hildegard Vieregg, 67–88. Munich: Iudicium, 1995.

Hackelsberger-Bergengruen, N. Luise, ed. *Briefwechsel Werner Bergengruen–Reinhold Schneider*. Freiburg im Breisgau: Herder, 1960.

Hadley, Michael. "Resistance in Exile: Publication, Context and Reception of Stefan Andres' 'Wir sind Utopia' (1942)." *Seminar* 19, no. 3 (1983): 157–76.

Haecker, Theodor. *Über den abendländischen Menschen*. Kolmar im Elsaß: Alsatia, c. 1944.

———. *Tag- und Nachtbücher 1939–1945*. Edited by Heinrich Wild. Munich: Kösel, 1947.

Haefs, Wilhelm. *Nationalsozialismus und Exil 1933–1945*. Munich: Carl Hanser, 2009.

Haegert, Wilhelm. Propaganda Ministry Report of January 13, 1940. In Reiner, *Ernst Wiechert im Dritten Reich*, 44–46.

Hagelstange, Rudolf. *Venezianisches Credo*. Munich: Insel, 1946.

———. "Die Form als erste Entscheidung." In *Mein Gedicht ist mein Messer: Lyriker zu ihren Gedichten*, edited by Hans Bender, 37–47. Munich: List, 1964.

Hall, Murray G. *Der Paul Zsolnay Verlag: Von der Gründung bis zur Rückkehr aus dem Exil*. Tübingen: Niemeyer, 1994.

———. "'Ich bitte um Nachsicht. . . .': Innere Emigration privat." In Holzner and Müller, *Zwischenwelt*, 393–416.

Hanimann, Willy A. *Studien zum historischen Roman (1933–1945)*. Bern: Lang, 1981.

Härtling, Peter "Friedrich Percyval Reck-Malleczewen: Tagebuch eines Verzweifelten." In Härtling, *Vergessene Bücher: Hinweise und Beispiele*, 133–42. Stuttgart: Goverts, 1966.

Hattwig, Jörg. *Das Dritte Reich im Werk Ernst Wiecherts: Geschichtsdenken, Selbstverständnis und literarische Praxis*. Frankfurt am Main: Lang, 1984.

Hauptlektorat Schöngeistiges Schrifttum. "Jahresbericht 1940." *Lektoren-Brief* 4, nos. 5–6 (1941): 7–8.

Hausenstein, Wilhelm. "Bücher—frei von Blut und Schande: Ein Wort an Thomas Mann." *Süddeutsche Zeitung* December 24, 1945. In Grosser, *Die große Kontroverse*, 72.

Haushofer, Albrecht. *Scipio: Ein Schauspiel in fünf Akten*. Berlin: Propyläen, 1934.

———. *Sulla: Ein Schauspiel in fünf Akten*. Berlin: Propyläen, 1938.

———. *Augustus: Ein Schauspiel in fünf Akten*. Berlin: Propyläen, 1939.

———. *Moabiter Sonette: Die letzten Gedichte Albrecht Haushofers*. Berlin: Privatdruck, 1945.

———. *Gesammelte Werke*. Teil I, *Dramen I*, edited by Hans-Edwin Friedrich and Wilhelm Haefs. Frankfurt am Main: Lang, 2014.

Hay, Gerhard, Hartmut Rambaldo, and Joachim W. Storck. *"Als der Krieg zu Ende war": Literarisch-politische Publizistik 1945–1950: Eine Ausstellung des Deutschen Literaturarchivs im Schiller-Nationalmuseum Marbach a.N.* Munich: Kösel, 1973.

Heilbron, John L. *Galileo*. New York: Oxford University Press, 2010.

Heine, Heinrich. *Almansor: Eine Tragödie*. In *Heinrich Heine: Historisch-kritische Gesamtausgabe der Werke*, edited by Manfred Windfuhr, vol. 5 (1994). Hamburg: Hoffmann and Campe, 1973–97.

Heinen, Nicolas. *Gertrud von le Fort: Einführung in Leben, Kunst und Gedankenwelt der Dichterin*. 2nd ed. Luxemburg: Éditions du Centre, 1960.

Heiseler, Bernt von. "Gertrud von le Fort." In Heiseler, *Ahnung und Aussage*, 162–69. Munich: Kösel & Pustet, 1939.

Henley, Grant. *Cultural Confessionalism: Literary Resistance and the Bekennende Kirche*. Oxford: Lang, 2007.

Hennecke, Hans. "Stefan Andres." In *Stefan Andres: Eine Einführung in sein Werk*, 7–43. Munich: Piper, 1962.

Henze, Helene. "Erika Mitterer." *Frankfurter Zeitung*, December 22, 1941.

Hiller, Kurt. "Zwischen den Dogmen." *Die neue Weltbühne* 4, no. 50 (December 12, 1935): 1580–84.

Hillesheim, Jürgen, and Elisabeth Michael. *Lexikon nationalsozialistischer Dichter: Biographien, Analysen, Bibliographien*. Würzburg: Königshausen and Neumann, 1993.

Hilton, Ian. "Gertrud von Le Fort." In *German Men of Letters*, vol. 2, edited by Alex Natan, 275–98. London: Wolff, 1966.

Hitler, Adolf. *Mein Kampf*. Munich: Eher, 1933.

Hocke, Gustav René. "Deutsche Kalligraphie oder Glanz und Elend der modernen Literatur." *Der Ruf* 1, no. 7 (1946): 9–10.

Hoffmann, Charles Wesley. *Opposition Poetry in Nazi Germany*. Berkeley: University of California Press, 1962.

Hoffmann, Daniel. "An den Grenzen des aufgeklärten Selbstbewusstseins: Elisabeth Langgässers Auseinandersetzung mit den Bedingungen menschlicher Existenz." In Schwab, *Eigensinn und Bindung*, 285–97.

Hoffmann, Fernand. "Zeitlose Ästhetik als Vorwand und Politik als Zweck—und etwas mehr: Zu der Novelle 'El Greco malt den Großinquisitor' von Stefan Andres." *Mitteilungen der Stefan-Andres-Gesellschaft* 8 (1987): 30–45.

Hofmann, Konrad, Reinhold Schneider, and Erik Wolf, eds. *Sieger in Fesseln: Christuszeugnisse aus Lagern und Gefängnissen*. Freiburg im Breisgau: Herder, 1947.

Hohendahl, Peter Uwe. "The Text as Cipher: Ernst Jünger's Novel 'On the Marble Cliffs.'" *Yearbook of Comparative Criticism* 1 (1968): 128–69.

Holzner, Johann. "Dialoge und Kontroversen mit der Moderne: Gedichte von Erika Mitterer." In Petrowsky and Österreichische Gesellschaft für Literatur, *Eine Dichterin*, 100–114.

Holzner, Johann, and Karl Müller, eds. *Zwischenwelt: Literatur der "Inneren Emigration" aus Österreich*. Jahrbuch der Theodor-Kramer-Gesellschaft 6. Vienna: Theodor-Kramer-Gesellschaft, 1998.

Hornung-Berk, Gerda. "Die schaffende Frau: Gertrud von le Fort." *Münchner Neueste Nachrichten* 203 (July 26, 1936): 28.

Hoth-Blattmann, Barbara, and Ekkehard Blattmann. "Grauen und Passion: Quellenstudien zu Reinhold Schneiders 'Las Casas vor Karl V.'" In Blattmann and Hoth-Blattmann, *Reinhold Schneider—Ich, Tod, Gott*, 261–402.

Hoyer, Franz A. "Die Wiedertäufer als Modell? Friedrich Percyval Reck-Malleczewen, *Bockselson*: Geschichte eines Massenwahns, Stuttgart 1968." *Frankfurter Hefte* 24 (1969): 524–26.

Huch, Ricarda. *Weiße Nächte: Novelle*. Zurich: Atlantis, 1943.

———. *Herbstfeuer*. Leipzig: Insel, 1944.

———. *Briefe an die Freunde*. Edited by Marie Baum. Berlin: Deutsche Buch-Gemeinschaft, 1960.

———. *Deutsche Geschichte*, vol. 1, *Römisches Reich Deutscher Nation*. Zurich: Manesse, 1987.

Hughes, Peter. "Dichtung, Wahrheit, Lüge: Fritz Recks 'Tagebuch eines Verzweifelten.'" *Variations: Literaturzeitschrift der Universität Zürich* 5: *Fälschungen/Faux/Fakes* (2000): 61–75.

Imhoff, Gérard. "Friedrich Reck-Malleczewen." In *Christen im Widerstand gegen das Dritte Reich*, edited by Joël Pottier, 354–67. Stuttgart: Burg, 1988.

Ives, Margaret. "Erika Mitterer as a Christian Writer: A Study of the Novel *Der Fürst der Welt* as a Precursor of the Later Poetry." In *Other Austrians: Post-1945 Austrian Women's Writing*, edited by Allyson Fiddler, 83–90. Bern: Lang, 1998.

Jelusich, Mirko. *Der Traum vom Reich: Roman*. Berlin: Safari, 1941.

Jens, Inge. *Dichter zwischen rechts und links: Die Geschichte der Sektion für Dichtkunst der Preußischen Akademie der Künste, dargestellt nach den Dokumenten*. Munich: Piper, 1971.

Jetter, Marianne R. *The "Island Motif" in the Prose Works of Ernst Wiechert*. Vancouver, BC: Continental Book Centre, 1957.

Jeziorkowski, Klaus. "El Greco malt den Großinquisitor." In *Interpretationen zu Stefan Andres verfaßt von einem Arbeitskreis*, edited by Ruppert Hirschenauer and Albrecht Weber, 51–94. Munich: Oldenbourg, 1969.

Jung, Edgar J. "Deutschland und die Konservative Revolution." In *Deutsche über Deutschland: Die Stimme des unbekannten Politikers*, edited by Edgar J. Jung, 369–83. Munich: Langen-Müller, 1932.

Jünger, Ernst. *In Stahlgewittern aus dem Tagebuch eines Stoßtruppführers*. Leisnig: Robert Meier, 1920.

———. *Der Kampf als inneres Erlebnis*. Berlin: Mittler, 1922.

————. *Feuer und Blut: Ein kleiner Ausschnitt aus einer großen Schlacht.* Magdeburg: Stahlhelm, 1925.

————. "Von den Wahlen." *Die Standarte* 1, no. 21 (August 19, 1926): 488. In Jünger, *Poltische Publizistik 1919 bis 1933*, 241–45.

————. "Der neue Nationalismus." *Die neue Front*, supplement to *Völkischer Beobachter* 40 (January 23–24, 1927). In Jünger, *Politische Publizistik 1919 bis 1933*, 285–91.

————. *Das abenteuerliche Herz: Figuren und Capriccios.* Hamburg: Hanseatische Verlagsanstalt, 1928.

————. *Der Arbeiter: Herrschaft und Gestalt.* Hamburg: Hanseatische Verlagsanstalt, 1932.

————. *Blätter und Steine.* Hamburg: Hanseatische Verlagsanstalt, 1934.

————. *Die totale Mobilmachung.* Berlin: Junker & Dünnhaupt, 1934.

————. *Über den Schmerz.* In *Blätter und Steine*, 157–216.

————. *Afrikanische Spiele.* Hamburg: Hanseatische Verlagsanstalt, 1936.

————. *Das abenteuerliche Herz: Figuren und Capriccios.* Revised edition. Hamburg: Hanseatische Verlagsanstalt, 1938.

————. "Violette Endivien." In *Das abenteuerliche Herz* (1938), 11–14. Also in *Sämtliche Werke*, vol. 9 (1999), 183–84.

————. *Auf den Marmorklippen: Erzählung.* Hamburg: Hanseatische Verlagsanstalt, 1939.

————. *Gärten und Straßen: Aus den Tagebüchern von 1939 und 1940.* Berlin: Mittler, 1942.

————. *Der Friede: Ein Wort an die Jugend Europas, ein Wort an die Jugend der Welt.* Bergisch-Gladbach: Heider, 1945.

————. "Ältere Herrn-Heroiker." *Frankfurter Rundschau*, March 10, 1973.

————. "Rückblick." In Jünger, *Ernst Jünger und Alfred Kubin: Eine Begegnung: Briefe*, 93–108. Berlin: Propyläen, 1975.

————. *Sämtliche Werke.* 22 vols. Stuttgart: Klett-Cotta, 1978–2003.

————. *Politische Publizistik 1919 bis 1933.* Edited by Sven Olaf Berggötz. Stuttgart: Klett-Cotta, 2001.

————. "Revolution und Idee." In Jünger, *Politische Publizistik 1919 bis 1933*, 33–37.

Jünger, Ernst, with Antonio Gnoli, and Franco Volpi. *Die kommenden Titanen: Gespräche.* Vienna: Karolinger, 2002.

Jünger, Friedrich Georg. *Der Taurus: Gedichte.* Hamburg: Hanseatische Verlagsanstalt, 1937.

Jungmichl, Johannes. *Nationalsozialistische Literaturlenkung und bibliothekarische Buchbesprechung.* Berlin: Deutscher Bibliotheksverband, Arbeitsstelle fur das Bibliothekswesen, 1974.

Kaempfer, Wolfgang. *Ernst Jünger.* Stuttgart: Metzler, 1981.

————. "Das schöne Böse: Zum ästhetischen Verfahren Ernst Jüngers in den Schriften der 30er Jahre im Hinblick auf Nietzsche, Sade, und Lautremont." *Recherches Germaniques* 14 (1984): 103–17.

Kalthoff, W. "Las Casas vor Karl V." *Deutsche Allgemeine Zeitung* (1938). Reproduced in *Das Inselschiff* 20 (1938/39): 92–93.

Kampmann, Theoderich, ed. *Die Welt Werner Bergengruens, mit einem Nachwort des Dichters.* Warendorf: Schnell, 1952.

Kappeler, Alphons. *Ein Fall von "Pseudologia phantastica" in der deutschen Literatur: Fritz Reck-Malleczewen: Mit Totalbibliographie.* 2 vols. Göppingen: Kümmerle 1975.

Kasack, Hermann. *Mosaiksteine: Beiträge zur Literatur und Kunst.* Frankfurt am Main: Suhrkamp, 1956.

Kaschnitz, Marie Luise. *Elissa: Roman.* Berlin: Universitas, 1937.

Kästner, Erich. *Das fliegende Klassenzimmer: Ein Roman für Kinder.* Stuttgart: Perthes 1933.

———. *Drei Männer im Schnee: Eine Erzählung.* Zurich: Rascher, 1934.

———. *Emil und die Zwillinge.* Zurich: Atrium, 1934.

———. *Lyrische Hausapotheke.* Basel: Atrium, 1936.

———. "Über das Verbrennen von Büchern (10.5.1958)." In *Erich Kästner: Gesammelte Schriften für Erwachsene,* vol. 8, 277–85. Munich: Knaur, 1969.

Keil, Wolfgang, ed. *Poetischer Einfall—politische Zensur: Kurzprosa von Stefan Andres aus den Jahren 1933 bis 1945.* Schweich: Stefan-Andres-Gesellschaft, 2011.

Keller, Ernst. "Der Tag des Gerichts: Werner Bergengruen." In Keller, *Nationalismus und Literatur: Langemarck, Weimar, Stalingrad,* 158–71. Bern: Francke, 1970.

Kershaw, Ian. *The Nazi Dictatorship.* London: Edward Arnold, 2000.

Kerssenbroch, Hermann von. *Hermanni a Kerssenbroch: Anabaptistici furoris: Monasterium inclitam Westphaliae Metropolim Evertentis: Historica narratio.* Edited by Heinrich Detmer. Münster: Theissing, 1899. http://www.archive.org/details/hermanniakersse00westgoog. Accessed July 10, 2014.

———. *Geschichte der Wiedertäufer zu Münster in Westfalen.* Translated by Simon Peter Widmann. Münster: Verlag der Aschendorffschen Verlagsbuchhandlung, 1929.

Kessels, Johannes. "Reinhold Schneider und die Herausgabe der Sammlung 'Das Gottesreich in der Zeit.'" In *Caritas '83—Jahrbuch des Deutschen Caritasverbandes,* Sonderdruck, edited by Deutscher Caritasverband, 305–42. Freiburg im Breisgau: Deutscher Caritasverband, 1983.

Ketelsen, Uwe-Karsten. *Literatur und Drittes Reich.* 2nd ed. Schernfeld: SH, 1994.

Keun, Irmgard. *Nach Mitternacht.* Amsterdam: Querido, 1937.

Kiesel, Helmuth. "Ernst Jüngers Marmor-Klippen: 'Renommier-' und 'Problem-'buch der 12 Jahre." *Internationales Archiv für Sozialgeschichte der deutschen Literatur* 14, no. 1 (1989): 126–64.

———, ed. *Ernst Jünger/Carl Schmitt: Briefe 1930–1983.* 2nd ed. Stuttgart: Klett-Cotta, 1999.

———. *Ernst Jünger: Die Biographie.* Munich: Siedler, 2007.

Kirshner, Sumner. "Some Documents Relating to Ernst Wiechert's 'Inward Emigration.'" *German Quarterly* 38, no. 1 (1965): 40.

————. *Ernst Wiechert's "Briefe an einen Werdenden" and "Ein deutsches Weihnachtsspiel,"* Monographic Supplement No. 4, vol. 34, no. 1 (March 1966), Research Studies, Washington State University Press. http://www.ernst-wiechert.de/Sumner_Kirshner_Briefe_von_ Ernst_Wiechert.htm. Accessed February 16, 2014.

Klapper, John. *Stefan Andres: Der christliche Humanist als Kritiker seiner Zeit.* Bern: Lang, 1998.

————. "Encouragement for the 'Other Germany'?: Stefan Andres' Publications in the *Krakauer Zeitung* 1940–1943." In *The Text and Its Context: Studies in Modern German Literature and Society,* edited by Nigel Harris and Joanne Sayner, 121–32. Frankfurt am Main: Lang, 2008.

————. "Cultural 'Diskontinuität' and Thematic Continuity: Ernst Wiechert after 1945." *German Life and Letters* 62, no. 4 (2009): 430–47.

————, ed. "Stefan Andres-Bibliographie." Stefan-Andres-Gesellschaft, 2009–. http://stefan-andres-gesellschaft.de/?page_id=25. Accessed December 18, 2014.

————. "'[. . .] um aus dem Vergangenen Gesetz und Maß des Gegenwärtigen herüberholen': Zur Einordnung von Stefan Andres' geschichtlicher Prosa im Dritten Reich." In *Mimesis, Mimikry, Simulatio: Tarnung und Aufdeckung in den Künsten vom 16. bis zum 21. Jahrhundert: Festschrift für Erwin Rotermund,* edited by Hanns-Werner Heister and Bernhard Spies, 61–73. Berlin: Weidler, 2013.

————. "Categories of the Nonconformist: The Historical Fiction of Inner Emigration." *German Life and Letters* 67, no. 2 (2014): 158–81.

Klein, Christian. "Nachwort." In Ernst Glaeser, *Ernst Glaeser, Jahrgang 1902: Roman,* edited by Christian Klein, 321–89. Göttingen: Wallstein, 2013.

Klein, Uwe. *Stefan Andres: Innere Emigration in Deutschland und im Exil.* PhD diss., University of Mainz, 1991.

Klemperer, Victor. *LTI: Notizbuch eines Philologen.* Berlin: Aufbau, 1947.

————. *Ich will Zeugnis ablegen bis zum letzten: Tagebücher 1933–1945.* Edited by Walter Nowojski. Berlin: Aufbau, 1995.

————. *I Shall Bear Witness: The Diaries of Victor Klemperer 1933–41,* translated by Martin Chalmers. London: Weidenfeld & Nicolson, 1998–99.

Klepper, Jochen. *Der Vater: Roman eines Soldatenkönigs.* Stuttgart: Deutsche Verlags-Anstalt, 1937.

————. *Gedichte: Olympische Sonette/Der König.* Berlin-Dahlem: Der Christliche Zeitschriftenverlag, 1947.

————. *Unter dem Schatten deiner Flügel: Aus den Tagebüchern der Jahre 1932–1942.* Edited by Hildegard Klepper. Stuttgart: Deutsche Verlags-Anstalt, 1956.

————. *Kyrie: Geistliche Lieder.* Witten: Eckart, 1957.

————. *Gast und Fremdling: Briefe an Freunde.* Edited by Eva-Juliane Meschke. Berlin: Eckart, 1960.

————. *Jochen Klepper: Briefwechsel 1925–1942.* Edited by Ernst G. Riemschneider. Stuttgart: Deutsche Verlags-Anstalt, 1973.

————. *Unter dem Schatten deiner Flügel: Aus den Tagebüchern der Jahre 1932–1942.* Stuttgart: Deutsche Verlags-Anstalt, 1983.

Klieneberger, H. R. *The Christian Writers of the Inner Emigration.* The Hague, Paris: Mouton, 1968.

————. "Reinhold Schneider." In Klieneberger, *Christian Writers of the Inner Emigration,* 44–80.

————. "Werner Bergengruen." In Klieneberger, *Christian Writers of the Inner Emigration,* 108–34.

Knapp, Friedrich. "*Der Kranz der Engel* und die Menschen." *Frankfurter Hefte* 2 (1947): 970–73.

Knes, Ulrike. "Frank Thiess: Ein Autor zwischen Realität und Selbststilisierung." In Holzner and Müller, *Zwischenwelt,* 47–72.

Koch, Hans-Albrecht, ed. *Rudolf Alexander Schröder (1878–1962).* Frankfurt am Main: Lang, 2013.

Koebner, Thomas. "Die Schuldfrage: Vergangenheitsverweigerung und Lebenslügen in der Diskussion 1945–1949." In Koebner, *Unbehauste: Zur deutschen Literatur in der Weimarer Republik, im Exil und in der Nachkriegszeit,* 320–51. Munich: text + kritik, 1992.

Koenigswald, Harald von. *Die Gewaltlosen: Dichtung im Widerstand gegen den Nationalsozialismus.* Herborn: Oranien, 1962.

Koepcke, Cordula. *Ricarda Huch: Ihr Leben und ihr Werk.* Frankfurt am Main: Insel, 1996.

Kolmar, Gertrud. *Die Frau und die Tiere: Gedichte.* Berlin: Jüdischer Buchverlag, 1938.

————. *Das lyrische Werk.* Edited by Regina Nörtemann. Göttingen: Wallstein, 2010.

Kramer, Heinrich. *Malleus maleficarum 1487: Mit Bulle und Approbatio.* Zurich: Olms, 1992.

Kranz, Gisbert. *Gertrud von le Fort: Leben und Werk in Daten, Bildern und Zeugnissen.* Frankfurt am Main: Insel, 1976; 3rd ed., 1995.

Krause, Tilman. *Mit Frankreich gegen das deutsche Sonderbewußtsein: Friedrich Sieburgs Wege und Wandlungen in diesem Jahrhundert.* Berlin: Akademie, 1993.

Krauss, Werner. *PLN: Die Passionen der halykonischen Seele.* Potsdam: Rütten & Loening, 1946.

Krenzlin, Leonore. "Auf der Suche nach einer veränderten Lebenshaltung: Ernst Wiechert: 'Das einfache Leben.'" In Bock and Hahn, *Erfahrung Nazideutschland,* 384–411.

————. "Autobiografie als Standortbestimmung: Ernst Wiecherts 'Wälder und Menschen' im Kontext der Entstehungszeit." In Pleßke and Weigelt, *Zuspruch und Tröstung,* 133–48.

Krohn, Claus Dieter, Erwin Rotermund, Lutz Winkler, and Wulf Koepke, eds. *Aspekte der künstlerischen Inneren Emigration 1933–1945.* Munich: text + kritik, 1994.

Kroll, Frank-Lothar, ed. *Wort und Dichtung als Zufluchtsstätte in schwerer Zeit.* Berlin: Gebr. Mann, 1996.

———. "Geschichtserfahrung und Gegenwartsdeutung bei Werner Bergengruen." In Kroll, *Wort und Dichtung*, 45–63.

———. *Dichtung als Kulturvermittlung: Der Schriftsteller Werner Bergengruen: Beiträge für Unterricht und Weiterbildung.* Filderstadt: Weinmann, 1997.

———, ed. *Flucht und Vertreibung in der Literatur nach 1945.* Berlin: Gebr. Mann, 1997.

———, ed. *Die totalitäre Erfahrung: Deutsche Literatur und Drittes Reich.* Berlin: Duncker & Humblot, 2003.

———. "Das Deutschlandbild Werner Bergengruens im Spiegel seiner Tagebücher." *Zuckmayer-Jahrbuch* 7 (2004): 187–210.

———. "Intellektueller Widerstand im Dritten Reich: Möglichkeiten und Grenzen." In Kroll and von Voss, *Schriftsteller und Widerstand*, 13–44.

Kroll, Frank-Lothar, and Rüdiger von Voss, eds. *Schriftsteller und Widerstand: Facetten und Probleme der Inneren Emigration.* Göttingen: Wallstein, 2012.

Krüger, Horst. "Zur Literaturgeschichte der Neuzeit." *Der Buchhändler im neuen Reich* 8, no. 3 (1943): 28–34. In Reiner, *Ernst Wiechert im Wandel der Zeiten*, 129.

———. "Ein Denkmal deutscher Innerlichkeit: Über Ernst Wiechert, *Das einfache Leben* (1939)." In *Romane von gestern—heute gelesen*, vol. 3, edited by M. Reich-Ranicki, 238–45. Frankfurt am Main: S. Fischer, 1990.

Kuckhoff, Adam. *Der Deutsche von Bayencourt.* Berlin: Rowohlt, 1937.

Kurz, Gerhard. "'Innere Emigration': Zur öffentlichen Kontroverse zwischen Walter v. Molo, Thomas Mann und Frank Thieß." In *Öffentlicher Sprachgebrauch: Praktische, theoretische und historische Perspektiven*, edited by Karin Böke, Matthias Jung, and Martin Wengeler, 221–35. Opladen: Westdeutscher Verlag, 1996.

Küsel, Herbert. "Dietrich Eckart: Geboren am 23. März 1868," *Frankfurter Zeitung*, Erstes Morgenblatt, March 23, 1943. In Küsel, *Zeitungs-Artikel*, 26–34. Heidelberg: Schneider, 1973.

Laack-Michel, Ursula. *Albrecht Haushofer und der Nationalsozialismus: Ein Beitrag zur Zeitgeschichte.* Stuttgart: Klett, 1974.

La Chevallerie, Eleonore von, ed. *Ausstellung im Juni 1981, veranstaltet von der Universität Würzburg aus Anlaß des 10. Todestages der Dichterin.* Würzburg: Fränkische Gesellschaftsdruckerei, 1981.

———, ed. *Gertrud von Le Fort: Wirken und Wirkung*, Ausstellungskatalog. Heidelberg: Universitätsbibliothek, 1983.

Lämmert, Eberhard. "Beherrschte Prosa: Poetische Lizenzen in Deutschland zwischen 1933 und 1945." *Neue Rundchau* 86 (1975): 404–21.

Landspersky, Otto. "Stefan Andres." In *Der Bamberger Dichterkreis 1936–1943*, edited by Wulf Segebrecht, 83–92. Bamberg: Staatsbibliothek, 1985.

Lange, Horst. *Schwarze Weide: Roman.* Hamburg, Leipzig: Goverts, 1937.

Langenbucher, Hellmuth. "Sinn und Unsinn der Buchproduktion." *Bücherkunde der Reichsstelle zur Förderung des Deutschen Schrifttums* 4, no. 3 (March 1937): 138.

———. "Neuerscheinungen 1937." *Nationalsozialistische Monatshefte* 8, no. 93 (December 1937): 1143–51.

———. *Volkhafte Dichtung der Zeit.* Berlin: Junker und Dünnehaupt, 1941.

Langenhorst, Georg. "Reinhard Schneider heute lesen?: Theologisch-literarische Annäherungen." In Emde and Schuster, *Wege zu Reinhold Schneider,* 1–30.

Langgässer, Elisabeth. *Rettung am Rhein: Drei Schicksalsläufe.* Salzburg: Otto Müller, 1938.

———. *Das unauslöschliche Siegel.* Hamburg: Claassen & Goverts, 1946.

———. *Das Christliche der christlichen Dichtung: Vorträge und Briefe.* Freiburg im Breisgau: Walter, 1961.

———. "Schriftsteller unter der Hitler-Diktatur." In Arnold, *Deutsche Literatur im Exil 1933–1945,* vol. 1, *Dokumente,* 280–85.

las Casas, Bartolomé de. *Brevísima relación de la destrucción de las Indias Occidentales.* Filadelfia: J. F. Hurtel, 1821.

le Fort, Gertrud von. *Hymnen an die Kirche.* Munich: Theatiner, 1924.

———. *Das Schweißtuch der Veronika,* vol. 1, *Der römische Brunnen.* Munich: Kösel & Pustet, 1928.

———. *Der Papst aus dem Ghetto: Die Legende des Geschlechtes Pier Leone.* Munich: Transmare Verlag, 1930.

———. *Die Letzte am Schafott: Novelle.* Munich: Kösel & Pustet, 1931.

———. *Hymnen an Deutschland.* Munich: Kösel & Pustet, 1932.

———. "Hymnen an Deutschland." *Völkischer Beobachter* 46 (August 23, 1933).

———. *Die Ewige Frau.* Munich: Kösel & Pustet, 1934.

———. *Das Reich des Kindes: Legende der letzten Karolinger.* Munich: Langen-Müller, 1934.

———. "Vermächtnisse." In *Mein Elternhaus: Bekenntnisse, Dank und Vermächtnis,* edited by Martin Warneck, 140–52. Berlin: Warneck, 1937.

———. *Die Magdeburgische Hochzeit.* Leipzig: Insel, 1938.

———. *Die Abberufung der Jungfrau von Barby: Erzählung.* Munich: Ehrenwirth, 1940.

———. "Das Gericht des Meeres: Erzählung." *Das Inselschiff* 22 (1941): 86–107. Republished as *Das Gericht des Meeres.* Leipzig: Insel, 1943.

———. *Das Schweißtuch der Veronika,* vol. 2, *Der Kranz der Engel.* Munich: Beckstein, 1946.

———. *Die Consolata.* Wiesbaden: Insel, 1947.

———. *Unser Weg durch die Nacht: Worte an meine Schweizer Freunde.* Wiesbaden: Insel, 1949.

———. "Behütete Quellen." In le Fort, *Werk und Bedeutung,* 5–6.

———. *Den Heimatlosen: Drei Gedichte.* Munich: Ehrenwirth, 1950.

———. *Werk und Bedeutung: "Der Kranz der Engel" im Widerstreit der Meinungen.* Munich: Ehrenwirth, 1950.

———. *Aufzeichnungen und Erinnerungen.* Einsiedeln: Benzinger, 1951.

———. "Vom Paradox des Christentums: Vorwort zu dem gleichnamigen Buch von Graham Greene." In le Fort, *Die Krone der Frau*, 42–43.

———. *Die Krone der Frau.* Edited by Bernt von Heiseler. Zurich: Arche, 1952.

———. *Die Unschuldigen: Dem Andenken der toten Kinder des Weltkrieges.* In le Fort, *Gelöschte Kerzen: Zwei Erzählungen.* Munich: Ehrenwirth, 1953. In le Fort, *Erzählende Schriften*, 3:413–57.

———. *The Song at the Scaffold.* London: Sheed & Ward, 1953.

———. *Am Tor des Himmels.* Wiesbaden: Insel, 1954. And in le Fort, *Erzählende Schriften* 3:459–522.

———. *Erzählende Schriften.* 3 vols. Munich: Ehrenwirth; Wiesbaden: Insel, 1956.

———. *Der Christ im Atomzeitalter.* Munich: Biehl, 1958.

———. "Autobiographische Skizze." In le Fort, *Die Frau und die Technik*, 31–43.

———. *Die Frau und die Technik.* Zurich: Arche, 1959.

———. "Über den historischen Roman." In le Fort, *Die Frau und die Technik*, 47–48.

———. *Das fremde Kind: Erzählung.* Frankfurt am Main: Insel, 1961.

———. *Die Tochter Jephtas.* Frankfurt am Main: Insel, 1964.

———. *Hälfte des Lebens: Erinnerungen.* Munich: Ehrenwirth, 1965.

———. *Der Dom: Erzählung.* Munich: Ehrenwirth, 1968.

Lehmann, Wilhelm. *Antwort des Schweigens.* Berlin: Widerstands-Verlag, 1935.

———. *Der Grüne Gott: Ein Versbuch.* Berlin: Otto Müller, 1942.

———. *Sämtliche Werke in drei Bänden.* Gütersloh: Mohn, 1962.

Lernet-Holenia, Alexander. *Der Mann im Hut: Roman.* Berlin: S. Fischer, 1937.

———. *Ein Traum in Rot: Roman.* Berlin: S. Fischer, 1939.

———. *Mars im Widder: Roman.* Stockholm: Bermann-Fischer, 1947.

———. *Mars im Widder.* Vienna: Zsolnay, 1976.

Lessing, Gotthold Ephraim. *Hamburgische Dramaturgie*, 2. Stück. In *Lessings Werke*, vol. 2, *Schriften I*, edited by Kurt Wölfel. Frankfurt am Main: Insel, 1967.

Lippe, George B. von der, and Viktoria M. Reck-Malleczewen, eds. *A History of the Münster Anabaptists: Inner Emigration and the Third Reich: A Critical Edition of Friedrich Reck-Malleczewen's 'Bockelson: A Tale of Mass Insanity'.* New York: Palgrave Macmillan, 2008.

Loerke, Oskar. *Der Silberdistelwald: Gedichte.* Berlin: S. Fischer, 1934.

———. *Der Wald der Welt: Gedichte.* Berlin: S. Fischer, 1936.

———. *Tagebücher 1903–1939.* Edited by Hermann Kasack. Heidelberg: Schneider, 1955.

———. *Sämtliche Gedichte.* 2 vols. Edited by Uwe Pörksen, Wolfgang Menzel, and Lutz Seiler. Göttingen: Wallstein, 2010.

Loesch, Ronald. "Werner Bergengruen." *Die Neue Literatur* 40 (1939): 175–189.

Loewy, Ernst. *Literatur unterm Hakenkreuz: Das Dritte Reich und seine Dichtung: Eine Dokumentation.* Frankfurt am Main: Europäische Verlags-Anstalt, 1966.

Lokatis, Siegfried. "Hanseatische Verlagsanstalt: Buchmarketing im 'Dritten Reich.'" *Archiv für Geschichte des Buchwesens* 38 (1992): 1–189.

——. *Hanseatische Verlagsanstalt: Politisches Buchmarketing im "Dritten Reich."* Frankfurt am Main: Buchhändler-Vereinigung, 1992.

Loose, Gerhard. *Ernst Jünger: Gestalt und Werk.* Frankfurt am Main: Klostermann, 1957.

——. *Ernst Jünger.* New York: Twayne, 1974.

Löwenthal, Richard. "Widerstand im totalen Staat." In Löwenthal and Mühlen, *Widerstand und Verweigerung in Deutschland,* 11–24.

Löwenthal, Richard, and P. von zur Mühlen, eds. *Widerstand und Verweigerung in Deutschland 1933–1945.* Bonn: Dietz, 1997.

Lukács, Georg. *Deutsche Literatur im Zeitalter des Imperialismus: Eine Übersicht ihrer Hauptströmungen.* Berlin: Aufbau-Verlag, 1950.

——. "Der Kampf zwischen Liberalismus und Demokratie im Spiegel des historischen Romans der deutschen Antifaschisten." In Arnold, *Deutsche Literatur im Exil 1933–1945,* vol. 2, *Materialien,* 173–99.

Magenau, Jörg. *Brüder unterm Sternenzelt: Friedrich Georg und Ernst Jünger, eine Biographie.* Stuttgart: Klett-Cotta, 2012.

Mallmann, Marion. *"Das Innere Reich": Analyse einer konservativen Kulturzeitschrift im Dritten Reich.* Bonn: Bouvier, 1978.

Mann, Heinrich. "Zola." In Heinrich Mann, *Geist und Tat: Franzosen 1780–1930,* 149–255. Frankfurt am Main: Suhrkamp, 1981.

Mann, Klaus. *Der Vulkan: Roman unter Emigranten.* Amsterdam: Querido, 1939.

Mann, Thomas. *Thomas Mann: Briefe 1937–1947.* Edited by Erika Mann. Frankfurt am Main: Fischer, 1979.

——. *Gesammelte Werke in Einzelbänden: Frankfurter Ausgabe.* Edited by Peter de Mendelssohn. Frankfurt am Main: S. Fischer, 1980–86.

——. "[An Eduard Korrodi]." In Mann, *Gesammelte Werke,* vol. 18, *An die gesittete Welt: Politische Schriften und Reden im Exil* (1986), 146–51.

——. "Schicksal und Aufgabe." In Mann, *Gesammelte Werke,* vol. 18, *An die gesittete Welt,* 643–66.

——. *Tagebücher 1944 bis 1.4.1946.* Edited by Peter de Mendelssohn and Inge Jens. Frankfurt am Main: Fischer, 1986.

——. "Warum ich nicht nach Deutschland zurückgehe." In Mann, *Gesammelte Werke,* vol. 18, *An die gesittete Welt,* 728–37.

——. *Tagebücher, 1933–1934.* Edited by Peter de Mendelssohn and Inge Jens. Frankfurt am Main: Fischer, 1997.

Mann, Thomas, Frank Thiess, and Walter von Molo. *Ein Streitgespräch über die äußere und die innere Emigration.* Dortmund: Crüwell, 1946.

Marcuse, Ludwig. "Die Anklage auf Flucht." *Das neue Tagebuch* 4, no. 6 (1936): 131–33.

Markowski, Bruno. "Hymnen an Deutschland." *Zeitschrift für Deutschland* 48 (1934): 198–206.

Martin, Elaine. "*Alle unsere Spiele* und die NS-Jahre: Interview mit Erika Mitterer-Petrowsky—Wien, den 3. und 4. Juni 1986." *Der literarische Zaunkönig*, no. 2 (2003): 28–38.

Martus, Steffen. *Ernst Jünger*. Stuttgart: Metzler, 2001.

Matthies, Kurt. "Hymnen an Deutschland." *Deutsches Volkstum* 15 (1933): 613–21.

Mayser, Erich. "Die Leidenschaft verzweifelter Verachtung." *Frankfurter Allgemeine Zeitung*, no. 177 (August 11, 1984).

McVeigh, Joseph G. "Continuity as Problem and Promise: Erika Mitterer's Writings after 1945." *Modern Austrian Literature* 12, nos. 3–4 (1979): 113–26.

———. *Kontinuität und Vergangenheitsbewältigung in der österreichischen Literatur nach 1945*. Vienna: Braumüller, 1988.

Meier, Peter. *Die Romane Werner Bergengruens*. Bern: Francke, 1967.

Meier, Pirmin A. *Form und Dissonanz: Reinhold Schneider als historiographischer Schriftsteller*. Frankfurt am Main: Lang, 1978.

Meyer, Jochen. "'Dank des Lebens': Erika Mitterers Briefwechsel in Gedichten mit Rainer Maria Rilke." In Petrowsky and Österreichische Gesellschaft für Literatur, *Eine Dichterin*, 83–99.

Meyerhofer, Nicholas J. *Gertrud von le Fort*. Berlin: Morgenbuch, 1993.

Michalak-Etzold, Magdalena. "Zusammenspiel von Innerer Emigration und Innerer Zensur." In Holzner and Müller, *Zwischenwelt*, 111–25.

Michels, Josef. "Der Fürst der Welt." *Völkischer Beobachter* 33 (February 2, 1941).

Mirbt, Karl-Wolfgang. *Methoden publizistischen Widerstandes im Dritten Reich, nachgewiesen an der "Deutschen Rundschau" Rudolf Pechels*. PhD diss., Freie Universität Berlin, 1958.

Mitchell, Allan. *The Devil's Captain: Ernst Jünger in Nazi Paris, 1941–44*. New York: Berghahn, 2011.

Mittenzwei, Werner. *Exil in der Schweiz: Kunst und Literatur im antifaschistischen Exil 1933–1945*, vol. 2. Frankfurt am Main: Röderberg, 1981.

Mitterer, Erika. *Dank des Lebens: Gedichte*. Frankfurt am Main: Rütten & Loening, 1930.

———. *Höhensonne*. Berlin: Deutsche Verlags-Anstalt, 1933.

———. *Gesang der Wandernden: Neue Gedichte*. Leipzig: Staackmann, 1935.

———. *Der Fürst der Welt*. Hamburg: Marion von Schröder, 1940.

———. *Begegnung im Süden*. Hamburg: Marion von Schröder, 1941.

———. *Die Seherin*. Hamburg: Marion von Schröder, 1942.

———. *Verdens Fyrste*. Oslo: Aschehoug, 1942.

———. *Wir sind allein: Ein Roman zwischen zwei Zeiten*. Vienna: Luckmann, 1945.

———. *Zwölf Gedichte 1933–1945*. Vienna: Luckmann, 1946.

———. *Die nackte Wahrheit: Roman.* Innsbruck: Osterreichische Verlags-Anstalt, 1951.

———. *Kleine Damengröße: Ein Roman im Schatten der Jugend.* Vienna: Luckmann, 1953.

———. *Arme Teufel* (1954). In *Erika Mitterer: Dramen III.*

———. *Verdunkelung* (1956). In *Erika Mitterer: Dramen I.*

———. *Tauschzentrale: Roman.* Vienna: Luckmann, 1958.

———. *Wähle die Welt!* (1959). In *Erika Mitterer: Dramen II.*

———. *Ein Bogen Seidenpapier* (1960). In *Erika Mitterer: Dramen I.*

———. *Der Fürst der Welt.* Berlin: Non Stop Bücherei, 1964.

———. *Entsühnung des Kain.* Einsiedeln: Johannes, 1974.

———. *Alle unsere Spiele.* Frankfurt am Main: Knecht, 1977.

———. *Das verhüllte Kreuz: Neue Gedichte.* Vienna: Niederösterreichisches Pressehaus, 1985.

———. *All Our Games.* Columbia, SC: Camden House, 1988.

———. *Der Fürst der Welt.* Edited by Roman Roček. Vienna: Böhlau, 1988; Berlin: Volk und Welt, 1988.

———. "Selbstporträt." *Modern Austrian Literature* 21, no. 2 (1988): 77–84.

———. "'Sie gehören doch auch zu uns. . . .': Zwischen Protest, Mitfühlen und Anpassung—Eine Schriftstellerin erinnert sich an 1938." *Die Presse*, January 30–31, 1988. http://www.erika-mitterer.org/dokumente/mitterer_gehoerenzuuns.pdf. Accessed February 20, 2014.

———. *Bibelgedichte—ein Vermächtnis.* Föhrenau: Stiglmayr, 1994.

———. *Das gesamte lyrische Werk.* Edited by Martin G. Petrowsky and Petra Sela. Vienna: Doppelpunkt, 2001.

———. *Dramen I (Verdunkelung, Ein Bogen Seidenpapier).* Edited by Martin G. Petrowsky and Petra Sela. Vienna: Doppelpunkt, 2001.

———. *Dramen II (Wähle die Welt, Wofür halten Sie mich?).* Edited by Martin G. Petrowsky and Petra Sela. Vienna: Doppelpunkt, 2002.

———. *Dramen III (Charlotte Corday, Arme Teufel).* Edited by Martin G. Petrowsky and Petra Sela. Vienna: Doppelpunkt, 2003.

———. *The Prince of Darkness.* Translated by Catherine Hunter. Riverside, CA: Ariadne, 2004.

———. *Der Fürst der Welt.* First complete revised edition. Vienna: Seifert, 2006.

Moeller van den Bruck, Arthur. *Das dritte Reich.* Hamburg: Hanseatische Verlagsanstalt, 1931.

Mohler, Armin, and Karlheinz Weißmann, eds. *Die Konservative Revolution in Deutschland 1918–1932: Ein Handbuch.* 6th ed. Graz: Ares, 2005.

Molo, Walter von. *Eugenio von Savoy: Heimlicher Kaiser des Reichs.* Berlin: Holle, 1936.

Möser, Gerlinde. "Spiegelbild einer Zeitenwende: Geschichtswissenschaftliche Betrachtung der Milieuschilderung im Roman 'Der Fürst der Welt.'" *Der literarische Zaunkönig*, no. 1 (2010): 39–43.

Moßmann, Manfred. "Stefan Andres' 'Der Palast des Marquis': Freiheit und Camouflage." *Mitteilungen der Stefan-Andres-Gesellschaft* 30 (2009): 17–21.

———. "Andres zwischen LTI und nationalem Wahn: Zu den Publikationen 'Sphinxe, Köpfe und Fische' und 'Der Tod als Instrukteur' in der Krakauer Zeitung." *Mitteilungen der Stefan-Andres-Gesellschaft* 33 (2012): 59–65.

Mühlberger, Günter, and Kurt Habitzel. "The German Historical Novel from 1780 to 1945: Utilising the Innsbruck Database." In *Travellers in Space and Time: The German Historical Novel*, edited by Osman Durrani and Julian Preece, 5–23. Amsterdam: Rodopi, 2001.

Mühleisen, Horst, and Hans Peter DesCoudres. *Bibliographie der Werke Ernst Jüngers*. 2nd ed. Stuttgart: Cotta, 1996.

Müller, Emil. "Die Motive für die Verhaftung Ernst Wiecherts." *Stuttgarter Zeitung* 27, no. 44/B (February 23, 1971): 21.

Müller, Erich. "Bockelson—eine deutsche Utopie." *Weiße Blätter*, July 6, 1937, 209–10.

Müller, Karl, and Johann Holzner. "Vorwort." In Holzner and Müller, *Zwischenwelt*, 8–22.

Müller, Karlheinz. *Elisabeth Langgässer: Eine biographische Skizze*. Darmstadt: Gesellschaft Hessischer Literaturfreunde, 1990.

Müller, Manfred. "Eine Flucht in Haß und Verzweiflung: Friedrich Reck-Malleczewen, ein Konservativer in der Inneren Emigration." *Frankfurter Rundschau* 26, no. 56 (March 7, 1970): 4–5.

Müller, Richard. *Eine Geschichte der Novemberrevolution: Vom Kaiserreich zur Republik—Die Novemberrevolution—Der Bürgerkrieg in Deutschland*. Berlin: Die Buchmacherei, 2011.

Müller-Gangloff, Erich. "Ein Dichter und Deuter der Zeit." *Berliner Hefte für geistiges Leben* 4, no. 2 (1949): 198–201.

Mulot, Arno. *Die deutsche Dichtung unserer Zeit*. 2nd ed. Stuttgart: Metzler, 1944.

Nagelschmidt, Ilse, Almut Constanze Nickel, and Jochanan Trilse-Finkelstein. *Dichten wider die Unzeit: Textkritische Beiträge zu Gertrud Kolmar*. Frankfurt am Main: Lang, 2013.

Neaman, Eliot Y. *A Dubious Past: Ernst Jünger and the Politics of Literature after Nazism*. Berkeley: University of California Press, 1999.

Nebel, Gerhard. "Ernst Jünger und die Anarchie." *Monatsschrift für das deutsche Geistesleben* 41, no. 11 (1939): 610–16.

Neuhaus, Stefan. *Das verschwiegene Werk: Erich Kästners Mitarbeit an Theaterstücken unter Pseudonym*. Würzburg: Königshausen & Neumann, 2000.

Neuwinger, Helmut. "Ernst Wiecherts Roman 'Das einfache Leben'—eine ländliche Idylle?" In Pleßke and Weigelt, *Zuspruch und Tröstung*, 149–73.

Nevin, Thomas. *Ernst Jünger and Germany: Into the Abyss, 1914–1945*. London: Constable, 1996.

The New English Bible: New Testament. Oxford: Oxford University Press and Cambridge University Press, 1961.

Nickel, Gunther. "Die Schwierigkeiten politischer Hermeneutik am Beispiel Friedrich Sieburgs." In Braun, Guntermann, and Gandner, *"Gerettet und zugleich von Scham verschlungen,"* 39–58.

Nicolin, Günther. "Stefan Andres als Internatsschüler am Collegium Josephinum (1918–1920)." *Mitteilungen der Stefan-Andres-Gesellschaft* 16 (1995): 47–62.

———, ed. *Ernst Jünger—Stefan Andres: Briefe 1937–1970.* Stuttgart: Klett-Cotta, 2007.

Niekisch, Ernst. *Widerstand: Ausgewählte Aufsätze aus seinen Blättern für sozialistische und nationalrevolutionäre Politik.* Krefeld: Sinus, 1982.

Nietzsche, Friedrich. *Der Wille zur Macht: Versuch einer Umwertung aller Werte.* Edited by Peter Gast, with Elisabeth Förster-Nietzsche. Frankfurt am Main: Insel, 1992.

Nijssen, Hub. *Der heimliche König: Leben und Werk von Peter Huchel.* Würzburg: Königshausen & Neumann, 1998.

Niven, Bill. "Ernst Wiechert and His Role between 1933 and 1945." *New German Studies* 16 (1990): 1–20.

N. N. "Aus der ersten Lese." *Das Deutsche Wort* 15 (1939): 322–24.

Noack, Paul. *Ernst Jünger: Eine Biographie.* Berlin: Fest, 1998.

Nordstrand, Karl O. "Stefan Andres und die 'innere Emigration.'" *Moderna Språk* 63, no. 3 (1969): 247–64.

———. "El Greco malt den Großinquisitor." In *Utopia und Welterfahrung: Stefan Andres und sein Werk im Gedächtnis seiner Freunde,* edited by Klaus Piper, 117–131. Munich: Piper, 1972.

Nyssen, Elke. *Geschichtsbewußtsein und Emigration: Der historische Roman der deutschen Antifaschisten 1933–1945.* Munich: Fink, 1974.

O'Boyle, Ita. "Gertrud von le Fort's *Die Letzte am Schafott.*" *German Life and Letters* 16 (1963): 98–104.

Oelze, Klaus-Dieter. *Das Feuilleton der Kölnischen Zeitung im Dritten Reich.* Frankfurt am Main: Lang, 1990.

Olschner, Leonard. "Absences of Time and History: Poetry of *Inner Emigration.*" In Donahue and Kirchner, *Flight of Fantasy,* 131–52.

Orendi, Diana. "Luise Rinser's Escape into 'Inner Emigration.'" In Donahue and Kirchner, *Flight of Fantasy,* 199–210.

Orlowski, Hubert. "Krakauer Zeitung 1939–1945: Nichtnationalsozialistische Literatur im Generalgouvernement?" In *"Das war ein Vorspiel nur. . . .": Berliner Colloquium zur Literaturpolitik im Dritten Reich,* edited by Eberhard Lämmert, 136–58. Berlin: Akademie der Künste, 1985.

Ortega y Gasset, José. *La rebelión de las masas.* Santiago: Moderna, 1932.

Otten, Karl. *Das leere Haus: Prosa jüdischer Dichter.* Stuttgart: Cotta, 1959.

Paetel, Karl O. *Deutsche innere Emigration: Antinationalsozialistische Zeugnisse aus Deutschland.* New York: Friedrich Krause, 1946.

————. "Eine ketzerische Huldigung." In Karl O. Paetel, *Bekenntnis zu Ernst Wiechert: Ein Gedenkbuch zum 60. Geburtstag des Dichters*, 170–79. Munich: Desch, 1947.

————. *Ernst Jünger: Weg und Wirkung: Eine Einführung.* Stuttgart: Klett, 1949.

————. *Ernst Jünger: Eine Bibliographie.* Stuttgart: Lutz & Meyer, 1953.

Parker, Stephen. "Collected—Recollected—Uncollected?: Peter Huchel's *Gesammelte Werke.*" *German Life and Letters* 40, no. 1 (1986/87): 49–70.

Payr, Bernhard. "Aufgaben des Amtes Schrifttumspflege." In *Die Welt des Buches: Eine Kunde vom Buch*, edited by Hellmuth Langenbucher, with Will Vesper, 203–7. Ebenhausen near Munich: Langewiesche-Brandt, 1938.

————. "Deutsch-französische Begegnungen im deutschen Roman 1937." *Völkischer Beobachter* 51, Norddeutsche Ausgabe (February 2, 1938).

————. "Gutachten für Verleger: Fritz Reck-Malleczewen: *Charlotte Corday.*" *Börsenblatt für den deutschen Buchhandel* 105, no. 67 (March 21, 1938): 1540.

————. "Mustergutachten." *Lektorenbrief* 2, no. 6 (1939): 8–10. In Reiner, *Ernst Wiechert im Dritten Reich*, 153–57. Also in *Bücherkunde* 6, no. 8 (1939): 419–21.

————. *Das Amt Schrifttumspflege: Eine Entwicklungsgeschichte und seine Organisation.* Berlin: Junker und Dunnhaupt, 1941.

Pechel, Rudolf. "Sibirien." *Deutsche Rundschau* 252 (1937): 172–75.

————. *Deutscher Widerstand.* Zurich: Rentsch, 1947.

————. *Zwischen den Zeilen: Der Kampf einer Zeitschrift für Freiheit und Recht 1932–1942.* Wiesentheid: Droemer, 1948.

–per. "Die Wiedertäufer zu Münster." *Frankfurter Zeitung* 81, no. 269 (May 30, 1937): 6.

Perels, Christoph. "Nachwort." In *Reinhold Schneider: Gesammelte Werke* 5, 408.

Peters, J. "Das Werk Ernst Wiecherts." *Die Bücherei* 7, nos. 1–2 (1940): 9.

Petersen, Jan. *Unsere Straße: Eine Chronik: Geschrieben im Herzen des faschistischen Deutschlands 1933/34.* Berlin: Dietz, 1947.

Petrowsky, Martin G. "Das Dritte Reich in der Literatur: Verschwiegen und verdrängt: Welche Rolle spielten die 'Vermittler?'" *Der literarische Zaunkönig*, no. 2 (2012): 26–33.

Petrowsky, Martin G., and Helga Abret, eds. *Dichtung im Schatten der großen Krisen: Erika Mitterers Werk im literaturhistorischen Kontext.* Vienna: Praesens, 2006.

Petrowsky, Martin G., and Österreichische Gesellschaft für Literatur, eds. *Eine Dichterin—ein Jahrhundert: Erika Mitterers Lebenswerk.* Vienna: Doppelpunkt, 2002.

Pflug-Franken, Hans. "Gertrud von Le Fort: Die Magdeburgische Hochzeit: Roman." *Die Literatur* 40 (1937–38): 752.

Philipp, Michael. "Distanz und Anpassung: Sozialgeschichtliche Aspekte der Inneren Emigration." In Krohn, Rotermund, Winkler, and Koepke, *Aspekte der künstlerischen Inneren Emigration 1933–1945*, 11–30.

Pike, David. *German Writers in Soviet Exile, 1933–1945*. Chapel Hill: University of North Carolina Press, 1982.

Plard, Henri. "Ex Ordine Shandytorum: Das Schlangensymbol in Ernst Jüngers Werk." In *Freundschaftliche Begegnungen: Festschrift für Ernst Jünger zum 60. Geburtstag*, edited by Armin Mohler, 95–116. Frankfurt am Main: Klostermann, 1955.

Pleßke, Hans-Martin. "Vom Wort als Macht des Herzens: Versuch über Ernst Wiechert." *Sinn und Form* 40, no. 4 (1988): 760–75.

———. *Der die Herzen bewegt: Ernst Wiechert, Dichter und Zeitzeuge aus Ostpreußen*. Hamburg: Landsmannschaft Ostpreußen, 2005.

Pleßke, Hans-Martin, and Klaus Weigelt, eds. *Zuspruch und Tröstung: Beiträge über Ernst Wiechert und sein Werk*. Frankfurt am Main: Rita G. Fischer, 1999.

Polt-Heinzl, Evelyne. "Ein Fürst und ein Herr der Welt: Zwei historische Romane von Erika Mitterer und Alma Johanna Koenig." In Petrowsky and Abret, *Dichtung im Schatten der großen Krisen*, 151–79.

Pongs, Hermann. "Rheinische Stammesseele in der Dichtung der Gegenwart." *Dichtung und Volkstum* 39 (1938): 123.

Pottier, Joël. "Gertrud von le Fort: Eine biographische Skizze." In *Deutsche christliche Dichterinnen des 20. Jahrhunderts: Gertrud von le Fort, Ruth Schaumann, Elisabeth Langgässer*, edited by Lothar Bossle and Joël Pottier, 22–49. Würzburg, Paderborn: Creator, 1990.

———. "Der Widerstand der deutschen christlichen Dichter gegen den Nationalsozialismus am Beispiel Gertrud von le Forts und Werner Bergengruens." In *". . . aus einer chaotischen Gegenwart hinaus . . .": Gedenkschrift für Hermann Kunisch*, edited by Lothar Bossle and Joël Pottier, 151–82. Paderborn: Bonifatius, 1996.

———. "Erlebte und gedeutete Geschichte: Gertrud von le Forts 'Weg durch die Nacht' im Dritten Reich." In Kroll, *Die totalitäre Erfahrung*, 153–69.

———. "Zwischen Ernst Troeltsch und Edith Stein: Gertrud von le Forts einsamer Weg." *Wiener Jahrbuch für Philosophie* 34, no. 2002 (2003): 185–225.

———. "Ein Anti-Claudel?: Gertrud von le Fort und der französische Renouveau catholique." In *Moderne und Antimoderne: Der "Renouveau catholique" und die deutsche Literatur*, edited by Wilhelm Kühlmann and Roman Luckscheiter, 489–509. Freiburg im Breisgau: Rombach, 2008.

———. "'Ich habe das Historische nie als eine Flucht aus der eigenen Zeit empfunden': Wahrnehmung und Deutung der Geschichte bei Gertrud von le Fort (1876–1971)." In *Freie Anerkennung übergeschichtlicher Bindungen: Katholische Geschichtswahrnehmung im deutschsprachigen Raum des 20. Jahrhunderts*, edited by Thomas Pittrof and Walter Schmitz, 367–80. Freiburg im Breisgau: Rombach, 2010.

Prümm, Karl. *Die Literatur des Soldatischen Nationalismus der 20er Jahre (1918–1933): Gruppenideologie und Epochenproblematik.* Kronberg, Tn.: Scriptor, 1974.

Puknat, Siegfried. "God, Man, and Society in the Recent Fiction of Ernst Wiechert." *German Life and Letters* 3, no. 3 (1949–50): 221–30.

———. "Max Picard and Ernst Wiechert." *Monatshefte für deutschen Unterricht, deutsche Sprache und Literatur* 42 (1950): 371–84.

Q. E. "Wo steht der Dichter Ernst Wiechert?" *Völkischer Beobachter* 48, nos. 108–109, Münchener Ausgabe, April 18, 1935. In Reiner, *Ernst Wiechert im Dritten Reich*, 66.

Ranke, Leopold von. *Deutsche Geschichte im Zeitalter der Reformation.* vol. 3. Berlin: Duncker und Humblot, 1840.

Reck-Malleczewen, Friedrich Percyval. *Frau Übersee.* Berlin: Mosse, 1918.

———. *Die Dame aus New York.* Berlin: Mosse, 1921.

———. *Phrygische Mützen.* Munich: Drei Masken, 1922.

———. *Die Siedlung Unitrusttown.* Berlin: Ullstein, 1925.

———. *Sif: Das Weib, das den Mord beging.* Munich: Drei Masken, 1926.

———. *Sven entdeckt das Paradies: Roman.* Berlin: Deutsche Buchgemeinschaft, 1928.

———. "Biographische Skizze." In *Obelisk-Almanach auf das Jahr 1930,* edited by Obelisk Almanach, 128–29. Berlin: Drei Masken, 1930.

———. *Bomben auf Monte Carlo.* Berlin: Scherl, 1930.

———. "Vom Reich der Deutschen." In *Was ist das Reich?: Eine Aussprache unter Deutschen,* edited by Fritz Buechner, 51–58. Oldenburg: Stalling, 1932.

———. *Acht Kapitel für die Deutschen.* Großschönau/Sachsen: Kaiser Verlag, 1934.

———. "Ewige Gironde." *Widerstand: Zeitschrift für nationalrevolutionäre Politik* 9, no. 9 (1934): 289–95.

———. *Ein Mannsbild namens Prack: Roman.* Berlin: Schützen, 1935.

———. *Sophie Dorothee: Mutter Friedrichs des Grossen.* Berlin: Schützen, 1936.

———. *Bockelson: Geschichte eines Massenwahns.* Berlin: Schützen, 1937.

———. *Charlotte Corday: Geschichte eines Attentats.* Berlin: Schützen, 1938.

———. *Diana Pontecorvo: Roman.* Berlin: Knaur, 1944.

———. *Bockelson: Geschichte eines Massenwahns.* Wiesentheid: Droemersche Verlagsanstalt, 1946.

———. *Das Ende der Termiten: Ein Versuch über die Biologie des Massenwahns,* Fragment. Lorch: Bürger, 1946.

———. *Tagebuch eines Verzweifelten.* Lorch: Bürger, 1947.

———. *Tagebuch eines Verzweifelten: Zeugnis einer inneren Emigration.* Stuttgart: Goverts, 1966.

———. *Bockelson: Geschichte eines Massenwahns.* Edited by Joachim Fest. Stuttgart: Goverts, 1968.

———. *Tagebuch eines Verzweifelten.* Edited by Bernt Engelmann. Berlin: Dietz, 1981.

———. *Tagebuch eines Verzweifelten*. Frankfurt am Main: Eichborn, 1994.

Reddemann, Karl Wilhelm. *Der Christ vor einer zertrümmerten Welt: Reinhold Schneider—ein Dichter antwortet der Zeit*. Freiburg im Breisgau: Herder, 1978.

Reifarth, Gert, and Philip Morrissey, eds. *Aesopic Voices: Re-framing Truth through Concealed Ways of Presentation in the 20th and 21st Centuries*. Newcastle upon Tyne: Cambridge Scholars Publishing, 2011.

Reiner, Guido. *Ernst-Wiechert-Bibliographie 1916–1971*. Teil 1, *Werke, Übersetzungen, Monographien und Dissertationen mit kritisch-analytischen Kurzbesprechungen*. Paris: Reiner, 1972.

———. *Ernst-Wiechert-Bibliographie*. Teil 2, *Ernst Wiechert im Dritten Reich: Eine Dokumentation: Mit einem Verzeichnis der Ernst-Wiechert-Manuskripte im Haus Königsberg*. Paris: Reiner, 1974.

———. *Ernst-Wiechert-Bibliographie*. Teil 3, *Ernst Wiechert im Urteil seiner Zeit: Literaturkritische Pressestimmen (1922–1975):* Paris: Reiner, 1976.

———. *Ernst-Wiechert-Bibliographie*. Teil 4, *Ernst Wiechert im Wandel der Zeiten: Literarische Beiträge 1920–1980:* Paris: Reiner, 1984.

———. "Ernst Wiechert und seine Freunde." In Reiner and Weigelt, *Ernst Wiechert heute*, 11–55.

Reiner, Guido, and Klaus Weigelt, eds. *Ernst Wiechert heute*. Frankfurt am Main: R. G. Fischer, 1993.

Reinhardt, Stefan. *Alfred Andersch: Eine Biographie*. Zurich: Diogenes, 1990.

Renner, Gerhard. "Frank Thiess: Ein 'freier Schriftsteller' im Nationalsozialismus." *Buchhandelsgeschichte* 2, no. 51, Beilage zum Börsenblatt für den deutschen Buchhandel (June 26, 1990): 41–51.

Rey, William. "Ernst Jünger and the Crisis of Civilization." *German Life and Letters* 5 (1951/52): 249–54.

Riccabona, Max von. "F. Reck-Malleczewen." *Der Monat* 18, no. 216 (1966): 94.

Richards, Donald Ray. *The German Bestseller in the Twentieth Century: A Complete Bibliography and Analysis, 1915–1940*. Bern: Lang, 1968.

Riegel, Paul, and Wolfgang van Rinsum. *Drittes Reich und Exil 1933–1945: Deutsche Literaturgeschichte*. vol. 10. Munich: dtv, 2004.

Ringshausen, Gerhard. "Der christliche Protest: Konfessionelle Dichtung und nonkonformes Schreiben im Dritten Reich." In Kroll and von Voss, *Schriftsteller und Widerstand*, 267–96.

———. "Regimekritik in der Erzählung *Der Palast des Marquis* von Stefan Andres," *Mitteilungen der Stefan-Andres-Gesellschaft* 35 (2014), 68–74.

Riordan, Colin. "Depictions of the State in Works of the *Inner Emigration*." In Donahue and Kirchner, *Flight of Fantasy*, 152–67.

Ritchie, James. M. *German Literature under National Socialism*. London: Croom Helm, 1983.

Roček, Roman. "Anstelle eines Nachworts: Rainer Maria Rilke—Erika Mitterer Briefwechsel in Gedichten." In *Erika Mitterer: Der Fürst der Welt*, edited by Roman Roček, 624–35. Vienna: Böhlau, 1988.

———. "Vorwort." In *Erika Mitterer: Der Fürst der Welt*, 5–10.

———. "Zwischen Subversion und Innerer Emigration: Alexander Lernet-Holenia und der Nationalsozialismus." In Holzner and Müller, *Zwischenwelt*, 181–211.

Roch, Herbert. "Ernst Jünger: Auf den Marmorklippen." *Das Deutsche Wort* 16, no. 1 (1940): 28.

Rosenberg, Alfred. *Der Mythus des 20. Jahrhunderts: Eine Wertung der seelisch-geistigen Gestaltenkämpfe unserer Zeit.* 3rd ed. Munich: Hoheneichen, 1932.

Rost, Nico. *Goethe in Dachau.* Frankfurt am Main: Fischer Taschenbuch Verlag, 1983.

Rotermund, Erwin. *Zwischen Exildichtung und innerer Emigration: Ernst Glaesers Erzählung "Der Pächter."* Munich: Fink, 1980.

———. *Artistik und Engagement: Aufsätze zur deutschen Literatur.* Würzburg: Koenigshausen & Neumann, 1994.

———. "Herbert Küsels 'Dietrich Eckart'-Artikel vom 23. März 1943: Ein Beitrag zur Hermenutik und Poetik der 'verdeckten Schreibweise' im 'Dritten Reich.'" In Rotermund, *Artistik und Engagement*, 239–48.

———. "Tarnung und Absicherung in Rudolf Pechels Aufsatz 'Sibirien' (1937): Eine Studie zur 'verdeckten Schreibweise' im 'Dritten Reich.'" In Rotermund, *Artistik und Engagement*, 225–38.

———. "Zu Joachim Günthers Publizistik im 'Dritten Reich.'" *Zeitschrift für Germanistik*, Neue Folge 9, no. 2 (1999): 330–43.

———. "Verklärung und Kritik: Bilder des preußischen Adels in der Literatur der Inneren Emigration (1933–1945), unter besonderer Berücksichtigung von Werner Bergengruen." *Literatur für Leser* 4 (2009): 221–32.

Rotermund, Erwin, and Heidrun Ehrke-Rotermund. "Literatur im 'Dritten Reich.'" In *Geschichte der deutschen Literatur vom 18. Jahrhundert bis zur Gegenwart*, vol. 3, part 1, *1918–1945*, 2nd ed., edited by Viktor Žmegač, 318–84. Königstein/Ts.: Athenäum, 1994.

———. "Getarnte Regimekritik in Stefan Andres' Kurzprosa der frühen Vierziger Jahre." In *Stefan Andres: Zeitzeuge des 20. Jahrhunderts*, edited by Michael Braun, Georg Guntermann, and Birgit Lermen, 105–21. Frankfurt am Main: Lang, 1999.

———. "Nachwort." In *Stefan Andres: Wir sind Utopia*, 275–314.

Rothe, Arnold. "Die *Marmorklippen* ohne Marmor." *Internationales Archiv für Sozialgeschichte der deutschen Literatur* 21, no. 1 (1966): 124–27.

Rüther, Günther, ed. *Literatur in der Diktatur: Schreiben im Nationalsozialismus und DDR-Sozialismus.* Paderborn: Schöningh, 1997.

S. "'Auf den Marmorklippen.'" *Hochland* 37, no. 1 (1939–40): 244–45.

Saile, Olaf. *Kepler: Roman einer Zeitwende.* Stuttgart: Behrendt, 1949.

Samhaber, Ernst. "Massenwahn." *Deutsche Zukunft* 6, no. 2 (January 9, 1938): 10–11.

Sarnetzki, Dettmar Heinrich. "Die Magdeburgische Hochzeit." *Das Inselschiff* 19 (1937/38): 188–89.

Sass, Maria. "Wer vergisst, hat vergebens gelebt: Vergangenheitsbewältigung in Erika Mitterers Roman 'Alle unsere Spiele.'" In Petrowsky and Abret, *Dichtung im Schatten der großen Krisen*, 275–92.

——. "Aspekte des Mythischen und des magischen Realismus in Erika Mitterers Roman 'Fürst der Welt.'" *Der literarische Zaunkönig*, no. 3 (2011): 32–52.

Saward, Helena M. "A Literature of Substitution: Vicarious Sacrifice in the Writings of Gertrud von le Fort." *German Life and Letters* 53 (2000): 179–200.

Schäfer, Eckart. "Die Indianer und der Humanismus: Die spanische Conquista in lateinischer Literatur: Mit einem Anhang zu Reinhold Schneiders 'Las Casas vor Karl V.'" In Blattmann and Hoth-Blattmann, *Reinhold Schneider—Ich, Tod, Gott*, 205–59.

Schäfer, Hans Dieter. *Wilhelm Lehmann: Studien zu seinem Leben und Werk*. Bonn: Bouvier, 1969.

——. "Die nichtfaschistische Literatur der 'jungen Generation' im nationalsozialistischen Deutschland." In Denkler and Prümm, *Die deutsche Literatur im Dritten Reich*, 459–503.

——. *Das gespaltene Bewußtsein: Über deutsche Kultur und Lebenswirklichkeit 1933–1945*. Munich: Hanser, 1981.

——. *Das gespaltene Bewußtsein: Vom Dritten Reich bis zu den langen fünfziger Jahren*. Göttingen: Wallstein, 2009.

Schelle, Hansjörg. *Ernst Jüngers "Marmor-Klippen": Eine kritische Interpretation*. Leiden: Brill, 1970.

Schenker, Anatol. *Der Jüdische Verlag 1902–1938: Zwischen Aufbruch, Blüte und Vernichtung*. Tübingen: Niemeyer, 2003.

Scherer, Bruno. *Tragik vor dem Kreuz: Leben und Geisteswelt Reinhold Schneiders*. Freiburg im Breisgau: Herder, 1966.

Schickert, Werner. "Erika Mitterer: *Der Fürst der Welt*: Roman." *Die Literatur* 43 (1940–41): 611.

Schmidt-Dengler, Wendelin. "Geschichte ohne Historie: Typologisches zum Roman 'Der Fürst der Welt.'" In Petrowsky and Österreichische Gesellschaft für Literatur, *Eine Dichterin*, 71–82.

——. "Geschichte bekommt Konturen." *Der literarische Zaunkönig*, no. 1 (2003): 5.

Schmitt, Franz Anselm, and Bruno Scherer, eds. *Reinhold Schneider: Leben und Werk in Dokumenten*. 2nd ed. Karlsruhe: Badenia, 1973.

Schmollinger, Annette. *"Intra muros et extra": Deutsche Literatur im Exil und in der inneren Emigration: Ein exemplarischer Vergleich*. Heidelberg: Winter, 1999.

Schneider, Reinhold. *Das Leiden des Camões: Oder Untergang und Vollendung der portugiesischen Macht*. Hellerau: Hegner, 1930.

——. *Innozenz der Dritte*. Cologne: Hegner, 1960 [1931].

——. *Philipp II oder Religion und Macht*. Leipzig: Hegner, 1931.

——. *Fichte: Der Weg zur Nation*. Munich: Langen, 1932.

———. "Der Wiedereintrittt in die Geschichte." *Der Tag*, December 31, 1933.

———. *Die Hohenzollern: Tragik und Königtum.* Leipzig: Hegner, 1933. 2nd ed., Cologne: Hegner, 1953.

———. "Der Tröster." *Hochland* 31, no. 2 (1933–34): 143–59.

———. "Die Rechtfertigung der Macht." *Europäische Revue* 11 (1935): 35–42.

———. "Die Warnung des Donoso Cortés." *Weiße Blätter*, January 1935, 13–20.

———, ed. *Gestalt und Seele: Das Werk des Malers Leo von König.* Leipzig: Insel, 1936.

———. *Das Inselreich: Gesetz und Größe der britischen Macht.* Leipzig: Insel, 1936.

———. *Kaiser Lothars Krone: Leben und Herrschaft Lothars von Supplinburg.* Leipzig: Insel, 1937.

———. *Las Casas vor Karl V.: Szenen aus der Konquistadorenzeit.* Leipzig: Insel, 1938.

———. "Die Magdeburgische Hochzeit." *Eckart* 14 (1938): 276–77.

———. *Sonette.* Leipzig: Insel, 1939.

———. *Dreißig Sonette.* Halle: Werkstätten der Stadt Halle, 1941.

———. *Das Gottesreich in der Zeit: Sonette und Aufsätze.* Reichshof: Udzialowa, 1942.

———. *Sonette—Auswahl.* Typecopy reproduction. Freiburg: Kirchliche Kriegshilfestelle, 1942.

———. *Jetzt ist der Heiligen Zeit.* Kolmar: Alsatia, 1943.

———. *Vor dem Grauen.* In *Die dunkle Nacht: 7 Erzählungen.* Kolmar: Alsatia, 1943.

———. *Die Waffen des Lichts.* Kolmar: Alsatia, 1944.

———. *Über den abendländischen Menschen.* Kolmar im Elsaß: Alsatia, c. 1944.

———. "Das Gottesreich in der Zeit." Essay. In *Gesammelte Werke*, vol. 10 (1978), 114–18.

———. *Die Verwaltung der Macht.* Freiburg im Breisgau: Herder, 1945.

———. "Persönlichkeit und Schicksal Philipps II von Spanien." In Schneider, *Weltreich und Gottesreich*, 41–108.

———. *Weltreich und Gottesreich: Drei Vorträge.* Munich: Schnell & Steiner, 1946.

———. *Die innere Befreiung: Gedenkwort zum 20. Juli.* Stuttgart: Hatje, 1947.

———. "Donoso Cortés." *Eckart* 22 (1952/53): 328–31.

———. *Der christliche Protest.* Zurich: Verlag der Arche, 1954.

———. *Verhüllter Tag.* Cologne: Hegner, 1954.

———. *Winter in Wien: Aus meinen Notizbüchern 1957/58.* Freiburg im Breisgau: Herder, 1958.

———. *Das Vaterunser.* Freiburg im Breisgau: Herder, 1960.

————. *Reinhold Schneider und Leopold Ziegler: Briefwechsel.* Munich: Kösel, 1960.

————. *Werner Bergengruen (1892–1964) Reinhold Schneider (1903–1958): Briefwechsel.* Edited by N. Luise Hackelsberger-Bergengruen. Freiburg im Breisgau: Herder, 1966.

————. *Gesammelte Werke.* 10 vols. Edited by Edwin Maria Landau. Frankfurt am Main: Insel, 1977–81.

————. *Der Friede der Welt.* Edited by Edwin Maria Landau. Frankfurt am Main: Suhrkamp, 1983.

————. *Tagebuch 1930–1935.* Edited by Josef Rast. Frankfurt am Main: Insel, 1983.

Schnell, Ralf. *Literarische innere Emigration 1933–1945.* Stuttgart: Metzler, 1976.

————. "Innere Emigration und kulturelle Dissidenz." In Löwenthal and Mühlen, *Widerstand und Verweigerung in Deutschland*, 211–25.

————. "Zwischen Anpassung und Widerstand: Zur Literatur der Inneren Emigration im Dritten Reich." In *Europäische Literatur gegen den Faschismus 1922–1945*, edited by Thomas Bremer, 15–32. Munich: C. H. Beck, 1986.

Schoeps, Karl-Heinz. *Literatur im Dritten Reich (1933–1945).* 2nd ed. Berlin: Weidler, 2000.

————. "Conservative Opposition: Friedrich Reck-Malleczewen's Antifascist Novel *Bockelson: A History of Mass Hysteria.*" In Donohue and Kirchner, *Flight of Fantasy*, 188–97.

————. *Literature and Film in the Third Reich.* Rochester, NY: Camden House, 2004.

Scholdt, Günter. "'Gescheitert an den Marmorklippen': Zur Kritik an Ernst Jüngers Widerstandsroman." *Zeitschrift für deutsche Philologie* 98 (1979): 543–77.

————. "Wiedertäufer und Drittes Reich: Zu einer Verschlüsselung im literarischen Widerstand." In *Literatur und Sprache im historischen Prozess: Vorträge des Deutschen Germanistentages in Aachen 1982*, vol. 1, edited by Thomas Cramer, 350–69. Tübingen: Niemeyer, 1983.

————. *Autoren über Hitler: Deutschsprachige Schriftsteller 1910–1945 und ihr Bild vom Führer.* Bonn: Bouvier, 1993.

————. "'Den Emigranten nach außen entsprechen die Emigranten im Innern': Kasacks Diktum und die Kritik an einem Begriff." In *Hermann Kasack—Leben und Werk: Symposium 1993 in Potsdam*, edited by Helmut John and Lonny Neumann, 99–109. Frankfurt am Main: Lang, 1994.

————. "'Ein Geruch von Blut und Schande': Zur Kritik an dem Begriff und an der Literatur über die Emigranten im Innern." *Wirtschaft und Wissenschaft* 1 (1994): 23–28.

————. "Kein Freispruch zweiter Klasse: Zur Bewertung nichtnazistischer Literatur im Dritten Reich." *Zuckmayer-Jahrbuch* 5 (2000): 127–77.

———. "Geschichte als Ausweg?: Zum Widerstandspotential literarischer Geschichtsdeutung in der 'Inneren Emigration.'" In Kroll and von Voss, *Schriftsteller und Widerstand*, 101–23.

Schonauer, Franz. *Deutsche Literatur im Dritten Reich: Versuch einer Darstellung in polemisch-didaktischer Absicht*. Freiburg im Breisgau: Walter, 1961.

———. "Der Schöngeist als Kollaborateur oder Wer war Friedrich Sieburg?" In Corino, *Intellektuelle im Bann des Nationalsozialismus*, 107–19.

Schröder, Jürgen. "Benn in den dreißiger Jahren." In Corino, *Intellektuelle im Bann des Nationalsozialismus*, 48–60.

———. "Gottfried Benn als Emigrant nach Innen." In Rüther, *Literatur in der Diktatur*, 131–44.

Schröder, Rudolf Alexander. "Dichtungen der Naturvölker" (1935). In *Gesammelte Werke*, vol. 2, 1127–43.

———. *Die Ballade vom Wandersmann*. Berlin: S. Fischer, 1937.

———. "Vom Beruf des Dichters in der Zeit: Rede bei einer Tagung junger Dichter 1947." In *Gesammelte Werke*, vol. 3, 43.

———. *Gesammelte Werke*. 5 vols. Berlin: Suhrkamp, 1952–65.

———. *Abendstunde: Ein Selbstbildnis in Gesprächen*. Edited by Lutz Besch. Zurich: Die Arche, 1960.

Schröter, Klaus. "Der historische Roman: Zur Kritik einer spätbürgerlichen Erscheinung." In Grimm and Hermand, *Exil und innere Emigration*, 111–51.

Schürr, Friedrich. *Miguel de Unamuno: Der Dichterphilosoph des tragischen Lenbensgefühls*. Bern: Francke, 1962.

Schuster, Ralf, ed. *Antwort in der Geschichte: Zu den Übergängen zwischen den Werkphasen bei Reinhold Schneider*. Tübingen: Narr, 2001.

Schwab, Hans-Rüdiger, ed. *Eigensinn und Bindung: Katholische deutsche Intellektuelle im 20. Jahrhundert*. Kevelaer: Butzon & Bercker, 2009.

Schwarz, E., ed. *Exil und Innere Emigration II: Internationale Tagung in St. Louis*. Frankfurt am Main: Athenäum, 1973.

Schwarz, Hans-Peter. *Der konservative Anarchist: Politik und Zeitkritik im Werk Ernst Jüngers*. Freiburg im Breisgau: Rombach, 1962.

Schwilk, Heimo. *Ernst Jünger—Ein Jahrhundertleben*. Munich: Piper, 2007.

———. *Ernst Jünger: Leben und Werk in Bildern und Texten*. 2nd ed. Stuttgart: Klett-Cotta, 2010.

Seidel, Eugen, and Ingeborg Seidel-Slotty. *Sprachwandel im Dritten Reich: Eine kritische Untersuchung faschistischer Einflüsse*. Halle: Verlag Sprache und Literatur, 1961.

Seidel, Ina. *Das Wunschkind*. Stuttgart: Deutsche Verlags-Anstalt, 1930.

———. *Der Weg ohne Wahl*. Stuttgart: Deutsche Verlags-Anstalt, 1933.

———. *Es werde Deutschland*. Frankfurt am Main: Societäts-Verlag, 1933.

———. *Robespierre*. Frankfurt am Main: Societäts-Verlag, 1935.

———. *Aus den schwarzen Wachstuchheften: Monologe, Notizen, Fragmente*. Edited by Christian Ferber. Stuttgart: Deutsche Verlags-Anstalt, 1980.

Siefken, Hinrich. "The Diarist Theodor Haecker: Tag- und Nachtbücher 1939–1945." *Oxford German Studies* 17 (1988): 118–31.

———. ed. *Theodor Haecker 1879–1945*, Marbacher Magazin 49 (Marbach am Neckar: Deutsche Schillergesellschaft, 1989): 89–92.

———. ed. *Die Weiße Rose und ihre Flugblätter: Dokumente, Texte, Lebensbilder, Erläuterungen.* Manchester: Manchester University Press, 1994.

———. "Totalitäre Erfahrungen aus der Sicht eines christlichen Essayisten: Theodor Haecker im Dritten Reich." In Kroll, *Die totalitäre Erfahrung,* 117–51.

Siefken, Hinrich, and Hildegard K. Vieregg, eds. *Resistance to National Socialism: Kunst und Widerstand: Forschungsergebnisse und Erfahrungsberichte.* Munich: Iudicium, 1995.

Sonntag, Holger. "'The Night Will Soon Be Ending': Jochen Klepper: A Luther Hymn-writer in Dark Times." *Logia: A Journal of Lutheran Theology* 18, no. 2 (2009): 31–40.

Speirs, Ronald. "The German Novel during the Third Reich." In *The Cambridge Companion to the Modern German Novel,* edited by Graham Bartram, 151–66. Cambridge: Cambridge University Press, 2004.

Spengler, Oswald. *Der Untergang des Abendlandes: Umrisse einer Morphologie der Weltgeschichte.* Edited by Anton Mirko Koktanek. Munich: Deutscher Taschenbuch-Verlag, 1979.

Spoerl, Heinrich. *Feuerzangenbowle: Eine Lausbüberei in der Kleinstadt.* Düsseldorf: Droste, 1933.

Staub, Norbert. *Wagnis ohne Welt: Ernst Jüngers Schrift "Das abenteuerliche Herz" und ihr Kontext.* Würzburg: Königshausen & Neumann, 2000.

Stauffacher, Werner. "Zwischen äußerer und innerer Emigration: Las Casas als Figur des Widerstandes bei Alfred Döblin und Reinhold Schneider." In *Christliches Exil und christlicher Widerstand: Ein Symposion an der Katholischen Universität Eichstätt 1985,* edited by Wolfgang Frühwald and Heinz Hürten, 394–406. Regensburg: Pustet, 1987.

Steinle, Jürgen. *Reinhold Schneider (1903–1958): Konservatives Denken zwischen Kulturkrise, Gewaltherrschaft und Restauration.* Aachen: Müller, 1992.

Sternberger, Dolf. *Dolf Sternberger: Schriften.* 12 vols. Frankfurt am Main: Insel, 1977–1996.

———. "Figuren der Fabel." *Frankfurter Zeitung,* December 25, 1941. In *Dolf Sternberger: Schriften,* 9:13–26.

———. "War das Sklavensprache?" *Frankfurter Allgemeine Zeitung,* July 8, 1961.

———. "Eine Muse konnte nicht schweigen: 'Auf den Marmorklippen' wiedergelesen." In *Dolf Sternberger: Schriften,* 8:306–23.

———. *Figuren der Fabel: Essays.* Frankfurt am Main: Suhrkamp, 1990.

Storck, Joachim W. "Anatomie einer Denunziation: Der 'Fall' Günter Eich." In *Widersprüche im Widersprechen: Historische und aktuelle Ansichten der Verneinung,* edited by Peter Rau, 156–81. Frankfurt am Main: Lang, 1996.

———. "Erika Mitterers Briefwechsel in Gedichten mit Rainer Maria Rilke und sein literarischer Kontext." In Petrowsky and Abret, *Dichtung im Schatten der großen Krisen*, 21–34.

Strauss, Leo. "Persecution and the Art of Writing." In Strauss, *Persecution and the Art of Writing*, 22–37. Chicago: University of Chicago Press, 1952.

Streim, Gregor. "Junge Völker und neue Technik: Zur Reisereportage im Dritten Reich, am Beispiel von Friedrich Sieburg, Heinrich Hauser und Margret Boveri." *Zeitschrift für Germanistik* 2 (1999): 344–59.

Strothmann, Dietrich. *Nationalsozialistische Literaturpolitik: Ein Beitrag zur Publizistik im Dritten Reich.* Bonn: Bouvier, 1960.

Suhrkamp, Peter. "Die Neue Rundschau." In Suhrkamp, *Die Stockholmer Neue Rundschau: Auswahl 1945/48*, 3–16. Frankfurt am Main: Suhrkamp, 1949.

Süskind, Wilhelm Emanuel. "Mut zum Unbedingten: Anmerkungen zu sechs neuen Romanen." *Die Literatur* 38 (1935–36): 271–73.

Tau, Max. "Als Lektor in der Emigration." In *Jahrbuch 1963: Deutsche Akademie für Sprache und Dichtung*, edited by Deutsche Akademie für Sprache und Dichtung, 85–94. Darmstadt: Lambert Schneider, 1964.

Thiede, Carsten Peter, ed. *Über Reinhold Schneider.* Frankfurt am Main: Suhrkamp, 1980.

Thiess, Frank. *Tsushima* Berlin: Zsolnay, 1936.

———. *The Voyage of Forgotten Men.* Indianapolis, IN: Bobbs Merrill, 1937.

———. *Das Reich der Dämonen: Der Roman eines Jahrtausends.* Berlin: Zsolnay, 1941.

———. "Hitlers Werk—eine erlösende Tat." *Neuer Hannoverscher Kurier,* June 21, 1946.

———. *Das Reich der Dämonen.* Hamburg: Krüger, 1946.

———. *Jahre des Unheils: Fragmente erlebter Geschichte.* Vienna: Zsolnay, 1972.

Thunecke, J., ed. *Leid der Worte: Panorama des literarischen Nationalsozialismus.* Bonn: Bouvier, 1987.

Tomko, Helena M. *Sacramental Realism: Gertrud von le Fort and German Catholic Literature in the Weimar Republic and Third Reich (1924–1946).* London: Maney Publishing, 2007.

Tornow, Ingo. *Erich Kästner und der Film.* Munich: Deutscher Taschenbuch Verlag, 1998.

Töteberg, Michael. "'Beim Film weiß man nie': Ein Autor scheitert an der Filmindustrie." In *Hans Fallada*, edited by Gustav Frank and Stefan Scherer, 40–50. Munich: text + kritik, 2013.

Tralow, Johannes. "Die Geschichte eines Massenwahns." *Süddeutsche Zeitung* (Munich) 2, no. 17 (September 26, 1946): 5.

Troeltsch, Ernst. *Glaubenslehre: Nach Heidelberger Vorlesungen aus den Jahren 1911 und 1912.* Munich: Duncker & Humblot, 1925.

Trott zu Solz, Heinrich von. "Nicht einmal: 'Der Fall Ernst Jünger.'" *Ausblick: Zeitfragen im Lichte der Weltmeinung* 1, no. 5 (July–August 1945): 123.

Uhde, Werner. "Las Casas." *Frankfurter Zeitung*, October 23, 1938, 8.

Unamuno, Miguel de. *Del sentimiento trágico de la vida en los hombres y en los pueblos*. Madrid: Renacimiento, 1913.

van Liere, Cornelis Geeraard. *Georg Hermann: Materialien zur Kenntnis seines Lebens und seines Werkes*. Amsterdam: Rodopi, 1974.

van Roon, Ger. *Neuordnung im Widerstand: Der Kreisauer Kreis innerhalb der deutschen Widerstandsbewegung*. Munich: Oldenbourg, 1967.

Vargas Machuca, Bernardo de. *Apologías y discursos de las conquistas occidentales por don Bernardo Vargas Machuca en controversia del tratado destruición de Las Indias escrito por don Fray Bartolomé de las Casas*. Madrid: Manuel Ginesta, 1879.

Vieregg, Axel. "The Truth about Peter Huchel?" *German Life and Letters* 41, no. 2 (1987/88): 159–83.

———. *Der eigenen Fehlbarkeit begegnet: Günter Eichs Realitäten*. Eggingen: Edition Isele, 1993.

Vieregg, Hildegard K. "Theodor Haecker: Christliche Existenz im totalitären Staat." In Schwab, *Eigensinn und Bindung*, 117–35.

Vietinghoff, Arnold von. "Werner Bergengruen 50 Jahre." *Völkischer Beobachter* 55, no. 259, Münchener Ausgabe (September 16, 1942).

Voigt, Klaus. *Zuflucht auf Widerruf: Exil in Italien 1933–1945*. vol. 1. Stuttgart: Klett-Cotta, 1989.

Volke, Werner, ed. *Gertrud von le Fort*. Marbacher Magazin 3. Marbach: Deutsche Schillergesellschaft, 1976.

Vondung, Klaus. "Der literarische Nationalismus: Ideologische, politische und sozial-historische Wirkungszusammenhänge." In Denkler and Prümm, *Die deutsche Literatur im Dritten Reich*, 44–65.

Wagener, Hans. *Stefan Andres*. Berlin: Colloquium 1974.

———. "Stefan Andres: Widerstand gegen die Sintflut." In Große, *Stefan Andres: Ein Reader*, 90–114.

———. "Stefan Andres: El Greco malt den Großinquisitor." In *Interpretationen: Erzählungen des 20 Jahrhunderts*, vol. 1, 219–30. Stuttgart: Reclam 1996.

Walberer, Ulrich, ed. *10. Mai 1933: Bücherverbrennung in Deutschland und die Folgen*. Frankfurt: Fischer-Taschenbuch-Verlag, 1983.

Wehdeking, Volker. "Zwischen Exil und 'vorgeschobenem Posten' der Kulturnation: Thomas Mann als Projektionsfigur für die im Land gebliebenen Nichtfaschisten." In Rüther, *Literatur in der Diktatur*, 145–62.

Weisenborn, Günther (under name Christian Munk). *Traum und Tarantel: Buch von der unruhigen Kreatur*. Dresden: Heyne, 1938.

———. *Der lautlose Aufstand: Bericht über die Widerstandsbewegung des deutschen Volkes 1933–1945*. Hamburg: Rowohlt, 1953.

Weiskopf, Franz Carl. "Hier spricht die deutsche Literatur!: Zweijahresbilanz der 'Verbrannten.'" In *Zur Tradition der sozialistischen Literatur in Deutschland: Eine Auswahl von Dokumenten*, edited by Deutsche Akademie der Künste, 663–68. Berlin: Aufbau-Verlag, 1967.

Wenzel, Walter. "Widerstandskämpfer des Geistes?" *Geist und Zeit* 1, no. 4 (1956): 133–38.

Westenfelder, Frank. *Genese, Problematik und Wirkung nationalsozialistischer Literatur am Beispiel des historischen Romans zwischen 1890 und 1945.* Frankfurt am Main: Lang, 1989.

Wiechert, Ernst. *Die Flucht* (under name Ernst Barany Bjell). Berlin: Concordia, Deutsche Verlags-Anstalt, 1916.

———. *Der Wald: Roman.* Berlin: Grote'sche Verlagsbuchhandlung, 1922. In *Sämtliche Werke*, vol. 1, 433–638.

———. *Der Totenwolf: Roman.* Regensburg: Habbel & Naumann, 1924. In *Sämtliche Werke*, vol. 2, 5–254.

———. *Der Knecht Gottes Andreas Nyland.* Berlin: G. Grote, 1926. In *Sämtliche Werke*, vol. 2, 254–634.

———. "Die Flucht ins Ewige: Novelle." *Westermanns Monatshefte 72*, vol. 143, no. 854 (1927): 185–93. In *Sämtliche Werke*, vol. 7, 181–207.

———. "Der Hauptmann von Kapernaum." *Europäische Revue* 5 (1929): 614–26. In *Sämtliche Werke*, vol. 7, 213–30.

———. "Der brennende Dornbusch." *Westermanns Monatshefte 77*, vol. 153, no. 913 (1932): 53–59. In *Sämtliche Werke*, vol. 7, 571–89.

———. "Die Gebärde" (1932). In *Die Gebärde—Der Fremde.* Zurich: Die Arche, 1946. In *Sämtliche Werke*, vol. 7, 605–12.

———. *Jedermann: Geschichte eines Namenlosen.* Munich: Langen-Müller, 1932. In *Sämtliche Werke*, vol. 3, 303–538.

———. "Lebensabriß" (1932). In *Sämtliche Werke*, vol. 10, 711–12.

———. *Die Magd des Jürgen Doskocil.* Munich: Langen-Müller, 1932. In *Sämtliche Werke*, vol. 4, 5–177.

———. "Der Dichter und die Jugend: Rede vor der Münchener Studentenschaft, 6. Juli 1933." In *Sämtliche Werke*, vol. 10, 349–67.

———. "Tobias: Novelle." *Hochland* 30, no. 2 (1932/33): 495–505. In *Sämtliche Werke*, vol. 7, 725–42.

———. "Hirtennovelle." *Das Innere Reich* 1, no. 7 (1934): 859–90. In *Sämtliche Werke*, vol. 6, 493–552.

———. *Die Majorin: Roman.* Munich: Langen-Müller, 1934. In *Sämtliche Werke*, vol. 4, 179–356.

———. "Der Dichter und die Zeit" (1935). *Das Wort* 2, nos. 4–5 (1937): 5–10. In *Sämtliche Werke*, vol. 10, 368–80.

———. *Wälder und Menschen: Eine Jugend.* Munich: Langen-Müller, 1936. In *Sämtliche Werke*, vol. 9, 5–196.

———. *Der weiße Büffel oder Von der großen Gerechtigkeit* (1937). Zurich: Rascher, 1946. In *Sämtliche Werke*, vol. 6, 553–625.

———. *Das einfache Leben.* Munich: Langen-Müller, 1939. In *Sämtliche Werke*, vol. 4, 357–726.

———. *Die Jeromin-Kinder*, vol. 1 (1940–41). Munich: Desch, 1945. In *Sämtliche Werke*, vol. 5, 5–520.

———. "Der reiche Mann und der arme Lazarus" (1946). In *Sämtliche Werke*, vol. 10, 631–55.

———. *Der Totenwald: Ein Bericht.* Munich: Rascher, 1946. In *Sämtliche Werke*, vol. 9, 197–329.

———. "Über Kunst und Künstler" (1946). In *Sämtliche Werke*, vol. 10, 412–55.

———. "Vom Wolf und vom Lamm" (1946). In *Sämtliche Werke*, vol. 10, 656–61.

———. *Die Furchen der Armen: Roman.* Second part of *Die Jeromin-Kinder.* Zurich: Rascher, 1947. In *Sämtliche Werke*, vol. 5, 521–978.

———. *Jahre und Zeiten: Erinnerungen.* Erlenbach-Zurich: Rentsch, 1949. In *Sämtliche Werke*, vol. 9, 331–800.

———. *The Earth Is Our Heritage.* London: Nevill, 1950.

———. *Missa sine nomine.* Munich: Desch, 1950. In *Sämtliche Werke*, vol. 6, 5–441.

———. *Sämtliche Werke in zehn Bänden.* Munich: Desch, 1957.

———. *The Simple Life.* London: Quartet, 1994.

Wiese, Benno von. "Gegen den Hitler in uns selbst." In *Romane von gestern heute gelesen*, edited by Marcel Reich-Ranicki, 61–68. Frankfurt am Main: Fischer, 1990.

Wiesner, Herbert. "'Innere Emigration': Die innerdeutsche Literatur im Widerstand 1933–1945." In *Handbuch der deutschen Gegenwartsliteratur*, 2nd ed., vol. 2, edited by Hermann Kunisch, 383–408. Munich: Nymphenburger Verlagshandlung, 1970.

Wilk, Werner. *Werner Bergengruen.* Berlin: Colloquium, 1968.

Williams, Jenny. *More Lives Than One: A Biography of Hans Fallada.* London: Libris, 1998.

Winkler, Eugen Gottlob. "Erzählende Literatur." *Hochland* 33, no. 2 (1935–36): 262–73.

Wipfelder, Hans-Jürgen. *Die Rechts- und Staatsauffassung im Werke Werner Bergengruens.* Zell am Main: Schmitt-Meyer, 1966.

Wirth, Günter. "Eine Stimme für die Gleichberechtigung der Völker: Reinhold Schneider, 'Las Casas vor Karl V.: Szenen aus der Konquistadorenzeit.'" In Bock and Hahn, *Erfahrung Nazideutschland*, 298–334.

———. "Geschichte in metaphorischer Gestalt: Jochen Klepper: 'Der Vater.'" In Bock and Hahn, *Erfahrung Nazideutschland*, 189–230.

Wolf, Yvonne. *Frank Thieß und der Nationalsozialismus: Ein konservativer Revolutionär als Dissident.* Tübingen: Niemeyer, 2003.

Woods, Roger. *Ernst Jünger and the Nature of Political Commitment.* Stuttgart: Hans-Dieter Heinz, 1982.

———. *The Conservative Revolution in the Weimar Republic.* Basingstoke, England: Macmillan, 1996.

Wulf, Joseph. *Literatur und Dichtung im Dritten Reich: Eine Dokumentation.* Frankfurt am Main: Ullstein, 1983.

Wunderlich, Eva C. "Gertrud von le Fort's Fight for the Living Spirit." *Germanic Review* 27 (1952): 298–313.

Zeile, Christine. "Friedrich Reck: Ein biographischer Essay." In Friedrich Reck, *Friedrich Reck-Malleczewen: Tagebuch eines Verzweifelten*, 250–98. Frankfurt am Main: Eichborn, 1994.

Zeller, Bernhard, ed. *Klassiker in finsteren Zeiten 1933–1945: Eine Ausstellung des Deutschen Literaturarchivs im Schiller-Nationalmuseum Marbach am Neckar*. vol. 1. Marbach: Deutsche Schillergesellschaft, 1983.

Zimmermann, Hans-Dieter. "'Innere Emigration': Ein historischer Begriff und seine Problematik." In Kroll and von Voss, *Schriftsteller und Widerstand*, 45–61.

———. "Reinhold Schneider—ein Dichter der Inneren Emigration?" In Kroll and von Voss, *Schriftsteller und Widerstand*, 353–67.

Zimmermann, Ingo, *Der späte Reinhold Schneider: Eine Studie*. Freiburg im Breisgau: Herder, 1973.

———. *Reinhold Schneider: Weg eines Schriftstellers*. Berlin: Union, 1982.

Ziolkowski, Theodore. "Form als Protest: Das Sonett in der Literatur des Exils und der Inneren Emigration." In Grimm and Hermand, *Exil und Innere Emigration*, 153–72.

Zöckler, Paul. "In Memoriam Friedrich Reck-Malleczewen." In *Friedrich Reck-Malleczewen, Bockelson: Geschichte eines Massenwahns*, vii–xxiv. Wiesentheid: Droemer, 1946.

Zuckmayer, Carl. *Geheimreport*. Edited by Gunther Nickel and Johanna

Index

Schneider, Reinhold,
 works by—*(cont'd)*
 vor Karl V., 45, 89, 91, 243, 249,
 252, 255–70 (the disputation,
 261–63; genesis and publication,
 255–57; imitation of Christ and the
 tragic sense of existence, 267–70;
 and Nazi Germany, 263–67;
 reception, 258–60; a story of
 conscience, 260–61; summary,
 257–58); *Das Leiden des Camões*,
 246; "Persönlichkeit und Schicksal
 Philipps II von Spanien," 274;
 Philipp II oder Religion und Macht,
 246–47, 272; "Die Rechtfertigung
 der Macht," 255, 275; *Sieger
 in Fesseln* (ed.), 274; *Sonette*,
 253–55, 274; *Sonette—Auswahl*,
 274; *Tagebuch 1930–1935*, 272,
 275; "Der Tröster," 249, 273;
 Das Vaterunser, 244, 252–53,
 274; *Verhüllter Tag*, 271; *Die
 Verwaltung der Macht*, 274; *Vor
 dem Grauen*, 251–52, 274; *Die
 Waffen des Lichts*, 274; *Weltreich
 und Gottesreich*, 274; "Der
 Wiedereintrittt in die Geschichte,"
 273; *Winter in Wien*, 271
Schnell, Ralf, 9, 17, 32, 37, 45, 50,
 52, 68, 99, 101, 135, 141, 169,
 200, 201, 209, 269, 276, 343
Schnurre, Wolfdietrich, 70
Schoeps, Karl-Heinz, 2, 8, 46, 98,
 207
Scholdt, Günter, 4–5, 9, 41, 53, 96,
 187, 203, 205, 206, 207, 209,
 295, 298, 311, 312, 313, 331,
 346, 386, 387
Scholl, Hans, 110
Schonauer, Franz, 37, 52, 102, 259–
 60, 276, 328, 345
Schönfeld, Herbert, 345
Schopenhauer, Arthur, 245, 272
Schreyvogl, Friedrich, 80
Schrifttumsabteilung/Department
 VIII (of Propaganda Ministry), 23,
 24, 26, 28, 111
Schröder, Jürgen, 101

Schröder, Rudolf Alexander, 6, 55,
 66–67, 72, 86, 98, 99, 343
Schröder, Rudolf Alexander,
 works by: *Abendstunde*, 98; *Die
 Ballade vom Wandersmann*, 67;
 "Christentum und Humanismus,"
 66; "Dichtungen der Naturvölker,"
 66, 98; "In memoriam Hugo
 von Hofmannsthal," 66; "Kunst
 und Religion," 66; "Shakespeare
 als Dichter des Abendlandes,"
 66; "Thomas Mann zum 60.
 Geburtstag," 66; "Vom Beruf des
 Dichters in der Zeit," 99
Schröder Verlag, Marion von, 358,
 359
Schröter, Klaus, 232, 241
"Schublade." *See* writing "for the
 drawer"
Schulze-Boysen, Harro, 57
Schünemann Verlag, 29
Schürr, Friedrich, 272
Schuster, Gerhard, 100, 101
Schuster, Ralf, 273, 277
Schützen-Verlag, 186
Schutzverband deutscher Schriftsteller,
 18, 110
Schwab, Hans-Rüdiger, 96
Schwarz, Hans-Peter, 309
Schwarzschild, Leopold, 284
Schwilk, Heimo, 308, 311
SD. *See* Sicherheitsdienst
Second Vatican Council, 146, 213,
 352
Segebrecht, Wulf, 169
Seghers, Anna, 17
Seidel, Eugen, 106
Seidel, Ina, 72, 74–75, 101, 350, 351
Seidel, Ina, works by: *Aus den
 schwarzen Wachstuchheften*, 101;
 Das Wunschkind, 75; *Der Weg ohne
 Wahl*, 75
Seidel-Slotty, Ingeborg, 106
Seiler, Lutz, 99
Sela, Petra, 377, 378, 379
Sender Freies Berlin, 51
Sicherheitsdienst (SD), 3, 27–28, 30,
 289

320–24; spiritual transformation, 317–20
Wiechert, Ernst, works by:"Der brennende Dornbusch," 318–19; "Der Dichter und die Jugend," 320–21; "Der Dichter und die Zeit," 321; *Das einfache Leben* (*The Simple Life*), 16, 29, 94, 117, 315, 316, 319, 320, 323, 324–41 (ambiguous cultural pessimism, 335–40; genesis and publication, 324–25; oppositional novel?, 329–35; reception, 327–29; summary, 325–27), 346, 385; *Die Flucht*, 316; *Die Furchen der Armen* (*Die Jeromin-Kinder* II), 344; *Die Gebärde*, 319, 342; "Der Hauptmann von Kapernaum," 318; "Hirtennovelle," 319–20, 336, 342; *Jahre und Zeiten*, 51, 324, 341; *Jedermann*, 318, 338, 342; *Die Jeromin-Kinder* I (*The Earth is our Heritage*), 83, 117, 324, 338; *Der Knecht Gottes Andreas Nyland*, 317; "Lebensabriß," 317; *Die Magd des Jürgen Doskocil*, 338; *Die Majorin*, 319, 320, 336, 338, 342; "Eine Mauer um uns baue. . . .," 334; *Missa sine nomine*, 234, 338; "Der reiche Mann und der arme Lazarus," 344; "Tobias," 319, 342; *Der Totenwald: Ein Bericht*, 7, 83, 323–24, 344; *Der Totenwolf*, 316–17, 330, 342; "Über Kunst und Künstler," 335; "Vom Wolf und vom Lamm," 344; *Der Wald*, 316–17, 330; *Wälder und Menschen*, 321–22; *Der weiße Büffel oder Von der großen Gerechtigkeit*, 89, 322, 339, 340, 341
Wiener Dichterkreis, 80

Wiese, Benno von, 8, 122, 130, 136
Wiesner, Herbert, 37, 52, 103, 328, 345
Wild, Heinrich, 96
Wilk, Werner, 122, 139
Williams, Jenny, 101
Winkler, Eugen Gottlob, 70, 96, 140
Winkler, Lutz, 52
Winnig, August, 120
Wipfelder, Hans-Jürgen, 140
Wirth, Günter, 96, 276
Wismann, Heinz, 24, 111
Wissenschaftlicher Beirat der Stefan-Andres-Gesellschaft, 169, 170
Wolf, Erik, 274
Wolf, Yvonne, 103
Wölfel, Kurt, 239
Woods, Roger, 45, 309
writing "for the drawer," 56, 83, 111, 324
Wulf, Joseph, 102
Wunderlich, Eva C., 240
Wust, Peter, 221

"young generation," 49, 69–73

Zeile, Christine, 179, 203, 204, 205
Zeller, Bernhard, 46
Zerkaulen, Heinrich, 145
Ziegler, Benno, 120
Ziegler, Leopold, 249, 259, 273, 275
Zimmermann, Hans-Dieter, 9, 53, 274
Zimmermann, Ingo, 274, 276
Ziolkowski, Theodore, 9, 98
Žmegač, Viktor, 45
Zöckler, Paul, 204, 206
ZsolnayVerlag, 29, 79, 378
Zuckmayer, Carl, 1, 7, 39, 53
Zweig, Arnold, 18, 20
Zweig, Stefan, 19, 350, 378